# Manuscript Illumination in the Modern Age

MARY AND LEIGH BLOCK MUSEUM OF ART

Northwestern University

Evanston, IL

This catalogue was published

in conjunction with the exhibition,

**Manuscript Illumination**

**in the Modern Age**

Mary and Leigh Block Museum of Art

January 11-March 4, 2001

SANDRA HINDMAN

MICHAEL CAMILLE

NINA ROWE

ROWAN WATSON

edited by

SANDRA HINDMAN

and NINA ROWE

Manuscript Illumination

in the Modern Age:

RECOVERY

AND

RECONSTRUCTION

DEDICATED TO SANDRA HINDMAN

Design by Diane Jaroch

Library of Congress Catalog Control
Number 00-136126

ISBN 0-941680-21-5

Printed in Singapore

CONTENTS

The search for new ideas and expanded modes of understanding leads to some unique perspectives and often surprising directions in thought and scholarship. The use of new technologies in support of research, the insights of a new generation of scholars and the reinterpretation of material previously thought fully discussed bring new perspectives on traditional subjects and challenge traditionally held beliefs. The museum is privileged to often be at the forefront of such a dialectical process with history and to provide an environment in which it can flourish. It is even more privileged to be able to make this research an integral part of the study, research, teaching and publishing associated with Northwestern.

Manuscript Illumination in the Modern Age is a unique curatorial endeavor addressing new ideas and perspectives on the vandalization and reconstitution of the illuminated manuscript in the 19th century in England and France and the first half of the 20th century in the United States. This book and the accompanying exhibition define the field of study for those who will follow. The ninety-three works in the exhibit illustrated throughout the text of this accompanying book are brought together by eighteen institutional and private lenders. Their generosity and trust in lending such superb and rare pieces spanning the past eight centuries is most appreciated.

Manuscript Illumination in the Modern Age would not have been possible without its pimary curator, Sandra Hindman. As a professor of art history at Northwestern, the former Chair of the Art History Department, and a scholar whose imminent knowledge of manuscripts is renowned, Sandra has been involved with the conceptualization and implementation of this book and the exhibition for more than six years. As Director of a university museum, one could not hope for a better collaborator/scholar/friend or teacher. Her inclusion of both Michael Camille and Rowan Watson brought to this endeavor two extraordinary scholars whose work is seminal to the definition of the field and to the results seen herein.

Nina Rowe, the 2000 Graduate Fellow of the Block Museum, deserves singular recognition in this book. Not only is she one of the four main scholars responsible for the text, she is also the co-editor of this book and has been involved in almost every phase of this project. From writing and editing the text to co-curating the exhibition to assisting in the design and implementation of the exhibition Nina, was involved in all aspects of Manuscript Illumination in the Modern Age. The quality and excellence of the project is, in great part, due to her efforts.

Throughout the period in which this book and the exhibition were conceived and organized, there have been three institutions that deserve special recognition and without whom Manuscript Illumination in the Modern Age would not have been possible. The Victoria and Albert Museum has offered constant support and encouragement. Rowan Watson, curator of an earlier exhibition entitled, Vandals and Enthusiasts, and Curator of Manuscripts at the National Art Library of the Victoria and Albert Museum is one of the authors and has been both a source of inspiration and a project advocate. He has been a pleasure to work with. So too, has the staff of the Pierpont Morgan Library in New York. Special thanks should be given to Roger Wieck, Curator, Medieval and Renaissance Manuscripts and William Voelkle, Curator of Medieval and Renaissance Manuscripts and department head. Russell Maylone, Curator of the Charles Deering McCormick Library of Special Collections at Northwestern University, has been a great friend of the museum and a true collaborator on this and other projects. He brings to the students, faculty and indeed all who do research at the university an immense and diverse resource from which to work. His knowledge of the collections and his desire to lend, share and collaborate are, and should be, renowned.

As with all of the exhibitions at the Block Museum of Art, a cacophony of patrons and friends have come together in support of a clearly extraordinary project with far-ranging impact. Early in the life of this project the National Endowment for the Arts, the Illinois Humanities Council and the Elizabeth F. Cheney Foundation provided needed support for travel, research and the beginning stages of the organization of the exhibition and book. Their wisdom and perseverance has been much appreciated. The Illinois Arts Council, a state agency, the Institute of Museum and Library Services, a federal agency and the Friends of the Mary and Leigh Block Museum of Art have provided additional support. Within Northwestern, this project could not have come to fruition without the assistance of President Henry Bienen, Provost Larry Dumas and Associate Provost Jean Shedd, the Judd A. and Marjorie Weinberg College of Arts and Sciences, Eric Sundquist, Dean, and the Department of Art History Chair, Hollis Clayson. Their support for all aspects of this project as well as for the collaboration between the museum and the art history department is of profound importance to this project and to future ones.

Presenting all phases of this project has been no small feat. The implementation of MIMA, as it has become affectionately known among the staff, has been possible because of the curatorial, registrarial and preparatory excellence of many at the Block. Mary Stewart, Assistant Director; Deb Wood, Assistant Curator; Brooke Dierkhising, Program Assistant and Registrar; Carole Towns, Business Manager; Dan Silverstein, Preparator; Dabney Hailey, Curatorial Assistant; Jane Friedman, Curatorial Assistant; Adeel Abbasi, Caroline Luther and Barry Kardon work-study students and the numerous docents of the museum have all been an amazing team that has lead to the success of the multiple aspects of the project.

It is incumbent upon me to recognize the numerous staff members of the lending institutions who have so graciously given of their time and energies to assist in bringing *Manuscript Illumination in the Modern Age* to fruition. They are listed by institutional affiliations. Brooklyn Museum of Art, Brooklyn, New York: Arnold L. Lehman, Director; Ellen Reeder, Deputy Director for Art; Dottie Canady, Assistant Registrar; Carnegie Museum of Art, Pittsburgh, Pennsylvania: Richard Armstrong, The Henry J. Heinz II Director; Allison Revello, Assistant Registrar; Monika Tomko, Registrar; Kroch Library, Cornell University, Ithaca, New York: Elaine Engst, Director of the Rare Books and Manuscript Collection; Katherine Reagan, Curator of Rare Books; Peter Martinez, Administrative Assistant; Oberlin College, Allen Memorial Art Museum, Oberlin, Ohio: Dr. Sharon Patton, Director; Lucille Stiger, Registrar; The Billy Graham Center Museum, Wheaton College, Wheaton, Illinois: James Stambaugh, Director; The Charles Deering McCormick Library of Special Collections, Northwestern University Evanston, Illinois: David Bishop, University Librarian; Lorraine Olley, Head of Preservation Department; The Cleveland Museum of Art, Cleveland, Ohio: Dr. Katherine Lee, Director; Mary Suzor, Chief Registrar; Diane De Grazia, The Clara T. Rankin Chief Curator; Ann Abid, Head Librarian; Joanne Fenn, Associate Registrar for Loans; Larry Sisson, Mellon Fellow Objects Conservator; The Free Library of Philadelphia Rare Book Division, Philadelphia, Pennsylvania: Elliot Shelkrot, Director; William Lang, Head of the Rare Book Department; The Lilly Library, Indiana University, Bloomington, Indiana: Joel, Silver, Acting Director; Sandra Taylor, Curator of Manuscripts; Lisa Browar, Librarian; Jim Canary, Head of Conservation; Lewis Johnson, Conservation Technician; The Medieval Institute, The University of Notre Dame, Notre Dame, Indiana: Dr. Jennifer Younger, Edward H. Alnold Director of University Libraries; Dr. Marina Smyth, Librarian; The Pierpont Morgan Library, New York, New York: Charles E. Pierce, Director; Lucy Eldridge, Registrar; Isabel Romano, Assistant to the Registrar; The Newberry Library, Chicago, Illinois: Charles Cullen, President; Mary Wyly, Associate Librarian; Susan Summerfield Duke, Program Assistant, Library Services; Susan Russick, Director of the Conservation Department; Paul Gehl, Custodian, John M. Wing Foundation on the History of Printing; The Toledo Museum of Art, Toledo, Ohio: Roger Berkowitz, Director; Patricia Whitesides, Registrar; University of Chicago Library, Chicago, Illinois: Martin Runkle, Director of the Library; Dr. Alice Schreyer, Curator of Special Collections; and Sherry Byrne, Preservation Librarian; University of Michigan, Ann Arbor, Michigan: William A. Gosling, Director of the Library; Anne Beaubien, Librarian; Victoria & Albert Museum, London: Dr. Alan Borg, CBE, FSA, Director; Dr.Timothy Stevens, Assistant Director (Collections); David Wright, Registrar; Catherine Kurtz, Registrar's Assistant; Janet Skidmore, Assistant Curator, Department of Prints, Drawings and Paintings, Head of Access; Iain K. Slessor, Deputy Security Adviser; Martin Durrant, Picture Library; and anonymous private lenders.

To all we say thanks!

DAVID MICKENBERG
*Director*
Mary and Leigh Block Museum of Art
Northwestern University

## LIST OF LENDERS

ALLEN MEMORIAL ART MUSEUM
Oberlin College
Oberlin, Ohio

THE BILLY GRAHAM CENTER MUSEUM
Wheaton College
Wheaton, Illinois

BROOKLYN MUSEUM OF ART
Brooklyn, New York

CARNEGIE MUSEUM OF ART
Pittsburgh, Pennsylvania

THE CHARLES DEERING MCCORMICK LIBRARY OF SPECIAL
COLLECTIONS
Northwestern University
Evanston, Illinois

THE CLEVELAND MUSEUM OF ART
Cleveland, Ohio

DIVISION OF RARE AND MANUSCRIPT COLLECTIONS
Cornell University Library
Ithaca, New York

THE LILLY LIBRARY
Indiana University
Bloomington, Indiana

THE NEWBERRY LIBRARY
Chicago, Illinois

THE PIERPONT MORGAN LIBRARY
New York, New York

RARE BOOK DEPARTMENT, THE FREE LIBRARY OF PHILADELPHIA
Philadelphia, Pennsylvania

THE TOLEDO MUSEUM OF ART
Toledo, Ohio

UNIVERSITY OF CHICAGO LIBRARY
Chicago, Illinois

UNIVERSITY LIBRARIES OF NOTRE DAME
Department of Special Collections
Notre Dame, Indiana

UNIVERSITY OF MICHIGAN LIBRARY
Ann Arbor, Michigan

VICTORIA & ALBERT MUSEUM
London

ANONYMOUS PRIVATE COLLECTORS

**FIGURES**

**PLATES**

1. Bury St. Edmunds Monastery, Scenes from the Life of Christ, single leaf from a Bible or psalter (England, twelfth century). New York: The Pierpont Morgan Library, M. 521.

2. Giulio Clovio, miniatures of Evangelists and decoration (Italy, sixteenth century); montage of fragments from Sistine Chapel choir books (nineteenth century). New York: The Pierpont Morgan Library, M. 270.

3. Simon Marmion, miniature of Virgin and Child (France, late fifteenth century); Attavante Attavanti, decorative border (Italy, early sixteenth century); montage of fragments (nineteenth century). Toledo, Ohio: The Toledo Museum of Art, Frederick B. and Kate L. Shoemaker Fund, 1939.501.

4. Don Silvestro dei Gherarducci, historiated initial C, cutout fragment from a gradual of San Michele a Murano, Venice (Florence, 1392–99). London: The Victoria and Albert Museum, PDP, 431.

5. Scenes from the Life of St. Bartholomew (Hungary, circa 1300–50), miniatures cut and reconfigured in an album. New York: The Pierpont Morgan Library, M.360, folio 20.

6. *The Woman Clothed with the Sun and the Dragon* (Lorraine, France, circa 1295), cutout fragment formerly in the Burckhardt-Wildt Album. Cleveland, Ohio: The Cleveland Museum of Art. Purchase John L. Severance Fund 1983.73.2a.

7. Historiated initials from a pocket Bible (France, circa 1250),assembled as a montage (nineteenth century). London: The Victoria and Albert Museum, PDP, E.2126-1909 to 2141-1909.

8. Master of the Geneva Latini or follower, the Annunciation and Adoration of the Magi (Rouen, 1480), miniatures; Niccolo da Bologna, heads in frames (Bologna, 1370); assembled as a montage (by O. Du Sartel [?], Paris [?], circa 1880). Private collection.

9. Henry Shaw, copy of a leaf from the *Howard Psalter* (BL Arundel MS 83, folio 14). (London, early 1860s). London: The Victoria and Albert Museum, PDP, 5863.

10. Initial R (nineteenth century), copied from a fifteenth-century choir book of San Marco (Florence: Museo di San Marco, Graduale B, inv. 516, c.3). London: The Victoria and Albert Museum, PDP, E.120-1996.

11. L with iris and butterfly from *Model Alphabet Book for Illuminators* (Paris, circa 1500 [?]). Baltimore: The Walters Art Gallery, W. 200, folio 17v.

12. Ernesto Sprega, historiated initial C with St. Lawrence and two angels (Siena, circa 1863). Copied from a fifteenth-century Siena choir book illuminated by Liberale da Verona. London: The Victoria and Albert Museum, PDP, 4596.

13. Ernesto Sprega, historiated initial L with the Miracle of the Loaves and Fishes (Siena, circa 1836), copied from a fifteenth-century Siena choir book illuminated by Liberale da Verona. London: The Victoria and Albert Museum, PDP, 4594.

14. John Obadiah Westwood, tracing of the Apocalypse for *Illuminated Illustrations of the Bible: Copied from Select Manuscripts of the Middle Ages* (London: William Smith, 1846). Los Angeles: The Getty Research Institute, 920003.

15. John Obadiah Westwood. Hand-colored proof for *Illuminated Illustrations of the Bible: Copied from Select Manuscripts of the Middle Ages* (London: William Smith, 1846). Los Angeles: The Getty Research Institute, 920003.

16. Caleb William Wing, historiated D, Christ calling Peter and Paul, copied from a north Italian choir book of the 1470s or 1480s (England, nineteenth century). London: The Victoria and Albert Museum, PDP, 4950.

17. Jean-François-Auguste Bastard d'Estang, *Peintures et ornements des manuscrits* (Paris: privately printed, 1837–46), "Ecritures dites visigothiques," chromolithographed plate. Fasc. 6, MSS Francais, VIIIe S (2e moitie) (texte latin).

18. Paul Lacroix, *Sciences et lettres au moyen âge et à l'époque de la renaissance* (Paris: Firmin-Didot, 1877), frontispiece and title page.

19. H. Bichard, copy of a circa 1527 illumination of Henri d'Albret, roi de Navarre, in BnF l'Arsenal MS 5096, folio 1 (France, nineteenth century). Private collection.

20. George Beck, St. Ulrich and St. Afra miniature (Augsburg, 1494–45), from a psalter, removed and overpainted (England [?], nineteenth century). London: The Victoria and Albert Museum, PDP, D.86-1892. 157

21. Spanish Forger, Seated Ruler with Two Women and a Standing Saint (France, nineteenth century). New York: The Pierpont Morgan Library, M.786c.

22. Garcia, watercolor copy of a fifteenth-century Burgundian manuscript (France, nineteenth century). Paris, private collection.

23. Owen Jones, preparatory artwork for the *The Victoria Psalter* (London, circa 1861). London: The Victoria and Albert Museum, NAL, L.458-1952.

24. Charles Fairfax Murray, portrait of William Morris, title page in *A Book of Verse*, by William Morris and others (London, 1870). London: The Victoria and Albert Museum, MSL 1953/131.

25. Lord Charles Thynne, Crucifixion, copied from the tenth- or eleventh-century *Beauvais Sacramentary* (England, before 1865). London: The Victoria and Albert Museum, PDP, 4392.

26. Augustus Welby Northmore Pugin, "The Shrine," illuminated page with list of reliquaries (England, 1832). London: The Victoria and Albert Museum, MSL 1961/5179.

27. Augustus Welby Northmore Pugin, "St. Margaret's Chapel" (England, 1833). London: The Victoria and Albert Museum, MSL 1969/5176.

28. James Orr Marples, illuminated address presented to Mrs. Matilda Madden (Liverpool, 1900). London: The Victoria and Albert Museum, MSL/1985/15.

29. Phoebe Traquaire, *The Dream* (Edinburgh, 1886–87). London: The Victoria and Albert Museum, 1936/1765, folio 2r.

30. Nuns of Maredret, Nuptial Mass (Belgium, 1914–15). New York: The Pierpont Morgan Library, MS M. 658, folios 9v–10r.

31. Illuminated leaf from a fifteenth-century Book of Hours affixed to the inside back cover of O. A. Bierstadt, *The Library of Robert Hoe* (New York, 1895). Baltimore: The Walters Art Gallery, MS W. 795 a.

32. Simon Bening, St. Gertrude of Nivelles, from *Hours of Albrecht of Brandenburg* (Flanders, sixteenth century). Pittsburgh: Carnegie Museum of Art, Bequest of Howard A. Noble, 1964, 64.11.6.

33. Master of the Cypresses, initial *T* with Benedictine monks singing (Spain, 1430s), from an album bought in Spain in 1849. Washington, D.C.: The National Gallery of Art, Rosenwald Collection. no. B23, 759.

34. Adoration of the Christ Child (Tours, France, circa 1480–90). Wheaton, Ill.: The Billy Graham Center Museum, 1290-2.

35. Bartholomaeus Horn, *Kurtze Unterweissung artlichs annd andeutlichs Schreibens* (Holy Roman Empire, late sixteenth to early seventeenth centuries). Chicago: The Newberry Library, Wing MS ZW 547.H782, folio 2v.

36. Caleb William Wing, Nativity from a book of miniatures (England, circa 1858). Bloomington, Ind.: The Lilly Library, Ricketts MSS 140, folio 9r.

37. Coella Lindsay Ricketts, copy of the *Book of Kells* (United States, late nineteenth to early twentieth centuries). Bloomington, Ind.: The Lilly Library, MS Ricketts MSS III, "The Book."

38. Coella Lindsay Ricketts, illuminated manuscript celebrating the seventieth birthday of Anton Hesing (United States, 1893). Chicago: The Newberry Library, Wing MS fZW 883. R42, folio 11r.

This publication commemorates an exhibition organized by the Mary and Leigh Block Museum at Northwestern University and presented in January 2001. Although in the past decade a large number of highly successful exhibitions have been devoted to manuscript illumination of different periods, there has never been an exhibition dealing with the rise of the appreciation of manuscript illumination in the modern age. By providing the prehistory of the contemporary interest in illumination, our exhibition seeks to address troubling questions that have gone largely unanswered for audiences of modern-day exhibitions: Why is this illumination cut from the page? Why is this page cut from the book? Why is this illumination pasted in another book? Or made into a collage? By whom? When? What about fakes and forgeries? Reproductions? Facsimiles? Remakes? Can we tell the difference? Were "they" aware of the difference? Many of these questions confront head-on the modern anxiety that museums—and, as a result, their public—sometimes display concerning the status of the "original."

Some of these issues were addressed in an exhibition by Rowan Watson, *Vandals and Enthusiasts.* That show, comprising 94 objects from the Victoria and Albert Museum, was held at that museum in winter 1995 and accompanied by a desktop-published catalogue, *Vandals and Enthusiasts Views of Illumination in the Nineteenth Century: An Exhibition Held in the Henry Cole Wing of the Victoria and Albert Museum 31 January–30 April 1995.* About half those works of art are included in the present exhibition. However, in this exhibition, they are accompanied by a large number of additional works, mostly from the United States, totaling 93 objects from European and American public collections.

The four authors who created this book had considerable intellectual input in all its parts; thus, individual authors are not cited for each chapter. Nevertheless, the division of labor can be summarized: The introduction was written by Michael Camille, Sandra Hindman, and Nina Rowe. Camille and Hindman, aided, especially in chapter 3, by Rowan Watson, are the primary authors of chapters 1, 2, and 3. ("Curiosities," "Specimens" and Reproductions). Chapter 4 (Revivals) was written by Watson, and chapter 5 (Reconstructions) by Rowe, who was also responsible for the bibliography. Christine Geisler Andrews, David Areford, and Rowe compiled the checklist, the lists of figures, and the notes. Without the active participation of graduate students, beginning in a seminar in 1996 cotaught by Camille and Hindman, the project would not have achieved its final form in the text presented here.

We are grateful to David Mickenberg, the director of the Mary and Leigh Block Museum, whose enthusiastic support of the project never waned and without whose support the project would not appear in its present form. We also thank Block Gallery interns Christine Geisler Andrews, David Areford, Jane Friedman, and Elizabeth Seaton, who worked efficiently in successive years on this project.

Other individuals deserving thanks include François Avril, Alice Beckwith, Christopher De Hamel, Roland Folter, Paul Gehl, Russell Maylone, Myra Orth, Lilian Randall, Saundra Taylor, William Voelkle, and Roger Wieck.

1.

Ludger Tom Ring the
Younger, *Open Missal*
(circa 1570), oil on oak
panel

**Manuscript Illumination at Beginning of the Twenty-First Century**

Today, manuscript illuminations are familiar to a wide range of audiences. They are treasured in the world's great national libraries and occasionally exhibited as museum objects. They are collected by a small international elite that acquires them through a worldwide auction market and a tiny network of specialist dealers. They are the subject of scholarly research by experts in manuscript illumination and historians more generally. They are also reproduced in everything from greeting cards, films, videos, and CD-ROMs—available to mass culture—to expensive facsimiles that cater to a deluxe market.

However, four hundred years ago manuscript illumination was almost forgotten, and the objects themselves neglected. But not quite. A painting of about 1570 that at first glance might seem to embody the triumph of panel painting over book painting is the work of the German, Ludger Tom Ring the Younger, who was active in Münster in the late sixteenth century (figure 1).[1] This tromp l'oeil image of an open missal, which makes visible the "Word of God" and whose text illusionistically reveals the incarnation of Christ in the "flesh" of the parchment (Luke 1:28–31), in fact shows the continuing power of the manuscript as an object well into the age of print. In a certain sense, this is a painting about the charisma of the parchment page. Likewise, four pages of engraved plates appearing in an edition printed in Ingolstadt in 1578, only a little more than a century after the invention of printing, constitute a remarkable attempt at the first facsimile edition of the great Carolingian manuscript *Prayerbook of Charles the Bald* (figure 2).[2] This edition suggests that there was much greater continuity between the handproduced manuscript and the printed book than has heretofore been realized. The story of attitudes toward manuscript illumination in the sixteenth and seventeenth centuries, merely hinted at by these two examples, still needs to be written. What our study explores is the historical trajectory of the recovery and reconstruction of manuscript illumination from the eighteenth century to today.

With the exception of the pioneering work of A. N. L. Munby's *Connoisseurs and Medieval Miniatures 1750–1850*,[3] this story is being told for the first time. Munby was a bibliographer and not an art historian, and his interests were

**2.**

*Liber precationum quas Carolus Calvus imperator* (1583), woodcut facsimile of the *Prayerbook of Charles the Bald*

predominantly with the collectors and not the objects themselves. His study re-mains indispensable since it lays out the English context of collecting. By contrast, our study is more expansive both geographically and chronologically, dealing not only with England but also with France and the United States. Our study is also driven by an art-historical interest in the material objects as repositories of memory and sites of reconstruction as well as cultural history—the politics of institutions that govern their potential recovery. Rather than being seen as a part of the Goth-ic Revival, or as a facet of medievalism, this material has its own trajectory and its autonomous history.[4] We envision the work presented here as a first step; it is a preliminary reconceptualization of a large body of material that merits much further study.

Manuscript illuminations have often come down to us divorced from their original context in the book, that is, not as wholes but as parts, and this is a crucial aspect of their history. Carl Nordenfalk first drew scholarly attention to this phenomenon in his exhibition catalogue of the Lessing J. Rosenwald illuminations at the National Gallery of Art (1975).[5] His fundamental catalogue lays out a model for treating the fragment as a part of a larger whole, the manuscript book. With the renewed interest in the history of collecting and connoisseurship, a number of more art-historical articles have opened up this subject for further reflection.[6] More recently, Christopher De Hamel has distinguished the vandalism and de-struction of manuscripts, tracing this impulse all the way back to the fifteenth cen-tury, and suggested that it fostered the appreciation of illumination.[7] Ironically, appreciation grew out of destruction. De Hamel's writings also bring to the surface a modern anxiety about the way manuscripts have been treated in the past that surely partly reflects his role as a scholar-expert for an auction house that promotes their sale in the present.

Roger Wieck and William Voelkle have recently traced a "short history on the collecting of single leaves," and Wieck himself explored this in greater depth in an important article.[8] Coming from their own vantage point as museum curators, they are concerned with a class of object—the fragment —particularly problematic for the modern scholar-librarian. The destruction and reconstitution of medieval illuminations are central aspects of their history, which we also deal with in depth. Usefully, they introduce the place of America in the narrative of manuscript collecting. Sharing many of the concerns of Wieck and Voelkle, in-cluding the incorporation of the United States in the twentieth century in the examination of this material, our study focuses not only on the collecting of man-uscript originals but the impact of their diffusion through reproduction.[9] From the outset of our narrative, which begins in the eighteenth century, we argue that the history of the reproduction of manuscripts is inseparable from the appreciation and collection of them as "originals."

Each chapter of our story takes as its title a word used by contemporaries to define manuscript illumination during the particular period the chapter describes. These titles collectively are redolent of the transformation that these objects un-derwent during the period covered.

Chapter 1, "Curiosities," provides an overview of how illuminated man-uscripts were viewed in the eighteenth century. The first section of chapter 1 deals with the antiquarian interest in manuscripts in the mid-eighteenth century, when they were used to define national, religious, and political identity differently in France and England. The second section discusses the collection of manuscripts in this period and examines the history of collecting in relation to the history of taste. In France, the powers of church and state held central positions in the construction of official history; England had already experienced its religious and social revolutions centuries before. Things medieval were thus already viewed with a sense of nostalgia and estrangement that did not emerge in France until after the 1789 Revolution. The final section of chapter 1 investigates the romantic views of Thomas Frognall Dibdin, whose eccentric bibliomania serves as a transition between the age of curiosity and the nineteenth-century age of the specimen.

Chapter 2, "Specimens," first calls attention to the status of the manuscript fragment as an object. The historical events that paved the way for this shift in status were the Napoleonic Wars and the Sack of Rome, which fractured the integrity of ancient collections and the books themselves contained within them. Curate-turned-dealer Abate Celotti and art-historian-amateur William Young Ottley in their collaborative landmark sales (1825 and 1838 respectively) attempted to market illuminations as specimens of Renaissance painting, concurrent with the rise of the history of art and its incipient periodization. The subsequent sections treat individual types of fragments and their reconstitution, which followed over the next decades: single leaves, cuttings, albums, extra-illustrated volumes, and collages. Our analyses of how these original specimens were collected, cut, and reconstituted through the nineteenth century culminates in the concoction of totally new objects by contemporary artists as "originals."

Chapter 3, "Reproductions," inserts the history of technologies of reproduction into the rise in interest in manuscripts during the nineteenth century. The first section covers a group of individuals—for example, Henry Shaw and C. W. Wing—who created modern illuminations that were handmade, exact copies of medieval and Renaissance illuminations in order to expand the canon of available "great" single leaves. A second section examines how the state sought to construct an ideal image of the French past using manuscript illuminations. Particular social groups, most significantly women, played a crucial role in this development. Subsequent sections look at how reproductive methods—wood and metal engraving, lithography, chromolithography, and photography—structure and present manuscript illumination to the modern public in new ways. By the end of the nineteenth century, the flourishing of a lucrative industry of fakes and forgeries, which constitute an entirely new category of "originals," is an index of the enormous impact reproductive technologies had on the status of manuscript illumination. Chapter 3 concludes with an examination of other new original forms, the gift book and the works of William Morris, which can no longer be described as reproductions or facsimiles—two modern forms of medievalizing books providing the inspiration for Morris's productions.

Chapter 4, "Revivals," turns to the morality of a specific milieu seen in terms of ideologies, institutions, and broader social attitudes. Focusing on England, the text charts the trajectory by which manuscript illumination became a discourse for negotiating religious tensions, as well as an agent for creating the politics of modern design under the influence of writers like John Ruskin. In the course of the century, manuscript illumination undergoes a radical transformation from being the domain of the gentleman connoisseur to being the medium of mass-marketed art practice. This chapter culminates with the role of manuscripts and cuttings in the wider morality of public education, explored through a study of a new institution specifically conceived to educate and edify a public, the South Kensington Museum (now Victoria and Albert Museum) in London, where illuminations were an integral part of its original mission.

Chapter 5, "Reconstructions," explores the early-twentieth-century American manifestation of the phenomena tracked in the first four chapters. The chapter examines the specifically American ways in which European fragments and objects were mediated to a New World audience. Traces of the idiosyncracies of collectors are more evident in the American material than in the European. Therefore, here we individually examine distinctive enthusiasts: J. P. Morgan, Henry Walters, Robert Hoe, John Frederick Lewis, and Robert Lehman. Chapter 5 then turns from the rarified world of the manuscript collectors to exhibitions and programs designed to use manuscript illumination to educate the public about the art of a distant and now alien culture. And, finally, modern illuminators in the United States are discussed. These individuals often found themselves catering to a market that had little historical knowledge of the Middle Ages but seemed to find illuminated ornament an appropriate and exotic adornment for commercial products ranging from calling cards to restaurant menus.

This study stops before the recent renascence of interest in manuscript illumination, which continues in our contemporary world. For example, the text does not deal with the powerful contributions of three or four generations of European and American scholars who have greatly enhanced our understanding of the production and reception of medieval manuscripts. Nor does the book cover recent public and private European and American collections and their impact.

The proliferation of high-quality photographic facsimiles likewise falls outside the scope of this study. Such a companion study would have to explore the shifting attitudes toward medieval illumination in different cultural contexts. An example of the transformation of a medieval manuscript through its reproduction is provided by the celebrated *Très riches heures* of Jean, duc de Berry, completed circa 1416.[10] When its famous calendar was reproduced in *Life* magazine in the United States on January 5, 1948, the February page was "doctored" to efface the genitals of the peasants warming themselves by the fire (figure 3). For the prudish, postwar, American audience, the licentiousness of the Middle Ages had to be censored. By contrast, in 1984 the more recent facsimile of the whole manuscript was marketed as an object reproducing every detail of the original with technological exactitude (figure 4).[11]

All technologies transform our perceptions and reconstitute objects of the past for new and different audiences. Because, in our computer age, the past is increasingly mediated through immaterial, electronically transmitted visual images, the material objects examined here take on an even more fundamental resonance, and strategies for their future circulation remain open-ended. New forms of visual communication currently under way—such as CD-ROMs, which allow us to turn the page virtually—are constantly reshaping and changing the way the past is viewed. But they also depend upon the past. Similarly, in this study the emphasis is on historical continuity. Manuscripts continued to be illuminated throughout the eighteenth and nineteenth centuries just as they were in the Middle Ages. Artist-publishers create new forms when they reproduce the fragmentary remains of old illuminated books. Advanced modern thinkers like John Ruskin and William Morris utilized manuscript illuminations in developing their ideas about the role of art in contemporary society. What links the manuscript book, the fragmented cutting, the gift book, the hand-painted calling card, and even the digitally scanned image of an illumination is a dynamic of recovery and reconstitution, a process joining past and present that is fundamental to all cultural practice.

**3.**

*Life* magazine,
January 5, 1948.
Reproduction of
February calendar
page from the
*Très Riches Heures*
of Jean, duc de Berry

**4.**

Facsimile of
*Très Riches Heures*
of Jean, duc de Berry
(Lucerne, 1984)

# ABBREVIATIONS

BIB. MUN.
Bibliothèque Muncipale

BL
British Library, London

BnF
Bibliothèque Nationale de France, Paris

BODL.
Bodleian Library, Oxford

BPL
Boston Public Library

CMA
Cleveland Museum of Art

FREE LIBRARY, LEWIS
Rare Book Department, Free Library of Philadelphia, John Frederick Lewis
Collection

LEHMAN
Metropolitan Museum of Art, New York, Robert Lehman Collection

LILLY, RICKETTS
Lilly Library, Ricketts Collections, Bloomington, Indiana

MORGAN
Pierpont Morgan Library, New York

NEWBERRY
Newberry Library, Chicago

ROSENWALD, LC
Library of Congress, Lessing J. Rosenwald Collection, Washington, D.C.

ROSENWALD, NGA
National Gallery of Art, Lessing J. Rosenwald Collection, Washington, D.C.

WALTERS
Walters Art Gallery, Baltimore

# Manuscript Illumination in the Modern Age

# "CURIOSITIES"

Appreciation of Manuscript Illumination in the Eighteenth Century

I n order to provide a prehistory of the appreciation of medieval illuminated manuscripts at the beginning of the nineteenth century, this chapter reviews the contributions of a selection of French and English scholars who laid the groundwork for a more comprehensive discovery of the Middle Ages. In the seventeenth and eighteenth centuries, notions of what was "medieval" were not yet well formed. Yet the research and publications of certain key scholars—antiquarians-cum-historians—during this period prepared the way for a richer understanding of the medieval period. The chapter also enables us to propose certain distinctions between England and France that remained pertinent throughout the nineteenth century, when the appreciation of medieval illuminated manuscripts evolved rapidly across many sectors of society.

Some research on the early appreciation of medieval manuscript illumination in France and England exists. Alan Noel Latimer Munby's classic monograph, *Connoisseurs and Medieval Miniatures, 1750–1850*, constitutes a basis for the study of England, but, as others have remarked, nothing comparable to Munby exists for France.[1] No comparative evaluation of the two countries

"[M]y history is better than other histories because it is more detailed and it represents a large number of images taken from originals of the same period as the events that they portray, from which we learn many things previously unknown, as much on history, as on dress, arms, and an infinity of other subjects."
—ABBÉ BERNARD DE MONTFAUCON

"[T]he engravings, which constitute an essential part of this work, are not the produce of modern invention . . . all the copies are made without the least unnecessary deviation. As specimens of the art of design they have nothing to recommend them to the modern eye, but as portraitures of the manners and usages of our ancestors, in times remote, they are exceedingly valuable."
—JOSEPH STRUTT

is available. Nor does any work focus specifically on the impact antiquarians have had on the study of medieval illuminated manuscripts. The most useful account that bears indirectly on this one is that by Francis Haskell.[2] While Haskell is not concerned specifically with the medieval illuminated manuscript, his claim underlies the driving conception of this book: "[I]f we are not unaware of just which pictures or sculptures or buildings were accessible to these and other historians, we shall often fail to understand the substance of their conclusions and hence the more valid theories that may be deduced from them."[3] The study of medieval manuscripts today has been shaped by the research of earlier eras.

**France**   The examination of early attitudes toward illumination in France is limited here to a consideration of four individuals: Jean Mabillon, Abbé Bernard de Montfaucon, Jean-Baptiste de La Curne de Sainte-Palaye, and Abbé Jean-Joseph Rive. Some of their contributions (for example, those of Rive) have yet to be systematically analyzed, although many primary and secondary sources are available. With the exception of Rive, who died shortly after the French Revolution, these men fit securely in the Old Regime, and they thoroughly subscribed to its traditional religious and political values. Mabillon and Montfaucon were much influenced by the Benedictine congregation of St.-Maur, in Paris, which spurred the leading scholarly reformation of the seventeenth and eighteenth centuries and undertook vast projects on the historical, ecclesiastical, and literary sources of Western Christendom. La Curne de Sainte-Palaye was brought up in the sphere of the monarchy, whose absolutist pretensions he wholeheartedly embraced in the wake of the turmoil French culture and politics experienced on the eve of the French Revolution. The four form a group whose interest in medieval manuscripts stems from the recognition of the role the Middle Ages played in the foundations of French monastic life and monarchical authority.

Each of these figures is a sort of archaeologist or excavator, uncovering widely diverse textual and pictorial sources. Together, they rediscovered a multitude of works from the Middle Ages long hidden away in libraries, and they disseminated these works in publications for a specific, if limited, audience. Their act of dissemination involved gathering and classification, as each treated the works as specimens of a particular subject—handwriting, French history, portraiture, social customs and mores, and so on. However, each, in different ways, either subjected these sources to a historical process that demonstrates increasing intellectual sophistication and scrutiny or reused them in telling ways that alter their historical validity. They were not discerning about the chronology of medieval art, nor did they prefer one period to another within the Middle Ages, and, again, this group antedates and is markedly distinct from what became known as the Gothic Revival. The vastness of the projects they undertook, which assured a kind of comprehensiveness—even if many projects never saw fruition in the forms the men envisioned—connect with the eighteenth-century encyclopedist tradition, which culminated in the work of Denis Diderot, although the secular, progressive spirit of the latter is quite distinctive.[4]

**Jean Mabillon,**   Brought up on the goals of the congregation of
**Diplomatics, and**   St.-Maur, Jean Mabillon (1632–1707) was one of its
**the Foundation**   intellectual leaders.[5] Admitted as a postulant to the
**of Medieval Studies**   Benedictine abbey of St.-Remy in Reims, after

short stays at various abbeys (St.-Niçaise, St.-Denis, Corbie, etc.) he ended up at the abbey of St.-Germain-des-Près in Paris, headquarters of the congregation. The Maurists were a reformed group of Benedictines with a history dating back to 1616. Centered at the abbey of St.-Germain-des-Près, the Maurists affirmed a strict return to the rules of St. Benedict, including compulsory manual labor, ritual recitation of the Divine Office during the canonical hours, obligatory observation of silence, and so forth. The Maurist movement is known primarily for its immense biblical and ecclesiastical scholarly contributions: its novices completed a six-year course of philosophical and theological study. Monumental historical projects they undertook include many sources still invaluable today, such as *Histoire literaire de la France, Recueil des historiens de Gaule et de la France,* and other such titles.[6] As editor of the collected works of two of the leaders of monasticism, Augustine and Bernard, and author of numerous other works of theological and biblical importance, Mabillon represents well the overall scholarly goals of the movement.

However, Mabillon's *De Re Diplomatica,* the grandfather of all paleography manuals, is wholly distinctive and is the greatest contribution that Mabillon as a diplomatist-paleographer made to the study of medieval manuscripts.[7]

Divided in six books, this work marks Mabillon as the "founder of the sciences of palaeography and diplomatics," the basic discipline of medieval studies.[8] The first four books of *De Re Diplomatica* mainly concern the study and classification of charters: book 1, how to determine their authenticity; book 2, their external characteristics; book 3, the authenticity and authority of Charlemagne's and Dagobert's charters; book 4, French royal palaces. Book 5 presents a chronological paleography manual with alphabets of different scripts and engraved examples accompanied by identifications and sometimes transcriptions. Using additional examples, mostly of charters, book 6 explores some of the principles laid out in the first five books.

Book 5, on paleography, represents the fruits of Mabillon's voyages throughout Europe, during which he consulted medieval manuscripts, and his years spent poring through monastic libraries at the foundations where he lived and worked (figure 5). Various plates in his book bear witness to his study of the manuscripts of St.-Remi, where he was a novice; Corbie, where he was a monk; St.-Denis, where he was guardian of the treasury; and St.-Germain, where he ended his career, becoming official historian at the headquarters of the congregation (he identifies some fragments as from "nostro St.-Germanus"); as well as his travels to Italy, especially Florence and Rome. He chose texts that interested him for other scholarly projects: Bernard and Augustine, whom he edited; Thomas à Kempis (plate 15); and liturgical texts such as *sacramentaries* and psalters (he prepared a *De Liturgica Gallicana*).[9] He was not much interested in the visual characteristics of script in general or in the long evolution of Gothic script; the entire period from the twelfth to the fifteenth centuries receives only two plates, each with sparse commentary. He was extremely interested in the difficult charter scripts that marked the period of early French kingship—especially the Merovingian dynasty.

*De Re Diplomatica* has often been praised for the fidelity of its engraved plates and its comprehensiveness, and Mabillon for his systematic classification of different scripts and his lasting contributions to their nomenclature. However, *De Re Diplomatica* has not previously been appreciated as a kind of protoscrapbook or album. In it, as in many other works on medieval manuscripts by eighteenth- and even nineteenth-century antiquarians, the samples of writing are extracted—cut out—from their sources with limited regard for their origins in a parent codex.

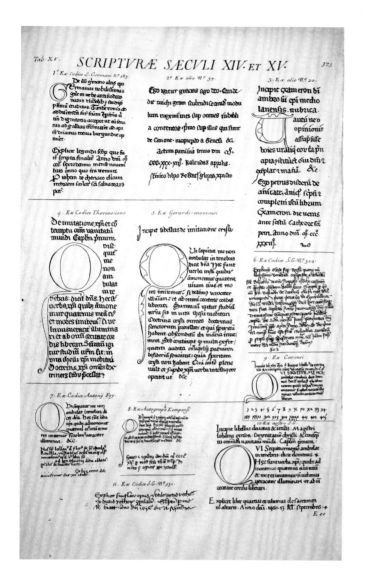

5.

Jean Mabillon,
*De Re Diplomatica* (1681),
tab. xv, page 373

6.

Pierre-Camille Le Moine,
*Essai sur l'état des
sciences et des arts en
Lorraine depuis le premier
duc hereditaire jusqu'au
règne de Charles III,
prouvé par les monuments*
(September 1761)

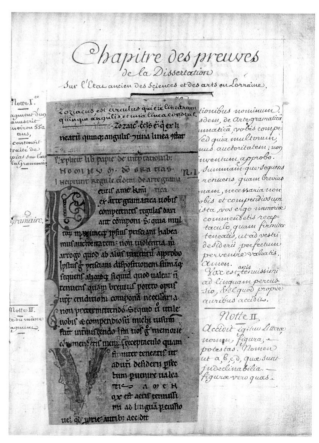

They are often pieced together on the surface of the page, in some cases even as a kind of collage (figure 5).[10]

The scrapbooklike effect of *De Re Diplomatica,* some of its pages awkwardly folded to accommodate specimens of special format, is more fully appreciated when it is compared with the actual manuscript scrapbook compiled by archivist-paleographer Pierre-Camille Le Moine (1723–circa 1789) in the eighteenth century: *Essai sur l'état des sciences et des arts.*[11] Archivist of the cathedral at Toul and author of the *Diplomatique pratique* (1765), Le Moine was undoubtedly influenced by Mabillon's groundbreaking work on charters in *De Re Diplomatica,* where Mabillon set out to provide a guide to the organization of archives. In the slightly earlier *Essai sur l'état des sciences et des arts,* which was never published, Le Moine used actual manuscript cuttings (probably taken from manuscripts in the cathedral library) as examples of scripts of different dates and as "monuments" that illustrate not only the regional history of Lorraine but also science and liberal arts, including "Grammar, Languages, Poetry, Dialectic, Physics, Rhetoric, Arithmetic . . . Music, Theology, Canon and Civil Law, Medicine, Architecture, Painting and Sculpture" (figure 6). As idiosyncratic as *Essai sur l'état des sciences et des arts* may initially seem, the work—in physical format and arrangement, language, use of cuttings, and classification—offers a manuscript analogue to *De Re Diplomatica.* Although it might appear that these scholars ignored manuscript illumination, they made a fundamental contribution in creating a scientific method with systematic tools to apply to the study of handwritten documents, including manuscript books.

## Bernard de Montfaucon and the French Monarchy

The idea of visual fragments of medieval manuscript material as *monumens* lies behind another great Maurist enterprise of the eighteenth century, *Les Monumens de la monarchie françoise* of Bernard de Montfaucon (1655–1741).[12] Unlike Mabillon, whose origins were modest, Montfaucon came from an ancient noble family of the Comté de Cominges; his father was sire of La Rochetaillade, a title he had inherited. Montfaucon was meant to follow in his father's footsteps, but, attracted to study from an early age, Montfaucon chose instead to become a Benedictine monk of the congregation of St.-Maur, like Mabillon, whom he knew and greatly admired. Before retiring near the end of his life to St.-Germain-des-Près in Paris, where he died and was buried, he spent many years traveling, especially throughout Italy, where he consulted numerous manuscripts; he published the results of his studies in his *Palaeographia Graeca,* a work that did for Greek manuscripts what Mabillon's *De Re Diplomatica* had accomplished for Latin.[13]

Montfaucon's corpus, *Les Monumens de la monarchie françoise,* betrays his own noble origins in its abiding interest in the Middle Ages as the privileged locus and site of origin for the French monarchy. Dedicated to Louis XV, who poses as an equestrian figure in the engraved frontispiece (figure 7), *Les Monumens* addresses the king as follows: "The reader will understand, Sire, that you follow in the footsteps of those who have merited public approbation, that you reunite in your person those virtues that distinguish them, and that you surpass them all in those qualities that characterize the greatest princes" ("Le lecteur s'appercevra d'abord, SIRE, que vous marches sur les traces de ceux qui ont mérité l'approbation publique que vous reunisse en Vous les vertus qui les distinguent, & que vous les surpassez tous dans celle qui caracterize les plus grans Princes").[14] Montfaucon claimed his written history was better than previous works because "it will represent a very large number of figures taken from originals of the time, which will

AU ROI.

S IRE.

*Le feul titre de cet Ouvrage eft un*
*engagement pour l'Auteur de le dédier*

*Louis Quinze*

teach things hitherto unknown as much on History as on the habits, arms, and an infinity of other subjects" ("qu'elle representera un très grand nombre de figures tirées des originaux au tems, qui apprendront bien des choses ci-devant inconnues, tant sur l'Histoire que sur les habits, les armes & une infinté d'autres sujets").[15]

The five volumes include 306 engraved plates, mostly full page, many double page, that comprise the *monumens* of French kingship from Charles Martel to Henri IV. Most of these representations are chosen from works roughly contemporary with the kings (and queens) they illustrate, and as many as half are taken from medieval manuscripts. However, in the prospectus he designed to elicit subscriptions, Montfaucon felt compelled to apologize for the preponderance of medieval images. He justifies the inclusion of crude medieval art from the barbarous centuries—a sort of entertaining spectacle—in the *interet de la nation,* contrasting *Les Monumens* with his earlier *l'Antiquité expliquée,* where elegant images from the more fashionable Greek and Roman eras appear. These statements clearly evoke a sense of the lack of appreciation of medieval art in Montfaucon's time. Even near the end of the century, around 1795, when Alexandre Lenoir's Musée des Monuments Français opened, this view of medieval art as debased persisted.[16] Here, the "Salle du 13e siècle," constructed with a low vault painted blue with gold stars, stained-glass windows removed from St.-Germain-des-Prés, and royal tombs, was criticized as the "damp, gloomy, ruinous assemblage of monkish horror," and one traveler wrote that it was "impossible to walk through this dark place of tombs without being seized by secret terror."[17]

Because of its poor reception, Monfaucon's *Les Monumens* was never completed. The project was meant to include four additional parts in more than eight volumes: part 2 on the church and its architecture; part 3, daily life, including dress, houses, games, and so on; part 4, war and duels; and part 5, funerals. In its proposed form, *Les Monumens* would have been one of the most comprehensive pictorial corpora of institutional and private life, extensively illustrated with images of the day.

**7.**

Bernard de Montfaucon, *Les monumens de la monarchie françoise* (1729–33), volume 1, frontispiece and dedication

**8.**

Bernard de Montfaucon. *Les monumens de la monarchie françoise* (1729–33), volume 1, plate 26, Charles the Bald presented with manuscript, from the Vivian Bible

In its final form, however, *Les Monumens* is a kind of chronicle of the "races" of French kings, a latter-day *Grandes chroniques de France* that appropriated many of the strategies of chronicle construction employed by medieval and Renaissance manuscripts. Between the royal dedication and frontispiece and the first of the images of Pepin is a *discours préliminaire* on the coronation of the first French kings. Illustrated with an engraved plate of the coronation of David copied from the *Paris Psalter* (volume 1, plate 1), this section records Gregory of Tour's account of the coronation practice of raising a newly crowned king on a shield. The sequence of images establishes a political program that flatters the dedicatee, Louis XV, who stands at the end of a long line beginning with King David and extending through the earliest French kings.

The subsequent reigns of the Carolingians and Ottonians, Lothaire and Charles the Bald, are illustrated with a presentation miniature from the *Vivian Bible* in which the secular canons present the book to Charles the Bald (figure 8). In the engraved plate, Montfaucon has transformed the image to suit eighteenth-century taste. But what is more interesting is how this image signals Montfaucon's relationship with Louis XV, since, as a Benedictine cleric, he was just like one of the secular canons as he presented his work to Louis XV. The large number of presentation images that follow, at least one for nearly each reign in *Les Monumens,*

is understandable not only because these are common pictures of the largesse of kings and the flattery of their subjects but also because they underscore the chroniclelike features of this work. The inclusion of illustrations of chivalric orders emphasizes further the chroniclelike character of the work as a testimony to French monarchy and patrimony: the Bourbon Ordre d'Ecu, the Ordre de St.-Michel, the Ordre du St.-Esprit, and the Angevin Ordre du Croissant are all present.

Nearly three-quarters of the plates in *Les Monumens* come not from the original manuscripts but from the copies of these sources then in the collection of François-Roger de Gaignières, whom Montfaucon graciously acknowledges in the preface.[18] Although not a Maurist himself, Gaignières was a friend of the elite circle of Benedictine scholars to which Montfaucon later belonged. Like Montfaucon, he grew up in the company of nobility: he was secretary-tutor for Henri de Lorraine, comte de Harcourt, before becoming equerry for Louis-Joseph de Lorraine, duc de Guise, then his aunt, Mademoiselle de Guise, who in 1679 named him governor of the town and principality of Joinville and had a royal pension bestowed on him. His historical interests were fueled by his study with Le Laboureur, a historian and genealogist.

Gaignières was not only an antiquarian but an assiduous collector who by the end of the seventeenth century had amassed a celebrated cabinet (*musée-bibliothèque*) of medieval and Renaissance high art and material culture. Described in 1713 in a guide to the city of Paris, the diverse collection included more than twenty-seven thousand items from the *bas siècles*—portraits, drawings of tombs, windows, and tapestries, paintings (Gaignières owned the famous portrait of King

John the Good in the Louvre), manuscripts and charters, game pieces and playing
cards, and drawings of costumes from the reign of St. Louis to the present. Notable for its conspicuous absence of antiquities and for its breadth as a pictorial
record of social life, Gaignière's collection contained many items we would not
think of as originals: a large number were copies after original monuments he assembled by visiting churches and monasteries with his manservant, paleographer
Barthélemy Remy, and his painter-engraver, L. Bourdan. Often these copies were
extracted from the larger context of the original monument—manuscript or sculpture—and reproduced in a different scale, but sometimes they were also transformed. The most famous example of transformation is the reproduction of the
bust-length portrait of John the Good represented full length. Thus, concern was
not for a faithful reproduction of the original but for the function the original could
serve as a document in the overall collection.

In 1710, Gaignières decided to assign his collections to the king, and
Clairambault, royal genealogist, took charge of negotiating the transaction, which
was completed in 1711 against a substantial counteroffer by William II, king of
England. Clairambault then proceeded to disburse the collection. The manuscripts
were divided between the Louvre and the then Bibliothèque du Roi and the
printed books between the Affaires Etrangères and the Bibliothèque du Roi. Many
of the portraits went to Estampes, while the costume portfolios went to Marly to
distract the king. On March 21, 1717, many pastels were sold, along with the
porcelains and the medals. Eventually, the Gaignières collection that went en bloc
to the Bibliothèque Nationale (Départment des Manuscrits et Estampes) comprised
2,407 volumes of manuscripts, 2,231 volumes of the history of costume, 31 portfolios on tombs and funeral monuments, 133 geographical cards, and 210 portraits.[19]

**La Curne de
Sainte-Palaye and a
New Pictorial
Self-Consciousness**

If Gaignières and Montfaucon appropriated medieval
imagery in a relatively naive manner, using it as transparent historical documentation partly in the service of
state, Jean-Baptiste de La Curne de Sainte-Palaye
(1697–1781) at midcentury represents a new, independ-
ent-minded approach toward medieval illumination.[20] As Haskell has observed,
when La Curne de Sainte-Palaye published images from a manuscript copy of
Froissart (one used earlier by Montfaucon), he remarked that "the painter had
confused the costumes of his own century with those of the times whose history
he was painting" ("le Peintre n'ait confondu les habillements de son siècle, avec
ceux du temps dont il peignoit l'histoire").[21] Such a comment throws into considerable doubt the status of Montfaucon's *Les Monumens* as a kind of real-life scrapbook of the French kings and queens. La Curne de Sainte-Palaye goes on to
remark that the painters of the Froissart manuscript were similar to painters "of the
old days who came after the invention of gunpowder and who almost never depicted the siege of Troy in their miniatures without adding some piece of our
own artillery."[22] These remarks are echoed almost verbatim in comments written
in an album of cutout illuminations (Paris: BnF, Estampes, D 1) from a chronicle
of ancient history, perhaps a Tite-Live, wrongly attributed to René d'Anjou as an
illuminator. The owner (one M. Dutertre)[23] wrote in the flyleaf of the album,
which he acquired on May 1, 1787:

The reproach that can be made about this painter-king is that he clothed his figures
in contemporary dress and used the Gothic architecture he had before his eyes to
represent the Rome and Carthage of Alexander, Augustus, and Julius Caesar in

Gothic monuments. He took even greater licence in his military compositions, where he placed a cannon from his own time . . . before the invention of gunpowder.

Le reproche qu'on peuvoir faire à ce roi peintre cest davoir habillé ses figures dans le costume de son tems et de s'etre servi de l'architecture gothique qu'il avoit sur ses yeux pour representer Rome ou Carthage dans les monumens gothiques sous Alexandre, Auguste, et Jules Cesar. Il a encore abusé d'un trop fort license dans ses compositions militaires en y placant du canon . . . avant que l'invention de la poudre en . . . sous son siècle.

These cuttings include an image of Notre Dame (folio 9) and a battle scene with cannons prominently displayed as ammunition (folio 6r).

La Curne de Sainte-Palaye's observation about pictorial anachronism, which the owner of the nineteenth-century album repeated, is not his only contribution to the field of medieval manuscript studies. He is credited with two other colossal projects, both incomplete at his death but both of which put him clearly in advance of his times. The first, a cataloguing project of the manuscripts at the Bibliothèque Nationale and other private and institutional collections, includes more than two thousand capsule descriptions.[24] They give complete physical descriptions of the codices, descriptions of the manuscripts and miniatures, original and later provenances, and manuscript comparisons. Too ambitious to serve as the official published catalogue of the collection, this project nevertheless signals La Curne de Sainte-Palaye's precocious interest in medieval manuscripts as sources in their own right. Here, he should be compared with his English counterpart Humphrey Wanley, who around the same time set out to catalogue the entire Harley collection of manuscripts in the British Museum.

The second project is his "Dictionnaire des antiquités françoises."[25] A guide to French society from the thirteenth to the seventeenth centuries, it includes articles on all topics, from fiefs and government to kings and nobility, medieval paleography, laws, finances, dress, money, and so forth. In this work, his scholarly interest looks forward to later English historical antiquarians like Strutt. However, his top-down approach, beginning with the highest level of state, remains characteristic of the French attitude toward the past.

**Abbé Jean-Joseph Rive and the Discovery of Illuminated Manuscripts as Objects**

History has not been kind to Abbé Jean-Joseph Rive (1730–91), born in Apt to an artisanal family of goldsmiths. He became an ecclesiastic, taught philosophy and physics in Avignon, and became curate at Mollèges near Arles before leaving these duties for Paris in 1767. Most of his career as a bibliophile, a bibliographer, and an antiquarian-scholar was spent as the librarian of the manuscript collection of the duc de La Vallière from 1768 to 1780, when his patron died. A self-declared "bibliognoste," Rive engaged in acerbic battles with many individuals such as De Bure, Le Long, Van Praet, and others. He seems to have quit his last position as the head of library of the marquis of Mejanes over irreconcilable differences, and he died of apoplexy in 1791.[26] Most modern sources, if they discuss him at all, criticize not only his difficult character but his inaccurate writing, faulty grammar, and awkward neologisms. Rive makes it into Munby's study on the basis of his impact on the history of collecting in England, where many of the duc de La Vallière's books ended up and where the paleographer Thomas Astle used Rive's writings for his work, *The Origins and Progress of Writing, as Well as Hieroglyphic as Elementary, Illustrated by Engravings Taken from Marbles, Manuscripts and Charters.* But Munby dismisses Rive as a "disagreeable, neurotic, quarrelsome man."[27]

With the exception of the attention Munby paid to Rive, the latter's fundamental contribution to the study of manuscript illumination has largely been overlooked. Rive breaks entirely with the eighteenth-century views of his predecessors. In 1782, he published a prospectus to attract subscribers for his projected *Essai sur l'art de vérifier l'age des miniatures.*[28] The seventy-page pamphlet announces a folio-format publication that was to include an essay, twenty-six hand-colored engraved plates from medieval and Renaissance manuscripts, and accompanying descriptions. Although the work attracted little interest and was thus never published, approximately forty copies of the engraved plates were made. Only one of these copies contains the handwritten, likely autograph, descriptions, written between 1783 and 1791, although the plates themselves must predate the sale of the duc de La Vallière's manuscripts, which figure prominently among the reproductions.[29]

Rive was a pioneer in two respects: first, his technique of cataloguing and, second, his awareness of the place of manuscript illumination in the history of painting. These points are clarified by the manuscript copy of *Essai sur l'art de vérifier* (British Library, MS Add. 15501), with Rive's notes on the plates.

Rive explains the purpose of his work, which bears primarily on the "Histoire de la peinture and de la calligraphie" in the prospectus: "to compare their different styles and degrees of beauty and to determine a part of the value of the manuscripts that they enrich" ("[D]e comparer leurs differents styles & desgrés de beauté, & de déterminer une partie de la valuer des manuscrits qu'elles enrichissen").[30] As an afterthought, he adds that the examples are also meant to touch on the history of "architecture, many other arts, customs, ecclesiastical, civil, and military dress, fashion, furniture, utensils, and weapons of the same centuries" ("[a]rchitecture, divers autres arts, des usages, des habillement ecclesiastiques, civils et militaires, des modes, des meubles, des ustensiles, et des instruments de guerre des memes siecles") and thus to furnish a sort of supplement to *Les Monumens* by Montfaucon.[31] As Munby realized, the explicit purpose of *Essai* is thus distinct from that of previous studies, which exploited manuscripts primarily as visual documents for ancillary fields or disciplines.

Equally distinctive is the list of instructions and questions Rive offers for the study of individual manuscripts—some of which are exceptionally probing even by the standards of modern scholarship:[32] Establish the author and text. Assess the physical attributes. Is the work by the author's hand, or a copy? If a copy, whom is it by and where was it written, and on what date? Is the date correct or incorrect? On what support is the manuscript written (the choices are parchment, vellum, human skin, Egyptian paper, palm leaves, linen or cotton paper, bamboo, silk, etc.)?

With what instrument is it written (stylus, *pinceau,* goose or roseau feather)? What color is the ink? What is the script? Is the scribe known as the writer of other manuscripts; did he sign the manuscript?

What is the reputation of the scribe? Who else employed the scribe? From what library or collection does the manuscript come before passing into the trade? Are there corrections? Do they derive from the author? What is the provenance? Does it carry armorial bearings or other marks of identification? Are there marginal corrections? If so, are they by the author or another "savant"; if another, who? Can this identity be verified? Has it been printed? Does the manuscript precede publication? What is the nature of the textual reading offered by the manuscript? Does it correspond with what we know about the author? Is the manuscript rare? If the manuscript is posterior to printing, is it unique? What is its cost?

Is the content original? If it is of an old text, has the style of writing been updated? What is the order of the books (for example, in a Bible)? Is it decorated with miniatures? By whom, when, and where were they executed, in what style, and with what pigments? Are the miniatures added later? What is their style? What is their *touche* (manner)? Are they highlighted in gold? Are they of the period, and, if so, how? Are they important for what they tell us of the manners and customs of their time?

Rive's awareness of and interest in technical exactitude with regard to the illustrations also distinguishes his work. In the prospectus, he testifies to the "most scrupulous exactness" ("fidelité la plus scrupuleuse") of his illustrations and notes that neither the engraver nor the painter were permitted the slightest variation from their models.[33] In referring proudly to the tracings taken directly from the originals, he offers to make them available to anyone who doubts the reliability of the plates. He further points out that the painter has added the colors with the manuscript models directly under his eyes, using the same colors and the same nuances. Several later publications describing Rive's work testify to the fidelity of the plates "avec une parfaite ressemblance à leurs originaux," as the *Journal de Paris* stated in 1783.[34] Such claims are not surprising to us, living in the age of mechanical reproduction, but they show Rive to be a long way from Mabillon, Montfaucon, Gaignières, and even La Cuyne de Sainte-Palaye, whose images are often fragmented, pieced together, out of scale, and sometimes startlingly modified.

Rive's assessment of what constitutes quality in art conforms with the tenets of eighteenth-century taste—especially his interest in the classical—and, in its more explicit statement of chronology, sets the stage for the early nineteenth century as well. Rive praised earlier and later art and neglected Gothic art. From the fifth century to the tenth century, he argued, miniatures preserve some beauty, especially insofar as they are still classical in appearance. Between the tenth and the mid–fourteenth century they are almost all *affreuses* (atrocious) and represent the barbarousness of the centuries when they were painted.[35] Only the later period, after 1350, was represented in Rive's plates. Indeed, the plates include reproductions of twenty-one miniatures from the fifteenth century, beginning with a miniature from the *Rohan Hours* (Paris: BnF, MS lat. 9471), then in the duc de La Vallière's collection (figure 9), and five miniatures from the sixteenth and seventeenth centuries, two miniatures from the *Salisbury Breviary,* others from René d'Anjou's *Roman de Coeur d'Amour Epris,* and still others from *deluxe* Pierre Salmon manuscripts.

Although Rive promised two sets of descriptions, one on diplomatics or paleography, the other on painting, only one set accompanies the British Library manuscript, and these appear to conform to the latter. Because of the brevity of the descriptions, it is impossible to judge whether Rive followed his own prescriptions. *Rohan Hours* is called "one of the most beautiful and richest manuscripts to

**9.**

Abbé Rive, prospectus for *Essai sur l'art de verifier l'age des miniatures* (1782), copy of John the Evangelist at his desk and God the Father with the saved from *Rohan Hours* have appeared in the fourteenth century" ("l'un des plus beaux et des plus riches qui ait paru dans le quatorzieme siecle").[36] The *Salisbury Breviary* boasts "cette superbe miniature," in a manuscript "of which there exist few or no manuscripts so magnificent by the innumerable quantity [of miniatures] and of ornament" ("qu'il existe peu ou point de MSS aussi magnifiques soit par la quantite innombrable et d'ornements").[37]

Sixteenth-century miniatures are said to come from "the good century of painting" ("le bon siecle de la peinture").[38] Mostly, with a few comments on style and quality, the descriptions function as labels, identifying the subject and sometimes giving the provenance ("from Gaignat to the duc de La Vallière, nos. 25–26"; "from the maison de Tremoille to the Duc de St. Aignan"). In spite of Rive's comments, the colors are not accurate, and gold leaf is not used.

Although nowhere in his *Essai sur l'art de vérifier* does Rive display an interest in the identities of the artists and their individual styles, a previously overlooked passage in his vitriolic *La Chasse aux bibliographes et antiquaires mal-advisés* suggests that he had an unusually precocious interest in the problems of attribution—a century before Morelli![39] Mostly an acerbic critique of the errors made by other scholars, *La Chasse* attacks Le Long for his description in his Bibliotheca Sacra of the Bible Historiale sold in the Gaignat sale and described as "painted on commission for King Charles V of France, and the painter who did the miniatures is Jan Van Eyck, painter of the King" ("peint par ordre de Charles V, Roi de France, et le Peintre qui en a exécuté les miniatures est Jean de Bruges [Jean Van-Eyck] Peintre du Roi").[40] He publishes the poem contained in the Bible (now in The Hague, Museum Meermanno-Westreenianum, MS 10 B 23), where Jehan Vaudetar, *servant du Roi,* takes credit for the paintings.[41] He then proceeds to point out the historical inconsistencies that make it impossible for Jan van Eyck to have painted the miniatures, and he concludes by stating that the manuscript "would have been sold at the Gaignat sale at a much higher price . . . if Jean de Bruges had really painted the miniatures in this Bible" ("auroit été vendue à la vente de Gaignat à un prix bien plus considerable . . . si Jean de Bruges eut peint réelement les miniatures de cette Bible").[42] In fact, it was sold for 399 pounds to the Dutch collector Meerman, who gave it to the Baron Westreenen, founder of the museum that bears their names. Although Rive drew the wrong conclusions when he suggested that the inscription might therefore be false, this passage confirms his interest in illuminations as paintings, or works of art, an interest that appears to be exceptional in France in the eighteenth century.

**England**        Bishop Thomas Percy (1738–1811) defined the antiquarian as "one who reverenced manuscripts," but early antiquarians in England were, like their French counterparts, far more concerned with monuments, coins, inscriptions, and the textual records of the nation and tended to relegate the pictorial products of the past to a second order of importance. Antiquarians were even viewed with disdain in many quarters as lacking taste and refinement in their search for the old. John Oldmixion, in his *An Essay on Criticism as It Regards Design, Thought and Expression, in Prose and Verse* (1728) was critical of rude and unpolished antiquarians and "dealers in records" such as manuscript illuminations for presenting "naked facts without Form or Order, without Ornament, or even Clothing."[43]

The study of manuscripts as repositories of art as well as literature was also just beginning. For example, Thomas Astle's *The Origins and Progress of Writing, as Well as Hieroglyphic as Elementary, Illustrated by Engravings Taken from Marbles, Man-*

*uscripts* and *Charters* of 1784 was an extensive early paleographic study of medieval manuscripts in English.[44] Yet it hardly mentions illumination at all, and when it does, the remarks are a summary of Abbé Rive's *Prospectus* with statements to the effect that from the tenth to the middle of the fourteenth century miniature painting was "very bad . . . and may be considered as so many monuments of the barbarity of these ages."[45]

Yet in other respects, England was in a better position than France to reassess the visual past. The establishment of the Society of Antiquaries in 1707 and the start of the first scholarly journal devoted to things from the past, *Archeologia,* in 1770 laid the foundation for a scholarly gentleman's approach to archeology that nonetheless had a far wider social base than in France. In 1807 the *Antiquarian Repertory* stated that "every man is naturally an antiquarian" and argued that "although it has long been the fashion to laugh at the study of Antiquities and to consider it the idle amusement of a few humdrum plodding fellows, who, wanting genius for nobler studies, busied themselves in heaping up illegible manuscripts" their study was in fact socially useful and could be practiced by "many social types, the clergyman, Man of Law, Statesman, legislator and man of pleasure."[46] How distinctive this view seems compared with the hierarchical attitudes toward antiquities in France, which were to be appreciated and collected primarily by the aristocracy.

In contrast with France, where the powers of church and state held such central positions in the construction of official history as in the cases of Mabillon and Montfaucon, England had already experienced its social revolutions and religious reformations centuries before. Medieval monuments were thus already viewed with a sense of estrangement and nostalgia that would not emerge in France until after the 1789 Revolution. Even more important, another more gradual but no less groundbreaking revolution—the industrial one—was rapidly transforming the English visual as well social landscape, creating a split between past and present, the handcrafted and the machine produced, that made it the seedbed of the Gothic Revival. This period also saw the establishment of major private and public collections of manuscripts and startlingly new intellectual attitudes toward manuscript illuminations as objects of both art and history. The two figures discussed here in detail, Joseph Strutt (1749–1802) and Richard Gough (1735–1809), were antiquarians who published groundbreaking works in this transitional period, influencing the next generation of scholars, collectors, and, in Strutt's case, the reading public more generally.

It can be argued that a previous generation of English bibliographers, paleographers, and antiquarians had laid the foundations for this new interest. Humphrey Wanley (1672–1726) was library keeper to the great collector Edward Harley, earl of Oxford, who in the space of ten years acquired twenty-five hundred "curious and rare manuscripts," including illuminated volumes. In the history of Anglo-Saxon scholarship and cataloguing, Wanley is well known, but in terms of the study of illuminated books, his letters and diaries reveal him to be far less interested in manuscripts as objects of artistic or national importance than in the role they might play in his patron's collection. He noted for example that on June 21, 1721, he showed Harley the *Lovel Lectionary* (British Library, MS Harley 7026), which has a signed miniature by the artist John Siferwas but which his employer did not purchase, "the whole being but a fragment, and the Pictures and Armes belonging to families not of his kindred."[47] This shows us how much aristocratic collectors were still seeking identity and continuity with their own family pasts and that librarians, such as Wanley, were more like elevated servants, bookkeepers rather than grounds-keepers, for the great lords. Wanley also worked as a librarian at the Bodleian Library, Oxford. One of his plans, although never executed, shows a new attitude to viewing manuscript fragments as documents. He "submitted to the Curators of the Bodleian a request to be allowed to remove all manuscript leaves used as pastedowns in printed books in the library so that they could be arranged to illustrate the development of writing."[48] While this might at first sound like a progressive thing to suggest, in current thinking it is not. Certainly it predates, by a remarkable span of time, the encyclopedic efforts of twentieth-century compilers of cuttings and pastedowns such as Otto F. Ege (see chapter 5), but it is by no means the desired way of dealing with these fragments today. It does not consider the book as a total historical object but, like the scrapbook approach of Mabillon and Le Moine in France, as a specimen that can be taken apart for its historical value. Rowan Watson has argued that "to remove a fragment from its binding is potentially to destroy the evidence."[49] However, considering that the Bodleian pastedowns remained unlisted until Neil R. Ker's *Fragments of Medieval Manuscripts Used as Pastedowns in Oxford Bindings with a Survey of Oxford Binding c.1515–1620* of 1954, Wanley was certainly ahead of his time in his appreciation of the intellectual value of the fragment—an aesthetic abhorrent to eighteenth-century taste.[50]

The antiquarian study of Anglo-Saxon language and literature, in which Wanley was also a pioneer, was a crucial impetus to the interest in images, since so many of the important English books of the eleventh century contained animated line drawings. One of the earliest facsimiles of a medieval manuscript was the copy of the Anglo-Saxon *Caedemon* manuscript in the Bodleian Library, Oxford (MS Junius XI; see figure 10), produced by Edward Rowe Mores in 1754.[51] It is described on the title page in Latin as designed to illustrate the manners, customs, and buildings of the Anglo-Saxons of the tenth century. In this, too, it presages a new appreciation of medieval manuscript illustrations as historical records, best exemplified in the work of Joseph Strutt.

**10.**

Edward Rowe Mores, *Figurae quaedam antiquae ex Caedmonis Monachi paraphraseos in Genesin exemplari pervetusto, in biblioteca Bodleiana, deliate* (1754), copy of miniatures of Genesis 5:9, the story of Enosh

Joseph Strutt
and Illuminating
History

The most important fact about Joseph Strutt that is not often emphasized is that he was an artist.[52] The son of a wealthy miller, he was apprenticed to an engraver and went on to become a student prizewinner at the Royal Academy, later exhibiting paintings there. In 1771, after being employed by a gentleman to make some drawings after manuscripts contained in the British Museum Reading Room, he resolved to make a study of medieval England using his own careful copies of details from illuminated manuscripts available to him in the newly accessible public collection. In a letter dated August 1, 1773, he wrote, "I would not only be a great Antiquary, but a refined Thinker: I would not only discover Antiquities, but would, by explaining their use, render them useful."

His first publication is in many ways an English Montfaucon in its emphasis upon royal representation and genealogy. *The Regal and Ecclesiastical Antiquities of England: Containing the Representations of All the English Monarchs from Edward the Confessor to Henry the Eighth, Together with Many of the Great Persons That Were Eminent under the Several Reigns, the Whole Carefully Collected from Antient Illuminated Manuscripts* is a slim volume reproducing sixty portraits of English kings from Edgar (A.D. 966) to Henry VIII.[53] Unlike Montfaucon, however, Strutt was careful to cite the sources for each engraving in a special tabulated index "for finding the Manuscripts mentioned in this book."[54] Moreover, he copied most of the illustrations from complete miniatures or even whole pages. Strutt also paid close attention to color, describing the exact shades of many of the garments as they appeared in the original illuminations. Strutt's text makes a real distinction between the engravings as "true" copies or "fac-similes" and the originals upon which they are based, though both are artisinal products of human labor. In this, he is typical of many eighteenth-century thinkers who were searching for optical truth, what Barbara Stafford has described as the Enlightenment distrust of "misleading appearances" and "the war against simulation" in a world of increasing "mechanical impressions, replicas and variants."[55]

Strutt's preface made clear that he wanted his readers to see these images as "useful—and pleasing to the curious, because these pictures are the most likely to contain the exact representation of the customs and manners of the earlier aera [sic] of our ancestors."[56] Like Montfaucon, he argued that "the authority [of the images] is undoubted since the illuminations were made in, or soon after, the reign of each particular monarch."[57] This assumption—that pictorial representations are an unmediated and more direct expression of the "real" than any textual document —has to be understood in terms of the vision-as-knowledge model projected by the Enlightenment, the rise of naturalism as the scopic regime of modernity, and a new interest in visual education through print and spectacle. Strutt saw his engravings not only as true records of past perceptions but also as models for future ones, providing artists of history paintings with proper, accurate sources for depicting the Middle Ages. He complained that "[h]itherto our artists have been extremely deficient in their delineations of early history."[58]

The documentation of historic dress was included in a list of objectives drafted by Humphrey Wanley for the foundation of the Society of Antiquaries around 1708, and Montfaucon had projected an illustrated history of dress that was never completed, but it was Strutt who many years later made this an actuality.[59] In *Regal and Ecclesiastical Antiquities* Strutt notes that, in the "statues and bas-reliefs of the Greeks and Romans," their "dress and customs    . . . become perfectly clear and intelligible to us," and his works document not just a royal lineage, as did Montfaucon's works, but the everyday life of the past.[60] Between 1774 and

1776 he published *Horda angel-cynnan; or, A Compleat View of the Manners, Custom, Arms, Habits &c. of the Inhabitants of England, from the Arrival of the Saxons, till the Reign of Henry the Eighth; with a Short Account of the Britons, during the Government of the Romans,* in three volumes reproducing hundreds of miniatures and details from a variety of manuscripts in the British Museum and Oxford and Cambridge libraries.[61] In the preface to the first volume, Strutt acknowledges his debt to "the celebrated Montfaucon." But he also makes a strange case for the logic of this method of using illuminations as historical records. He argues that the

total want of proper taste in collecting of antiquities and application to the study of them are owing to the ignorant errors committed by the unlearned illuminators of old MSS. and so far were they from having the least idea of any thing more antient [*sic*] than the manners and customs of their own particular times, that not only things of a century earlier than their own aera [*sic*], are confounded together, but even representations of the remotest periods of history.[62]

Echoing La Curne de Saint-Palaye's remarks around the same time about the lack of any sense of historical distance on the part of medieval artists, Strutt turned this lack into what he called a "lucky circumstance."[63] Aware of what Erwin Panofsky later was to call the "principle of disjunction," Strutt made the sophisticated argument that these very anachronisms enabled the modern observer to see "the undoubted characteristics of the customs of that period in which each illuminator or designer lived."[64] *A Compleat View* was like a view through a picture window onto the medieval world.

Strutt was aware that art had a history and that styles changed over time, although in tune with most of his contemporaries he saw this development as a single ascending line rising toward the Vasarian heights of Italian High Renaissance painting. To the third volume of *A Compleat View,* Strutt appended "A short account of the rise and progress of the art of design in England."[65] This reveals his inability to deal with or appreciate earlier medieval styles of manuscript painting, such as the Evangelist portraits in the eighth-century Lindisfarne Gospels. According to Strutt's account, "in these rude and ancient delineations we find no great idea of grace, nor the least mark of genius besides the evident disproportion."[66] He could only admire this art when it came closest to his own classical tastes in folds of drapery and delicate William Blake–like colors, such as in the marginal drawings of Matthew Paris, "an accurate and ingenious designer as well as a great and faithful historian."[67] He also admired, precisely because they were subtle wash drawings rather than fully illuminated, the marginal images in the *Queen Mary Psalter* (British Library, MS Royal 19 B. XV), as demonstrated by a series of manuscript notes preserved in Oxford in a volume belonging to Francis Douce (Bodleian Library, MS Douce e. 18) and called by him "Mr. Strutt's account of the Mss. that have illuminations, as they occur in various English libraries." Strutt here describes the famous psalter as "a very beautiful ms. with many curious drawings relative to ancient habits."[68]

In his next publications, the two large quarto volumes of *The Chronicle of England,* published in 1777 and 1778, Strutt went even further in "improving" the figures that he copied from his manuscript sources, making Anglo-Saxons appear as classical figures in a pastoral idyll.[69] Because of lack of funds and support, only two of the six volumes originally planned for the survey of English history were ever completed. Strutt's subsequent influence rests on two later works, published toward the end of his life on his return to London after a period of financial difficulty, bad health, and forced seclusion—*Dresses and Habits of the English People* (1796–99) and *Sports and Pastimes of the People of England* (1801), both of which claimed to reproduce exact copies from the original sources.[70] But Strutt isolates miniatures and even single objects from medieval miniatures and makes a kind of specimenlike layout of them, cutting out a Saxon mantle from one manuscript and laying it like a vignette at the bottom of the page, where he reproduces the calendar scene from another manuscript (see plate 5 in *Dresses and Habits*). Even more remarkable is the "collage" entitled *Funereal Habits and Saxon Ornaments,* which Strutt engraved from isolated details of Anglo-Saxon crowns and hats that he laid out in a concocted composition using sleeping figures from other manuscripts and encasing the whole lot in a frame made of twelfth-century-looking dragons (figure 11). In this respect, he was doing in the simulacral realm of print what some collectors were to do a decade or so later to actual manuscripts—cutting them up and pasting them into new collages more compatible with their own contemporary tastes (see chapter 2).

Even when he does not fragment miniatures, he redeploys them. For example, with the famous image from Matthew Paris's chronicle (British Library, MS Royal 14 CVII) showing the monk-artist outside the border kneeling before a vast seated Virgin and Child, Strutt eliminated the figure of Matthew entirely and desacralized the image so that the caption states "A Queen of the 13th century in her habit of state" (figures 12 and 13). England's Protestantism had enormous influence on the way the "popish" past was filtered down, and Strutt's de-Catholicizing of the Middle Ages was crucial to his success. Although Strutt always emphasized the accuracy of his engravings, stating that they "are faithfully copied from the originals, without additional folds being made to the draperies or the least deviation from the form of the garments" (reminiscent of Rive's remarks on the accuracy of plates in his *Essai*), he confessed to "grouping them as pleasingly as the nature of the subject would admit."[71] This peculiar interest in both exactitude and refashioning is seen in the Matthew Paris reproduction, which belies the still-strong Italianate fashion that permeated English taste in the late eighteenth century. Strutt turned Matthew Paris's Gothic Virgin into a Raphael Madonna. But Strutt's adaptations are essential assimilations of the medieval past rather than negative alterations.

Strutt reveals a new fascination with the formal features of medieval draftsmanship precisely because he is an artist, not only an antiquarian. In his chapter "A Short Account of the Rise and Progress of the Arts of Design in England," he describes something new—delight. He remarks, "I myself can look over these slight sketches with infinite pleasure, and though I am sensible how much better they might be made, yet I can easily discover therein the marks of an original genius laboring under a vast disadvantage, namely the want of better cultivation."[72] The Gothic Revival could never have taken place had not eighteenth-century authors and artists first gathered medieval representations and then fashioned them in their own image. Strutt played a crucial role in this, not least because his versions of medieval manuscript images, unlike those in French publications, were relatively inexpensive.[73]

*Sports and Pastimes of the People of England,* according to Strutt's son, "attracted the notice and admiration of readers of almost every class."[74] His books were translated into French at an early date. Unlike the French publications of the same era, which were wholly concerned with manuscripts as diplomatic and scholarly objects, Strutt helped popularize manuscripts in the public imagination. Opening a "window onto the Middle Ages"—Roy Strong's felicitous phrase—Strutt selected illustrations that displayed all levels of society, the lives and habits of common rustics as well as kings.[75]

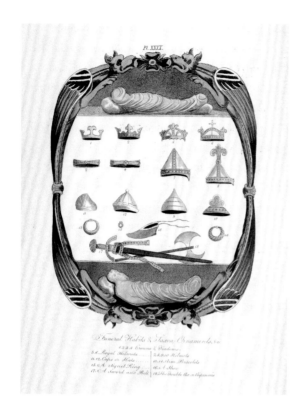

11.

Joseph Strutt,
*A Complete View of the
Dress and Habits of
the People of England*,
volume 1 (1796–99),
plate 29, "Funereal
Habits and Saxon
Ornaments"

12.

Matthew Paris,
*Chronicle*, self-portrait,
Matthew Paris praying
to the Virgin and Child

13.

Joseph Strutt,
*A Complete View of
the Dress and Habits of
the People of England*,
volume 2 (1796–99),
plate 44, "A Queen of
the Thirteenth Century
in Her Habit of State"

When, in 1845, the great French iconographer Victor Didron wrote the article "Miniatures in Manuscripts" in the second volume of the French equivalent of *Archeologia, Annales Archeologiques,* he stated that miniatures were like stained-glass windows on parchment ("Comme les miniatures ne sont que des vitraux sur parchemin)."[76] But the French scholar, writing well into the Gothic Revival proper, when forms themselves had overtaken history as the focus for fascination, was saying not that they were windows *onto* a past civilization in the Strutt tradition but that, in their transparency and light, they were like Gothic stained-glass windows. This shows how quickly Montfaucon's approach was superseded in France, which was never the case in England with Strutt's historicism. Fifty years after the publication of Montfaucon's *Les Monumens,* the work already had the status of a rare book—in the duc de La Vallière sale *Les Monumens* realized the same price as a fifteenth-century illuminated manuscript chronicle.

The democratic historicism of Strutt and his generation was to leave its mark on the different directions of English and French medievalism for more than a century and instill the notion that English medieval manuscripts are full of imagery that is "common" or "realistic" compared with the always more refined French "courtly" style. This view has influenced the way the history of manuscript illumination has been constructed even to the present day.

One aspect of Strutt's volumes that links directly to French thought is the encyclopedic tradition, demonstrated by his isolation of individual details on one page in an effort at almost taxonomic classification. For example, in the *Sports and Pastimes* volume, Strutt shows the different types of bows used in archery; this approach increases in frequency in his later works.[77] Strutt was here treating the things in medieval manuscripts as scientific specimens of natural history, which can be dissected and analyzed and compared with others of their class or genus in layouts that go back to seventeenth-century natural-history books. The whole effort is encyclopedic—bringing together from a variety of sources visual evidence from the past.

In Paris in the 1790s the only contemporary manifestation of the medieval past that was open to a wider public and that comes close to Strutt's magnificent series of volumes in its historical breadth and nationalistic zeal was not a publication but a place—Lenoir's Musée des Monuments Français.[78] Lenoir compared his museum to a book in which the visitor could read the history of France from sculptural and architectural fragments salvaged from the vandalism of the Revolution. Arranged in chronological order, these monuments, Lenoir hoped, would be studied objectively. By contrast, Strutt's creations were part of a cultural continuity, providing a comfortable link with "Merry Olde England," which helped construct it as a mythical era of social harmony and clearly visualized, class-stratified distinctions at the very moment of revolutionary fear and crisis. Whereas the French peasant was literally to tear Montfaucon's world apart, breaking tombs and burning the Gothic monuments of monarchy, including manuscripts, the English peasant, in Strutt's delicate little engravings after the *Queen Mary Psalter,* was put comfortably in his proper, medieval place.

As the first panoramic accounts of costume, Strutt's volumes were often reprinted and even plagiarized by subsequent historians, and they are by no means overlooked by medievalists today. Reproductions from them appear in history books published in the 1990s by historians who still, rather naively, like Montfaucon, think a picture is not only worth a thousand words but can be a view onto historical experience. Two centuries ago, both artist and antiquary felt no such qualms about making the past live again in images. As Roy Strong has suggested,

"A full-length book on Strutt is a desideratum, as he emerges as an influential but totally neglected figure in the history of art in Britain."[79]

**Richard Gough's Presentation of the Illuminated Manuscript as a Unique Object**

Richard Gough was a more traditional antiquarian, whose inheritance of a fortune as a young man, in the words of the *Dictionary of National Biography*, "qualified him for the labours of an antiquary, whose researches rarely receive adequate remuneration."[80] Educated but not graduating from Corpus Christi College in Cambridge, he was elected a fellow of the Society of Antiquaries in 1767 and was its director from 1771 to 1797.

Among Gough's numerous contributions to the study of English topography and history was *Sepulchral Monuments of Great Britain; Applied to Illustrate the History of Families, Manners, Habits and Arts at the Different Periods from the Norman Conquest to the Seventeenth Century* (1786).[81] Also an important collector of illuminated manuscripts, which he eventually bequeathed to the Bodleian Library in Oxford, Gough is the author of the first monograph in English devoted to an illuminated manuscript: *An Account of a Rich Illuminated Missal Executed for John, Duke of Bedford, Regent of France under Henry VI and Afterwards in the Possession of the Late Duchess of Portland* (1794).[82] As the monograph's title implies, this manuscript, like many in the opening years of the century, was famous not so much for its intrinsic merit as a work of illumination and calligraphy but for its association with certain elite owners. The *Bedford Hours* (British Library, MS Add. 18850) was created between 1423 and 1430 for John, duke of Bedford, regent of France, and his first wife, Anne of Burgundy, whose portraits appear within. Given to Henry VI in 1430, it later belonged to Henri II of France and his queen, Catherine de Médici, and was in England again when it was bought from Francis, wife of Sir Robert Worsley, by Edward Harley, second earl of Oxford.[83] This was when the portrait of the duke of Bedford was engraved by George Vertue to illustrate the third edition of Rapin's *History of England* (figure 14).

Munby recounts the vicissitudes by which the *Bedford "Missal,"* the misnomer by which it was known for eighty years (lot 2,951 in the catalogue of the Portland Museum) was sold by Skinner and Company in May 1786. At this moment, the manuscript left the curiosity cabinet for the library, purchased for the large sum of 213 pounds and 3 shillings by the bookseller James Edwards, who was an important manuscript collector of a new social class, "his majesty declining the competition."[84] But as Munby assiduously notes, this price was not extravagant, considering that at the duc de La Vallière sale three years previously, the *Bedford Hours*'s companion volume, the *Bedford Breviary* (now Paris: BnF, MS lat. 17294), sold for 5,000 pounds. This was equal to only one-third the price attained by a seventeenth-century manuscript, the *Guirlande de Julie* (Paris: BnF, fr. n.a. 19735) penned by the royal calligrapher Nicolas Jarry and with decoration added by Nicolas Robert.[85]

More important than the sale of the manuscript to Edwards was its becoming the subject of Gough's research. With eighty-three quarto pages and four plates, Gough's folio-by-folio account is careful to note the exact location of miniatures and even the subjects of the complex borders of this richly illuminated volume. The manuscript that was described in such detail by Gough was perhaps the first illuminated book to become a national celebrity through its sale, like the *Luttrell Psalter* when it was "saved" for the country in 1929.[86]

**14.**

**Richard Gough,
*An Account of
a Rich Illuminated
Missal Executed
for John Duke of
Bedford* (1794),
page 11**

But why did this particular French manuscript have such importance for an English audience? Intense hostility between France and Great Britain marked the early fifteenth century, as it did the late eighteenth, and here was a book full of images showing the English victorious over the French, made for the man who ruled Paris as regent and could hire the best artists of the time to portray him. Although Gough noted the hands of "various artists, probably French or Flemish," the fact that these were naturalistic portraits, almost like contextualized portrait miniatures, so much sought after at the time, is also significant.[87] The manuscript's value as a monument of art and a work of particularly English nationalistic concerns (with a veiled reference to the deleterious effects that social revolutions have upon books) is made clear in a note that Gough appended to a special vellum copy of his catalogue (with colored plates and costing an amazing twelve pounds, twelve shillings), which he presented to its less-than-noble owner James Edwards:

Preserve, Sir, this splendid monument of the arts in the 15th century, and precious memorial of one of the most illustrious in the catalogue of English Worthies; to remain either a heir-loom in your own family, or as a deposit in some of our national collection. And it may survive to the latest posterity secure from the ravages of Time, or the far worse havoc of Political Frenzy.[88]

When Thomas Frognall Dibdin reproduced the famous portrait of the duke in his *Bibliographical Decameron* of 1817, he criticized the earlier plate in

Gough's book as being "only in outline." He went on to decry the use of hand-colored engravings, which he considered "the sorriest possible representations of the originals." "Who, of the modern sons of men," waxes Dibdin, "could successfully imitate the delicate hues, the radiant colors, and the dazzling gold, of this wonderful volume?! The attempt would either be folly or madness. Therefore, it is, that one sober tint, either *brown* or *black,* is more satisfactory than the piebald colors of an indifferent modern illuminator."[89] In championing the minuteness and delicacy of his own engraver, a Mr. Lewis, who had executed the plates in the *Bibliographical Decameron,* Dibdin was also making an important value judgment about the superiority of mechanically produced, well-executed, but, above all, accurate facsimiles over badly illuminated, hand-painted originals. Another thrill that this manuscript gave Dibdin was that Mr. Edwards had obtained it "against the bidding of his present majesty" and that the latter was twice or thrice offered fifty guineas for it, which he declined. "To an Englishman" concludes Dibdin "the BEDFORD MISSAL is the proudest and most interesting monument existing of the early art of book-illumination!"[90]

That the dedication page of *Bedford Hours* was one of the most famous images from a medieval manuscript circulating in various reproductions should not surprise us, since the notion of noble patrons being dedicatees of books was still part of publishing. As Montfaucon had dedicated *Les Monumens* to Louis XV (figure 7), Strutt dedicated the first volume of *A Complete View* to "Her Grace Margaret Cavendish, Duchess Dowager of Portland." Gough dedicated his vellum copy of the description of the missal to the London bookseller James Edwards (later immortalized in Dibdin's works as Rinaldo, "the wealthy, the fortunate and the heroic"). This intermingling of aristocratic and nationalistic desire propelled English interest in medieval manuscripts in this period. Strutt had also announced that in his *Compleat View of the Manners,* "I present to my countryman the portrait of their great ancestors."[91]

No longer "curious" relics of the barbarous past, illuminated manuscripts both in France and England became, in the course of the eighteenth century, powerful symbols of patriotism and continuity in the present. In this sense, they were the domain not only of antiquarian-scholars, who sought to understand and explain them as objects from the past, but also of collectors, who through acquisition, possession, and appreciation began to view them as objects of artistic value.

## COLLECTING MANUSCRIPTS AND THE HISTORY OF TASTE

> There are only a few manuscripts, and these are really curious.
>
> *Les manuscrits n'y sont pas en petit nombre, et il y en a de fort curieux.*
>
> —CATALOGUE DES LIVRES, IMPRIMES ET MANUSCRITS, PRINCE DE SOUBISE
>
> I set little store by a collection of manuscripts.
>
> —LETTER FROM HORACE WALPOLE TO WILLIAM COLE

Since they were first made, beautifully illuminated manuscripts had been the prerogative and property of powerful institutions and individuals, never having much mass appeal when compared with medieval painting on walls and panels. There were a number of medieval "collectors" like Charles V (died 1380), who built the library in the Louvre, and his younger brother, Jean, duc de Berry (died 1416), who seem to have accumulated both contemporary and earlier illuminated volumes purely for their own delight.[92] But despite continuities such as this, the medieval book, after a lapse of three centuries, constituted a wholly unfamiliar and even strange or curious object for the educated eighteenth-century beholder. It was not so much that the texts being printed rather than copied were so different (people still owned

Bibles and prayer books as well as hand-painted volumes of various kinds) but that
the visual expectations of elite culture were totally suffused with a neoclassical
taste that relegated medieval images to the realm of the barbaric. Things Gothic,
often called "curious" in contemporary sources, must have seemed as "primitive"
and ugly to the eyes of eighteenth-century connoisseurs as did African tribal art to
the eyes of the nineteenth-century bourgeoisie.

The *Encyclopédie* explained the term *curieux:* "[A] painting enthusiast
*curieux* is someone who collects drawings, paintings, prints, marbles, bronzes,
medals, vases, etc. This taste is known as curiosity. Not everyone who indulges in
this is a connoisseur; and this is why enthusiasts are so often figures of fun, in
common with all those who talk about things they do not understand."[93]

Today, there is a great separation between books and other types of objects. For the most part, medieval manuscripts are kept in libraries, while paintings
and statues are in museums. But the word "museum" originally indicated a library,
and in the Latin dictionary *Orbis sensualium pictus* of 1658, the word appears with
an illustration of a man reading in a room filled with books.[94] In a dictionary of
1706, "museum" is defined as "a Study, or Library; also a College, or Publick
Place for the Resort of Learned men."

Many famous libraries housed, in addition to manuscripts, curiosity cabinets such as that at the Bibliothèque Ste.-Genevieve in Paris.[95] Here the book was
viewed as having unique and almost magical power, seen not as a work of human
artifice so much as a marvel. The *Wunderkammer* made all things equal and did
not seek to classify things historically, which is why the curiosity cabinet went out
of fashion in the second half of the eighteenth century as a new urge for order
and systematization took hold.[96]

**France**        Eighteenth-century France set the stage for nineteenth-
attitudes toward illuminated manuscripts. The story
turns upon three related phenomena: (1) the shift in ownership of a large number
of notable private collections; (2) the impact of the French Revolution on the
availability of manuscripts; and (3) the formation of a national institutional library.
The story does not stand entirely on its own but is linked to the history of the
contributions of antiquarian-scholars during the same period, as outlined in the
preceding section. These phenomena, together with the publications discussed earlier, brought manuscripts into the public domain more than ever before and, inevitably, changed the perception of them.

Significant private collections were formed and dispersed in the eighteenth century between the 1706 sale, by private treaty, of the library of Menars
(the former library of Jacques-Auguste de Thou, ancestor of the king's librarian) to
the duc de Rohan and the 1789 public auction of the Rohan-Soubise library.[97]
Between those dates, especially the years from about 1760 to 1790, sometimes vast
collections of French bibliophiles changed hands—Jean-Baptiste Colbert (sale 1726
to 1727), Chatre du Cange (sale 1733), J.-B. Denis Guyon de Sardière (sale 1759),
Jean-Louis Gaignat (sale 1769), Louis-César de La Baume Le Blanc, the duc de La
Vallière (sales 1768, 1773, 1777, 1784, 1768), Charles de Rohan, the prince de
Soubise (sale 1789), and Antoine-René de Voyer d'Argenson, marquis de Paulmy.
Most of these collectors are relatively well documented, and many have been
studied recently.[98] However, any serious account of their relative interests in and
attitude toward manuscripts within the framework of their overall collections is
virtually absent.

For England, Bernard Quaritch gives as an example of a typical eighteenth-century collector Sir John Thorold (1734–1815), whose library included many great first editions but who owned no manuscripts and no miniatures (the example of Francis Douce comes slightly later). But no such generalization exists for France.[99] Even though prizing certain sorts of printed books more highly than manuscripts, each of the French collectors included medieval illuminated manuscripts in his collection (although none is recorded to have owned single leaves or isolated miniatures). Nevertheless, none of these collectors can be said to be primarily interested in manuscripts, since manuscripts occupy only a tiny part—between about a half of 1 percent and 1 percent—of their overall collections: for example, Guyon de Sardière had 39 manuscripts out of 2,550 books; Charles de Rohan had 45 manuscripts out of 8,302 books; and the most assiduous collector of manuscripts, the duc de La Vallière, had about 200 or 300 manuscripts out of more than 32,000 volumes.[100] Not surprisingly, in sales throughout the eighteenth century, printed exemplars, sometimes on vellum and occasionally illuminated, were much more highly valued than manuscripts. At the sale of the library of the duc de La Vallière, the Fust and Schoefer Bible (lot 28) sold for sixty times the price realized by a thirteenth-century portable illuminated Parisian Bible (lot 25) and ten times the price of an illuminated chronicle by Jean de Coucy (lot 445).[101]

Nonetheless, certain common characteristics define this select group of collectors and their interest in manuscripts. For these men, all of whom have illustrious noble origins, manuscript acquisition was tied to class, lineage, and patrimony. These issues determined not only their ability to purchase but their interest in certain sorts of material, individual differences among the collectors notwithstanding. Thus, provenance was important—whom the manuscript was made for and who owned it previously—accounting in part for the focus on historical works apparent in Montfaucon, Gaignières, and La Curne de Sainte-Palaye. Belles lettres emerges strongly as a category, surpassing others into which sales were normally divided: in addition to belles lettres (2,150 to 4,467 items, or more than half the total lots in the duc de La Vallière sale), the categories are theology, jurisprudence, science and arts, and history. The categories reflect interest in the origins of a French national culture, not only historical but linguistic, accounting for the concentration on texts of French romance, chivalry, and chronicles. A focus on French sixteenth-century and later material over "Gothic" items grows out of historical perceptions concerning antiquity and the Renaissance, perceived as the centuries of culture opposed to the intervening "barbarous" era. For the most part, artistic merit—style and attribution—is of no relevance; rarely are the illuminations described from any perspective other than their documentary value, a characteristic that unites collectors and antiquarian-scholars. On the other hand, the interest in textual studies appears already to be relatively sophisticated.

**J.-B. Denis Guyon de Sardière and the *Eclarissements* of Illuminated Manuscripts**

The sale catalogue of the collection of J.-B. Denis Guyon de Sardière reinforces these distinctions.[102] The introduction to the catalogue underscores the importance of provenance. It recounts that Guyon de Sardière acquired many of his manuscripts at the sale of the Bibliothèque d'Anet in 1724, a collection that itself had a distinguished lineage going back to the royal line in the sixteenth century. It was initially formed by Diane de Poitiers, at the château built for her by Henri II; from her, it passed to the house of Vendôme; then, after the death in 1718 of Marie-Anne de Bourbon, widow of the last duc de Vendôme, it entered the house of Condé.

Finally, when Madame Anne de Bavière, widow of Henri Jules de Bourbon, prince de Condé and heir of his daughter, died on February 23, 1723, the library was sold.[103]

Manuscripts get unusually full play in the catalogue, which perhaps provides the most extensive published descriptions to appear in a French auction catalogue of that time. The introduction states that, since manuscripts are less well known than printed books, additional *éclarissements* are included to supplement the otherwise brief entries.[104]

Here, too, the interest in princely provenance is evident. Among the illuminated manuscripts are the Bible Historiale of Jean, duc de Berry; the collected works of Adenet le Roi, made for Marie de Brabant (Paris: Arsenal MS 3142); a copy of the *Roman de la Rose;* and *Les Voyages et les aventures de Charles Magius* (BnF, Estampes AD 134). The entry on Marie de Brabant's manuscript is typical. It gives the identity of the patron and her lineage: "Marie de Brabant, queen of France, and a lady named Blanche, whom Fauchet called a great lady [this was Blanche d'Artois, sister of the comte d'Artois]" ("Marie de Brabant, Reine de France, & une Dame nommee Blanche, que Fauchet appelle une grande Dame [c'etoit Blanche d'Artois, soeur de comte d'Artois]"). It identifies many of the texts, often with their incipits: *Les Enfances Ogier le Danois, Les Romans de Berrin et de Berthe a grans pies, de Buenon de Commarchis, Li Reclus de Moliens,* and finally *Les fables d'Esope . . . par Marie.*

The catalogue briefly discusses the texts; for example, "Guy, count of Flanders, commissioned this poet to remake the history of knighthood that jongleurs had falsified; to obey the count's orders, Adenet consulted the chronicles of St. Denis that Nicolas de Reims, a monk of that Abbey, had given him" ("Guy, comte de Flandres, engagea ce Poete a reformer l'histoire de Chevalier, que les jongleurs avoient falsifiee; Andans, pour obeir aux ordres de ce Comte, consultera les Chroniques de S. Denys, que dans Nicolas de Reims, Religieux de cette Abbaye, lui communiqua"). Or for Marie de France:

The fables were translated from English and put into French verse by Marie simply because she was French. She understood this translation, said Monsieur L'Abbé Massieu, for the love of Count William. We don't really know which Count William she was speaking of.

Les fables de Esope ont ete traduites de l'Anglois & ises en vers Francois par Marie, simplement parcequ'elle etoit Francoise. Elle entreprit cette traduction, dit M. l'Abbé Massieu, p. 158, comme elle le dit elle meme "Pour l'amour du comte Guillaume. . . ." On ne sait pas bien quel est ce Comte Guillaume dont elle parle.[105]

Although this deluxe manuscript—subsequently acquired by the duc de La Vallière, then by the marquis de Paulmy, before going to the Arsenal, where it is today—is illuminated with more than two hundred miniatures, the illuminations are not so much as mentioned in the sale catalogue.[106]

Philological interest also underlies the discussion in the entry on *Roman de la Rose,* which dismisses the miniatures that "only have merit because of their age" ("n'ont que le merite de l'antiquité"). Citing an eighteenth-century publication (1753) on the works of S. Evremond that calls attention to the frequent modernization of language in early printed editions of medieval texts, the entry goes on to note that in their transmission manuscripts also were modified—"Il a meme remarque qu'il y a des MSS qui ont ete alteres aussibien que les Imprimés"— and laments that "it is difficult to find among these manuscripts those that have escaped the indifferent diligence of revisers . . . who believed they were making the text better when in fact they were spoiling it" ("il est tres difficile d'en trouver

qui aient echappe a la diligence indiferete de ces riviseurs. Ils on cru rendre l'ouvrage meilleur & ils n'ont fait que le gater").[107] Compared with the sparse discussions of illumination, such comments on textual issues are relatively sophisticated.

As though earlier "Gothic" pictures don't count for much, illuminations
are described in the entries on later sixteenth- and seventeenth-century manuscripts: *Chevaliers de Ste. Esprit,* made for Henri III, and *Les Voyages et les aventures de
Charles Magius.*[108] The very inclusion of these manuscripts is in keeping with the
concentration on postmedieval material as well as on belles lettres and *histoire.* Yet
the comments focus primarily on history. The frontispiece is identified as "une
grande mignature, qui represente la disposition de la Chapelle ou ce Prince fit la
ceremonie de la premiere promotion de l'Ordre du Saint-Esprit." After a description of the portraits of the king, the entry concludes that "the calligraphy is beautiful, the portraits, vignettes, and arms and miniatures are well drawn and well
painted" ("[l]'ecriture en est belle, les Portraits, les Vignettes et les armes en
mignatures sont bien dessinées & bien peintes"). Occupying the largest space in the
catalogue is *Les Voyages et les aventures de Charles Magius;* the text states that the
"drawings and plans designate the locales, ports, and places he visited, which he
painted in reduced scale in 1578" ("desseins et Plans desdites Places, Ports & lieux
ou il a passe, qu'il a fait peindre & reduire en petit en 1578"; see figure 15). Three
and a half pages follow, describing all the pictures. Travel was a crucial aesthetic
and educational experience for the eighteenth-century gentleman, and this interest
undoubtedly had its impact on taste in manuscript collection. Charles Magius's
richly illuminated manuscript with its detailed topographies of Italian sites offered
a kind of grand tour in miniature.

**15.**

*Les Voyages et les
aventures de Charles
Magius, noble venitien
depuis que les turcs
attacquerent et prirent
l'Ile de Cypre sur les
Venitiens* (1571 [1578]),
plate 2

**The Duc de
La Vallière's
Cabinet des Rares**

The most celebrated French collection of the eighteenth century was that of flamboyant Duc Louis-
César de la Baume le Blanc de La Vallièr (1708–80).[109]
Great-nephew of the duchess of this name and last heir
of the ancient house of Touraine, he was exceedingly rich. He collected more
than 32,000 books.

In the first sale of his collection, 5,468 volumes were sold.[110] The second
part of the collection contained the less expensive books: an astonishing 26,748
items were sold en bloc by the bookseller Jean-Luc Nyon to the marquis de Paulmy. Abbé Rive, the duc de La Vallière's librarian of twelve years, found this portion of the library just as rare as the first.[111]

As it was constituted between 1735 and 1768, the duc de La Vallière's extensive library was housed in the château of Montrouge in the south of Paris. His
so-called second library, formed with the intervention and assistance of Rive between 1768 and 1780, was kept in the duc de La Vallière's Parisian hotel on the
rue du Bac. It became a well-known gathering place for intellectuals, including
such figures as Voltaire.

"Attach yourselves to parchments: demand impressions on parchment—
manuscripts and books printed on parchment" ("Attache-toi aux vélins: demande
des impressions sur vélin, des manuscrits, des livres imprimés sur vélin") was Rive's
recommendation to the bookseller Joseph David, a friend and colleague from Aix
from whom Rive presumably sought manuscripts for his employer.[112] In his role as
librarian-adviser to the duke, Rive most likely would have spoken the same words
to the duc de La Vallière himself, although it is not certain whether Rive inspired
the duc de La Vallière's fascination with manuscripts or, alternatively, the duke's
already formidable manuscript collection offered Rive an unparalleled opportunity
for a new field of bibliomania, which became the basis of his foundational last
writings. The former is the more likely case, for in 1759, long before Rive came
to work for him, the duc de La Vallière had purchased the collection of Guyon de
Sardière, which included many important manuscripts. However, he had not yet
made an impact at the Gaignat sale in 1769, where he bought heavily,
especially illuminated manuscripts, one year after Rive took over as librarian.

Estimates of the number of illuminated manuscripts the duc de La Vallière eventually counted among the books in his library range from two hundred
to five hundred, but there is unanimity on the importance of his manuscripts,
housed separately in a so-called *cabinet des rares,* apparently located on the second
floor of the duc de La Vallière's town house, not far from his bedroom.[113] *Cabinet
des rares* is an interesting phrase, suggesting that this portion of the duc de La Vallière's library, isolated from the rest, had a separate status in the library, which
Rive bragged was "the most curious in Europe" ("la plus curieuse de l'Europe").[114]
Precisely how the manuscripts were stored or displayed is not known, but the
idea that the duc de La Vallière had a sort of curiosity cabinet, a kind of museum
rather than a library in the modern sense, is reiterated in a nineteenth-century
review of his sale that notes he enriched his *musée* with major collections of
manuscripts, that "he spared nothing, not effort, pains, or money, in order to acquire [them], and in this period, sometimes called the golden age of curiosity,
such occasions were frequent" ("il n'avait jamais rien épargne, ni soins, ni peines,
ni argent pour à querir, et l'on sait qu'à cette epoque, l'age d'or de la *Curiosité,* les
occasions étaient fréquentes").[115] It is tempting to make the link between Rive's
use of the adjective *curieuse* to describe the library of the duc de La Vallière and
the unusual presence of manuscripts, rivaled only by one other collection in Paris,

that of Gaston de Préfond, which Rive did not consider much competition on the Parisian market, since the latter always tried to buy *a bon compte* (so cheaply).[116]

The list of the paintings the duc de La Vallière owned adds credibility to the view that his manuscript collection was a "curious" part of his larger private museum.[117] "Early" art is entirely absent; there are no Flemish, Italian, or French primitives, and very few religious paintings figure among the works, except for a group of three paintings by Cornelis Van Poelenburgh (1586–1667) and a Madonna and Child by Adriaan Van der Werff (1659–1722). The paintings owned by the duc de La Vallière include stylish French artists—Charles Coypel (1694–1752), Le Nain (1588–1648), Robert Tournières (1667 or 1668–1752). His collection focuses, however, on secular Dutch and Flemish baroque art: two portraits by Rembrandt (1606–69), three genre scenes by Teniers (1610–90), a genre painting by Gerard Terborch (1617–81), two landscapes by Philips Wouwerman (1619–68), and a genre scene by Jan Steen (1626–79). In the sale of the duc de La Valliere's paintings, those by Van der Werff fetched the largest sum but perhaps less because of their subject than their provenance, since they came from the illustrious collection of the duc de Choiseul, a fact noted in the catalogue.[118] In any event, the duc de La Valliere's painting cabinet reveals that, for this genre, his taste had little to do with the "Gothic" or the "curious."

Much has been made of the huge sum the books fetched at the duc de La Vallière sale, but less than a century after the sale the astronomical prices were already regarded as cheap.[119] Sale prices confirm the relative disinterest in manuscripts compared with printed books, the greater value of Renaissance and later manuscripts relative to "Gothic" curiosities, and the interest in history and belles lettres. Nicolas Jensen and Orosius had similarly high prices (680 and 336 pounds respectively).[120] A manuscript version of the *Chronique de Jean de Coucy,* dated 1422, with six miniatures cost 445 pounds, and other chronicles also sold for strong prices.[121] Astonishingly, a five-volume set of Montfaucon cost the same as a fifteenth-century illuminated manuscript. Twice as much was Gaguin's edition of the *Grandes Chroniques. The Bedford Hours,* Daniel Rabel's illuminated album, and Nicolas Jarry's *Guirlande de Julie* (5,000, 7,000, and 14,510 pounds respectively) show the pricing variation.

Under the direction of its greatest eighteenth-century director, Abbé Bignon, the Bibliothèque Nationale bought many of its greatest manuscripts at the duc de La Vallière sale. Not only was *Rohan Hours* (Paris: BnF, MS lat. 9471) bought at the sale but also many historical and literary works; René d'Anjou's *Le Livre du cœur d'amour épris* (Paris: BnF, MS fr. 24399), a translation of Boccaccio's *Filostrato* (Paris: BnF, MS fr. 25228), *Dialogues of Pierre Salmon* (Paris: BnF, MS fr. 23279), and *Guirlande de Julie* are only a few examples. The duc de La Vallière sale is also important in that it shows that in France by the end of the eighteenth century there was a conscious move to appropriate French patrimony for the state.

### The Prince de Soubise and His Mutilated "Curious" Manuscripts

Having been acquired over two centuries, the collection of Charles de Rohan, the prince de Soubise, fits the general pattern. It was already celebrated in 1679, when the catalogue was first printed.[122] After that, it was bought from the heirs by Monsieur Le Président de Menars and then from his heirs by Monsieur Le Cardinal de Rohan, Armand Gaston. The library is praised as including all that the scholars of the fourteenth, fifteenth, and sixteenth centuries wrote to restore or clarify the text of these authors. . . . There are no small number of manuscripts, and there are some very curious ones. Unfortunately, some of them have only survived after having been neglected, allowing the ignorant to cut out miniatures to give to children.

tout ce que les Savans des 14, 15 & 16 siecles ont écrit pour restituer ou eclaircir le texte de ces auteurs. . . . Les manuscrits n'y sont pas en petit nombre, & il y en a de fort curieux. Malheureusement quelques-uns n'y sont parvenus qu'apres avoir ete livres a un abandon qui a permis a designorans d'en couper des miniatures pour donner a des enfans.

This is the first published reference to cuttings in eighteenth-century France, although Francis Douce bought cuttings as early as 1784, and Daniel Burckhardt-Wildt may have bought some of his cuttings in Paris in the 1790s (see chapter 2).

**The Marquis of Paulmy and the Foundation Voyer of the Bibliothèque de l'Arsenal**

From a noble family that extends back to the fourteenth century, Antoine-René de d'Argenson (1722–87) formed a library to rival that of the duc de La Vallière.[124] Antoine-René, the younger marquis de Paulmy, enjoyed a career in government in the ministry, succeeding his uncle as minister of war (until 1758), then ambassador to Poland (to 1766), then Venice (to 1770). As minister of war, he put together a significant collection of maps and plans. In 1770, he abandoned government service altogether to concentrate on the formation and study of his library and to undertake a career as a scholar. Unlike the flamboyant duc de La Vallière, the marquis de Paulmy was more interested in documentation, less concerned with condition, not attracted by fine bindings, and interested in many other "curiosities," including medals (he had 11,000) and prints (592 portfolios). At his death, the sheer volume of his library was daunting with its 160,000 printed books and 2,512 manuscripts (including modern manuscripts). Known as the *vrai fondateur de la Bibliothèque de l'Arsenal* (true founder of the Bibliothèque de l'Arsenal), the marquis created the library in the Arsenal, selling his collection to the comte d'Artois in 1785, ensuring its eventual gift to the Arsenal, which became a public institution on April 28, 1797.[125]

What he shares with the duc de La Vallière is an interest in manuscripts, which developed at an early date, as is evident in a letter of 1750 in which he notes in a catalogue of the city of Berne that "looking through this catalogue you will see that it contains the titles of several very curious manuscripts" ("vous verrés en parcourant le catalogue qu'il contient le titre de plusieurs manuscrits très curieux"). He goes on to say that the librarian has offered to let him copy some manuscripts secretly. In 1755, the manuscripts in the marquis de Paulmy's library were referred to admiringly in a letter written by Voltaire.

Acquired over a number of years, the marquis de Paulmy's manuscripts came from important sources. From the comte d'Argenson, by the terms of whose will he could choose 1,000 volumes, he acquired 512 works, of which at least 40 manuscripts from the dukes of Burgundy are included, many illuminated. He also acquired en bloc the "lesser" library of the duc de La Vallière, the manuscripts of La Curne de Sainte-Palaye, the library of Joseph-Louis, baron d'Heiss, and the twelfth-century manuscripts of the monastery of Fontenay.[126]

Texts motivated the marquis de Paulmy, not pictures. His extraordinary collection of romances was to form the basis of a projected sixty-five-volume work, *Bibliothèque universelle des romans,* which sets out views about romances.[127] He calls romances "the first books of all nations" ("les primiers Livres de toutes les nations"). They include "the oldest, most extensive, and richest line of our literature" ("la branche . . . la plus ancienne, la plus etendue et la plus riche de notre litterature").[128] Most interesting are his comments on history: "The romance has this advantage over history, that it depicts manners as it describes events, that it develops and distinguishes characters, and that it represents the whole nation in the narrative of certain citizens . . . romances form the true body of history" ("Le Roman a cet avantage sur l'Histoire, qu'il peint les moeurs en decrivant les faits; qu'il developpe & nuance les caracteres; et qu'il represente toute une nation, dans les recit des avantures de quelques citoyens . . . les Romans, forment le veritable corps de l'Histoire").[129]

Among the manuscripts owned by the marquis de Paulmy are the French Bible of Acre (MS 5211), Frère Laurent's *Somme le Roi* (MS 6229) from A. Picard's collection, the *Equestrian Armorial of the Golden Fleece* (MS 4790) from the Baron d'Heiss collection, and Guillaume Bude's *De L'Institution du prince* (MS 5103). These books were housed in the Arsenal, the building that the marquis de Paulmy renovated for this very purpose.

**From Bibliothèque du Roi to Bibliothèque Nationale**

The strengthening of the Bibliothèque du Roi emerges against the background of these developments.[130] Under the enlightened leadership of Jean-Baptiste Colbert (1664–83), who enriched its holdings through acquisition and purchase, strengthened its central administration, and practiced a political policy that began to place the library at the center of cultural life, the library grew more in stature than it had since François I. Colbert was followed by Abbé de Louvois (1684–1718), then by Abbé Jean-Paul Bignon (1719–41). The latter not only moved the library into its present quarters, he enhanced its cataloguing system, expanded its collections through private purchases (he bought the huge library of Colbert, for example), set up a better system of library administration, and perfected the process of the *dépot légal*. Under Louis XIV and especially under Louis XV, the library "was opened up not just to privileged scholars but to a wider public."[131] The founding of the Cabinet des Médailles, the opening of the Cabinet des Estampes, the situation of the Département des Manuscrits, policies of enrichment and cataloguing—these ensured that the Bibliothèque du Roi became the Bibliothèque Nationale in 1795, at the height of the French Revolution.

**England**

The radical transformation in taste that occurred in England between the middle of the eighteenth century and the opening years of the nineteenth, during which things "Gothic" became, like primitivism in the twentieth-century, highly visible and fashionable, can be partly gauged by the changing perception of the *Bedford Hours*. In 1749, the famous presentation page (figure 14) could still be described as belonging to "a curious prayer book."[132] The manuscript went unmentioned in the diaries of Humphrey Wanley, librarian to Edward Harley, earl of Oxford. This was probably because it was an item in a curiosity cabinet rather than a library proper, one of 4,156 objects that were later auctioned in the sale of the Portland Museum along with shells, insects, and Queen Elizabeth's buttons. Thomas Astle, in his *Origins and Progress of Writing* had called the *Lambeth Apocalypse* "a curious example of the manner of painting in the fourteenth century."[133]

16.

**Gothic Room,
Strawberry Hill,
engraving
(circa 1750)**

The transition from the curiosity cabinet, where odd things from all ages, natural and manufactured, are deposited together, to the "period room" effect, where a whole era's historical ambience can be evoked through objects, was exemplified by Horace Walpole's Gothic library at Strawberry Hill, where medieval manuscripts played the role of decorative props. In his 1762 *Anecdotes of Painting,* Walpole repeated the Vasarian model of Italian superiority and reveled in denigrating medieval art.[134] The few manuscripts he owned were in the High Renaissance style associated with Giulio Clovio. "'I set little store by a collection of manuscripts," he wrote to William Cole in July 1782.[135] Walpole, educated at Eton and Cambridge, made his grand tour and returned in 1741 to a seat in Parliament as the earl of Orford. Part of a society of aristocrats grouped around the *Gentleman's Magazine,* he purchased Strawberry Hill in 1757 with its Gothic-style library (figure 16). Not simply studying the medieval past as an antiquarian but seeking to re-create the taste and picturesque effects he saw in medieval things, Walpole used fragments of stained glass to effect "Gothic gloom." In the "glass closet" were a few illuminated manuscripts, books of drawings by Vertue, and other antiquaries.[136] His desire to recapture a pure English style of architecture "before Art and Palladio had reached the land" was part of a sharp shift in taste toward nationalistic styles and away from Italianate forms. In 1800 another famous English collector, Sir John Soane, fit an exotic monk's cell in his London house with manuscripts and jumbled fragments of sculpture from medieval buildings.[137] Neither Walpole nor Soane used manuscripts to learn about the past but rather to create an idea of the past in the present.[138]

### William Hunter and the Economics of English Taste

William Hunter (1718–83), author of *The Anatomy of the Human Gravid Uterus* (1774) and a consultant obstetrician to Queen Caroline, consort to George III, had "refined appreciation of the visual arts as a patron and collector."[139] He, too, collected all sorts of things—books, paintings, coins, shells, archeological and ethnographic material from the South Seas brought back by Captain James Cook—which filled the museum he established at his house on Great Windmill Street in London. The 250 manuscripts that Hunter collected were not, like so many book repositories of his time, sold in public auction but ended up augmenting a public institution as Sir Hans Sloane's manuscripts had done in forming the nucleus of the British Museum collections in 1753.[140] Together with funds for building a new museum, Hunter left his collections to his old university, Glasgow. In this respect, in spite of his much more modest origins, he is the English equivalent of the marquis de Paulmy, whose collection founded the Arsenal.

When most of his contemporaries were collecting printed books and paying vast sums at auction for early Caxtons, Hunter was picking up manuscripts for a few shillings. In the words of Neil R. Ker, "They were an unfashionable line."[141] Copies of theological texts had even depreciated in value by the 1760s. At the famous sale of Jean-Louis Gaignat in 1769, Hunter bought 150 early printed books and a dozen manuscripts through his Paris agent Dessain. Competing with the absurdly rich duc de La Vallière, Hunter obtained 214 lots for less than a thousand pounds. This included a late-twelfth-century English psalter (Glasgow University Library, MS Hunter 229), which must have seemed an oddity at the time (hence overlooked by the duc de La Vallière) but which is one of the most important manuscripts of the period. In Ker's valuable assessment of Hunter as a collector of medieval books, he argues that manuscripts like this have given the physician "a false reputation as an *amateur des livres*. . . . [For e]xcept on this occasion Hunter did not go in much for picture books."[142] Ker is probably correct, since Hunter's fascination seems to have been with scholastic works, Greek texts, and, especially, in the light of his own interests, medical manuscripts, of which he had twenty-four. Many of these were not elaborately illuminated and, with the exception of the medical tracts, were obtained at the sales of Thomas Martin (in 1773 and 1774), the Greek scholar-reverend Caesar de Missy (in 1776), and Pieter Burmann in Leiden (in 1779).

But in other respects, Hunter's tastes were more in tune with his times. He was proud of his fifteenth-century illuminated books, such as the magnificent three-volume French manuscript of the *Vita Christi* of Ludolphus of Saxony (Glasgow University Library, MSS Hunter 36–39), which brought 220 pounds at the Gaignat sale.

Hunter's minutely documented sales records show how booksellers and collectors broke up manuscripts into more than one part.[143] Hunter rebound in a single volume what had appeared as two separate items sold by the dealer Thomas Osborne. Another manuscript he bought was rebound as three separate manuscripts (Glasgow University Library, MSS Hunter 426–28) and two printed volumes. Hunter was in many ways typical of the educated gentleman collector of his generation, but he was only one of a group of collectors who were making the most of the French collections' being dispersed owing to the Revolution, like the *Biblioteca Parisiana* brought to London for sale by James Edwards. Hunter went against the grain of his age in preferring the model of nature to antique models, an anticlassicism that helps explain his interest in medieval art.

A contemporary of Hunter's who should really be considered as part of the French movement was Count MacCarthy-Reagh, an Irishman resident in Toulouse who became a French subject in 1789.[144] His library is interesting because it shows not only how unscrupulous collectors could take advantage of political turmoil and the corrupt state of ecclesiastical foundations to gain treasures but also how many great books were in these decades moving from France to England. For example, MacCarthy-Reagh persuaded the canons of Albi Cathedral to part with important illuminated manuscripts like the Priscian made for King

Robert of Sicily, which belonged to Jean, duc de Berry, in exchange for some
modern printed books! At the sale of MacCarthy-Reagh infamous library in 1815,
this volume was bought by Dr. Charles Burney; he bequeathed it to the British
Library, where it is now MS Burney 275.[145] But already in 1789, Leigh and Sotheby had sold some of the MacCarthy Reagh books when they held a sale of "a
very elegant and curious cabinet of books lately imported from France . . . together with a considerable number of manuscripts, both on vellum and paper, the
greater part of which contain elegant paintings and illuminations." Among these
treasures was "a very ancient psalter, with illuminated miniatures in the initials"
and what the catalogue described as "a Bible written in the 13th century, with 156
miniatures in the coarse manner of that age." They were both bought, the first for
eight shillings, six pence, and the second for seven pounds, by the second important English collector who deserves a more detailed treatment here, Francis Douce.

**Francis Douce
and Manuscript
Illuminations as
Popular Culture**

Francis Douce (1757–1834) was a neurotic, hyper-
sensitive bibliographer who amassed over his life time
—in addition to thirteen thousand printed books—
four hundred manuscripts; medieval ivories; paintings
and drawings, especially of the northern schools; what
his diary of accessions lists as "an ancient rolling pin," "a piece of the outer painted coating of a human mummy," a "Gnostic crocodile," and a plaster cast of a
hermaphrodite.[146] But his curiosity cabinet was not so much a showcase of the
strange as a laboratory for cultural history. Although he did not publish much after
a vicious review of his first publication, *Illustrations of Shakespeare, and of Ancient
Manners: With Dissertations on the Clown and Fools* (1807), his interest in things, in
the manifestations of social history through material culture, was remarkable for his
time.[147] In 1807, rather late in his life, he joined the staff of the British Museum,
where he worked on the catalogues of the Landsdowne and Harleian manuscripts
until disagreements with the trustees about poor working conditions led him to
resign. A large inheritance in 1823 did not seem to raise his spirits, although it allowed him to expand his museum from his London house to larger premises and
then to buy very expensive fifteenth-century manuscripts, like the *Hours of Engel-
bert of Nassau* (Oxford: Bodleian Library, MSS Douce 219–20) for seventy pounds
and later the lavish *Roman de la Rose,* with illuminations by Robinet Testard (Oxford: Bodleian Library, MS Douce 195), for eighty-four pounds, which had been
in the collection of MacCarthy-Reagh. For all this fascination with manuscripts,
Douce, like his contemporaries, was still obsessed by early printed editions and
incunabula, which continued to bring higher prices than manuscripts at auction.
Sometimes, even modern printed books were sought. In January 1805, as his
"Collecta" (a list he kept of all his acquisitions and exchanges) shows, he exchang-
ed an important illuminated copy of Boccaccio's *De casibus* in French, for which
he had paid the high price of fifteen guineas in 1799, for a recently published volume of *Travels in Egypt* by Baron Denon (1802) and a map of the Cape of Good
Hope by John Barrow.[148]

As the 1984 Bodleian exhibition catalogue makes plain, Douce's attitude
toward cuttings and the mutilation of manuscripts was ambivalent. He constructed
an *Alphabet of Fools* from initial letters and borders, mostly from printed books
(Oxford: Bodleian Library, Douce Portfolio 133). He certainly bought cuttings and
fragments as early as 1786, and he later "mutilated" some of his manuscripts to enrich his scrapbook. Three Douce manuscripts have had miniatures restored to
them in recent years from Douce's albums.[149] Yet he noted of one of his own

manuscripts (Douce 372), "The ignorant and wanton spoliation of this still valuable MS. is much to be regretted."[150]

Douce seems to have favored things English and French over those Italian, which is unusual for the time. Traceable early acquisitions (1789–1800) are predominantly fourteenth- and fifteenth-century English and French books, many illuminated. At his death his 420 manuscripts all went to the Bodleian Library, Oxford, to the vexation of Sir Frederic Madden of the British Museum. The copious notebooks and annotations pasted to many of these manuscripts reveal that Douce's intellectual interests were broad. Among his notebooks is *An Index of Christian Iconography* (Oxford: Bodleian Library, MS Douce e. 2), which is an early instance of the use of this term long before it was popularized by Didron and Emile Mâle in France. Also significant was his study of early vernacular rather than Latin culture. He was interested in Anglo-Norman and Middle English literature, especially chivalric romances and drama. A friend of Walter Scott, to whom he gave advice about Scott's medievalizing historical novels, Douce was part of the early Romantic revival of the cult and literature of chivalry. He owned one of the most important early collections of medieval ivory carvings, again mostly because of the romance subjects they depicted. His obituary in the *Gentleman's Magazine* lists Douce's particular subjects of study as "the history of the arts, manners, customs, superstitions, fictions, popular sports and games" of all people and all ages.[151]

Such themes were often illustrated in the borders of manuscripts. If Montfaucon and Strutt had sought depictions of kings in early manuscripts, Douce delighted in the very different image of the fool. He published articles on the history of the fool in *Archeologia,* an interest that must have made every psalter he owned, especially the great *Ormesby Psalter* (Oxford: Bodleian Library, MS Douce 366), with its startling image of the fool addressing Christ in Psalm 52, especially resonant. He purchased the tiny two-volume *Ghent Psalter* in November 1832 (Oxford: Bodleian Library, MSS Douce 5–6), noting in his "Collecta," "Beautiful small Horae 2 vols (grotesques) Payne." But his taste for the grotesque was more serious than that of his friend Dibdin and unparalleled among contemporary French collectors. It was an interest in what Francis Haskell calls "the alternative tradition" in European culture—what today we might call popular culture—which was not fully realizable in Strutt's volumes, with their emphasis upon manners and deportment. Douce was more like the forebear of Thomas Wright, whose *History of Caricature and the Grotesque* did not appear until 1865, and, in France, of the great realist critic Champfleury, whose *Histoire de la caricature du moyen âge et sous la renaissance* was not published until 1867.[152] As an old man, Douce was described by T. F. Dibdin in his *Bibliophobia* (1832) as a Prospero with his "enchanter's wand."[153] If Douce had been the Prospero in the tempestuous drama of this period of manuscript collecting, Dibdin was to play its Caliban.

**Thomas Frognall Dibdin's Bibliomania and the Romance of Illuminated Manuscripts**

The importance of the Reverend Thomas Frognall Dibdin (1776–1847) lies not only in his publication *Bibliographical Decameron* of 1817, which contains the first account of the history of manuscript illumination for the general reader, but in his flamboyant role as a collector and the popularizer of the notion of bibliomania, or "book madness," itself.[154] More than an antiquarian, he was, to use a twentieth-century term, a fetishist, fascinated not only by medieval books as objects but by their "curious scripts," "gleam of jewel-like illumination," "sensuous parchment feel," and "smell of old leather."[155] In his *Reminiscences of a Literary Life,* published in his sad days of financial decline in 1836, when his contemporaries were already beginning to label him a snob, a sycophant, a pedant, and, worst of all, "the world's worst bibliographer," Dibdin admitted to catching the disease of medievalism in his student days at Oxford, looking out of the window upon "Gothic battlements."[156]

Perhaps today this remarkable writer can be seen more sympathetically. If the antiquarian seems all mind, Dibdin brings some of the sensational physicality of the early Romantic sensibility to the study of manuscript illumination. He did not simply examine the Middle Ages at a distance; he sought to live it, not as Strutt had done in the simulacrum of the page itself but in "the Cabinet," "The Drawing Room," and "The Alcove" of the stately home. These are the various chapter titles in *Bibliomania or Book Madness,* first published in 1809.[157] This work made a name for Dibdin, but before this he had published more serious bibliographical works: *An Introduction to the Knowledge of Rare and Valuable Editions of the Greek and Roman Classics* (1802) and an edition of Joseph Ames's *Typographical Antiquities* (1810–19), which was, like most of his books, lavishly illustrated and beautifully printed.[158] A second, enlarged edition of *Bibliomania,* published in 1811, had the subtitle *A Bibliographical Romance* and appeared as a lavishly illustrated novel, with vignettes at the bottom of pages in addition to full-page woodblock engravings.[159]

Dibdin was not a member of the aristocracy like so many of his bibliomaniacal friends with whom he founded the Roxburghe Club; rather, he was but a humble clergyman, earning a small living from Exning in Suffolk. His clerical duties occupied him only on Sundays, and, until parishioners of his later parish of Marleybone complained, he spent most of his time following his literary pursuits. The rambling structure of *Bibliomania,* written in the form of delightful dialogue between characters like Lysander and his college master Philemon, with footnotes often filling three-quarters of each page, includes among its topics the history of snuffboxes, corporal punishment in public schools, and the history of book collecting. At this stage, Dibdin seems to have been no more sophisticated in his knowledge or understanding of the art of manuscript illumination than most of his predecessors. For example, discussing the thirteenth-century illuminations of a manuscript by the twelfth-century historian Gerald of Wales, Lysander states, "The art of book illumination in this country was then sufficiently barbarous, if at all known."[160]

Less than a decade later, Dibdin gave a far more positive and detailed history of manuscript illumination in the opening chapter of the similarly whimsical dramatic discourse of the *Bibliographical Decameron; or Ten Days Pleasant Discourse upon Illuminated Manuscripts, and Subjects Connected with Early Engraving, Typography and Bibliography.*[161] The first chapter, or "First Day," opens with a "brief view of the progress of the Arts of Design and Composition, in illuminated MSS. from the Vth to the XVIth century inclusively" and runs to more than two hundred pages.[162] The contents are organized not chronologically but by type of manuscript— Bibles, missals, heraldry, chronicles, and so on—and it begins with an account of a beautifully illuminated late-fifteenth-century manuscript of Boccaccio's *Decameron* in the library of Mr. Coke at Holkham, who allowed facsimile drawings to be made of a number of the portrait initials that Dibdin reproduces. He was very aware of the position of images in his books, instructing the reader to look to the side or up to see a particularly fine engraving. In one case, he states that "the OPPOSITE PLATE will convince the reader (although it have only the degree of colouring which good engraving and good printing can give it)" (figure 17). Dibdin continuously laments the inadequacies of printing "to convey the extreme

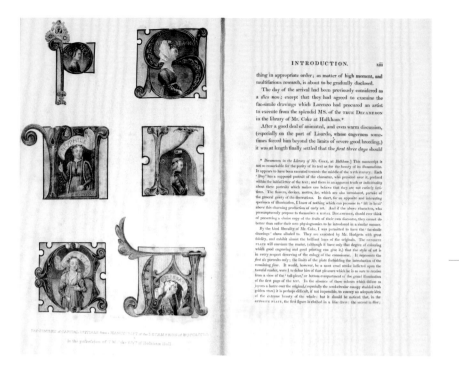

17.

Thomas Frognall Dibdin,
*Bibliographical Decameron;
or Ten Days of Pleasant
Discourse upon Illuminated
Manuscripts*, volume I
(1817), page xiii and facing
page

beauty of the whole."[163] A few pages later in a long footnote eulogy to Strutt, he
criticizes the latter's burin as being "rapid rather than vigorous" and states that he
was "not interested in drawing per se."[164] He then goes on to attack the "scur-
rilous, saucy but not unsagacious" Abbé Rive, criticizing him for describing manuscript illuminations from the tenth through the fourteenth centuries as "almost
entirely frightful, portraying the barbarity of the period in which they were executed." Dibdin hopes that "the reader will learn a different lesson from the pages
of this work."[165] With sixty illustrations and fourteen full-page plates, Dibdin's
short account presented some of the very first reproductions from medieval manuscripts to a wider public. There were fifty copies printed on large paper, in addition to a large press run on ordinary stock, and Didbin relates that 4,500 pounds
were spent on its production.

Despite the enormous costs of its printing, the *Bibliographical Decameron*
was a financial success. At an elaborately staged dinner on December 9, 1817, Didbin invited a dozen of his Roxburghe Club friends for whom he printed the two-
page "Order of Revels," inviting them as "book knights" to make toasts to past
authors and eat a Middle English menu. On this same occasion, he also burned all
the exquisitely engraved woodblocks used in the production of the *Decameron*.
The reason for this ruthless destruction was, according to Dibdin himself, that "the
property of the work was in a measure *secured* by it."[166] No reprint was possible.
In destroying his own print technology, Dibdin made each beautifully crafted and
citron-morocco-bound set of three volumes into a unique manuscriptlike object.
Some of these volumes were indeed to become the repository of extra illustration
—that is, more engravings and actual fragments of important illuminated leaves and
cuttings. One such exceptional extra-illustrated copy of the *Decameron* sold in New
York in 1960. It had 547 miniatures stuck into it, many highly valuable ones, including a William de Brailes leaf, now in the Pierpont Morgan Library (M. 913
–14; see figure 18). Lamentably dismantled without photographic record, this
extra-illustrated copy would have allowed a fascinating glimpse of the intersection
of collecting, scholarship, and printing and medieval manuscript illumination in
nineteenth-century England.

18.

**William de Brailes,
Scenes from the Infancy
of Christ (England, circa
1240), cut from a
prayerbook and pasted
into an extra-illuminated
Thomas Frognall Dibdin,**
*Bibliographical Decameron*

The *Bibliographical Decameron* is remarkable in terms of the changing tastes of the period; Dibdin is sensitive to and appreciates works of Romanesque and Gothic manuscript illumination that would, only a few years previously, have been seen as mere curiosities. The author tells us that the gesticulating actor from a twelfth-century manuscript of the *Comedies of Terence* in the Bodleian Library (MS Douce 347) was made from a tracing by his own hand. Strutt, too—and Rive—probably used this method, still common practice until fairly recently in some manuscript rooms.

Initial letters and individual figures are often isolated in the reproductions, such as the Elizabeth and Mary from a psalter in the Gough collection, also at Oxford, which Dibdin describes as "not a little grotesque but the folds of the drapery are managed with considerable attention to elegance and ease."[167] Yet Dibdin was one of the first writers to discuss and even reproduce in accurate outline twelfth-century hybrid initials. Moreover, he seemed to enjoy the "ease and whimsicality" of their monstrous intertwined forms.[168] The taste for these "fanciful ornaments" was part of the Romantic interest in the grotesque, which reached its height in England and France a few decades later. This also explains, as Munby notes, Dibdin's fascination with hitherto neglected genres of the medieval book, such as bestiaries.[169] Certainly even when he gets to the masterpieces of Renaissance illumination that both he and his readers could appreciate more easily—such as the missal of Cardinal della Rovere (figure 63), which takes up fifteen pages of the book, far more than any other —the decorative elements and grotesques (in the true sense of sixteenth-century *groteschi* ornament) are given fullest descriptions.

Dibdin also had some strong views on how gender affected appreciation of medieval art: "The Athelstan-book of the Gospels . . . dismally barbarous in the ornamental part: I fear the female part of my audience would not scruple to express their surprise, or even loathing, at the sight of those apple-green, and smoke-dried old figures intended to represent the Evangelists."[170] This odd bibliographical attitude seems to have rubbed off on Dibdin's modern commentator, Munby, who quotes this passage but earlier describes the miniatures of the missal of Cardinal della Rovere as "delicate—not to say effeminate."[171] The fact that interest in manuscript illumination in this period is almost exclusively a male concern (like most collecting) is another difference between this and the subsequent period of the Victorian fascination with manuscripts. In the repartee of Dibdin's dramatis personae, Belinda, the female participant is often presented as the delicate but naive sensibility (made to admire "the perfection of the headdresses" in a manuscript of Christine de Pisan's collected works [British Library, MS Harley 4431]) as opposed to the more learned interests of her male colleagues, a dichotomy that was to run its course through to Ruskin.[172]

The weight given to Renaissance manuscript illumination in Dibdin's account was not only a response to the taste of his time but to the fact that many of the books he mentions were owned by wealthy collectors or had just been purchased for them with his help. Many had been sold at the recent James Edwards sale—for example, the *Hours of Ferdinand I, King of Naples* (Berlin, Kupferstichkabinett, MS 78 D 14), for which Dibdin himself had paid 125 pounds and then, after having a plate engraved from it for his book, passed it to the marquis of Douglas for the same sum.[173] Dibdin's luxurious bibliophilic pleasures finally led him to financial ruin, and in 1817 he was forced to sell his own library.[174] The sale catalogue reveals that he owned no lavish illuminated codices himself at this date but that his fascinating collection included old catalogues and important printed books.[175]

The golden era of early-nineteenth-century book collecting, when great libraries were being assembled and crises on the Continent led to a massive influx of treasures from French monastic and princely collections into Regency London and when legendary bookmen like Richard Heber, Francis Douce, and William Young Ottley fought bibliomaniacal battles, was drawing to a close. In the 1830s Dibdin documented this decline, which paralleled his own personal plummet in fortunes, producing the pamphlet *Bibliophobia: Remarks on the Present Languid and Depressed State of Literature and the Book Trade.*[176] This pamphlet attributed the decline in bibliomania to the business slump created by the reform bill and an epidemic of cholera that made people wary of handling dusty old volumes that might carry infection. For all his romance, Dibdin, like Douce and Hunter, was a man of the eighteenth century, rooted in a sensibility that would vanish in the coming decades of the Gothic Revival proper. His crucial role in the foundation of the Roxburghe Club, which later, under Sir Frederic Madden and Thomas Wright, was to resuscitate interest in early printers and fine manuscripts, was clouded by criticisms of its exclusive nature. Introducing the negative attitude toward Dibdin as a frivolous figure of fun, which was to increase after his death, the periodical the *Museum* in 1823 wrote that Roxburghe Club members "are, for the most part, a set of persons of no true taste, of no proper notion of learning and its uses—very considerable persons in point of wealth, but very so-so *in point of intellect.*" From an earnest Victorian point of view, it is easy to castigate Dibdin as an amateur, but in his own terms he represents exactly that which the museum condems—a lover amorous of a certain class of objects that he helped redefine.

In many respects, Dibdin exemplifies the transition from the century that used "curious" manuscript illuminations as documents to the century that began to awaken to them as "specimens" of artistic merit. His interlocutors view works from the past in terms of their own desires, making the *Bibliographical Decameron* one of the few dramatized studies of medieval art ever written. In a specimen of Italian illumination in a service book, the chatter turns to the possible uses of manuscript illumination in the present day, which anticipates so many of the themes that carry through the nineteenth and into the twentieth centuries:

> ALMANSA. I am quite charmed with such specimens; and wish in my heart that some Girolamo, of the present day, would introduce the portraits of your MAJESTY and Privy Council, here solemnly assembled, within the graceful curvatures of a capital *C* or *D*.
>
> LISARDO. The thought is not very extravagant, my Almansa! Let us have our *family Bible* illustrated with a similar ornament. Yet tell me—are these beautiful initials the exclusive decoration of *Church Service Books?*
>
> PHILEMON. By no means. For see, what a lovely illustration of an *O*, from a MS. of Horace (once the property of Ferdinand I, King of Naples) does the following specimen exhibit! I know nothing that exceeds it.
>
> LORENZO. You are right. The composition is indeed delicious.
>
> PHILEMON. Let me now, as the last specimen to be adduced, present you with something of rather a whimsical, if not monstrous, appearance; but it brings down our illustrations toward the middle of the sixteenth century, we may fairly close the discussion on this branch of the subject. Observe, I entreat you, what a striking *melange* the following *P* exhibits!
>
> BELINDA. Extraordinary indeed! The Gothic age seems revived in it.[177]

Significantly, the letter *P* in which Belinda sees the Gothic age revived is, as Philemon is quick to point out, a sixteenth-century product of the time of François I (figure 19). It reminds us again how the history of the reception and collecting of illuminated manuscripts over the course of the nineteenth century, charted in the rest of this book, was not exactly parallel to the Gothic Revival proper. Yet such passages make apparent Dibdin's acute awareness of the tastes and interests that shaped his age. Passages of delightful repartee over the pretty letters seen out of context and painted in books are both Dibdin's inevitable response to an already existing market in cuttings, discussed in the next chapter, and perhaps even a stimulus to the continued practice of dismemberment of manuscripts throughout the nineteenth century. In another footnote, Dibdin describes how his friend "Mr. Ottley absolutely revels in the possession of the most splendid ancient fragments of books of this description, obtained by him in Italy, from monasteries and other individuals."[178] And indeed, Dibdin possessed cuttings from manuscripts of the then-fashionable Italian Renaissance and also medieval works—the taste for which would grow over the course of the nineteenth century (figure 20, plate 1). The text and the plates of Dibdin's *Bibliographical Decameron* are thus perhaps a primer not only in the social world of manuscript collecting and enthusiasm but also in manuscript cutting, reproducing, and re-creating.

**19.**

**Thomas Frognall Dibdin,
*Bibliographical Decameron;
or Ten Days of Pleasant
Discourse upon Illuminated
Manuscripts*, volume 1
(1817), page cviii, full page
with illuminated *P***

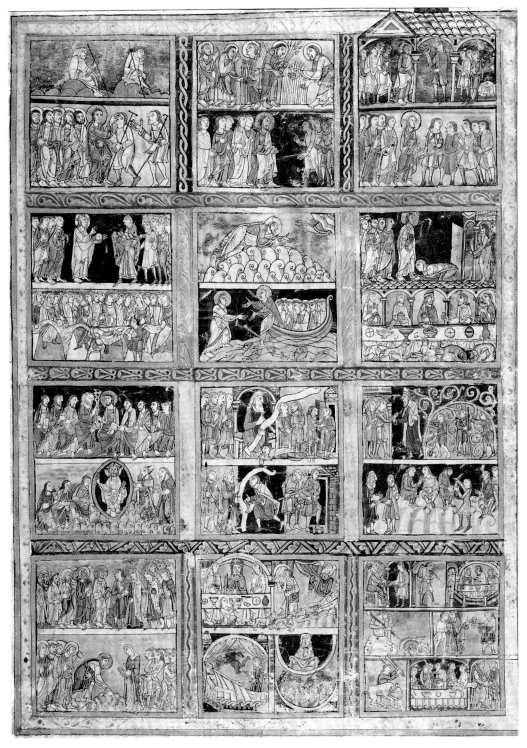

20.

Bury St. Edmunds
Monastery, scenes from the
Life of Christ (England,
circa 1155–60), single leaf
from a Bible or psalter

# "SPECIMENS"

Transformations of Illuminated Manuscripts in the Nineteenth Century

## The French Revolution and

## the Sack of Rome

**T**wo important events occurred in the
decade of the 1790s that significantly
changed the status of illuminated
manuscripts, certainly in France but probably also throughout Europe. First, the
beginning of the French Revolution in
1789, which dramatically redefined the roles of the
church and the state, led to the confiscation of cultural
property that had previously belonged to religious
foundations and to the nobility. The Commission of
Monuments was set up to counter widespread local and
national vandalism during the Reign of Terror. In fact,
the word "vandal" to describe a person who destroys
cultural property was a neologism coined as a direct
result of the French Revolution. The result was that a
huge number of manuscripts, previously the property of
the church and the nobility, was taken over by the State
and ended up not only in the Bibliothèque Nationale
but also in regional municipal libraries throughout
France. Second, Napoleon's military conquests under
the Directory from about 1794, when he was named
chief of the Italian army, led to widespread confiscation
of foreign cultural property not only in Italy but also in
Germany, Belgium, Austria, and the Netherlands. A
commission also oversaw his "artistic conquests" and

[T]hese specimens
are, in many cases,
found in a more
perfect state of
preservation than
the frescoes and
other large works
of painting remain-
ing to us of the
same periods . . .
so that whatever
performances of
this kind now
remain to us, merit
also our regard as
the *monuments of
a lost Art.*

—WILLIAM YOUNG OTTLEY,
SALE CATALOGUE,
CHRISTIE'S, LONDON
MAY 26, 1825

brought cultural treasures from all over Europe into France, where they were at once installed and displayed for public viewing. Each of these episodes impacted the availability of art in the public and private domains. In the public domain, the holdings of libraries and museums swelled immeasurably. In the private domain, in more subtle, less easily measurable ways, the greater visibility of art—the widespread perception of mutilation and fragmentation of public monuments and even whole libraries—coupled with the implicit licence to uprising and violence must have altered attitudes toward manuscripts and even eventually facilitated their fragmentation.

As Emmet Kennedy has argued, the Commission of Monuments, which was organized in October 1790, regulated the conservation and destruction of cultural monuments.[2] By directives passed in 1792, it was to conserve "all monuments prior to the year 1300 . . . because of the costumes . . . , all beautiful monuments, . . . any monument which sheds light on the history  and epochs of art or on mores."[3] Including four individuals whose careers were directly related to books (the librarians Hubert-Pascal Ameilhon and Abbé Gaspard-Michel Leblond, the archivist Dom Poirier, and the bookseller-publisher Guillaume Debure l'Aîné), this group of twenty-five inspectors was responsible for the donations that, it has been estimated, increased by fivefold the holdings of the Bibliothèque Nationale. The order that went out on November 14, 1789 (two weeks after the decree that church property be confiscated), for monastic and chapter libraries to deposit catalogues of their holdings with the royal court is usually seen as underlying a move toward a national catalogue. But it also inevitably made possible the peaceful seizure and subsequent accurate inventorying of property.

"Entire cartloads of material" were wheeled into the courtyard of the building on the rue Vivienne, increasing the holdings of manuscripts alone by more than fifteen thousand items.[4] In 1795 to 1796, nine thousand manuscripts came from the library of St.-Germain-des-Près; in 1796, nineteen hundred manuscripts from the Sorbonne, and still more from the abbey of St.-Victor. The Bibliothèque Nationale took in manuscripts from Notre-Dame de Paris, the Ste.-Chapelle, as well as many local parishes and convents, such as the convent of the Capucines on the rue St.-Honoré, the convent of the Carmelites, the parish church of St.-Bartholomew, and so forth. Regional churches and monasteries, such as Chartres Cathedral, the cathedral of Metz, the abbey of St.-Medard of Soissons, and so on, sometimes quasi forcibly joined local entities in turning over their treasures, not so much because the commission feared their destruction but because they wished to ensure a centralization of patrimony. (In the words of Dom Poirier, "Manuscripts before the eleventh century are only usually found in cathedrals and in the ancient Benedictine abbeys" ["Les manuscrits antérieurs au XIe siècle ne se trouvent communément que dans les ci-devant cathédrales et dans les anciennes abbayes des benedictines"]). Particularly interesting is the case of the city of Toulouse: searching for an appropriate gift for Napoleon on the birth of his son in 1811, Toulouse chose the *Godescalc Evangelistary,* a manuscript made for Charlemagne in 781 to 783, "a fitting gift for an emperor who in 1804 had declared 'Je suis Charlemagne.'" Napoleon placed the manuscript in the Louvre itself, although it was subsequently transferred to the Bibliothèque Nationale.[5]

Surely this strategy of "adoption" was better than the alternative expressed by two important figures of the era, both directly involved in the confiscation of property, Urbain Domergue and Abbé Grégoire. Domergue exclaimed, "Our libraries also have their counterrevolutionaries; I vote their deportation. Let us channel the poison of our books about theology, mysticism, royalism, feudalism and oppressive legislation to the enemies' camp." Along similar lines, Grégoire proposed that the "index of reason" would be to reduce the national collection from ten million to five million books, and to sell or trade the rest at home or abroad, thus creating new libraries for the underprivileged.

Going hand in hand with the confiscation of property during the French Revolution was the appropriation of artistic monuments from abroad. These were more than war spoils; they were widely regarded—not just by politicians who had a stake in influential propaganda—as rightful cultural property of Frenchmen and Frenchwomen. Thus, in 1796, Napoleon wrote "all men of genius, all those who have attained distinction in the republic of letters[,] are French no matter in what country they may have been born."[6] In a petition that French artists sent to the Directory, they recommended the appropriation of foreign art: "[T]he French people . . . naturally endowed with exquisite sensitivity, will . . . by seeing the models from antiquity, train its feeling and its critical sense. . . . The French Republic, by its strength and superiority of its enlightenment and its artists, is the only country in the world which can give a safe home to these masterpieces."[7]

And what monuments came; the *Apollo Belvedere,* the winged lion from San Marco in Venice, Raphael's *St. Cecilia* are only three of the large-scale sculptures and paintings. Plans that never came to fruition even envisaged the exportation of virtually unmovable treasures, such as Trajan's Column and Raphael's Vatican frescoes. For manuscripts, the story is initially less spectacular, but it is no less awesome from the perspective of artistic importance and quantity. As Marie-Pierre Lafitte and François Dupuigrenet have independently pointed out, the Bibliothèque Nationale had no official role in the seizures and no commissioner to represent its special interests; it nonetheless benefited substantially, if indirectly, from the spoils from abroad.[8] In 1794, when the Commission Temporaire des Arts was assigned the charge of overseeing paintings in occupied countries, the commissioners received specific instructions from the Bibliothèque Nationale:

In general, take all the manuscripts dealing with history, those by classical Greek and Latin authors, and those of poets in various languages. Do not bother with manuscripts by the church fathers and theologians, at least those that are not old enough to contribute to the study of the history of diplomatics . . . except those that are perfectly executed, enriched with miniatures or which have particular merit.

Prendre generalement tous les manuscrits d'histoire, d'auteurs classiques grecs et latins, de poetes en quelque langue qu'ils soient. Négliger les manuscrits des Pères de l'Eglise et des theologians, à moins qu'ils ne soient assez anciens pour servir a l'histoire de la diplomatique . . . on en except ceux qui sont partfaitement executes, enrichis de miniatures ou qui ont quelque merite particulier.[9]

Other scholars have called the interest "archaeological," pointing out that Italian patrimony, codices by Leonardo and Galileo, were spared in favor of other sorts of manuscripts.

The spoils were abundant. Lafitte has precisely chronicled the seizures: in Milan, Bologna, Rome, and Modena in 1796; in Polirone, Massa and Carrara, Verona, Rome, Mantua, and San Daniele in Friuli in 1797; in Venice, Padua, and Treviso in 1797; in Rome and Turin in 1798; and in Florence in 1799. The personal library of Pius VI was seized in 1798. All total, more than sixteen hundred manuscripts went from Italy to France, including great works of Italian literature, such as a celebrated illuminated copy of Dante's *Divine Comedy* (BnF, MS ital. 78) and Petrarch's *Triumphs* (BnF, MS ital. 545), both from Pope Pius's library. By the terms of the armistice and the resulting restitution, some of these manuscripts found their way back to Italy (to Bologna, Milan, Monza, Turin, and so on), but many, many others did not.[10]

Not just Italy but Belgium, the Netherlands, Austria, and Germany yielded tribute to Napoleon's armies, sometimes before Napoleon received the Italian spoils. Thus, in 1794 and 1795, art treasures from Burgundian holdings in Brussels arrived under the direction of Leblond, who was sent by the Comite d'Instruction Publique to Brussels; these treasures included deluxe illuminated manuscripts made under the patronage of the dukes of Burgundy, Philip the Good, and Charles the Bold.[11] But Leblond preferred manuscripts of the tenth century and earlier. Given a free rein, the curator of the Bibliothèque de l'Arsenal in Paris chose Carolingian manuscripts rather than late-medieval works.[12] In 1802, manuscripts and incunables from Trier, Coblenz, Cologne, Bonn, and Mainz arrived, and the famous library of the duke of Brunswick near Wolfenbüttel was sent to Paris.[13] And so it went until the terms of the 1814 Convention of Paris outlined the means for restitution, and many national treasures were returned to their countries of origin. Yet sentiments concerning the return of artworks ran high in Paris, so much so that the popular press took to recounting the situation with fervor:

The stripping of the Louvre is the chief cause of public irritation at present. . . . I have seen several French Ladies in passing along the galleries suddenly break into extravagant fits of rage and lamentation; they gather round the Apollo to take their last farewell . . . there is so much passion in their looks, their language and their sighs.[14]

Even after restitution, by the end of this period the Bibliothèque Nationale's holdings of printed books and manuscripts had increased fivefold, as mentioned above. An intriguing question emerges: Did French interest in illuminated manuscripts as spoils subsequently heighten an awareness of them as more than curiosities, or were the new attitudes developed in the course of the eighteenth century responsible for their changed reception?

## ABATE CELOTTI, WILLIAM YOUNG OTTLEY, AND THE FIRST-EVER SALE OF CUTTINGS

The Napoleonic Wars had a marked impact on the art market not only in France but also in England. In the decade of the 1790s and at least through the first quarter of the nineteenth century, dealers and collectors from throughout Europe flocked to Italy to profit from the increased availability of art. Political treaties, private bargaining between wealthy families and collector-dealers, the suppression of churches and monasteries in Tuscany and their consequent looting, the demands of Napoleon's armies for money—these factors fed the trade in works of art. In Rome and other Italian cities, such as Genoa and Florence, a large resident colony of collector-dealers exploited the situation. Soldiers, politicians, collectors, artists, and dealers preyed on Italy's art treasures. Diverse sources, from guidebooks to sale catalogues, attribute the plundering of art to the disasters of war and give a vivid idea of the extent of the circulation of artworks. By the time of the Battle of Waterloo, after nearly a quarter century of plundering, travel guides warned, "Since the late system of spoliation has taken place in Italy, the connoisseur in painting and sculpture will find little to detain him, I fear, in many of those cities, where weeks were scarcely sufficient to satisfy his ardent curiosity" (1814). If Italy was desolated, however, riches could now be admired at home, the recurring theme being that of rescue. For example, an 1825 account of William Young Ottley's house by J. S. Sartain, who was employed to engrave the plates for the former's *Early Florentine School,* describes the smaller gallery . . . the walls of which were covered from floor to ceiling with pictures by the old pre-Raphaelite artists, which Mr. Ottley had collected in Italy during the latter part of the last century. Most of them were taken from churches during the occupation by the French soldiery, and but for Mr. Ottley's intervention might have been destroyed.[15]

In the history manuscript illumination, two figures stand out during this period: Abate Luigi Celotti (born around 1768; died around 1846) and William Young Ottley (1771–1836).[16] The somewhat mysterious cleric-turned-art-dealer Luigi Celotti organized the first-ever exclusive sale of single leaves and cuttings in London at Christie's on May 26, 1825 (the second part of the sale occurred May 3, 1826, also at Christie's), called "Illumined Miniature Paintings of the Greatest Beauty, and of Exquisite Finishing, Taken from the Choral Books of the Papal Chapel in the Vatican, during the French Revolution; and Subsequently Collected and Brought to This Country by the Abate Celotti" (figure 21).[17] The rhetoric here blames the looting of the Vatican by Napoleon's philistine troops for the fragmentary state of the miniatures and for their dispersal. This may be true—though it should be noted that not all Sistine Chapel manuscripts suffered this fate, some being rescued in 1798 by the cardinal of Toledo—but the idea was an excellent marketing device. Prospective buyers were encouraged to acquire leaves from the hallowed sanctuary of High Renaissance art, rescuing the art from all that was undesirable in politics—that is, French Republicans.[18] Those manuscripts not sent to Toledo were exported by Celotti.

The facts about Celotti's life are disappointingly sparse. In his capacity as secretary and librarian for Count Giovanni Barbarigo in Venice from 1801, Celotti

**21.**

*A Catalogue of a Highly Valuable and Extremely Curious Collection of Illumined Miniature Paintings* London: Christie's, May 26, 1825, title page

A

# CATALOGUE

OF A

HIGHLY VALUABLE AND EXTREMELY CURIOUS COLLECTION OF

## ILLUMINED

# MINIATURE PAINTINGS,

OF THE GREATEST BEAUTY, AND OF EXQUISITE FINISHING,

*Taken from the Choral Books of the Papal Chapel in the Vatican, during the French Revolution ; and subsequently collected and brought to this Country by the*

### ABATE CELOTTI.

The above Collection is highly important for the illustration of the Art of Painting in Italy during the fifteenth and following centuries ; exhibiting, besides many fine productions of the Miniaturists, whose names have not been preserved by any Biographer, presumed specimens of the early masters, Francesco Squarcione and Giovanni Bellini ; and undoubted chef d'œuvres of Girolamo de' Libri, and his disciple Giulio Clovio, who brought the Art to the highest perfection, as also by some other great Painters who lived after Clovio's time. The whole are described in a Catalogue, drawn in Chronological series by a gentleman well conversant in the History of early Italian Art.

WHICH

## Will be Sold by Auction,

# BY MR. CHRISTIE,

AT HIS GREAT ROOM,

### NO. 8, KING STREET, ST. JAMES'S SQUARE,

On THURSDAY, MAY 26th, 1825,

AT ONE PRECISELY.

May be Viewed two days preceding, and Catalogues had (at One Shilling each) of Mr. CHRISTIE, 8, *King Street, St. James's Square.*

must have had ready entry into Italian collections. He thus bought the libraries of many private collectors, such as Don Tomaso da Lucca, as well as those belonging to the "illustrious families Nani, Guadenigo, and Mocenigo of Venice, Maffei of Verona, and Salviati of Rome."[19] In addition, with the suppression of many Italian monasteries and convents during the French occupation, he was able to purchase books and manuscripts from the monastic libraries of Santa Giustina at Padua, San Giorgio Maggiore in Venice, San Michele of Murano, San Benedetto in Polirone, and the Jesuits College in Agen.[20] During three sales of his properties in 1825, more than four thousand books and manuscripts were auctioned. Four years earlier, he had already sold the Saibanti and Canonici manuscripts in London.[21] And in the early years of the nineteenth century, he organized picture sales. Although he consigned nearly all the manuscripts to Sotheby's, he turned to Christie's to handle the auction of his miniature paintings, apparently because this firm was better known among picture dealers.[22]

Written in 1825, the catalogue of the Celotti sale of miniatures was evidently aimed at a picture-buying audience. Christie's employed William Young Ottley to write the catalogue. A new breed of antiquarian, this artist-connoisseur-historian had trained at the Royal Academy and had spent ten years in Italy, where he must have encountered Celotti; his publications on Italian art, particularly on Italian primitives, were already well known and widely respected. In fact, the title page of the catalogue implied that Ottley, "a gentleman well conversant in the History of early Italian Art," legitimized the project. Leaving no doubt as to his participation, Ottley signed the introduction. Called an "advertisement," the introduction made clear that these miniature paintings were to be considered alongside "frescoes and other large works of painting remaining to us of the same periods" as superior examples of the "style of Art that prevailed at the time."[23] Ottley's frequent references to Giorgio Vasari (1511–74), whose paradigm of the history of art he largely adopted, and his eagerness to relate miniature painters, such as Giulio Clovio, to monumental painters, such as Michelangelo, Raphael, and Giulio Romano, provide clear examples of his strategy. He also called attention to the additional importance of miniature paintings, when compared with the monumental arts, by noting their

more perfect state of preservation. . . . To this may be added that the processes which were resorted to by the ancient Illuminists, in preparing and laying on the different metals used in decorating their paintings, and in mixing their colours, have long ceased to be remembered; so that whatever performances of this kind now remain to us, merit also our regard as the *monuments of a lost Art.*[24]

Parenthetically, illumination was a new category of art in the nineteenth century. Earlier, the word had been used the indicate the coloring of maps and prints, with no systematic artistic connotations.[25]

Organized in chronological order "as best calculated to render the whole illustrative of the progress of the Art," with detailed historical notes, attributions to major artists, and often-elaborate descriptions, the catalogue displayed an unprecedented degree of sophistication that reinforced the perception of illuminations as legitimate examples of the "Art of Painting in Italy."[26] Two hundred seventy-six individual items were sold in ninety-seven lots, but the bulk of the catalogue focuses on the last sixty-eight lots, each of which is a single work, mostly framed and glazed. Before these, the first twenty-nine lots, largely cuttings, identified generically as "Illuminations from Monastic Choral Books," are often sparsely described, giving the subject only or a rough date (for example, "circa 1600") and rarely include attributions ("by an unknown artist"), except for the last lot (lot 28, "believed to be by Girolamo de' Libri, in his latter manner"). Among these lots, bargains could be had: typical are five (historiated) initials, St. Lawrence, St. John, and so on (lot 6, one pound, nine shillings);

nine (historiated) initials by an unknown artist, fifteenth century (lot 7, two pounds, two shillings); and four initials, two with figures of prophets (one signed "B.F.") and two with arabesques (lot 16, three pounds, twelve shillings). Picture dealers bought sparsely during this part of the sale. For about six shillings, a buyer could obtain a richly illuminated fifteenth-century cutting.

Following this initial group came the most interesting portion of the sale, "Miniatures from the Choral Books of the Pontifical Chapel in the Vatican." These single lots are organized under the reigns of the different popes, and, when known, the artist working for that pontiff is identified in the catalogue entry. The popes cited range from Innocent VIII (died in 1492) to Innocent XI (died 1689). In between are miniatures that belonged to intervening popes: Leo X (died 1521), Clement VII (died 1534), Paul III (died 1549), Paul IV (died 1559), Pius IV, Pius V (died 1572), Gregory XIII (died 1583), Urban VIII (died 1644), Alexander VII (died 1667), Innocent XI (died 1689). The artists highlighted in this part of the sale include Andrea Mantegna (lots 33–40); Girolamo de' Libri, "the master of Don Giulio Clovio" (lots 54–56); Apollonius de Bonfratelli "in imitation of that of Michelangiolo" (lots 80 and 82–85); and "the celebrated Miniature painter" Giulio Clovio (lots 86–90). Lesser-known artists, who have virtually disappeared from the annals of modern art history, are also cited by name, such as "Ant. Maria Antonotius Auximas . . . a disciple of Pietro da Cortona" (lots 91–94), Magdalena Corvia (lot 95), and Joann. frid. Heribach (lot 96). Ottley's attempt to market illumination like monumental painting—not only by attribution but by papal patronage, along the lines of the way the High Renaissance painters were grouped—is significant. Little effort was made to interest bibliophiles in this sale; instead, the overwhelming focus was on attracting those who wanted specimens of the "Art of Painting."

Other characteristics of the sale confirm its presentation of illuminations in the manner that Old Master paintings were presented. Nearly all the works in this part of the sale are single lots—one great picture, frequently framed, sometimes glazed (the entries specify "with plate glass")—and they are often presented as pictorial collages, entirely void of text (though the word "collage" is not used, and the component parts of the illuminations are described in detail). For example, here is the description of the collage in the Pierpont Morgan Library (M. 270), lot 87 (figure 22, plate 2):

Another [pasteboard], height 16 1/4, width 11; also containing figures of the four Evangelists; among which that of St. John is remarkable for its elegance. Upon the border, which is richly embellished like the last described, with flowers, birds, butterflies, &c., painted on a gold ground, are three small compartments, representing the Annunciation of the Virgin, and a half-figure of the Almighty, which are tastefully painted in chiaro scuro, heightened with gold; and at the bottom are the Arms of the Pontiff, supported by two little Angels, in the drawing of which Clovio has sufficiently evinced his well-known predilection for the style of Michelangiolo.[27]

Even when the works were not framed and glazed, their dimensions were routinely given (as is customary in descriptions of paintings), as though they were paintings suitable for framing. Discussed further in the section on collage, two illuminations fortuitously survive in the early-nineteenth-century frames they had in the Celotti sale. These were acquired at a later date by George Salting and in 1910 bequeathed by him to the Victoria and Albert Museum (PDP. E.4577–1910 and E.4578–1910). Examination of one of these pastiches (figure 23) shows that the painted frame presents a kind of illusionistic continuation of the collage, rather like the integrated frames of Italian Renaissance altarpieces. Just who did the framing—even whose idea it was—is unknown, but certainly this strategy is a unique, hitherto unobserved, feature of the Celotti sale, and it was apparently successful.

**22.**

**Giulio Clovio,
miniatures of Evangelists
and decoration (Italy,
sixteenth century),
montage of fragments,
from Sistine Chapel
choir books (nineteenth
century)**

23.

Miniature of decollation of
St. Paul and decoration
(Italy, early sixteenth century),
montage of fragments from
Sistine Chapel choir books
(nineteenth century)

The success of this part of the Celotti sale can be measured by the relatively high prices paid, which were comparable to those paid for Old Master
paintings and far in excess of the prices of illuminated manuscripts. In line with
the contemporary Vasarian paradigm of taste, sixteenth-century miniatures by
well-known painters fetched the highest prices. For example, a large miniature of
"unparalleled magnificence" of the Crucifixion, which was signed by Apollonius
de Bonfratelli, set the record for the sale at 91 pounds (lot 85). A Crucifixion
attributed to Clovio, now at the Brooklyn Museum, realized the second-highest
price at 38 pounds, 17 shillings (lot 89; figure 24). Comparable prices were paid
for other works by Bonfratelli, whose many signed full-page miniatures realized
the highest prices overall, and by Clovio, whose miniatures ranged from 16
pounds, 16 shillings, to 38 pounds, 17 shillings. A montage attributed to Clovio,
now in the Art Institute of Chicago, was sold for 16 pounds, 16 shillings (Chicago
Art Institute, 1982.438). A miniature by Girolamo de Libri, whom Vasari identified as the teacher of Clovio, brought a similarly high price of 17 pounds, 66
shillings (lot 56), and two miniatures by an artist "of superior talent" whose style
was related to Andrea Mantega's were sold for 38
pounds, 10 shillings, and 29 pounds, 8 shillings (lots 38
and 40). The entire sale made nearly 800 pounds.

At the same time, Italian paintings, referred
to at the time as "primitives" or "Pre-Raphaelites,"
sold for ridiculously small sums: one year earlier, in
1824, Filippo Lippi's *Christ Bearing the Cross* went for
7 pounds; Giotto's *Death of the Virgin* for 18 guineas;
and early Italian school *Marriage at Cana* for 3 pounds,
10 shillings, the same price realized by various works
by Masaccio.[28] These prices fall well below those that
important illuminations made in the Celotti sale.
The situation had not changed much by midcentury,
when, between 1847 and 1850, many of Ottley's
primitives were auctioned off and bought in (that is,
they did not realize their reserves and, therefore, went
unsold in the rooms). Sales of manuscripts from the
same years show that extraordinary works, such as
the twelfth-century picture cycle of the life of
St. Edmund, sold for 168 pounds, a richly illuminated
Burgundian copy of Christine de Pizan's *Epistre Othéa* sold for 136 pounds, 10
shillings, and a prayer book illuminated by Nicolas Jarry sold for 101 pounds.[29]
However, many other illuminated manuscripts could be bought for well under
100 pounds, often for fewer than 10 pounds.

**24.**

**Giulio Clovio,
Crucifixion,
(Italy, sixteenth
century)**

Yet while the prices of miniatures in the second part of the Celotti sale
seem high when compared with those of fully illuminated deluxe manuscripts
or Italian primitives, they were still cheap for the buyer who really wanted a
Raphael, Michelangelo, or Carracci. Anything between the period of Raphael and
Carracci was well over a 100 pounds. The cheapest Raphael to appear on the
market in the entire nineteenth century appears to have been the Orléans Pietà
which cost 131 pounds, 15 shillings, in 1831 (now in Fenway Court Museum,
Boston), and in 1839 the National Gallery in London bought William Beckford's
*St. Catherine* for $6,000.

Prosperous dealers of Old Master paintings turned up at the Celotti sale
and bought heavily. One-quarter of the lots, or twenty-four miniatures (mostly in

the second half of the sale), were acquired by Anthony Molteno (died circa 1846), a collector and dealer of prints and drawings and an associate of the celebrated London firm Colnaghi's, which handled fine paintings. Molteno set all the records at the sale and obtained every high-priced miniature. William Manson (died 1852), whose father was a book dealer and who would later join forces with James Christie but at this time was an independent picture dealer, bought ten lots. Among London booksellers, only Robert Triphook successfully purchased a few relatively inexpensive items. The big book dealers like Payne and Foss were conspicuously absent, although they did attend the Ottley sale a little more than a decade later, when interest in cuttings had grown substantially among various sectors of the art-buying public. Other buyers included connoisseurs and collectors. For example, Ottley himself, who had amassed a major collection of Italian paintings and was also an important collector-dealer of prints and drawings, bought fifteen lots in his own name, and he subsequently owned many of the illuminations purchased by Molteno, who might have been purchasing for him.

A puzzling detail results when prices paid at the Celotti sale are calculated on the basis of two extant annotated catalogues, one including the names of buyers. One catalogue belonged to Manson, the other to John William Bradley (but at a later date). The Bradley catalogue has two sets of prices. The first is in black ink and conforms exactly with the prices in the Manson catalogue. The second set, added in red, shows higher prices, mostly of those items purchased by Molteno and Manson. This suggests that either Bradley had access to the resale prices of Molteno and Manson (both dealers) or that the miniatures brought even higher prices at resale, in an after-sale ring. (A ring, now illegal, consists of a group of buyers who, by arrangement, conspire to keep prices low during a sale but who then hold a postsale auction among themselves; in this case, Ottley joined Molteno and Manson.) Whatever the circumstances, the final prices, according to Bradley's copy of the catalogue, were even higher than those officially recorded. For example, the highest-priced miniature, the Brooklyn Museum *Crucifixion,* brought 52 pounds, 10 shillings, instead of 38 pounds, 17 shillings, and the Art Institute montage 21 pounds instead of 16 pounds, 16 shillings.

William Young Ottley, the author of the Celotti catalogue and a major buyer at the sale, whose own sale of cuttings took place in 1838, offers an opportunity to explore the intersecting worlds of taste, scholarship, art making, and the market around 1800.[30] Son of Richard Ottley and Sarah Elizabeth Young, Ottley had independent means, the family money coming from plantations in the colonies. He began to study art under George Cuitt, perfecting a personal style rather like the neoclassical art of John Flaxman or Henry Fuseli, and in 1789 he entered the Royal Academy. From 1791 to 1799, Ottley resided in Italy, mostly in Rome, where he purchased many works of art—prints, drawings, and Old Master paintings. Apparently, during these years he also worked as a copyist for Jean Baptiste Louis Georges Seroux d'Agincourt, whose monumental opus, *Histoire de l'art par les monumens depuis sa décadence au IVe siècle jusqu'à son renouvellement au XVIe,* eventually appeared in 1823, although it was completed much earlier.[31] In France and England, Seroux d'Agincourt and Ottley, respectively, are pioneer historians of the history of Italian art before Raphael.

Upon his return from Italy, Ottley became known as an authority on art and collecting. Beginning in 1833, after he lost his income following the Emancipation Act, which freed the slaves, for the last three years of his life Ottley was keeper of the Print Room in the British Museum. His predecessor at the British Museum, John Thomas Smith (1816–33), praised him: "Mr. Ottley is a gentleman better qualified than any I know to speak of works of art, more particularly those of the ancient schools of Italy."

Through his publications, Ottley became a recognized expert on Italian art, including draftsmanship and printmaking. Two works are worth studying in some detail. In 1826, Ottley published *A Series of Plates Engraved after the Paintings and Sculptures of the most Eminent Masters of the Early Florentine School; intended to illustrate the history of the restoration of the arts of design in Italy* (figure 25). Dedicated to John Flaxman, this work "is intended to illustrate the history of the revival and gradual advancement of the arts of design in Italy, during the thirteenth, fourteenth, and fifteenth centuries."[32] The drawings in it were made between 1792 and 1798, that is, during Ottley's years in Rome. Not surprisingly, Ottley puts Leonardo, Fra Bartolommeo, Michelangelo, and Raphael at the pinnacle of the arts of design. However, he attempts to resurrect the efforts of their predecessors, who for "three centuries preceding that epoch . . . solidly laid" the foundation, "firmly fixed" the scaffolding, and even "in great measure erected" the superstructure.[33] Starting with an unknown artist of the Greek school ("barbarous style"), Ottley proceeds through Cimabue, Nicola Pisano, and Giotto, "one of the greatest geniuses that ever lived."[34] Gaddi, Orcagna, Donatello, and Signorelli are all characterized as antecedents who inspired Michelangelo, whereas Masaccio is seen as inspiring Raphael.

Ottley's second work is even more interesting: *The Italian School of Design: Being a Series of Fac-similes of Original Drawings by the most Eminent Painters and Sculptors in Italy; with biographical notices of the artists, and observations on their works* (which came out in parts between 1808 and 1823).[35] The facsimiles engraved by Ottley himself, illustrating some eighty drawings from his own collection, won this work high praise, and it was described as one of "the most sumptuous books on the fine arts ever produced."[36] (The function of Ottley's book, providing examples for the education of artists, anticipates the works treated in chapter 3.) Ottley's book is important because it shows how he viewed medieval painting in stark contrast to Renaissance painting:

Although during the darker century of the middle ages, the arts of painting and sculpture remained sunk in a state of torpor, they were never wholly lost, either among the Greeks or the Italians. The idolatry and magnificence of Pagan worship were not entirely set aside, ere the Christian church began to encourage the introduction of pictures and images within its sanctuaries: the hermit in his cell, the monk in his cloister, illumined the missal, or traced the memorial of passing events; and thus during a protracted period of anarchy and tumult, the germs of art and literature were kept alive. . . . Such was more especially the condition of painting, from the age of Constantine till the thirteenth century; insomuch as . . . it would be impossible to decide whether any work . . . should be ascribed to the sixth century, the ninth or the twelfth.[37]

Using the same figures and commenting on or glossing Vasari's text, Ottley himself became somewhat of a latter-day Vasari, for whom the "golden era of painting" had its beginnings with Leonardo.

Ottley was not an isolated case. Other important collectors in England and on the Continent participated in the rehabilitation of the Italian primitives that had begun at the end of the eighteenth century. Edward Solly (1776–1844), a banker in Berlin and Hamburg, formed a collection before 1821 (now the core of the early paintings collection in Berlin), when it was acquired by William III, king of Prussia.[38] Solly was one of the first to appreciate fully northern primitives, buying the wings of the Ghent altarpiece around 1816. Another collector was William Roscoe, whose catalogue, compiled in 1816, includes thirty-two Italian primi-

**25.**

**William Young Ottley, *A Series of Plates Engraved after the Paintings and Sculptures of the Most Eminent Masters of the Early Florentine School* (London, 1826), unnumbered final plate**

54

GROUPS PAINTED BY MICHELANGIOLO BUONAROTI 1508–1511, IN THE SISTINE CHAPEL AT ROME UNDER THE FIGURE OF THE PROPHET
JONAS, AND WHICH HE AFTERWARDS OBLITERATED, IN ORDER TO MAKE ROOM FOR THE UPPER PART OF THE CELEBRATED LAST JUDGMENT: UNMINDFUL PERHAPS, THAT
IN SO DOING, HE RENDERED IMPERFECT HIS GENEALOGICAL SERIES SHEWING THE DESCENT OF CHRIST FROM ABRAHAM.

DRAWN BY WILLIAM YOUNG OTTLEY, AND ENGRAVED UNDER HIS DIRECTION UPON THE
AUTHORITY OF A DRAWING OF THE EARLY PART OF THE 16ᵗʰ CENTURY, IN THE POSSESSION OF SAMUEL ROGERS ESQ.

TO WHOM THIS PLATE IS RESPECTFULLY INSCRIBED.

tives.[39] Historian of Lorenzo de' Medici, and thus exceptional in his interest in the quattrocento, Roscoe, like Ottley, valued primitives as "specimens" in a vision of progress toward a golden age. As Roscoe put it: "[T]he following works . . . have been collected . . . chiefly for the purpose of illustrating, by a reference to original and authentic sources, the rise and progress of the arts in modern times. . . . They are therefore not wholly to be judged of by their positive merits, but by a reference to the age in which they were produced."[40] Their views were shared by Fuseli: the period from Cimabue was the "stage of missal painting . . . its taste continued, though in degrees less shocking, to the time of Michelangelo and Raphael."[41] Deposited at the Walker Art Gallery in Liverpool in 1893, Roscoe's collection was given to the gallery in 1948.

Another interesting art collector was William Thomas Horner Fox-Strangeways (1795–1865), a diplomat, whose collection is now divided between Christ Church, Oxford (gifts of 1828 and 1834), and the Ashmolean Museum (gift of 1850), half of the nearly one hundred pictures being primitives.[42] By the time of Fox-Strangeways's letters, the taste for artists of the "good epoch"—Raphael, Correggio, and so on—had reached sufficient proportions to support a market in copying, about which Fox-Strangeways writes in considerable detail. In August 1826, he made several visits to the Italian studios of copyists, declaring that a certain Wallis's "copies of Raphael are decided failures."[43] He then visited one Cozi, who showed him "another copy of the Ezekiel done to imitate the original *exactly* with an old cracked varnish & a faded look about some of the clouds & mounted in an old frame."[44] Concerning the National Gallery, Fox-Strangeways wrote: "If I had capital I would lay out £5000 sterl. in pictures and make a perfect historical collection from Cimabue to Mengs & sell it for double to the National Gallery for they by [*sic*] nothing."[45]

Among the few historical commentators on attitudes toward Italian primitives in English collections during the early nineteenth century is Dr. Gustav Friedrich Waagen (1744–1868), director of the Royal Gallery in Berlin, who has been called the "first professional art historian."[46] In his *Works of Art and Artists in England* (1838), Waagen recounts a dinner he enjoyed at Ottley's, who apparently had become an intimate friend. Waagen admits that he went early "in order to examine more at leisure his collection of paintings of the Tuscan school, from the thirteenth to the fifteenth centuries." But he was treated to an array of medieval fragments as well—including early pieces such as Ottley's mid-twelfth-century work from Bury St. Edmunds (figure 26, plate 1).[47] Struck by Waagen's interest in his collection of cuttings, Ottley confessed that "nobody has paid so much attention to them as myself." After dinner, Waagen says,

a new pleasure was prepared for me. Mr. Ottley fetched his portfolios with ancient miniatures, of which he certainly has 1000, from the eleventh to the seventeenth century . . . the Italian is by far the richest. With the exception of a few, they are cut out of old MSS in parchment. By being thus detached from the documents to which they originally belonged, they are unfortunately deprived of the principal means of ascertaining the place and time of their origin. The number of those that are interesting and beautiful is considerable.[48]

## COLLECTORS OF MANUSCRIPTS AND ILLUMINATIONS

The collector of illuminations did not exist in the eighteenth century, which witnessed instead the formation and dispersal of great libraries by ardent bibliophiles. In contrast, the early nineteenth century saw the bifurcation of manuscript appreciation into, on the one hand, the continuation of the eighteenth-century tradition

of appreciating medieval manuscripts primarily as historical "curiosities" or patrimony and, on the other hand, the emergence of a new breed of manuscript collector, interested not in the whole book but in fragments from it as specimens of
artistic style and calligraphy. The vast number of nineteenth-century bibliophiles
are too numerous to deal with here and have been amply studied elsewhere; a few
are worth mentioning. In England were Sir John Soane (1753–1837), William
Beckford (1760–1844), and the redoubtable Sir Thomas Phillipps (1792–1872). In
France, the outstanding bibliophiles included the Firmin-Didot family, especially
Ambroise Firmin-Didot (1790–1876), who amassed about 375 manuscripts among
the more than 2,000 books sold at his six sales. (See chapter 3 for the Firmin-Didot family's contribution as publishers and collectors.) Encouraged by the Celotti
sale, collectors interested in independent manuscript illuminations (single leaves,
cuttings, collages, and so on) from England include the poet Samuel Rogers (1763–
1855); Charles Brinsley Marley (1831–1921), whose collection of 245 illuminations
went en bloc to the Fitzwilliam Museum in Cambridge; Lord John Northwick
(1769-1859); and the Australian George Salting (1835–1909), who lived in London.
In France were the architect Hippolyte Destailleur (1822–93), many of whose
fragments went to the Bibliothèque Nationale (Dep. Estampes); Comte Horace de
Viel-Castel (1802–64), whose collection was bequeathed to the Louvre; and the
Viennese Frederic Spitzer (1815–90). The collector of manuscripts, as distinct
from the collector exclusively interested in fragments from manuscripts, heralds a
larger cultural development—the nascent Gothic Revival movement in England.

Illuminated manuscripts had a place as the natural accoutrement for buildings in the Gothic style. Whether the London clergyman Anthony Mathew (1733–
1824), whose wife held a literary salon, owned illuminated manuscripts for the
Gothic library designed for him by John Flaxman and Edward Oram is not known.
Sir John Soane acquired some expensive illuminated manuscripts—referred to as
"sundry relics and Missals"—in 1800 as the appropriate decoration for a Gothic
monk's cell and oratory, with its monastic ruins and monk's tomb, in his London
house.[49] Soane was in fact suspicious of the Gothic Revival enthusiasms that developed in the 1820s as an architectural movement.[50] Illuminated manuscripts were
specifically the props of the "Gothick mystery" interlude in the palace he was
building in London's Lincoln's Inn Fields. Soane's one venture in Gothic was for
a private client, the duke of Buckinghamshire: a Gothic interior was the appropriate setting for the library at Stowe (Buckinghamshire) in 1805, recently enriched
with the Irish and "Saxon" manuscripts of the antiquary Thomas Astle (died 1803),
though the model followed was the sixteenth-century Gothic of Henry VII's
chapel at Westminster Abbey.[51] One or two illuminated manuscripts were selected
as furniture that suited the rococo extravaganza of Horace Walpole's elaborately
Gothic edifice at Strawberry Hill. They were in the High Renaissance style associated in the nineteenth century with Giulio Clovio, as part of exotic conceits for
which Walpole's house and collection were famous.[52]

William Beckford, author in 1786 of the popular Gothic tale, *Vathek,* had
illuminated manuscripts in his collection, housed at his neo-Gothic Fonthill Abbey.[53]
Before selling the abbey and its collection in 1823, he had amassed a number of
medieval illuminated prayer books, including one of the thirteenth century "in a
style that would have honoured Giotto." His manuscripts were kept in the Edward
III gallery of his library, and were a natural adjunct to portraits of medieval figures
from whom he claimed descent. Early-sixteenth-century manuscripts were deemed
"sufficiently gothic," as he said in 1815, and a necessary part of a library in the
Gothic style.

Beckford continued to collect illuminated manuscripts after 1823. By that time collections of a connoisseur commonly included one or two illuminated manuscripts. Popular access to such artifacts was minimal, and the exclusive quality of illumination was often an attraction to the collector. Beckford, after all, had been relieved that the *Bedford Hours,* a national heirloom after Richard Gough's 1794 monograph on it (discussed in the chapter 1), had not gone to a "plebeian" buyer at the 1815 Edwards sale (the successful bidder, the marquis of Blandford, had beaten off an attempt by John North to buy the work) and regretted that another manuscript prayer book, "The best for good taste that I have seen in my life," had been acquired by North, a mere corn dealer of East Acton.[54]

That illuminated manuscripts were particularly appropriate as possessions of aristocrats—or at least an aristocracy of connoisseurs—was a common idea throughout the nineteenth century. Armor, like illuminated manuscripts, was a suitable prop for people who saw their social position reaffirmed by an appeal to an ancient lineage. The supposedly medieval ritual for the coronation of Queen Victoria was not enacted as planned in 1838, so in Ayreshire the following August, the thirteenth earl of Eglinton organized a celebrated tournament that took place in the rain in front of his tenants and a large number of visitors.[55] Here, a political point was being made about the proper nature of the monarchy and its relations with the aristocracy. Related concerns lay behind the 110 or so festivals devoted to medieval and Renaissance themes among the 350 that Wolfgang Hartmann has identified as being held in northern Europe between 1791 and 1939; the past was being represented to make statements about the relation of the festival organizers (usually a potentate, city council, or society) to that past and to affirm beliefs about their status and relation to authority.[56] Artifacts like medieval manuscripts were among the useful props and sources.

At Middle Hill, the omnivorous collector Sir Thomas Phillipps amassed, through "great dragnet operations," often by buying entire collections en bloc, the largest private collection of manuscripts of the nineteenth century.[57] The vastness of his collection is measured in part by the fact that it took nearly a century to disperse in direct sales to governments, institutions, and private individuals as well as some twenty public auctions.[58] Phillipps was a pro-reform radical in the 1820s, an opponent of free trade in the 1840s. His largely historical taste in collecting may be attributed to his dislike of High Church Puseyites matched only by his hatred of Chartists, Roman Catholics, foreign Catholic countries, and Napoleon III. In 1839, medieval liturgical and biblical works were "thinly represented" in the list of his collection made when Chartists from Birmingham threatened to ransack Middle Hill. Interestingly, however, by 1872 prejudice against liturgical works had abated, and Phillipps's collection then contained "an embarrassingly large number of fifteenth-century books decorated with miniatures," many of them devotional or liturgical, evidently antiquarian or art-historical documents rather than treasured repositories of pure spirituality.[59] Collectors of this kind reflect the various political positions of their class. The richly illuminated manuscripts Phillipps owned makes surprising the critique that "Phillipps's artistic appreciation was nil," but his overriding interest in manuscripts as documentation makes him exemplary of the continuing bibliophilic obsessions of the previous century.[60]

Illumination became most popular around 1860. This popularity is evidenced by the high prices fetched at sales featuring major illuminated manuscripts. The decade of 1850 to 1860 was the high point of the growth of the national collection at the British Museum Library, its purchase grant raised from a mere seven hundred pounds in 1837 to three thousand pounds by 1850. The Treasury looked with more sympathy at requests for help in special cases. Having failed to gain support for the purchase of the Stowe manuscripts in 1846, the library was successful in gaining a Treasury grant of three thousand pounds in 1852 to acquire at last the collection of Sir John Tobin of Liverpool, which included the most celebrated manuscript of nineteenth-century England, the *Bedford Hours.*[61]

A distinct group was formed not by collectors of manuscripts but around the collecting of fragments, a group clearly distinguishable and increasingly numerous after midcentury. Some of these collectors, like Samuel Rogers and Robert Stayner Holford, were primarily picture collectors, supplementing their paintings with illuminations and benefiting from the glut of cuttings on the market in England in the aftermath of the Celotti and Ottley sales. They are distinguished from a second group of collectors of fragments, among whom Spitzer and Salting may be regarded as more typical, who come out of the late-nineteenth-century interest in decorative arts and ornament. Only with the rise of the interest in ornament can Gothic or earlier art achieve a place of pride next to High Renaissance figures like Clovio.

Robert Stayner Holford (1808–92) was a major English collector whose extensive collections of manuscripts were described in Waagen's *Treasures of Art in Great Britain.*[62] In addition to some of the finest illuminated manuscripts, most of which were bought by American collectors earlier this century, such as the twelfth-century *Miracles of St. Edmund,* which Holford bought for three hundred pounds in 1841, were more than sixty single-leaf miniatures. These were mostly obtained from Ottley's 1838 sale and were from Italian choir books.[63]

Just as Holford represents a more open-minded and serious midcentury collector of manuscripts in his taste for earlier Gothic and even Romanesque manuscript illustration, his cuttings, too, were more varied. He owned one of four twelfth-century leaves from the *Eadwine Psalter* (Pierpont Morgan Library, MS M. 521), which Ottley had correctly described as English and which would have been viewed with disdain as a mere curiosity a generation earlier. Waagen described Holford's collection as "as valuable as any to be found in public museums."

Samuel Rogers is another important English art collector. A banker's son, he sought and achieved fame as a poet (*The Pleasures of Memory,* a work that went through fifteen editions by 1806).[64] Rogers is regarded as one of the first connoisseurs. His house on St. James Street, overlooking Green Park, was decorated by Flaxman and Stothard under his personal supervision. There he housed his collection of pictures, engravings, antiquities, and books. Rogers's eclectic tastes are evident in the title of the sale catalogue: *Catalogue of the Very Celebrated Collection of Works of Art, the Property of Samuel Rogers, Esq., Deceased; Comprising Ancient and Modern Pictures; Drawings and Engravings; Egyptian, Greek, and Roman Antiquities; Greek Vases; Marbles, Bronzes, and Terra-Cottas, and Coins; Also, the Extensive Library; Copies of Rogers's Poems, Illustrated; the Small Service of Plate and Wine.*[65] Lots 981 and 984 to 1010, many with multiple items, represent the illuminations he had amassed and include the famous *St. Michael* illumination from Fouquet's *Hours of Etienne Chevalier,* now in the British Library. Attributions are rare in the short catalogue entries; they are restricted to works by Bonfratelli, following the taste of the Celotti and Ottley sales. One lot (1006), later to be incorporated in an album anachronistically known as the *Rogers's Album* (British Library, MS Add. 21412), is described as a "collection of ninety-two exquisite arabesque illuminated borders" executed for Cardinal Antonio de Pallavicini and termed by Dr. Waagen "[a]mong the most magnificent and the richest monuments of this period" in his discussion of Ottley's collection. This group of borders fetched two and a half times the price of the Fouquet (forty versus sixteen pounds).

Born in New South Wales of a merchant family, from whom he enjoyed an inheritance of some thirty thousand pounds annually, George Salting apparently spent all his time searching for art treasures.[66] Interested the ornamentation and decoration of objects, what would now be termed the "minor arts," Salting represents a different sort of collector than Holford or Rogers. He collected Italian and Spanish majolica, enamels, jewelry and metals, small sculptures, works of art from the Middle Ages, Japanese art, and, above all, Chinese porcelain. He was such an avid collector of the latter that he eventually lacked space for his purchases, lending his collection of Oriental porcelain to the Victoria and Albert Museum, where he began to send new purchases directly. His interest in "things medieval," complemented by his eye for decoration and ornament, led him to medieval illuminations, and he bought heavily at the Spitzer sale, spending more than forty thousand pounds, some on illuminations. For example, he acquired two collages from the Celotti sale (see figure 23) and four illuminations attributed to the Dunois Master (Jean de Haincelin?).

Frederic Spitzer came from his native Vienna to Paris in 1852, where he arrived without a fortune. He appears to have made his money partly through commerce in art, buying and selling off as he built his vast collection. Spitzer's taste, like Salting's, was eclectic, and it formed around "things medieval," as is evident in the Musée des Arts Industriels that he opened in a private hotel in Paris on the rue Villejust in 1878. Systematically, almost encyclopedically, organized, Spitzer's museum-mansion included whole rooms devoted to ivories and boxwood sculpture, religious goldsmithery, Italian art, including manuscripts, medals, and plaquettes, with a small collection of Greek art to remind the viewer that the Renaissance goes hand in hand with antiquity and armor. It was in the second room, with the enamels and French furniture, that most of Spitzer's thirty-one illuminations, and some of his forty manuscripts, were kept. Spitzer's sale in 1893—called *la plus grande vente du siècle,* with its catalogue in four thick volumes—brought in just over 9 million francs.[67] His manuscripts are now widely dispersed (the *Conradin Bible* in the Walters Art Gallery; *DeBuz Hours* at Harvard University; and so on). His illuminations show his taste to be diverse. He owned sixteen single sheets from the *Juvenel des Ursins Hours* illuminated by the Dunois Master; three collages, one that includes a Flemish Marmionesque Virgin surrounded by Italianate medallions (figure 26, plate 3); and two others from the ubiquitous Ottley Collection (see figure 23) bought by George Salting and later bequeathed to the Victoria and Albert Museum.

## THE ART OF "SPLENDID ANCIENT FRAGMENTS"

Dibdin's *Bibliographical Decameron* (1817) celebrates how "[m]y friend Mr. Ottley absolutely revels in the possession of the most splendid ancient fragments of books of this description," but discussing how recently many of these had been excised from manuscripts, the bibliophile adds the sly comment "as no *names* are here mentioned, this general observation will remain *stingless.*"[68] This suggests that there already existed some unease about taking a knife or scissors to books, but there is little evidence that this practice was denounced during the first half of the nineteenth century. It is not until 1860 that Henry Lucien, author of *Hints on Illuminating,* uses the term "vandal" to describe the habit.[69] As mentioned earlier, the term "vandal" had been coined to describe those who wreaked destruction on churches and other monuments during the French Revolution. Ironically, the Revolution also popularized the practice of vandalizing manuscripts for their pictorial treasures and made it possible for Ottley to write of cuttings as the "monuments of a lost art."[70]

26.

Simon Marmion, miniature of Virgin and Child (France, late fifteenth century); Attavante Attavanti, decorative frame (Italy, early sixteenth century), montage of fragments (nineteenth century)

Modern scholars also tend to feel uneasy about the creating and collecting of cuttings. These are "activities which art historians approach with some ambivalence," according to Roger Wieck, pointing to our modern fear of "breaking apart" the complete art object.[71] By contrast, nineteenth-century art enthusiasts thought nothing of altering older artifacts to suit their tastes. Collectors would have viewed what we see as vandalism and mutilation as exactly the opposite: by isolating the painting from the rest of the book, they were elevating the work of the anonymous medieval illuminator to the status of the great masters. Perhaps censorious attitudes toward past perpetrators of this type need reevaluation; the obsession with the totality of a sacred original as a unique, inviolable object was not shared by our forebears. Moreover, the restoration and re-creation that are viewed with disdain for a manuscript leaf are deemed quite normal for a Gothic cathedral or an oil painting.

In the realm of medieval architecture, the most obvious example, "restorers" like Viollet-le-Duc rebuilt monuments such as Carcassonne and totally transformed churches and cathedrals like Vézelay and Notre-Dame to suit their own vision of the Middle Ages. Rowan Watson has pointed out how virtuoso Victorian goldsmiths often "improved" and repaired medieval metalwork and how furniture was constructed from fragments.[72] Today, most of the medieval objects displayed in the Victoria and Albert Museum and the Metropolitan Museum of Art are incomplete fragments that were saved by being reconfigured and changed, broken apart and refashioned, to fit into the taste and collector's cabinet of subsequent generations.[73] Sometimes, after the "derestoration" of an object to get to the "real" thing, not much is left. Once it is accepted that there is no such thing as a pure and original artwork, only the constant transformation of objects that are refashioned both conceptually and physically over time to suit different audience expectations, the history of the cutting up of manuscripts by collectors and dealers through the nineteenth century can be seen not so much as a shameful but as a reconstitutive act.

The practice of cutting up manuscripts was not new in the nineteenth century, but its popularity blossomed in this period, partly owing to the increasing interest in gathering "specimens" of things medieval. But it can also be seen as part of a wider phenomenon of fragmentation and re-creation of the past in the period that shaped European culture more generally. Munby alerts us to another, more practical reason for dealers jettisoning the vast pages and heavy bindings of Italian antiphonals and bringing home only the salable initials. Anyone importing books made before 1801 into England from the Continent had to pay an import duty of six pounds, ten shillings, per hundredweight.[74]

Whereas in the nineteenth century illuminated manuscripts were cut up and reconstituted because they were seen as valuable objects that could be made even more attractive and salable when framed as isolated paintings, in earlier centuries medieval manuscripts were commonly cut up for precisely the opposite reason: their lack of value. Christopher De Hamel has pointed to the sixteenth century as a period when, especially after the arrival of printing, thousands of cutout leaves of manuscripts were used as binders' waste: "sewing guards, flyleaves and as the wrappers of bookbindings."[75] The remarkable quality of some pastedowns recently discovered in old bindings by scholars such as Neil R. Ker and others also reveals how little value subsequent generations attributed to "old things" whether script or picture.[76] Even in the later nineteenth century, Leopold Delisle discovered leaves cut from manuscripts in the library of St.-Martin of Tour among the piles of fragments stocked by *bouquinistes* in their stalls on the banks of the Seine.[77]

The Middle Ages was, in Karl Morrison's words "intolerant of the frag-mentary, indeed unwilling for a fragment that could not be worked into a greater context, to survive."⁷⁸ The transformation of medieval manuscript fragments into objects of artistic value, ordered in portfolios, framed together on walls, rearranged in albums and collages, preciously preserved in extra-illustrated volumes, suggests that nineteenth-century collectors shared this attitude. But on another level, the notion that a small cutout piece of a larger whole could be appreciated as valuable in itself, as a specimen of style or of the art of a particular period, is more recent—an idea alien to the Middle Ages and one that seems to have its origins in the nineteenth century.

The following discussion separates single leaves, initials, albums, extra-illustrated volumes, and collages. Obviously, these categories overlap, and many objects are cuttings that are remade when collaged together with others (see figures 22, 23, and 26, plates 2 and 3). But this order preserves something of a historical trajectory in the sense that miniatures and initials first have to be excised before they can be collected and rearranged. Also there is a difference between single leaves, which are to some extent coherent pieces of a book, and fragments such as initials, which were meant to be viewed as part of a sequence of letters spelling a word. The cutout framed miniature is in a more ambiguous category, since it can be seen both as something complete in itself, as a picture, and as a fragment of a larger whole.

### BREAKING THE BOOK: THE STATUS OF THE SINGLE LEAF

The collecting of single leaves of illuminated manuscripts as opposed to complete volumes can be traced back to the fifteenth century.⁷⁹ Netherlandish illuminators of this period produced single pictures that could be sold separately, inserted in Books of Hours, pinned on the wall as devotional images, or even mounted on wood and lacquered.⁸⁰ On his travels in the Netherlands, Albrecht Dürer bought a miniature of Christ from the illuminator Susanna Horenbout (1503–45), probably a genre of what was called *illuminure* that was never meant to be part of a book. These exam-ples, as well as some illuminations by the famed Simon Bening (1483 or 1484–1561), perhaps should not be thought of as single leaves at all but as paintings that happen to be on parchment, like the limnings popular at the English court.

There is a vast difference, however, between a miniature that was pro-duced as a single independent object for sale and a leaf that has been excised from what was once a larger whole. A Book of Hours with full-page miniatures by Jean Bourdichon (1457–1521), probably made for Henry VII, was broken up in Eng-land sometime before 1700, though most of the parent manuscript is still in the British Library (MS Royal, 2 D XL). Understanding the motives for making inde-pendent pictures out of such leaves is not difficult, as they contain single large images with blank versos, constructed in Bourdichon's highly naturalistic style. Because of their thick, illusionistically painted frame borders, in a sense they are already framed and ready to be viewed as separate pictures, just as they were in the subsequent centuries of their dispersal and sale. Significantly, illuminators like Bourdichon, Simon Marmion, and, most obviously, Fouquet, all fifteenth-century artists whose small-scale work was later cut out of context, also produced monu-mental paintings. In addition to being mounted on wooden supports, such isolated miniature leaves were often later glazed to appear more like varnished panel paintings.

The beginnings of this practice of dismembering books for their paintings coincides with the beginning of the interest in illuminated manuscripts as works of art in the late eighteenth century. The most famous case is undoubtedly that of *Hours of Etienne Chevalier,* painted by Jean Fouquet around 1455 and, according to François Avril and Nicole Reynaud, "one of the most celebrated illuminated manuscripts in the world" (figure 27).[81] They go on to say, however, that "manuscript" is today not the right word, since in the eighteenth century someone cut out each full-page miniature right down to the frame. At the time of the French Revolution, this manuscript, which had been copied by Gaignières and illustrated as a historical example in Montfaucon's *Les Monumens de la monarchie françoise* (1729–33), entered the possession of the dealer Peter Birmann (1758–1844). Birmann was one of the first specialist dealers in manuscript illumination as well as the compiler of the Burckhardt-Wildt album, discussed below. Fouquet's miniatures were probably removed in the 1790s, pasted on panels of wood, and some of them then framed in a noted Parisian atelier. It used to be thought that the text pages were discarded as worthless, but recently a bifolium of the text from the Hours reappeared in a private Swiss collection and was sold at Sotheby's in 1981.[82] Making miniatures into small panel paintings

went beyond cutting them out. Before framing them, someone clumsily covered up the words of text with fragments from either later fifteenth-century borders or decorative motifs cut from seventeenth-century manuscripts made in the Benedictine monastery of the congregation of St.-Maur, at the abbey of St.-Germain-des-Près, whose library had been pillaged in 1792. In 1803, forty of the newly constructed "paintings" from the *Hours of Etienne Chevalier* were sold in Basel by the banker and picture-collector Georges Brentano for 5,000 gold francs. In 1891, these were resold by Brentano's son to the duc d'Aumale (for 250,000 francs), who placed them in the collections at Chantilly. Seven other leaves were in different sales during the nineteenth and twentieth centuries, mostly in England, and are now in the Louvre, the British Library, the Metropolitan Museum in New York, and the Wildenstein Collection at the Musée Marmottan, Paris.[83]

An English example of this practice of around the same date is John Gower's manuscript *Confessio Amantis,* now in the Pierpont Morgan Library (MS M. 126; see figure 28). It had belonged successively to two eighteenth-century antiquarians, Peter le Neve (1661–1729) and Thomas Martin of Palgrave (1697–1771), who clearly appreciated it for its literary text and not its 108 miniatures. At the death of Martin, chemist named Thomas Worth bought the manuscript and cut out nine miniatures and sold them to Sir John Fenn, "another antiquary with an eye for a miniature."[84] The mutilated book was purchased by Brigg Price Fountain of Narford, at whose 1902 sale it was acquired by Quaritch (and subsequently by J. P. Morgan). The Pierpont Morgan Library has since been able to acquire the missing miniatures at the 1926 sale of Fenn's great-nephew. An interesting hypothesis sees Fenn's activity in extracting the miniatures as part of his scholarly intention to copy and engrave them for his antiquarian work. In this respect the history

Upon the poynt of his bileue
The people thought to releue
And tes him self to be ded
Wher is now such another hed
Which wold for the lynes dye
And natheles in som partie
It onst a kynnes seete stere
That he his seete men forbere
And eck toward his enemyes
Fuloffte he may deserue prys
To take of pite remembrance
Wher that he mighte do vengeance
For whom a kinge hath the victoire
And thanne he dubbe into memoire
To do pite in stede of wreche
Ne may not faile of thilke speche
Wherof Arisce the worldes fame
So wide aprince aworthy name fo

Hic ponit exemplum de victorioso
principe pietate erga aduersarios suos
Et narrat quod cum pompeius Romanoz
inparator regem Armenie aduersariu
suu in bello victum cepisset captumq̃ vin
culis alligatum Rome tenuisset tiranni
die iracundie stimulos post ponens pietatis
mansuetudinem opatus est dicit enim
q̃ nobilius est regem facere quam deponere
sup quo dam Regem absq̃ ulla redempc̃i
one non solum a vinculiis ab soluit sed
ad sui Regni culmen gratuita voluntate
coronatum restituit

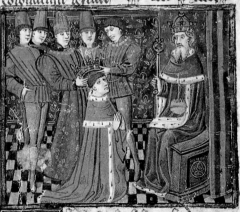

Lite solũ whilom the pompeie
De whom that fame moste alere
A were he hadde in Armenie

May in this wilde feld aplayne
So sitte it wel a kynge to haue
Pite for this walter to lede
And seide how thei be dede goke
Todeus Which were in his Retue
Kyng of Athenis the Tiree
A were he hadde ayein Dorence
And for to take his euidence
What shal he falle of the bataile
Ne thought he wolde him self consaile
With Apollo in whom he triste
Thurgh whos answere thus he wiste
Of tho poyntes thei he muste chese
Or that he wolde his lady lese
And in bataile him self dele
Or elles the secund were
Of seen his people discounfit
But he which pite hath parfit

of manuscript reproductions is linked to the activity of cutting up manuscripts in a previously unrealized way.

This practice of cutting out folios obviously increased during the nineteenth century with two important sales consisting solely of single leaves taking place in England: the already-discussed Celotti sale in 1825 and the sale of Ottley's leaves in 1838.[85] The cutting up of manuscripts was surely stimulated by the market. S. Hindman has observed of the Spitzer sale in Paris in 1893: "[T]he prices realized reveal at once that single leaves were incredibly expensive when compared with entire manuscripts."[86] The English collector George Salting paid the enormous sum of six thousand francs for a pair of Italian Renaissance miniatures made for Pope Clement VII, about the same price as a whole manuscript, the thirteenth-century *Conradin Bible* (figures 32 and 128), now in Baltimore (Walters Art Gallery, MS W. 152). Throughout the century tastes and prices continued to valorize the Italian over the French and the Renaissance over the Gothic in the realm of miniature as much as panel painting. Two major nineteenth-century collectors of cuttings in England, Sir Richard Wallace (1819–90), whose thirty-two examples form part of the Wallace Collection in London, and the artist Charles Fairfax Murray (1849–1919), focused on Italian examples.[87] When later in the century the taste for Van Eyck and Flemish manuscripts of the fifteenth century was nascent, Ghent-Bruges Books of Hours were cut up, the text discarded, to function as isolated devotional miniatures. Six small illuminations from a Book of Hours by the French painter Simon Marmion, in the Masson collection and now in the Ecole des Beaux-Arts, Paris, were cut out of their larger pages to create multiple meditative images.[88]

The single leaf made its appearance in the public museum as well as private collections. Spitzer's Musée des Arts Industriels, opened in Paris from 1878, was one of the many places to see displays of single-leaf cuttings framed like paintings. Another museum in Paris was the Musée de Cluny, which displayed both manuscripts and single leaves in cases in its various period rooms from its opening in 1853.[89] The Victoria and Albert Museum bought cuttings as part of its educational project from 1855. Today, the best place to see how the private collector and museum might have displayed framed cuttings during the last century is the collection of Georges Wildenstein, who donated his 220 examples to the Musée Marmottan in Paris. This includes large initials from Italian choir books but also smaller framed miniatures from thirteenth- and fourteenth-century manuscripts. Some have been framed to become miniature altarpieces—as three miniatures by Bulbil and the Master of the *Murano Gradual* —and others are elaborately organized groups of cuttings framed together.[90]

As the century progressed, so did the notion that art should be not only pleasurable but also useful. Ruskin's important contribution to the history of manuscript studies—his championing of earlier thirteenth-century Gothic art and illumination above the classicism of Giulio Clovio and Renaissance art, which he hated with a passion—has been overshadowed by the notorious entries in his diary describing his destruction of manuscripts. His entry under December 30, 1853, reads, "Set some papers in order and cut some leaves from large missal; took me till 12 o'clock." On January 1 he "put two pages of missal in frame" and on January 3 "cut missal up in evening—hard work."[91] Ruskin's comments have to be seen not only in terms of how they reflect attitudes toward collecting but also in a very different current of the period: the democratization of manuscript illumination through its use as an example of handcrafted art and decorative design (see chapter 3). Nonetheless, Ruskin's aims were part of a serious effort at education, and as he wrote, "There are literally thousands of manuscripts in the libraries of England . . . of which a few leaves, dispersed among [the] parish school, would do more to educate the children of the poor than all the catechisms that ever tortured them."[92] However, as well as donating manuscript leaves to the Ruskin School of Drawing, which he had established at Oxford, and to a working men's museum near Sheffield, he gave three leaves of his most precious Gothic manuscript, the *Isabella Psalter* (Cambridge Fitzwilliam Museum MS 300) to his American friend Charles Eliot Norton. Another of his treasures, the multivolume *Beaupré Antiphoner* (circa 1290), is today in pieces (figure 29). Christopher De Hamel has come to the defense of Ruskin—the "unjustified hero of manuscript breakers"—noting that of almost a hundred illuminated manuscripts personally owned by him, Ruskin removed and gave away only four sample leaves from books that had already been partially dismembered by the bookseller John Boykett Jarman.[93] Not a "snipper-out of miniatures," Ruskin separated only whole leaves, and the single collage of miniatures, now at Bembridge (figure 44), presents no evidence of Ruskin's having actually done the cutting. This attempt to rehabilitate Ruskin suggests an important distinction between the removal of a whole page from a book and the taking apart of that page, either for its miniatures or, as was more common, its illuminated initials.

## Breaking the Page: The Nature of the Cutout Initial

The cutout initial *C* depicting a prophet (figure 30, plate 4) is typical of the high-quality Italian illumination that was appreciated by Victorian collectors in the wake of the new interest in the so-called "Italian primitives," especially Giotto. Choir books made for San Michele a Murano in Venice in the 1390s, illuminated by Don Silvestro dei Gherarducci, a monk of the Camaldolese order who worked in the monastery of Santa Maria degli Angeli in Florence, were widely dispersed in the nineteenth century. Before 1799 William Young Ottley acquired initials like this directly from the monks of Santa Maria degli Angeli in Florence, where manuscripts had been systematically dismembered to provide "specimens." In his *Lives of the Painters,* Vasari had mentioned Don Silvestro dei Gherarducci as an important illuminator of choir books, which gave these cuttings the added luster of a name. Dibdin in his usual poetic vein describes how "Choral, or Church-Service Books are the very seed-plot, or nursery-ground, of such whimsical decorations. In these books, Giotto, Cimabue, and a hundred other graphic constellations of various degrees of magnitude and lustre, diffused their grateful light."[94] By this date Ottley and others were looking for additional earlier "Gothic" names and not only Vasari's Giulio Clovio.

Choir books such as graduals and antiphonals were especially prone to dismemberment. They were bulky and unwieldy, containing liturgical and musical material that might no longer be used; moreover, the vast size of the folios made even an initial into something large enough to be thought of as a painting. While the tiny initials from a thirteenth-century Bible would make little sense framed and isolated (however, see figure 45), the enormous and elaborate initials from Italian choir books were ideally collectible as isolated units. Although one might argue, as Waagen did, that this destroys their original locus, the illumination of such books was done after the text was written, and isolated initials can be found in fourteenth-century model books and pattern books, suggesting that already in their own period of production they could have an autonomous quality. Illuminations were sometimes cut out of earlier manuscripts and put into newly written books, a practice

**29.**

Historiated initial O,
Betrayal of Christ,
single leaf from the
*Beaupré Antiphoner*
(Flanders, circa 1290)

**30.**

**Don Silvestro dei Gherarducci, historiated initial C, cutout fragment from a gradual of San Michele a Murano, Venice (Florence, 1392-99)**

that occurred in monastic foundations, where a ready-made supply of initials was at hand. De Hamel's examples include the Brigettine nuns of Syon Abbey in England and the Dominican nuns of Poissy in France, who in the sixteenth century cut out initials from mid-thirteenth-century Bibles and borders from around 1400 to decorate their books.[95]

This reuse within the same monastic context has to be distinguished from the vandalism that ripped initials from many books in Oxford and Cambridge libraries. Sir Robert Cotton (died 1631) used initials cut from illuminated books for decorative purposes.[96] There are other examples of manuscripts losing initials in the eighteenth century, including the great *Conradin Bible* now in the Walters Art Gallery (figures 31, 32, and 128). It is harder to classify the decorative reuse of initials created by Philip Hanrott's children and their cousin Esther Cory, who circa 1828 cut out the beautiful initials from their father's *Carmelite Missal* of circa 1400 to spell out messages and their names in medieval letters (figure 33). This has to be seen as part of the craze for alphabets, scrapbooks, and collages, in which even the not-so-well-off could construct their own little collections. The *Carmelite Missal* as painstakingly reconstructed by Margaret Rickert is now considered a crucial work of London manuscript illumination.[97]

The Victorians loved tiny things, what Susan Stewart has called the collector's fascination with "the miniature" as a category not of painting but of objects in general, including shells, flowers, jewels, doll's houses, names inscribed on grains of rice, and so on.[98] Commodification and industrialization only increased this interest in owning scaled-down things. The cutout fragment in the form of an initial or a miniature fit well in the bijoux world of the nineteenth-century parlor with its clutter of prints, embroideries, watercolors, and butterflies. Kept in portfolios rather than framed at this date, the initial was a tiny specimen, not unlike a pressed flower or butterfly that would have been pored over in the delightful solitude of contemplation. But the manuscript fragment was also deemed to be useful, as John Ruskin was later to argue, in teaching poor children.

**31.**

**Four fragments from**
*Conradin Bible*

**32.**

*Conradin Bible*
(Italy, thirteenth century),
God speaks to Moses
in the wilderness

**33.**

Hanrott, "Signatures,"
initial letters from the
*Carmelite Missal* reconfigured to spell the names
of the members of Philip
A. Hanrott's family

Not only private collectors but public institutions like the Victoria and Albert Museum were buying these initials, as examples of medieval art, from the middle of the century. Colonel Stranges's catalogue of the museum states, "The damage having been done it is now possible to preserve carefully such relics as may still be found."[99] This use of the word "relics" is interesting, since the ways of collecting and exhibiting relics—the fragmented bones and body bits of saints—during the Middle Ages were similar to the ways of collecting and exhibiting fragmented bodies of books in the nineteenth century. But whereas the relic embodied the sacred aura of the saint's incorruptible and still powerful divinity, the cutout initial embodied the increasingly sacralized and transcendent notion of "art"—the artist's name that came to be worshiped as the religion of art replaced the old faith. Even initials had their "signatures." One of the San Michele a Murano fragments, now in Kansas City, had the forged signature of the miniaturist Don Silvestro dei Gherarducci on it, possibly added by none other than Ottley himself (figure 34). Paradoxically, our modern attitude toward the pristine original has resulted in the "restoration"—that is, removal—of Gherarducci's forged signature, thereby returning the leaf to its original status but erasing evidence of its nineteenth-century history.

Another stimulus to the collecting of manuscript fragments was the rise of the study of art history itself. A good example of this is the Liverpool historian William Roscoe (1753–1831), who, in addition to gathering an important collection of Italian primitives, also collected cuttings. One of these was a large initial by Don Silvestro dei Gherarducci depicting the birth of St. John the Baptist, which he obtained from Ottley's collection and which is now in the Walker Art Gallery.[100] Roscoe's aim to write the "Historical Sketch of the State of the Arts in the Middle Ages" came to nothing after the failure of his bank in 1816 forced him to sell his collection. As Munby describes, Roscoe was not a very advanced connoisseur for his times; his chapter on art in *The Life of Lorenzo de' Medici* (1796) repeats the usual clichés about the barbarous Dark Ages, describing tenth-century miniatures in the Laurentian Library in Florence as "perverse distortions of nature."[101] Roscoe never visited Italy, and all his information came from books like Vasari's and from his own familiarity with manuscripts like those of his friend Thomas Coke, whose important collection at Holkham Hall Roscoe began to catalogue in his retirement.

That Roscoe did not travel is interesting, considering that the importance of travel, travel writing, and guidebooks is an unwritten episode in the historiography of art history. As an extension of the grand tour, continental journeys continued to be crucial, especially for English collectors. It is hard for us to imagine today how easy it was for the tourist to take away souvenirs that were hundreds of years old. Visitors to the monastery in Zwolle in the eighteenth century could leave their names in the six-volume Dutch Bible kept in the chapter house and take leaves or initials as mementos of their visit (figure 35).[102] Ruskin wrote to his friend Sir Charles Newton, who was traveling on the Continent, "But if you come across any very interesting MS—interesting I mean in *art,* for I don't care about old texts—and can secure it for me, I will instantly reimburse you to the extent of 50 pounds, only I should expect a great deal for that price out of those old convent lumber rooms."[103]

Another example of the importance of travel and scholarly publications, is James Dennistoun (1803–55), a Scottish antiquary and scholar who traveled extensively in Italy for twelve years, collecting paintings but also single leaves and fragments for a projected study he was writing on the history of medieval Italian art.[104] He recorded where he bought many cuttings in Padua, Verona, and Milan, including three initials from an antiphonary now in the Breslauer collection ob-

34.

Don Silvestro dei Gherarducci,
historiated initial *M*,
St. James and St. Andrew
(Italy, fourteenth century),
cutout fragment with forged
signature added in nineteenth
century (photo taken before
cleaning)

tained in Lucca directly from the monastery in 1838.[105] The same year he received a French miniature as a gift from Celotti, of which he wrote, "the long contorted figures of which afford a perfect specimen of the French style."[106] Once again, this word "specimen" is used to describe the object of delight and study, fitting it into a history of artistic forms.

One can understand how cuttings could provide easily accessible and classifiable specimens of this kind, examples of the art of different periods and centers, for those who, like Dennistoun, were beginning work in a totally unmapped field of study, without the aid of photographs that later made Berenson's connoisseurship possible. Dennistoun was able to label his initials "Lombardo-Venetian" or "passing from the manner of Beato-Angelico into that introduced by Domenico Ghirlandaio." The earliest recorded acquisition of a medieval manuscript by the Victoria and Albert Museum is a cutout historiated initial from a fifteenth-century Italian manuscript (figure 36), which came from the Dennistoun collection at his death in 1855 and was bought by the museum for four pounds, fourteen shillings, six pence. The initial M—again from a choir book—has an interesting iconography with Christ crucified, a bishop catching his blood in a chalice. Perhaps in this case it was the imagery rather than the style that attracted the art historian to this piece. Dennistoun never completed his projected work on Italian painting, passing on his notes to his friend Lord Lindsay, earl of Crawford, who incorporated them in his *Sketches of the History of Christian Art* (1847).[107] This may account for the new interest in Byzantine and trecento painting in Lindsay's work, which was well in advance of its time.[108] Dennistoun owned a Crucifixion by Fra Angelico, who was a crucial artist in the rising appreciation of earlier religious art in England.

**35.**

**Moses with the Tablets of the Law, cutting from the Zwolle Bible**

The taste for the initial isolated from its page was to wane, especially in the second half of the century when the real mania for calligraphy and illuminated alphabets meant that people wanted specimens of script as well as "art." Ruskin and others championed the integration of the arts in the Middle Ages, and although Ruskin cut up his beloved *Beaupré Antiphoner*, he nonetheless reproduced not isolated initials but whole pages from it in his own publication as specimens of design. Roger Wieck has drawn attention to some Italian leaves in the Pierpont Morgan Library that show this new preference for the whole rather than the fragment. Of the twenty-two cuttings that Morgan bought in 1909, a number of initials have been knifed out without any regard for the foliate borders or tendrils attached to them. "Later, while he or another still had access to the choir books themselves, some entire leaves were excised and the historiated initials reinserted into their holes."[109]

## REMAKING THE BOOK: THE FORMATION OF THE ALBUM

Nineteenth-century collectors often gathered their cuttings into albums or scrapbooks of different sizes or types, comparable to the sorts of albums or portfolios in which prints and drawings were also collected from at least the sixteenth century. Although no sixteenth-century albums of cutout miniatures have been traced (the

possible exception is a reference to one such album containing a miniature by the
illuminator Simon Bening of Bruges in Albrecht of Brandenburg's collection,
just a few years after Bening's death), there are albums recorded from at least the
seventeenth century. One of these is the exquisite album of fourteenth-century
Hungarian miniatures from the Life of Christ that belonged to Giovanni Battista
Saluzzo (1579–1642), who in 1630 presented it to his brother Angelo Saluzzo (died
1638), now divided between New York, Pierpont Morgan Library (MS M. 360
and MS M. 360c), and Rome, Vatican Library (MS 8541; see figure 37, plate 5).[110]
In the 1930s, Sir Kenneth Clark recomposed the album he bought from his aunt
that had been made up initially by James Dennistoun in the nineteenth century,
but by Clark's time such albums were no longer fashionable (figure 38).

Any study of these albums has become increasingly difficult for two reasons. First, the exigencies of the market, which places a value on a single cutting
far in excess of the value of an unbroken album, encourages their disassembly, as
has occurred in recent years with at least two famous examples, the Burckhardt-
Wildt and the Dennistoun-Clark albums (both dispersed in London, Sotheby's,
April 25, 1983, and July 3, 1984). Second, the policies of institutions also encourage their dismantling, as has occurred with both the Rogers album and the Rothschild-Ascott album in the British Library (MSS Add. S 35254 and 60630). In
seeking to preserve properly works of art on paper, conservationists often remove
manuscript cuttings from the old, acidic paper or card, to which they were hinged
with destructive animal glues, and remount them with new museum matts in
archival environments outside the original physical context. This procedure, of
course, destroys the form of the original album. Often, as is the case with another
category of medieval manuscripts, pastedowns and binding fragments, the history
of which is likewise erased by their undocumented removal—the dismantling of
albums, without appropriate record-keeping, will ultimately destroy part of the
history of collecting.

No systematic study of manuscript albums has ever been undertaken,
although some interesting research exists concerning related albums of prints and
drawings. Such a study would have to consider when, why, by whom, and how
miniatures were gathered into albums. In posing these questions, the multiple purposes albums served at different moments in time would likely also emerge. Albums
of works in other media provide some clues.

One of the most famous albums was put together by Giorgio Vasari,
mannerist painter and biographer of Italian Renaissance artists, whose work was so
influential in the history of collecting illuminated miniatures. Vasari intended his
Libro de' Disegni, a now-dispersed collection of some eight or more volumes, as a
sort of pictorial complement to his Lives of the Artists.[111] He assembled his drawings
on large sheets united with architectural frames he drew himself, and sometimes
with portraits of the artists drawn in cartouches in the frames. Vasari's sheets were
supposed to illustrate the history of Italian painting from its origins in the trecento
with Cimabue and Giotto to its climax with Michelangelo and his successors in
Vasari's own lifetime, as his own comments at the beginning of the book indicate:
"There remains for me to say of Cimabue that in the beginning of our book,
where I have put together drawings from the own hand of all those who have
made drawings from his time to ours . . . it is seen how much excellence was given by his work to draughtsmanship" (figure 39).[112] The Libro was known in some
form to Ottley who even owned drawings from it and who refers to it as a paradigm for collecting examples from the Italian schools.[113]

**37.**

Scenes from the Life of
Saint Bartholomew
(Hungary, circa 1300–50),
miniatures, cut and
reconfigured in an album

**38.**

James Dennistoun
Album, outer cover

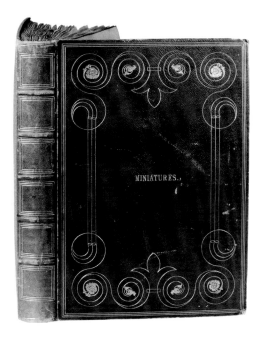

**39.**

**Giorgio Vasari,**
*Libro de' Disegni*
**(Italy, sixteenth century),
with drawings by
Giorgio Vasari,
Filippino Lippi, and
Sandro Botticelli**

Vasari's album tracing a history of art through drawings is not wholly unique, but different organizational schemes characterize other surviving albums of prints and drawings. Many of these are reviewed by Peter Parshall in an important study on print collecting.[114] A collector-cum-art-dealer in Nuremberg, William Imhoff kept twenty-nine albums mostly of prints and drawings by Albrecht Dürer arranged by size and including notes on their authorship, condition, and financial value. Other German collections, such as that of the Nuremberg collector Paul Praun, were arranged by artist and national school.[115] Inventories of Antwerp collections reveal that prints were also classified in albums in the sixteenth century by subject (classical, biblical, architectural, and so on). The immense collection of Ferdinand of Tyrol was arranged both by artist and subject.

Unlike many albums of manuscript cuttings that have been dispersed without record, or whose histories are obscure, the Burckhardt-Wildt album offers the opportunity for a fascinating case study because its physical description, acquisition, and dispersal can all be reconstructed in detail. Its approximately 475 illuminated cuttings on 53 folios were put together in Paris in the 1790s—that is, during the period of the chaotic vandalism that characterized the Reign of Terror and the Sack of Rome—by Peter Birmann, the Swiss art dealer and landscape painter in Basel who also marketed the Fouquet miniatures around the same time as the Burckhardt-Wildt album. Birmann sold the album, ready-made, to Daniel Burckhardt-Wildt (1759–1819) of Basel, a collector who also frequented Paris, where from the 1770s he bought works of art in a wide variety of media, including prints, paintings, drawings, marbles, and bronzes. Burckhardt-Wildt thus had a wide-ranging taste for the "curious" similar to that of other eighteenth-century gentlemen-collectors like the duc de La Vallière and the marquis de Paulmy. Unlike these aristocratic amateurs, however, Burckhardt-Wildt came from a family whose members had been merchants since the sixteenth century, and he himself was a silk ribbon manufacturer and a minor artist.

It is difficult to discern any clear logic to the organization of the Burckhardt-Wildt album. It includes mostly French cuttings (a few Greco-Italian miniatures and a few Flemish miniatures) from a variety of types of manuscripts (Books of Hours, chronicles, and literary works) and widely ranging in date—from the thirteenth to the sixteenth centuries. Diverse cuttings are often clustered together on a single page, unusually without regard for common provenance. For today's viewers, the most spectacular illuminations are a complete set of Apocalypse miniatures, once thought to be English but now assumed to be French, that occupy the first six folios of the manuscript and that, along with the two Greek miniatures, are the earliest illuminations in the album (figure 40, plate 6). Although these wonderful miniatures were kept together in the front of the album, they were not mounted in textual order (for example, folio 40 of the original manuscript is on folio 6 of the album, whereas folio 46 of the original manuscript is on folio 1). After this group, the album skips around in a rather helter-skelter fashion between fragments mostly from Books of Hours and from some secular texts.

An inserted price list made up by Birmann (and fortuitously still with the album, which remained in the same family for nearly two centuries, after which it was taken apart and sold in London at Sotheby's in 1982) gives some sense of how the whole collection was conceived. At the top of the itemized list of the prices Birmann charged Burckhardt-Wildt, appears a title: "Samlung Uhr, alter Kloster Zeichnungen en Miniature, welche H. Peter Birman anno 1796 in Paris eingekauft." The phrase, "old drawings and miniatures from cloisters," clearly stresses the religious content that does, in fact, prevail in the album. On its last folio, functioning

40.

*The Woman Clothed with
the Sun and the Dragon*
(Lorraine, France, circa 1295),
cutout fragment formerly in
Burckhardt-Wildt album

as a kind of pictorial colophon, is a striking collage of a cross, made up of 52 bits
and pieces of decorated borders (perhaps the residue of the fragments pasted into
the album, many of which had their border decoration removed). (see figure 41.)
This imaginative image underscores the idea that the album contains religious fragments. What must have encouraged the mutilation of these manuscripts—their acquisition and their rearrangement by Birmann—is the confiscation and destruction
of church property that was taking place everywhere in Paris at that very moment.

Birmann's itemized price list also offers the first real opportunity to compare the relative values of cuttings at the very end of the eighteenth century as a
means of assessing taste for different types of illumination. While the results are un-
expected to anyone familiar with today's markets, they are in line with the study
of eighteenth-century appreciation of manuscript books. For example, the interest
in belles lettres and chronicles is borne out in the prices for miniatures from Vincent of Beauvais's chronicle, *Speculum historiale,* valued at fifteen bogen each (folio
31, lot 129), compared with only six bogen each for the cuttings from the Apocalypse or the two Greco-Italian miniatures. The low value placed on the Apocalypse leaves reminds us that William Hunter had successfully acquired the twelfth-
century *Hunterian Psalter*—similarly undervalued—in a Paris sale just a few years
before. Earlier art, as Rive had insisted, was "barbarous." Miniatures from a chronicle of the Hundred Years' War were listed at about the same value (sixteen bogen)
as those from Vincent of Beauvais, although they are painted in watercolor wash
and on paper (folio 41, lot 153). Most surprising, however, are the values of leaves
from Books of Hours: small ones were appraised at only eight bogen, but larger
ones, including illuminated printed cuttings, cost upward of fifteen bogen, two and
a half times an Apocalypse leaf. This is perhaps because illuminated printed books
continued to be more highly sought after than manuscripts in sales of the period.

Quite different from the Burckhardt-Wildt album is the album of cuttings that James Dennistoun compiled on three grand tours mostly between 1836
and 1839.[116] Educated in Edinburgh and Glasgow, Dennistoun is best known to art

historians for his discovery of the art of Piero della Francesca, highlighted in his book *Memoirs of the Dukes of Urbino, illustrating the Arms, Arts, and Literature of Italy from 1440 to 1630.*[117] He became interested in antiquities during his first grand tour in 1825 to 1826, and although he kept a journal of his travels, the entries come to an end before he began to buy Italian miniatures. However, the idea that he was putting together a prehistory of Italian painting using illuminations is suggested through correspondence to David Laing. In 1848, he wrote: "I have . . . got together a very interesting series of miniature illuminations, illustrating the various schools from about 1000 to the days of Raffael after which this, the parent of oil painting, fell into disuse—now of all the rarities in art the rarest and most prized."[118] In the same letter, Dennistoun explained his picture collecting activity: "I have got now a small but very choice collection of Cabinet pictures, collected chiefly with the object of illustrating the progress of painting from the 13th through the successive schools down to modern times . . . but my favourite style goes back to the 14th and 15th."[119] Like Vasari in his *Libro,* then, Dennistoun wished to document a history of Italian art, and he chose illuminations as the particular medium he collected.

Waagen characterized works in the Dennistoun album as "ecclesiastical productions of the 13th to 16th century," in this respect like the Burckhardt-Wildt album with its primarily religious subject matter.[120] However, Dennistoun's red morocco album, though full of cuttings from choir books, is, in fact, entirely different from the Burckhardt-Wildt album, and it bears out many of the goals Dennistoun expressed in his correspondence with Laing.

*53.*

It should be pointed out that, although acquired by Sir Kenneth Clark (from Mrs. Henson, Dennistoun's granddaughter and the wife of the bishop of Durham in 1930; they were apparently called "Uncle Denny's scraps"), in whose sale fragments from the album appeared, the Dennistoun album was no longer complete at that date. A more thorough study would be necessary to reconstruct the album, but some items were sold after Dennistoun's death (Christie's June 14, 1855, lots 44, 46–47, and 115). As mentioned above, the earliest recorded acquisition of a medieval miniature by the Victoria and Albert Museum, an initial *M* of Christ crucified, a bishop, elders, and two beggars (PDP no. 2991; in 1855 for four pounds, fourteen shillings, 6 pence; see figure 36) comes from the sale of Dennistoun's miniatures held just after his death in 1855.[121] A miniature now attributed to Liberale of Verona was acquired by the Barber Institute, University of Birmingham, when consigned by Clark for sale on February 2, 1960 (London: Sotheby's, lot 250, as Sano di Pietro).[122] Clark sold other miniatures from the album as well (June 18, 1962).[123] And a number of whole album leaves were excised at an unknown date.

Clark not only sold some of the miniatures, or framed them separately, but he remounted those he kept in a two-volume album of completely different design and format in quarter vellum over paper boards with "Italian Miniatures. I"

**41.**

**Burckhardt-Wildt Album, pictorial colophon assembled in the nineteenth century**

and "Italian Miniatures. II" embossed on the spines. The order of the miniatures in the two-volume Clark set—not recorded in the sale catalogue—was completely different from Dennistoun's order and deserves to be further studied. Accurate cataloguing by Christopher De Hamel permits a partial reconstruction of each and furthers the understanding of their relationship one to the other.

Dennistoun mounted approximately sixty miniatures in his album, which he arranged roughly chronologically, by national school, regional style, and artist. What is extraordinary about the album is the way he mounted the pictures on hinges that allow them to be flipped up and that, when the flap is lifted, reveal a handwritten text below where Dennistoun wrote his comments, often on attribution and sometimes on provenance. The earliest fragments, Dennistoun 1 (St. Luke) and 2 (St. John), are early-fourteenth-century Greek miniatures (only the St. John was sold in the Clark sale, lot 90), which Dennistoun optimistically identified as "Greek school 10th century" and noted that they were "acquired in Geneva." Under the St. Luke he wrote, "The school and period of art to which I have assigned them are confirmed by a facsimile and description of a St. Luke much resembling this, in Agincourt *Storia dell'arte,* Vol. vi. p. 149 and plate 47." A few other fragments represent other artistic traditions. There are German examples, including two important early Gothic miniatures (Dennistoun 3 and 5, called "Byzantine School of Cologne? 12th Century," Clark lot 77, and Dennistoun 49, Clark lot 112; and Dennistoun 50, "Georg Penz, pupil of Albrecht Dürer," Clark 117) and Flemish examples (Dennistoun 34–36, "Three Flemish miniatures, School of Vaneyck, 15th century," Clark lot 105). Dennistoun acquired the German miniatures in Munich between 1836 and 1839, which indicates what kinds of miniatures were available on the market there, but wrote "the old German painters are not to my taste."[124]

What Dennistoun was most attracted to was Italian painting before Raphael, which he avidly bought throughout Italy, in Florence, Lucca, Siena, Gubbio, Verona, and Milan. In Florence in 1838, he met Abate Celotti, who gave him a fourteenth-century French miniature to add to his collection (not in the album).[125] Examination of Dennistoun's comments in the album show that for his time he displayed an extraordinary acumen about Italian art. Dennistoun 10 and 11 (Clark lot 78) are "cut out of a choral book or graduale in the cathedral of Florence, where I bought them in 1837. They seem to be monastic work, and are quite in the style of Giottino, the grandson & pupil of Giotto." These are followed by a set of four cuttings (Dennistoun 16–19; Clark lot 80) of the same age as the earlier set, "but the style imitates rather that of the Gaddis, the best pupils of Giotto who somewhat enlarged his manner." Then come two cuttings of the martyrdom of St. Agatha (Dennistoun 8–9; Clark lots 81–82), mounted consecutively with the comments that one is "very inferior . . . illustrates the differences between the handiwork of an artist, and a monk," and the second he gives to "School of Giotto." He calls a set of Venetian miniatures "Lombardo-Venetian," an extraordinary distinction for the time (Dennistoun 23–24, 25–27; Clark lots 83–84). Thirty-nine miniatures come from Lucca in 1838. Dennistoun writes:

On the invasion of Italy by the revolutionary armies of France, these beautiful books were plundered, and fell into the hands of some boors, who proceeded to cut up the broad parchment leaves, wherewith to cover their flasks of olive oil. Fortunately someone rather less barbarous rescued these initials by crudely cutting them out, without the slightest regard to the elegant borders, which are crudely mangled. The collection thus saved was bought by me at Lucca in 1838.

Others are "by some pupil of Taddeo Bartolo" (Dennistoun 74, 104; Clark lot 95) or in the "style of design in the convents after Beato Angelico de Fiesole" (Dennistoun 34, Clark lot 96), or "showy specimen of the Florentine School while passing from the manner of Beato Angelico that was introduced by Dominico Ghirlandaio" (Dennistoun 35, Clark lot 98), or "exhibit various styles . . . in Lombardy, previous to Leonardo da Vinci" (Dennistoun 37–39; Clark lot 101).

Following some illuminated copies after frescoes in the Vatican Loggia by Raphael (Dennistoun 53, Clark lot 116) came an illumination of the Annunciation by Giulio Clovio (Dennistoun 54; not in the Clark sale). Dennistoun's comments show that he was affected by the widespread cult of admiration for Clovio characteristic of nineteenth-century taste:

> . . . scarcely marred by a slight fading of the colours, the consequence of long exposure to the Italian light in a frame. It hung at the bed-head of the late Cardinal Albania, where it was always considered a precious work of Clovio, pupil of Giulio Romano and the finest miniature painter of Italy.[126]

Unlike other contemporary albums that were to be arranged in a more haphazard fashion, Dennistoun's album merits a close look partly because it so closely parallels more widespread attitudes toward taste in nineteenth-century England.[127] In 1836, when a commission in charge of recommending purchases of art works urged the National Gallery, which owned only four Pre-Raphaelite paintings, to buy early Italian pictures, Sir Robert Peel retorted: "I think we should not collect curiosities." Then in 1853, when Dennistoun was called before a similar committee charged with setting the basis for purchases at the National Gallery, he recommended that it purchase "works of the best age . . . the period between 1450 and 1540." When pressed about the lack of public interest in these works, he suggested to the committee that taste can be "corrected" through a very brief acquaintance with those pictures and finally added that "the National Gallery of pictures should contain specimens of what ought to be avoided, as well as what ought to be followed, in so far as regards the gradual progress of art. But true Pre-Raphaelite pictures, when good, show much to be admired."[128]

Dennistoun's album, then, even if it served primarily his own education instead of the larger viewing public's, contained such "specimens," works that enabled him to chart the idea of progress in Italian painting in four periods: first, the Byzantine, or stationary period; second, the medieval, or the age of sentiment; third, the Italian primitives, as the epoch of effort; and fourth 1490 to 1520, the age of mastery. In this, Dennistoun is a true follower of slightly earlier collectors of the revolutionary period, such as Ottley and Roscoe, and scholars such as Seroux d'Agincourt.

A whole manuscript, the *Ghislieri Hours,* rather than a cutting or an illuminated sheet, might be considered Dennistoun's finest purchase. He bought the manuscript in 1838 and sold it to Lord Ashburnham in 1847 (British Library, MS Yates Thompson 29).[129] It is no wonder *Ghislieri Hours* appealed to Dennistoun. It contains inserted miniatures of superior quality, two signed by Amico Aspertini and Pietro Perugino, one attributed to Lorenzo Costa, and another by an unknown Bolognese artist.

One other sort of album is relatively common, the album formed from single manuscripts. As Roger Wieck pointed out, one of the earliest extant albums of miniatures comes from a *legendarium,* a picture book of the lives of Christ and the saints, which was given by Giovanni Battista Saluzzo (1579–1642), the Genoese ambassador to France, to a relative of his, Angelo Saluzzo, in Rome in 1630 (see figure 37, plate 5).[130] Saluzzo took the quadripartite miniatures, divided them into four cuttings each, mounted them in an album with Latin distichs below and Italian ones above (and a brief note to the reader at the end indicating that "distichs pure and singular . . . will please at least by their brevity. . . . Calliope has her praise also in small things").

From the bookseller Bernard Rosenthal, Lessing J. Rosenwald bought a bound volume containing a group of thirteen cuttings from one choir book, presumably made in the mid–fifteenth century for Seville Cathedral and illuminated by the Master of the Cypresses (Pedro da Toledo), plus one small illumination by Simon Bening. Inside the front cover is a pencil annotation in the hand of W. Sterling: "I bought these cuttings from a Spanish *Libros Deloro* at Madrid in 1849" (on this album see also chapter 5). Still others include an album of thirty-four miniatures from a manuscript of the prose Lancelot illuminated by the Dunois Master, owned by Joachim Napoleon, fifth prince Murat (1856–1932), then by Wynn Jeudwine, who removed the miniatures and described them.[131] Related to these are albums in which the miniatures are not remounted on card or paper but tipped in as picture leaves into a binding; this is the case with, for example, a manuscript of leaves from a Book of Hours in the Blackburn Museum and Art Gallery (MS 20984) and of a universal chronicle in Paris (BnF, MS n.a. 14285).

An album of a different sort, and earlier, is Thomas Astle's collection of some 152 folios of leaves comprising Stowe manuscript 1061 in the British Library (for other albums by paleographers, see Taupier, the French writing master [Paris: BnF, MS n.a. fr. 1456]). This is the same Astle whose *Origin and Progress of Writing* plundered Rive's *Essai,* and folios 131 to 152 consist of Rive's plates (for Astle and Rive, see chapter 1). However, many other items—text leaves (one from a late-thirteenth-century Lancelot manuscript, folio 120) and a surprisingly large number of Cotton manuscript fragments—are included. A paleographer, Astle was evidently more interested in script than decoration, if we are to judge by the examples he included in his album, an observation that is confirmed by his *Origin and Progress of Writing,* which devotes only a few perfunctory pages to "Paintings, Ornaments, and Illuminations."[132] When he discusses illuminations, such as on folio 20, where he reproduces the St. Luke page of the Augustine Gospels, his inscription focuses on pure description. The middle section of the Stowe manuscript contains a large number of Victorian facsimiles of Cotton, Harley, and Lambeth manuscripts, evincing the nineteenth-century attitude that facsimiles were coevals of originals, indeed originals in their own right.

It was the William Young Ottley sale in 1838, however, that appears to have ushered in the real craze for albums in nineteenth-century England. Whether Ottley himself kept his miniatures in albums is unknown (if we are to believe Waagen, they were in portfolios, like prints or drawings), but the sale of his nearly one thousand cuttings, single leaves, and collages must have flooded the market. Everybody bought—private collectors, like Rodd, Sneyd, Rogers, Fuller, and Northwick, and booksellers, like Payne and Foss. Active buyers included John Thomas Payne and Henry Foss, prominent booksellers in London who ran their century-and-a-half-old firm (Payne and Foss, founded about 1740; broken up 1850) in partnership.[133] Specialists in illuminated manuscripts, classics, Aldines, and so on, they are said to have virtually shaped the important libraries of Grenville and Holford. An album they put together after the Ottley sale went to Robert Holford in 1845, from whom it then went to Sir George Holford, before its eventual sale (and dispersal) at the latter's sale (London: Sotheby's, July 12, 1927).[134]

A number of similar albums compiled from Ottley's leaves entered the British Library at various dates: the Rothschild-Ascott album, with forty-two cuttings, all from the Ottley sale (MS Add. 60630, purchased 1979); the Rogers album, with 110 cuttings, many of illuminated borders (MS Add. 21412), apparently not put together by Rogers himself but by someone after his sale (London: Christie's, April 28, 1856); the album of Robert Curzon (1810–73), with 58 cuttings (MS Add. 39636), bequeathed to his wife, Baroness Zouche of Harynworth (1860–1917); the album of John Malcolm of Poltalloch (1833–circa 1896) of about 20 cuttings plus a large number of borders. Two other volumes were bound by Charles Lewis, circa 1840—one of 97 cuttings from the sale of N. P. Simes (1886, 1095), another of 80 cuttings belonging to Thomas Bateman (1821–61; sale 1893, 1152). Three others, containing 59, 32, and 103 cuttings respectively, were in the sale of J. M. Gutch (London, March 16, 1858, 1830–32). Finally an album of cuttings plus three portfolios of miniatures were in Edward Hailstone's (1818–90) sale, London, February 4, 1891 (1465–68). None of these albums readily reveal any particular organizing principle; they are literally scrapbooks full of pretty pictures, and they often recount in a brief narrative Celotti's fabulous tribute brought from Italy. Owned by bibliophiles, not picture collectors (except Rogers and Holford, who also collected pictures), these albums suggest that cuttings collected and displayed in this way had come to be regarded as a requisite component of a nineteenth-century book collection.

### RE-CREATING THE BOOK: THE EXTRA-ILLUSTRATED VOLUME

The idea of the album took on a related form in the extra-illustrated volume, an activity that was also called grangerization. Named after James Granger in 1769 (and recently summarized, with interesting examples, by Roger Wieck), this practice entails placing extraneous leaves from other origins in a host volume.[135] There are medieval precedents for extra illustration. Owners often inserted devotional images—hand-colored prints or miniatures, even dried flowers, pilgrims' badges, and other flat memorabilia—into the flyleaves of their books. Some centers, like Bruges, supplied single leaves for the export trade, but this phenomenon does not really count as grangerization, because the manuscript volume was prepared in advance to receive extraneous illustration. Two fifteenth-century examples of collectors of the medieval phenomenon of grangerization are Hartman Schedel and Jacopo Rubieri.

Hartman Schedel was the Nuremberg physician and humanist most noted for his compilation of the *Nuremberg Chronicle* but also renowned as a collector. He pasted more than 120 prints, and sometimes miniatures, into volumes in his large library—both manuscripts and incunabula. In some examples, fugitive prints function primarily as ornament. However, others relate to their texts, often in interesting ways. For example, Schedel used a drawing of a playing card by the Master of the Banderoles, the figure of a king, as the frontispiece to Robert Gaguin's *Compendium de origine et gestis Francorum*. He appended the handwritten title "Most Christian King of France" to the engraving, and he painted, or had painted, a red frame around the image. He again used engravings by the Master of the Banderole, this time from his figure alphabet, as the headings for an index to Pliny's *Naturalis historia*.[136]

Jacopo Rubieri, a little-known Italian jurist, kept a written record of the cases he tried and of the proceedings of church councils he attended in five manuscripts (for example, Ravenna, Bibl. Classense, Cod. 450, 374, 485I/II, and Pesaro, Bibl. Oliveriana, Cod. 98). Forty-six hand-colored prints were removed from one of these manuscripts between 1937 and 1939 during a conservation project of the Vatican Library. Most of these prints are votive images, including pictures of

St. Roch, St. George, St. Christopher, Simon of Trent, and so on, purchased at various churches and cathedrals during Rubieri's journeys. Rubieri evidently used these manuscript volumes as albums for the collection he made as a kind of pilgrim.

The examples of Schedel and Rubieri indicate that supplemental illustrations usually reflect the content of the host volume in some way, and examination of nineteenth-century grangerized books bears this out. For example, a copy of Dibdin's *Bibliographical Decameron* was sold in New York in 1960. Divided into an impressive twelve volumes instead of the customary paltry three and bound in a deluxe binding by Rivière, this copy had the huge number of five hundred forty-seven interleaved illuminations, one of the favorite topics of the book. It was bought by a bookseller, and its miniatures were dispersed: two sheets by William de Brailes went to the Pierpont Morgan Library (MS M. 913, 914; see figure 18); another miniature went to the Metropolitan Museum of Art.[137] A copy of Henry Shaw's *Illuminated Ornaments* (London, 1833) is another example, containing thirty-seven historiated initials, six cuttings from borders, and seventy-seven illuminated initials; in other words, it contained examples of ornament like those reproduced by Shaw. These were pasted on the rectos of thirty-four leaves of thick paper bound into the back of the book. The Shaw volume was successively in the collections of John Lomax (1803–86) of Clayton Hall, Lancashire (January 5, 1842), who must have been responsible for its grangerization; then W. O. Wade; then C. W. Dyson Perrins, in whose sale it was (London, November 29, 1960, lot 151). After that, it was bought by the London bookseller Alan Thomas and ultimately dispersed at his sale (Sotheby's, London, June 21–22, 1993, lots 29 and 30, initials; lot 397, album). Bound by Charles Lewis in 1838, this volume displays many miniatures with sister leaves in the Holford and Northwick collections. It also includes the requisite description from a bookseller's catalogue on the inside front cover, describing the contents as "cut out of altar service books (particularly that of Como) during the French invasion of Italy."

Two interleaved books compiled by William Roscoe were meant to illustrate his idea of history. In a copy of Joseph Strutt's *Biographical Dictionary of Engravers,* no longer extant, he added original and reproduced works of the artists. Then, later, he interleaved a copy of Abate Luigi Lanzi's *Storia pittorica dell'Italia* (Bassano, 1795–96), now in the Liverpool Library.[138] Other interesting grangerized copies are of William Blades's *Enemies of Books* and are today in the Free Library of Philadelphia (see chapter 5).

How common the practice of grangerizing was may never be known, especially as extra-illustrated volumes are now consistently broken apart because they are of little interest to the modern collector and more valuable to the trade when marketed piecemeal. A deluxe exemplar of Dibdin's *Bibliomania* in the 1842 edition, printed on special pink paper and originally owned by its publisher-collector Henry G. Bohn, has recently come to light. It was grangerized not by its first owner but probably around 1883, and the original single volume was turned into three fat volumes with the addition of hundreds of engraved portraits and autographs, as well as eleven illuminations. The research of Roland Folter, to whom we are especially grateful for generously bringing the work to our attention, suggests that a Chicago book collector, Edward G. Asay, whose bookplate appears on an extra flyleaf in the first volume, was responsible for adding the extra illustrations. Among these added illuminations (of which four are medieval) are eleven miniatures attributed to the skillful illuminator Caleb William Wing (see chapter 3). This newly recovered copy of *Bibliomania* confirms the hypothesis that the practice of grangerizing was most frequently associated with books on books, transforming volumes by authors such as Shaw, Westwood, Dibdin, and Blades into hybrid exemplars like printed scrapbooks, which occupy a gray area between the manuscript and the printed book. If Asay indeed grangerized the work, the status of a nineteenth-century illuminator like Wing was assured on both sides of the Atlantic in his own lifetime.

## RE-CREATING THE PAGE: CUTTINGS AS COLLAGE

Most collages of manuscript illumination share one feature, the elimination of the text, and so they fit, in part, with impulses to transform illumination into picture painting. This is superficially true, but what marks collage especially as a nineteenth-century re-creation is the kind of picture painting that collage emulated.

Of the dozen or so collages recorded as having survived from the period, three types are distinguishable, each responding to a different taste in picture collecting during the century. The first group, those in the Celotti sale, reveals an attempt to make illumination into monumental wall painting of the "golden era of painting"—that is from Raphael to the Carracci. A second group, including an example made by or for John Ruskin, documents the renewed scholarly and commercial interest in the primitives, particularly their altarpieces—northern and southern—that accelerated only well after midcentury. A third group, comprising the collages from the Du Sartel sale in Paris and Albert Racinet's examples at the end of the nineteenth century, represents a response to the popular reproductive techniques of chromolithography (or color lithography), whose colors the collages attempted to replicate and whose own composite technique they sought to imitate.

Whereas approximately eight collages from the Celotti sale can still be identified, many more existed. It is therefore possible that their composite parts have been dismantled as they were "restored" into independent cuttings and fugitive border fragments. This is the case with a border fragment from the Curzon album (British Library, MS Add. 35254 P), which once surrounded a Crucifixion in the Brooklyn Museum (inv.11.499; see figure 24). It may also be the case with miniatures of the four Evangelists, once in Lord Northwick's collection and now dispersed (private collection; a sister cutting is in the Free Library of Philadelphia). These may originally have formed a pasteboard montage like those at the Art Institute of Chicago and the Pierpont Morgan Library (see figure 22, plate 2).[139] Those that exist share the following characteristics: a central miniature or cluster of miniatures, cut away from the surrounding text, is united by pasting strips of border decoration composed of cartouches and usually with other ornament either in the form of pediments or a quasi-architectural armature. In fact, "pasteboard"—the term used most frequently in the Celotti sale—best describes the final form. Others are identified simply as a frame, with multiple borders, and a miniature. In no instance does the Celotti sale catalogue specify whether these composite parts come from the same or different volumes. They are described as integral paintings.

The collages from the Art Institute of Chicago and from the Pierpont Morgan Library, both from the Celotti sale, exhibit some of the aesthetics of this early period (figure 22, plate 2). They are remarkably similar works, both being composite pasteboards of fragments from choir books created for Pope Gregory XIII. The Chicago collage is made up of six cuttings, which include four miniatures of the Evangelists grouped in the center, a full-page trompe l'oeil border, and an architectural cartouche enclosing a nineteenth-century inscription: GREGORIUS XIII PONT. OPT. MAX. Although the inscription dates later, it records an original provenance that is confirmed at the bottom of the border by the arms of Pope Gregory XIII, a dragon in an escutcheon, upheld by two putti and surrounded by the papal tiara and keys. Three cartouches in the margins display figures of the theological and cardinal virtues: on the left, Faith holding up a chalice and a host in one hand and a book in the other, with Hope, hands raised in prayer; at the right, Fortitude holding a broken column over her head and trampling broken columns at her feet, with Prudence, a book in one hand and a serpent entwined around the other; and, at the top, Charity supporting three children, Justice with scales and a sword in opposite hands, and Temperance pouring water into a jug of wine.

The New York collage (figure 22, plate 2) is a virtual twin of the Chicago one. Like the Art Institute montage, it is made up of six parchment cuttings, consisting of four separate miniatures of the Evangelists, a floral border with three oval medallions and the papal arms of Gregory XIII, and an architectural cartouche with a nineteenth-century inscription similar to that on the Chicago collage. In the New York example, the four Evangelists are mounted in a different order, and the *camaieu d'or* cartouches depict different subjects (the Annunciation on the left and right and a half-length figure of God the Father as the "Ancient of Days" above), but the overall conception is comparable. These fragments have a complex relationship with their parent manuscript, which must have been an impressive service book made for Pope Gregory XIII, most likely an evangelistary that included the readings from the Gospels appropriate for the feasts of the liturgical year as recited by the celebrant at the Mass.

With the elimination of the text, these collages transform the fragments from illustrations in books to independent paintings. But what is most interesting is how Celotti (and Ottley?) accomplished this and what pictorial models they had in mind when they composed the collages. An imitator of Michelangelo, though working on a small scale, Clovio—the artist to whom these collages were attributed in the Celotti sale and to whom they are traditionally still attributed—employed monumental, dramatically foreshortened figures, rendered in the pastel tones of fresco that readily recall Michelangelo's project in the Sistine Chapel. In fact, the Evangelists as they appear when cut away from their surrounding text, turned in three-quarter poses and facing architectural columns and pilasters, resemble remarkably the figures of the prophets and the Sibyls painted around the Sistine Chapel ceiling (figure 42). Below Michelangelo's figures appear entablatures bearing inscriptions surrounded by painted stucco ornament often composed of volutes. Surely these inscriptions offered the models for the similarly composed nineteenth-century inscriptions added by Celotti to the Chicago and New York collages. The additional volutes on which the cutout fragments of the Evangelists appear to rest in both collages, as though suspended in space but anchored to an architectural support, appear also beneath the prophets and Sibyls. Even the painted framing devices made up of egg-and-dart motifs among others in the Sistine Chapel ceiling are like the frames that set off the various parts of the collages. Here is it important to know what parts of the pasteboard (in addition to the inscription) date from the nineteenth century. The cutout fragments are all neatly arranged in a composition on a painted liquid gold ground that enhances the illusion of three-dimensionality and suggests that the miniatures, especially the Evangelists, jut out in space.

The New York collage, then, simulates the illusionistic painted program of the Sistine Chapel ceiling, combining simulated architecture and sculpture with the armature of the wall. Considering how much was made by collectors and antiquarians of the period of the Celotti sale of the "good epoch" of painting beginning with Raphael, not surprisingly the construction of the collages reveals an aesthetic that values such art. Only the trompe l'oeil floral border framing the page gently reminds the viewer of its origin in a book.

Another group of collages from the Celotti sale evokes a slightly different aesthetic of High Renaissance and mannerist painting. Nineteen composite lots in the Celotti sale come from service books made for Pope Clement VII, whose mottoes, emblems, and name appear on most of the surviving examples. Dated circa 1523, when Clement VII was elected, these composite leaves are credited to an "unknown painter" in the Celotti catalogue, but they have been subsequently attributed to various hands—Vincent Raymond, a French artist working for the popes in Rome; Blasius, a Florentine miniaturist cited in documents during these years; and Jacopo del Giallo, an artist praised by Vasari. Representing a wide variety of subjects, including numerous martyrdoms as well as Christological events, these miniatures probably come from one of two missals cited in inventories in the Sistine Chapel (MSS A.I.9 and A.I.14). They differ from the collages formed from Pope Gregory XIII's evangelistary in that they each include one large central narrative scene surrounded by separate panels of border decoration, sometimes four, sometimes as many as eight. Clement's papal tiara and arms are centrally located at the bottom of each composite sheet, and figural medallions decorate the margins, which are in turn filled with dense gold ornamental decoration, rather like painted *groteschi*.

Comparison of the composite in the Victoria and Albert Museum depicting the beheading of St. Paul (figure 23) with painted decoration in the gallery of the Palazzo Farnese in Rome painted by Annibale Carracci between 1597 and 1604 suggests that Celotti (and Ottley) also looked toward baroque illusionism for further inspiration in constructing their collages. In Carracci's ceiling, the central fresco paintings are presented as simulated easel paintings rather like the simulated easel paintings at the center of the Victoria and Albert collages (see figure 43). Along the curved panels of the vault and the lateral walls in the Palazzo Farnese, illusionistically painted medallions punctuate the rectangular paintings, similar to the medallions that decorate the panels of the collages. In the ceiling, the overall design is secured along the lateral walls by an elaborately painted architectural framework made up of gilded cornices, pilasters, and entablatures strikingly like the illuminated panels surrounding the central miniature in the collage. The finishing touch Celotti added to these collages—architectural painted frames decorated with rosettes at their four corners—also recalls painted architectural decoration in the Farnese gallery. At once more ornate and flatter—in fact, more classical—the Farnese ceiling, like the collages from Clement VII's service books, represented the most sought-after art of the revolutionary period, which may explain why Celotti turned to it for inspiration as he conjectured how best to make a market for the looted miniatures.[140]

Against the background of the art market, Celotti's (and Ottley's) decisions about how to compose their collages make even more sense. Whereas there was virtually no active market for Italian primitives before midcentury (most of Ottley's Italian primitives bought in during two sales in the 1830s and 1840s), the market actively supported the "good epoch," which included anything that was Raphaelesque. From this date, by bequest or by purchase, Italian and Flemish primitives start to enter the National Gallery.

The situation was similar in France. The earliest French primitives acquired by the Louvre, apart from those of John the Good, appear to be the 1835 portraits by Fouquet, and active acquisitions of French primitives only postdate midcentury.

**42.**

**Michelangelo, prophet Zachariah (Rome, 1508–12), spandrel of Sistine Chapel ceiling**

**43.**

**Annibale Carracci, Palazzo Farnese ceiling (Rome, 1597–1600)**

The second group of collages depends on an awareness of the aesthetic of the primitive, especially the altarpiece, with or without movable wing, that entered the public arena through the marketplace and the museum after midcentury. Although there is no secure independent means of dating examples from this group (since they are not easily identifiable in sales catalogues, which would provide a *terminus ante*), they therefore most likely were put together after midcentury. One little-known example from the Toledo Museum of Art can be seen as transitional (figure 26, plate 3). The borders, attributed to the Florentine illuminator Attavante Attavanti (Florence was also little prized before midcentury, Rome being preferred)—a collaborator of Domenico Ghirlandaio and one of the few illuminators, apart from Clovio, praised by Vasari—recall borders of the Victoria and Albert collages. The center, however, resembles an independent easel painting, a primitive of the type current throughout the fifteenth century in works by Robert Campin, Roger van der Weyden, Petrus Christus, and Hans Memling. Here, an illumination close to the style of Franco-Flemish painter-illuminator Simon Marmion (died 1489) has been laid down on a simulated marble stele serving as a kind of altarpiece against a Florentine landscape. Typically, in manuscripts by Attavante this flat space presents an inscription that serves as a rubric or title: for example, "Here begins the Ordo. . . ." The effect is very odd not only because of the anachronistic mixing of styles but also because the relationship of the viewer to the spatial fields is so peculiar, as comparisons with "original" fifteenth-century illuminations of approximately the same date and milieu make clear. Sold in the Spitzer sale in 1893, the work postdates about 1850, when the taste for primitives had changed.

A more typical example from the latter half of the nineteenth century, composed of French (and Italian) cuttings, John Ruskin gave to the Bembridge School (Lancaster: Ruskin Library, RF 194). A closely related example is composed of pieces from an Italian psalter. In Ruskin's example, a scene of the Presentation in the Temple, very close to the style of Jean Bourdichon and cut around its rectangular frame, is placed in the center of a pasteboard and surrounded by scenes from another French Book of Hours, these in arched frames (figure 44). As though forming a *predella*, five miniatures decorate the lowest row below the large miniature. Next to the central illuminations are two vertical rows of miniatures on either side (twelve in total). At the top are two more miniatures. The seams give the impression that the bottom horizontal panel is fixed in place and that the outermost vertical panel is hinged as in an altarpiece with movable wings. The whole is then united by a border decoration of large besants and rosettes applied wallpaper style to the surface of the pasteboard (the cuttings are mounted on top of this design).[141] Very similar is the group of cuttings by two Florentine painters, Giovanni di Antonio Varnucci (1416–57) and Ricciardo di ser Nanni (active 1430–80), so similar that they may even have been put together by the same individual.

Collages not only responded to the taste for late-medieval painting, they also reflected burgeoning interest in other medieval art forms, like stained glass. For example, fragments from a pocket Bible made in France, circa 1250, are arranged in a collage structured like a Gothic stained-glass window that reflects the Victorian taste for miniaturization. This inventive collage also recalls Didron's characterization that miniatures were like stained-glass windows on parchment (see chapter 1), a view echoed in Ruskin's famous remark that a "well-illustrated Missal is a fairy cathedral full of painted windows." The luminous properties of miniature painting, especially works from the thirteenth century, like stained glass, remind us that the monumental medium of glass painting was undergoing a simultaneous revival (figure 45, plate 7).[142]

98

**44.**

**Scenes from the Life of Christ, from fifteenth-century French Books of Hours, assembled as a montage (nineteenth century)**

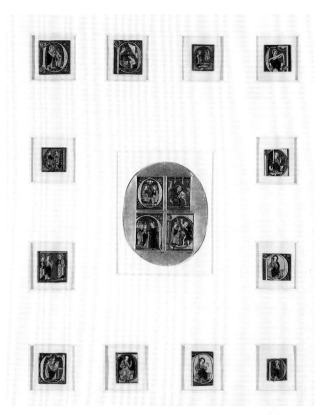

**45.**

Historiated initials from
a pocket Bible (France,
circa 1250), assembled as
a montage (nineteenth
century)

**46.**

Master of the Geneva Latini
or follower, the Annunciation
and Adoration of the Magi
(Rouen, 1480), miniatures;
Niccolo da Bologna, heads
in frames (Bologna, 1370);
assembled as a montage
(by O. Du Sartel[?], Paris[?],
circa 1880)

A third group of collages, including those in the Du Sartel sale and those reproduced by Albert Racinet, imitate the new reproductive technique of chromolithography begun circa 1840 (see chapter 3).[143] One particularly interesting case is the composite picture in figure 46, plate 8 (United States, private collection). Two full-page miniatures, probably painted in Rouen in about 1480 by an artist related to the Master of the Geneva Latini, are juxtaposed to form a kind of diptych, along the lines of the previous Ruskinian examples. Historiated initials, painted by Niccolò di Giacomo da Bologna around 1370 and from a fragmentary manuscript by Johannes Andreae, entitled *Novella super III–IV Decretalium,* are used to created a border around the miniatures. These initials depict figures involved in canon-law decrees, a priest with a pyx, a hooded flagellant, a knight with a sword, a bishop with a monstrance, and a man with a bag of money. Additional decorated initials and fragments of border decoration come from an early-fifteenth-century Parisian Book of Hours.

The Victorian painter who composed this collage was mindful of how he could reconstitute the images to create an aesthetically pleasing, independent painting, and the choices he made were creative. In arranging the historiated initials along the two vertical borders of the collage, he deliberately chose initials with figures that face the miniatures. He selected full-page miniatures in which the Virgin faces inward in both cases. To harmonize further the overall scheme, he painted a new sky above each of the miniatures, which he in turn carefully cut out and attached over these areas. He also painted strips of black around the miniatures, over which the outer edges of the miniatures rest (and float), as well as strips of black around the outer border itself. Painted strips in other colors—green, brown, and yellow—set off the miniatures from the inner border and set off the historiated initials from the outer border.

The overall result is surprisingly effective and strikingly three-dimensional. The different parts of the painting are situated in different depths of field from one another and from the viewer. The composite follows the rules set up by Racinet, who, although a skilled and prolific copyist of medieval illuminations, made his reputation through chromolithographic illustrations. In his most famous work, *Ornement Polychrome* (Paris, 1873, second edition in 1875, and second series of 120 plates in folio in 1885–87), Racinet laid out the principles of chromatics, relying heavily on a work by Dr. Ernest Brücke on the physiology of colors: "The advancing colors are red, orange, and yellow . . . the retreating colors are the various categories of blue . . . green is advancing in relation to blue and especially to ultramarine; it is retreating in comparison with red, orange, and yellow."[144] These principles have been followed exactly in the Du Sartel collage. Around the borders, green, brown, and yellow, as well as black, are employed. To enhance the "retreat" of the blue, Du Sartel's assistant expanded the area of the sky. Whereas Celotti had used Renaissance painting as the armature for his collages, Du Sartel had them outlined with ornament that appears also in Racinet's book but that recalls the ornament used on his Sevres porcelain (Du Sartel was the director of the Sevres Museum). In fact, in a recent meeting with the Du Sartel heirs, we may have uncovered the name of the helper charged with painting ornamental borders on china, on the one hand, and ornamental borders on illuminated collages, on the other hand (see figure 47). The result, as with many chromolitho-

**47.**

**Sèvres porcelain, white fan-shaped jardinière (1760)**

**48.**

**Monks at the door of
their cavern-monastery
(Megaspelaeon,
Greece), stereopticon**

graphic images, is rather like a picture seen through a stereopticon, an apparatus that offered a popular pastime as viewers traveled the world over with such pictures (figure 48). The aesthetic is wholly unlike the Ruskin or Celotti collages that predate it.

In this last example, the impact of reproductive techniques upon the composition and presentation of original-manuscript material is striking. The fragment, from being a "monument of a lost art" at the beginning of the century, has become something quite different and of its own time by the century's end. The early-nineteenth-century fragment retained its integrity, even when recombined, and imitated a Renaissance aesthetic. By contrast, by the end of the century, manuscript illumination had itself become a modern art form, and even the collaged construction erased the integrity of the individual fragment through the exploitation of contemporary reproductive techniques. The story of specimens outlined in this chapter is thus synchronic with the story of reproductions, which is the subject of the next chapter. The popularity of manuscript illumination in the modern age is best understood within this framework, in which the fragmentary remains of the medieval past intersect with modern attempts to recapture history through reproduction.

# REPRODUCTIONS

Transmission of Manuscript Illumination in the Nineteenth Century

Today, we tend to distinguish very sharply between the reproduction and the original. This distinction did not hold in the nineteenth century. For this reason, this chapter is organized so as to bring out the fascinating overlaps and intersections between handmade and mechanically reproduced copies of illuminated manuscripts. At the time when the objects in each of these categories were created, they were regarded as facsimiles and sometimes were considered to be originals in their own right. But one of our main objectives in this chapter is also to show the ways in which techniques of reproduction intersected with strategies of reception and the uses of manuscript illumination among various social groups in the nineteenth century.

The chapter is framed around three overarching themes. The first section will focus on artistic production in France and England, on artists and publishers whose varying roles in the development of the reproduction and the dissemination of manuscript material are crucial. The second section revisits the theme of cultural property in France previously discussed in chapter 2. Here, the imperial appropriation of manuscript illumination continues under Napoleon III, with particular focus on how royal and religious revivals influenced new forms of reproduction. This section concludes with an exploration of how manuscript material was used to construct popular notions of national identity and memory, as well as ideas about gender, in the second half of the nineteenth century. The third section focuses on the changing forms of reproduction, which made a wider public appreciation of medieval manuscript illumination possible. Fundamental to this explosion of interest in manuscript illumination was the reproductive technique of photography, which had a far-reaching impact on the public appeal and accessibility of medieval manuscripts. The eventual emergence of the "fake" or forgery as a deceptive form of reproduction quite distinct from nineteenth-century original illumination, or handmade facsimiles, is dependent on the very trajectory outlined here. While new reproductive techniques made forgeries possible, they also stimulated significant transformations in original book design and appreciation, best exemplified in the pioneering work of William Morris, whose contribution concludes this chapter.

## THE ARTIST-PUBLISHER AND THE MAKING OF THE FACSIMILE

**What Is a Facsimile?**
The word "facsimile," according to the *Oxford English Dictionary,* originally meant the act of transcribing a written copy.[1] By the eighteenth century there are references to drawings being copied *per factum simile*—meaning to make an exact likeness. In the nineteenth century, artists who copied medieval manuscripts were called "facsimilists." It is important to recognize that facsimiles have always been a part of manuscript culture, since the copying and duplication of texts and images from one manuscript to another, from model to copy, was standard practice throughout the Middle Ages. Jonathan Alexander has used the word "facsimile" to describe "historicist copies made of earlier works as opposed to replicas produced at the same time or after only a short interval," citing a fifteenth-century case of the *Notitia Dignitatum* made for a bishop of Padua from a fifth-century model in 1436.[2] The important word here is "historicist." For unlike the copies or duplicates made in the illuminator's workshop, the facsimile is more self-consciously copied from a historical source, and is divorced from contemporary production. Additionally, the fact that illuminated manuscript models of herbals were used by early woodcutters in Lyons and Besançon to make their blocks means that these early incunabula should not be considered print facsimiles of manuscript originals, because they totally reshape and omit aspects of the manuscript model in the process of copying. Rather than seeking to preserve the signs of manuscript culture, they erase them.

The first facsimiles in the proper sense are, as Alexander points out, the replicas of earlier treasured codices made for the proto-humanists of the fifteenth century, since it was only with the onset of the Renaissance that a sense of the historicity, the otherness of the past, opened up the gap between now and then that the facsimile could fill. The urge to produce modern copies of illuminated manuscripts grew only in the eighteenth century, when interest in these objects as collectible items really blossomed. As we would expect, the earliest reproductions from medieval manuscripts aimed to produce "specimens" of text for study by antiquarians, such as the copperplates of early English charters made for Richard Rawlinson (1690–1755) and bequeathed to the Bodleian Library in Oxford. Rawlinson exhibited and circulated these at the annual meetings of the Society of Antiquaries, which played a major role in the early reproduction of medieval artifacts in England. The first miniature Rawlinson had reproduced was an Evangelist portrait from a tenth-century Gospel book in St. John's College, Oxford (MS 194), which he had engraved in 1754. In the same year Edward Rowe Mores published what Munby calls "the earliest substantial facsimile of an English manuscript," fifteen engraved plates after the Anglo-Saxon Caedmon manuscript, which is also in

Oxford (Bodleian Library, MS Junius XI; see figure 10).[3] These scholarly reproductions are manifestations of the same historical urge that made Strutt's and
Montfaucon's volumes so important, but, like them, reveal little interest in pictorial elements for their own sake, the pictures serving only as illustrations of national
manners and sentiments (see chapter 1).

Both handmade illumination and mechanical reproduction of illuminated
manuscripts have to be considered as works of artistic production. Even today the
makers of expensive facsimiles advertise that their products are a combination of
"electronics and the Old Crafts" of the hand. The nineteenth century's most important and avid collector of illuminated books, Sir Thomas Phillipps, had professional illuminators copy both manuscripts and printed books for his collection. In
1865, his fellow collector John Camden Hotten sent Phillipps a "very cleverly executed facsimile of *Reynolds Herauldry of North Wales.*" In the accompanying letter,
Hotten states that he had borrowed the book from its owner for a fortnight and
that "I got my facsimilist to put forth his very best efforts in producing a copy."
Another letter, this time from Phillipps to Hotten, speaks about a further occasion
of copying a printed leaf: "I have received your . . . facsimile this morning and
fortunately I had the Book itself in my house so that I could immediately compare
it. Your copy is wonderfully exact and without the original anybody might be
deceived. . . . Your worm holes are very neatly executed, but your rotten corner,
if it is an *imitation,* is admirable. I have several printed books I should like to have
perfected by imitation."[4]

In this way, collectors like Phillipps could supplement their collection
of originals and printed works with cleverly executed copies. Such a practice was
only possible because during this period the exemplary status of the object, its
standing for a particular period or style, often mattered more than its authenticity.
Moreover, copies were not looked down upon as inferior in the way they have
come to be seen by modern eyes. This accounts for the popularity in both Europe
and the United States of museums and exhibitions that displayed plaster casts of
notable artworks. Originally exhibiting copies of Greco-Roman works, these
displays broadened to cover medieval statues as well, as in the Musée de Petits-
Augustins, which eventually became the Musée des Monuments Français.[5] In England, the Royal Architectural Museum, founded by Sir George Gilbert Scott in
1852, and later to form part of the Cast Court of the Victoria and Albert Museum,
provided those who were unable to visit the great cathedrals with plaster of Paris
details of medieval monuments from which they could learn architectural history.
Education was an important impetus for nineteenth-century notions of art and had
its impact too on the production of facsimiles of medieval manuscript illumination,
which began entering museum collections during this period (see chapter 4).

The popular appreciation of medieval illuminations was stimulated
not by handmade copies, which remained unique and expensive objects, but by
continual experimentation with those processes that made multiple copies of the
same image available to a wide audience. Strutt's volumes, discussed in the first
chapter, had used engravings to reproduce images for historical purposes, but it is
only with the works of Dibdin in the early nineteenth century that the creation of
facsimiles becomes a matter of art. This is partly because of Dibdin's interest in
printing techniques and the lavish care which he took in the quality of reproductions in his *Bibliographical Decameron* (also discussed in chapter 1). Dibdin concludes
the first day of the *Decameron* with a plea that the British Museum publish a series
of facsimiles of the illuminated manuscripts held in national collections, arguing
that "I auger well . . . that very many years will not elapse before we receive some

specimen, or specimens, in the way of *graphic illustration*, of the beautiful, curious, extraordinary, or instructive exhibitions of ancient art which that Repository contains."[6] This prediction, written in 1817, was not to be fulfilled until nearly a century later, when the British Museum published the first of its *Reproductions from Illuminated Manuscripts,* in 1907.[7]

The continuing impulse to reproduce medieval manuscripts throughout the nineteenth century accompanied, and gained momentum from, extensive experimentation with three technical processes—woodcut and metal engraving, lithography and chromolithography, and photography—sometimes used in combination with each other.

Up until the beginning of the nineteenth century, the traditional methods of printing images had remained more or less the same for four hundred years— the woodblock and the copperplate.[8] Woodcuts are prints made by cutting or chipping away the background on a wooden block, leaving a design raised in relief to take ink, but early in the century several innovations fundamentally changed the character of the woodcut. The artist Thomas Berwick, for example, began printing woodblock engravings, in which the lines were cut with an engraver's burin into the end-grain of a very hard block of wood in an intaglio process, yielding an extremely fine quality of line. Wood engraving became a preferred technique in book production of the first half of the nineteenth century, when book designers repeatedly experimented with the aesthetics of the wood-engraving juxtaposed with the text type on the page. This helped stimulate a taste for illustrated books in the period, which, along with the magnificent creations of William Blake, likewise encouraged people to look back at the illustrated books of earlier eras. With regard to engraving, an intaglio technique dating back to the Renaissance, the introduction of zinc plates, as opposed to copper ones, extended the life of the plate and consequently the size of the edition that could be printed from it.

Even more than the changes wrought by improvements to these traditional methods, lithography, invented by Alois Senefelder in 1796, had a marked impact on printed illustrations because it offered virtually unlimited possibilities of reproduction; it has been estimated that a single lithographic stone could yield nearly fifteen thousand draws without any loss of clarity in detail. The process of lithography entails drawing directly on a stone or sometimes a metal plate with a greasy pigment, which is then fixed with nitric acid. In printing, the stone is wet with water, and printing ink applied to the stone is held by the greasy areas, while the nongreasy (blank) areas, which hold moisture, repel the ink. The stone's inked surface is then printed on paper. The fact that the artist required no special technical skill with the medium itself, unlike with the processes of woodcuts or engravings, represented another advantage of lithography. In 1836, a variant of lithography, called chromolithography, was patented in Paris by Godefroy Engelmann. The invention of chromolithography, in which each color of a reproduced image is printed with a different stone, up to eighteen stones in all being used, inaugurated a fertile period of experimentation with color printing that continued throughout the century.[9] It was chromolithography that not only virtually made the careers of publishers such as Léon Curmer and Ambroise Firmin-Didot but also created a thriving market for drawings copied from manuscripts by facsimilists—nineteenth-century illuminators—for transfer to the lithographic plates.

It is probably not an overstatement to claim that the invention and perfection of photography—the heliograph, the daguerreotype, and the calotype, among other variations—did for the reproduction of images in the nineteenth century and afterward what Gutenberg's invention of printing had done for the reproduction of the written word in the fifteenth century.[10] A photograph (from the Greek *phos* for "light" and *graphos* for "drawing") is an image formed by the action of light falling on a sensitized surface, which can be "developed" and "fixed." Photography provided a new measure of reality and visual truth, replacing the relative uniqueness of the hand-rendered visual image with a purely mechanically produced one that had the potential for exact and infinite repetition. Photography eventually eliminated altogether the need for the copyist, although in the beginning facsimilists could take on piecework coloring in black-and-white photographs, and photography ultimately changed the word "facsimile" from the active sense it had earlier in the century ("to facsimile") to a passive noun ("a facsimile"). Photography all but put facsimilists out of work, except in the case of consciously retrospective practices that catered to a new taste for the deluxe handmade object in the early twentieth century, as represented by the artist-illuminator Alberto Sangorski.

**Henry Shaw: Facsimiles as Originals**

Born in London, Henry Shaw (1800–73) had a long career as an architectural draftsman, engraver, antiquarian, and illuminator.[11] He participated in the publication of at least nineteen works, mostly for William Pickering of the Chiswick, Press between 1823 and 1866.[12] He apparently began his career in association with John Lutton, for whom he supplied the drawings for the *Cathedral Antiquities of England.* He then published his first independent work in 1823, *A Series of Details of Gothic Architecture.* Architecture, furniture, tile pavements, metalwork, stained glass, heraldry, and costume captured his attention, and he completed the preparatory drawings for publications on all these subjects. While he contributed the drawings or engraved the plates for these volumes himself, he often collaborated with others who wrote the commentaries, such as Sir Samuel Rush Meyrich (for example, on furniture), John Gough Nichols, and Thomas Moule (on architecture). In 1833 he was elected a member of the Society of Antiquaries.

Two works on illuminated manuscripts stand out among Shaw's many publications. Published near the beginning of his career, the first, *Illuminated Ornaments Selected from Manuscripts of the Middle Ages* (London: William Pickering, 1830–33), incorporates a historical commentary by Sir Frederic Madden (1801–73), Keeper of Manuscripts at the British Museum from 1837.[13] More than thirty years later, in 1866, Shaw returned to the subject of illuminated manuscripts in the second publication, *A Handbook of the Art of Illumination as Practised during the Middle Ages.* Whereas the former work focuses mainly on the ornamental and decorative features of manuscripts, the latter brings to bear Shaw's extensive experience as a copyist and a contemporary illuminator. Composed of sixteen plates reproducing works from the ninth to the sixteenth centuries, his *Handbook* includes "a description of the metals, pigments, and processes employed by the artists at different periods." For this latter work, he composed his own commentary.

Of primary interest to us here is Shaw's *Illuminated Ornaments.* Released in sets of five illustrations at a time over a twelve-month period, three separate editions of *Illuminated Ornaments* were advertised by the publisher, William Pickering, for the printer, Charles Whittingham, of the Chiswick Press.[14] Sets of uncolored woodblock prints cost three shillings and sixpence, colored prints cost seven shillings and sixpence, and imperial quarto copies that promised to be richer in color, opacity, and the quality of the gold were priced at fifteen shillings.[15] Nordenfalk has suggested that stencils were used for coloring all but the imperial quarto imprints, but Beckwith notes that certain individualistic features of many of the copies suggest instead that they may all have been done by hand.[16] Approximately two hundred to three hundred copies of all three editions are thought to have been published.

*Illuminated Ornaments* offered a compact handbook on illuminated manuscripts that the public at large could afford. Shaw, probably closely guided by Madden, selected fifty-nine examples of ornament for *Illuminated Ornaments,* beginning with a rare fragmentary Greek Gospel book and extending to the seventeenth century with cuttings from the Barberini choir book. Most of the examples illustrate manuscripts in the British Museum, but at least five private collections are also represented (Ottley, Richard Griffin Neville Braybrooke, Francis Douce, William Pickering, and Thomas Willement). What is unusual for the time is the focus on ornament, which Madden excuses on partially practical grounds. He explains that the high cost of hand coloring and the difficulty in rendering faithfully the originals (citing the unsuccessful efforts of Abbé Rive) led them instead to trace the history of the "humbler branch of art" (as opposed to, say, panel paintings), which readers might nevertheless admire (pp. 1–2). It is also worth pointing out that Madden and Shaw display a precocious interest in illuminated incunabula, including works by Fust and Schoefer of Mainz and Nicolas Jensen of Venice, which has gone unnoticed. The complexity of the paleographic descriptions Madden provided testifies to the high level of his scholarship. For example, he provides codicological information far in advance of his time, when he notes with some consistency whether the manuscript is fragmentary or incomplete at beginning and end. He also usually provides citations of previous publications, noting the particular purpose the manuscript serves in the earlier study. He offers much information on provenance, especially of English families, describing the arms, the heraldry, and tracing previous ownership. Finally, he includes some physical descriptions on the size of the volume and the place of illustrations within it.

In keeping with the Vasarian paradigm, characteristic of the beginning of the nineteenth century (and most evident in the Celotti sale), Madden and Shaw preferred High Renaissance examples of manuscript illumination. They outline a model for the history of the development of illumination that typifies the state of manuscript studies in England in the first third of the nineteenth century. They cite the great skill of Carolingian scribes and decorators well-versed in the forms of antiquity, praise the invention of initials *historiées,* wonder at the intricacy of Irish and Hiberno-Saxon examples, and comment on the monumentality of twelfth-century Romanesque books. They exhibit a nationalistic streak in lamenting the absence of British examples from the earlier discussions by Seroux d'Agincourt and Dibdin. They echo most antiquarians before John Ruskin in their depreciation of Gothic art, which was redeemed by artists of the fifteenth century who "made rapid strides toward the perfection [found] . . . in the subsequent age" (p. 13). For Madden and Shaw, the art of illumination "received new life in Italy" through the agency of Cimabue and Giotto, who contributed to the "improvement of taste" (p. 12). But it was the sixteenth century that witnessed the final "triumph of art" under Leonardo da Vinci, Raphael, Giulio Romano, and the ubiquitous Giulio Clovio, when "miniature painting attained a new degree of lustre and dignity from its being practised by artists who were also renowned for works executed on a grander scale." (p. 15).

The published edition of Shaw's *Illuminated Ornaments* is considered a landmark in the history of color facsimiles in England because it introduced a fashion for deluxe reproductions of illuminated manuscripts and set a high standard for their illustration and description.[17] There also exists a version of this famous work, however, that was drawn and painted entirely by hand (Art Institute of Chicago, acc. no. 19.791). The Chicago manuscript has escaped notice altogether, since it was not recorded by De Ricci in his census of manuscripts in the United States, and it apparently does not appear in the sales of the extensive collection of its previous owner, the bibliophile Sir Thomas Brooke.[18] This manuscript version of *Illuminated Ornaments* is a large folio volume comprising 2 parchment flyleaves, plus 125 parchment leaves, of which 63 display illuminations that are seamlessly set into the larger sheets.[19] The illuminations are the same size as those in the printed version, and both printed and hand-done facsimiles are identical in scale to the originals (unless otherwise noted by Madden) and were probably traced from the actual manuscripts. The manuscript version is still preserved in its original binding of thick red velvet over a thin wood backing, the upper and lower covers decorated with brass (or gilded?) Celtic-style incised corner guards. The edges are goffered and gilt.

Although described in a late-nineteenth- or early-twentieth-century hand on the front pastedown as *The Original 63 Drawings by Henry Shaw in Gold Silver and Colours from which Pickering Published the Work "Illuminated Ornaments of Middle Ages," 1833,* the manuscript, in fact, differs from the published work in ways that reflect Shaw's interests and abilities as an illuminator and which suggest that the manuscript cannot be a preparatory maquette for the printed edition. It must instead be a lavish one-of-a-kind gift book made by Shaw for one of his friends or associates. Differences between the printed version and the manuscript include many details that, when the manuscript is consulted, lead us, first, to appreciate Shaw's skill and interests as an illuminator and, second, to understand somewhat better the aims of the printed edition. For example, comparison between the manuscript copies of the Greek Gospel leaves and the plates in the printed edition (plates 1–4, folios 5–11; from British Library, MS Add. 5111) reveals that the irregular shape of the pages was regularized in the printed copy, the imperfections (mostly holes) in the sheets were colored in with gold, and the text was "completed." In several instances, Shaw omitted the text altogether, or included only a fragment of it, whereas the entire text was usually reproduced in the printed version (for example, plate 17, folio 37, of a Romanesque Bible; from British Library, MS 2803; and plate 46, folio 97, of a Latin breviary; from British Library, MS Royal 2 B. XV). In this respect Shaw resembles other nineteenth-century copyists, like the infamous Caleb William Wing, discussed below, whose skills as illuminators far exceeded their abilities as calligraphers capable of accurately reproducing historic handwritings.

Shaw's attention to detail in the manuscript confirms his considerable skill as an illuminator. For example, in the fragments reproduced from two royal charters, he imitated the toolwork in the backgrounds of the miniatures (plate 25, folio 53; from British Library, MS Royal 20 D. X). In the borders of two white vine miniatures, he carefully added vinelike sprays around the initials, omitted in the printed copy (plate 35, folio 73; from British Library, MSS Harley 3109, 4902). Unlike Comte Jean-François-Auguste Bastard d'Estang, and to a much greater extent than John Obadiah Westwood, Shaw was evidently attracted to the aesthetic of the collage, of which important examples put together from High Renaissance cuttings had been sold in the Celotti sale only a few years before *Illuminated Ornaments* was published (see chapter 2). In eliminating the text in the copy of a breviary, for example, Shaw composed a sort of collage in which an artfully arranged pattern of borders and initials occupies the text block. Ornament from an illuminated copy of the *Decretals* published by Fust and Schoefer forms a similar overall decorative pattern, executed to scale over two pages in the manuscript and reduced and combined on one page in the printed version (figures 49 and 50). Madden attentively specifies in his accompanying notice that the scale has been changed: "In the original, the scroll and letters here copied are of a size a third larger" (under notice XXIII). The aesthetic of the collage, which fabricates a new, independent work of art out of discrete miniatures and bits of ornament, manifests a radically different attitude than we now have toward the historical integrity of the "original." It is tempting to understand the manipulation of an object or objects, which the collage achieves, as a procedure fostered by new technologies. In chromolithography the object was dissected for printing from multiple stones or plates inked with different colors, then reassembled when printed on the surface of the page. Even facsimile printing itself opened up the possibilities of rearrangement and adjustment. Whatever the underlying reasons, the popularity of the collage persisted through the nineteenth century.

As an antiquarian-illuminator Shaw became one of the most skillful and prolific copyists of his generation. Rowan Watson has recently called attention to unpublished material concerning Shaw's activity as a copyist, noting that he was employed by John Ruskin, among others, to make copies of works in the British Museum and that he himself hired assistants to help him undertake these copies.[20] As an entrepreneur, who set out to establish a market for his copies, Shaw was remarkably successful. A telling sequence of events in the 1850s and 1860s documents the interrelationship between his activities as a copyist and an engraver, the status of the market, and the needs of the newly opened South Kensington Museum.

In 1855, the South Kensington Museum had declared its intention to begin to acquire illuminations as part of its teaching mission to make artifacts available to students as models for design (see chapter 4).[21] Acquisitions of single leaves and cuttings by the museum can be traced from that year under the direction of its first curator, J. C. Robinson.[22] Evidently already well aware of the South Kensington Museum's holdings in the field of manuscript illumination, Shaw wrote the museum's librarian in 1864, urging that the museum round out its collection by the purchase of facsimiles because the range of illumination available for students was far too narrow:

[T]he specimens at present in the collection have been taken from one class of manuscripts, large choral books . . . examples of Italian and German art of the 15th and 16th centuries. . . . Would it not be advisable to supply . . . your deficiencies by carefully executed fac-similes of a page or two of the most choice manuscripts. . . . These fac-similes would have an advantage . . . over the originals from their freshness and completeness deteriorated from constant use, exposure or ill treatment.[23]

However, the South Kensington Museum does not seem to have responded immediately to Shaw's recommendation. Two years later, in 1866, Shaw mounted an exhibition of eighty-nine examples of his copies (he called them "illuminated drawings") at an art gallery located at 196 Piccadilly. In the catalogue he wrote to accompany the exhibition, he again underscored the pedagogical value his copies might have, using language similar to that he had used in his 1864 letter:

[F]or the purposes of instruction, these copies may, in many cases, be considered more satisfactory than the original drawings. The best preserved volumes have almost invariably suffered, to some extent, from frequent use, while many, especially those of an early date, show evidences of extensive deterioration, both from use and abuse.[24]

Later in the year, on June 6, 1866, Shaw's "illuminated drawings" were sold by Christie's, which used the same brochure he wrote for his exhibition as

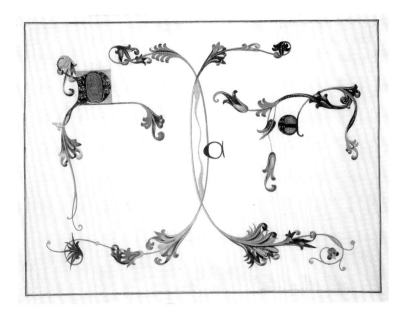

**49.**

Henry Shaw,
"Illuminated Ornaments
Selected from Manuscripts
of the Middle Ages . . ."
manuscript (before 1832)

**50.**

Henry Shaw,
*Illuminated Ornaments
Selected from Manuscripts
of the Middle Ages*
(London, 1830–33),
plate 37

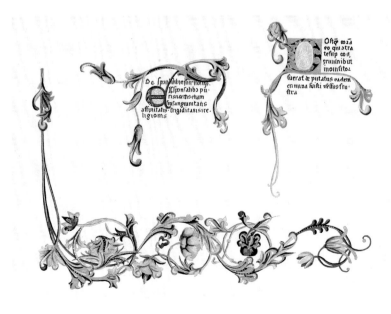

the sale catalogue; Christie's reset the title page and added a few items at the end.[25]
Perhaps Shaw intended his group of illuminated leaves, accompanied by the title
page "Choice Leaves from Rare Illuminated Manuscripts," to serve as a model for
a third book of illuminated manuscripts that was never published.[26] By this time,
the South Kensington Museum must have taken Shaw's comments very seriously,
for it purchased almost his entire collection of illuminated drawings at the 1866
sale (only thirteen items went to other buyers, who included Sotheran and Whitehead; and Whitehead's purchases later entered the museum).[27] The extraordinary
sums paid for these items underscore how in the nineteenth century there was no
chasm separating "facsimiles" and "originals." For example, in 1866, the same year
as the Shaw sale, the South Kensington Museum acquired a portfolio of medieval
illuminations, comprising twelve items in all (including a miniature now attributed
to Domenico Morone), for only fifteen pounds; whereas it paid forty-two pounds
for three of Shaw's originals after borders attributed to Apollonius Bonfratelli.[28] In
1860, the museum had paid only twelve pounds for a large original work, an altar
card attributed to Giulio Clovio.[29]

Although Shaw included some examples of ornament, such as frames and
decorated initials, in his set of "illuminated drawings," especially from the early
centuries before about 1200, he also included many full-page illuminations (items
listed include facsimiles from a Turonian Bible, the Harley Gospels, the *Epistre* of
Richard II, the *Bedford Psalter,* the *Prayerbook of Henry VI,* the *Roman de la Rose,*
and so on), thus distinguishing this set from his earlier efforts focused on ornament.
Shaw's remarkable skill as a facsimilist is evident in the diversity of styles he was
able to imitate effectively, ranging from those of the Insular Lindesfarne Gospels
(figure 51), to that of the English Gothic *Howard Psalter* (figure 52, plate 9), to the
Renaissance styles such as appear in border frames said to have been done by Bonfratelli (figure 53).

**51.**

Henry Shaw,
copy of a "carpet page"
from the *Lindisfarne
Gospels*

**52.**

Henry Shaw,
copy of a leaf from the
*Howard Psalter*

**53.**

**Henry Shaw,
copy of border frame and
ornament from a 1564
manuscript illuminated by
Appollonius de Bonfratelli**

**The Arundel Society: Facsimiles as Illustrations**

Founded in 1849, the Arundel Society, also called the Society for Promoting the Knowledge of Art, was named in honor of Thomas Howard Arundel (died 1646), whose own fame rests on his patronage of the arts and his fine collections, including his library, given to the Royal Society and subsequently bequeathed to the British Museum (in 1831), forming the Arundel Collection.[30] The aims of the society, published in the *London Times* on February 24, 1849, at the time of its foundation, were to "promote the knowledge of art by the publication of literary compositions which may illustrate the principles or the history of art in any of its branches . . . and by the publication of engravings of important examples of architecture, sculpture, painting, or ornamental design." The announcement continues in expressing the hope that the society will have an impact on the "improvement in the public taste." It concludes with a reassurance that "some of the most influential and classic patrons of art and literature" are members of its council [Samuel Rogers, John Ruskin, Charles Eastlake] and a reminder that the society's prospectus is posted at Colnaghi's, thereby linking the trade with its didactic pursuits. Subscription cost one guinea, and within a few years the society's membership had swelled to between five hundred and six hundred individuals, each of whom received an annual publication as a benefit of membership.

Whereas the prospectus emphasized literary publications, as well as reproductions of works of art from all fields, in fact, most of the society's publications focused on Italian Renaissance art. For our purposes, one of the most interesting features of the society is its self-consciousness about the different reproductive techniques available for its facsimiles: "by adopting . . . different processes invented or perfected by the scientific and mechanical genius of the age, more adequate expressions both of form and colour might now . . . be obtained than was possible with the limited means in use at any former period."[31] The Arundel Society's first publications were all devoted to Fra Angelico: an account of his life and works, followed by copperplate engravings of his frescoes in the chapel of Nicholas V in the Vatican (1849–50, 1850–51, 1851–52).[32] Then, in 1851, begins a series of publications of Giotto's frescoes in the Arena Chapel (to 1856), never before reproduced as an ensemble, and all executed in wood engravings, along with (in 1854) "A Notice of Giotto and His Works in Padua" by John Ruskin.[33] Just how varied the publications of the society were in these years, in subject and in technique, is evident by its publication in 1855 of the "Notices on Sculpture in Ivory," with nine photographic illustrations.[34] Copper engravings, wood engravings, and photography were all used in the early years of the society's activity.

In 1856, under the influence and patronage of Sir Austin Henry Layard (1817–94)—a well-known archaeologist, connoisseur, art critic, and adviser, then trustee, of the National Gallery of Art—the society turned to the expensive procedure of chromolithography for the reproduction of frescoes.[35] Its experiment with the new technique paid off. By 1863, when its membership had reached more than 1,600, the society was obliged to restrict subscriptions (it considered 1,500 the maximum number of chromolithographic prints to be pulled from a set of stones), and it set up different classes of memberships. Then, evidently cognizant of the interest the facsimiles had aroused among the public who wanted cheap art, and eager not to turn away potential subscribers, the society expanded its list of publications, producing two per year. Color made possible, of course, the reproduction of works of art in their full splendor, and it is evident that the chromolithographs of the society were marketed as "art": the society sold frames to accompany them; they were hung on walls, decorated sideboards, and were placed upon the altars of

117

churches. In this way, the medium of fresco underwent a process of reconstitution, not unlike what manuscript illumination had undergone, a fragmentation that turned fresco into easel painting.

In 1862, under the patronage of one of its members, Count Cottrell (or Cotterell, 1801–74),[36] who apparently had executed the illuminated copies after the originals, the society produced an alphabet book, *An Alphabet. Capital Letters Selected from the Illuminations of Italian Choral Books of the Fifteenth and Sixteenth Centuries. Engraved in Outline with One Letter Printed in Colours.*[37] This project probably reverts to the society's initial interest in Fra Angelico, since the frontispiece reproduced in color was attributed to this celebrated Florentine painter (figure 54). A large group of other initials in *An Alphabet* also come from choir books in the convent of San Marco in Florence and are said to be based on designs by Fra Angelico executed by his elder brother Benedetto da Mugello (letters *E* to *H, K, M* and *N,* and *R* through *T;* see figure 55, plate 10). Other initials are from choir books in the Communal Library of Siena by Giovanni di Paolo di Neri (*A* and *I*), the Piccolomini Library in the Duomo of Siena by Liberale da Verona (*B* to *D* and *L*), and the Duomo in Florence by unknown artists (*O* to *Q,* and *U* to *Z*). When Frederick W. Maynard, secretary of the society, published his *Descriptive Notice of the Drawings and Publications of the Arundel Society for 1849 to 1868 Inclusive,* he noted that "among the Society's collection are several coloured drawings of letters from which the outlines were taken."[38] In fact, these facsimiles copy only the initials from openings in the choir books, and they are surrounded by border decoration extracted and rearranged in a new composition on a page. The text has been entirely suppressed.

Two points are worth making about *An Alphabet.* First, in presenting isolated illuminated letters (as Dibdin had described them in the *Bibliographical Decameron* and as Dennistoun had arranged them in his album), the Arundel Society thought nothing of treating illuminated manuscripts as fragments; indeed, it hardly seems aware that this is the case. Second, by choosing the format of an alphabet book, the society responded to Victorian interest in such books (the first one is evidently one produced by Henry Shaw),

**56.**

**A Model Alphabet Book for illuminators (Paris, circa 1500[?]), L with iris and butterfly manuscript**

which must have been used partly for teaching illumination. But the alphabet book itself represents a reprise of earlier medieval and Renaissance forms, the scribe's and decorator's model books. Examples of these include an illuminated model book manuscript in the Walters Art Gallery (Baltimore: Walters Art Gallery, W. 200; see figure 56, plate 11), or the Renaissance model book by the scribe Guinifortus de Vicomerchato of Milan (figure 151) from the Ricketts collection in the Lilly Library (Bloomington: Lilly Library, MS Ricketts I, no. 240), among many others.[39] Here nineteenth-century reconstitution appears at its most interesting, as it reshapes an earlier genre to serve purposes similar to what the original form had served.

Perhaps the success of *An Alphabet* prompted the Arundel Society to produce additional facsimiles of illuminated letters shortly thereafter, because in 1863 and 1864 the society issued in its "Occasional Publications" three chromolithographs of letters from *An Alphabet,* all taken from manuscripts painted by Liberale da Verona in the Duomo of Siena: *C* (*St. Lawrence;* see figure 57, plate 12), *L* (*Miracle of the Loaves and Fishes;* see figure 58, plate 13), and *D* (*Christ's Entry into Jerusalem;*

**54.**

**Arundel Society,
*An Alphabet: Capital
Letters Selected from
the Illuminations
of Italian Choral Books
of the Fifteenth and
Sixteenth Centuries.
Engraved in Outline
with One Letter Printed
in Colours* (London,
1862), frontispiece**

**55.**

Initial *R*
(nineteenth century)
copied from a
fifteenth-century choir
book of San Marco

**57.**

**Ernesto Sprega,
historiated initial C,
St. Lawrence with two
angels. Copied from a
fifteenth-century Siena
choir book by Liberale
da Verona**

**58.**

Ernesto Sprega,
historiated initial *L*,
Miracle of the
Loaves and Fishes.
Copied from a
fifteenth-century
Siena choir book by
Liberale da Verona

**59.**

Ernesto Sprega,
historiated initial *D*,
Christ's Entry into
Jerusalem. Copied
from a fifteenth-
century Siena choir
book by Liberale da
Verona

see figure 59).⁴⁰ The society doubtless reused the "coloured drawings" referred to
by Maynard. All three "coloured drawings" were by the evidently gifted Ernesto
Sprega, who was also known as a restorer of frescoes, having restored the Raphael
rooms in the Vatican, as well as frescoes in the Villa di Belcaro in Siena.⁴¹ Perhaps
Sprega was responsible for the entire series of letters, in which case he was a versa-
tile copyist, easily shifting styles between the quattrocento and cinquecento, between Fra Angelico and Liberale da Verona. By this time the coffers of the society
were full enough to warrant an outlay of seventy-two pounds, nineteen shillings,
and sixpence for the cost of the chromolithograph of the letter *D* (from *Christ's
Entry into Jerusalem*), copies of which sold for one pound, four shillings.⁴² In the
first year the society took in thirty-eight pounds and in the second fifty-five
pounds from its publication of this letter, turning a nice profit of a little more than
twenty-one pounds.

The story does not end there, however, for in 1866 the society sold all
three "coloured drawings" to the South Kensington Museum, each for fifteen
pounds.⁴³ The high price paid by the museum for these illuminations is in line
with the prices paid for Shaw's drawings around the same time. The reason for
purchasing Sprega's illuminations was undoubtedly the same one that had prompted the museum's acquisition of Shaw's examples: namely, to fill out gaps in its
collection for teaching purposes. This response of the South Kensington Museum
to the Arundel Society affirms the close relationship that existed between the two
institutions in the 1860s, with both serving common roles as educators. That
Shaw's and Sprega's copies are both called "coloured drawings" reminds us once
again that the distinction between "original" and "facsimile" is blurred during this
period. Shaw's and Sprega's copies made directly from the originals are considered,
like their sources, to be "drawings" or originals, whereas the chromolithographs
made after them are "facsimiles" and the artist of the preparatory drawing is called
the "facsimilist."

The remaining drawings of illuminated letters, including a few that were
not used (PDP E. 123-1996 to E. 127-1996), stayed in the Arundel Society's collection until they were deposited in the National Gallery of Art in 1889 or 1895.
Then, in 1899, they were made a gift to the National Gallery, which in 1906 deposited them in the Victoria and Albert Museum, to which they were finally made
an outright gift in 1996 (PDP E. 120-1996 to E. 133-1996). Facsimiles for the
plates *F, O, P, Q,* and *T* through *Z* are not among them. The exceptional quality,
as well as the character of the decoration combined with the letter, of these
"drawings" merit further study.

In 1869 the society switched to the use of photography, a move that was
reviewed with approbation in the *Art Journal* of that year.⁴⁴ Apparently, the society
had become so popular that there was an increasing demand for its out-of-print
engravings and chromolithographs. To meet this demand, in keeping with its desire "to preserve the record and diffuse a knowledge of the more important remains of painting and sculpture," the society decided to photograph works it had
previously chromolithographed. It promised members that the photo would be
taken from the original drawing and reassured them that if they already possessed
the chromolithograph, they should consider themselves as having the "deluxe version." At the same time, the society reaffirmed its complementary goals to publish,
and thereby preserve a record of, works that might otherwise perish, and to promote art education among the people, the subject of the next chapter.

**John Obadiah Westwood: Facsimiles and Exactitude**

John Obadiah Westwood (1805–93) was a self-taught paleographer and entomologist whose knowledge of Anglo-Saxon and early medieval manuscripts was exceptional for his time. After publishing *Paleographia Sacra Pictoria* (1843–45) with a series of high-quality chromolithographed plates, he focused on producing two books of facsimiles from illuminated manuscripts. The second of these to be published, *Fac-similes of the Miniatures and Ornaments of Anglo-Saxon and Irish Manuscripts* (1868), exemplifies Westwood's Anglo-Saxon interests, and contains at the end of the introduction a reference to the work of the French publisher, the Comte Auguste de Bastard d'Estang.

In almost every instance the facsimiles from the original MSS for this work have been executed by myself, with the most scrupulous care, the majority having been made with the assistance of a magnifying glass, and the plates have been produced under my especial direction and constant supervision, so that I may in conclusion venture to express the hope that my work may be regarded as a humble rival of the grand but enormously expensive work of Count Bastard on the miniatures and ornaments of early French MSS.[45]

Westwood's other book of facsimiles, *Illuminated Illustrations of the Bible Copied from Select Manuscripts of the Middle Ages,* is more interesting. It was originally published in 1846 by William Smith of Fleet Street in 13 parts, at a price of 13 shillings per part. The low price of the publication, especially compared to the lavish expense of Bastard d'Estang's project, is remarked upon by Westwood, who emphasizes in his preface that:

The object of the present work is to endeavor to present in as cheap of form as possible a series of fac-similes of Miniatures illustrative of the events recorded in Holy Writ, copied from some of the more select Illuminated manuscripts of the Middle Ages contained in our public libraries and other sources.[46]

A unique extra-illustrated copy of this work that belonged to Westwood exists at the J. Paul Getty Center (Research Institute, 920003). This beautiful extra-illustrated copy contains six leaves from medieval manuscripts, thirty-six original drawings, and forty hand-colored or color-printed plates in a morocco binding. Westwood wrote in an inscription on the front flyleaf:

This large paper copy (of which six only were printed) contains the original tracings from which I drew the subjects on the zinc plates—also the only set of proofs on India paper which were taken—and six very beautiful painted missal illuminations (two of which are copied in the work), namely the Purification of the Virgin, the Adoration of the Magi, the Murder of the Innocents, the Baptism of Christ, the Descent of the Holy Spirit, the Virgilia mortuorium at the end of the volume . . . . The binding is copied from a Grolier-bound volume in the British Museum and is a very elaborate piece of work.

This book is remarkable for two reasons. First, it preserves an exceptional illustrated record of the technical process of its creation, from Westwood's drawings for the zinc plates, to his proofs taken from the plates and printed on India paper, to the final hand-colored engravings (figures 60, 61, and 62, plates 14, 15), and finally to the insertion of original medieval illuminations within the modern volume. Second, it shows just how complex a facsimile could be, for Westwood's hybrid copy is, at the same time, an extra-illustrated volume, like an album, containing fifteenth-century illuminations alongside nineteenth-century drawings and proofs, and a facsimile of printed reproductions taken from original manuscripts. It was as though in this special volume Westwood was still clinging to the residual aura of the medieval manuscript book in the age of print, despite the fact that he success-

**60.**

John Obadiah Westwood, tracing of the Apocalypse for *Illuminated Illustrations of the Bible* (London, 1846)

**61.**

John Obadiah Westwood, India-ink proof of the Apocalypse for *Illuminated Illustrations of the Bible* (London, 1846)

**62.**

John Obadiah Westwood, hand-colored proof for *Illuminated Illustrations of the Bible* (London, 1846)

fully marketed the work as an inexpensive illustrated Bible rather than as a collection of facsimiles from illuminated manuscripts.

The images in Westwood's *Illuminated Illustrations of the Bible* are arranged in order chronologically according to the story of the Bible from the Creation to the Apocalypse, but the images do not all come from biblical manuscripts. Most of the illustrations are taken from manuscripts in the British Museum, and each illustration is accompanied by a biblical quotation. Although there are some pastiche effects, with borders added from elsewhere providing some frames, there is an effort to explain the miniatures in their original context. For example, alongside the Annunciation from the collection of Rev. Mr. Delafosse, Westwood adds, "In the original the two figures before us occupy two pages facing each other, so that when the book is opened, the two drawings form a wide continuous miniature."[47] Westwood quotes the remarks of Dr. Waagen as to the preeminence of the English school in the art of manuscript illumination, and opines that "England is intrinsically very poor in the productions of middle-age art" due to iconoclasm and "ignorant church wardens."[48] Westwood, then, sees his facsimiles as substitutes for a lost monumental art. His book is a good example of the creation of something new from composite parts taken from elsewhere. Hardly a facsimile proper, since no medieval Bible contains such an odd amalgam of images, Westwood's *Illuminated Illustrations of the Bible* is a Victorian reimagining of a medieval manuscript for the pious art-loving public, and simultaneously a precursor to the gift book.

## Caleb William Wing: Facsimiles and Virtuosity

The career of Caleb William Wing (1801–75) reflects the diverse activities of a nineteenth-century manuscript illuminator who was a restorer, a teacher, a facsimilist, and a printmaker. Wing is best known as a restorer of illumination in original manuscripts, particularly those of the collector John Boykett Jarman (died 1864), whose "beautiful collection of Illuminated Missals and Books of Hours" was badly damaged in a flood, probably in 1846.[49] Janet Backhouse has reconstructed in considerable detail Wing's association with Jarman, showing that he skillfully retouched damaged volumes (e.g., British Library, MS Egerton 2973, among others). But Wing apparently also added illuminations to volumes where none previously existed, and he painted a vast number of modern copies—some sixty sets of loose miniatures are described in the 1864 sale of Jarman's collection.[50] His considerable skill as a copyist can partly be judged from the copy he made directly from the Della Rovere Missal before it was badly damaged in the flood (lot 96, Jarman sale, eventually to J. Pierpont Morgan, MS M. 306). Wing's copy was acquired by the Victoria and Albert Museum (PDP, D. 310-1899; see figures 63 and 64).

Quite apart from his association with Jarman, Wing earned his living as a maker of facsimiles of manuscripts, some of which he sold on his own account, while others entered the trade and could be acquired from picture dealers. The South Kensington Museum bought directly from him, in 1870 purchasing for five pounds a full-page letter *B* copied from a twelfth-century Beatus (British Library, MS Arundel 157, folio 19). The museum also bought Wing's facsimiles through Colnaghi's, in 1866 purchasing for three pounds, three shillings a Crucifixion he copied from a sixteenth-century Netherlandish Book of Hours, and for three pounds a historiated *D* copied from a late-fifteenth-century north Italian choir book (figure 65, plate 16).[51] That Wing was regarded as "collectible" is suggested by the large number of his illuminations owned by Jarman, and by the purchase of his facsimiles to round out the collection at the Victoria and Albert Museum. The

collector Lord Aldenham (1819–1907)[52] acquired a sheet by him—featuring the
Descent from the Cross—at the Jarman sale for two pounds. He also executed
copies for others, specifically for Henry Noel Humphreys,[53] and worked too as an
engraver and lithographer.

Wing was a prolific and capable copyist, and his productions have only
just begun to attract the attention they deserve. One hitherto unpublished work is
a partial facsimile he did relatively early in his
career of the famous *Roman de la Rose* that was
readily accessible to him in the British Library
(MS Harley 4425). Made to order for Octave
Delepierre, who hand wrote a colophon (dated
May 1, 1848, London) to the manuscript, this
work is interesting because it records the collaboration between Wing and the celebrated
French calligrapher Midolle, who executed the
ornamental frames—unfortunately left incomplete—for the miniatures. Intriguing also is
the function the facsimile evidently served:
Delepierre himself hand wrote "all the passages
relative to the *Roman de la Rose*" in other contemporary works. To this end, he includes
excerpted passages from Martin le Franc's
*Le Champion des dames,* among numerous other

texts. More than many other Wing productions, which are sometimes difficult to
distinguish from originals, this manuscript reveals a nineteenth-century taste. On
the title page, the cartouche with the title of the work lifts up to reveal a painted
copy of Titian's *Reclining Venus.* Inserted in the back of the volume are other nineteenth-century reprises of earlier paintings (Chicago: Newberry Library, MS Case
Y 7675.R 7184; see figure 66).

At the beginning of the 1859 holiday season, Wing appeared in Brighton
offering drawing classes for young ladies, evidently an activity which he and his
daughters felt had some financial prospects. That teaching of this kind was sought
after in this fashionable resort is suggested by the prospectus of a competitor, Frederick Curtis, "teacher of drawing, illuminating and designing," issued in Brighton
in the early 1860s.[54] Wing came from a precarious world of artists who had to
struggle to make a living, turning their hand to a variety of activities in order to
survive. In this he resembled Noel Humphreys, of whom we get a rare glimpse
working late into the night to meet a publisher's deadline and getting help from
his wife and young children—an important corrective to the conventional view of
Humphreys as the artist-writer in charge of his own destiny.[55] Wing's obituary in
the *Academy* reveals the admiration of his contemporaries: "ILLUMINATIVE Art
has lost one of its most skillful and experienced exponents in the late Mr. C. W.
Wing, known during the last thirty years at the British Museum as the best facsimile copyist of ancient illuminations."[56]

It is tempting to see Wing's teaching activity as directly related to the
craze for do-it-yourself manuals and classes for amateur illuminators. In turn, this
do-it-yourself craze intersects with a more scholarly interest in techniques of illumination around the same time. For example, one fascinating Victorian scholar,
Mrs. Mary P. Merrifield (1804–89), intriguingly also of Brighton, took a special
interest in the techniques of painting, similar to the enthusiasm of Wing and
Curtis. Her two volumes of original texts describing artists' techniques included

 us deus misericordiam tua
in medio templi tui. secundu
nomen tuum deus ita 7 laus
tua in fines terre iustitia plena
est dextera tua. ps. Magn

63.

Francesco Bettini,
Presentation of
Christ in the Temple,
single leaf from the
*Della Rovere Missal*
(Italy, late fifteenth
century), historiated *S*,
water damaged

**65.**

Caleb William Wing,
historiated *D*, Christ calling
Peter and Paul copied
from a north Italian choir
book of the 1470s or 1480s

**66.**

Illuminations by
Caleb William Wing,
calligraphy by Midolle,
facsimile of the *Roman de la
Rose* manuscript (England,
circa 1880s), title page
with central medallion lifted

recipes she collected from many early tracts on manuscript illumination from all over Europe.[57] Merrifield's research did much to further scholarly understanding of the structure of manuscript illuminations as objects. As related in her work's preface, she had been "honoured by Her Majesty's Government with a commission to proceed to the North of Italy, for the purpose of collecting MSS relative to the technical part of painting."[58] She also had access to some of the leading private collections of her day and mentions the beautiful album of "Mr. Rogers the poet, whose elegant and correct taste is well known. The volume, formed at great expense, consists of miniatures from different works and different countries; and it is scarcely possible to see more exquisite specimens of the art."[59] Even for the careful historian, such as Mrs. Merrifield, the concocted album was as much, if not more useful, than the complete manuscript. Like her fellow female medievalist Mrs. Anna Jameson (1794–1860), who was more a pioneer of medieval iconography generally, Mrs. Merrifield confirms how involved women had become, not only in the actual making of illuminations, but in historical research into the fine arts of the past.[60] Though still barred from university education at Oxford and Cambridge and from the learned societies of the British establishment, women were active both as producers and consumers of the manuscript image, perhaps more than has hitherto been noticed.

## Comte Auguste de Bastard d'Estang: Facsimiles as Monuments

Comte Auguste de Bastard d'Estang (1792–1883) inaugurated the grandest project for the reproduction of illuminated manuscripts in the entire nineteenth century, *Peintures et ornements des manuscrits, classés dans un ordre chronologique.*[61] His long labors began under the auspicious regime of the July Monarchy (1830–48), which, under the Orléanist prince Louis-Philippe, aimed to ensure the protection of France's artistic patrimony by creating institutions such as the Comité des Arts et Monuments and the Commission des Monuments Historiques under Viollet-le-Duc. At the beginning of the July Monarchy, Bastard had taken up the project of reproducing the outstanding miniatures from the library of Jean, duc de Berry, under the title *Librairie du duc de Berry,* but the French minister of the interior, Adolphe Thiers, proposed that Bastard extend his work to produce a general history of manuscripts from the sixth through the sixteenth centuries. The radical innovation of this project in the 1830s is hard to appreciate today, but it has to be seen as part of the daring first phase of efforts to recover the cultural heritage of the past at this time. In France, this project was sanctioned at the highest levels of the government, while in England similar efforts were confined to amateurs. Whereas the Arundel Society had struggled to become self-supporting through a program of subscriptions and sales to a popular audience, Bastard received close to one million francs from the French government in an unprecedented intervention; the funds were allocated by the Ministry of Instruction to encourage the advancement of science and letters, and by the Ministry of the Interior to encourage the advancement of the fine arts. From the beginning the project was one that united paleographic, historical, and artistic interests. In 1847 the government was contributing 180,000 francs per year, one-sixth of its yearly disposable operating budget.

Bastard's declared aims in carrying out this high-profile and prestigious publication of the nation's cultural patrimony were sophisticated and ambitious, and he aimed to do for manuscript painting what Seroux d'Agincourt had done in the late eighteenth century for architecture in his *Histoire de l'Art par les monuments.*[62] Echoing the sentiments of Westwood, Bastard's first professed aim was to investigate and publicize the art-historical value of miniatures which were, because of the destruction and decay of monumental and wall paintings, "the only monuments of French painting that remained unaltered to the present day."[63] In this respect he wrote of filling in "a large lacunae in the History of Art." Auguste de Bastard also proclaimed that the illuminations reproduced in these volumes would be useful for archaeological and historical research into earlier periods of Christian Europe. The words he used to articulate this goal remind one of the efforts of his own compatriot Montfaucon and also of Joseph Strutt: "coutumes, moeurs et usages,—arts et métiers,—costumes,—iconographie,—histoire naturelle,—symbolique chrétienne." Miniatures provided an "inexhaustible mine of varied documents." "But Bastard's goal is also reminiscent of discussions before the Commission of the National Gallery of Art in London in the 1830s about whether or not to purchase "specimens" of painting before Raphael, thus constructing a complete history of painting. Auguste de Bastard viewed his project not just as a historical survey, but as a practical aid to artists and restorers of monuments such as stained-glass windows, sculptures, and wall paintings. "Inspired by these facsimiles of illuminations," states Bastard, "they might thus avoid archeological error."[64] Jocelyn Bouquillard has published letters between Bastard and the inspector of monuments, Prosper Mérimée, confirming how closely national efforts at restoration were linked to those of reproduction.[65] No such comprehensive project for manuscript illumination existed in England, where reproduction also addressed a much more popular audience.

Bastard's painstaking techniques were aimed at producing the most faithful facsimile possible. His products are remarkable even by today's standards, and this is partly because he, like Shaw, did not fully do away with the concept of handmade or manuscript work in making reproductions. Lithography had been developed in France under the Restoration (1815–30) and proved immediately successful because it was quicker and cheaper than engraving, while at the same time allowing greater exactitude through its ability to reproduce subtler gradations of tone and a greater variety of line. Godefroy Engelmann had created a process of fully automated color lithography in 1836, but Bastard, again like Shaw, disdained this practice, calling the facsimiles produced by this method "shoddy" ("livres de pacotile"). Because Bastard preferred to retain a larger degree of manual control, his atelier in the rue St.-Dominique-St.-Germain was basically an artist's or craft atelier whose thirty employees (many of them Polish immigrants) were carefully trained artists rather than mere mechanical copyists. Bastard had the contours of the miniatures printed from a stone and then had each plate colored by hand. Artists would also add gold or platinum powder or leaf in an effort to recreate the exact appearance of the original in its current state of preservation.

The project was to be published in installments, with an accompanying three volumes of textual description in folio size. By 1848, when a disastrous fire halted publication and destroyed the plates for the three text volumes, twenty installments of eight plates each had already been published. Those volumes extant in libraries today preserve the opening plates of the paleographical examples of Roman, Merovingian, and Carolingian scripts down to the Capetian periods (figure 67, plate 17). The edition was intended to include not only French illuminations but also an extra section on non-French illuminations for those copies of *Peintures et ornements* destined for foreign governments. In this respect the publication was as much a bespoke trade as medieval manuscript production, with a very small print run and very few actual copies available at an enormous cost. The French government was the principal subscriber, taking sixty-six of the planned

**67.**

Jean-François-Auguste
Bastard d'Estang,
*Peintures et ornements
des manuscrits*
(Paris, 1837–46),
"Ecritures dites
visigothiques"

seventy-five copies for distribution to various municipal libraries throughout France, with the remaining nine copies destined for foreign governments.[66] The exorbitant cost of *Peintures et ornements,* which ironically made each volume more expensive than many illuminated manuscripts available on the market, was a result of the paper costs, as well as the application of precious metals and the hand painting of each plate, which ended up costing one hundred francs apiece. Each *livraison* (installment) of eight plates, two of paleographic examples and six of miniatures, cost five hundred francs without and seven hundred fifty with gold leaf. One full volume was made up of twenty *livraisons* or one hundred sixty plates, totaling the vast sum of fifteen thousand francs for a complete set with gold leaf.

Although Jacques-Charles Brunet in his famous *Manuel de libraire et de l'amateur de livres* of 1842 initially called Bastard's *Peintures et ornements* a masterpiece and a "sumptuous work,"[67] in 1860, after the disruption of the project and in a very different, more turbulent political climate, he criticized its exorbitant cost.[68] Bastard was to spend the rest of his life trying to regain government support for the project, but was never again able to produce the labor-intensive facsimiles he had earlier published and had to be content with black-and-white reproductions. Michel Hennin in his *Les Monuments et l'histoire de France* (1857) attacked Bastard for his folly and suggested the money would have been better spent on the collection of "real" manuscripts. Indeed, such"originals"—even richly illuminated ones —could be bought for several hundred francs.[69] Criticizing Bastard for never producing the explanatory text or describing which manuscripts were drawn upon in making his images, Hennin concluded that it would be better to produce facsimiles of one or two manuscripts from the Middle Ages than to reproduce all these fragments from so many different examples. What had seemed in the 1830s like a wonderfully progressive and encyclopedic museum of manuscript monuments appeared, only three decades later, after revolutions and upheavals in the very notion of what constituted French national identity, to be a mere collection of fragments.

It should not come as a surprise to find Bastard's enthusiasm for manuscripts reflected in his interest in collecting examples of them from different periods and countries. He owned a famous manuscript of miniatures of the Life of Christ (Morgan MS, M. 44; see figure 68), which he reproduced in *Peintures et ornements*. This manuscript has an illustrious pedigree from the duc de La Vallière to Bastard d'Estang to Firmin-Didot to Spitzer to J. Pierpont Morgan. Bastard also acquired the famous Conradin Bible (Walters MS, W. 152; see figures 31, 32, and 128), from which he may even have extracted cuttings, since it is recorded as having 120 miniatures in his description and only 103 miniatures when it was purchased by Walters (for further discussion, see chapter 5). Throughout the century, as we have seen, there remained an intimate relationship between those who collected and those who reproduced manuscript illuminations.

**68.**

Scenes from the Life of Christ, Christ in Majesty (France, circa 1200)

**Léon Curmer: Facsimiles and the Roman Catholic Church**

In the work of Léon Curmer (1801–70), imagery derived from illumination penetrated religious publishing in France.[70] The son of a sheet merchant, Curmer can be described as one of the earliest editors in the modern sense. His career spanned both the July Monarchy and the Second Empire (1851–70), during which he became the most important publisher of reproductions of illuminated manuscripts. Most of his early books were illustrated by wood engravings, influenced by Berwick, and integrating text and image. For his later publications, he relied on a perfected version of chromolithography. Unlike many of his contemporary editors, Curmer gave full credit to all his engravers and artists and made sure they were decently paid. The main framework for understanding Curmer's enterprise is the revival of Catholicism and its impact on religious publishing during this turbulent period.

The decade from 1840 to 1850 can be characterized as a period when the general aim of popular devotional publishing was to teach the catechism to children and to purvey in a simplified fashion the essentials of the faith. The marketing of the cult of the "Infant Jesus" with images that would today be considered overly sentimental and sugary, if not wholly fitting the category of "kitsch," dates from the years 1850 to 1870. An outburst by the Abbé Sagette in *Essai sur l'art chrétien* (1853) was directed against the bad taste of such devotional images; they were perverting taste, weakening piety, and sometimes insulting Christian sentiments and dogma.[71] At midcentury, there was little to suggest that mass-distributed religious images, which were issued in enormous quantities by publishers like Charles Letaille, made any reference to illumination. The period was characterized by the products of, for example, the Düsseldorf-based Société pour la Propagande des Bonnes Gravures Religieuses, which was founded in 1842 and had opened a Paris branch by the early 1850s. The 1856 catalogue of the society's agents, Schulgen and Schwan in the rue St.-Sulpice, Paris, promoted works by Overbeck and other

Nazarene painters who worked in a sentimental, saccharine figurative style that to-day looks like a dilution of a too-pagan Raphael by the meek, saintly simplicity of Fra Angelico. Pictures could be had for as little as twenty-five centimes each; illumination was at the top of the range, a chromolithographed Book of Hours being available at one hundred francs (about four pounds sterling).[72]

As if responding to the anxieties of the Abbé Sagette, Curmer gave religious publishing a style based on medieval illumination that was of impeccably good taste. Curmer's deluxe publications of the 1850s and 1860s exploited illuminated manuscripts as never before for religious ends. He typified the successful entrepreneurial publisher who managed to survive in the publishing revolution of the 1830s and 1840s, when new reproduction and distribution methods allowed cheap illustrated works and color printing to flourish. Curmer's submission to the jury of the 1839 Exhibition showed him defining the new role of the publisher: he was a business entrepreneur who coordinated the work of machines and a host of specialists to realize publishing ideas. His method is demonstrated by the successful catalogue of social types, *Les français peints par eux-mêmes* (1841–42), in which he took a wildly successful publishing genre—the *physiologies,* cheap booklets published by the Maison Aubert describing various types of people in amusing ways and illustrated by Daumier and others—and made a success of it in a more expensive format, issuing monthly fascicules with colored pictures. He then adapted the formula used in this work to a series of monumental publications focusing on illuminated manuscripts. The first was his *Imitation de Jésus Christ,* published between 1856 and 1858 in fifty fascicules that appeared on the tenth, twentieth, and thirtieth day of each month for three francs, fifty centimes, apiece.[73] The publication by fascicules of the *Grandes heures de la reine Anne de Bretagne* (i.e., the *Anne of Brittany Hours*), was announced in April 1859 and completed in August 1861 (figure 69). Curmer repeated the formula in his monumental work *Les Evangiles des Dimanches et fêtes de l'année,* issued in seventy-six fascicules between April 1862 and January 1864. The *Jehan Foucquet, Heures de Maistre Etienne Chevalier* was likewise announced as a work to appear in sixty fascicules at six francs each and was issued at a rate of four a month from 1864 to 1866.[74] This serial form of publication had been common since the 1830s, as it also was in England with Shaw and Westwood, but Curmer used it for a novel kind of production. His approach can be paralleled by, for example, Henri Reiss in Vienna, who in 1861 began to publish a magnificent *Missale romanum* in ten fascicules; the deluxe edition with miniatures in gold, silver, and colors reproduced works by miniaturists from medieval Flanders (thus claiming Flemish art for the German school), southern Germany, and the lower Rhineland. Reiss's work was directed by a "Committee of scholars and archaeologists," revealing a concern for academic respectability similar to Curmer's.[75]

The print runs of Curmer's works were similar to those of expensive facsimiles today: the *Anne of Brittany Hours* had 850 subscribers, and the *Evangiles* had 550. Reprintings took the numbers beyond this,[76] and the makeup of the books allowed their constituent parts to be issued separately. The *Histoire de l'ornementation des manuscrits* by Ferdinand Denis, which came with its own title page in the *Imitation de Jésus Christ* of 1856 to 1858, was still being issued as a limited edition of six hundred copies by Edouard Rouveyre in 1880. The various ornaments for the texts were also probably reused in other publications, and other images from these works could be published separately. Plain copies of borders from the *Imitation de Jésus Christ* were sold at one franc, fifty centimes, for do-it-yourself coloring, while a cheap version of the *Jehan Foucquet* was issued as a *petit missel illustré* from

LISTE
DES
SOUSCRIPTEURS
AU LIVRE D'HEURES
DE LA REINE ANNE DE BRETAGNE

1 S. M. NAPOLÉON III, EMPEREUR DES FRANÇAIS. 58
2 S. M. L'IMPÉRATRICE DES FRANÇAIS. 355
3 S. A. I. LE PRINCE J. NAPOLÉON. 362
4 S. A. I. Mᵐᵉ LA PRINCESSE MARIE-CLOTILDE NAPOLÉON. 356
5 S. A. I. LA PRINCESSE MATHILDE NAPOLÉON. 357
6 SA SAINTETÉ PIE IX, SOUVERAIN PONTIFE. 392
7 S. M. ALEXANDRE II, EMPEREUR DE TOUTES LES RUSSIES. 315
8 S. M. ISABELLE II, REINE D'ESPAGNE. 353
9 S. M. MARIE FERDINAND, ROI D'ESPAGNE. 344
10/11/12 S. M. LA REINE MARIE-CHRISTINE DE BOURBON 413/414/415
13 S. M. LÉOPOLD Iᵉʳ, ROI DES BELGES. 304

**69.**

Anne of Brittany at Prayer, from *Le Livre d'heures de la Reine Anne de Bretagne* (Paris, 1861)

**70.**

Appendix, subscription list from *Le Livre d'heures de la Reine Anne de Bretagne* (Paris, 1861)

April 16, 1864, in fifty fascicules, with outlines to be colored by the "dames et demoiselles" who subscribed. It was not so much the prestige publications, but their ancillary offshoots in other publications and the reuse of plates in other contexts, which contributed to Curmer's commercial success.

Curmer stressed the technical triumphs involved in the publication of these magnificent works. The work of printers, engravers, and lithographers was acknowledged with unrestrained praise—not since Gutenberg, it was claimed, had such excellence been seen. The appendix of the *Evangiles* of 1862 to 1864 listed all those who had drawn, decorated, and colored the images. In fact, Curmer's enterprise points to the existence of an army of illuminators preparing images for chromolithography that compares with the one working for Auguste de Bastard on his *Peintures et ornements de manuscrits.* In thanking the participants, Curmer was stressing the benefits of the new technology of chromolithographic printing. Another technological marvel was the use of photographic images in his production processes. The appendices of the *Imitation de Jésus Christ* had pasted-in photographs of seventeenth-century engravings, as did those of the *Evangiles.* Quite apart from this, photography had become a method used to copy manuscript illuminations, as Curmer describes in volume 2, the appendix, of the *Evangiles.* The Bibliothèque Impériale had not been able to provide facilities for photographing the most deluxe manuscripts stored in the *Réserve,* and Curmer thus regretted that pages of the *Aragon Hours* and the *Bedford [Salisbury] Breviary* had been printed from hand copies. By contrast, he reported that the *Réserve* had been thrown open to him for hand copies to be reproduced in the *Imitation* of 1856 to 1858, but photography was not then involved. The Musée des Souverains in the Louvre, the Brera Library in Milan, and the Marciana Library (Biblioteca San Marco) in Venice had all welcomed photographers. In the latter institution, even the great *Grimani Breviary* was made available to photographers. In these instances, "the accomplished hand of the colorist intervened to complete this marvel of photographic reproduction" ("la main habile du coloriste est venue compléter ce prodige de la reproduction photographique").

For these publications, Curmer had texts provided by the Abbé Delaunay, the curé of St. Etienne du Mont, who had been designated for the task by the archbishop of Paris. Religious orthodoxy was thus guaranteed. This was important, since all the publications were designed as working books for the devout. The *Imitation de Jésus Christ* had a detailed table of contents to guide the reader. The *Evangiles* and the *Jehan Foucquet* were organized as functional prayer books, and to enhance its accessibility, the text of the *Anne of Brittany Hours* was printed in a French translation.[77] All three publications could be used for personal devotions, and the first two had introductory pages for the insertion of "souvenirs de famille"; like the Victorian family Bible, they were intended to be family heirlooms. Curmer was able to print a letter from Pope Pius IX as a preface to the *Jehan Foucquet* (figure 71). The pope welcomed its publication in a world where greed and corruption distanced people from God, and in which the goal of Art as representing the Beautiful and the Good was ignored. The pope commented that the inspection of the pages was sufficient to inspire disgust with common, vulgar religious engravings and to lead the soul toward love of celestial things. Abbé Sagette would have agreed.

Curmer matched this religious respectability with academic credentials: his works acknowledge the help of the major scholars of the time, from Auguste de Bastard, Horace de Viel-Castel, and Léon Laborde in France to Henry Coxe, Frederic Madden, and Anthony Panizzi in England. Ferdinand Denis was called on to provide historical texts, and the professor of botany at the Sorbonne provided a treatise on the flowers for which the *Anne of Brittany Hours* was famous. But perhaps the most striking aspect of these works was their patronage. The *Anne of Brittany Hours,* the *Evangiles,* and the *Jehan Foucquet* each carried subscription lists that began with Napoleon III, the empress, and members of the royal and noble families of Europe, not to mention the pope and senior politicians. The subscription list of the *Anne of Brittany Hours* is perhaps the most impressive one (figure 70).[78] The publication was presented as being carried out in the shadow of Napoleon III; he and the empress headed up the list of subscribers, followed by their three children, who were in turn followed by Pope Pius IX, Tsar Alexander

**71.**

*Oeuvre de Jehan Fouqet. Heures de Maistre Estienne Chevalier. Texte restitué par M. l'abbé Delaunay, curé de St. Etienne du Mont (Paris, 1866)*

II of Russia, the monarchs of Spain and Belgium, the duc d'Aumale, and the duc
de Montpensier. Thereafter, the list includes senior members of the French government and Catholic clergy, followed by subscribers in alphabetical order.

What kind of art history was promulgated by these publications?
Curmer's flair for satisfying the expectations and prejudices of his readership makes
his publications worth examining for evidence of the views of illumination held in
mid-nineteenth-century France. Ferdinand Denis provided the necessary slant in
his historical account published with the *Imitation de Jésus Christ* (1856–58). He
called attention to monarchs who directly oversaw the production of their illuminated manuscripts, such as Charlemagne and Charles V in particular, as well as the
fifteenth-century prince René d'Anjou, who was himself an illuminator. Denis
made the point that the Englishman Alcuin's Anglo-Saxon illumination was by no
means the only determinant of style in the Carolingian lands.[79] The art of illumination, which reached its golden age in the fifteenth century, declined as it became
secularized. (Denis had had a contrary view in Arsennes's manual of 1833, when he
held that illumination developed only when applied to secular works from the
thirteenth century.) In contrast to England, where the reputation of Giulio Clovio
still held sway, Italian illumination is mentioned only in passing. Denis's narrative
stresses the excellence of French work done in Paris around 1400, and it then
traces a line of development that extends from Fouquet, who surpassed Van Eyck,
the supposed illuminator of the *Bedford Breviary,* to the seventeenth- and eighteenth-
century illuminators working for Louis XIV and his successors.

It is easy today to be seduced by Curmer's presentation of his wares. He
evidently knew his market, and geared his publications to appeal to his audience's
views of the world. Though he displayed his works at the great exhibitions, they
were praised in purely conventional terms. In 1855, the exhibition jury declared
that Curmer should be judged on his past output, since "he had not done much
recently." In 1862 he was one of thirty printers from France who received medals,
his specialty being described as "Imitation of Manuscripts, by chromolithography."
The report for the British government on the 1867 Paris exhibition admired the
"large, costly and highly illuminated editions," which were "superbly decorated,"
but commented that the most remarkable fact was that Curmer could number
eight hundred subscribers to his *Evangiles,* a work which cost twenty pounds in
English money.[80]

**Godefroy Engelmann,**
**Ambroise**
**Firmin-Didot, and**
**Pierre-Jules Hetzel:**
**Facsimiles for**
**the Populace**

In France, gift books were the near-exclusive province
of the "inventor" of chromolithography, Godefroy
Engelmann (1788–1839), who with his son, (Godefroy
II (1814–97), founded the Société Engelmann, Père et
Fils, in 1837, which became Engelmann et Graf in
1842, when Auguste Graf joined the company.[81] The
most ambitious historicist use of the new medium of
lithography in the nineteenth century was Nodier and Taylor's *Voyages pittoresques
de la France* published between 1820 and 1878—an attempt not only to record but
to recreate the appearance of medieval monuments and buildings throughout the
country.[82] The lithographic plates for this vast project were produced at Mulhouse
and Paris by Godefroy Engelmann, who had established himself as the leading ex-
ponent of the new medium from 1815. The problems of creating manuscript facsimiles were different from allowing young artists like Gèricault and Delacroix to
evoke monastic ruins in Romantic light and shade, since this called for color and
for exact replication of the style of the original. One of the earliest and most suc-

cessful facsimiles produced by Engelmann *fils* and Graf, dating from 1853, was of a fourteenth-century Neapolitan manuscript which was on display at the Musée des Souverains, the *Statuts de l'Ordre du St. Esprit* (Paris: BnF MS fr. 4274). The reasons for this unusual manuscript being reproduced at such great expense lie perhaps in its belonging to that repository of the relics of monarchy, its appeal as a series of images of secular authority and power, and its dazzling display of heraldry, which was much enjoyed and studied at the time by amateurs as well as by the nobility. The manuscript's dedication page, featuring the Trinity with impressive figures of King Louis d'Anjou and Queen Jeanne in prayer, suggest the appeal of the manuscript for its nineteenth-century audience (figure 72).

According to the *Grand Dictionnaire universel du XIXe siècle,* a facsimile was a *reproduction exacte,* and this is what people who could afford these lavishly crafted objects were buying, ironically—as in other instances noted earlier—often

paying more for them than for actual medieval manuscripts. Such a lavish facsimile, which was still basically produced by hand, was still beyond the means of most people, and it was only after the midcentury in France, as the technical process of chromolithography was further mechanized and the process became standardized, that books reproducing not whole manuscripts in facsimile, but isolated pages and miniatures from them, became fashionable. This fragmentation of the manuscript page in reproduction is related directly to manuscripts' being cut up and collected, as described in the previous chapter. But it is also part of a general movement toward fragmentation that can be seen in the sculptural cast museums of the period and the Musée de Cluny in Paris, which showed the fragmentary remains of statues and paintings destroyed by revolutions, neglect, or just time.[83]

One of the most important exponents of the historical book filled with chromolithographed images was Paul Lacroix (1806–84; also

72.

*Statuts de l'Ordre de Saint-Esprit au droit desir* (Paris, 1853), plate 1

known as "Bibliophile Jacob"), who edited a number of large-scale studies of medieval art and life under the direction of the publisher Ambroise Firmin-Didot, the head of a family of important scholar-printers of the period.[84] In 1849, Lacroix and Ferdinand Séré published *Le Moyen Age et la Renaissance,* which contained a long section on manuscript illumination by the expert Champollion-Figeac.[85] Most of the examples in this work were taken from the Bibliothèque Nationale and other national collections, although a number are captioned as being in the "Bibl. Ambroise Firmin-Didot," the publisher of the volumes.[86] Lacroix was a "public servant" himself, being the conservator of the Bibliothèque de l'Arsenal. His vast work filled five quarto volumes and had, in Lacroix's own words, "taken its place in the library of the amateur, not only in France but also among foreigners; it has become celebrated." These words appear in the preface to the second French edition produced twenty years after the first; this second edition was shortened considerably and was aimed at a different audience "in a form more simple, easier, and more pleasing; within the reach of youth who desire to learn without weariness or irksomeness, of females interested in grave authors, of the family that loves to assemble round a book altogether instructive and attractive."[87] Indeed, in the same preface, Lacroix makes an interesting observation about the educational use of images as compared to texts:

The numerous illustrations that adorn the work will engage the eye, while the text will speak to the intelligence. The designs in chromolithography are executed by M. Kellerhoven, who for several years has made the art one of a high order, worthy to shine among the finest works of our greatest painters, as is proved by his "Chefs-d'oeuvre of the Great Masters," "Lives of the Saints," and "Legend of St. Ursula."[88]

Lacroix's crusade to educate a broad spectrum of the population about the medieval past comes across further in the preface to his volume dealing with medieval learning, *Sciences et Lettres au moyen âge et à l'époque de la Renaissance* (1877).[89] Here Lacroix gives a long eulogy to his "excellent and venerable friend," the savant M. Ambroise Firmin-Didot, just deceased, who had given Lacroix the good advice to "leave to others the profundity of minute erudition . . . great success awaits less the learned than the vulgarizers."[90] Lacroix's superb volumes are still reprinted today (without the expensive chromolithographs, of course), a testament to the belief of both author and printer that the Middle Ages appeal to a broad public in word and image. The *Sciences et Lettres* images also offer insight into the processes underlying Lacroix's creation. This volume features thirteen full-page chromolithographs, mostly copied from medieval and Renaissance manuscripts, interspersed with smaller isolated designs in the cheaper medium of wood engravings, which could be set together with the text on most of the pages. The illustrations are beautifully executed by four artists named in red on the title page: "Compère, Daumont, Pralon et Werner" (figure 73, plate 18).

In the Firmin-Didot archives, we were lucky enough to come across some of the preliminary watercolor drawings for the color lithographs of Lacroix's volumes—works which have fascinating links to the Spanish Forger (discussed below) who may have worked on this project and there learned to make his hand a "medieval" one. One watercolor (figure 74, plate 19) features a miniature of Henri d'Albret, king of Navarre, in a garden, copied from a manuscript in the Bibliothèque de l'Arsenal (BnF, Bibl. de l'Arsenal, MS 5096, folio 1). The watercolor is signed by one A. Bichard, while the lithographed work within the book bears the inscription "Pralon." Adolphe-Alphonse Gery-Bichard, an "engraver and illustrator" known for doing frontispieces and illustrations, was active in France in the 1880s and 1890s.[91] There is also record of an Antoine Pralon, designated as a "lithographer of reproductions," who did copies of works by Fouquet and Memling, and was active in Paris between 1865 and 1882.[92] While Bichard is the artist who created the hand-copied watercolor remarkable for its assiduous fidelity to its manuscript model, it is the master of mechanized color reproduction, Pralon, who gains honor within Lacroix's mass-produced volume. Pralon's signature appears in the lower-left corner of the book's frontispiece, and his name is featured boldly on the book's title page (figure 73).[93]

Other works in Ambroise Firmin-Didot's collection suggest his personal appreciation for medievalizing products made possible through the technology of the day. His library housed a richly bound, three-volume set containing photographs of miniatures from famous manuscripts such as the *Grimani Breviary* (Venice: Biblioteca S. Marco) and the *Salisbury Breviary* (Paris, BnF) that had been hand colored by modern artists.[94] He also owned meticulously hand-copied miniatures from works including, again, the celebrated *Grimani Breviary,* some of these signed by an Italian painter named Prosdocimi.[95] The scene of the Queen of Sheba before Solomon copied from this manuscript (figure 75) was also reproduced in Lacroix's

**73.**

Paul Lacroix,
*Sciences et lettres au
moyen âge et à l'époque
de la renaissance*
(Paris, 1877),
frontispiece and
title page

**74.**

H. Bichard, copy of
circa 1527 illumination
of Henri d'Albret,
roi de Navarre
(France, nineteenth
century)

*Moeurs et usages au moyen âge* (1871). Firmin-Didot's involvement with experiments in reproductive technology is suggested by an item that appears in the sale of his library (lot 66), a fourth volume of the famous Curmer facsimile of Fouquet's oeuvre, described as:

1. Le portrait du pape Pie IX, photographie admirablement colorie par un des eleves de l'Adademie de France a Rome; 2 et 3. Deux epreuves, de ton different, du portrait de Fouquet; 4, une epreuve, d'un ton different de celui du tirage entier, de la planche des Antiquites judaiques representant l'Entree d'Antiochus IV a Jerusalem; 5 a 8, deux photographies et deux epreuves du tirage en chromolithographie, de ton different, de la sainte Vierge, sous les traits d'Agnes Sorel, d'apres un des panneaux du diptyque de Melun.[96]

The sale catalogue entry credits four artists for the copies after originals: M. Hendshel for the works in Frankfurt, M. Gewundel for those in Munich, and all the others were executed by MM. Lavril and A. Racinet *père* (figure 76). Whether this "Album," as it is titled on the spine, belonged to Curmer first and was then acquired by Firmin-Didot, its existence clearly suggests the common interests of the two publishers in technical experimentation with the reproduction of works of art. Further witness to nineteenth-century reproductive techniques is found in a set of nine watercolors now divided between the Rosenwald Collection, Washington, D.C. (discussed further in chapter 5), and the Bibliothèque Nationale in Paris (figure 77). These grisaille and gold miniatures, executed in a late-fifteenth-century Flemish style, copy—but also modify—elements of illuminations within a manuscript created for Louis of Bruges (BnF, MS fr. 181). Wieck has demonstrated that these nineteenth-century works were not forgeries (a class of object discussed further below). Rather, they were copies made from tracings of the original miniatures—a step in the process of creating Georges Hurtrel's 1870 facsimile of the Louis of Bruges manuscript.[97] Purchased as originals in the twentieth century, these works now stand as relics of an antique mode of reproductive technology.

**75.**

Handmade copy of illumination in the *Grimani Breviary*, Queen of Sheba before Solomon, (France, nineteenth century)

The young publisher Pierre-Jules Hetzel in 1838 published the first of a new kind of prayer book, the *Heures Royales,* with an imprimatur from the archbishop of Paris dated November 1837. This was a self-consciously artistic production: the names of the chief designers and the page references of their contributions were given at the back of the book, as were the names of the engravers. The Gothic frames and borders were the work of Daniel Ramée, while the drawings and figures were done by Gérard-Séguin. The latter was a minor painter of religious scenes; the architect Ramée, on the other hand, was a medieval enthusiast, noted in 1833 for marketing casts of thirteenth-century sculptures. The *Heures Royales* is arranged to facilitate contemplation of the images as works of art, while at the same time allowing perusal for devotional purposes; the message of the prayers is read into the medieval images. The effect was intensified when the publisher Léon Curmer, who seems to have acquired the remaining stock of the book in 1840, added illuminated ornament printed by chromolithography to the book. Curmer issued the work with a new title page, "Heures Nouvelles—L. Curmer, 1840," decorated by a floral il-

**76.**

**Proof portrait of
Jean Fouquet, from an
album of experiments
in reproductive
technology connected
to the chromolitho-
graphed facsimile of
*Hours of Etienne
Chevalier* (1864–66)**

**77.**

**Georges Hurtrel,
*Four Scenes from the
Life of Christ* and *Four
Scenes from the Legends
of Judas and Pilate*
(Paris, nineteenth
century), preparatory
miniatures for facsimile**

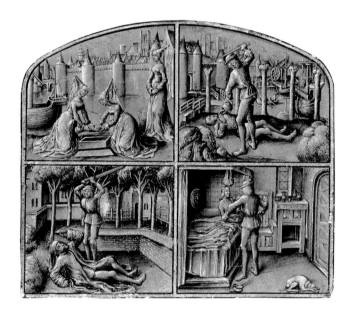

luminated border in which two monks are praying (figure 78); four other chromolithographed illuminated pages were added with rich floral borders that took French manuscripts of the early fifteenth century as their model. At a later date, in 1842, steel-engraved illustrations with medieval floral borders by André Féart were added to at least one copy.[98] The Book of Hours of Hetzel and Curmer was the earliest and most lavish of a type of book that was to make the fortune of a number of publishers. From the early 1840s, these books were produced in large quantities by publishers such as Alfred Mame in Tours and Martial Ardant Frères in Limoges, to be given as presents at baptisms, weddings, confirmations, and other significant moments in the life of the Catholic bourgeoisie. These works appear in the *de luxe* account published for the 1867 Exposition Universelle, *Alfred Mame et Fils, Notices et Specimens* (Tours, 1867), where, with beautifully printed breviaries and missals, are pages from extravagantly ornamented *Livres de Marriage, Livres d'Heures,* and a more modest *Paroissien* decorated in illuminated styles by H. Catenacci, H. Giacomelli, and others.[99] Publishers offered such books in simple formats or in lavish bindings that could be specially ordered. It was works of this kind that, in France, definitively linked medieval style to Catholic piety, a link which flourishes even today.

Hetzel's publication was at the forefront of an invasion of religious publishing in illuminated styles. A work like Théophile Fragonard's *Evangiles de Notre Seigneur Jésus-Christ* (Paris: J.-J. Dubochet, 1837) had lithographed borders in black and white imitating French fifteenth-century Books of Hours.

78.

*Heures Nouvelles*
(Paris, circa 1837
and circa 1842),
title page

Fragonard was one of that army of draftsmen called into being by the explosion in the 1830s of books, magazines, and prints illustrated by the new technologies of lithography and of wood engravings that could be integrated with type. Publishers such as Curmer relied on their services, but while many such draftsmen aspired to the status of artists, few gained admittance to the roll of those showing their work in the Salon. The presence of styles based on medieval illumination in this milieu is seen in works like Fragonard's *Vie de Jésus-Christ* (Paris: Challamel & Cie, 1840); the initials are in simple medieval styles, and if the floral ornament satisfied the nineteenth-century desire for realism, it also has the unmistakable mark of floral ornament found in late medieval illuminated books.

The circulation of prints that matched religious texts with medieval illumination is shown by the sheets of Mademoiselle Aline Guilbert, "Libraire, 21 bis Quai Voltaire" in Paris, who designed, engraved, and hand colored prayers around 1838, when she issued a set of them with the title page "Prières, fac-simile du 9e au 15e siècle." Most of her illumination is copied from manuscripts in the Bibliothèque Royale—a fifteenth-century humanistic Petrarch, the *Salisbury Breviary*, and *Histoire des Juifs* of the fourteenth century—but there are also sheets in decorative styles of the 1830s, one of them based on fifteenth-century flower and acanthus borders; another sheet reproduces a page from a late-fifteenth-century Rouen or Paris psalter from the collection of the Comte Lanjuinais. That Guilbert survived commercially is suggested by a reference at the end of the nineteenth century to a Book of Hours she had made that was published by Gruel and Engelmann.[100]

Like the popular Books of Hours of the fifteenth century, in which families also recorded momentous life and death events, these chromolithographed medievalizing prayer books served the nineteenth-century French market for pretty and affordable *livres des famille*.

## The State, the Individual, and the Refashioning of the Manuscript Book

**Manuscripts and Emperors: The Musée des Souverains**

After his coup d'état of 1852, Louis-Napoleon, who soon became Emperor Napoleon III, decided that the Louvre should house the Musée des Souverains—a kind of living Montfaucon (see chapter 1)—in which objects that had belonged to the monarchs of France would be brought together for a display "of great interest for art and for history" ("d'un grand intérêt pour l'art et pour l'histoire"). The chosen site was significant. The museum was to be set up in the Throne Room that Napoleon Bonaparte had ordered when restoring the Louvre in 1804. Louis-Philippe after 1830 had made Versailles the site for the display of the history of France and his place within it by commissioning a series of paintings of selected glorious moments in the country's past. Napoleon III from 1852 developed the Louvre as an expression of imperial power.[101]

The new museum was arranged to show the succession of dynasties that had ruled France and brought it to greatness, from the Merovingians to the Napoleonic dynasty. Napoleon III decreed that objects were to be gathered from public collections all over France. The artist and the historian—and above all the general public—could learn about France's past and its present from the artifacts gathered there. There were 408 registered objects in the display, and 240 of them related to Napoleon I, from his pistols and a copy of Ossian's works to locks of his hair and the crown given by the city of Cherbourg for his coffin when his remains were brought back to France in 1840.[102] Illuminated manuscripts made for medieval emperors and kings and now displayed in a public museum were intended to present Napoleon III as the natural heir to the history of France and the culminating point of all French culture; continuity from Charlemagne to Napoleon III was assumed.

The manuscripts were probably the most striking objects displayed in the Musée des Souverains, rivaled only by the suits of armor that Napoleon III was so keen on collecting and by some of the larger pieces of metalwork.[103] These manuscripts included Books of Hours dating from the late fifteenth to the seventeenth centuries, notably the celebrated *Anne of Brittany Hours* (Delisle remembered in 1907 with emotion the day he was sent to retrieve it for the Bibliothèque Nationale in 1871), as well as two thirteenth-century psalters associated with St. Louis. The fourteenth century was represented by part of a Bible made for Charles V of France and by the *Statuts de l'Ordre du St. Esprit* set up by Louis d'Anjou, the Angevin king of Naples, in 1352 (discussed earlier). The inclusion of a work done for a minor potentate from southern Italy in this roll call of French monarchs no doubt suited the imperial horizons of the Musée des Souverains and may have underlined the historical precedents for Napoleon III's support of the nationalist movement in Italy. But pride of place was given to Carolingian works: the Bible of Charles the Bald, the psalter of Charles the Bald, and the evangeliary of Charlemagne. The catalogue of the museum, with its lengthy description of the manuscripts, was priced at one franc, fifty centimes, which shows it was intended to be

widely circulated.[104] All in all, the Musée des Souverains canonized illumination as
an art with royal and imperial associations. Illumination could be presented as a
kind of art that flattered the pretensions to cultural hegemony of the Catholic
bourgeoisie; it was French, traditional, and Catholic, and it was associated with
the great figures of France's past in a particularly intimate way. In an age of shifting values, illumination could represent the enduring and unchanging character of
France's imperial, Christian mission and its artistic culture.

**Illumination and Legitimist Sentiment:** *Chambord Missal* **and the** *Gallois Hours*

If the prominent display of illuminated manuscripts
in the Louvre appropriated royalist icons for Napoleon
III's imperialist purposes, there were also groups of
royalists who used newly fabricated illuminated manuscripts to assert their own legitimacy. For in the
nineteenth century a close link existed between illumination and piety, a piety that was anti-Republican
and Legitimist (the term given to supporters of the Bourbon line deposed and ex-
iled by the July Revolution of 1830). A graphic illustration of this was the illuminated missal given by noble ladies of Legitimist sympathies to the comte de
Chambord when he became head of the house of Bourbon on the death of his
uncle, Louis Antoine, in June 1844 (figure 79).[105] Each leaf was financed by a lady
whose heraldic arms were represented and whose name was given at the bottom
of each page. The decoration varies from facsimiles of fourteenth- and fifteenth-
century styles, some of them with Renaissance elements, to elaborate flower
pieces and floral designs coupled with sweetly smiling angels. The miniatures have
a definite political message. In one picture, the nation bestows on the young duc
de Bordeaux (as he was known as a child) the château of Chambord; another
scene shows the Louis IV (Louis d'Outremer) returning from exile in England in
936, a reference to an episode in French history when a monarch was invited
from abroad to unite the French people. Henri IV, who united France after the
sixteenth-century Wars of Religion, is depicted several times. Joan of Arc is likewise referred to on several pages. In one, she leads Charles VII to his coronation
in Reims, the scene artfully suggesting that the Dames Légitimistes de France
were surrogates for the Maid of Orléans. There is no hint here of the evidence
seized on by Republicans, published by Quicherat in 1841 and popularized by
Henri Martin in succeeding editions of his *Histoire de France,* that Joan had been
betrayed by the king of France himself.[106] The missal's binding in rich ruby-red
velvet with gilt ornament was done by Gruel in imitation of princely bindings of
the Renaissance. The whole work served to remind Chambord of his historic
role, which was to return to France and unite the French under a sacral kingship
on the medieval model.

The Dames Légitimistes de France were a well-organized group who
made several gifts to Chambord and his family, the most celebrated being the
Froment-Meurice heavily ornamented, silver-gilt, neo-Gothic *mobilier de toilette*
(dressing table and attendant furnishings), which was financed by public subscription for the marriage of his sister to the future duke of Parma, and shown at the
Great Exhibition of 1851.[107] Gothic was the natural style for the Legitimist nobility
that retreated to the countryside after 1830 and shunned contact with the July
Monarchy and the Second Empire of Napoleon III; nostalgia for the chivalry of
ancient France made them notable builders of neo-Gothic châteaux, particularly
in the west of France.[108] The Gothic style in the manuscript context of the *Chambord Missal* carried an overt political message for its Legitimist patrons: the book

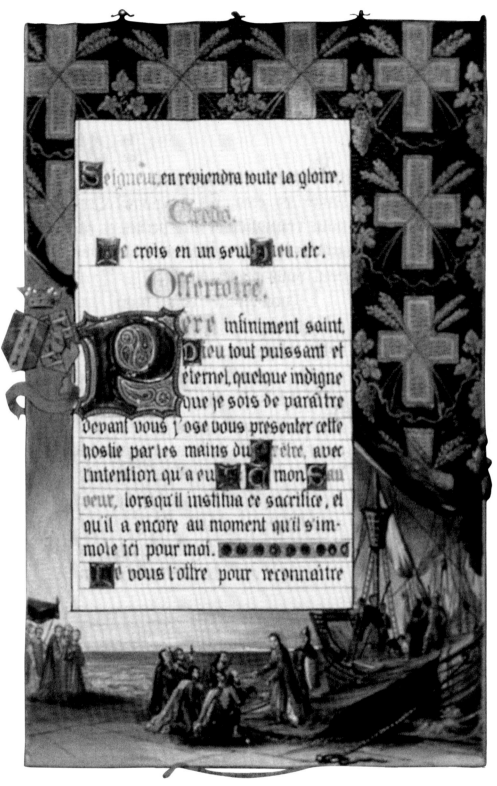

**79.**

*Chambord Missal*
*(Paris, 1844)*

was a call to reinstate a united and traditional France under a king who was the direct heir of a sanctified royal line that stretched back to a mythic Middle Ages— a period when each class in the social hierarchy knew its place and duties, and all placed their trust in God for the destiny of France.

The gift of a prayer book, such as that made to the comte de Chambord, was a public act. A work that was rather more private in character shows illumination used in a similar way. Louis-Jules Gallois (1800–67) in 1838 commissioned an illuminated manuscript Book of Hours in memory of his wife, Adèle Lecamus (figure 80). The work was sufficiently complete in 1843 to be presented to Pope Gregory XVI, whose indulgence is bound into the work. The book has a title page dated 1840, the title appearing as a panel against a scene of a city in a landscape in evident imitation of manuscripts of the Ghent-Bruges style of the early sixteenth century. The book's elaborate calendar pages, as well as the profuse illuminated borders and miniatures, are in styles that range from exact copies of conventional marginal ornament in fifteenth-century French manuscripts to figural scenes that might be either of a medieval or Re-naissance character or else in the treacle-laced style of nineteenth-century religious art. Two of the miniaturists signed their names, Auguste Ledoux (1816–69) dating work between 1839 and 1841, and Charles Leblanc (1815–77), whose contributions were undated. The binding, dated 1840, was by the "Relieur du Roi," Alphonse Simier, and incorpo-rated extraordinarily rich covers and spine made up by the celebrated jeweler François Mellerio (died 1843). The binding and title page are decked out with the arms of Gallois and of his wife.[109]

**80.**

*Gallois Hours*
**(Paris, 1838–42, 1850)**

The *Gallois Hours* was a highly tenden-tious document. We learn about the genesis of the work from illuminated pages inserted into the book after 1850. These pages describe the making of the book, which was said to have taken fourteen years to complete and to have occupied twenty-two artists and one scribe. There was already a claim for nobility of a kind in the earlier part of the book, in that Adèle Lecamus was portrayed as Anne of Brittany, the queen who united Brittany to the French crown by marrying two French kings in succession: the portrait following is that by Bourdichon in the early-sixteenth-century *Anne of Brittany Hours,* a manuscript whose decorative bor-ders of flowers on a gold ground are copied in the *Gallois Hours.* The additional pages provide an abstract of documents intended to prove that Gallois was de-scended from the family of "Gallois dite de Naives," which can be traced in Lor-raine in the sixteenth and seventeenth centuries. Pelletier's *Nobiliaire ou armorial général de la Lorraine* of 1758 described how one Antoine Gallois of Naives was given letters of nobility by the duc de Lorraine in 1536, and it was this title, "Comte de Naives," that Louis-Jules Gallois succeeded in acquiring from Leopold, archduke of Austria, grand duke of Tuscany, on November 28, 1842. By that date, Gallois was already using the arms described by Pelletier as granted to the family in 1536—they figure in Gallois's manuscript before the granting of the title in 1842. The pages added after 1850 finally claim that Gallois's ancestors were knights of the Order of Malta, a crusading order based in Malta from 1530 with a venerable medieval history.

The display of heraldic arms in the *Gallois Hours* is worth considering. Obsession with rank is doubtless endemic in societies where aristocracies owe their power to a king or emperor, and in France it can be traced back to the Middle Ages; rank, after all, was the source of exemption from specific kinds of duties and taxes, quite apart from guaranteeing social status. The insistence on title and pedigree shown in the *Gallois Hours* is of a different order, however, and reflects the uncertainties of a whole class of French society. The law court that guaranteed title had been finally abolished by the 1832 edition of the Code Pénal, the collection of laws first promulgated in 1810 on which the legal system of France was based since the Napoleonic reforms. After 1832, there was no authority to prevent the capricious adoption of titles by unsuitable persons. Only historical documentary proof could give a title such as the "Comte de Naives" any credibility.

The story of the Salle des Croisades at Versailles demonstrates the problem. If the Galerie des Batailles was Louis-Philippe's official version of French history and of the king's role as its representative, the Salle des Croisades was the sphere of the nobility in general. The heraldic arms of all whose families had been crusaders in the Middle Ages were to be displayed. The gallery opened in 1839; two series of heraldic shields were displayed, the authenticity of each supported by the evidence of medieval chronicles, medieval charters, or archival documents. On the basis of this research some 306 shields were admitted, representing some 100 family names that still survived in the 1830s. However, claims by aspirant descendants were enormous: the gallery had to be closed in 1841 to admit over twice the number of arms, so that when it opened again some 690 shields were displayed. A mechanism had to be set up to judge the validity of the arms claimed, the Archives Générales de la Noblesse, and this was presided over by M. Lacabane, president of the Ecole des Chartes and the head of the Cabinet des Manuscrits in the Bibliothèque Royale. From at least the 1860s, this association had an office for authenticating proof of nobility. Documents that supported a family's link with crusading or noble ancestors became highly valuable. They were wrenched from libraries and archive repositories; originals had the names of ancestors of nineteenth-century aspirants inserted and were even forged. Eugène Henri Courtois and Paul Letellier made up "crusader charters" that would allow supposedly ancient and learned families to be included in the Salle des Croisades.[110] Just as Louis-Philippe underscored his line of descent from thirteenth-century kings by building, in 1840, a Gothic chapel in memory of St. Louis outside Tunis (where Louis had died while on a crusade in 1277), and Louis-Jules Gallois claimed attachment to the values of medieval France, royalist and Catholic, with his investment in a Book of Hours, the public at large now inserted itself into French history. The background to such investment in an imagined past was a response to the highly polarized and uncertain nature of French society in the mid–nineteenth century. It can be compared, for example, with the mania in Germany for titles in the 1840s, or the huge growth in England of works that concerned status and its historical justification. John Burke's *Genealogical and Heraldic Dictionary of the Peerage and Baronetage* first appeared in 1826, and by the time of its twenty-first edition in 1859 had become an annual publication, a status matched by John Debrett's *Peerage,* which first came out in 1803.[111] The market in England for these spectacular publishing successes was matched by that in France for the *Annuaire de la pairie et de la noblesse de France* and the *Almanach de noblesse.*

It is likely that the *Gallois Hours* was not an uncommon kind of production. Less luxurious printed versions certainly were produced in very large numbers. A Book of Hours issued by Curmer in about 1840, printed on vellum but illuminated by Gérard-Séguin and Charles Auguste Questel (1807–88), was given a luxury binding similar to that of the *Gallois Hours* by Simier, with jeweled covers by Desiré Froment-Meurice: the work was a gift to the duc de Chartres, grandson of Louis-Philippe.[112] The illuminated manuscript as testament to social status was, thus, by the mid–nineteenth century, available to several levels of French society. The very rich could have them made by hand, whereas the less rich could choose from a variety of formats in the catalogues of Mame & Companie or Martial Ardant Frères.[113] If today we know more about the medieval illuminated manuscripts owned by the highest nineteenth-century aristocracy, the duc d'Aumale owning the *Très Riches Heures*, for example, and the duc de Chartres a large number of very high-quality medieval illuminated manuscripts, we should bear in mind that they were also proud of owning *modern* illuminated works such as the *Gallois Hours*. It was the duc de Chartres's *modern* Book of Hours that was selected for the exhibition of French art that accompanied the 1900 Great Exhibition in Paris.[114] There is a suggestion here that, as in England, modern illumination was considered the equal of medieval illumination, the excellence of the practice rather than age dictating value.

**Women and the Cult of Illumination in Later-Nineteenth-Century France: L'Art Féminin par Excellence**

From the 1830s, there are indications that illumination was engaged in as an amateur art practice, no doubt alongside the drawing and painting that were part of the education of the respectable classes. An amateur market was served by the engravings, sold either colored or uncolored, of Aline Guilbert in the 1830s. Victor Hugo's daughter appears to have done illuminations in the mid-1830s. Another example of an amateur illuminator is the poet Lamartine's wife, who decorated some of her husband's manuscripts in the 1840s with illuminated borders in a pastiche fifteenth-century style. Laure Burnouf was likewise an amateur illuminator, which, according to her husband, Leopold Delisle, gave her special insight into medieval illumination.[115] But until the last decades of the century in France, illumination was largely a professional activity. The manuscript prayer books of the comte de Chambord and Louis-Jules Gallois of the 1840s were produced by professionals. The chromolithographic process, which was widely used in the printing trade from the early 1860s, needed people whose skills were the same as those of the illuminator to make the colored pictures for lithographic printing, and it is to this area that we should look to find out who made the illuminated facsimiles of manuscripts like the early-fifteenth-century *Pontifical-Missal* copied in 1837 by "M.B." and destroyed when the Paris Hôtel de Ville was gutted by fire in 1871.[116] Auguste de Bastard, of course, employed a team of such professionals for his magnum opus in the 1840s and afterward, as did Curmer. Some of these artists were women—a Mademoiselle d'Aligny was employed by Curmer[117]—but on the whole female labor was used for unskilled jobs, such as the coloring of engravings and images of piety. Lagrange in 1860 mentioned *ouvrières enlumineuses* employed by the hundreds in the book trade but seems to refer to the matter of coloring binding covers rather than illumination proper.[118] The illuminated address so popular in England (see chapter 4) did not have the same status in France; the equivalent was the diploma that Henri Bouchot described as flourishing after 1855. These often adopted styles based on

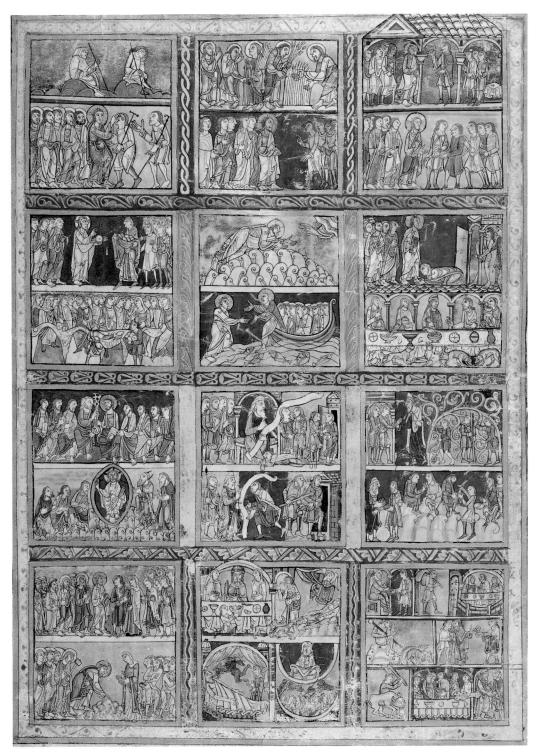

PLATE 1.

Bury St. Edmunds Monastery,
scenes from the Life of Christ
(England, circa 1155–60),
single leaf from a Bible

DEI MATER
ALMA
FVNDA NOS IN PACE
FELIX COELI PORTA

PLATE 3.

**Simon Marmion, miniature of Virgin and Child (France, late fifteenth century), and Attavante Attavanti, decorative border (Italy, early sixteenth century), montage of fragments (nineteenth century)**

PLATE 4.

**Don Silvestro dei
Gherarducci, gradual for
San Michele a Murano,
Venice (Florence, 1392–99),
historiated initial C,
cutout fragment**

PLATE 5.

Scenes from the life
of Saint Bartholomew
(Hungary, circa 1300–50),
miniatures, cut and
reconfigured in an album

PLATE 6.

*The Woman Clothed with*
*the Sun and the Dragon*
**(Lorraine, France, circa 1295),**
**cutout fragment formerly**
**in the Burckhardt-Wildt album**

PLATE 7.

**Historiated initials
from a pocket Bible
(France, circa 1250),
assembled as a montage
(nineteenth century)**

PLATE 8.

Master of the Geneva Latini
or follower, the Annunciation
and adoration of the Magi
(Rouen, 1480), miniatures;
Niccolo da Bologna, heads in
frames (Bologna, 1370);
assembled as a montage
(by O. DuSartel [?], Paris [?],
circa 1880)

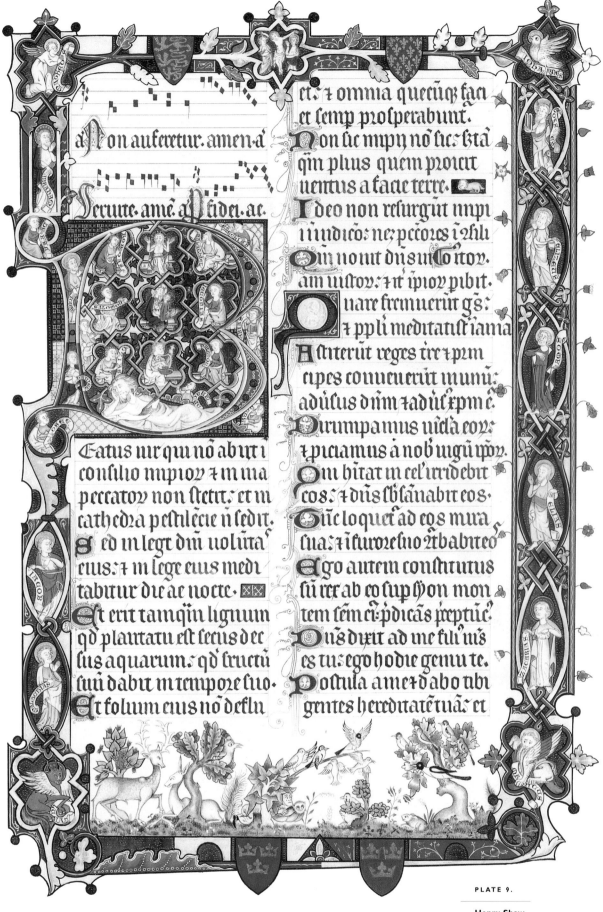

PLATE 9.

Henry Shaw,
copy of a leaf from the
*Howard Psalter*

PLATE 10.

Initial *R* copied from a
fifteenth century choir book
of San Marco

PLATE 11.

**Model Alphabet Book
for Illuminators
(Paris, circa 1500[?]),**
*L* with iris and butterfly

Ernesto Sprega fece

4594

39 K 4/4

PLATE 12.

Ernesto Sprega,
historiated initial C,
St. Lawrence with two
angels. Copied from
a fifteenth-century
Siena choir book
by Liberale da Verona

Ernesto Sprega,
historiated initial *L*,
Miracle of the Loaves
and Fishes. Copied
from a fifteenth-century
Siena choir book by
Liberale da Verona

PLATE 16.

Caleb William Wing,
Christ calling Peter and Paul
(England, nineteenth
century), historiated *D*,
copied from a north Italian
choir book (1470s or 1480s)

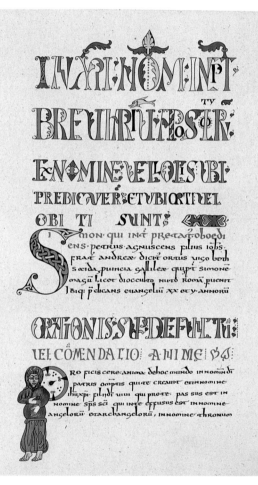

PLATE 18.

Paul Lacroix,
*Sciences et lettres au moyen
âge et à l'époque de la
renaissance* (Paris, 1877),
frontispiece and title page

PLATE 19.

H. Bichard,
copy of a circa 1527
illumination of Henri d'Albret,
roi de Navarre, (France,
nineteenth century)

Pefchier et tresame filz
pour la grant affection
et amour paternelle g
jay atoy · Je me voeul
travellier desarpre aulaines petites
Remonstrances et enseignemens que

PLATE 22.

Garcia, watercolor copy
of fifteenth-century
Burgundian manuscript

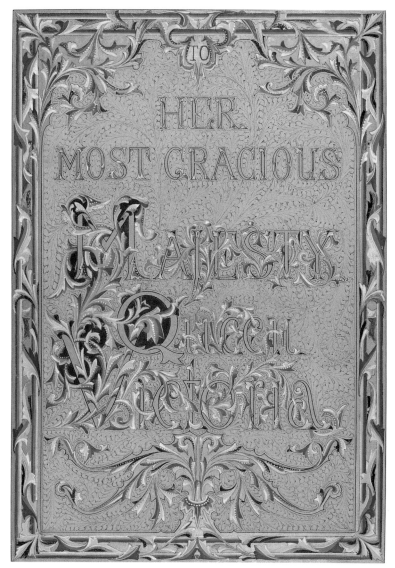

PLATE 23.

Owen Jones,
preparatory artwork for
*Victoria Psalter*
(London, circa 1861)

PLATE 24.

Charles Fairfax Murray,
portrait of William Morris,
title page in *A Book of Verse*
(London, 1870), by William
Morris and others

PLATE 25.

**Lord Charles Thynne,
Crucifixion,
copied from** *Beauvais
Sacramentery*

PLATE 26.

**Augustus Welby
Northmore Pugin,
"The Shrine"
(England, 1832),
illuminated page with
list of reliquaries**

THE END

PLATE 27.

**Augustus Welby
Northmore Pugin,
"St. Margaret's Chapel"
(England, 1833),
"Saint Margaret"**

PLATE 28.

**James Orr Marples,
illuminated address presented
to Mrs. Matilda Madden
(Liverpool, 1900)**

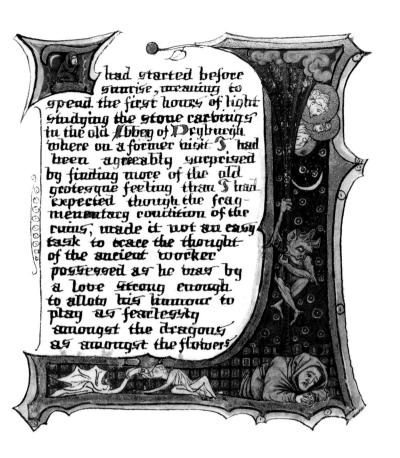

PLATE 29.

Phoebe Traquaire,
*The Dream*
(Edinburgh, 1886–87)

PLATE 30.

Nuns of Maredret,
Nuptial Mass
(Belgium, 1914–15),
illuminated manuscript

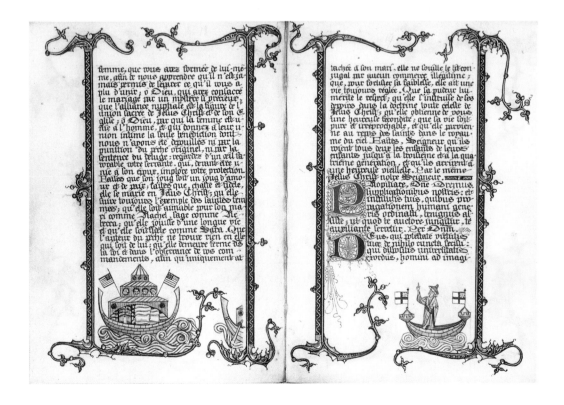

PLATE 31.

Illuminated leaf from a
Book of Hours affixed to
inside of back cover of
Oscar Albert Bierstadt,
*The Library of Robert Hoe*
(New York, 1895)

Master of the Cypresses,
Benedictine monks singing
(Spain, 1430s),
initial *T*,
from an album bought in
Spain in 1849

DEVS · IN · AV ·

PLATE 34.

Adoration of the
Christ Child (Tours, France,
circa 1480–90)

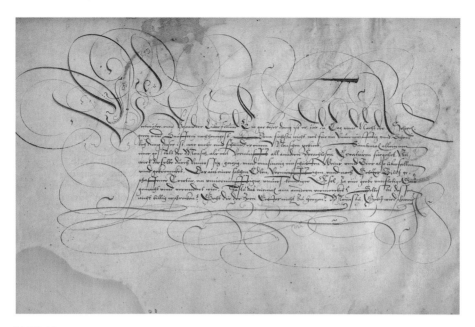

PLATE 35.

Bartholomaeus Horn,
*Kurtze Unterweissung artlichs
annd andeutlichs Schreibens,*
(Holy Roman Empire,
Italy, sixteenth or seventeenth
century)

PLATE 36.

Caleb William Wing
Nativity, (England, circa 1858)

PLATE 37.

Coella Lindsay Ricketts,
Copy of *Book of Kells*
(United States, twentieth
century)

**PLATE 38.**

**Coella Lindsay Ricketts,
illuminated manuscript
celebrating the seventieth
birthday of Anton Hesing
(United States, 1893)**

illumination but were the work of professional graphic designers. On the whole, they adapted designs from medieval illuminated borders and vignettes into fashionable modern styles. A famous work like Eugène Grasset's *Histoire des quatre fils Aymon* (1882) follows the layout of a medieval illuminated manuscript and uses a "Merovingian" style redolent of *Japonisme* and the emerging Art Nouveau used for celebrated posters of the day. The allusion was to modern art rather than medieval art.[119] There are indications that the making of illuminated manuscripts for the church was not uncommon in the last third of the nineteenth century. One major undertaking was a series of three illuminated manuscripts made in Strasbourg in 1879, comprising a history of the church and saints in Alsace and copies of a bull of Pius IX. These were the work of Jean-Michel Gustave Keller, chaplain to the Filles de la Charité de Strasbourg, and Victor Weckerlin, a *peintre enlumineur en vitraux* based near Mulhouse.[120] Perhaps an office book for St.-Rémi completed by Alphonse Lesoeur of Reims in 1882 to 1886 was characteristic of what churches were providing for themselves.[121]

A new phenomenon in the 1880s and 1890s in France was the sudden emergence of amateur illumination as a flourishing activity. As in the England of the 1860s (see chapter 4), illumination was presented as a "charming art" to be revived as a modern school. An article in the *Gazette de l'Hôtel Drouot* in 1891 talked of illumination as an art that needed to be resurrected. The fact that this was said in the magazine of an auction house surely shows that it was a market thought worth developing. André Girodie in 1898 talked of a new fashion whereby a missal had to be entirely painted and written by its owner.[122] Similar to the activity of Wing in Brighton in previous decades (as well as others in England; see chapter 4), in late-nineteenth-century France a body of teachers emerged to guide enthusiasts. The Mesdemoiselles Rabeau were described as *professeurs d'enluminure* in 1888, and the same title was given to Lucien-Adolphe Foucher: teaching no doubt was the chief means by which these people earned their living. Madame Louise Rousseau was a prodigious producer of models for students to follow, as was J. van Driesten. Madame C. Mermet published a *Missel de Première Communion, de Confirmation et de Marriage* in various states for coloring and also hired out models. Magazines such as *L'Enlumineur* (1889–1900) and *Le Coloriste-Enlumineur* (1894–95) both published outlines that could be made up into missals and prayer books. Ernest Guillot provided elaborate color-printed examples of medieval lettering and ornament for students.[123] But the works that dominated the revival were those of Karl Robert and Albert Labitte, authors of manuals and aids for illumination.[124]

Prominent among the publishers that catered to this demand was Henri Laurens, who specialized in practical books on art and illustrated books; his series on art and the French provinces, supplying a heritage and nostalgia market in the last decades of the nineteenth century, was particularly successful.[125] The range of Laurens's aids for illumination, from complete books to sheets with outlines for coloring, is striking. Another publisher, Turgis, was also a color printer and could no doubt produce colored images of medieval illumination without trouble as a sideline to other work. The business of van Driesten and Labitte was broad enough to allow them to publish a magazine, *L'Enlumineur: L'Art dans la famille,* to publicize and sell their wares, from 1889 to 1900. The publisher Desclée produced a magnificent journal in 1894 to 1895, *Le Coloriste-Enlumineur* (figure 81), published for the Société de St. Augustin in Paris. Desclée had made a fortune from religious publishing and indeed had financed the building of a new monastery, Maredsous, near Namur in Belgium, from the late 1870s—where illumination was among the

81.

*Le Coloriste Enlumineur*
**(Paris, 1894),
model for illuminating
Joan of Arc**

arts practiced. Desclée's journal promoted art and craft activities alongside illumination, discussing enamels and painting on glass and silk.[126]

With these works, which sought to promote illumination as much as an activity as an object of veneration, came other publications more directly aimed at those concerned with illumination as an object of connoisseurship. Lecoy de la Marche's *Les Manuscrits et la miniature* (Paris: A. Quantin, 1884) aimed to situate illumination in an art-historical context. According to de la Marche, Fouquet was "less idealist than the Italian school, less original than the English school, less sentimental than the German school," but was superior by the nature of his compositions and by his taste, demonstrating the reason and clarity "that are the appanage of our nation." De la Marche's discussion of "our national art" is replete with references to archival sources and to academic literature, though he regrets that this "charming art of illumination or miniature painting" still lacked the studies that would make it a serious archaeological subject. He refers to the small illuminated images that Marie-Antoinette brought to Versailles from Vienna. Similar works done by contemporary enthusiasts he characterizes as "more zealous than enlightened"; his reference to "the glorious heroine" Joan of Arc shows he shared something in common with the conservative Catholicism of his day.[127] The major point here is that the contemporary revival is cast aside, and further archival research is recommended.

Labitte, who had worked in the book trade and collaborated with Henri Laurens in 1893, became the editor and publisher of *Le Manuscrit. Revue spéciale de documents-manuscrits, livres, chartes autographes etc.* in 1894. Aimed at the book trade and at the interested public who wanted to keep abreast of academic literature, the magazine proposed to reveal to the man of taste the unknown treasures of private and public libraries in France. Léopold Delisle acted as its consultant editor and supplied articles, as did many of the outstanding scholars of the day—Count Paul Durrieu, Camille Couderc, and A. Claudin among them. The enterprise did assume a link with contemporary practice, however. A glowing account of an illuminated manuscript of 1843 made by the De Pape brothers in Bruges, "Album historique de l'Eglise de Jérusalem, Bruges," was given in the second volume. The magazine supported the Société des Miniaturistes et Enlumineurs de France, which held its first exhibition in 1894 at the Grande Gallerie of Georges Petit. Collectors lent their manuscripts—Labitte himself lent some thirteenth-century Bibles and fifteenth-century Books of Hours from his own collection—but in general, only medieval work, fragments as well as books, and illumination of the sixteenth, seventeenth, and eighteenth centuries was reviewed by the magazine. Despite Labitte's appeals for the foundation of a modern school of illumination, only a few examples of contemporary work, such as copies of twelfth-century Greek miniatures, and illuminations by A. Fouché, were mentioned.[128]

Though based in amateur practice, illumination continued to be accepted as an exhibitable art form. The "Noir et Blanc" exhibitions in Paris opened a section for illumination in 1892. The success of the missal of Madame Marie Noblot there led her admirers back home in Nancy to hope for the reestablishment of a school of illumination in the city: it was hoped that Madame Noblot would increase the number of her pupils and ensure that illumination became "a feminine art par excellence" (*l'art féminin par excellence*) and replace the current passion for painting flowers on plates.[129] In 1908, the Société de la Miniature, de l'Aquarelle et des Arts Précieux, under the presidency of a celebrated "aquarelliste-enlumineur," Horace de Callias, held an exhibition, possibly one of a series, in the Georges Petit gallery. The exhibitors were nearly all women. The work of some was praised for being traditional, or *d'une distinction toute aristocratique,* while others were congratulated for "the good taste of their modernism." The arbiter of this taste was L. A. Foucher, *l'enlumineur le plus sérieux qui soit,* mentioned as the outstanding master.[130]

A number of themes appear regularly in discussions of illumination at the time of its revival from the 1880s. All the manuals, and perhaps most explicitly the magazines *L'Enlumineur* and *Le Coloriste-Enlumineur,* assumed that illumination was a private, domestic activity. Labitte's *L'Art de l'enluminure* of 1893 allowed that screens, menus, and even a fashion accoutrement such as a fan might be illuminated, even in the successful Art Nouveau style, but the religious nature of the activity always predominated: illumination was a communing with the Sacred in the bosom of the family. And as such it was an activity led by women. Karl Robert is typical in his insistence on the suitability of illumination for women. The work required patience and conscientiousness—men had a "too animated temperament" ("tempérament toujours plus enfièvré"). Women, he held, had done most miniatures in the medieval period, but were unable to sign their names on account of the strictness of their religious vows.[131] Illumination was a religious art, to be practiced by those wanting to conserve elements of their religious education, and to be used for the production of Books of Hours, canon tables for the altar, images for wedding presents, and souvenirs for First Communion. The models to be followed were modern works by Mademoiselles Rabeau, Books of Hours by respected illuminators like Aline Guilbert, and the works of Geoffroy Tory, Lucas Cranach, and Albrecht Dürer. Labitte shared Karl Robert's approach. He stated that female fingers had "a particular aptitude to bring to illumination an admirable lightness, delicacy and grace," and referred to many women of the day who had distinguished themselves in this art. The magazine *L'Enlumineur* similarly assumed a feminine readership: the cover until 1891 showed a woman in fifteenth-century dress painting at an easel.

The insistence on the national character of illumination is striking in this context. France's defeat by the forces of Prussia in 1870 to 1871 (with the destruction of illuminated manuscripts in libraries in Strasbourg, Chartres, and elsewhere), the loss of Alsace-Lorraine, and the civil war associated with the Commune (in which the Paris Hôtel de Ville was burned down and the Louvre library damaged by fire), quite apart from notions of "degeneracy" harbored by critics of the flamboyant social life of the metropolis, made illumination appear safely and reassuringly traditional, with a direct link to a period of France's greatness. When political debate was conducted with a rhetoric appealing to France's immediate or distant past, and when contemporary loyalties were expressed in terms of admiration for figures as various as Vercingetorix, Clovis, Charlemagne, Joan of Arc, or Voltaire,[132] it is not surprising that illumination was unable to escape association with the political complexions put on specific historical moments. Illumination was concerned above all with the making of devotional works and liturgical apparatus, and for most Catholics, it was among the art forms that gave "the most tangible proof of the genius of Christian civilization and [were] brought forward to oppose with vehemence the mediocrity of contemporary society spawned by the French Revolution."[133]

An instance of the use of illumination to make a specific political point is seen in Du Cleuziou's *L'Art national* (1883). Henri Raison Du Cleuziou (1833–97) was an antiquary and draftsman who founded a Legitimist magazine in 1861, *La Jeune France,*[134] and published sentimental illustrated works about the Paris that Baron Haussmann was destroying as he replanned the capital in the 1860s. For his *L'Art national* he produced a lithographed cover with a colorful border of acanthus scrolls in fifteenth-century Renaissance style, the French tricolor flag standing proudly within it. Given that the work was a call to patriotism and national revival in art after France's defeat by the Prussians, illumination was proposed as a national symbol. The text was a call, after recent disasters, to reclaim a national patrimony and "to soak ourselves in the fountains where our ancestors drank." It does not in fact discuss illumination, though thirteenth-century art in general is seen as precursor to a sixteenth-century Renaissance that was totally French and glorious and that owed nothing to Italy. France, and Paris in particular, was presented as the center of all human development. There is the same Francocentric approach as in Du Cleuziou's work of 1887, *La Création de l'Homme,* in which the prehistoric sites around Paris are made the key to tracing the development of Neanderthal and Cro-Magnon humans in Europe as a whole. (The remark of Curmer's expert, Ferdinand Denis, in 1858 that Paris must have had a Carolingian scriptorium and illuminating school, contrary to any evidence, shows a similar assumption.)[135] Several decades after Du Cleuziou, a similar set of ideas—the centrality of Paris and France to developments in art, the appeal to periods when French art was held to provide a European standard—motivated Marius Vachon. In 1916, Vachon published a tirade against weaknesses in the provision for art that had allowed Germany to overtake France and thus challenge her in World War I. According to Vachon, international styles like Art Nouveau and Impressionism had seduced France from the art that was the source of her strength, particularly that of the twelfth and thirteenth centuries, when the Gothic style had been imitated all over Christendom, and of the eighteenth century, when the art of the *ancien régime* was the standard all over Europe.[136]

The attitudes revealed by Du Cleuziou and Vachon show a climate in which illumination could be prized as a fundamentalist art that was Christian and French. After the death of the comte de Chambord in 1883, monarchists may have had to accept the 1789 Revolution and abandon interpretations of that event as a betrayal of France's real nature.[137] The Third Republic sought to establish its own identity in historical terms, promoting the celebration of Voltaire's centenary in 1878, making the "Marseillaise" the national anthem in 1879, and choosing the 14th of July as a national holiday in 1880, as part of a program of modernization. At the same time, the monarchist Right adopted a populist nationalism as a means of combating a perceived decadence; mass pilgrimages to Patay, Lourdes, Domrémy (the birthplace of Joan of Arc), and other places drew crowds that could number several hundred thousand people, and the cult of the Sacré Coeur saw a meteoric development in the wake the defeat of 1870 to 1871.[138] We see a clash of cultures, for instance, when the Catholic Assembly in 1888 applauded the wish of the Catholic Congress of Lille the previous year to fight the planned celebrations of the 1789 centenary: it was the France of St. Louis, Joan of Arc, and the Sacré Coeur that should concern French Catholics.[139] The dispute about the proposal to establish a national day of celebration in memory of Joan of Arc, proposed from 1878 by the duchess de Chevreuse on behalf of the Comité des Femmes de France, and coming to a head in 1894, was another instance of such a clash.[140]

As a fundamentalist art practice, illumination suited the agenda of such Catholic activists. It may not be without significance that ephemeral religious images that directly copy fifteenth-century illuminated ornament are securely dated to just this period, the last decades of the nineteenth century.[141] The *Coloriste-Enlumineur* clearly promoted illumination as a type of art production intimately bound to traditional French ideals (figure 81). This magazine was published on a monthly basis from 1894 for the Société de St. Augustin, an organ of a congregation known as the Augustinians of the Assumption. The Assumptionists, as they were called, promoted a Catholicism loyal to Rome and virulently hostile to liberal republicanism and socialism. They maintained a huge publishing program aimed at family circles and factories. The order was banned from France in 1900 on the grounds that it was amassing money for a royalist movement to overthrow the Republic. That illumination was included in the activities proposed by the Assumptionists for good Catholic families reveals its "fundamentalist" (or "intégriste," as the French would say) nature very clearly.

The role of manuscript reproductions in relation to the complexities of the French political arena, however, cannot be understood without appreciating developments in the mechanics of reproduction itself, the types of reproductions that were marketed, and the public to whom they were aimed.

## THE PUBLIC AND THE MASS CONSUMPTION OF ILLUMINATED MANUSCRIPTS

**Photography: The Explosion of Manuscript Images**

In 1882 there is an interesting use of the word "facsimile," describing a work of art as "the work of the artist who adapts, and not of the photographer who facsimiles." This indicates that the new medium had already become associated not only with the accurate reproduction of nature, but with the reproduction of works of art. Earlier manuscript connoisseurs like Gustav Waagen (1794–1868) had rejected the use of photography as a tool in studying art and manuscripts, arguing that only the original gave access to the "truth" of the object.[142] However, it soon became clear that one great potential of the new medium was in making reproductions. This was underlined by one of the inventors of photography, William Henry Fox Talbot, who described how the reproduction of works of art by "photogenic drawing" was capable of reproducing the page of a manuscript, a drawing, or a lithograph with the quality of a reproduction in facsimile.[143] It was not until the 1870s that techniques employing photography, photogravure, and heliogravure began to take over from steel and wood engravings and lithographs in the mass-produced book. For study purposes, photographs themselves had become indispensable tools for academics and art historians. But when photography was allied with printing in the process of heliogravure, perfected in 1854, a new type of facsimile became possible. In this process, a transparent photographic positive of a manuscript image was used in etching a copper plate, that was then printed by traditional means, making it possible to get the same rich tonal effects as lithography through a mechanical light-sensitive process rather than by laborious handwork. A lithographically produced facsimile and a heliogravure can both be classed as printed reproductions of medieval images, but one is privileged by its photographic origins as more "real." Reproductions of manuscript illuminations well known today, like the *Très Riches Heures,* first appeared in heliogravure plates in the *Gazette des Beaux-Arts* of 1884 in an article by Leopold Delisle,[144] and the Bibliothèque Nationale began to issue facsimiles of its Greek manuscripts in the 1890s using the same method.

The value of having manuscripts fully reproduced in photographs became apparent after the disastrous fire that ravaged the Biblioteca Nazionale in Turin in January 1904. Only those pages from destroyed masterpieces like the Hours by Van Eyck (Turin: Biblioteca Nazionale, MSS K.IV.29) which had already been photographed were left to the gaze of posterity.[145] This disaster, along with a fire at the Vatican Library, led to the establishment of international commissions to plan large-scale photographic campaigns, while in France, the Société Française de Reproductions de Manuscrits à Peintures was founded in 1911. In England the Roxburghe Club, active from 1814 to the present day, continued to publish exemplary scholarly facsimiles of medieval manuscripts and distributed them through its antiquarian, pseudo-medievalizing network of a private club, but it used modern photographic processes to create the facsimiles.[146]

A good example of the reception and transformation of a famous medieval manuscript during the course of the nineteenth century under the dual influence of photography and ideology is the Manesse Codex, a famous volume of German love poetry with 137 full-page miniatures.[147] The manuscript had been stolen from Heidelberg in 1621 during the Thirty Years' War, and in 1871, after the peace settlement of the Franco-Prussian War, Kaiser Wilhelm I made a claim to the codex, along with works that had been taken from Germany by Napoleon's troops in 1797. In 1886, to celebrate the jubilee year, Heidelberg University asked the Bibliothèque Nationale for permission to make a photographic facsimile of the Manesse Codex. The French agreed, on the condition that two copies of the facsimile be deposited in their national library. Until this time, the only reproductions of the Manesse Codex had been in Mathieu's unfinished lithographic facsimile *Minnesänger aus der Zeit der Hohenstaufen Fac-simile der Pariser Handschrift* of 1850, and in some line engravings made for a German thesis of 1856.[148] The manuscript had become a crucial foundational symbol for the newly unified German state, a *Volksbuch* containing the greatest poetry and images of the origins of German language and life. A Heidelberg book dealer, K. J. Trübner, who had acquired the facsimile, now sought to retrieve the original. In a settlement of 1888, the Bibliothèque Nationale gave him the manuscript together with 150,000 francs in exchange for his outstanding collection of 166 manuscripts formerly owned by Lord Ashburnham (1797–1878), which the latter had formed from the libraries of Libri and Barrois.[149] When in 1888 the manuscript itself was finally returned to Heidelberg, the Bibliothèque Nationale retained a beautiful phototype facsimile of it.[150] This facsimile is a very early example of a "true" reproduction, containing all the blank folios, stains, and damaged areas, as well as the famous illuminations and text, in an attempt to stand in for the lost, returned object. The story of the Manesse Codex shows how much facsimiles served not only to preserve artworks of the past, but to stimulate national interest in collecting and retaining them. In this narrative, it was the promulgation of reproductions of the manuscript that had helped create a desire for the retrieval of the original manuscript as a monument of German patrimony and, thus, led to its ultimate return.

**Fakes and Forgeries: The Exploitation of Manuscript Images**

The virtuoso products of C. W. Wing (died 1875), which self-consciously drew attention to themselves as modern works and were often inserted alongside "original" medieval miniatures, were discussed earlier not as fakes but as examples of Victorian manuscript illumination. The category of the fake brings with it all kinds of epistemological and aesthetic problems. A faked medieval manuscript is a conscious attempt to deceive the viewer or buyer into believing it is something which it is not—a medieval artifact. For a long time viewed with horror, fakes are viewed today as more than "false" objects. They are cultural products like any others and reveal interesting historical evidence of their time of production and reception. Fakes are now both exhibited and collected as such and are studied as useful indices of the ever-changing history of taste.[151] In terms of manuscript illumination, they are for our purposes a fascinating index of the rise in status of manuscript painting during the nineteenth century, since in 1800 we know of no consciously faked manuscript paintings that are not repairs or remakes, whereas by 1900 there were already in Paris a number of specialists at work producing "medieval" manuscripts and cuttings for a market of eager collectors. Since there can be no market for forgeries of objects that do not already have enhanced value and collectibility, fake manuscript illuminations were relative latecomers on the European and American art scene. (The production of false documents, by contrast, goes back to the Middle Ages itself.)[152] As we have already seen, illuminated manuscripts and cuttings were sought-after only by a small and select group of collectors in the early nineteenth century and, moreover, did not fetch high prices compared to printed books. This hardly made it lucrative to produce painstaking forgeries by hand. By contrast, Gothic ivory carvings, which were already collectible luxury items in private collections in both France and England by the late eighteenth century, were being reproduced for the market by the early nineteenth century, when salesrooms were flooded with dubious ivory diptychs and statues.[153] Ivories are to some extent a special case, however. Already mass-produced and duplicated in a semi-industrial way in fourteenth-century Paris, ivories were easier for the modern forger to produce in variants and versions of well-known and accepted masterpieces. It was only after the publication of books reproducing miniatures from illuminated manuscripts reached a wider audience in the second half of the nineteenth century that there came to exist a sufficiently rich visual pool of sources to serve as a context in which fake manuscript illuminations could circulate profitably as authentic medieval products.

Illuminated books are highly wrought and complex objects that are the work of more than one individual and are far more difficult to imitate than, say, a small Gothic ivory figure or a wooden statue, whose weathered appearance could easily be simulated with a bit of rough treatment. There was always the problem of the text, as well as of the parchment support. The forger of manuscripts could not easily use modern materials. This meant that rather than creating a totally new object, the forger of manuscript illuminations often adapted or added to an existing shell of a medieval manuscript which had been damaged—such was the case with Wing—or where spaces had been left for miniatures that were never completed. In this respect, many of the objects we might regard as fakes are only partially so, having a text portion or sometimes borders that are "authentic." The rise in the value of fragments and cuttings made things simpler for the forger. Cuttings, unlike complete codices, were not only easier to create, but the availability of old parchment in choir books and bindings provided a ready supply of supports on which the forger could work. Most of the illuminated fakes known today are either inserted into already existing medieval manuscripts or are single-leaf cuttings, painted on medieval parchment whose original text or music has been scraped off.

If a reproduction is a copy that is meant to be easily distinguishable from the original and which points to an object elsewhere, then the fake is meant to be autonomous. But of course, no image exists separate from other images, and part of the fascination with fakes lies in understanding the sources on which they were based. In this respect the study of fakes is intimately bound up with the study of reproduction and facsimiles, especially in the realm of manuscript illumination. The work of the most famous producer of fake medieval manuscripts and cuttings, the so-called Spanish Forger, is such a case where the reproduction of manuscripts as originals and as copies overlaps. Count Paul Durrieu (1855–1925), warning buyers to suspect illuminated images of tournaments, royal entries, feasts, and women in medieval costume with forced smiles and "mouths that were too pretty," mentioned a workshop in Siena that had supplied the market with "French primitives" from about 1870. It was pointed out to him on one occasion in 1894 that the modern work to be sold at the Hôtel Drouet that he, Durrieu, had thought might mislead was not intended to deceive.[154] The work of the forgers was highly admired; it was thought to be only the honor of accomplished practitioners such as the collector Du Sartel that prevented them flooding the market with undetectable forgeries.[155]

The amassing of original illuminated manuscripts, cuttings from illuminated manuscripts, and hand-executed facsimiles of illuminated manuscripts as sources for design students makes it less surprising that an intermediate category of illuminated manuscript should exist in the Victoria and Albert collection and else-

where. This was the *improved* illuminated manuscript, retouched to make it a fitting guide for the modern student. The leaf from the psalter of 1494 to 1495 illuminated by Georg Beck for the church of Saints Ulrich and Affra in Augsburg likely was cut from its parent volume after the abbey's secularization in 1802 (figure 82, plate 20). At some point during the nineteenth century, the work has overpainted extensively. Perhaps this was done to deceive; perhaps this was done in good faith— simply an act of beautification.[156] Such improved works had already been acquired by Robinson from Entres in Munich, in 1857.[157] The architect William Burgess may have been typical in improving his medieval illuminated books to accord with contemporary taste; he had the faces of a fourteenth-century *Roman de la Rose* bought from Quaritch's in 1874 repainted by an illuminator, Horatio W. Lonsdale, and noted this within the volume.[158] In the same year, G. A. Audsley exhibited modern restorations next to original fourteenth-century initials at the Liverpool Art Club to

**82.**

**George Beck, Saints Ulrich and Afra (Augsburg, 1494–45), miniature, from a psalter, removed and overpainted (England [?], nineteenth century)**

indicate the original state of the colors—and no doubt to display his skill as an illuminator.[159] Firmin-Didot claims to have sent his illuminated manuscripts off for restoration before the multiple sales of his collection,[160] and a number of manuscripts once owned by this collector can be shown to be retouched.

One of the most successful, skillful, and prolific forgers of all time, the so-called Spanish Forger, worked, most probably in Paris, between the 1890s and the 1920s.[161] Even before the development of scientific techniques for the analysis of artworks, scholars recognized the flood of false "medieval" works circulating the market. We have already mentioned Durrieu's warning.[162] In 1914 two specific works by the Spanish Forger were exposed by Salomon Reinach and Henry Omont. But it was the curator of manuscripts at the Pierpont Morgan Library, Belle da Costa Greene (discussed further in chapter 5), who first assembled an oeuvre for this artist, which by 1939 had fourteen items.[163] As of 1988 no less than 65 panel paintings, 154 single leaves or cuttings, and 7 complete manuscripts have been attributed to him, and more surface each year. In recent decades, scientific studies have offered incontrovertible proof of the modern date of works by the Spanish Forger and others. Neutron activation analysis and neutron autoradiogra-

phy reveal that the Forger consistently used a green pigment containing copper arsenite that was not available until around the year 1814.[164] And the analysis of suspicious miniatures in a Book of Hours in the Pierpont Morgan Library (M. 54) that appeared to be a genuine work of the fifteenth century showed that the manuscript's borders contained pigments used by the medieval artist (white azurite for blue; malachite for green), while the principle illuminations were made up of pigments only available to the modern master (artificial ultramarine and emerald green; compare figures 83 and 84).[165]

Returning to the oeuvre of the Spanish Forger, two-thirds of his works have secular subject matter: scenes of chivalry, courtly love, and aristocratic pastimes like falconry and feasting; these suited the medievalizing tastes of the period, which increasingly came to think of the Middle Ages as an age of chivalry rather than an age of faith. It may be significant that the Forger was working in the very decades when the French philologist Gaston Paris "invented" the term "courtly love" to enhance the secular vision of the French Middle Ages as progressive and civilized.[166] The Forger also produced pairs of miniatures, on the model perhaps of paired prints, which have strange juxtapositions of sacred and secular figures. A leaf in the Pierpont Morgan Library (M. 786 c; see figure 85, plate 21) shows a nimbed saint standing alongside two elegant courtly ladies and a seated ruler—a composition that is impossible to imagine in a medieval context. This image also reveals the Forger's typical stylistic features: hard, angular outlines; overelaborate costumes, often with plunging necklines; and theatrical spatial configurations; but soft, almost sentimental facial expressions. This example is also significant in that it has an elaborately arched and illusionistically painted frame, presumably created to suggest not that the image was once part of a manuscript book, but that it is an autonomous painting. The Spanish Forger gave his clientele exactly the kinds of pictures they wanted, framed "scenes" which could previously only be constructed by dismembering manuscripts and cutting out actual medieval illuminations from their context. The appearance of rubbed-out musical notation and script on the reverse of many cuttings that the Forger created out of old Spanish choir book

83.

Autoradiograph of Christ driving demons from Mary Magdalene, exposure begun twenty-two days after irradiation for five days (United States, twentieth century)

84.

A forger, Christ driving demons from Mary Magdalene (France, nineteenth century), illumination added to fifteenth-century French Book of Hours

**85.**

**Spanish Forger, Seated Ruler with Two Women and a Standing Saint (France, nineteenth century)**

fragments suggests that he knew enough about manuscripts to create a suitably "old" feel to them. But the fact that his juxtapositions of text and picture often make no liturgical or textual sense shows how single-mindedly the audience for these things was concerned with art and art alone. The Spanish Forger even went so far as to create manuscript fragments, cuttings which include a dozen large historiated initials, of a type common in late-fifteenth-century choir books.[167] These depict secular music being performed by courtiers in a garden setting. The public's taste for cuttings in particular was predominantly for secular rather than religious scenes. To meet this demand, the Spanish Forger and others produced images of courtship and feasting, often in pairs of leaves, which had no textual source or literary analogues. These efforts were inspired by the tradition of manuscript images as "slices of medieval life" that went back to Joseph Strutt (see chapter 1).

But the Forger also created works for lovers of books (figure 86). One recently discovered example of a Book of Hours is especially interesting for what it reveals about the Forger's creativity. The skeleton of the manuscript was written and decorated in Tournai in the fifteenth century. It was bound by a northern French binder, Robier Plourins, who signed the panel-stamped binding. But it must have remained unfinished, because there is no evidence that the surface under the miniatures was scraped. Its cycle of illumination includes the following pictures: the Crucifixion introducing the Hours of the Cross, the Coronation of a French King at the Hours of the Holy Spirit, the Marriage of Mary and Joseph at the Hours of the Virgin, a Jousting Match between David and Goliath at the seven penitential psalms, and the Funeral of a French King at the Office of the Dead. Especially interesting is the coronation scene, in which the king receives the *main de justice* and the scepter while a dove descends bearing the holy ampule, a sign that French kings were divinely appointed. The funeral scene derives from an engraving of the funeral of Anne of Brittany in Lacroix's *Vie militaire et religieuse au Moyen-Âge et á l'époque de la renaissance* (1873). This inventive cycle reminds us that the eighteenth and nineteenth centuries used medieval illumination to bolster national identity and to champion legitimist claims. Unusual too, even comical, is

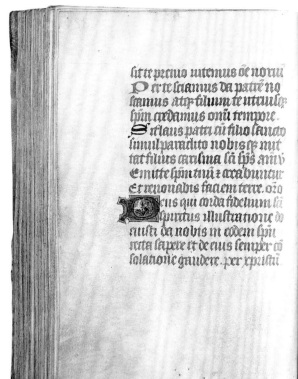

the scene of King David and the giant Goliath, which the Forger has transformed into a theatrical display of chivalric life. An inscription in the Book of Hours, "Abbé J. Degout curé doyen de Mormant en Brie, 1886" (localities approximately twenty miles from Paris), contributes further data that may one day help circumscribe the Forger's career.

The Spanish Forger was so named by Belle da Costa Greene because one of his panels had been attributed, wrongly as it turned out, to a fifteenth-century Spanish painter. The majority of his works were thought of as French, however. This is partly due to the fact that most of them first appeared on the Paris art market, at the beginning of the twentieth century. But it is also because, as Voelkle points out, most of his sources were taken from French publications on medieval art and culture by Paul Lacroix (compare figures 87 and 88). Lacroix's lavishly illustrated volumes, published by the Parisian house of Firmin-Didot, began with *Les arts au moyen âge et à l'époque de la renaissance* (1869) and ended with *Louis XII et Anne de Bretagne* (1882). Although these books followed the tradition of using manuscript illustrations as records of life and manners à la Strutt, they were far more deluxe productions.[168] Utilizing chromolithography, they had beautiful full-page illustrations from famous manuscripts in the Bibliothèque Nationale and other libraries, as well as numerous wood engravings placed within the text. It seems that the Forger used these small line engravings for compositional devices but was stylistically influenced by the color lithographs. As Voelkle suggests, the Forger not only lifted iconographical motifs, figure groups, and even whole compositions from Lacroix's publications, but to some extent replicated even the patina, metallic colors, and surface effect of their chromolithographed plates.[169]

It is important to remember that most people had little chance to examine manuscript illuminations in large numbers, and this made lithographic reproductions the chief source of familiarity with medieval illuminations in the late nineteenth century. While we might laugh today at the thought that anyone could ever have taken the sweet cloying faces, coquettish female types, and mixed-up

86.

**Spanish Forger, David and Goliath (nineteenth century) added to a fifteenth-century French Book of Hours**

87.

(opposite page, left) **Spanish Forger, hunt of the unicorn Annunciation (France, nineteenth century), added to a fifteenth-century French antiphonary**

88.

(opposite page, right) **Paul Lacroix, *Les Arts au moyen âge et a l'époque de la renaissance* (Paris, 1877), page 463, figure 337** secular and sacred compositions of the Spanish Forger's images as genuine, this is only because the advent of mass photographic reproduction has made our subtle distinctions between styles of art possible. Today it is hard to imagine what exact period the Forger was trying to replicate, since he combines sources such as late-fifteenth-century Italian spatial models with Flemish and French panel paintings. In fact, it is clear that the bulk of his forgery business consisted of panel paintings, which were far more sought after—especially in France, where, after the exhibition of French Primitives in 1904, the search for the French national roots of the Renaissance was all the rage.[170] Whereas the forger of a painting often seeks to imitate the style of a particular artist and pass this work off as genuine, the Spanish Forger was working under the stylistic cover of the anonymity and conformity of the late-medieval manuscript illuminator's workshop, in which figure styles and compositional models were repeated, interchangeable, and passed around for generations through model books. However, it is exactly the neutrality and homogeneity in medieval manuscript production that the Forger was unable to carry off. Being a late-nineteenth-century Romantic individualist, he was unable to subsume his own personal characteristics to the model from which he was copying. He combines and adapts his sources in far more radical ways than medieval illuminators had done. His own peculiar traits—pursed lips and dimpled cheeks—emerge as "personal" in a way that would not occur in the work of a fifteenth-century illuminator. As Voelkle puts it, his "style [has] an individuality and personality which makes his work easy to recognize."[171] Among the qualities of this artist which suggest he had a professional knowledge of the book trade are his capacity to reverse compositions and to combine elements from different sources. Voelkle notes that he has "the skill of an illustrator" in this respect.[172] Evidence suggests that the Forger's knowledge of the illustrated volumes by Paul Lacroix was far more intimate than previously imagined, and he might have been involved in the making of the chromolithographic reproductions themselves. What better way to learn how to make medieval manuscripts than to copy them for the purposes of

reproduction? Watercolor copies of some of the full-page miniatures from a Burgundian manuscript, very close to the Spanish Forger in style, have recently come
to light in the Firmin-Didot Archives (figure 89, plate 22). One work, signed by
the artist "Garcia," has the same suave redefinition of lines and figures that appears
in the works of the Spanish Forger. The discovery of this piece bolsters the long-
suspected link between the Forger and the famous publisher Firmin-Didot.

There are works which predate this now eminently collectable artist,
suggesting that in the third quarter of the nineteenth century the line between a
remake and a fake had already become blurred. The small Book of Hours in the
Pierpont Morgan Library (discussed earlier in relation to technical analysis), for example, was originally lacking its miniatures, but had a beautifully written text for
the use of Coutances and elaborate borders painted in the early fifteenth century.
Six full-page miniatures and twelve calendar illustrations were added by someone,
again using printed sources from Lacroix—this time his *Moeurs, Usages et costumes
au moyen âge* (Paris, 1871)—to create a unique calendar cycle of games and pastimes, including blindman's buff for August and a snowball fight for December
(figure 90).[173] This volume was purchased by Richard Bennett of Manchester in
1895 as an original and bought by Pierpont Morgan in 1900. The Pierpont Morgan Library owns another modern creation—a single leaf of the *Life of St. Louis in
Eight Scenes* (M.786b; see figure 91) which used Montfaucon's *Les Monumens de la
monarchie françoise* as its model.[174] Clearly the production of forgeries, which was
centered in Paris, was motivated partly by a need to fill in gaps of French history,
responding thus to nationalistic themes, which made both St. Louis and especially
Joan of Arc popular subjects for fakes.[175] Another miniature, this one of Joan of
Arc returning to Charles VII after the Liberation of Orléans, is significant because
it was reproduced in Lacroix's *Vie Militaire et religieuse au moyen âge*.[176] Does this
not suggest that, when it was impossible to find certain iconographic subjects in
the original documents, "new" images might have been produced specifically for
the purpose of reproduction in Lacroix's volume? This once again places the very
earliest examples of forgers in the orbit of Firmin-Didot. Another manuscript page
by the same illuminator, once again produced for a specific political purpose, was
shown as early as 1893 to be a forgery.[177] This particular miniature had been reproduced in an edition of Froissart's chronicles printed in Paris in 1881, which is
where its inauthenticity was first detected. Once again this suggests that the relationship between the print shops and the Forger's workshop was a close one.

It is worth commenting here on the popularity of Joan of Arc as a subject for fakes. The *Coloriste-Enlumineur* in 1894 published scenes from the life of
Joan of Arc for illumination, and reproduced in color an illuminated picture of
Joan first hearing the voices that established her mission to liberate France (figure
81). In terms of the late-nineteenth-century debate about Joan, such an image
proposed a view of French history in which God's guiding hand was paramount:
this was not the Joan, representative of the People, who liberated the national
territory despite royal betrayal, but the messenger of God sent to restore the
monarchy and throw foreigners from France. By the 1890s, Joan of Arc had been
appropriated by conservative Catholic circles, to the extent that in 1894 soldiers
were forbidden to attend in uniform rallies and pilgrimages dedicated to her.[178]
Even earlier, Joan of Arc had become a political icon for anti-republican Catholics.
In 1876, Henri Wallon had produced a book reproducing fifteenth-century miniatures that portrayed her, and Pope Pius IX congratulated the author for reminding
France of the simple, pious girl who had restored to France her legitimate king.[179]
Joan was certainly among the most favored subjects for illumination at this time.

GARCIA.

**89.**

Garcia,
watercolor copy of
fifteenth-century
Burgundian manuscript

**90.**

A Forger,
snowball fight, December
calendar page, (France,
nineteenth century),
added to a fifteenth-
century French Book of
Hours

**91.**

A Forger,
*Life of Saint Louis*
(France, nineteenth
century)

Labitte reproduced miniatures of Joan of Arc illuminated by Charles Gilbert, curator of the museum in Toul, and referred to others done by the same artist.[180] In 1904 Durrieu referred to an invasion of fake portraits of the maid of Orléans. Distinguished connoisseurs such as Georges Spetz acquired illuminated portraits of Joan. And even as art historians challenged the authenticity of such works, Catholic circles embraced them as true medieval pieces.[181] These fakes were the icons of a specific political current, one rabidly hostile to the Third Republic and nurturing an ideal of a Catholic and monarchist France expressed in terms of St. Louis, Joan of Arc, and the inspired leadership of a feudal aristocracy.[182]

The way in which forgers utilized what seem to us today inappropriate historical characters such as Joan of Arc and even Christopher Columbus should not obscure the fact that these images represented the Middle Ages as people then wanted to see it. Sometimes, these distortions go beyond the nubile saints and risqué courtly encounters of the Spanish Forger, however, into more disturbing territory. One example is an unusual Book of Hours in the Bibliothèque Nationale whose miniatures are clearly fakes added in the same period as the Spanish Forger or perhaps even earlier. Here, rather than the sweet and sentimental imagery of the late nineteenth century, we witness its virulent anti-Semitism (BnF, Smith Lesoeuf 317; see figure 92). The images of a group of hideously depicted Jews crucifying a Christian child (32v.) and stealing the bleeding Host (13v.) are strongly marked by the kind of hook-nosed, leering caricatures that are found less often in fifteenth-century manuscripts than in the anti-Dreyfus cartoons and newspaper propaganda of the 1890s (figure 93).[183]

It is perhaps ironic, given our current fascination with "medievalism" rather than the medieval, and with simulation rather than representation in the contemporary art world, that a cutting by an individual "master" like the Spanish Forger can today be collectible as a fake. Nonetheless, in the context of the history of the collecting and appreciation of manuscript illumination the fake is perhaps the most significant clue to the vast change in status of illumination in the course of the nineteenth century. As more fakes come to light, we will understand far more completely not only what earlier audiences expected but also what they concocted the Middle Ages to be.

92.

A Forger, *Jews attacking the Host* (France, nineteenth century), from a Book of Hours

93.

"Eugène-Henri Brisson, Premier of France Seduced by Jews," *L'Antijuif* (September 22, 1898)

**The Gift Books of
Henry Noel
Humphreys
and Owen Jones:
The Ornamentation
of Sentiment**

Beginning in the 1840s, with the perfection of chromolithography in England, and continuing through the 1860s, several key individuals sustained the publication of illuminated gift books that were splendidly decorated with chromolithographs and skillfully set in letterpress, often in Gothic type.[184] Chief among them were two contemporaries and collaborators, the architect Owen Jones (1809–74) and the author-turned-book designer Henry Noel Humphreys (1810–79).[185] The illuminated gift book, a relatively cheap publication in which text and colored illustration were combined, was actually a kind of stand-in for a medieval manuscript. It was not, properly speaking, a facsimile, because its illustrations did not copy from "old Missals," as Humphreys was to brag in *Parables of Our Lord* (1847), but invented new designs.[186] In this sense, the gift book also played an important role in the Gothic Revival, which was to bring English book design to the forefront with William Morris and the Arts and Crafts movement near the end of the century.

The popularity of the gift book is directly linked to two related phenomena, both exemplified in publications of the 1840s by Humphreys: the scholarly expansion of the canon of medieval illumination and the training of "modern" illuminators, previously discussed. Between 1844 and 1849, Humphreys wrote *Illuminated Books of the Middle Ages,* a work issued in twelve parts at 21 shillings per part over five years. Owen Jones supplied the chromolithographs. What distinguished *Illuminated Books* from its predecessors—by Shaw and Madden, by Westwood, by Thomas Astle—was its scope. Humphreys's account of the history of illumination extended from Byzantium to the eighteenth century, when illumination died out, only to be revived in the 1820s. Whereas Shaw and Madden had favored High Renaissance illumination and extolled the virtues of Clovio, and Westwood had expressed a nationalistic bias, Humphreys paid equal attention to all schools, and he showed a new emphasis on Gothic illumination, which Ruskin was later to favor. The accompanying color work is impressive; Owen Jones's chromolithographs required between eight and twelve press runs. Humphreys's appendix lists the 463 manuscripts he consulted, arranged by date and nationality.[187] *Illuminated Books* confirms that scholarship by midcentury was adopting a broader, more diverse history of illumination, examples of which served as inspiration for gift books.

In 1849 Humphreys published a second, related gift book, this time more explicitly aimed at the amateur illuminator, *The Art of Illumination and Missal Painting: A Guide to Modern Illuminators,* briefly mentioned earlier.[188] This work included twelve chromolithographs printed in up to fourteen colors, with the same plates provided a second time in outline "to be coloured by the student according to the theories developed in the Work" (figures 94 and 95).[189] *The Art of Illumination* is also of interest because in it Humphreys included an explanation of the qualities he believed were required of an illuminator:

He must be acquainted with Botany, and also [must] possess a knowledge of what may be termed the poetry of flowers . . . their association, their symbolism, and their properties. Entomology too. . . . In short, Natural History in general . . . [and] the history of decorative art. . . . [The illuminator] must be a poet too . . . [and know the] symbolism of early Christianity . . . song of the Troubadour . . . [and] Romances of the age of Chivalry. . . . Finally, the illuminator must have an artistic dream of excellence.[190]

Humphreys could well be describing himself.

**94.**

Henry Noel Humphreys,
chromolithographed
plate of King David,
*The Art of Illumination
and Missal Painting:
A Guide to Modern
Illuminators* (London, 1849)

**95.**

Henry Noel Humphreys,
outline drawing
model of King David,
*The Art of Illumination
and Missal Painting. A Guide
to Modern Illuminators*
(London, 1849)

What is interesting about gift books, then, is their artful medievalism. In 1845, *The Book of Common Prayer* illuminated by Owen Jones included wood-engraved borders on each of its five hundred pages, eight four- and five-color chomolithographed illuminated title pages, four full-page woodcut plates, and thirty-seven wood engravings. Beckwith has pointed out that because *The Book of Common Prayer* was the English answer to the Latin liturgical and lay texts of Catholicism, it presented a "logical choice for honoring with ornament."[191] The print run of four thousand copies by the London publisher John Murray anticipated the book's success. Its illustration has features typical of Owen Jones's gift books, thirteen of which were published between 1844 and 1851. It includes, for example, a

**96.**

**Owen Jones,
"Evening Prayer" in
The Book of Common
Prayer (London, 1850)**

five-color chromolithograph of an angel praying as an illustration of "Evening Prayer" (figure 96). The angel itself resembles a picture from the Pre-Raphaelite circle more than anything in manuscript illumination, and its surrounding border makes allusion to Flemish fifteenth-century floral borders without, however, evoking any single model.[192] The diverse ornament presented on each decorated text page reveals the widest variety of sources, from Anglo-Saxon to English Gothic and fifteenth-century Flemish and French, and even includes orientalizing motifs. Jones radically altered his manuscript models in redesigning them, and no direct source can therefore be identified. His work in progress can be seen from a preparatory drawing he did for the chromolithographs of the *Victoria Psalter,* published in London in 1861 (figure 97, plate 23). He made his attitude toward copying explicit in the mission statement accompanying the folio edition of the *Grammar of Ornament* (first published, Day and Son, 1856):

I have ventured to hope that, in thus bringing into immediate juxtaposition the many forms of beauty which every style of ornament presents, I might aid in arresting that unfortunate tendency of our time to be content with copying, whilst the fashion lasts, the forms peculiar to any bygone age.[193]

Humphreys's gift books (at least fifteen were published in the 1840s) are every bit as eclectic, and allusive, in their use of medieval sources as those of Jones, but they raise the genre to a new height of design through Humphreys's own skill as an illuminator. Two books are typical: *Parables of Our Lord* and *Miracles of Our Lord.*[194] Using chromolithographic plates of up to twelve colors, Humphreys pioneered the design of the double-page opening, another way in which the gift book is like a manuscript. His borders in *Parables of Our Lord* show an awareness of the *Anne of Brittany Hours* (reproduced by Longman's for an illuminated calendar in 1845), as well as Flemish and French ornament of the fifteenth century. The sources for some of his figures of standing saints, which appear in the lateral borders of each page in the *Miracles* volume, were engravings by Martin Schongauer, whom he credited in an appended section.[195] Bright rich coloring, alternating with more subdued tones on the subsequent double opening, is typical of Humphreys's well-crafted, aesthetically beautiful productions, which were mass-marketed by Longman's on both sides of the Atlantic.

Printed on stout paper boards to withstand the multiple runs required of the press, gift books posed certain technical problems of presentation, which led to the creation of elaborate protective bindings. Owen Jones mass-produced embossed leather bindings to house his *Victoria Psalter* (figure 98). In keeping with the predominating Victorian *horror vacuii,* his cover features an allover vegetal ornament that evokes the modernized medieval motifs adorning the pages within. Bookmak-

97.

Owen Jones,
preparatory artwork
for *The Victoria Psalter*

98.

Owen Jones,
*The Victoria Psalter*
(London, 1861)

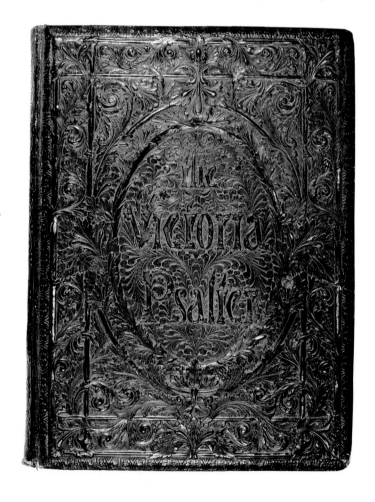

ers of the period also innovated the papier-mâché and plaster binding. These bold, heavy bindings were built up on a metal framework, produced in up to 1,000 copies from complex molds, and then painted and gilded. For *Parables,* Humphreys designed a binding of plump foliate and floral motifs arranged in rectangular panels and set off in the center by a title carved on swirling banderoles, with rosettes at the four corners containing symbols of the four Evangelists. For *Miracles,* he based his design for the upper cover, which includes carved roundels of six of Christ's miracles, on the Romanesque manuscript of the psalter of Queen Melisende in the British Museum (figure 99). Ironically, it can now be shown that the *Melisende Psalter* cover is itself a nineteenth-century re-creation.[196] Even when the manuscript sources are evident, these bindings, which combine the aesthetic of the fifteenth-century panel-stamped binding with architectural decoration, are thoroughly Victorian in conception, like the gift books they envelop.

The Victorian taste for the modern illuminated manuscript was kept alive by Alberto Sangorski (1862–1932), a former jeweler and numismatist-turned-illuminator, who produced many richly illuminated manuscripts by hand. Each of these florid and colorful one-off works echoed the aesthetic less of original illumination than of nineteenth-century reconfigurations of medieval ornament such as those found in the gift books of Jones and Humphreys. Most of Sangorski's books were bound by the company Sangorski and Sutcliff and were made for the American market (apparently the most luxurious—the property of a wealthy world traveler—went down with its owner on the *Titanic*). A volume of John Keats's *Odes* in a jeweled binding is typical of Sangorski's productions (figure 100).

**The Manuscript as Utopia: William Morris**

William Morris (1834–96), the central figure in the English Arts and Crafts movement and a leading proponent of socialism, was neither a facsimilist nor a forger.[197] Instead, he was a new breed of nineteenth-century artist-illuminator-publisher, whose work stands at the end of a long development in the nineteenth century and validates modernist notions of original craftsmanship. Significantly, he reacted outspokenly against the very forms of mechanical reproduction we have outlined so far. For Morris, the medieval manuscript—like his revivalist designs of wallpaper, stained glass, printed textiles, and carpets, like his celebrated Kelmscott Press—represented an object around which a call to social reform could be mounted. In Morris's utopian vision of society, all crafts, including the book arts, were to be handmade and "unspoiled by the sordidness of commercialism," just like they had been in the Middle Ages.

Born in 1834 into an affluent family, Morris entered Marlborough College, and later Exeter College, Oxford, where he studied ecclesiastical architecture, archaeology, and medieval history. Perhaps the most profound influence of his college years, however, was the friendship he developed with Edward Burne-Jones, and the "Set" or "Brotherhood" they formed, under the assumed patronage of Sir Galahad, with others interested in medieval romance and chivalry. In 1856 Morris entered the office of the Gothic Revivalist architect G. E. Street, but his stay there was short-lived. He was determined to become an author-artist, and his first published work, *The Defense of Guenevere,* dates from 1858. Just a few years later, in 1861, Morris established his famous interior decorating and design firm (Morris, Marshall and Faulkner), with Ford Maddox Brown, Dante Gabriel Rossetti, Burne-Jones, and Philip Webb. The next year, in 1862, the firm exhibited stained glass, furniture, embroideries, and wallpaper at the International Exposition in South Kensington. From 1870 to 1875, Morris was occupied with his projects

**99.**

**Henry Noel Humphreys,**
*Miracles of Our Lord,*
**binding (London, 1848)**

**100.**

**Sangorski & Sutcliff,**
**jeweled binding for**
*Some Odes by John Keats*
**(England, twentieth**
**century)**

for calligraphic manuscripts. By 1877 he had turned to public affairs, founding the Society for the Protection of Ancient Buildings and delivering the first of many public lectures. In 1883 he published a collection of lectures on art, including "Hopes and Fears for Art"—in which he declared that "real art is the expression by man of his pleasure in labour"—and the next year he joined the Democratic Federation.[198] Only in 1891, five years before his death, did Morris found the Kelmscott Press, which issued sixty-six books, all designed by himself.

Even if Morris, like Humphreys and Owen Jones, rejected mere copying and avidly studied original medieval manuscripts, his illuminated manuscripts are so highly original that they bear little resemblance to what had gone before him, either in the nineteenth century or the Middle Ages. Indeed, Nash calls attention to the interesting fact that he did not own a single illuminating manual among his vast library.[199] Between 1870 and 1875, Morris wrote and illuminated, or had illuminated in collaborative projects, twenty-one manuscript books. He had already tried his hand at illumination in 1857 in a heavily Gothicizing version of the Brothers Grimm's "Iron Man" (J. Paul Getty, Wormsley Library), and two other

examples of early experimentation survive from this period.[200] The lettering in these youthful works is often called "amateurish," but the half-decade of his concentrated efforts does reveal his mastery of five Renaissance-inspired scripts from italic to roman minuscule (he did own writing manuals by the sixteenth-century Renaissance calligraphers Arrighi and Tagliente) and his versatility as an illuminator (his floral designs, especially, are of infinite variety).[201] Many of his calligraphic manuscripts betray his fascination with Icelandic sagas, some of which he translated. One such work is likely the first manuscript he created (circa 1869–70), "The Story of the Dwellers at Eyr" (Oxford: Bodleian Library, MS Eng. Mis. C. 265).[202] In the manuscript he made of another of his translations, The Story of Kormak (1871), he left room for illuminations and sketched in the ornament, but the work was never colored (figure 101).[203] Here, the double-columned format and wide margins demonstrate Morris's enthusiasm for the aesthetic of the medieval page. His last two callligraphic manuscripts, Horace's Odes (Bodleian Library, MS lat. Class. E. 38) and Virgil's Aeneid (private collection), are generally regarded as his masterpieces. Appropriately, the lettering

101.

**William Morris,**
**The Story of Kormak**
**(England, 1871)**

he used for these classical texts drew inspiration partly from humanist manuscripts of the Italian Renaissance.[204]

But Morris did not solely rely on the classics—either of the north or the south—for inspiration for his illuminated works. Some of his volumes contained writings of his own creation. In A Book of Verse (London: Victoria and Albert Museum, NAL L.131-1953)—a work Morris presented to his lifelong friend Giorgiana Burne-Jones—he illuminated twenty-five of his own poems. Morris's first dated manuscript (August 26, 1870), and one of the few he completed, A Book of Verse is an extraordinary accomplishment and already foreshadows Morris's contribution to manuscript illumination.[205] It was a collaborative project. Burne-Jones contributed the first miniature to illustrate "The Youths" (figure 102), and Charles Fairfax Murray painted the rest. George Wardle, the director of Morris's design firm,

THE TWO SIDES OF THE RIVER

THE YOUTHS

O winter, O white winter, wert thou gone
No more within the wilds were I alone
Leaping with bent bow over stock and stone!

No more alone my love the lamp should burn,
Watching the weary spindle twist and turn,
Or oër the web hold back her tears and yearn
O winter, O white winter, wert thou gone!

THE MAIDENS

Sweet thoughts fly swifter than the drifting snow,
And with the twisting thread sweet longings grow,
And oër the web sweet pictures come and go
For no white winter are we long alone.

102.

Edward Burne-Jones,
"The Youths," from
*A Book of Verse*
(London, 1870),
by William Morris
and others

103.

Charles Fairfax Murray,
portrait of
William Morris,
title page in
*A Book of Verse*
(London, 1870),
by William Morris and
others

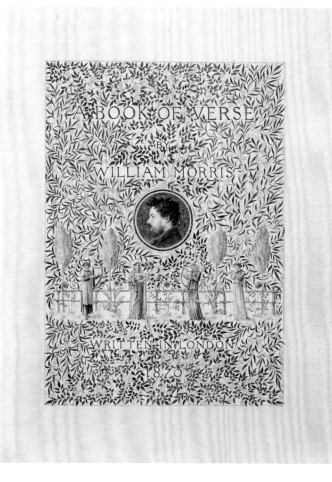

drew the ornaments for the first ten pages, and according to the colophon he "did all the colored letters both big and little." Morris took over the ornament from page 11 to the end (there are fifty-five pages in all). He also did the whimsical figures with musical instruments on the title page, where Fairfax Murray executed a striking portrait roundel of Morris copied from a photograph (figure 103, plate 24). And, of course, Morris executed the calligraphy, a flat Italianate italic he was also to employ in his second manuscript, *The Story of the Volsungs and Niblungs* (Bodleian Library, MS Eng. Misc. d. 268).[206] The delicate floral ornament interacting with the fine italic, the verdant greens (especially of the frontispiece), the Pre-Raphaelite style illustrations, and Morris's verses (two poems are translations from the Icelandic) create a pleasing harmonic whole, the "modernity" of which scholars have noted and praised.[207] Together the team of artist-friends produced a truly unique gift book, a thoroughly nineteenth-century manuscript. How little these works may have been appreciated in Morris's own lifetime is suggested by George Bernard Shaw's remark, when Morris exhibited several of his manuscripts at the first exhibition in 1888 of the Arts and Crafts Exhibitions Society. Shaw wrote bitingly in *The World:* "The decorative diagonal strokes [referring no doubt to Morris's special uneven version of italic writing, perfected in *Three Icelandic Sagas* (1873–74; Cambridge: Fitzwilliam Museum, MS 270)], suggest the conventional representation of a shower, as affected by artists who design advertisements for macintoshes."[208]

Morris is well known for his lecture, "The Ideal Book," delivered in 1893.[209] Here the designer-visionary expounds upon the virtues of clarity of typeface, correct spacing of words, and proportionate margins. Morris's remarks about medieval illumination included in "Some Thoughts on the Ornamented Manuscripts of the Middle Ages" (first published 1934), however, have received little attention, but shed light on his own calligraphic exercises. Here the famous quote appears: "If I were asked to say what is at once the most important production of Art and the thing most longed for, I should answer, A beautiful House; and if I were further asked to name the production next in importance . . . I should answer A beautiful book."[210] Morris then proceeds to launch a harsh attack on books and readers of the modern era, books because they are superabundant and shoddily made and readers because they do not respect the book when they "dog-ear its leaves . . . and so maul it."[211] For Morris, the Middle Ages was a utopia to be respected, even revered, where art and craft happily coexisted. He is quick to warn that medieval art was not "the outcome of religion, or rather, ecclesiasticism," and includes an implicit critique that extends from Horace Walpole to Henry Noel Humphreys about those among his contemporaries who insist on describing medieval illumination as mere "missal painting."[212] The medieval artist, according to Morris, "working as a free-workman, or artist . . . was free to develop both his love for ornament and his love for story to the full."[213] Morris explains the preponderance of religious subject matter by pointing out that, while the medieval artist might have been religious, he was an artist and "first of all a man." A survey of the major schools of art concludes Morris's account of medieval illumination. Not surprisingly, given his own calligraphic interests, he focuses on the harmony of the decorated page, the accomplished union of calligraphy and ornament, which he finds in Irish, Anglo-Saxon, and French and German Romanesque illumination.[214] In a complete departure from his predecessors such as Celotti, Ottley, and Dennistoun, among others, he deplores later manuscript illumination, which he maintains "has now gone off the road of logical consistency; for divorce has taken place between the picture work and the ornament." While he could admit the high quality of illuminations from this period, he dismisses the artists who did them as "men employed to fill up a space, and having no interest in their work save livelihood." Morris's views may be idiosyncratic, but they are also an index of how much the taste for High Renaissance painting had changed by the end of the nineteenth century, a phenomenon we have witnessed elsewhere, as in the altered interest in models for collages (see chapter 2). These remarks are interesting not only for what they confirm about Morris's own aesthetic in making manuscripts— his interest in the union of calligraphy and ornament, his concern with the choice of texts (the "story"), his belief in collaboration—but they also help differentiate his medievalism from that of other social reformers, like Ruskin, who nevertheless exercised a profound influence on him. Morris's medievalism gave him a model for artisanship, and, in turn, his own experience as a craftsman then made him a socialist.[215]

Though this is not the place for a review of the contributions of Morris's Kelmscott Press, founded in 1891 and the subject of extensive scholarship else-where, it is important to point out that Morris's views on printing resembled his utopian views on manuscript illumination. In an extraordinarily modern move that anticipates Curt Bühler and other twentieth-century scholars,[216] Morris commented that early printed books of the incunabulum period were not so different from the manuscripts they supplanted: "The difference between the printed book and the written one was very little indeed."[217] Rather than producing facsimiles of the books of early printers—which he studied and even collected—he set out, just as he had done through his calligraphy projects, to imitate their craftsmanship. To this end, he invented and had cast Renaissance-like fonts and produced high-quality handmade paper. He purchased and used a hand press for his small exclusive editions, for which he bought special ink and vellum (from Germany and Italy, respectively). He printed a few copies of each work on vellum, and even finished his imprints by hand with painted and drawn initials.

Up until about 1891, Morris, who "possessed a library of higher quality than any major English literary figure," showed little interest in acquiring medieval manuscripts.[218] But around the time he founded the Kelmscott Press, he began to purchase them in earnest, perhaps realizing that manuscripts were the natural complement to his collection of incunabula. His acquisitions included no Italian humanist manuscripts; instead they focus on English and Continental Gothic ex-amples: the *Windmill Psalter, Tiptoft Missal, Huntington Psalter,* a psalter from Beauvais, other thirteenth-century English, Flemish, and French psalters, and finally a bestiary and a *Roman de la Rose.*[219] Morris's telling descriptions of these manuscripts further confirm his views of medieval manuscripts, already discussed. About an English thirteenth-century psalter probably made for William the Baron of Vescy (Pierpont Morgan Library, MS. M. 100), he wrote: "Though this book is without figure-work the extraordinary beauty and invention of the ornament make it most interesting . . . thoroughly characteristic of English work."[220] About a late-thirteenth-century psalter from northern France (Pierpont Morgan Library, MS. M. 98), "This book has a complete and satisfactory scheme of ornament, which is nowhere departed from, and the colour of which is thoroughly harmonious."[221] Then, of another psalter, this one from Beauvais (Pierpont Morgan Library, MS. M. 101): "These ten leaves of designs . . . are of the best French work, at once el-egant and serious. The historiated letters are clear and bright in colour . . . there is a particular charm about these letters, which take up a good space on the page. . . . The writing . . . is big, and bold, and as good as can be."[222] Nowhere is Morris concerned with pictures, their symbolism or subject matter; his interest here, as with his own calligraphic manuscripts and the productions of his private press, lies in the nature and quality of the ornament as evidence of the craftsmanship that preceded his time and that his era should emulate. The work of William Morris is unimaginable without the prehistory of reproductions outlined in this chapter. He represents the culmination of a tradition but at the same time radically breaks with that tradition in his commitment to a craftsmanship that no longer reproduces the Middle Ages but recasts it in a modern age.

R E V I V A L S

Morality and Manuscript Illumination in Nineteenth-Century England

## Gentlemen's Gothick and

## Social Distinction

The flirtation with Gothic style by architects of the generation of James Gibbs (1682–1754), William Kent (1685–1748), and Batty Langley (1696–1751) prompted no general reevaluation of medieval artifacts. An antiquarian like William Stukeley (1687–1765), scouring the countryside for the prehistoric remains of British ancestors and druids, eventually came to rest in York Minster, one of the greatest medieval cathedrals, in 1740, declaring it superior even to St. Peter's in Rome and the Pantheon. He had some affection for medieval artifacts—he owned a number, including Limoges enamels—and accepted that such objects might be useful for modern ornamental purposes. But illuminated manuscripts apparently had no place in his collection. The vogue for neo-Gothic mystery novels of the kind satirized in Jane Austen's *Northanger Abbey* (1818) brought with it no general interest in medieval objects. However, one or two enthusiasts responded to neo-Gothic passions by turning to medieval books. Sir John Soane, for example, no friend of the Gothic Revival enthusiasms of the 1820s, acquired some illuminated manuscripts for the monk's cell and oratory in the palace he constructed in Lincoln's Inn Fields. Collectively referred to as "missals" on account of their illumination, they were the appropriate furniture for monastic ruins and a monk's tomb in the basement. The collector William Beckford, author of the wildly successful Gothic horror novel *Vathek* (1786), acquired an early-sixteenth-century manuscript of a kind we would immediately categorize today as Renaissance; his comment that it was "sufficiently gothic to please me" was perhaps a response to its nature as a Book of Hours. The manuscripts he included in the fabled art collection he put together in his neo-Gothic Fonthill Abbey, sold in 1823, were objects of connoisseurship and exotica, to be judged by art-historical criteria. Thus a thirteenth-century prayer book was "in a style that would have honoured Giotto." The works were valued as illustrating a traditional view of painting, as described by Vasari, by which Giotto liberated Italian painting from the yoke of Byzantine art, allowing the full flowering of a Renaissance in the sixteenth century. Horace Walpole likewise included one or two illuminated manuscripts as exotica for his collection, housed in the Rococo extravaganza of his elaborately Gothic edifice at Strawberry Hill. Here, they had the additional advantage of functioning as personal heirlooms: they were kept in the Edward III gallery of his library and were a natural adjunct to portraits of medieval figures from whom he claimed descent.[1]

Miniatures from illuminated manuscripts were acknowledged as the source of images in works on costume. William Camden's *Remaines concerning Brittaine* (1607) in 1609 had commented on their usefulness. A host of books from Strutt's *Horda Angel-cynnan* of 1776 to James Planché's popular volume on British costume of 1834 were to acknowledge them as a source. These works fueled the cult of history painting that was proposed as an indigenous national school independent of foreign—above all French—influence. In this context, illuminated manuscripts had the character of an archaeological resource, gaining value only on account of the subjects shown in miniatures. It became conventional to commend manuscripts with illuminated images as useful in illustrating the customs and manners of remote periods, particularly for works that could not easily be described with the terminology associated with Renaissance art. Richard Gough's monograph of 1794 on the *Bedford Hours*, produced for the duke of Bedford in Paris in the 1430s when he was regent of Henry VI for his lands in France, had no vocabulary to describe this sumptuous work (now British Library MS Add. 18850). Its illumination could find no niche in conventional accounts of painting and its history: its value lay in the association with a great figure of English history (one who had defeated the French in a way that Gough's compatriots were failing to do in the 1790s). Gough's work made the manuscript a national heirloom; it joined the *Aethelwold Benedictional*, a magnificent tenth-century manuscript, as a work inextricably linked with a glorious national past, one heightened by its residing in the collection of the duke of Devonshire, the manuscript never mentioned in the nineteenth-century without the name of its illustrious owner.[2] Some connoisseurs saw themselves as guardians of a national history as well as of standards of taste: Beckford was relieved that the *Bedford Hours* had not fallen into "dirty plebeian hands" at the Edwards sale in 1815 (the successful bidder, the marquess of Blandford, had beaten off an attempt by John North to buy the work), just as he regretted that another manuscript prayer book, "the best for good taste that I have seen in my life," had been acquired by North, a mere corn dealer of East Acton.[3] The marketing language of Ottley, both for his own sales and Celotti's sale in 1825, aimed to flatter the highly conservative prejudices of collectors such as Beckford. Ottley's introduction to Celotti's sale catalogue appealed to connoisseurs to save works rescued from the sanctum of the High Renaissance, the Sistine Chapel in Rome, from the fury of disorderly troops who were not only French but also Republican.

A collector like Robert Curzon, whose family had resurrected the title of Baron Zouche in 1810, was doubtless sympathetic to such appeals.4 In 1833 and

1834 he traveled in Egypt, Syria, and Greece in a search for early texts of the Bible. These, with a wide range of illuminated works, were a natural complement to his collection of over seventy-five pieces of armor, all of them forgeries, in his appropriately named Baron's Hall at his seat, Parham Park, Sussex. The 1838 painting of the Young England enthusiast Daniel Maclise, *Merry Christmas in the Baron's Hall*, in which the baron entertains his squires and serfs as the benevolent overlord, seems to characterize his world. Curzon voted systematically against the reform of Parliament in 1832.[5] His was the world of the Young England movement, a romantically inspired program that stressed the social obligations of a country gentry toward their feudal subordinates; its political complexion was established in Parliament by the young Disraeli, whose philosophy of benign paternalism, based on medieval example, was the expression in England of a reaction to social change found throughout Europe from the late eighteenth century.

Curzon was probably more characteristic of early collectors of illuminated manuscripts than, say, Francis Douce (1757–1834), a radical in politics and an admirer of Napoleon; if the bulk of his manuscript collection was acquired for scholarly purposes connected with interests in literary and political history, he showed no restraint in acquiring beautifully illuminated Books of Hours, mostly of a luxurious late-fifteenth- or sixteenth-century kind favored by connoisseurs of the day.

Sir Thomas Phillipps, who amassed at Middle Hill the greatest private collection of manuscripts of the nineteenth century, may have been similar to Douce in outlook, but he initially avoided works with too close an association with medieval religion. He was a pro-reform radical in the 1820s, an opponent of free trade in the 1840s; his dislike of High Church Anglicanism was matched only by his hatred of Chartists, Roman Catholics, foreign Catholic countries, and Napoleon III. Before midcentury, his collection was largely historical. Medieval liturgical and biblical works were "thinly represented" in the list made when Chartists from Birmingham threatened in 1839; by 1872 liturgical works were eminently collectible, and his collection contained "an embarrassingly large number of fifteenth-century books decorated with miniatures," very many of them devotional or liturgical, evidently antiquarian or art-historical documents rather than treasured repositories of pure spirituality. Phillipps's collecting seems to mirror the growing acceptance of illumination as a worthy form of art.

An opportunity to gain a collective view of manuscripts is provided by the "loan exhibition" of works of art that opened in the South Kensington Museum in June 1862. This was the first time that such objects had been included en masse in an art exhibition. Over thirty-five collectors lent works for the section of the exhibition devoted to illuminated manuscripts. If the Reverend John Fuller Russell's High Church interests are revealed by his correspondence in *The Ecclesiologist* and by Waagen's description of his collection, he was no doubt in the same category as Sir Baronet William Lawson, Bart. (1796–1865), whose third son, William, became a Catholic priest and whose three daughters all became nuns, or the Benedictine monk, the Reverend W. Ryan of St. Mary's, Warwick Bridge, Carlisle. Rather different was Sir William Tite (1798–1873), the antiquarian, a man who in 1865 opposed Scott's proposal to build a Gothic building for the Treasury and who was Liberal member of Parliament for Bath from 1855. A collector of a similar antiquarian background was Austin Henry Layard (1817–94), excavator of Nineveh and Liberal member of Parliament; his enthusiasm for Italian Renaissance art is seen in his loan of illuminated initials from Pisa. Robert Holroyd, whose huge collection of manuscripts and works of art was eventually housed in the sumptuous Dorchester Palace, which he built in London's Park Lane, was a member of Parliament of conservative persuasion from 1854 to 1872. Munby characterized him and his friend Walter Sneyd, another collector of manuscripts well represented in the 1862 exhibition, as "products of [the] romantic medievalism" of the Eglinton tournament generation. This generation was characterized by those who responded to the call of the thirteenth earl of Eglinton, who in a fury at the lack of medieval pomp at Victoria's coronation in 1837, had organized a tournament that took place under the rain in Ayrshire in front of his tenants and a host of visitors—the armor-clad aristocrats became immersed in mud, to the delight of cartoonists.[6]

The years around 1860 represent a watermark in the reception of illuminated manuscripts in Britain. What follows investigates the background to this "domestication" of an art that was exclusive and foreign in the years between Beckford's sale in 1823 and the mass marketing of illumination in the 1860s.

**High Church Gothick and Religious Controversy**
The link of High Church Anglicanism with illumination is worth considering. For most of the nineteenth century, any illuminated manuscript that had the slightest association with religion was known as a "missal," a word that immediately associated it with the Roman Catholic Church. The success of the Oxford Movement in the 1830s, with its emphasis on personal devotions (including fasting, frequent communion, confession, and penance), disciplined prayer for the laity, a committed sacramental priesthood, and regular church attendance for all classes, created a climate in which medieval illuminated prayer books might be valued. If John Henry Newman, who ceded to Rome in 1845, and John Keble, the leaders of the new devotion, did not engage with historical artifacts, their followers certainly did. Many of the early authorities on illumination were Catholic. William Maskell, the author of the first serious histories of Anglican ritual and liturgy, became a Catholic in 1850. His *Ancient Liturgy of the Church of England according to the Uses of Sarum, Bangor, York and Hereford and the Modern Roman Liturgy* (1844) made him an authority on missals, Books of Hours, and the like, as well as on illumination; his collection of illuminated manuscripts was celebrated. Daniel Rock, chaplain to the Catholic earl of Shrewsbury, produced the influential *Church of Our Fathers* (1849–53); like Maskell, he was recruited in the early 1870s to produce catalogues of medieval applied art for the South Kensington Museum. Of the same ilk was Frederick Husenbeth (1796–1872), ordained a Catholic priest in 1820; as an authority on medieval liturgical practices, he advised collectors such as Dawson Turner in the 1840s.

Of paramount concern to the Oxford Movement, and to the Anglo-Catholic tendency within the Church of England that it gave way to, was the provision of churches for the sprawling suburbs of industrial centers. These were essential for the promotion of religion as an instrument to fight social deprivation. It was feared that Low Church missions in deprived areas were taking the lead, thus stealing the role traditionally reserved for the classes from which High Church enthusiasts were recruited. Beyond this, Roman Catholics were considered more advanced in providing for the urban poor. A rallying point for High Church sympathizers was the Camden Society in Cambridge, founded in the early 1840s and known as the Ecclesiological Society from 1845. Matters relating to the building and equipping of new churches dominated its journal, *The Ecclesiologist*, and there was much discussion of, and advertisements for, fittings and liturgical equipment copied from medieval models. Illuminated manuscripts were referred to occasionally, usually as an iconographic source. And yet it was among the architects associated with the group that illumination began to be prized as a contemporary activity: William Morris executed his first illuminated manuscripts when working in the offices of the Gothic Revival architect George Edmund Street, while the architect William Burgess, an energetic collector of manuscripts, in 1859 recommended thirteenth-century illumination to his students as a source for architectural ornament. On hearing a lecture by Digby Wyatt in 1860 on illumination, Burgess went so far as to propose that illumination be revived to make service books in cathedrals.[7]

Along with other articles needed in churches, illumination became a matter of contemporary production as well as of guidance in matters of design—and it was carried out within an environment of High Church supporters, many of whom seceded to Rome. Common to them was a nostalgia for a lost world of solidarity between hierarchically ordered classes expressed in collective worship and loyalty to tradition; a society of deference was held up in contrast to a socially and

morally dislocated present. Lord Charles Thynne, the second son of the marquess of Bath, is a revealing example. He occupied an exulted position in British society: apart from his noble birth, he was Canon of Canterbury Cathedral. In explaining to his parishioners in 1853 why he had left the Anglican Church for that of Rome (the former had no clear answers on matters concerning the role of the priest, such as confession and penance), he made clear his romantic vision of the place of the Church in British history. The cathedrals and parish churches of England, "even now the boast and glory of our country," had altars that were deserted, because in rejecting Catholic unity and Catholic practice there had been a rupture with the way our fathers had worshiped God; there were quotations from Roman Catholic prayers to the Virgin Mary and to saints, whose power to intercede with God on behalf of the individual penitent was the major as-

104.

**Lord Charles Thynne, Crucifixion, copied from the tenth- or eleventh-century *Beauvais Sacramentary***

sumption of the medieval Book of Hours. Thynne hoped that "our country [may regain] her lost inheritance," a phrase that echoes Newman's description of pre-Reformation liturgical practices lost "through inadvertence." In showing concern not only with traditional, that is to say pre-Reformation, forms of worship but also with the notion of continuity of authority that went back to the time of the Apostles, Thynne was as well echoing Anglo-Catholic concerns. It is difficult not to link his evident skill as an illuminator to those views: in executing superb facsimiles of a leaf from the early-fourteenth-century English *Howard Psalter* in the British Museum, the tenth-century King Edgar's Charter in Winchester Cathedral, or the early-eleventh-century *Beauvais Sacramentary* (figure 104, plate 25), he was reproducing powerful icons of religion and history that were politically constructed.[8]

It is worth comparing Thynne's practice as an illuminator—the pieces known by him apparently all date from the 1860s—to that of the architect and designer Augustus Welby Northmore Pugin, a Roman Catholic from 1828. Pugin's celebrated *Contrasts* (1836) was among a number of works that presented medieval society as a pious, mutually supportive, and caring community, comparing it with the harsh industrial society of the nineteenth century, where greed, ugliness, mate-

Parish Church 1830

Ecclesia Parochialis MCCCCXXX

105.

Augustus Welby
Northmore Pugin,
sketchbook for *Contrasts*
(England, 1836),
contrasting pair 3,
"Contrasted Ecclesi-
astical Architecture 1
(exteriors)"

rialism, and the cruel social provision of the workhouse was the norm. A sketch-book for the project shows how Pugin came up with comparative schema. In each pair, neoclassical style represents debased modern taste that came with the Reforma-tion and the introduction of "paganism" into architecture; Gothic style, conversely, heralds the higher moral state associated with Catholicism (figure 105). Pugin here was claiming for Catholicism ideas current with other non-Catholic thinkers of his time and earlier who had stressed the benevolent, paternal nature of feudal society, where lords protected the well-being of their subjects.[9] He is not known to have owned any medieval manuscripts.[10] The drawing books that he completed for sev-eral of his projects make clear that he was expert at illuminating and that he had studied medieval manuscripts closely. Completed in 1832, "The Shrine" contained finished drawings for the imaginary reconstruction of the thirteenth-century shrine of St. Edmund, Archbishop of Canterbury, in the abbey of Pontigny in France (figure 106, plate 26). The title page has illumination in colors that recall thirteenth- and fourteenth-century Italian manuscripts, and the catalogue of relics has a pass-able interpretation of a fourteenth-century initial. A similar volume of 1833, recording an imaginary project for a chapel dedicated to St. Margaret, has decora-tion on the last leaf reminiscent of thirteenth-century Italian illumination and also initials clearly based on twelfth-century Anglo-Norman models (figure 107, plate 27).[11] Both volumes show that Pugin had experimented with a variety of different kinds of lettering found in medieval manuscripts. It is striking that the work of Pugin generally contains few references to illumination (other than using minia-tures as iconographic sources). His work on decorative motifs, *Floriated Ornament*, contains only very generalized approximations to what was common in late-medieval manuscripts—the lack of direct reference to the floriated ornament of medieval illuminating styles is striking. The illustrations he contributed to Husen-beth's *Missal for the Use of the Laity* (London: Charles Dolman, 1838) are pictorial and without any reference to medieval illumination. Pugin's use of illumination was functional in that it was restricted to the role prescribed for it by medieval tra-dition, that is to say, to the decoration of books. The dedication to his patron, the earl of Shrewsbury, in *An Apology for the Revival of Christian Architecture in England* (1843), was set in Gothic type and printed in red and black; the initial letter was illuminated and historiated.[12] It was again appropriate that the copy of Pugin's *Contrasts* (1836) given to the Pope had illuminated decoration, with well-executed,

VIII

ic seqitur catalogus
sanctarum reliquiarũ
capsæ pertinentium

i Feretrum
ij Reliquiarium auratum cum gemmis
iij Reliquiarium eburneum argento ornatum
iiij Baculum pastorale
v Crux Sti Edmundi
vi Annulus pontificalis
vij Crux aurata cum gemmis
viij Mitra Stola Manipulum

106.

Augustus Welby
Northmore Pugin,
"The Shrine"
(England, 1832),
illuminated page with
list of reliquaries

107.

Augustus Welby
Northmore Pugin,
"St. Margaret's Chapel"
(England, 1833)

THE END

pen-flourished initials in imitation of late-medieval example. Pugin's principle of "Fitness for Purpose" led to the use of illumination, for example, to provide elaborate decorative initials in letters to his colleagues or to inscribe books. An example of the latter dates from 1843. When a guest of his patron, Washington Hibbert, at Alton Towers, Pugin obligingly illuminated a dedication inscription for the gift of a guidebook given by Hibbert to another guest, the comte de Chambord. It is tempting to associate Pugin with a major illuminated work, unfortunately undated and unsigned, made for a St. Cuthbert's College at Ushaw, a building that he had designed. The manuscript, a list of benefactors known as the *Liber Vitae*, has numerous miniatures as vignettes in borders that are faithful copies of northern French illuminated ornament of the fifteenth century: there are acanthus scrolls with schematic flowers and compartments of flowers and berries on gold grounds. If the manuscript can be associated with Pugin (the volume was added to until the 1890s), it would show that Pugin was thinking in terms of illuminated manuscripts as the fitting accoutrements of the churches he designed.[13]

Pugin's use of illumination shows the rigor of the designer using styles in a consistent and appropriate manner. Rather different is the work of Ambrose Lisle Phillipps, a Catholic acquaintance of Pugin's and the protector of a community of Trappist monks in Leicestershire. His translation of the Elisabeth of Hungary chronicle (from the French version of Montalembert) was dedicated to Queen Victoria when published in 1839. A special title page was provided, a hand-colored lithograph in a fourteenth-century English style of illumination: the inclusion of grotesque heads with animal legs, with its implied acceptance of the bawdy, secular element in medieval art, at once shows a perspective that differs from that of Pugin, as does the reference in the introduction to the "material evils that existed during the middle ages." Phillipps used illumination to underline the sanctity of a medieval saint—a woman who achieved sainthood within marriage—while recognizing the benefits of living in the nineteenth century. Phillipps's presentation of St. Elisabeth was to become the center of a debate about the role of women as wives. The radical anti-Catholic Charles Kingsley doubtless had Phillipps's version in mind when he referred in 1848 to "softened and sentimentalised . . . Romish" versions of the story that undermined domestic purity and Protestantism. Catholicism and its art, including illumination, were roundly dismissed.[14]

The response of people such as Kingsley perhaps induced Cardinal Newman to distance himself from any association with medieval styles. He mistrusted Pugin's passion for steps to the altar and chancel screens; his predilection was for the baroque classicism that characterized the Rome of the sixteenth-century saint Philip Neri, whose Oratory congregation Newman helped to bring to Britain. Within Anglican and Nonconformist circles, the matter of style became potent in the 1840s: if Ritualists and Anglo-Catholics championed Gothic architecture and design, the Baptist minister Charles Spurgeon declared in 1861 that "Every Baptist place of worship should be Grecian, never Gothic" with an emphasis intended to stamp out earlier interest with the Gothic. The character of Mr. Slope in Trollope's novel *Barchester Towers* (1857) provides a caricature of the Low Church position: "[Mr. Slope's] gall rises at a new church with a high pitched roof; a full-breasted black silk waistcoat is with him a symbol of Satan; and a profane jest would not, in his view, more foully desecrate the Church seat of a Christian, than a Book of Prayer *printed with red letters, and ornamented with a cross on the back.*" This was not an environment in which illumination could be admired. Neither did the newly established Roman Catholicism find it useful—it needed reference to an uncontested style that was august and classical, as even its first primate, the flamboyant Cardinal Wiseman, saw in 1849 and 1850. It was in Anglo-Catholic rather than Roman Catholic circles that illumination was nurtured.[15]

Continuity between the Oxford Movement and the Anglo-Catholicism of the mid–nineteenth century can be provided by considering John Keble, a fellow of Oriel College in Oxford and from 1836 a parish priest in Hampshire. His work *The Christian Year*, first published in 1827, was the equivalent of a medieval Book of Hours in providing a structured sequence of poems of a religious nature for Sundays and holy days of the year. These poems, designed to guide a series of inner reflections, proved a tremendous publishing success. Many editions from the 1840s were published in the highly decorated covers and illustrations; illuminated versions were available.[16] Keble died in 1866, but his prestige can be gauged from the fact that an Oxford college was raised in his memory in 1870. Its library opened in 1878. Keble did not apparently own any illuminated manuscripts, but the place of such objects in High Church circles is revealed by the stream of illuminated manuscripts bequeathed to the college in memory of Keble after 1881: the collection is distinguished among nineteenth-century institutional collections for its richly illuminated Books of Hours, missals, breviaries, and other liturgical works, and its nature explained by the "ideological and personal connections between the benefactors and founders" of the college.[17]

The link between High Church sympathies and illumination is demonstrated by the work of an early and very proficient illuminator, Louisa Strange (1788–1862), the wife of Sir Thomas Strange (died 1841). An illuminated book of poems given to her daughter Isabel in 1840 on her marriage to Alexander Trotter includes illumination in a regency style, but also copies of fifteenth-century illuminated ornament. The inclusion of a poem describing Charles I as a martyr indicates High Church sympathies, and this is confirmed by the family's association with Legitimist circles in Paris in 1830. The Strange family had a house in Boulogne; there was much embarrassment when in 1831 they were asked to attend municipal celebrations commemorating the beheading of Louis XVI. Lady Strange was called on at a later period to add miniatures to some treasured late-medieval manuscripts in the Boulogne Bibliothèque Municipale, a gesture of respect for her skill and perhaps the political correctness of her art.[18]

Another opportunity to examine the place of illumination in High Church circles relates directly to John Keble. Charlotte M. Yonge was the outstanding novelist of the High Church movement and submitted to Keble for approval everything she wrote. She achieved literary fame with *The Heir of Redcliffe* in 1853, an account of a search for a contemporary spirituality seen in terms of medieval chivalry. William Morris and Dante Gabriel Rosetti were enchanted by the novel, Morris being a confirmed Anglo-Catholic on going to university at Oxford; it was said to have been the preferred reading of wounded officers during the Crimean War. In one of Yonge's novels, *The Trial* (1864), a rather dangerous widow (dangerous as in being a woman with worldly experience and unattached) is discovered illuminating a copy of the Magna Carta, a constitutional document not much admired in High Church circles—the usual correlation of illumination with a sphere of calm, meditative spirituality was breached to warn the reader of evil. Charlotte Yonge was the acknowledged "headmistress" of a group of young women from High Church families who called themselves the Goslings, whose manuscript journal the *Barnacle*, issued between 1863 and 1867, contained discussion of illumination and its history.[19]

Anglo-Catholics had prescriptive principles concerning the role of women. Charlotte Yonge insisted on the place of women within the family unit;

she and Keble equated parenthood with priesthood. The introduction of "sister-hoods," communities of women devoted to a spiritual way of life, was an exten-sion of the idea. Wackerbarth was typical of High Church divines in his alarm that Low Church missionaries were seizing the initiative in promoting religion among the urban masses and longed for an appropriate response to combat social works of "Tridentine Sectaries," as he called Roman Catholic activists. Pusey, Keble, and Newman had all in the 1830s been struck by the example of the good works of the Soeurs de Charité and the St. Vincent de Paul organizations in Catholic France. The first Anglican sisterhood was founded as a memorial to the poet lau-reate Robert Southey (died 1843). Prompted by the example of the Catholic Sis-ters of Mercy, who in 1839 established convents in Bermondsey and Birmingham, prominent members of the Church of England met in 1844 to discuss the founda-tion of sisterhoods. William Gladstone, then president of the Board of Trade and a member of Sir Robert Peel's cabinet, was unable to attend but took a close inter-est. Their purposes were to live under a religious rule; to visit the poor in their own homes; to visit hospitals, prisons, and workhouses; to feed, clothe, and in-struct destitute children; and to help to bury the dead. The first sisterhood, the Sisterhood of the Holy Cross, was established in 1845 in Park Village West, near Albany Street, between the elegant John Nash buildings around London's Re-gent's Park and the slums of Camden Town. In 1850 they moved to a new Gothic building in Osnaburgh Street, Munster Square, where their lives were governed by a translation of the medieval *Sarum Breviary*. Other communities in Wantage (where from 1890 a printing press was installed to produce plain chant), Ascot, Hastings, Oxford, and West Malvern were established by 1851.[20]

A driving force in the movement was Priscilla Lydia Sellon, who arranged for her nuns to act as nurses in the Crimea and who in 1856 was responsible for organizing the sisterhoods into a coherent structure. The significance of all this for our theme is that illumination became one of the activities that nuns in the strictest houses of the order were to practice. The sisters from Devonport, for instance, going to the Crimea to nurse war casualties in 1854, took prayer books that were illuminated.[21]

**Gothick Nature and Anti-Catholic Sentiment**

The link between Anglo-Catholic sisterhoods and illu-mination did not go unnoticed. In 1850, when anti-Catholic feeling was at its height, *Punch* published an illustrated article, "The Convent of the Belgravians," in which the sisterhoods were shown as frequented by well-born, fastidiously ele-gant young ladies (the illustration shows one carefully tying on her bonnet in front of an illuminated initial whose sanctity is punctured by a goose climbing up the side). "The time of the nuns will be devoted to the charities of life by making morning calls, and occasionally visiting soup kitchens and model lodging houses in a properly appointed carriage, or, if they walk, attended by a footman. Otherwise, their leisure will be employed in illuminating books of devotion" (figure 108). The same association of High Church loyalties and illumination is seen in Punch's mocking cartoon of a High Church divine teaching a boy about an elaborately drawn illuminated letter (figure 109). Initials copied from medieval illuminated books were used in the magazine to stigmatize convents, Catholics, and Papist for-eigners and appeared in conjunction with the caricatures of medieval clothes and medieval armor that ridiculed the pretensions of heroic antireform politicians and Catholics.[22]

* To prevent mistakes, the unilluminated are apprised, that this is simply the letter A.

108.

"Convent of the Belgravians," from *Punch* magazine (1850)

109.

A clergyman teaching a boy about an elaborately drawn illuminated letter *A*, from *Punch* magazine (1851)

This idea that illumination was associated with the Church of England's accommodation with Catholicism was further developed in *Punch*'s attack on Pre-Raphaelite painting. Richard Doyle dismissed Pre-Raphaelite paintings at the Royal Academy as un-British and foreign. They had "a certain Quaintness that do smack of church-window and illuminated Missals." The similarity to illumination was sufficient by way of dismissal.[23] Charles Dickens made Catholicism, High Church Anglicanism, and neofeudal conservatism his target in grouping together Pugin, the Oxford Movement, and Disraeli's Young England movement in a diatribe against Millais's picture *Christ in the Carpenter's Shop* in the 1850 Royal Academy exhibition. Ralph Wornum referred to the Pre-Raphaelites as the "Young England School."[24] Ruskin initially assumed the Catholic allegiance of the Pre-Raphaelites, though evidence for this did not go beyond the fact that Rosetti's mother and sister attended Christchurch in Albany Street, London, where the vicar, William Dodsworth, the spiritual leader of the first Anglican sisterhood, had made the daring political act of placing flowers on the altar, the first Anglican church of the time in London where this is recorded. Pre-Raphaelite painters did indeed make frequent reference to medieval manuscripts, though their concern was more a search for historical exactitude than proselytizing zeal; on the whole they used the works of Henry Noel Humphreys rather than spending hours in the British Museum Library or Bodleian Library reading rooms.[25]

A picture that reflects the mood of Anglo-Catholicism was Charles Allston Collins's *Convent Thoughts*, displayed in the 1851 Royal Academy exhibition (figure 110). It showed a nun in a walled garden, surrounded by flowers; she interrupts reading a Book of Hours to examine a passionflower. Ruskin declared he had no particular sympathy with this "lady in white," made a joke about goldfish, but praised the study of the flowers greatly. The picture was parodied in *Punch*:

CONVENT THOUGHTS.

there, the passionflower is taken to represent not Christ's Crucifixion but opposition to life in a convent; the flowers, maintained *Punch*, suggested not sanctity but
nature, which is to be preferred to the "legend of a saint" represented by the illuminated manuscript in her hand; the enclosing wall and the passionflower, *Punch* concluded, relate to the woman's frustration at being prevented from adopting a conventional woman's role as a wife, mother, and doer of good works (figure 111).[26]

  *Punch*'s comments on *Convent Thoughts* oppose illumination and nature.
This polarity is of some significance. *Punch* as a whole equated illumination with
the Catholicism that threatened to undermine the British way of life. If illumination for *Punch* was High Church, Anglo-Catholic, and even Catholic, the nature
set up in opposition to it can be read as the "man-in-the-street" view of art.
Vaughan has described how the construction of the idea of a British School in the
1820s was centered on the idea of nature, with Gainsborough, Wilson, and Hoga-
rth becoming its Old Masters as the historical painting of Joshua Reynolds and
his followers was put to one side. An indigenous art that owed nothing to foreign
work was sought. The neoclassicism of Revolutionary France was thus to be rejected; genre and landscape painting in England in the 1820s were to be the marks
of the British school, a view no doubt endorsed by the classes in which amateur
watercolor landscape painting flourished. Characteristic of these views were the
ideas, for example, in Allan Cunningham's *Lives of the Most Eminent British Painters,
Sculptors and Architects*, published first in 1829 to 1832 but much reprinted thereafter, which struggled to find a tradition of British art independent of foreign influence. As regarded the early period, the poor standard in medieval religious art
was attributed to the fact that the pre-Reformation Catholic Church employed
foreigners rather than Englishmen. The chauvinistic Sarsfield Taylor was to use the
same argument for kings from Henry VIII to Charles I who unpatriotically hin-
dered the emergence of a national school; the Romans had debauched the native
Britons, but for the medieval period, he could point to the reign of Edward III as
marking a height of native excellence, before the decadence associated with Tudor
patronage of foreigners.[27] There was a real problem, at the level of society at

which these books were aimed, concerning historical justification. To be acceptable beyond those with High Church sympathies, illumination had to divest itself in some measure of its foreign and Catholic associations.

Curators and scholars seeking a wider audience for illuminated manuscripts began to refer to the appearance of naturalism in works on illumination in the 1830s and 1840s, as if claiming parity for illumination with painting and ridding it of its Catholic associations. Frederic Madden in 1833 describes it as a feature of the fifteenth century, while Henry Noel Humphreys in 1849 attributed it to the late fourteenth or early fifteenth century; Richard Holmes, of the Manuscripts Department of the British Museum Library, stated in 1862 that "the spread of taste and knowledge made the study of nature the chief aim of the illuminator" in the thirteenth century.[28] In his historical account of medieval illumination, Matthew Digby Wyatt in 1860 refers to naturalism incidentally, but the theme is taken up enthusiastically by Edwin Jewitt in one of the earliest do-it-yourself illuminating manuals dependent upon Digby Wyatt's work of the same year. Wyatt's book of 1860 stressed the importance of following nature for *contemporary* illumination, as if to show it as a respectable art practice devoid of association with Catholicism of any kind.[29] The *Art Journal* in 1849, in its first major article "The Illuminated Literature of the Present Day," extols the work of fifteenth-century illuminators as adopting decorations "consisting almost entirely of sprigs of wild flowers, closely painted from nature, and placed upon a field of gold." This valuing of naturalism, defined as the lifelike representation of natural phenomena, especially flowers but also landscape, might be expected in an environment where watercolor drawing of flowers and landscapes was much practiced as an amateur art, as the illustrations in the *Barnacle* magazine make clear.

Flowers were frequently taken as the subject for illuminated pictures, a tendency doubtless encouraged by the popularity of the famous *Anne of Brittany Hours* with its highly naturalistic depiction of plants, flowers, and herbs—one of the earliest popular color publications had been a calendar of 1845 with colored reproductions from the manuscript. At a popular level, the association of illumination with naturalism allowed its inclusion with respectable amateur activity, so that, for example, the frontispiece of William Randle Harrison's *Suggestions for Illuminating* of 1863 (figure 112) was based on a highly realistic flower painting (and the text recommends the *Anne of Brittany Hours* as a model).

112.

**W. Randle Harrison, *Suggestions for Illuminating* (1871)**

Claims of naturalism enabled illumination to be considered British. Against a rather different background, Charles Blanc in France in 1861 was keen to advance the notion that French illuminators copied nature, though here to promote the idea of a native Renaissance independent of Italian influence.[30]

The singling out of naturalism in late-medieval illumination in the rhetoric of nineteenth-century commentators seems perverse today. There are undoubtedly elements of realism in illuminated ornament and miniatures from the late fourteenth century, but usually within a context of extreme stylization, at least until the borders of the so-called Ghent-Bruges school from the 1480s and its French and Italian equivalents. The illustrations for the seventh edition of Bradley's *Manual of Illumination* (1861) include nothing in this style, preferring conventional and highly stylized acanthus and patterns as models: yet the *Manchester Weekly Express* in

September 1861 could refer in a review to "the fervent love and pursuit of nature" which the practice of illuminating encouraged. The appeal to naturalism represented an effort to fit illumination into a scheme of development used by art-historical narratives based on other media. If the work of Fouquet satisfied the eye of those trained in classical and neoclassical art, the miniatures in the huge numbers of late-medieval Books of Hours in the nineteenth-century book trade can hardly match the naturalism achieved by nineteenth-century painters. William Morris, who perused illuminated manuscripts from his undergraduate days in Oxford and reproduced a thirteenth-century manuscript in his earliest painting (1858), based his great cycle of pattern designs on natural forms and on their historical representation. His mature illuminated works of the 1870s reinterpret plant forms in a way that owes nothing to medieval illuminated ornament. However much he adored medieval illumination, it had little to offer the new avant-garde aesthetic destined for the top end of the design market.[31] The promotion of illumination as in some way "naturalistic" is surely an effort to divorce it from unwanted foreign and Catholic associations and to allow it to flourish as an acceptable object of admiration.

## ILLUMINATION AS DESIGN

**Manufacturing Modernity for Illumination**    Much of the early promotion of illumination was by people involved in the promotion of the new category of "design," that is to say, art made relevant to manufacture. This was true of Henry Noel Humphreys, Owen Jones, Matthew Digby Wyatt, and even Henry Shaw. When illumination was approached as a source of design, there was no complication of having to adjust to a view of art in which Raphael was the summit toward which medieval art strived, or indeed of coming to terms with a discourse in which national traits and qualities were in competition.[32]

Even here, illumination had to shed its association with Catholicism. The plethora of gift books that emanated from publishers like Longman in the 1840s, though parading as illuminated books, in fact avoid too close imitation of medieval styles (see chapter 3).[33] This is particularly striking in the case of books by Owen Jones and Noel Humphreys. The latter, in *Parables of Our Lord* (1847), stresses that his designs were new rather than "embroidery borrowed from old Missals," and that they were appropriate for the text—the *Art-Union* was able to commend them for their "tasteful simplicity." Reviews in the *Art-Union* and its successor, the *Art Journal*, constantly stress, before the 1860s, the use of publications reproducing medieval illumination for design and ornament. The fascicules of *Illuminated Books of the Middle Ages* in 1849 were reviewed as "full of suggestive ideas for ornamental work"; a review of both gift books and facsimiles produced in the 1840s talked of them as "of immeasurable service . . . to the student of design" as well as others. True to its mission to help artists in practical ways, the *Art Journal* went on to recommend these illuminated works to architects as a source of ornament for the restoration of buildings; Humphreys's *Illuminated Books of the Middle Ages* (1849) was "a fund of ornament . . . of eminent service . . . to the modern artist," as well as ornamental designers of every class. The *Art Journal*, which accepted medievalism with difficulty in the mid–nineteenth century, could accept Humphreys *Parables of Our Lord* as a gift book made "as elegant as modern art can bestow," just as it warned the Illuminating Art Union in 1859 to develop a modern style and not merely copy medieval example.[34] In the first substantial account for practitioners, *The Art of Illumination and Missal Painting* (London: H.G. Bohn, 1849), Noel

Humphreys appended a lengthy text to a discussion of each medieval work illustrated, headed "Suggestions for applying the style . . . to modern illumination." The modernity was again a badge of respectability; to characterize illumination under the rubric of design and ornament was to make it modern.

Defense of the new art of illumination against un-British associations was led by those prominent in the movement for design education. One such was Noel Humphreys. In a chromolithographed illuminated gift book of 1848, *Miracles of Our Lord* (figure 99), he had to argue for the appropriateness of ornament based on medieval illumination. "Designated as this interesting branch of study has often been by the name of 'Romanism,' it is perhaps not difficult to account for the indifference or hostility with which, till lately, it has been viewed," claimed Humphreys. He cited the reaction of Thomas Arnold (died 1842), headmaster of Rugby School and prominent Anglican of Low Church persuasion, to the pictures by the sixteenth-century Italian artist Nicolo Circignani, known as Il Pomarancio, in the church of San Stefano Rotondo in Rome. No art lover, Arnold had approved of these scenes of gruesome martyrdoms: "the contemplation of suffering for Christ's sake is a thing most needful for us in our days. . . . And, therefore, pictures of martyrdoms are, I think, very wholesome, not to be sneezed at." It is not inconceivable that in defending illumination in this roundabout way, Humphreys had Charles Dickens in mind. The latter had probably been led to the San Stefano Rotondo in Rome by Murray's guide of 1843, where the paintings were described as "displeasing to the eye and imagination, without having any recommendations as works of art." Dickens, in his column in the *Daily News* describing his visit to Rome in early 1846, had mentioned the paintings as "hideous . . . such a panorama of horror and butchery no man could imagine in his sleep, though he were to eat a whole pig, raw, for supper."[35] Humphreys's defense illustrates the "cultural edginess" that governed attitudes to art at the time, a fear of seeming politically incorrect before a popular audience.[36] John Obadiah Westwood, in his *Illuminated Illustrations of the Bible Copied from Select Manuscripts of the Middle Ages* (London: William Smith, 1846), went out of his way to stress that although many of the miniatures had been copied "from prayer books devoted to the service of the Roman Catholic Church," great care had been taken to select *appropriate* subjects to illustrate stories from the Bible (and *not* miniatures with "compositions devoted to the Virgin Mary and the legends of the Church"). Appropriateness and suitability for function were among the founding principles of the design reform movement.

By 1853, Pre-Raphaelite painters on the whole had abandoned the religious subjects that allowed their pictures to be attacked as Catholic or High Church—by 1853 scenes of contemporary life dominated their output. *Punch* could even reverse its view and hail them as champions opposing revivalist High Church heresies.[37] In 1855, the South Kensington Museum, as part of its declared aim of providing an encyclopedic account of the history of ornament, made its first acquisitions of illumination, reinforcing the neutral quality of illumination a source for design. The work that underpinned the educational movement led by the museum, Owen Jones's *Grammar of Ornament* (1859), promoted the autonomy of design by surveying ornament from every known society on the basis of equality (figure 149). Medieval illuminated ornament from all European countries was necessarily included, even if the essential Britishness of ornament in England had to be stressed (the remarks take their cue from architecture but by association were applied to illumination): "Early English ornament is the most perfect in principle and in execution, of the Gothic period. There is as much elegance and refinement in modulations of form as there is in the ornament of the Greeks. It is always in perfect harmony with structural features, and always grows naturally from them. It fulfils every one of the conditions which we desire to find in a perfect style of Art." Illumination was now safely English. If the excellence of the art and illumination of Edward III's reign had long been trumpeted by chauvinistic accounts of artistic development, such as that of Sarsfield Taylor in the 1840s, it now became possible to construct a complete history of illumination that was indigenous. The Reverend William Loftie (1839–1911), author of many tourist guides and editor of the successful "Art at Home" series in the 1870s, insisted in 1876 that "we had a school of art in England in the 12th and 13th centuries such as we have never had since"; the beauty of thirteenth-century English illumination "can hardly be exceeded"; he was also pleased to show that Anglo-Saxon illuminators surpassed those in Ireland responsible for the *Book of Kells*.[38] For the designer, this latter manuscript represented a peak of achievement uncomplicated by its national origin—Digby Wyatt, "one of the most accomplished living artists," had broken down in despair when trying to copy some of its ornament.[39] As illumination became considered a national art, any hint of Irish origins had to be explained away. Made acceptable as design, illumination could be incorporated into national history. It was under the banner of "Design" that the effusion of historicist revivals of historical styles took place in the mid–nineteenth century: it was the mission of the design movement to apply standards to the styles and ensure that "unacceptable taste" did not intrude. All the styles had to be shorn of unwanted associations to be made fit for their contemporary function. Illumination had to prove itself both as design and as a national art, with the result that the rhetoric of naturalism and Englishness has to be invoked. By 1874, the *Art Journal* had no doubt that "the vigour and bold character of English illumination" became lost as foreign schools were imitated in the fifteenth century.[40] If this represents the "naturalization" of illumination, part of the credit must go to John Ruskin, the greatest art critic of nineteenth-century Britain.

**John Ruskin's Moral Rejuvenation of Illumination**

On the whole, Ruskin was hostile to the kind of illumination purveyed by the gift books of the 1840s. His dismissal of the illuminated books in embossed covers of the kind shown in Holman Hunt's picture *The Awakening Conscience*, exhibited at the 1854 Royal Academy exhibition, was damning: they were "vain and useless . . . new . . . marked with no happy wearing of beloved leaves"—they were books acquired for show and not for reading.[41] Pugin had endowed Gothic style with the moral purpose of medieval Christendom, just as Alexis-François Rio (1797–1874) in his work *L'Art Chrétien* (1836), translated into English in 1837, had described the thirteenth and fourteenth centuries as the height of Christian art, when the artist's workshop was also an oratory and the quality of production governed by the quality of faith.[42] Ruskin's espousal of thirteenth- and fourteenth-century illumination was similarly to infuse it with moral qualities, but ones in line with his philosophy rather than with the sectarian religious positions of Pugin and Rio.

In *Praeterita*, the autobiography written toward the end of his active life, Ruskin dated his interest in illumination to his first acquisition, made in 1850 or 1851, of a fourteenth-century Book of Hours. "The new worlds which every leaf of this book opened to me . . . cannot be told . . . a well-illuminated Missal is a fairy cathedral full of painted windows" (see also the discussion in chapter 3).[43] After inspecting the collection of the duke of Hamilton in 1853, Ruskin worked systematically through the holdings of the British Museum—he was not the sort of man to be content with using published facsimiles. In the third volume of *Modern Painters*, a work originally undertaken to defend Turner, Ruskin founds a view of art upon the illumination of the period 1200 to 1350. The received view of the period obeyed Vasari in talking of a renewal of art at the time of Giotto in fourteenth-century Italy and of subsequent progress to the perfection of Leonardo, Michelangelo, and Raphael in the sixteenth century—by this model the illuminator Giulio Clovio, a colleague of Raphael, represented the high point of illumination. This was the scheme adhered to by Madden and Shaw in *Illuminated Ornaments* (1833); Digby Wyatt in *The Art of Illuminating* (1860) is less insistent, finding merit at any period after "the miserably low pitch" of the twelfth century, but he does not alter the scheme. To these canonical views, Ruskin in 1856 sets up the period 1200 to 1500, and more particularly 1250 to 1350, as the summit of achievement, modern art after 1500 going "downward."

For Ruskin, illumination provided an agenda for *action*. He thus maintained the approach of Humphreys, Jones, Wyatt, and others for whom the introduction of the art was to help modern practitioners. In volume 3 of *Modern Painters*, published in 1856, he discussed the decorative use made by thirteenth- and fourteenth-century illuminators of ornament based on botanical forms: understanding of botanical science enabled illuminators to create decoration that was truthful and expressive. There was a "peculiar modification of natural forms for decorative purposes . . . seen in its perfection"; there was an understanding of the natural and a translation into a formal decorative scheme revealing "the expanding power of joyful vegetative youth." Examples given were of thirteenth- and fourteenth-century ornament, which surely to late-twentieth-century eyes looks abstract and schematic, aware as we are today of how they were produced serially by rote and paid for by the dozen or gross (figure 113). Their abstract character is explained by the symbolic nature of medieval art at this time: Ruskin refers to a "crisis of change in the spirit of medieval art" around 1400, when the symbolic character of art became increasingly invaded by a spirit of imitation, a spirit which developed into the Renaissance. The depiction of rocks in landscape, schematized or natural, was another feature of illumination to illustrate Ruskin's theme. He was elaborating the theme explored in volume 3 of *The Stones of Venice* (1852): here

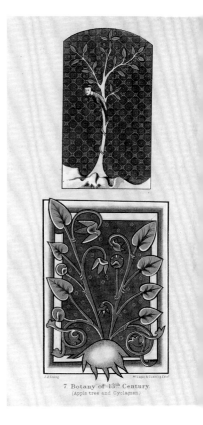

113.

John Ruskin, "Botany of the Thirteenth Century— Apple Tree and Cyclamen," from *The Works of John Ruskin* (1903–12)

Ruskin compared the chaste, restrained abstract ornament of fourteenth-century French illumination with the wanton "luxurious curvature" of a fifteenth-century Italian border—luxury led to moral depravity.[44]

Ruskin established illumination as a specific category of art governed by its own laws. He had little sympathy with its function as a resource for the rigid program of outline drawing and shading that was the basis of the art education of the South Kensington Museum, a dehumanizing process based on prescriptive exercises carried out with military precision that contrasted with his own drawing method founded on representation of light and shade. In lectures in 1854, he described fourteenth-century illumination in terms of graduated color within an outline and without shadow. Though he protested against the appropriation of illumination by those engaged in the popular pastime of flower painting, he insisted that in illumination "there might be as much perception of nature in working out these mere outlines as in working out a fully shadowed drawing." The importance of illumination was such that Ruskin had to expand his definition of nature to include it.[45]

Linked to Ruskin's notion of illumination was a specific idea about the nature of the illuminator himself. Like the Gothic mason described in *The Nature of the Gothic*, the illuminator was taken as the model of the free worker, directly in control of his work and finding reward in the exercise of his art, and above all free of the constraints associated with nineteenth-century factory employment.[46] Just as a mason had to be found to match Ruskin's theories—James O'Shea was called from Cork to decorate in situ the windows of the Oxford Museum in 1870—so illuminators had to be conjured up. Throughout his active life, Ruskin spent large amounts of his own considerable fortune in employing people to copy works of art, from frescos to buildings and manuscripts, that were either in danger or of which he needed copies for teaching. Where manuscripts were concerned, those copyists were illuminators. Thus Henry Swan, a former student at the Working Men's College (he introduced the bicycle into England), was employed to copy manuscripts in 1855, one of them to be sent to the celebrated reformer Octavia Hill. J. J. Laing similarly made copies for Ruskin—his expertise led him to cooperate with the publication of Bradley's illuminating manual in 1861. In 1855, Ruskin actually talked of founding a school of copyists with William Ward, one of his students from the Working Men's College, where he had taught since 1854. His notion was to set up a community of art workers to copy manuscripts and make facsimiles of old pictures and buildings. It was to be a "Protestant Convent Plan"—the choice of words bears an obvious reference to Anglican nunneries. The same idea lay behind his plan to set up the Guild of St. George. Established in 1870 in the industrial suburbs of Sheffield, the guild, with its museum and teaching program, created a community of copyists. Ruskin considered his relations with the guild a spiritual pact, but he also paid them for copies between 1870 and 1890.[47]

Ruskin's correspondence likewise shows him encouraging friends in both drawing and illuminating. It is clear that he conceived it as particularly suitable for women. He wrote to Lady Trevelyan in 1854 that sign writers and above all young ladies should be taught illumination; all prayer books ought to be written by hand. Ruskin's correspondence with Louise, marchioness of Waterford, refers to drawing rather than illumination when art is mentioned, but it must be more than a coincidence that this devout woman of High Church loyalties is revealed as an accomplished illuminator with the publication in 1884 of her *Life Songs, Being Original Poems Illustrated and Illuminated by Louisa Marchioness of Waterford*.[48] At the Architectural Museum in November and December 1854, Ruskin developed his theme, proposing, with the enthusiasm of the recent convert, that shop fronts might be systematically decorated with illuminated letters. That illuminated styles were actually used in this way is suggested by Willis Brooks's insistence in 1864 that the calligraphy of painters and glaziers on the fronts and signboards of shops and public houses could in no way be admitted to the category of illumination.[49] Ruskin's dispatch of Henry Swan to give lessons in illumination to Adelaide Anne Proctor again shows Ruskin's promotion of this womanly art. Behind all this was the idea that the skill could be developed as a means of providing people with a livelihood. That these ideas had some currency is indicated by the fact that the *Illuminator's Magazine* of 1862 found it necessary to insist that proper illumination could only ever be executed by amateurs on account of the time needed "for the minute manipulation of highly-finished illuminations."

Ruskin's educational work—teaching at the Working Men's College in 1854 to 1858, at the Winnington girls' school in the 1860s, and at Oxford as Slade Professor in the 1870s—all involved the use of copies of images. He took great care at Oxford to provide teaching materials for students. Facsimiles of manuscripts as well as leaves of originals were selected and dispatched to the Oxford school and to the Guild of St. George in Sheffield. Oxford received leaves from his precious thirteenth-century *St. Louis Psalter*. Quite apart from his own ventures in Oxford and Sheffield, Ruskin provided thirteen other schools with materials for art education. The girls at Cork High School had to copy for him initials from facsimiles of the *Book of Kells*. Here and in other cases, Ruskin's presentation of illumination was clearly driven by a moral purpose. Ruskin aimed "to put the narcissism of an alienated class to use and, at the same time, foster cultural discrimination in artisans and labourers"; in the *Fors Clavigera* letters addressed to the working classes, Ruskin made clear his aim to merge education with religious observance and prevent the corruption involved when education became entertainment.[50]

William Morris, an avid reader of Ruskin since his undergraduate days, developed the idea that men's labor should be under their own control. His vision of the medieval craftsman as someone gaining satisfaction from control of the process of manufacture parallels Ruskin's view. Morris was a prolific illuminator himself, a means of investigating the processes used by medieval illuminators and of providing fitting vehicles for his favorite texts. He was at one with Ruskin in presenting the medieval illuminator as a free workman, operating within a tradition policed by the craft guilds that were the guarantors of the skill, invention, and beauty of the finished work. Like Ruskin, he distanced himself from popular illumination: the cult of missal painting was "sham gothic." He shared Ruskin's belief in the virtues of copying. In an address of 1880 as president of the Birmingham Society of Arts, he talked of the kind of museum that should be founded. There was to be a library, to include illuminated manuscripts; these and other things were to be the basis of a school of copying. As a graphic designer, Morris's work owed little to illumination, and the practical applications of his floral designs were wallpaper and curtains rather than illustration and facsimile: society was not to be saved by the practice of an art form but by new forms of cooperative organization that brought dignity, satisfaction, and profit to the worker.[51]

The much-quoted anecdote about Ruskin, to the effect that he spent evenings in 1853 cutting up missals ("hard work") appears shocking today, but it is totally explicable in an environment where it was axiomatic that exposure to art promoted the moral rejuvenation of society: it was a "shame to see a work of art put into a book," according to Ruskin, because it limited the potential exposure of contemporaries to this improving art.[52]

**Mass Marketing Illumination**

The practice of illuminating flourished at levels of society with which Ruskin and Morris had little experience. Charlotte, queen of George III, was much given to copying out texts and decorating them. Her daughter, Princess Elizabeth, when married to the *landgraf* of Hesse-Homburg, decorated in watercolor a text of a prayer book composed in the sixteenth century for Queen Elizabeth I. The decoration is Regency in style, based on palmettes, tightly rolled acanthus leaves, and crowns. Victoria's daughters were all taught drawing as part of a training in art considered integral to a good education. The eldest, Victoria (the princess royal, born 1840) was illuminating from at least the age of fifteen, under the instruction of Albert Warren, a pupil of Owen Jones and doubtless recommended by him. The princess royal's younger sister, Princess Alice (born 1843), was particularly expert and continued to produce illuminated sheets in Germany after her marriage in 1862 to Prince Louis, later grand duke of Hesse-Darmstadt.[53]

Queen Victoria, for all her medieval enthusiasms (as, for example, the famous medieval ball of 1842, in which she and Albert represented Edward III and his queen, Philippa of Hainault), was no sympathizer with High Church values. That illumination was chosen as a pursuit for her children in the 1850s was a powerful endorsement of its respectability. The royal example contributed to a view of illumination as an area of private experience, of intimacy and femininity; illuminated works were carefully displayed so that discreet glimpses might be had to advertise the rich inner life and artistic sensibilities of the owner. The carefully composed photograph of the boudoir of a young woman, possibly in Muckross House, Ireland, attributed to the Honorable Henry Herbert (1840–1901) and datable to circa 1860, shows illumination as suitable decoration for the most private of all domestic spaces (figure 114).[54] Literary allusions make the same point. In Menella Bute Smedley's novel of 1864, *Linnet's Trial*, the young Rose Forrester, discovering that the attractive Mr. Brandon is interested in the worldly widow, Mrs. Damer, composes herself; her brother, who has freed himself from parental control to become a respectable artist and sculptor, has a wife who comforts Rose: in conversation, the former admits she would rather die happy than learn a disagreeable truth. Rose retorts that the words "the truth shall make you free" are the greatest in the Bible: "That shall be the text which I choose to illuminate and hang up in my bedroom and look at every day."[55] Illumination is represented as intensely personal, characteristic of the bedroom and boudoir rather than the social areas of the house; it guaranteed the deeply felt nature and authenticity of the sentiments contained in the text. The remark of a minor novelist emphasizes the position of illumination as denoting honesty, sincerity, humility, and gentility—and the context juxtaposes this to the worldliness and material ambition of an irresponsible young man and a widow, the latter almost dangerous by definition. The illuminated manuscript becomes a convenient shorthand in a picture by an artist named Oakley (known as "La Port"), a piece that portrays the last moments of Prince Albert on his deathbed in 1861: while doctors and the prince of Wales, holding his father's hand, crowd on the left side of the bed, Victoria and her children make a group on the right, where an opened prayer book illuminated in gold and red lies on a stool (figure 115). The chief female mourners are thus circled around an illuminated manuscript at a moment of national crisis. Queen Victoria objected to the distribution of an image depicting such an intimate moment and tried to prevent the Art Union from circulating colored lithographic copies in 1869. The use of the illuminated manuscript to characterize the intimate quality of the scene and the heartfelt nature of sentiments experienced was doubtless understood by those who paid one pound, one shilling, for their copy.[56]

**114.**

**Honorable Henry Herbert,**
***Boudoir of a Young Woman***
**(circa 1860)**

Of all the hobbies proposed to nineteenth-century consumers, illumination had the advantage of signifying morality and gentility. The commercial potential of these associations were soon to be exploited. Printing was being promoted
as a suitable occupation for women in the 1860s. Illumination was linked to the
celebrated Victoria Press, funded and established in 1860 by Emily Faithful, daughter of Ferdinand Faithful, rector of Headley in Surrey. The venture was supported
by a number of women who were seeking means of improving the position of
women both legally and by providing channels for financial independence. In 1862,
Emily Faithful was granted the title "Printer and Publisher in Ordinary to Her
Majesty" after the publication of *Victoria Regia*, an anthology edited by Adelaide
Anne Proctor, the protégé of Ruskin. Major publications of the press were two
illuminated works, *Te Deum Laudamus* in 1863 (figure 116) and thirty-eight texts in
1872. The illumination was by Esther Faithful Fleet (1823–1908), elder sister of
Emily Faithful and wife of John George Fleet (1818–1902), a sugar merchant.[57] The
whole episode reveals both the extent to which illumination was practiced and its
powerful attachment with feminine pursuits.

The case of David Laurent de Lara is particularly revealing of the environment in which the exploitation of illumination for commercial purposes took place.
The author, in 1850, of one of the earliest illuminating manuals, he had evidently
been called on to teach members of the royal family by 1857, when he was styling
himself "Illuminating artist to the Queen." In 1854, he was advertising courses in
illuminating and lithography: instruction cost one guinea, after which he undertook
to provide employment—"fifty hands immediately in request." His first illuminating
manual had been published by Ackermann and Company, the print seller, which
invested in the publication as a means of selling artists' materials, including those
for illumination. The second edition of 1857, though published by Ackermann's,
makes clear that Laurent de Lara was using the manual to sell his own materials as
well. Later editions were issued by a book publisher—Longman's—rather than a
print dealer, and here the whole marketing effort could be directed at selling Laurent de Lara's wares. His major enterprise was the Illuminating Art Union of London, established in 1857 (figure 117). The organization was described as being in

199

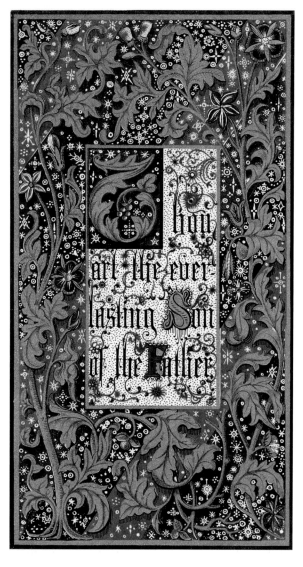

**116.**

Esther Faithful Fleet,
*Te Deum Laudamus*
(London, 1863)

**117.**

David Laurent de Lara,
*Elementary instruction
in the art of illuminating and
missal painting on vellum*
(London, 1857),
penultimate opening

## ILLUMINATING ART SOCIETY.

### (ESTABLISHED 1857.)

For promoting and encouraging the MEDIÆVAL STYLE OF ILLUMINATING ON VELLUM, adaptable for Modern purposes, either Sacred or Secular, by *Annual Exhibitions*, and by publishing one or more Subjects yearly from the Chromo-Lithographic Press, for distribution among its Members.

**Annual Subscription, £2 2s.,**

*(Or £1 1s. if the Number of Members shall exceed Five Hundred.)*

The following distinguished Ladies have consented to enrol their Names as Members and Patronesses :—

THE VISCOUNTESS DUNGARVAN.
THE VISCOUNTESS OF COMBERMERE.
LAURA COUNTESS OF ANTRIM.
BARONESS DE ROTHSCHILD.
LADY NAAS.
LADY DE ROTHSCHILD.
LADY A. LOFTUS.
LADY K. LOFTUS.
LADY ELLEN MACDONNELL.
LADY LOUISA BOYLE.
MRS. WILKINSON.
MRS. CHAUNCY.
MISS DE ROTHSCHILD.
MISS LAURA LANE FOX, &c.

Detailed Prospectuses may be had for Four Stamps.

D. LAURENT DE LARA,
*Manager.*

3, Torrington Square, Russell Square.

The following "ILLUMINATIONS" are to be had on *hire* at the Gallery of Arts, 3, Torrington Square,

| | |
|---|---|
| **Subscription Annually** | **£3 13 6** |
| **Half-yearly** | **2 0 0** |
| **Quarterly** | **1 5 0** |

A splendid assortment of "VELLUM ILLUMINATIONS" are constantly kept on Stock for Sale or Hire to copy from, a pencil outline of each being published at 6d. or 1s. each.

THE ILLUMINATED CHESS BOARD.
THOMPSON'S SEASONS (Three Subjects).
THE LORD'S PRAYER.
THE CREED (Three Subjects).
POESY.
DAVID WITH THE HEAD OF GOLIATH.
DAVID IN PRAYER.
THE ADORATION OF THE MAGI.
THE 67TH PSALM—"Deus misereatur."
SONNET—"It is all a Dream."
Initials P.
Do. Q.
Do. O.
Do. J.
Do. B.
Do. D.

Pencil outlines of the same on Drawing Boards or Vellum, from 6d. to 1s. each. Vellum extra.

*Subscriptions to be paid in advance by Post Office Order to D. Laurent de Lara.*

the care of "lady patronesses" who had entrusted the management of the enterprise to Laurent de Lara—these ladies evidently did not share the view of the *Athenaeum* and others who declared him ignorant of the subject he professed. The patronesses included two viscountesses, one countess, Baroness de Rothschild, Lady de Roth-schild, Lady Naas, and a bevy of noble ladies; by 1863, there were five countesses, three viscountesses, and an even longer list of female noble patrons. The Union boasted over three thousand pupils, "many from the aristocracy"; the annual sub-scription was two guineas, dropping to one guinea by 1863. The *Art Journal* noticed with approval the Union's first annual exhibition in 1859. According to the *Art Journal*, there was already a large demand "among the higher classes of society" for illuminated works: the aim was to increase demand to provide employment "for numbers of highly educated females who, from their social position, are unfit for any menial occupation and whose talents entitle them to be employed in a high-er sphere of labour, suitable to their education, and answering to the purpose of creating a livelihood or increasing a scanty income." The aim to enable "gentle-women of limited income and respectable females in the middle classes of society" to obtain a means of livelihood was applauded. The exhibition, of some eighty pieces, was highly praised, though the illuminators were warned not merely to imitate medieval example, but to create a modern school of illumination. The *Art Journal* found it necessary to comment that Roman Catholics could have their missals illuminated but that "the revived art of illuminating is in no respect or degree restricted to religious subjects, or preeminently associated with them; and missals have not a shadow of a claim upon it in preference to any other class of works."

The *Art Journal* was here doubt-less echoing the publicity issued by Lau-rent de Lara. The survival of the Union indicates its success in its first years, prof-its apparently coming from subscriptions and from the sale and hire of sets of illu-minating colors in boxes, such as the one preserved in Baltimore (Walter's Art Gallery acc. no. 66.2; see figure 118) and outlines for illuminating. Examples of his output can be seen in an illuminated book with the text of Psalm 119 (Victoria and Albert Museum II.RC.J.30; see figure 119). The book consists of twenty-three sheets in what was once a handsome morocco binding; each sheet has gaudy illu-mination in a pastiche of fifteenth-century styles with an admixture of floral ele-ments that look characteristically Victorian; the "off-the-shelf" quality of the work is indicated by the presentation page, where the words "Presented by" and "To" are illuminated, while the names of the giver (Mary S. Phillips) and the recipient (Lewis Phillips) are entered later in ink, and in a conventional copperplate hand. The British Library copy of the work (BL 3090.3.31) has a dedicated title page, printed, dedicating the work to Viscountess Combermere, but the sheets are all printed outlines, each with a small element illuminated in color as a guide to the women assigned to work on the sheet. Laurent de Lara evidently printed numbers of these sheets in outline, each with a guide for coloring, and employed young women to illuminate them to any customer's requirements. It seems likely that Laurent de Lara was in fact running a sweatshop, where "students" paid for their

**118.**

**Boxed set of paints for illuminating (England, nineteenth century), from the London firm George Rowney & Co.**

training and then provided cheap labor for the multiple copies of sheets required for chromolithographic printing or single copies of fully illuminated sheets on order. It was probably to Laurent de Lara that Willis Brooks was referring in 1864 when he spoke of "ladies in depressed circumstances" who were paid "worse than starvation [wages]" by "an adventurer ignorant of the very rudiments of the art he professes to teach." The printers William Day and Son in 1854 had protested Laurent de Lara's methods, which debased the skill needed for the production of chromolithographs, in the columns of *The Athenaeum*. The editor of the magazine regretted that Laurent de Lara's response was too offensive to be printed.[58]

The experience of Laurent de Lara indicates a developing market for illumination. Larger, more firmly based businesses were to become interested in the market in the 1860s. The commercial environment, in particular the marketing possibilities offered by the telegraph, the new railway network, and the new technology of color printing, was favorable. The 1851 Great Exhibition had provided a lesson. Cynics forecasting civil disorder were confounded; those arguing that exposure to art promoted social cohesion were thoroughly vindicated. It gave an indication of the benefits, commercial as well as cultural, of exhibition going. Some nine million people had visited London between May and October, all needing souvenirs and distraction in the capital, and all responding to the same message about what constituted taste and how the individual might gain it. From early in 1858, a rerun was being organized for 1861—and ultimately took place in 1862.

Illumination barely figured in the 1851 exhibition—the medieval court to which Pugin contributed might seem today a landmark in the revival

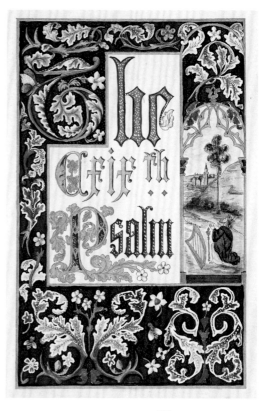

119.

David Laurent de Lara,
*Psalm 119*
(England, 1866)

of interest in medieval artifacts, but it raised difficult questions about its suitability on ideological grounds. The *Times* had to be warned not to make this element of "Papist art" in the showpiece of the Protestant nation the butt of an anti-Catholic campaign. Illumination did not figure in the medieval court, but there were incidental references to it elsewhere. Exhibits in class 17 of the 1851 exhibition show illumination as a style used by designers and printers for stationery and the decoration of book bindings; a designer like Arthur Harrison of Brighton boasted a facsimile of an illuminated prayer by Henry VII among a host of framed medieval heraldic devices.[59]

There was no reason in 1858, when publicity for another Great Exhibition was circulated, to doubt that the capital would see the kind of crowds it had witnessed in 1851. As an occasion for entertainments and selling merchandise from souvenirs to books, the Great Exhibition of 1862 was possibly a more carefully planned affair. Illumination was now respectable and eminently marketable: access to it could be promoted beyond the circle of connoisseurs who collected it or those able to afford expensive works that reproduced in color illuminated manuscripts. Illumination was exactly the kind of little-known art that could be launched in this environment, one that recent advances in printing technology allowed to be reproduced cheaply and in bulk. The catalogue of the 1862 Great Exhibition reproduced a full-page illustration from the Psalms of David printed by

Low and Sampson, a work illustrated with designs by John Franklin in medieval illuminated styles. A large number of printed works reproducing illumination were exhibited, as were examples of medieval and modern illumination. Christopher Dresser, then a teacher at the South Kensington art school, reviewed a whole series of printed illuminated books on display. The *Illuminator's Magazine* for 1862 (a publication significantly subtitled *A Journal of Ecclesiastical Decoration and All the Higher Branches of General Ornament*) reviewed the work of contemporary illuminators. Although it reflected that "illuminative work by English artists is disappointing, and not enough considering its popularity," it described with approval, among other pieces, a calendar by Miss Louisa Wing, the daughter of Caleb William Wing.[60] After 1862, examples of illumination, both printed and manuscript, were regularly displayed at exhibitions. Marcus Ward's address to Sir Benjamin Guinness of 1865 went to the Paris Exposition Universelle of 1867, as did other works this illuminator made for the prince of Wales and the earl of Hillsborough (figure 120). The revived art of illumination in England was fit to be exhibited with Auguste de Bastard's copies of historic illuminated manuscripts.

Early works on illumination were not aimed at a mass market. The large —and expensive—works of Noel Humphreys, Owen Jones, Digby Wyatt, and Tymms mentioned earlier were clearly intended for practicing or aspiring designers and artists. The first account giving advice on illuminating, Noel Humphreys's *Art of Illumination and Missal Painting*, was a more modest affair, advertised by Joseph Cundall at a guinea in December 1848 and sold by Bohn in January 1849 at the same price with a set of outlines for coloring. Bohn was profiting here from Cundall's bankruptcy, having acquired his stock and rights. Even more slight was

David Laurent de Lara's *Elementary Instruction in the Art of Illumination and Missal Painting on Vellum*, published by Ackermann and Company, in 1850 at six shillings; a second edition at the same price appeared in 1857. The work of Digby Wyatt and Tymms, *Art of Illuminating as Practised in Europe from the Earliest Times*, dated 1860 but ready for the Christmas market in 1859, was intended for students and connoisseurs. A landmark in terms of the scholarship of its introduction and the encyclopedic coverage of medieval styles of ornament from the Insular period to the sixteenth century and later, it was a textbook to stand beside Owen Jones's *Grammar of Ornament*, and adopted the approach of the design reformer in providing a series of ornamental details which could be copied and made into complete compositions by the illuminator.

The small-format publication on the model of Laurent de Lara's manual was aimed at a rather different reader, in particular the amateur and above all the female amateur. In the 1860s, such works sold for as little as one shilling. As publishing ventures, they were financed by the major stationers and color manufacturers in London. Jabez Barnard, "manufacturing artists' colourman," produced Edwin Jewitt's *Manual of Illuminated Missal Painting* (1860), Henry Montanelli Lucien's *Hints on Illuminating* (1860), William Randle Harrison's *Suggestions for Illuminating* (1863), Albert Warren's *Guide to Beginners in the Art of Illumination* (1861), as well as the *Amateur Illuminator's Magazine and Journal of Miniature Painting* (1861–62), issued monthly in parts; they also produced pattern books for illuminators by F. G. Wood, Victor Touche, and others. Winsor and Newton produced what was to be among the most long lasting, John William Bradley's *Manual of Illumination* (1865), at one shilling; by 1863 the eleventh edition had appeared. Rowney and Company produced a work by the architects William and George Audsley, *Guide to the Art of Illuminating and Missal Painting* (1861) in formats costing from one shilling to two shillings and sixpence. Day and Son recycled sections of their 1860 publication, the monumental *Art of Illuminating as Practised in Europe from the Earliest Times*, under the titles *What Illuminating Was* and *What Illumination Should Be* in 1865 at one shilling and sixpence. These works, with color plates and selling at between one and two shillings, were published in multiple editions until the middle of the 1860s. They had greater lasting power than similar works produced by those in the book trade: Edward and F. N. Spon, "scientific booksellers," according to the *Post Office Directory*, published Delamotte's *Primer of the Art of Illumination* in 1860 with some alphabet books for use as models, but the venture did not last to 1861; the publisher Longman, on the other hand, with greater capital resources, published their version of the genre until at least 1863, when the seventh edition of Laurent de Lara's *Elementary Instruction in the Art of Illuminating and Missal Painting* saw the light of day.

The bulk of publishing of this kind appears to have been in the 1860s, the works of Mrs. Charles Cooper and the architects W. J. and G. A. Audsley in 1868 coming at the end of an impressive run. There was a smaller market for these manuals in the 1870s; earlier manuals continued to be reprinted, but new ventures were rare. Marcus Ward of Belfast published in 1873 an illuminating manual, *A Practical Treatise on the Art of Illuminating*. He had been active as an illuminator in Ireland in the 1860s, training a team of artists to produce copies of chronicles and documents "for various members of the British Royal family, and for the nobility and gentry of the United Kingdom." His commercial success relied on publishing, particularly of children's books, all illustrated and many decorated in illuminated styles; a lucrative contract was a series of drawing books by Vere Foster which were adopted by the national education system in Ireland. Printed ephemera were probably an important part of his business: a sheet for illuminating printed in calligraphic type with a Celtic pen-work initial and borders based on medieval acanthus designs likely stand as an example of a what must have characterized illumination for many people. As with most publishers of illuminating manuals in the 1860s, Ward's publications were only an element of his interest in illumination.[61]

The initial investments for almost all of these manuals were made in the eighteen months or so before the opening of the Great Exhibition of 1862, making it possible that this, together with the continuing development of the Christmas shopping market, was at the back of their producers' minds. The manuals themselves are the tip of an iceberg, the visible remains of a huge marketing operation that comprised books (which can be fairly easily traced today in that they appear in library catalogues); ephemeral publications, such as single sheets; almanacs and so forth; and artists' materials, from special papers and prepared sheets of vellum to a huge range of pigments, in boxed sets or singly. Behind this, there was another phenomenon: the appearance of teaching classes offered at all levels of society. Laurent de Lara has been mentioned—Richard Thomson in 1857 declared that his publications were designed to lead students to the teacher. Caleb William Wing, celebrated today as a restorer of manuscripts and maker of facsimiles, was probably typical of many minor artists involved with illumination in giving lessons —he is seen advertising classes during the holiday season in fashionable Brighton in 1859; Frederick Curtis, "teacher of drawing, illuminating and designing," was proposing similar classes in Brighton at the same time.[62]

The *London Review* for September 1861 referred to illumination as "a charming female accomplishment," and *Building News* of October in the same year described it as "an elegant occupation for the fairer half of mankind." The link between illumination and femininity went further than its suitability as a drawing room pursuit. The art had a particular relevance for color printing, one which Laurent de Lara appears to have been exploiting. Chromolithography had been perfected since Owen Jones's works in the 1830s, but only in the 1860s did it become widely used in the printing industry. Chromolithographic printing processes required skills which were those of the illuminator. The printed image needed colored artwork as the first stage in the process, and each color required a separate printing stone with the necessary pigment applied to the appropriate area of the image involved. Women were particularly suited for this labor-intensive work: it was genteel, and women were cheaper to employ. The nascent South Kensington Museum as early as 1852 had classes in chromolithography "for female students only"; the students were to provide illustrations for a catalogue of the museum's collections, "thus aiding the production of a useful work . . . acquiring the knowledge of an art peculiarly suitable to them, and for which there is an increasing public demand."[63]

An indication of the range of work undertaken by a woman not inconceivably trained by the South Kensington system is seen in the album of a professional illuminator and decorative artist, one Miss A. E. Gimingham (figure 121).[64] The album contains printed trade cards, sketches of work done, printed and manuscript designs either done by Miss Gimingham or collected by her for reference, as well as catalogues of suppliers of colors and stationery. Dated pieces range from the 1840s to the 1870s. There is a private view card for the exhibition of Sir George Hayter's picture of the christening of the prince of Wales in 1842, with Gothic letters decorated with pen work flourishing, printed in gold and other colors, and with an elaborate illuminated frame; a similar invitation to see the picture of the Nativity of Our Lord by Pierre Van Schendel was printed in medieval letters with floral ornament. The trade card of A. and F. Sewell, Upholsterers and Decorative Painters, was printed in blue and gold with an extravagant illuminated initial and floral ornament. A label for paper, "Thick satin superfine cream laid, five quires," was printed in two colors with illumination worthy of Owen Jones. The small trade card of Edward A. Jones, House Decorator, of Bedford Square, London, has rich borders with geometric and spiral designs in red, blue, green, and gold. Most impressive is the card chromolithographically printed by "Engelmann et Graf" for the "Papeteries Marion" in London and Paris, "Maison spéciale pour les beaux papiers élégament ornés d'emblèmes de chiffres ou d'armoiries, et Pendules," replete with illuminated floral designs and medieval dragons. Such pieces represent commercial use of illuminated styles to create an exclusive aura for goods and services sold.

Illumination found a special role after the early 1860s in the illuminated address (figures 122, 123 and plate 28). These colorful documents testify to a widespread adoption of illumination as a veritable folk art, one which proclaimed the sincerity, honesty, and moral virtue of both giver and receiver. They were offered by tenants to a landlord when he became of age, married, or returned from the

121.

Miss A. E. Gimingham,
sheet from an album
(England, circa 1860–80)

wars; they were presented by employees to factory owners as they retired; they were dedicated by members of a party to a member of Parliament; they were handed over to a retiring magistrate by his colleagues; they greeted senior bureaucrats when they made official visits to hospitals or schools. At the time of Queen Victoria's jubilee of 1887, over two thousand were sent to Victoria from all over the British Isles and the British Empire; a larger number was sent for the 1897 jubilee. The addresses could be major works. That commissioned from Lewis Foreman Day by the Royal Society of Arts and sent to the queen in 1887 cost thirty-one pounds, fifteen shillings, sixpence. Henry Shaw was reported to have excelled in them. Edward Offer in 1875 could talk of a career of nearly forty years of "illuminating testimonials and addresses" in London, producing over four hundred of them. The *Art Journal* praised Offer's designs in 1868, commenting "this is an age of 'testimonials' of every description." Offer mentioned that he began his career working on chromolithographs for the catalogue of the Great Exhibition in 1851, again showing the related nature of illumination and the printing industry.[65]

The makers of illuminated addresses advertised their skills in the London *Post Office Directories* under the rubric "Illuminator." They were almost invariably engaged in trades relating to stationery and printing. By 1914, companies such as Blades, East and Blades, Smith, Kay and Company, and Waterlow Brothers, each with several retail outlets in London, dominated production. Its commercial associations meant that illumination had to be re-created as an artistic pursuit. In the 1860s, the *Art Journal* had encouraged illumination and its contemporary uses; by 1882 it deprecated modern illumination and pointed to medieval works as models of excellence.[66] Margaret Armour in *The Studio* of 1896–97 made an impassioned

122.

Illuminated address,
presented to William Reed
by the employees of
Messers Edward Shaw &
Company, Flax Spinning Mills
(Celbridge, County Kildare,
Ireland, 1877)

123.

James Orr Marples,
illuminated address presented
to Mrs. Matilda Madden
(Liverpool, 1900)

plea for artistic standards to be applied—her remarks reveal the concern of those
associated with the Arts and Crafts movement to reform taste in society at large:
"The illumination of addresses to eminent people, or for public functions such as
jubilees, 'freedoms' of cities, welcomes, majorities, testimonials, etc. . . . [is an]
outlet [that] might attract many genuine artists, were it not given over to 'ticket-
writers' and such avowed tradesmen. The commissioning of illuminated addresses
is largely in civic hands . . . vulgarity creeps in at every point, in the crudeness of a
tint, the hardness of a contour, the falseness of a balance, the unlovely sweep
of a line. But the most debasing touch of all is the substitution of photographs for
miniatures." Illuminators of whom she approved included Edmond G. Reuter,
W. B. Macdougall and E. Clegg, and Phoebe Traquaire. Traquaire's work was
shown at the exhibitions of the Arts and Crafts Exhibition Society. Indeed, Ruskin
too esteemed her artistry. When she sent illuminations, including *The Dream*, to
the critic, he held onto them, finally returning the pieces with a note reading:
"At last I return the beautiful leaves I could not resolve to part with" (figure 124,
plate 29).

Edward Johnston eventually redefined the nature of illumination and
calligraphy by careful examination of medieval practice; art of this kind was established at the heart of the Arts and Crafts movement, properly endowing it with
the ruralizing, homely design philosophy that proclaimed emancipation from historicism and aesthetic exoticism. Johnston also established illumination and calligraphy as an aspect of art school training. Introduced to the subject by the architect
W. H. Cowlinshaw, he began teaching at the Central School of Arts and Crafts
in 1899 and at the Royal College of Art from 1900. Lettering was his primary
concern, but illumination was a major part of the work of his followers, and classes in it became part of the standard diet of those art schools oriented toward the
Arts and Crafts until the 1950s.

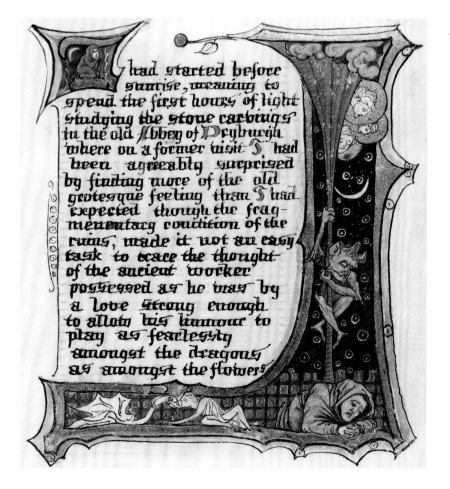

124.

Phoebe Traquaire,
*The Dream*
(Edinburgh, 1886–87)

## ILLUMINATION AS EDUCATION: THE GROWTH OF
## THE SOUTH KENSINGTON COLLECTION

The foundation of what became known as the South Kensington Museum in the wake of the Great Exhibition of 1851 was part of a major educational project funded by the British government. The aim was on the one hand to provide source materials for those involved in manufacture, and on the other to encourage more discerning consumption by the education of public taste. Attached to the nascent museum was an a school for art teachers, the head of a national network of over eighty art schools throughout the British Isles by 1861. Under Henry Cole and, until 1863, J. C. Robinson, the museum set out to compile an encyclopedia of art and design in any available medium, from original works of art to plaster casts, electrotypes, photographs, pictures of famous monuments or decorative schemes commissioned from artists, facsimiles of paintings and ornament of all kinds, and publications. The Great Exhibition of 1851 had included printing and books as a category of artifacts displayed, making it natural for the museum to collect materials that documented the  history of the way books had been decorated in the past. Before examining the nature of what was collected by way of illumination, it is worth seeing what possibilities there were, in the nineteenth century, of seeing original illuminated works.[67]

In practice, access to the collections of the British Museum Library, and other repositories such as the Bodleian Library in Oxford, was confined to the "more respectable classes." Provision for those termed artisans was felt to be deficient by those in government circles. The foundation of the South Kensington Museum and its library was designed to remedy the situation. By the 1860s, most national libraries had put restrictions upon access to their most famous manuscripts. The British Museum protected its greatest works by placing them in the category of "select" manuscripts. Despite the cheerful assertion of Mrs. Cooper, the author of an illuminating manual of 1868, that Sir Frederic Madden always gave permission when asked, this represented an effort to curb demand. Copying of manuscripts by the public was allowed at the discretion of staff at the British Museum by 1866. As regards exhibitions, the British Museum had a temporary display of manuscripts in 1851 but a permanent one only from 1859—historical works vastly outnumbered illuminated ones, though more were included in the 1860s.[68]

It was from the 1850s that illuminated manuscripts began to be shown in art exhibitions. A few cutout miniatures from the collections of William Roscoe and William Young Ottley were included among the Old Masters displayed at the 1857 Manchester Art Treasures exhibition. In 1861, the Society of Antiquaries of London organized a large exhibition of illuminated manuscripts on its own, though this was for the fellows of the society and their guests. The decision whether to deviate from custom and admit women was left to the society's executive committee, another indication of the assumed link between illumination and femininity.[69] The queen and the archbishop of Canterbury were among the lenders. The "loan exhibition" of 1862 has already been mentioned. The first public exhibition devoted solely to manuscripts was that of the Burlington Fine Arts Club in 1874. William Bragge lent some eighty-four manuscripts; other collectors included the Reverend Russell Fuller and John Malcolm of Polltaloch.[70] Rather more ambitious was the exhibition organized by the Liverpool Arts Club in 1876. Though the Liverpool Free Library and Lambeth Palace Library lent works, most were from private owners, including the Reverend Purbrick of Stonyhurst College, the earl of Derby, Henry Yates Thompson, and the Athenaeum Club. Private collectors such as John

Newton and Joseph Mayer lent both original works and a number of illuminated copies.[71] In 1886, another major exhibition devoted exclusively to manuscripts was held at the Burlington Fine Arts Club.[72] In the autumn of 1896, there was an exhibition of illuminated manuscripts at the South Kensington Museum. The duke of Devonshire lent his *Aethelwold Benedictional*, and the earl of Crawford his copy of *The Siege of Troy* by John Lydgate and "an ancient *Sarum Missal*"; included as well were twelfth-century works from the collection of William Morris, a Bestiary, and the *Huntington Psalter*. The notable art collectors George Salting and David Currie were also lenders. The display of Romanesque manuscripts was appropriate in a museum devoted to providing a complete account of design and the applied arts. Apart from the South Kensington exhibition of 1896, pride of place was inevitably given to fifteenth- and sixteenth-century illumination from France and Italy: Don Silvestro dei Gherarducci and Giulio Clovio were the heroes, the names of famous connoisseurs and collectors such as Ottley and Samuel Rogers mentioned in the catalogues. The Burlington Arts Club exhibition of 1908 was designed to break this mold, in emulation of the display of illuminated French manuscripts in the 1904 Paris exhibition of "Primitifs français": apart from French and Italian manuscripts, Sydney Cockerell included over eighty manuscripts to document "all the stages of the national style" in Britain from the tenth to the fifteenth centuries. As much as anything, this exhibition marked a watershed and a break with nineteenth-century attitudes. Roger Fry in the *Burlington Magazine* pronounced that the high point of illumination was the twelfth century, the fifteenth century showing a "steady loss of artistic control," liable to produce works "as bad in taste and as deliberately vulgar as anything the mid-Victorian epoch discovered."[73]

The exhibition-going public thus had periodic access to illuminated manuscripts. But the enthusiast also had access to a collection of illuminated manuscripts in South Kensington, provided for them through the Board of Trade and its successor from 1856, the Committee of Council on Education. Illumination had a minor but assured place among material collected by the museum in its first years. In 1855, referring to illumination, the museum declared that "it possessed as yet no characteristic specimens; it is intended, however, to collect a limited series." Illumination was included among the graphic arts, along with prints and typography. Apart from work of this kind displayed permanently in the museum that opened its doors in 1857, there were five distinct sets of "illuminated, engraved and typographic ornament . . . comprising several hundred specimens . . . mounted in glazed frames" which, as part of the museum's mission, were being circulated from town to town on loan. The museum's first catalogue, published in 1860, refers to these frames in general terms, but also describes individually four pieces acquired by Robinson. These were art objects rather than study pieces for design students, and they reflected Robinson's passion for High Renaissance art. There was a leaf from an early-fifteenth-century Italian choir book, a mid-seventeenth-century montage of fragments from a choir book made for Pope Urban VII, a mid-seventeenth-century leaf from the text of the oath taken by Giovanni Batista Vitturi on becoming a councilor in Venice, and a sixteenth-century altar card. The first three were works from famous collections, those of Dennistoun, Ottley, and Rogers respectively; the last was a work attributable to Giulio Clovio.[74]

Robinson made a clear distinction between these pieces, bought on the London art market and all except one from famous collections, and the mass of cuttings that he acquired after 1855. The bulk of these, which were both of complete leaves and of details cut from leaves, he acquired when in Germany in 1857 and 1858, from dealers such as Joseph Entres (1804–70) in Munich, Selb and Heberle in Cologne, Kruchen in Bonn, and Heinrich Karl Nold (1824–1903) in Nuremberg. The situation in these cities was apparently the same as in Paris, where Delisle described finding leaves cut from illuminated manuscripts from the St.-Martin-de-Tours library among the piles of illuminated leaves held by *bouquinistes* on the banks of the Seine.[75] Complete illuminated manuscripts were also acquired for the South Kensington Museum, but it is striking that until the 1880s, they were acquired for their bindings, this having been one of the categories of objects of the 1851 Great Exhibition that influenced the museum's early categorization of its artifacts—the only exception to this were two large north Italian choir books of the late fifteenth century, works that since the days of Dibden and Ottley had had such prestige with connoisseurs.[76]

Acquisitions of single leaves and fragments were made regularly throughout the nineteenth century; by 1900, there were almost two thousand pieces.[77] Some were bought individually, but ready-made collections were usually acquired. As much as two-thirds of the collection consisted of details of ornament or initials cut from complete folia, usually costing between a few shillings and ten pounds, the rest being complete folia cut from codices. Only in the 1890s did prestigious pieces with a recognized art-historical interest join the collection. Examples of these are a leaf from a mid-thirteenth-century German psalter once in the Ottley collection, acquired in 1893 for twenty-one pounds; the initial signed by Girolamo da Cremona, acquired in 1894 for one hundred pounds; and the *Eadwine Psalter* leaf of circa 1155 to 1160.[78]

In keeping with what was being done with other kinds of objects, facsimiles were acquired as much as originals. From the time of J. C. Robinson's control of acquisitions, there was a conflict between collecting "master-pieces," works of art, and models from which students and the public might learn the history of the various media comprehended by the term "decorative art." Robinson collected four pieces, mentioned previously, that represented artistic excellence. It seems that on the whole, the fragments acquired by him were by nature of examples rather than works of art—he was ever aware of the British Museum's role to acquire important and complete illuminated works. On Robinson's departure from the museum in 1863, Henry Shaw was asked, as an outside expert, to evaluate the illuminations collection. The employment of Shaw was doubtless an implied criticism of J. C. Robinson, who, before losing his post as curator in 1863, had built up the collection. Shaw's verdict was that examples other than German and Italian choir books of the fifteenth and sixteenth centuries were lacking, so that many schools of excellence in Europe were not represented. Shaw proposed to make good the gaps in the collection by handmade facsimiles of the best manuscripts in other repositories; he held that facsimiles "would in many cases have an advantage as objects for study over the originals from their freshness and completeness, as the latter have too generally become more or less deteriorated from constant use, exposure or ill treatment"—the copy in effect was superior to the original after the modern artist had interpreted it, the copy providing the standard for judging the original. Whereas Robinson had acquired small cuttings with details of ornament and initials as study materials for students, Shaw proposed to supply a survey of major illuminated works of art. Shaw's offer was not taken up at once. The museum preferred to wait until after Shaw's sale of facsimiles at Christie's in 1866, when it ordered from Shaw further copies of a large number of pieces described in the catalogue (see figures 51–53, plate 9 and the discussion in chapter 3).

In collecting facsimiles, the museum was acting in the same way as, for example, the Germanische Nationalmuseum in Nuremberg, which sought encyclopedic coverage of important German manuscripts by commissioning copies of works held in other repositories; some were fully illuminated facsimiles, others reproduced only the miniatures in outline—the comment that the latter were mere model sheets hints that illuminated copies were a superior form of art.[79] After acquiring the Shaw facsimiles, the museum continued to buy reproductions of this kind. The names of those supplying them give us an insight, as do the works of Curmer, into a community of minor artists across Europe who before the advent of color printing and photography earned their living by taking commissions for facsimiles and reproductions of famous works of art and architecture. Of facsimiles where we can attach a name, the museum bought from C. W. Wing and Lord Thynne, as mentioned previously, but also from Ludwig Gruner, the Director of the Dresden Academy, Georg Fuchs, C. H. Ruhl, Ernesto Sprega, and Marianecci.

With original illuminated manuscripts, cuttings from illuminated manuscripts, and hand-executed facsimiles of illuminated manuscripts, the museum also acquired *improved* illuminated manuscripts, leaves that had been retouched to make them a fitting guide for the modern student. The leaf from the psalter of 1494 to 1495 illuminated by Georg Beck for the church of Saints Ulrich and Affra in Augsburg (figure 82, plate 20) was probably cut from its parent volume after the abbey's secularization in 1802. Before it was acquired by the Victoria and Albert Museum in 1892, the surface was considerably improved by overpainting. It is impossible to know whether such overpainting was done to deceive or whether it was done to make it worthy of what the nineteenth century demanded of fifteenth-century German illumination. There is no indication that the museum was aware of the overpainting. At twenty-eight pounds, the piece cost the museum only twice the price of a well-executed facsimile.[80] Such improved works had already been acquired by Robinson from Entres, the sculptor and dealer in Munich, in 1857.[81] William Burgess, the architect, may have been typical in improving his medieval illuminated books to achieve the standard expected of illumination: he was perfectly content to have the faces of a fourteenth-century *Roman de la Rose* bought from Quaritch's in 1874 repainted by an illuminator, Horatio W. Lonsdale, and annotated the book to this effect.[82] In the same year, G. A. Audsley was rather more archaeologically correct in showing modern restorations next to original fourteenth-century initials in the Liverpool Art Club exhibition to indicate the original state of the colors—and no doubt to show his skill as an illuminator as well, though this was also shown by illuminations from his *Sermon on the Mount* (London: Day and Son, 1861) that were also displayed.[83] Given the role of the museum's collection as a source for design students, the acquisition of works overpainted was probably not considered problematic: it hardly affected the status of any piece as a guide for students.

After about 1900, the original pieces of illumination within the Victoria and Albert Museum were grouped together, distinguished from the copies as a separate category for the first time. Copies and originals had been circulated throughout the nineteenth century, but the circulating collection from 1908 was made up only of originals.[83] It was revealing of a new respect for original pieces that the justification for the acquisition of facsimiles bought at Sotheby's on March 11, 1899 was that such pieces would save wear on original illumination in the collection.[85]

The system of art education established by Cole and based on the South Kensington Museum grew rapidly. There were eighty-seven art schools in the

British Isles by 1861. By 1899 there were sixteen hundred of them recognized by the government department that ran the museum. The 120,771 students under instruction in that year, as in previous and succeeding ones, were all exposed to the notion that illumination was a major source of ideas for design and art generally. Perhaps not all saw materials from the illuminations collection that was circulated throughout the country. But generations of art students who had then to earn their living took it as axiomatic that the medieval art of illumination had contemporary relevance. The Victoria and Albert Museum possesses a watercolor copy of illuminated ornament, similar to the adornment found in late-fifteenth-century choir books (Victoria and Albert Museum, PDP 173). It is possible that this piece was copied from a fragment in the collection of the South Kensington Museum, a German leaf from the *Mainz Antiphoner* (Victoria and Albert Museum, PDP 4051).

In the reading rooms of the library in South Kensington (where the title National Art Library was increasingly adopted from 1870), "illuminations" were regularly requested beyond the circle of student-teachers based there. The figures of "applications for special permissions" are small, but they give an idea of the relative popularity of different classes of material within the museum. There were two applications for special permissions in 1867 (as against ninety-three to copy plaster casts, twenty-nine for furniture, and sixteen for enamels), thirty in 1868 (as against eighty-six for jewelry, thirty-five for furniture, thirty for Abyssinian objects, and sixty-seven for Mulready sketches), twenty-one in 1869 (as against thirty-six for furniture, twenty-nine for sketches by Mulready, twenty-one for the Raphael cartoons, and twelve for book bindings), and seven in 1870 (as against seventeen for furniture, fifteen for fans, thirteen for plaster casts, twelve for lace, and five for the Raphael cartoons).[86] Illuminations had thus matched the Raphael cartoons in 1869 and outperformed them in 1870. Until the 1920s, the collection of original illuminated works was to grow in the museum, now named the Victoria and Albert Museum, largely to facilitate circulation to art schools. But increasingly, individual manuscripts of artistic excellence, complete codices and not fragments, were acquired, of the kind the South Kensington curators had left for the British Museum Library before the 1890s. A growing body of scholarly articles and books, mostly illustrated, established the notion of the illuminated manuscript as a source for the history of art rather than a source of design or an improving recreation.

# RECONSTRUCTIONS

Recuperation of Manuscript Illumination in
Nineteenth- and Twentieth-Century America

Curiosities, specimens, reproductions, and revivals . . . over the course of the eighteenth and nineteenth centuries we have seen shifting attitudes toward and uses of illumination in France and England. In those countries, political, social, and religious agendas often drove

the attitude toward illuminated works. Illumination functioned as a marker of bygone golden eras in their national histories. But what could such Old World works mean in America, where all medieval and Renaissance objects were imported relics from a remote continent and historical period?[1]

Whereas other sections of this study are organized around different classes of objects and phenomena, our study here focuses primarily on individuals, for on the American stage, it was individual men and women who affected awareness of manuscript illumination, both within the rarefied world of art connoisseurship and in the spheres of public education and mass production.[2] Our first section examines specific collectors of manuscripts and cuttings, each exemplifying a distinctive attitude toward the relationship of the single leaf or cutting to the integral manuscript. New World money allowed these enthusiasts to collect relics of the Middle Ages and Renaissance, tokens of the past that lent an aura of authority and tradition to drawing rooms on this side of the Atlantic. But illumination did not long remain within the oak-paneled rooms of America's elite. Our next section examines the exhibitions of manuscript illumina-

> Who knows but one day or other the Apollo and the Laocoön may attract the future ages in our Capitol; and the horses of St. Mark's leave the banks of the Seine for the shores of the Potomac.
> —LETTER FROM ROBERT GILMORE JR., PARIS

tion and ornament that brought the medieval world to the doorsteps of urban and rural New World citizens alike. These public displays were designed to educate democratically the wider American populace about a remote European past. The final section of this chapter examines the way that medieval ornament was embraced by designers and artists in this country. Although lacking indigenous roots in the United States, and intimately associated with European institutions of church and state, illuminated styles came to connote present-day institutional authority even as they conjured a remote and mysterious age.

## ILLUMINATION TRAVERSES THE OCEAN

**Robert Gilmore Jr. and Illumination as Cabinet Curiosity**

Sources on pre–Civil War amateurs of art in the United States include only scattered references to a taste for the medieval, and apparently there is no evidence of collectors whose primary interest lay in illuminations. The case of Robert Gilmore Jr. (1774–1848), like his English contemporaries Rogers and Holford, seems typical of the early-nineteenth-century interest in collecting works of all kinds—paintings, casts, drawings, engravings, books, minerals and other scientific specimens, as well as a few manuscripts.[3] Gilmore was born to a Scottish émigré in Baltimore and educated in private schools in Amsterdam and on the east coast of the United States. As a young man of means, he was able to undertake the coming-of-age rite of his European counterparts, the grand tour. Returning home an avowed enthusiast of the arts and sciences, he began to amass (and sell) Old Master paintings—generously attributed to the likes of Holbein, Raphael, Leonardo, the Carracci, Hals, Rubens, and Canaletto—along with American works. Supplementing his art collection were the some two thousand volumes of his library, which, in the spirit of Horace Walpole, he housed in a neo-Gothic room complete with stained-glass windows. Among his bibliographic holdings were an estimated twelve illuminated manuscripts, two of which have been identified—an early-fifteenth-century Book of Hours by a follower of the Boucicaut Master (Library of Congress Rare Books and Special Collections, MS 56) and a thirteenth-century English Bible (Princeton University Library, MS Garrett 28), both richly painted.[4] While antebellum America had few dealers specializing in rare books or paintings from Europe, Gilmore did acquire his Book of Hours in his native land—in Charleston in 1807. This acquisition may have been the earliest purchase of an illuminated manuscript within the United States.[5] For Gilmore, medieval books were one of a range of effects collected as markers of Old World gentility. For a class of Americans who equated education with European cultivation, illuminated works functioned as trophies heralding refined taste.

**John Pierpont Morgan and Illumination as Booty**

The Pierpont Morgan Library... houses both the most extensive and the most beautifully selected series of manuscripts existing on the American Continent, and it may truthfully claim

On the whole, the great collectors of France and England tended to have gained their wealth the old-fashioned way—they inherited centuries-old family fortunes. In distinction, the late-nineteenth-century boom in industry in the United States helped generate a fresh breed of financial leaders of the New World. These Gilded Age magnates suddenly found themselves in a position to outbid a fading gentry in the auction rooms of Europe.[6]

The unchallenged leader in this program of cultural transfer was John Pierpont Morgan (1837–

1913). Echoing Napoleon's sackings, which had opened the way for the movement of Italian art to France and England, Morgan, an emperor of the New World armed with fistfuls of gold, sacked the auction rooms of London and transported Europe's treasures across the Atlantic.[7] In addition to outstanding medieval objects, Renaissance paintings, and works on paper, Morgan acquired some 670 manuscripts, creating a rare-books library that challenged the greatest princely and public collections of France and England.

J. P. Morgan was born in 1837 to a wealthy Hartford, Connecticut, family. His father, Junius Spencer Morgan, directed a powerful London-based company, George Peabody and Company, specializing in American securities. In 1854 the family moved to London and J. P. Morgan was sent first to boarding school in Switzerland and then to university at Göttingen. In 1861, at age twenty-four, he returned to the United States and became head of the American branch of his father's prosperous bank. Establishing his own firm, which was to become J. P. Morgan and Company, in the 1880s and 1890s, the steel, coal, and railroad magnate garnered such economic strength that he twice staved off major economic depressions in America.[8]

At his father's death in 1890, Morgan, then fifty-three years old, inherited a $12.4 million fortune and soon aggressively began to amass art. As a collector, Morgan stands as a transitional figure between the Old World and the New. This American with European breeding divided his time between handsomely appointed London and New York residences and, scorning the avant-garde artistic styles of his day, surrounded himself with treasures formerly in the possession of the secular and ecclesiastical princes of the medieval and Renaissance past. As to illuminated works, although the European market for cuttings of miniatures had been long established by the time that he started collecting, Morgan was primarily interested in whole manuscripts. It is worth observing, however, that Morgan did not hesitate to buy single leaves when examples of high artistic quality came on the market, a point made by Roger Wieck, who offers the related observation that Morgan's immense wealth allowed him to prefer the complete manuscript to the cutting.[9] We further suggest that Morgan took special interest in single folia exemplifying styles for which he did not possess a manuscript exemplar.

Echoing Bonaparte's sacking of the Vatican libraries, Morgan, as commander of the economic order of tomorrow, bolstered his prestige by amassing a library attesting to the greatness of an Old World yesterday. It is suggestive that Morgan's first major manuscript purchase was a work intimately associated with the grandest sovereignty of the early Middle Ages, the Holy Roman Empire. In 1899 he acquired the ninth-century Lindau Gospels (M. 1; see figure 145).[10] The manuscript itself, created at the monastery of St. Gall, is written in Caroline minuscule and features ornate openings for each Gospel book as well as canon tables written in gold on purple-dyed parchment. More splendid still is the bejeweled gilt silver treasure binding that houses these luxurious leaves.

If not of imperial provenance, other works in Morgan's collection also bore impressive pedigrees. In 1900, Morgan purchased Theodore Irwin's books and manuscripts, a collection that included the Ottonian *Golden Gospels*, formerly belonging to the duke of Hamilton (Morgan, MS M. 23), and an early-fifteenth-century French Apocalypse made for Jean, duc de Berry (Morgan, MS M. 133). Two years later, he bought the 700-volume library of Richard Bennett. The collection included 110 illuminated manuscripts (mainly of the fifteenth century), 29 of which had been formerly in the collection of the medievalizing designer William Morris (see chapter 3).[11] Among other outstanding works in the Bennett holdings was a volume of thirty miniatures from the Life of Christ (Morgan, MS M. 44), produced in France circa 1200 (figure 68). The work features a series of illuminations entirely free of text that probably originally functioned as the preface to a psalter but that had been rebound by the late eighteenth century as an autonomous work. The volume, transformed in the modern period to suit the tastes of an audience captivated by medieval pictures rather than texts, had previously passed through the hands of some of the most notable collectors of manuscripts—the duc de La Vallière, Jean-François-Auguste Bastard d'Estang (who not only reproduced four of the images in his *Peintures et ornements des manuscrits* but also created a facsimile of the work *Histoire de Jésus-Christ en figures, gouaches du XIIe siècle*), and Ambroise Firmin-Didot.[12]

Given the political and religious ideological functions to which manuscripts had been put in Europe, it comes as little surprise that Old World scholars and enthusiasts of illumination were often outraged at Morgan's massive appropriation of their cultural patrimony.[13] In the early years of his collecting, Morgan housed the bulk of his manuscript holdings in London. But in 1913 he began to move his precious books across the sea to New York, and deposited them in the library of his newly built mansion on Madison and Thirty-sixth Street.

In a review of M. R. James's 1906 catalogue of the Morgan collection, Léopold Delisle, manuscript scholar and *administrateur général* at the Bibliothèque Nationale, comments upon the remarkable movement of works across the ocean:

The taste for illuminated manuscripts has, at this time, changed in ways that could not have been foreseen only a few years ago. It has been acquired by Americans to such an extent that European markets are threatened by the possible emigration of the majority of manuscripts overseas.

Le goût des anciens manuscrits à peintures a pris, en ce moment, des développements qu'on ne pouvait pas prévoir il y a quelques années. Il a pénétré en Amérique . . . et l'Europe est menacée de voir émigrer au-delà de l'Atlantique la plupart des vieux livres d'art qui se présentent sur les marchés de l'ancien monde.

Delisle goes on, however, to commend Morgan for making his treasures available to a broad audience through publications and for allowing first-hand inspection of the works.[14]

Indeed, the New World Napoleon was acutely aware of his obligation to the scholarly community and the general public of Europe. In tune with Morgan's sense of responsibility and respect for the European attachment to patrimony, in 1929 the collector's son, J. P. Morgan Jr., facilitated the retention of the celebrated *Luttrell Psalter* in its native England. This fourteenth-century manuscript, held to be a national treasure from the time that Strutt reproduced its marginal images of farming life in his *Complete Views of the Dress and Habits of the People of England* (1796–99), had been lent to the British Museum in the closing years of the nineteenth century by its then owner, the Weld family. When, in 1929, the book was made available for sale, Morgan Jr. lent the necessary funds to the museum free of interest, feeling that the prized manuscript should never be allowed to leave its native country. Subsequently, the acquisition of the *Luttrell Psalter* became a national cause célèbre in England. The British Museum encouraged public donations toward the purchase of the manuscript, insisting that the loss of this work would be "nothing short of a national disgrace."[15]

The exercise of such munificence was a Morgan family tradition. In 1913, Morgan Sr. left his art collection and library—valued at roughly $60 million— to his son, with the stipulation that the holdings should, in some unspecified way, be made permanently available "for the instruction and pleasure of the American people." About 40 percent of Morgan's art objects—between six thousand and eight thousand works—were given to the Metropolitan Museum. The books and manuscripts, at the recommendation of Morgan's personal librarian, Belle da Costa Greene (1879–1950), remained intact as a collection and, in 1924 the Pierpont Morgan Library was established as an institution for the public with Greene as director.

Greene had been in Morgan's service since 1905, when the magnate had hired her to be his own personal Abbé Rive.[16] She became her boss's personal confidante and trusted agent, and together they sought to amass such treasures that Morgan's library would surpass even the Bibliothèque Nationale and the British Museum.

But while Morgan had fashioned himself as an American emperor of taste, Greene was carrying on a masquerade of her own. As recent scholarship shows, not only did she fabricate the details of her childhood and education, but on the question of her race, she also managed to deceive the elites and intellectuals with whom she hobnobbed. While publicly she would attribute her dark complexion to a Portuguese grandmother, in truth she was the daughter of the first African-American to graduate from Harvard University. Born in Washington, D.C., Belle moved to Manhattan with her family when she was in her early teens. She attended Teachers College but appears not to have graduated and in her early twenties was working as a clerk at the Princeton University Library. It was there that she met Morgan's nephew, who introduced her to his uncle, then on the lookout for a librarian.

Tales of Greene's flamboyance abound. The haute couture gowns she wore to work, her sharp wit, and her romantic liaisons with Bernard Berenson and other art-world luminaries are documented in contemporary accounts. But she is also renowned for the excellence of her connoisseur's eye and the aggressiveness with which she built up the Morgan collection, regularly traveling overseas to secure treasures for the library. During her tenure the Morgans gained some of their greatest masterpieces, including the Gospels of Matilda of Tuscany (Morgan, MS M. 492; purchased 1912), the thirteenth-century English Apocalypse known as the *Morgan Apocalypse* (Morgan, MS M. 524; purchased 1908), and the *Da Costa Hours of Simon Bening* (Morgan, MS M. 399; purchased 1910). After Morgan Sr.'s death, Greene developed the Morgan Library into an institution to serve both the general public and the scholarly community. She organized graduate studies, lectures, and exhibitions and in her twenty-six years as director the library held forty-six public exhibitions (some of the earliest of which are discussed later). Given her own lifelong deception, it is compelling that one of the many projects she undertook was the attempt to lay bare the identity of the late-nineteenth-century French master of the fake illumination, the so-called Spanish Forger (see chapter 3).

Correspondence in the Pierpont Morgan Library shows Greene to have been responsible for one particularly unusual purchase. In 1921 she recommended the acquisition of a manuscript illuminated by the nuns at the abbey of Maredret in the Ardennes, in Belgium, between 1914 and 1915 (Morgan, MS M. 658; see figures 125 and 126, plate 30).[17] Richly ornamented, the work presents a curious amalgam. A handwritten letter to Greene from one of the nuns, Sister Marie

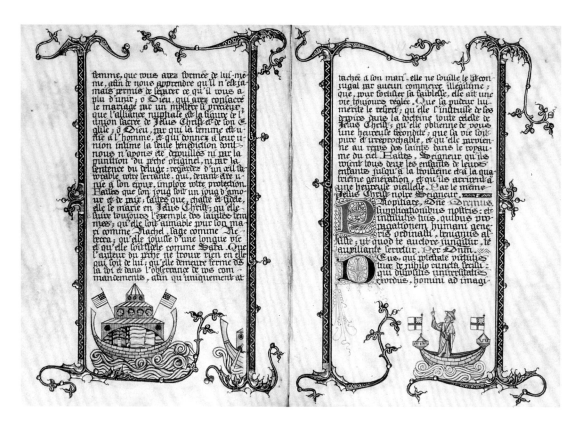

**125–126.**

**Nuns of Maredret,**
**Nuptial Mass**
**(Belgium, 1914–15),**
**illuminated manuscript**

Madelaine Kerger, explicates the work. As stated in a colophon on folio 13, the sisters at Maredret were busy illuminating the manuscript in the opening years of World War I. When the Germans invaded Belgium, the nuns continued their work in secret, hiding the book away because they feared discovery.

Many of the work's illuminations, executed in a fourteenth-century style, present scenes appropriate to the book's text, a Nuptial Mass written in both Latin and French. The folia are filled with matrimonial images of biblical figures and medieval saints, many of which were copied from photographs of original manuscripts. Curiously, however, images of the contemporary war invade the book's margins. The opening folio, for example, presents a large-scale image of St. Albert and St. Elizabeth praying to the Trinity against a background of burnished patterned gold, while below stands a personification of Belgium as a herald bearing the flags of the Allies (folio 1v). The facing page features an initial with the warrior St. Michael with a bas-de-page image of a battalion of mounted soldiers dressed in mail, led by a standing soldier holding in one hand a Belgian flag and in the other a shield that bears the date of the Belgian entry into the war—August 3, 1914 (folio 2v). On a subsequent page we see American ships, floating upon a fourteenth-century-style sea, bringing supplies to Belgium (folios 9v–10r; see figure 125, plate 30). More startling still is the folio featuring alleluia prayers for the Nuptial Mass set to music, beneath which appears an archer dressed as a medieval peasant shooting arrows at zeppelins flying through the air (folios 5r–6r; see figure 126).[18]

In this hybrid manuscript, with its infantrymen garbed as fourteenth-century knights waging the first modern war, the contemporary and the medieval are collapsed into one another. Its compelling juxtapositions suggest an analogy to the Morgans and their collecting. The nuns of Maredret embraced a medieval mode of living, ordering their time according to the precepts of the sixth-century Benedictine rule, but their daily existence was inextricably bound up with the contingencies of the modern world. The Morgan lifestyle and fortune, on the other hand, were engendered by the technology of the modern world; yet the robber baron and his heirs enclosed their domestic lives within an aesthetic sphere of treasures from the medieval and Renaissance past.

**Henry Walters and Illumination as Objet d'Art**

Like Morgan, Henry Walters (1848–1931) tended to acquire whole manuscripts instead of single leaves and, indeed, the two collectors often competed for works in European sale rooms. Starting in the 1890s, Walters transported across the Atlantic more than 700 manuscripts, along with some 340 medieval and Renaissance ivories and small-scale sculptures, not to mention roughly 2,300 other works spanning in date from 3000 B.C.E. to the modern period. Although his reconstruction of a gentlemanly library in the New World is similar to Morgan's activity, Walters's approach to illumination is distinctive. As Wieck recently observed, the Baltimore collector exhibited a particular predilection for jewel-like manuscripts, each treasured as an integral work of art.[19]

Henry Walters's taste for manuscripts can be seen as one facet of his deep-rooted francophilia and early exposure to the art market of Paris.[20] At the outbreak of the Civil War, when Henry was fourteen years old, his father, a Southern sympathizer, moved the family from Baltimore to Paris. With the restoration of peace in 1865, Henry returned to America and gained a bachelor of arts from Loyola College in Baltimore in 1869, a master's from Georgetown in 1871, and finally, a second bachelor's degree in science in 1873.

In his long stays abroad—both during and after the Civil War—Henry's father, William Walters (1819–94), who had made his fortune as a railroad magnate, ardently sought out contemporary paintings and, in his early-adult years, Henry participated in his father's collecting activities. Although William Walters displayed no interest in medieval objects or manuscripts—favoring instead works by currently fashionable late-eighteenth- and nineteenth-century painters as well as Far Eastern and French porcelains—the catalogue of his paintings and sculpture collection reflects an appreciation for the medievalizing publications of his day. The work, issued in 975 copies, some of which were hand illuminated, was designed in a style inspired by William Morris's Kelmscott Press books.[21]

William Walters's taste for collecting was passed on to his son. Early on, it seems, Henry bought a few medieval manuscripts, including a modest late-fifteenth-century Book of Hours created at a northern French atelier, which he purchased for thirty-five dollars (Walters Art Gallery, MS W. 236). But only at his father's death in 1894 did Henry, armed with a fortune gained through investment in the railroad, turn away from the acquisition of works by modern painters and toward luxury objects of the medieval age. In the opening decades of the twentieth century he began collecting exquisite treasury works, such as the early-fourteenth-century Rhenish, silver-gilt chalice with scenes from the Life of Christ (Walters Art Gallery 44.376) and the fourteenth-century German ivory diptych panel, also with episodes from Christ's life (Walters Art Gallery 71.156).[22] During this same period, Walters started to amass works from the leading booksellers of Europe. On his annual trips to Europe, he personally met with dealers of Paris, London, Florence, and Munich—sometimes purchasing as many as 40 manuscripts in a single visit. By the end of his life, the Baltimore enthusiast had acquired more than 730 medieval and later manuscripts, a collection complemented by more than 1,200 incunabula.

The strength of the Walters manuscript collection is in books for private devotion, particularly Books of Hours. In keeping with his Parisian coming-of-age, Walters favored works of French origin, but he also collected important examples from Belgium and Holland. Among his Books of Hours are works now considered masterpieces of their genre, such as the Hours by the Master of the Munich Golden Legend (Walters Art Gallery, MS 288) and the *Bourges Hours* attributed to Jean Colombe and his circle (Walters Art Gallery, MS W. 213).[23] It is impossible to learn the prices he paid; in an interesting spin on the nineteenth-century tendency toward scissors wielding, Walters habitually snipped off the price column of his invoices.

Drawn to the medieval book as integral object, Walters took a particular interest in bindings. He developed a close relationship with the Parisian binder Léon Gruel (1841–1923), who created antiquarian and modern covers for many of Walters's manuscripts and books. Gruel seems to have on occasion re-created his medieval objects to suit the tastes of his modern clientele, removing damaged leaves before rebinding to give his stock a fresh appearance.[24] Though not primarily a dealer, he apparently also acted as art agent for Walters; Gruel and his stepfather and business partner, Jean Engelmann (son of the lithographer Godefroy Engelmann, discussed in chapter 3), jointly owned manuscripts which they sold to Walters.[25]

But two productions by another Parisian binder, Charles Meunier, bring the Walters passion for the object most vividly to life. Published in 1895, O. A. Bierstadt's *Library of Robert Hoe* details the holdings of one of the earliest and most important rare book and manuscript collectors in the United States (discussed below). Walters, or his trusted art agent and family friend George A. Lucas, chose to have this publication itself transformed into an exquisite medievalizing object. In 1899 Lucas acquired a pair of miniatures from a Book of Hours made in the workshop of the early-fifteenth-century Boucicaut Master, from the dealer Seligman, for the high price of two hundred francs.[26] He then had the Paris binder Meunier affix the precious leaves to the upper and lower inside covers of a gilt-

**127.**

**Illuminated leaf from a Book of Hours affixed to inside back cover of O. A. Bierstadt,** *The Library of Robert Hoe* **(New York, 1895)**

tooled, green morocco binding (Walters Art Gallery, MS 795a,b; see figure 127, plate 31), creating a new luxury binding for the Hoe catalogue.[27] In the same period, Lucas had Meunier create a similar binding for another important book that documented the developing class of the American manuscript connoisseur, the catalogue for the 1892 exhibition of illuminated manuscripts at the Grolier Club (also to be discussed later; Walters Art Gallery, MS W. 781a, b).[28] These two Meunier creations —pastiches incorporating genuine medieval illuminations within nineteenth-century medievalizing bindings— enshrined two of the most important and representative books documenting the then-inchoate American enthusiasm for medieval manuscripts.[29]

Aiming to foster a broader knowledge of art, Walters (like Morgan) left his collection to his native city, and, in 1934, the Walters Art Gallery was opened as an institution for the education of the public and the development of scholarship.[30] As the Morgan Library had its Belle da Costa Greene, Baltimore could boast its own queen of the manuscript room, Dorothy Miner. This first Keeper of the Manuscripts at the Walters came from an academic family in New York. She attended the Horace Mann school for girls and then Barnard College. In the late 1920s, she studied illuminated manuscripts at the University of London and then at Columbia University under Meyer Shapiro. Miner, similar to her mentor Greene at the Morgan, was a key figure in making manuscripts available to students, scholars, the academic community, and the general public. A scholar in her own right, she published close to ninety articles, books, and reviews in her lifetime, primarily on manuscripts and early printed books and focusing on works in the Walters collection.[31]

The works collected by Walters attest to his love of the medieval object, and the ongoing activities of the institution bearing his name continue his commitment to the manuscript as integral whole.[32] A striking example of this activity is the Walters Art Gallery's effort to collect the disparate fragments of the Conradin Bible. In 1905, Walters purchased this extensively ornamented thirteenth-century Italian manuscript (Walters Art Gallery, MS W. 152; see figure 32).[33] A favorite of nineteenth-century illumination enthusiasts, the work was at one time in the hands of Bastard d'Estang, who reproduced two of its images in *Peintures et ornements des manuscrits* (Paris, 1837–46). Subsequently, it passed to the collection of Frederic Spitzer and, in 1893, was featured in the six-volume folio sale catalogue of his collection, accompanied by a scholarly analysis by Léopold Delisle. In 1902 it was owned by the Munich book dealer Jacques Rosenthal and then went to Leo Olschki of Florence, from whom Walters bought it in 1905.[34] The manuscript had long been in a fragmentary state, missing not only excised miniatures, but also many undecorated text pages. By the time Walters acquired it, it had been re-

biblica se
lecta

Anno tertio regni io-
achim regis iuda.
uenit nabuchodo-
nosor rex babi-
llonis ierlm.
obsedit eam. Et tradidit dominus in ma-
nu eius ioachym regem iuda. et partem ua-
sorum domus dei. q asportauit eam in ter-
ram sennaar in domum dei sui. q uasa in-
tulit in domo thesauri dei sui. Et ait
affanaz spoto eunuchorum suorum ut in-
duceret de filiis irl'. et de semine regio
q tirannor pueros. in quibus nulla esset
macula. Decoros forma. erruditos in o'i
sapientia. plenos sciencia et erudi-
tos disciplina. et qui possent stare in
palatio regis. ut doceret eos litteras et lin-
gua chaldeor. Et constituit eis rex anno-
nam p singulos dies de cibis suis. et de
uino un bibebat ipse. ut enutriti tribus annis postea starent in conspectu regis.
Fuerunt ergo inter eos de filiis iuda.
daniel. annanias. misael. azarias.
Et imposuit eis spdotus eunuchor
noua. danieli baltasar. annanie. si-
drac. misaeli misaac. misle. Et aza-
rie abdenago. Preposuit aut daniel in
corde suo. ne pollueret de mensa regis.
neque de uino potus eius. Et rogauit
eunuchor spdotum ne contaminaretur.
Dedit aut deus danieli gratiam et misericordiam in conspectu principis eunuchor. Et a-
it princeps eunuchor ad danielem. Timeo
ego dominum meum regem q constituit uo-
bis cibum et potum. Qui si uideret uultus
uestros macilentiores ceteris adole-
scentulis coeuis uestris. condemnabitis
caput meum regi. Et dixit daniel ad ma-
lasar. quem constituerat princeps eunuchor sup daniele. annania. misael.
et azaria. Tempta nos obscero seruos
tuos diebus decem et dentur nobis legumina ad uescendum et aqua ad bibendum.

et contemplare uultus nostros. et uultus
puerorum q uescuntur cibo regio et sicut
uideris. Sic facies cum seruis tuis. Qui
audito sermone huiusmodi. temptauit
eos diebus decem. Post aut dies decem appa-
ruerunt uultus eorum meliores. et corpu-
lentiores. pre omnibus pueris q uescebaan-
tur cibo regio. Porro uas lasar tolle-
bat cibaria. et uinum potus eorum dabat
que eis legumina. Pueris aut his dedit deus scienciam. et disciplinam in omni
libro et sapientia. Danieli aut intelli-
gentia omnium uisionum et somniorum. Com-
pletisq diebus post quos dixerat rex
ut introducerent. introduxit eos spdotus
eunuchor in conspectu nabuchodonosor. Cumque locutus eis fuisset rex non in-
uenit tales de uniuersis ut daniel. annanias. misael et azarias. et steterunt in conspectu regis. omne uerbum sapientie et intelli-
gentie. q sciscitatus est ab eis rex. inue-
nit in eis decuplum super cunctos ariolos.
et magos qui erant in uniuerso regno eius.
fuit aut daniel usque ad annum primum
cyri regis.

II

In anno secundo regni nabuchodonosor
uidit nabuchodonosor somnium et
exterritus est spiritus eius. et somnium eius
fugit ab eo. Precepit aut rex ut con-
uocarentur arioli. et magi et malefici.
et chaldei ut indicarent regi somnia
sua. Qui cum uenissent steterunt cora re-
ge. et ait ad eos rex. Vidi somnium.
et mente confusus ignoro quid uiderim.
Responderuntque regi chaldei syriace. Rex
in sempiternum uiue. Dic somnium seruis
tuis et interpretationem eius indicabimus
tibi. Et respondens rex ait chaldeis. Ser-
mo recessit a me. nisi indicaueritis
mihi somnium. et coniecturas eius peribi-
tis uos et domus uestre publicabuntur.
Si aut somnium et coniecturam eius naran-
ueritis. premia et dona et honorem multum
accipietis a me. Somnium ergo et interpretationem eius indicate mihi. Responderunt secundo
atque dixerunt. Rex somnium dicat
seruis suis et interpretationem illius indicabi-

bound to appear as though it were a complete work.[35] A previous owner had even employed a scribe to insert the title "Biblica Selecta" at the top of the first folio (figure 128) and had a cul-de-lampe inserted at the bottom of a leaf of the text of Lamentations (fol 146v).

The stylistically unique and intensely colored figures from the Conradin Bible must have held particular appeal for nineteenth-century enthusiasts anxious to amass rare specimens of a lost art. Although it seems the manuscript was already in an abbreviated form when Bastard d'Estang owned it, the comte, or some subsequent owner, removed even more of its brilliantly painted illuminations peopled with energetic figures. A note by Bastard's secretary (transcribed by Delisle) tallies a total of 120 miniatures, although the manuscript included only 103 illuminations when Walters purchased it. In the late 1960s Dorothy Miner asserted that roughly 23 of the manuscript's large miniatures had been excised over the years, but recent scholarship suggests the total number of missing illuminations comes closer to 60.[36] In 1966, 5 miniatures were recovered and purchased from the estate of Grete Ring, who had acquired them at a sale in Holland in 1901.[37] In 1981, 30 fragments of the lost portions of the Bible were auctioned at Sotheby's London.[38] Among the works in this sale were 6 interesting cuttings, now in a private collection in Italy (figure 31). This group includes a figure of a dragon—a motif recurring throughout the manuscript—and initials adorned with a gesticulating figure of Jeremiah looking up toward heaven, a fool holding a pot and sponging his own face, and an imposing image of Solomon holding a sword.[39] Under the leadership of Lilian Randall, other cuttings offered at Sotheby's were acquired for the Walters Art Gallery, reuniting the fragments with their parent manuscript.[40] In its efforts to reconstitute the disparate pieces of the Conradin Bible, the Walters Art Gallery is, in effect, undoing the nineteenth-century past—reconstructing a medieval puzzle and recuperating a rare medieval object.

## The Robert Hoe Sale and Illumination as American Prerogative

The earliest American collectors of medieval manuscripts did their purchasing in Europe. Morgan and Walters (as well as others in a select group of collectors in this country) either went abroad themselves or had agents travel to the book-buying capitals of London, Paris, Munich, and Florence. A crucial event that marked the new development of an American supply of and demand for European bibliophilic treasures was the auction of the library of Robert Hoe. Held by the Anderson Auction Company of New York, it lasted seventy-nine sessions between 1911 and 1912, and shocked bibliophiles and the general public alike on both sides of the Atlantic for three interrelated reasons.

First, the works sold fetched unprecedentedly high prices—in the final tally, the 14,588 lots went for $1,932,056.60, more than the combined totals of the sales of the four most valuable English libraries and a sum surpassed only a half century later in the Streeter sale of 1966 through 1969. Second, the Hoe sale demonstrated that collections in the United States had grown to the point that some of the most coveted works of European patrimony were now held by Americans. Finally, this sale was the first public occasion for which substantial numbers of European dealers crossed the Atlantic to bid on Old World treasures.

The Hoe family gained its wealth developing and manufacturing high-speed printing equipment for the expanding book and newspaper trades of the nineteenth century. Robert Hoe III (1839–1909) entered the well-established family business and became head of the firm of R. Hoe and Company in 1886. Under his leadership, the company developed increasingly faster machines as well as presses able to create color illustrations in newspapers. Hoe's interest in rare books and manuscripts would seem to have developed as an outgrowth of the family business of printing the written word. Concomitant to his collecting activity, Hoe took an interest in the history of the book in general, and in 1884, he and eight other enthusiasts founded the Grolier Club for bibliophiles. Hoe served as the club's first president and established the Club Bindery, designed specifically to serve the needs of members.[42]

It was in the 1880s and 1890s that Hoe avidly began to collect books and manuscripts. Through the British agents Bernard and Alfred Quaritch and Ernest Maggs, he purchased heavily at the Beckford (1882–83) and Ashburnham sales (1891 and 1897–98) and assembled a library of riches that rivaled those of his greatest European counterparts. Indeed, Hoe's collection can be compared with that of the duc de La Vallière, amassed a century and a half earlier. Similar to the duc's library, Hoe's expansive holdings covered a wide range of topics—from literature to history to religious works—including many outstanding examples of luxury early-printed books. Again, analogous to La Vallière, illuminated works constituted only a small portion of Hoe's overall holdings; only two hundred of the more than twenty-one thousand volumes in the collection were Western illuminated manuscripts. Among those works, however, were multiple examples of treasured, sumptuously adorned volumes, the majority of which were fifteenth-century French, Flemish, and Italian Books of Hours.[43]

Hoe died in 1909. In his will he stipulated that his library be sold and that the funds be returned to his estate. He left it to executors to select a site for the sale—London, Paris, or New York, whichever was considered potentially most profitable. Until that time, only a handful of important libraries had been sold in the United States (such as the sale of the library of Brayton Ives), and none had attracted many European buyers. The estate, however, recognizing the increasing power or even dominance of Americans in the sale rooms of Europe, settled upon New York as a venue, and after considerable jockeying, the Anderson Auction Company gained the privilege of holding the event.[44]

Until the sale, the Hoe collection had gained little publicity.[45] But in the weeks leading up to the event and throughout the multisession auction, the press was filled with news of the unprecedented presence of European dealers in the United States—including Quaritch and Maggs from London, Madame Théophile Bélin of Paris, and Ludwig Baer of Frankfurt—and avidly documented the astounding prices fetched. Often reported on the front page of the *New York Times*, prices realized for the first round of sales in April and May 1911 totaled $997,366, more than twice the amount seen from the sales of the famous Ashburnham library in 1891 and 1897–98.

Manuscript sales began on the sixth evening of the auction. By that time Henry E. Huntington of California had already broken the existing record for a price realized for a book (until then held by Morgan), paying $50,000 for a Gutenberg Bible printed on vellum; and Morgan had made an impressive showing, offering $42,800 for a nearly perfect 1485 Caxton edition of Malory's translation of *Le Morte d'Arthur*. Sustaining the excitement of the previous days, the manuscript sale had a remarkable start. During the first hour of bidding, ten of the richest works brought in a total of $123,000. Among the buyers was Thirza Benson, granddaughter of Robert Hoe, who paid $24,000 for a Book of Hours created for Anne de Beaujeu, daughter of Louis XI and regent of France in the late fifteenth century.[46] The highest bid of the evening was cast by another Hoe family member. Robert Hoe's son, Arthur, acting on behalf of New York collector Cortland Field Bishop, paid $33,000 for the *Pembroke Hours*. This mid-fifteenth-century manuscript had been created for Sir William Herbert, a partisan of Richard III in the War of the Roses, and contained additional leaves which had been inserted in the sixteenth century.[47]

Another flamboyant American presence at this session (as well as at the sale as a whole) was George D. Smith. More than half of the twenty-seven manuscripts singled out in the *New York Times* report on the morning following the sale had been bought by this New York dealer, often bidding on behalf of Huntington.[48] Most of the works acquired by Smith in this first manuscript session were fifteenth-century French Books of Hours for which he paid, at the low end, roughly $1,500 and at the high end $11,650.[49]

Outbid in many instances by new American money, European dealers did manage to secure some gems. Quaritch acquired a fifteenth-century French Book of Hours, probably from Angers, for what was considered a bargain at $975; Baer of Frankfurt gained a richly illuminated sixteenth-century Book of Hours believed to have been the work of Geoffroy Tory, formerly in the collection of

**129.**

"Ariadne Seated Crying at the Edge of the Water" (nineteenth century [?]) in manuscript of Ovid, *Epistolae Herodium*

the duc de La Vallière, among other esteemed collectors, for $11,000; and Madame Bélin of Paris acquired two celebrated manuscripts, the first a fifteenth-century French volume of Josephus's *History of the Jewish People*, formerly in the Ashburnham collection, for $8,200, and the second the *Burgundian Mirouer Historial de France*, for $6,000.[50] The work purchased by Baer passed first to Cortland Bishop and then to Lessing J. Rosenwald (discussed later) who gave it to the Library of Congress (Rosenwald, LC MS 1318). However, the other prized manuscripts acquired by foreign dealers apparently remained in Europe once rescued from American hands.

During this first manuscript session of the Hoe sale, the contest between Americans and Europeans had manifested itself only in increasingly competitive bids. In the days following the manuscript session, however, hostility between the two groups sharpened in the confrontation between dealers Ludwig Baer of Frankfurt and George D. Smith of New York over the authenticity of a manuscript. The piece in question was a manuscript featuring a French translation of Ovid's *Epistolae Heroidum*, purchased by Smith for ten thousand dollars (figure 129).[51] The catalogue issued by the Anderson Auction Company maintained that the work had been produced for Anne of Brittany and Louis XII in the closing years of the fifteenth century, that the manuscript's twenty-one miniatures were "painted in the best style of the French Renaissance and . . . are undoubtedly portraits from life." But six days after the spectacular night of manuscript sales, the front page of the *New York Times* reported a statement by Dr. Baer questioning the authenticity of both a putative sixteenth-century French binding and the miniatures in the Ovid manuscript.[52] Although he accepted the text as the product of a fifteenth-century scriptorium, Baer was skeptical of the book's purported royal provenance. More damning still, the German dealer suggested that the miniatures in the manuscript were not genuine, but rather the work of an artist of around 1840 who worked in the Nazarene style, perhaps Schnorr von Carollsfeld. Stating that European dealers "who have so much opportunity for studying manuscripts . . . in libraries" would never be taken in by modern fabrications, Baer implied that the high prices paid at the Hoe sale were an index of American naïveté.

Responses to Baer's accusation were quick to follow. Scoffing at Baer's comments, Smith maintained the absolute authenticity of the work and suggested that his German rival made his statement out of disappointment at his failure to gain the chief treasures of the collection: "[T]here is no reason to suppose that there is any foundation for Dr. Baer's contention. He and the other foreign buyers came over here expecting to take their pick of the great Hoe library and they failed to carry off the prizes. They are sore, that's all."⁵³ Commenting upon the events in a piece appearing the following day, W. N. C. Carlton of the Newberry Library stated, "Certain foreign representatives came over to the sale with the idea that they would show us Americans a few things and just wade in and 'clean us up.' Well they didn't, did they? Perhaps they are a little bit piqued over their failure."⁵⁴

The dispute ultimately ended with a whimper. First, a column-long article in the *New York Times* announced that Baer and Smith were to have a conference. The following day a brief notice, hidden on page 10 of the paper, stated that the conference had taken place, but the promised "statement to clear up the whole matter" was not forthcoming.⁵⁵ Today, the present owner, the Huntington Library, accepts the manuscript as a genuine work of the turn of the sixteenth century in France, though with faces and hands heavily repainted in the eighteenth century. Nicole Reynaud attributes the illuminations to Robinet Testard.⁵⁶ The controversy surrounding the miniatures in the Ovid manuscript attests to the state of manuscript connoisseurship at the beginning of the twentieth century. Fifty years earlier, illuminations by modern artists, in some cases, had enjoyed greater esteem than did genuine medieval works. But by the period of the Hoe sale, the market for and study of illuminations—as well as developments in reproductive technology, among other factors—had generated distinctive categories of "fake" and "original."

Although the Hoe sale heralded a new age in which American collectors and dealers could assert their presence upon the world stage, a handful of works in the collection of the printing mogul suggest the endurance of earlier attitudes toward miniatures. Among his extensive bibliographic holdings, Hoe kept five albums of cuttings, some of which functioned as integral luxury objects created to suit nineteenth-century taste. One of the most deluxe of those volumes contained a series of thirty-two historiated initials "apparently cut from church-service books, neatly mounted on black cardboard."⁵⁷ The leaves appear within a luxury binding fit with two fourteenth-century French ivories representing biblical scenes. Another volume containing forty-six miniatures "unfortunately . . . cut following the external line of the design, [some of which were] . . . somewhat rubbed and restored" are housed in an ornate binding featuring richly gilt-tooled dentelle borders and gilt edges.⁵⁸ But cuttings in Hoe's holdings were not limited to the albums of specimens so treasured by nineteenth-century enthusiasts. Toward the end of the Hoe sales, a volume was put on the block that contained eighteen miniatures on paper "copied by order of the Abbé Rive from the most beautiful manuscripts of the XIVth to the XVIIth century in the library of the duc de La Vallière and in the Royal Library" (see chapter 1).⁵⁹ These miniatures created for the never-realized *Essai sur l'art de vérifier* had at some time during the previous century and a half found their way across the ocean to the shelves of one of the grandest libraries of the New World. Interestingly, though other nineteenth-century copies of medieval manuscripts in the Hoe sale fetched prices upward of one hundred dollars, the Rive miniatures sold for a mere forty-five dollars. Perhaps they were considered scraps of an aborted *ancien régime* project, curiosities of little interest to citizens of the modern world.

### Susan Minns and Illumination Repatriated

The 1922 auction of the collection of Susan Minns (1840–1938) serves as an interesting follow-up to the Hoe sale. Over the course of her lifetime, this New England Brahmin, scientist, and collector-philanthropist gathered a huge collection of works relating to the Dance of Death, dating from the Middle Ages to the modern period. Minns had been one of the first woman students at the Massachusetts Institute of Technology, where she studied botany,

**130.**

"Allegory of Death" (France, sixteenth century), death leading a youth into the jaws of hell, from a Book of Hours

laying the foundation for a lifelong interest in natural science. She wrote and illustrated a book on the silkworm and the culture of silk in North America, and used her family wealth to encourage scholarly study, donating funds to MIT, Princeton, and the Marine Biological Institute at Woods Hole.

Minns began to collect works featuring the Dance of Death when she was a girl, first becoming aware of the theme through woodcuts in illustrated books.[60] From prints her interest expanded to include manuscripts and printed books, as well as paintings, drawings, bookplates, coins and medallions, and even a few photographs. Hunting down pieces herself, and with the help of agents, she ultimately amassed 1,020 works presenting the *Danse Macabre*, the largest private collection ever dealing with the subject. While her bibliographic holdings consisted mostly of printed books (many produced by early Parisian printers), she also owned twenty-one medieval and Renaissance manuscripts. Those select specimens, mostly French and mostly dating to the end of the Middle Ages, were richly illuminated and of high quality.

One piece, formerly owned by Ambroise Firmin-Didot and then Pierre Gélis-Didot, was a circa-1515 French Book of Hours with marginal images of the Dance of Death and one large miniature of Death escorting a youth into the fiery jaws of hell (figure 130).[61] Minns possessed further manuscripts with impressive provenances. One tiny Office of the Dead, probably of the early thirteenth century, was adorned with Burgundian arms between two skulls and bones and featured eight full-page miniatures of the Dance of Death.[62] Another richly illuminated work, a mid-fifteenth-century Boethius, *De Consolatione Philosophiae*, was originally created for a member of the Rohan-Visconti clan and later entered the collection of Guyon de Sardière.[63]

231

After almost seventy years of purchasing specimens specific to her beloved theme, in 1922 Minns chose to sell her collection at auction, offering as justification, "I have had the pleasure of collecting. Let others have the same."[64] One of the "others" who quickly took interest in the holdings was the library of the University of Louvain.[65] This library had had a valuable collection of books, paintings, and other works relating to the very subject of the Dance of Death, but these holdings had been destroyed during the 1914 German bombing of Louvain. Soon after arrangements had been made for the Minns sale at the American Art Association, Minns announced that she would donate $12,500 so that the Belgian university could purchase the articles they desired. She gave another $2,500 to the new Louvain library (also built with American assistance).[66] Through this act of philanthropy, the American collector ensured the safe return of her specimens of early books to the Old World.

## John Frederick Lewis and Illumination as Class Distinction

[Columbus] discovered a Utopia which should become an asylum for the oppressed of all nations ... whose inhabitants descended not from learned and skilled ancestors, yet in the ages to come, were to be distinguished in letters, adept in art.[67]

—JOHN FREDERICK LEWIS

The likes of Morgan and Walters, educated and professionally active abroad, had emulated their noble predecessors by reconstructing and enshrining the medieval past in gentlemanly libraries. The Hoe sale had heralded the strength of a rising market for illumination in the United States. Against this background, John Frederick Lewis (1860–1932) appeared as an exemplar of a new strain of collector, negotiating himself between the European past and an American future. Lewis was born in Philadelphia to a family with ties to the shipping industry. Following his graduation from high school he pursued a career in law and developed a particular expertise in admiralty legislation. With wealth gained through his marriage in 1895 to Anne H. Rush Baker of Philadelphia, starting at the age of thirty-five, he found himself in a position to indulge his longstanding interest in the arts and the history of the book. Initially he was drawn to the earliest form of the written word, collecting cuneiform tablets, cylinders, and wheels, and taking both a historical and a connoisseur's interest in printmaking. By the time of his death, Lewis had amassed printed works that spanned the fifteenth through nineteenth centuries and had given talks on block books, engravings, mezzotints, and lesser-known forms of printmaking.[68] Lewis's interest in texts and images came together in his enthusiasm for medieval manuscripts—an enthusiasm he fostered by connecting himself to leading book dealers and purchasing at important auctions such as the Hoe sale.[69]

Actively engaging in the manuscript market in the first few decades of the twentieth century, Lewis put together an outstanding collection. The bulk of those works date to the fifteenth century and are of French, Flemish, German, and Italian origin. Many of the Lewis manuscripts have distinguished provenances which not only attest to their luxury but also evince current trends and nineteenth-century attitudes toward illuminated manuscripts. For example, Lewis purchased an outstanding circa 1475 Sienese Book of Hours, formerly in the Dance of Death collection of Susan Minns (Free Library, Lewis MS 118).[70] He also bought a sixteenth-century Franco-Flemish Book of Hours (Free Library, Lewis MS 108) that had appeared in the sale of Guyon de Sardière in 1759, was purchased by the duc de La Vallière, was on the London market in the nineteenth century, and then entered the collection of Robert Hoe. Further, Lewis owned a sixteenth-century Book of Hours (Free Library, Lewis MS 125), formerly in the collection of John Ruskin, which, interestingly, had every one of its large miniatures excised.[71] Another Book of Hours, dated 1537, is filled with the modern illuminations of Caleb William Wing (Free Library, Lewis MS 125). This work has the distinction of having inspired particular scorn from Frederic Madden at the 1864 sale of the library of its mid-nineteenth-century owner, John Boykett Jarman (discussed in chapter 3).[72]

Bolstering Lewis's manuscript library was a group of roughly two thousand cuttings and single leaves purchased between 1910 and 1926. In the spirit of the Victoria and Albert Museum, Lewis, intent upon amassing holdings that demonstrated the history of illumination, acquired an encyclopedic collection of works ranging from the twelfth to nineteenth centuries and representing almost every European country. He purchased most of those fragments from book dealers who, by that time, had long been catering to the market for cuttings. Lewis stored the pieces in the manner of print collectors, mounting them on mats and presumably storing them in drawers or boxes. This enthusiast of woodcuts and engravings seems to have regarded his collection of illuminated fragments as an extension of his larger holdings of works on paper. In effect, his collection as a whole, housed within the walls of his Philadelphia residence, reconstructs the entire European history of the book and its adornment.

Lewis's expansive interest and taste is demonstrated by the diversity of countries represented in his collection of fragments.[73] Italian works constitute the greatest number of illuminations. Important pieces among these holdings include, for example, a late-fourteenth-century Sienese leaf from an antiphonal with an historiated initial *S* depicting St. Lawrence holding a chalice and wafer, given to Lippo Vanni (Free Library, Lewis M 69:13; see figure 131).[74] But Lewis's holdings represented almost every European land, including Bohemia, the Byzantine Empire, Spain, Portugal, and Slavonic centers. Among his roughly thirty Byzantine works are two particularly important fragments, one representing John the Evangelist, the other Moses (Free Library, Lewis 44:27–28; see figure 132). The leaves had been cut from an imperial Greek lectionary of the twelfth century now in the National Museum at Palermo (MS 1), from which about a quarter of the miniatures have been excised.[75] A penciled inscription on the Moses folio reading "Greek manuscrite—XI cen." suggests that the leaves passed through the hands of a French dealer, anxious to attract an English-speaking buyer. How they arrived in America is unknown, but a handwritten note by Lewis on the back of this same folio indicates that previously the works were owned by the Boston collector Thomas F. Richardson.

And Lewis's eclectic taste was not limited to European works. In 1926 he visited a show of eastern art at the Sesquicentennial Exhibition in Philadelphia, which solidified his already mounting taste for Arabic, Persian, and Indian manuscripts and miniatures. One of the earliest American collectors to take an interest in eastern manuscripts, he amassed an outstanding collection of works of diverse origins, the breakdown of his holdings being thirty-five Arabic, fifty-two Persian, ten Turkish, three Hindustani, eight Sanskrit, one Nepalese, four Pali, one Siamese, eleven Armenian, one Coptic, thirteen Ethiopic, ten Hebrew, one Samaritan, two Syriac. In addition to these codices, he owned one Egyptian papyrus of the *Book of the Dead* and more than twelve hundred Persian, Mughal, and Rajput miniatures.[76] The collection includes twenty-one copies of the Koran, most of them richly adorned, and important Indo-Persian miniatures, such as those accompanying *The History of the Mughal Emperor Jahangir* (Free Library, Lewis MS 44). Ac-

**131.**

Attributed to
Lippo Vanni,
antiphonal leaf with
St. Lawrence holding
a chalice and wafer
(Siena, late fourteenth
century)

**132.**

Moses
(Constantinople,
twelfth century),
from a lectionary

cording to his son, Lewis pursued these eastern manuscripts not only because he
was dazzled by their sheer beauty, but also because he recognized that competition
was inflating wildly the prices of Western manuscripts.

In contrast to Morgan and Walters, whose passions for illumination were
tokens of their aspirations to reconstruct the ethos of the European gentlemanly
library in the New World, Lewis took an active interest both in the development
of a school of contemporary American painters and in the history of his country.[77]
His concern with the former is evident from an involvement with the Philadelphia
Academy of Fine Arts that ultimately resulted in his presidency of the school. Interestingly, connected to that post is an exchange of letters between Lewis and the
eccentric local collector Albert C. Barnes addressing current debates about the future of art.[78] Lewis's broad enthusiasm for the history of the United States is manifest not only in his extensive portrait collection of American figures, but also in
his involvement with historical associations of his city. As a public figure, he gave
orations such as the 1904 speech delivered at the United Italian Society of Philadelphia in which he proudly expounded upon the unique virtues of the United
States, where "a new race was to arise" and "the worm-eaten traditions of the
Old World, which imprisoned the body and confined the mind," would never
prevail.[79] Morgan and Walters fashioned themselves as European gentlemen who
happened to abide upon the western shores of the Atlantic; Lewis, a man of more
modest origins, embraced his American identity and sought to distinguish his
world from an oppressive, socially static Europe.

But whereas Lewis the public individual may have cherished the possibilities open to people like himself in America, Lewis the collector seems to have
embraced some of the practices of the Victorian Old World. The Rare Book Department of the Free Library in Philadelphia possesses many volumes formerly in
his collection which are, in varying degrees, extra-illustrated. At least one of those
volumes, a copy of William Blades's 1880 publication *The Enemies of Books* (AL
025.8 B562), was filled with pasted-in fragments at the time Lewis acquired it,
suggesting his taste for and interest in the amusing pastimes of European ladies and
gentlemen of the previous century. This volume is particularly interesting as an
ironic example of one of the very phenomena it criticizes.[80] In the text, Blades bemoans the crimes committed against books by the likes of fire and water and is
particularly scornful of their abuse at the hands of ignorant collectors who cut up
volumes to decorate other works in their libraries. The chapter devoted to the
hazards of fire, for example, is adorned with a charred manuscript leaf; the chapter
on "Ignorance" is illustrated with a leaf from a Book of Hours from which the
miniatures have been sloppily excised (figure 133). A similar fragment is pasted into
the section on "Collectors," which also features a pen-and-ink drawing of a di-
sheveled gentleman of the nineteenth century, slouched in a chair (figure 134).[81]

Although we know that Lewis's most lavishly extra-illustrated volume of
Blades had been doctored at the time of purchase, there remains tantalizing evidence that our Philadelphia collector himself engaged in the Victorian hobby of
book adornment. There exist eleven extra-illustrated volumes, formerly in Lewis's
collection and now at the Free Library, which feature glued-in text leaves from an
early-fifteenth-century French Book of Hours.[82] A comparison of text block, page
size, calligraphy, and ornament suggests that the leaves come from the same parent
manuscript. This observation is unequivocally cemented by the fact that the catch
phrase on a folio in one volume, Madan Falconer's *Books in Manuscript* (AL 091
M261), matches the first line on a leaf in a different volume, Henry Shaw's *The Art
of Illumination* (AL 096 Sh2). Further evidence that it was Lewis himself who broke

54 ENEMIES OF BOOKS.

Lamport Hall in 1867 by Mr. Edmonds, are too well-known and too recent to need description. In this case mere chance seems to have led to the preservation of works, the very existence of which set the ears of all lovers of Shakespeare a tingling.

In the summer of 1877, a gentleman with whom I was well acquainted, took lodgings in Preston-street, Brighton. The morning after his arrival, he found in the W.C. some leaves of an old black-letter book. He asked permission to retain them, and enquired if there were any more where they came from. Two or three other fragments were found, and the landlady stated that her father, who was fond of antiquities, had at one time a chest full of old black-letter books; that, upon his death, they were preserved till she was tired of seeing them, and then, supposing them of no value, she had used them for waste; that for two years and a half they had served for various household purposes, but she had just come to the end of

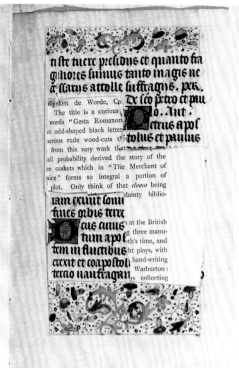

133.

"Ignorance"
in an extra-illustrated
**William Blades,**
*The Enemies of Books*

134.

"Collectors"
in an extra-illustrated
**William Blades**
*The Enemies of Books*

*A Book Collector - Drawing by T. Uwins. R.A.- 1830 →*

COLLECTORS. 101

entirely or of the greatest rarity; when you find the Colophon from the end or the "insignum typographi" from the first leaf of a rare "fifteener" pasted down with dozens of others varying in value, you cannot bless the memory of the antiquarian shoemaker, John Bagford. His portrait, a half-length, painted by Howard, was engraved by Vertue, and re-engraved for the Bibliographical Decameron. (See Frontispiece.)

A bad example often finds imitators, and every season there crop up for public sale one or two such collections formed by bibliomaniacs who, although calling themselves bibliophiles, ought really to be ranked among the worst enemies of books.

The following is copied from a trade catalogue dated April, 1880, and affords a fair idea of the extent to which these heartless destroyers will go:—

"MISSAL ILLUMINATIONS.
FIFTY DIFFERENT CAPITAL LETTERS *on* VELLUM; *all in rich Gold and Colours. Many*

up the manuscript is found first in the fact that notes in Lewis's hand, identifying the date and locale of the manuscript, appear at the bottom of most leaves, and second in that a sister leaf is found among Lewis's collection of matted fragments.

If Lewis displayed some attitudes toward the reuse of manuscripts reminiscent of his European forebears, at times his taste too conformed to that of the Victorians. Like many before him, he purchased leaves from the hand of the Spanish Forger (discussed in chapter 3). Among the seven folia in this group, for example, is a historiated initial *G* with a female saint, attendant, and reliquary in a boat (figure 135). As often in the Forger's oeuvre, the scene matches no standard medieval iconography and the sweet-faced ladies depicted sport daring décolletage. Lewis seems, nevertheless, to have accepted the illumination as a genuine work of the Middle Ages, for he stored it with a leaf by the Forger whose mat bears the note "French XII or XIII century," written in Lewis's own hand.[83] Status as a proud and forward-looking citizen of the cultural center of Philadelphia notwithstanding, Lewis exhibited the tastes and habits of his European forebears. The American of the future found the means to assert his gentility through a Victorian enthusiasm for the medieval.

**Robert Lehman and the Return to Illumination as Panel Painting**

The collectors examined thus far are united by their common interest in the medieval codex. Morgan and Walters occupied themselves with amassing impressive libraries, and Hoe and Lewis admired illumination primarily as an aspect of the history of the written word. Robert Lehman (1891–1969), however, like a latter-day Ottley, was representative of American collectors primarily interested in paintings, not books (see chapter 2). For Lehman, miniatures served to supplement the family holdings in panel paintings and objets d'art.

**135.**

**Spanish Forger, Historiated initial *G*, with female saint, attendant and a reliquary in a boat**

The Lehman family gained its fortune through its prestigious private banking and investment firm, Lehman Brothers. The first Lehmans came to America from Bavaria in the mid–nineteenth century and settled in Alabama. Starting out in retail, the clan soon entered the business of commodity and cotton brokerage and established a New York office. In the early years of the twentieth century, Robert Lehman's father, along with other family members of his generation, shifted the focus of the firm to investment banking. Embracing the opportunities of the expanding market economy of the time, Lehman Brothers underwrote the first mail-order chain, Sears, Roebuck and Company, as well as the future five-and-dime giant F. W. Woolworth. Under Robert Lehman's leadership in the 1920s and 1930s, the firm recognized the wealth to be gained in America's developing consumer, travel, and entertainment industries—subsidizing department stores like Macy's, backing the passenger aviation industry in its infancy, and investing in both radio and motion pictures.

Robert Lehman's parents, Philip and Carrie, started actively collecting European paintings in 1905, favoring High Renaissance and baroque works. As an undergraduate at Yale, Robert studied the trecento and quattrocento paintings in the James Jackson Jarves Collection, housed in the University Art Gallery, and developed a particular taste for Sienese works. Upon his graduation in 1913, Robert did not immediately enter the family business but rather was entrusted by his parents with the primary responsibility of enriching their art collection. With his parents' confidence (and checkbook), Robert Lehman purchased from dealers in Europe and those recently established in New York and consulted with the leading experts of the day in the developing field of connoisseurship, including Bernard Berenson, Richard Offner, Max Friedländer, and Raymond van Marle. Thanks to his careful researches and astute purchases, by the late 1920s the Lehman family had amassed more than eighty Italian primitives as well as outstanding works by Flemish masters, including Hans Memling, Petrus Christus, and Gerard David.[84]

Robert Lehman's holdings of miniatures can be seen as an expansion of the taste for primitive painting he developed during his time at Yale and indulged in his purchases of the subsequent years. In the 1920s, Lehman began to acquire single leaves and cuttings, the bulk of them fourteenth- and fifteenth-century central Italian works, along with exquisite examples of French and Flemish illuminations of the fifteenth and sixteenth centuries. For example, historiated initials, like the one ascribed to Lorenzo Monaco of Christ at the Last Judgment or another by Girolamo da Cremona featuring Christ entering Jerusalem, function as supplements to the panel paintings by Italian Renaissance masters acquired during the same decades.[85]

Given that many of the Lehman miniatures were bought already mounted, as though they were small-scale panel paintings, it should come as no surprise that Lehman did much of his buying from paintings and objects dealers. In Paris, he frequented the shop of Les Frères Kalebdjian on the rue de la Paix. From this Armenian art dealer, Lehman acquired thirty-three separate works (evidently more than from any other dealer) from France, Italy, Holland, and Flanders that ranged in date from the twelfth through sixteenth centuries.[86] Kalebdjian also sold ivories and other medieval and Renaissance precious objects, packaged in custom-made silk and velvet cases. Again purchasing outside the sphere of the book world, Lehman bought four of his best illuminations from the Parisian agent of the fine-art dealer Colnaghi, Bernard D'Hendecourt, and in the 1920s acquired works that appeared in the Madame Fould and Edouard Kann sales in Paris.[87]

The family also had ties to the Italian fine-art market. Around 1916, Philip Lehman had purchased from the Florentine dealer Luigi Grassi a Giovanni

Bellini Madonna and Child (Lehman 1975, 1.81)[88] and a Virgin Annunciate, now given to the mid-fifteenth-century painter Andrea Delitio (Lehman 1975, 1.29).[89] Interestingly, it was from this same dealer that Robert Lehman later purchased a large (ten-inch by six-inch) Flemish miniature of the Holy Face, today attributed to Gerard David.[90] The miniature may have originally appeared in the 1486 *Escorial Hours*, which is currently in Madrid, but when Lehman purchased the cutting, it had been trimmed to the edges of its painted border, mounted, partially covered with a gumlike glaze, and framed with an elaborate floriated border reminiscent of the designs of William Morris. This miniature transformed into a panel painting would have fit in easily with the collection of Flemish primitives already gathered by Philip Lehman, including a pair of triptych wings featuring a Christ bearing the Cross and the Resurrection by David.[91]

Although Robert Lehman collected his miniatures predominantly from objects and paintings dealers, he also was a customer at Maggs Brothers in London and Leo S. Olschki in Florence, two of the few book dealers of the time who tended to keep a stock of illuminated cuttings on hand.[92] From Olschki, Lehman purchased one of his most impressive Italian leaves, a mid-fifteenth-century miniature of a figure preaching, held to be St. Bernardino of Siena (figure 136).[93] The cutting is striking for its very unilluminationlike qualities. The isolated figure is asymmetrical and addresses an implied audience outside the picture frame, and the background is a flat blue, without any indication of the saint's distinctive location. Further, the image is free—or had been trimmed of—all ornamental border. On the reverse, written in an early hand, is a note attributing the work to the fifteenth-century Sienese painter Lorenzo di Pietro, known as Vecchietta (1412–80), best known for the monumental frescoes in the sacristy of the Ospedale di Santa Maria della Scala in Siena. The piece, however, is now given to Vecchietta's Sienese follower, Francesco di Giorgio. Lehman happened to own a signed drawing by this artist that conveys a grandeur similar to that of the illumination.[94] The spontaneity of the St. Bernadino image apparently led Lehman to accept the scholarly suggestion that the piece had been painted on the scene during a sermon at the Piazza del Campo of Siena in 1450—a proposition that renders the artist a kind of quattrocento antecedent to the French and American masters of the nineteenth century that Lehman also came to collect.[95]

Further works in the Lehman holdings attest to the variation in fortunes of folia that made the journey across the Atlantic. Lehman owned two leaves— a Pietà and an image of St. Bridget—that had been cut from the *Hours of Cardinal Albrecht of Brandenburg* (1490–1545), illuminated by Simon Bening around 1522 to 1523.[96] Although this two-volume Book of Hours still retains fifty full-page miniatures, in the nineteenth century the book seems to have fallen victim to enthusiasts or dealers hungry for works by Flemish masters, for folia from this manuscript surfaced in Rome and in 1856 were purchased by Frederick, marquis of Londonberry. These "Londonberry leaves" are now dispersed. While the Pietà and St. Bridget entered Lehman's New York drawing room, a leaf presenting St. Gertrude of Nivelles (figure 137, plate 32) found its way to the American industrial heartland. This impressive folio was acquired by Howard A. Noble, a native of Pittsburgh who worked for Steel and Company, a local firm established by his father.[97] As recently as 1988 two other leaves from the Londonberry group—one featuring a Presentation in the Temple, the other St. Odilia—were offered at Sotheby's.[98] It is easy to see how the St. Gertrude image would have appealed to a market for cuttings-cum-paintings. The piece is dominated by the monumental form of the saint spinning, impervious to the rats and mice—representing the devil—that surround

**136.**

**Francesco di Giorgio,
St. Bernardino preaching
from a pulpit
(Italy, circa 1470–75)**

her, and in the frame, against the backdrop of a rolling landscape, are two miracles
from the saint's life. The pathos and naturalism of the work as a whole are characteristic of the altarpieces produced in early-sixteenth-century Bruges.

Given the affinity in taste and attitudes toward miniatures between
Celotti and Ottley on the one hand and Lehman on the other, it is not surprising
that Lehman actually owned cuttings that had passed through the hands of the
pioneers of the single-leaf trade. Indeed, Lehman at one time owned at least ten
pieces formerly in Ottley's collection, works that the early connoisseur had acquired from Celotti's 1825 sale and that had come on the market in 1925 and 1928
at the Lord Northwick sales.[99] Most of these holdings were historiated initials cut
from fifteenth-century Italian choral books, but also included was a collage. The
work is a pastiche of early-sixteenth-century fragments, at one time given to Attavante Attavanti, presenting an image of the Crucifixion with a distant view of Florence in the background, framed by two rows of ornamental borders bearing the
armorials, devices, and mottoes of a pope, presumably Leo X.[100] Just as Celotti's
and Ottley's early-nineteenth-century market, with a taste for Renaissance works,
snatched up collages which, both physically and conceptually, divorced illumination from its original-manuscript context, so too, a century later, those very same
works came to augment Lehman's exquisite collection of paintings. But comparison of Lehman to Celotti and Ottley brings to the fore a distinction which highlights the changes that had occurred over the century that divided the collectors.
Whereas Ottley's discussion of Italian primitives—in his sale catalogues, and particularly in his publications on art—regarded trecento and quattrocento paintings primarily as a preview to the High Renaissance works of Leonardo, Michelangelo,
and Raphael, in his own publication on the family holdings, Lehman considered

137.

Simon Bening,
St. Gertrude of Nivelles
(Flanders, sixteenth
century), from *Hours of
Albrecht of Brandenburg*

the works of the fourteenth and fifteenth centuries, particularly of Siena, as the
highlights of the family collection, the apex of excellence rather than a prelude.[101]

**Seymour De Ricci's
Census and
Illumination as
American
National Treasure**

The massive transfer of illuminated manuscripts (as
well as other works of art) from Europe to the United
States in the decades between the 1890s and the 1920s
made clear the need for a catalogue of these new
national treasures. In 1925 the Library of Congress,
with the support of the American Council of Learned

Studies, set out to compile a comprehensive survey of all the manuscript holdings
in this country. The project was carried out by Seymour De Ricci, a French bibliographer alert to the effects of American buying on the European market, assisted
by W. J. Wilson.[102] Questionnaires were sent to all known American collectors—
from the Morgans on Madison Avenue to the humblest midwestern amateurs—
who responded with descriptions of their holdings, in varying degrees of detail.
De Ricci also visited many of the public and private libraries of the United States,
personally inspecting the European treasures in their new adoptive homes. After
his six years of study and four trips across the country, the first *Census of Medieval
and Renaissance Manuscripts in the United States and Canada* was published.[103] This
opus amounts to a reconstruction of the European-style catalogue in America, collectively treating the holdings in this country as one massive collaged library.

The closing observation in De Ricci's preface leads us to our next area of
investigation. He observes that "private ownership of early manuscripts is essentially a transitory feature of book-collecting. Nearly all valuable manuscripts in private
hands are destined in the near future to become public property."[104] The expecta-

tion, then, was that America would follow the pattern of Europe, where huge private libraries, such as those of the duc de La Vallière and Douce ended up in public collections. Indeed, as we will soon see, manuscripts did not long remain within the private salons of the cultivated collectors of the New World.[108]

## ILLUMINATION CONFRONTS A NEW WORLD PUBLIC

> I believe . . . that great public collections will be formed by individual exertions and that in time America will rival the "old world" in Art-Treasures.
>
> —JAMES JACKSON JARVES, ART HINTS, 1855

**Background: America Encounters the Medieval**

The rarefied world of collecting is only one aspect of the story of illumination in the United States. Around the turn of the century two distinctively America tendencies laid the groundwork for programs aimed at educating the broad American public about illumination. The first was a developing sense of moral obligation among the philanthropic rich to share artistic treasures with the public. The second was a rising American interest in the general history and culture of the Middle Ages.

**Primitives Come to Broadway but Play to an Empty House**

To tell the story of the development of a public interest in illumination, we must turn back to the mid-nineteenth century, when there were few European works on public view in this country, medieval or otherwise. One of the earliest collectors to transfer European paintings to the United States, and apparently the first to encourage public edification through exposure to such works, was Thomas Jefferson Bryan (1802–70).[105] Bryan was born to a wealthy Philadelphia family. In 1823, after completing his education at Harvard, he moved to Europe and settled there for roughly thirty years. Spending most of his time in Paris, he built a collection of approximately 230 paintings dating from the thirteenth century to his own age that included works of the Italian, Spanish, French, Flemish, and English schools. In keeping with the mid-nineteenth-century European taste for primitives, he also acquired a few trecento and quattrocento works.[106] Bryan, however, apparently was not personally drawn to such early works. Rather, in the spirit of Ottley's writings on the development of the Italian school, he seems to have purchased them to function as exemplars of the state of painting in the period before the High Renaissance.

Having amassed a collection boasting specimens of every era of European painting from the pre-Renaissance on, Bryan brought his holdings back to this country with the aim of establishing a national gallery of art for the education of the American public. Initially, he brought his works to Philadelphia, but his native city dismissed his offer of sale and the collector was forced to find an alternative exhibition venue. In 1852 he opened the Bryan Gallery of Christian Art on the second floor of his New York residence at Thirteenth Street and Broadway. There the works remained for the next eleven years. Within the gallery hung paintings generously attributed to masters including Giotto and Duccio as well as Dürer, Van Eyck, Mantegna, and Velásquez. Of the 230 works shown, only 23 were given to pre-1500 artists, and the collection contains no miniatures at all. Indeed, the catalogue for the exhibition, written by the journalist Richard Grant White and Bryan, adopts a familiar tone, scorning the depth to which art had sunk during the "Dark Ages" of the pre-Renaissance period and committing itself to determining a master's hand behind each work.[107] In 1864 Bryan left the paintings to the New York Historical Society, where they attracted little attention.[108]

Like Bryan, James Jackson Jarves (1818–88) aimed to educate his compatriots to the history of European painting. He distinguished himself, however, by devoting his attention specifically to Italian primitives.[109] Born in Boston to a family that had gained its fortune in the sale of glass, around 1850 Jarves and his wife moved to Europe, first living in Paris and then settling in Florence. In Italy, Jarves traveled in refined Anglo-American expatriate circles, befriended such advocates of Gothic Revivalism as John Ruskin, and corresponded with like-minded American intellectuals such as the medieval enthusiast and professor of fine arts at Harvard Charles Eliot Norton. He amassed a collection of primitives that included works by Taddeo and Agnolo Gaddi, Gentile da Fabriano, Sassetta, Giovanni di Paolo, and Ghirlandaio. Bemoaning the low state of American taste and knowledge of European culture, Jarves, like Bryan, transported his collection to his native land in the hope of establishing a national gallery there. The goal, however, was never realized. The paintings were first shown in New York between 1860 and 1861 in a newly constructed, marble Institute of Fine Arts on Broadway between Houston and Bleeker. Jarves subsequently offered the works to Boston and to New York, but was refused in both instances. Under financial duress, the collector lent the pictures to the newly built Yale Art Gallery. In 1871 the works were bought by the university for $22,000, a fraction of the $60,000 Jarves claimed to have paid for the paintings. They aroused little enthusiasm and hung in New Haven for almost fifty years before they gained the esteem of the scholarly community.[110]

Despite his enthusiasm for primitives, Jarves exhibited almost no interest in illumination. He seems to have purchased no cuttings or manuscripts himself, and in his three written works on the history of art, he virtually disregards illumination. Neither *Art Hints* (1855), a book baldly dependent upon Ruskin, nor *Art Studies: The "Old Masters" of Italy* (1861) makes any mention of illumination whatsoever.[111] In *Art Thoughts: The Experiences and Observations of an American Amateur in Europe* (1869) Jarves does finally mention medieval manuscripts. This work is broader in scope than Jarves's previous studies and includes discussion of subjects from "The Pagan and Christian Religious Idea in Art" to "The Arts of Japan and China." In "French Art," four particular manuscripts are discussed—one of the eighth century, one of the ninth, and two dating to the thirteenth—all within the space of a single paragraph. Jarves's assessment is largely negative. In the "Heures de l'Empereur Charlemagne," he discerns the influence of "degenerate Byzantine models." Maintaining that the work "is scarcely better than the picture hieroglyphics on skins done by American Indians," he asserts that it "betrays the final stages of decay of an illustrative and decorative art of a superior character which had preceded it."[112] Such remarks are striking, particularly in contrast to the esteem with which such Carolingian manuscripts were held during the very same period at the Musée des Souverains (see chapter 3). For Jarves, illumination functioned as a prelude to a golden age: "In the best MSS of the medieval epoch may be detected the germs of leading characteristics of subsequent styles of painting"— a statement that echoes the sentiments of Ottley and, later, Bryan in their discussions of Italian primitives.[113]

Ultimately, Bryan and Jarves failed to spur native taste for early European painting in the third quarter of the nineteenth century in America, and in this period, there was apparently no effort to educate the American public to medieval illumination. The lack of enthusiasm for the ornamented page in the United States stands in stark contrast to the contemporary rage for medievalizing works, such as the gift book, across the sea in France and England. An America struggling with its own political and social reconstruction following the Civil War preferred a pastiched hybrid image of the European past, one in which manuscripts initially played little part.

**The Middle Ages Meets the Heartland** Early interest in the Middle Ages in this country was not focused on medieval artworks. Those Americans who could travel to Europe, similar to eighteenth-century Europeans, tended to view the period before the Renaissance as a chaotic and uncivilized age.[114] By the mid–nineteenth century, however, a broad taste for medieval and other historiating ornamental styles was in evidence, adorning architecture as well as mass-produced household products. Many Americans came to associate Romanesque and Gothic styles with chivalry, virtue, and Christian moral standing. Ketchup bottles and glasses, creamers and jugs, even cast-iron stoves and furniture were produced in medievalizing styles, sometimes interspersed with classically inspired figures or acanthus leaves. An unsystematic jumble of ornament was happily mixed and matched in a society that saw the European past as exotic, romantic, and remote.[115]

But the medieval was not merely a dialect within the language of ornament of the nineteenth-century American designer. Similar to European uses of illumination, Americans conceptualized the Middle Ages to suit larger social and religious agendas of the day. Indeed, on the remote terrain of the New World, it seems that Americans could exercise even broader freedoms than their European counterparts in the cooption of the Middle Ages. T. J. Jackson Lears maintains that starting around the 1880s, many of the educated bourgeoisie of America, dismayed with an overcivilized culture, created a fantasy of the medieval period as a respite from a modern world committed to material progress.[116] In "The Virgin and the Dynamo" Henry Adams, obsessed with a "feminine" Middle Ages, denounced what he saw as the contemporary American social and ethnic muddle accompanying industrial development in favor of what he imagined to be a simpler, faith-filled world of the thirteenth century.[117] Late Gilded Age professionals, disturbed by rising class conflict and social dislocation, embraced medieval revivalist ideologues like Ruskin and Morris with their critique of capitalism.[118] In a similar vein, university intellectuals like Charles Eliot Norton valorized the religious faith and communal pride of the medieval artisan, and such views were popularized in the widely circulated magazines produced by advocates of the Arts and Crafts movement in this country.[119] Mass-market magazines too brought both historical and fictionalized accounts of a pre-Renaissance world peopled by "pure" and "honest" characters with childlike irrational values to the living rooms of middle America.[120]

**Fragments Collaged at the Cloisters** As we have seen in our discussion of Bryan and Jarves, mid-nineteenth-century Americans had little interest in pre-Renaissance paintings. In subsequent decades, the public collections established in major urban centers—the Metropolitan Museum of Art, the National Gallery, the Art Institute of Chicago—expended little energy on the exhibition of medieval pieces. At this early stage, such galleries mostly exhibited plaster casts and second-rate Old Master paintings, directing public attention toward antiquity and the Renaissance, not the period in between. Only toward the end of the century did institutions, on the East Coast and in the Midwest, amass select medieval objects, fragments of a European past that by the 1880s had at last begun to capture the public imagination in the United States.

The Cloisters, now a branch of the Metropolitan Museum, was originally a private collection of French and Spanish medieval works collected by the American sculptor George Grey Barnard. In the first decade of the twentieth century, Barnard, living in France and finding himself in financial straits, discovered a lucrative sideline. He gathered stone fragments from abandoned churches and abbeys ruined during the French Revolution and its aftermath and sold them to dealers and wealthy medieval enthusiasts in Paris. Keeping select works for himself, the sculptor soon began to export medieval stonework fragments to his homeland, hoping to develop a New World audience for the arts and techniques of the Middle Ages. Similar to Bryan and Jarves before him, however, Barnard was unable to interest an American museum in his hoard of European treasures. He thereupon opened his own private museum, Barnard's Cloisters, in a small brick building in New York's Washington Heights in 1914. Barnard dressed his guards as monks, filled the air with incense, and piped in evocative music, aiming to reconstruct a lost medieval world on the shores of the Hudson.

Purchasing the collection for the Metropolitan Museum in 1925, John D. Rockefeller Jr. sought to create a more historically accurate reconstruction of the Middle Ages.[121] But though the Cloisters museum created by the philanthropist, which opened to the public in 1938, was designed to be historically coherent, it remained a reconstructed New World pastiche. The structure incorporates cloisters from four different southern French abbeys, ranging in date from the twelfth to the late fifteenth centuries, and a late-Gothic arcade from the Lorraine region with such pieces as a carved arch and a fountain from various other ruined monasteries from France and Spain. Such fragments from sacred structures are presented adjacent to master exemplars of secular arts, such as the *Unicorn Tapestry* series. In contrast to Lenoir's Musée des Monuments Français or the Musée des Souverains, each with the agenda of presenting the glory of a former France, the small Cloisters museum attempts to present a complete history of medieval art; historical periods, geographic regions, and functionally distinct works are collapsed into one medleylike crash course in the European past. In the style of the collaged manuscript fragments assembled in the nineteenth century (see chapter 2), this museum assembles genuine medieval fragments into a whole that never existed in the Middle Ages.

**Institutionalization:**
**Illumination and**
**Its Urban Audience**

**Ladies and**
**Gentlemen Savor**
**the Old World**

The exhibition and study of manuscript illumination in the United States followed a pattern already set in Europe, if at an accelerated pace. On both sides of the Atlantic, initially a small circle of the wealthy and educated amassed specimens of this art, and subsequently their holdings were made available to the public. By the turn of the twentieth century, a United States negotiating its political, economic, and cultural position on the world stage was keen to construct a comprehensive vision of the European cultural past.

The 1890 exhibition of panel paintings and manuscripts held at the Union League Club was paradigmatic of the attitudes toward and the narrow audience for medieval manuscripts in late-nineteenth-century America. Whereas London's South Kensington Museum had been encouraging the study of illuminations since the 1860s, New York's keepers of manuscripts reserved their treasures for the eyes of elite society. Although the Union League Club was founded as a gathering place for reformist members of the new Republican Party supporting Unionism, and although the club had been instrumental in the founding of the

Metropolitan Museum of Art, this circle of New York socialites nonetheless sponsored periodic art exhibitions open exclusively to club members and their guests.[122]

In 1890, the Union League Club took advantage of the medieval holdings of its members in an exhibition of "Illuminated Books and Manuscripts, Old Master and Modern Master Paintings."[123] Exhibited beside seventeenth-century Dutch, eighteenth-century, and modern landscape painting, illuminated manuscripts served as a prelude to the later pieces. The exhibition opened with works including a thirteenth- or fourteenth-century English Bible, continued with the *Pembroke Hours* (which, as we have seen, was to gain attention again at the Hoe sale of 1911), and moved to a Gutenberg Bible and other early examples of printing. The show then continued with paintings given to masters like Rembrandt, van Goyen, and Reynolds, and closed with modern paintings by both European and American artists.

Not surprisingly, the catalogue descriptions of the exhibition's miniatures smack of French and English attitudes at the beginning of the century: "While the drawing of the figures shows a certain amount of crudity, there is, nevertheless, a quaint simplicity about them which give them a distinct charm."[124] Marveling at the minuteness of the calligraphy in a Gothic manuscript, the catalogue continues, "It is a wonderful specimen of the skill and patience shown by the mediaeval monks."[125] In the late nineteenth century, just as oils by Dutch masters had become requisite adornment for the refined sitting room (on both sides of the Atlantic), so too illuminated manuscripts functioned as conversation pieces to be treasured by gentlemen and ladies of taste. Together, these European specimens spanning the thirteenth to the nineteenth centuries construct a history of development of painting at the same time that they educate a select public to the parlor room favorites of the age.

But the gentlemen of the New World were becoming acutely aware of European developments in the study of manuscripts. In 1884 nine bibliophilic members of New York society (including Robert Hoe III) had established the Grolier Club as a kind of New World analog to the Roxburghe Club, devoted to "the literary study and promotion of the arts pertaining to the production of books."[126] This group sponsored exhibitions and lectures and issued publications principally on the history of the artistic aspects of the book and printing. During its first decade of existence, the club held two shows of illuminated works (and did not hold another manuscript show until 1968).[127] Similar to the case at the Union League Club, these exhibitions were open to club members (limited in 1889 to a quota of roughly 250) and to their invited guests.[128] Examination of the deluxe catalogue made to accompany the second manuscript exhibition at the Grolier Club, in 1892, suggests that America's early bibliophiles had by that time begun both to encourage the acquisition of works that would represent a broad spectrum of the history of illumination and to educate high society to the current state of knowledge about the production and technical aspects of the art of the medieval book.

The 1892 exhibition showcased the holdings of the Grolier Club members. The 137 works displayed included 94 medieval and Renaissance manuscripts, 21 printed books with illuminations, and 16 Persian and Indian manuscripts.[129] Although the exhibition featured a handful of thirteenth- and fourteenth-century manuscripts, the majority of works displayed were of a later date. Indeed, almost half the Western manuscripts in the show were richly illuminated Books of Hours of the fifteenth and sixteenth centuries (many of them, incidentally, drawn from the Hoe collection). Limited by the holdings of collectors in this country, the Grolier Club was in a position to display a dazzling array of late specimens but did not have the objects available to offer a comprehensive vision of the historical development of manuscript illumination.

But if the taste among American manuscript collectors at late century tended toward fifteenth- and sixteenth-century works, the Grolier Club was nonetheless committed to educating its audience to a full history of the medieval book. The extensive introductory text of the show's limited-edition catalogue dwells less upon the beauty of the late-medieval volumes displayed at the club than upon a broad overview of the history and technology of manuscripts. This text is divided into five sections: "Vellum and Parchment," "The Writing and the Materials Employed by the Calligrapher," "Initial Letters and Ornaments," "The Miniaturist," and "The Patron and Collector of Manuscripts" (a particularly appropriate section given the venue). In short, the Grolier Club exhibition did not limit its interest to a connoisseur's admiration of its gems of medieval painting. Rather, its aim was to suggest the entire historical milieu of European manuscript production and use for its elite New World audience. Thus the exhibition demonstrates a move away from an American taste for miniatures as delectable accoutrements of the well-appointed libraries of the elite and toward a comprehensive history of illumination for a New World audience, limited though this audience may have been.

## Scholars Scrutinize the Past

Manuscripts remained the preserve of elite connoisseurs for about two decades following the Grolier Club show. But in the opening years of the twentieth century, East Coast universities began to sponsor exhibitions of medieval books designed to educate the public to this growing area of academic study. Such exhibitions attest to the incipient American scholarly interest in the historical development of illumination. During the first twenty years of the new century, the same period during which the Metropolitan Museum held three separate exhibitions of J. P. Morgan's medieval luxury objects (in 1908, 1910, and 1914), interested laypeople could flock to the ivy-covered towers of universities like Columbia and Princeton to enrich with painted images their mental reconstructions of a remote medieval Europe.

In the fall of 1906, J. P. Morgan lent Columbia University selections from his rarest and most important holdings of illuminated manuscripts. Included in the show were the thirteenth-century English *Huntingfield Psalter* (Morgan, MS M. 43), a volume of the histories of Jehan de Courcy illuminated around 1470 in Bruges by Philippe de Mazerolles (Morgan, MS M. 214), and a sixteenth-century poem on the Passion of Christ executed for François I featuring an image of the king, flanked by courtiers, accepting the manuscript from the kneeling author (Morgan, MS M. 147).[130] Over the course of twenty-six days, twelve thousand visitors—an unprecedented number for such an event in this country—visited Columbia to view Morgan's superb examples of illumination.

Although Columbia exhibited specimens spanning more than eight centuries, the small size of the show left viewers more dazzled by the splendid individual pieces than educated to a comprehensive history of illumination. Ten years later, however, Princeton University held an exhibition expressly designed to present a complete vision of the development of the medieval book and its adornment. In the 1930s Princeton was to become a haven for German and Central European intellectuals of all casts, fleeing the mounting anti-Jewish policies of their homelands. But already within the first decades of the twentieth century, a school of American medievalists was taking root at the university. Charles Rufus Morey

(1879–1955), the scholar who first conceived of the Index of Christian Art and was a founding member of the *Art Bulletin*, helped to establish the study of medieval art at Princeton and was instrumental in the actualization of an exhibition of manuscripts at the university library in 1916.

The brochure that Morey wrote to accompany the show makes plain that this professor's primary goal was the education of students and of the broader public.[131] The entire conceptualization of the exhibition was distinguished from the earlier shows at the Union League Club, the Grolier Club, and even Columbia. Rather than exposing the public to outstanding specimens of a lost art, the Princeton show used a combination of facsimiles and original works to reconstruct the trajectory of the development of medieval painting. Images from facsimiles, such as Westwood's *Anglo-Saxon and Irish Manuscripts* (London, 1868), or more recent scholarly analyses, such as Hieber's *Die Miniaturen des frühen Mittelalters* (Munich, 1912), were displayed alongside original works from the thirteenth and subsequent centuries.

Such university exhibitions are particularly notable because they mark an important shift in the conceptualization of medieval artistic achievement. Whereas the Grolier exhibition echoed the early nineteenth-century taste for illumination of the fifteenth and early sixteenth centuries, the text accompanying the Princeton exhibition specifically celebrated the achievement of artists from the fourth through fourteenth centuries. In fact, Morey even pointedly disparages the illumination of the fifteenth and sixteenth centuries, condemning the works for the very qualities for which they were so celebrated less than one hundred years earlier: "Subsequent examples show the decadence of the art . . . [it] becomes a mere imitation of easel painting."[132]

**The Public Lines Up**    By the beginning of the 1930s, New York's museum-attending population was in a position to piece together a conceptual and visual image of the remote Middle Ages from the stone and luxury fragments then on view at the Metropolitan Museum itself, the specimens at the Cloisters, and the touring Guelph Treasure, exhibited at venues on the East Coast and in the Midwest.[133] However, no comprehensive major exhibition of illuminated works had as yet been seen in the United States. In the years between the turn of the century and the Great Depression, J. P. Morgan and subsequently his son, each aided by Belle da Costa Greene, amassed a collection of manuscripts that featured representatives of all medieval eras, and, in 1934 the Pierpont Morgan Library and the New York Public Library jointly launched an exhibition of Morgan manuscripts ranging from the ninth through the sixteenth centuries (figure 138). The exhibition presented 162 manuscripts and cuttings, including such masterpieces as the Lindau Gospels (Morgan, MS M. 1), the *Gospel Book of Judith of Flanders* (Morgan, MS M. 708–9), the *Life of St. Edmund* (Morgan, MS M. 736), the *Morgan Picture Book* (Morgan, MS M. 638), the *Windmill Psalter* (Morgan, MS M. 102), and the *Farnese Hours* by Giulio Clovio (Morgan, MS M. 69).

Two discrete and complementary catalogues for the exhibition were produced, one by the New York Public Library, the other by the Pierpont Morgan Library. In the first, Charles F. McCombs, of the New York Public Library, presented a historically complete vision of illumination to a general audience. In the second, Charks Rufus Morey offered readers his scholarly conceptualization of the development of medieval painting.

McCombs's primary purpose was to draw attention to Morgan's success in bringing earlier medieval manuscripts to this country. He begins by asserting

the historical importance of illumination, citing Sydney Cockerell's statement in
the Burlington Fine Arts Club catalogue: "[until recently] professed students of art,
with a few notable exceptions, have chosen to regard them [illuminations] as
interesting toys, quite outside the scope of their more serious investigations."[134]
McCombs goes on to celebrate the recent recognition of the beauty and importance of earlier medieval illumination, repeatedly maintaining that the work of the
thirteenth and early fourteenth centuries presents the height of perfection of the
art. Further, he adopts the formulation Morey had already used in his essay accompanying the Princeton exhibition—that is, McCombs asserts that the late fifteenth
and early sixteenth centuries present a period of decline in which the images abandoned their status as adornment and assumed the position of autonomous illustration. McCombs then presents his readers with a sketch of some recent scholarly
insights on key elements of illumination, medieval book production, and the function of illuminated manuscripts. Finally he discusses workshops, various supports,
and bindings, and closes with explications of individual manuscripts.

The volume produced by the Morgan Library for the same exhibition
takes an even more markedly academic approach. The catalogue opens with an
essay by Morey that lays out an elaborate conceptualization of the development of
style in medieval illumination.[135] He discerns three distinctive artistic tendencies in
the early Middle Ages. The first current he describes is a residual three-dimensional Hellenism evident in late-antique manuscripts such as the *Vatican Virgil*. A
second tendency appears in "Oriental" manuscripts and is characterized by a two-
dimensional, decorative quality. A third approach is found in works from northern
Europe, where "barbarian" interlaced animal ornament dominates artistic production. In Morey's schema, during the ninth century these three tendencies—along
with a fourth, linear approach that develops at Rémois workshops—come together
in varying proportions at the distinctive Carolingian schools of illumination across
the Holy Roman Empire. Throughout this bookish text, Morey repeatedly cites
scholars such as Franz Wickhoff, M. R. James, and A. M. Friend (incidentally,
Morey's student at Princeton).[136] His argument had originally been published in
the journal *The Arts* in 1925. Its reprinting as the introduction to a book whose
numerous reproductions of illuminations lent it the possibility of appealing to a
general audience suggests that the Morgan Library was determined to circulate the
discoveries of American manuscript experts to a broad public. In the United

States, scholarship—not aesthetic appreciation—was becoming the glue that bound
together the illuminated bits of the European past.

**Lessing J. Rosenwald
Invites America In**

In the early part of the twentieth century, the United
States was without national holdings in illuminated
works analogous to those of the Bibliothèque Na-
tionale or the British Library. At the Library of Congress, early efforts in the
acquisition of medieval manuscripts were directed toward paleographic samples
more than ornamented codices.[137] But Lessing J. Rosenwald (1891–1979), philanthropist and collector primarily of printed books and prints, apparently recognized
the place of illumination in the history of the illustrated book and applied himself
to the acquisition of single leaves and cuttings to supplement his huge donations
of printed material to the national collection. If Rosenwald's donation of illuminations to the National Gallery casts a glance back to our discussion of the realm of
the private collector, this benefactor's attitudes and activities root him firmly
among the trends toward increased public knowledge of miniatures.[138]

Lessing J. Rosenwald was born in Chicago. His father, Julius Rosenwald,
was an early developer and later president of Sears, Roebuck and Company, then
a Chicago-based mail-order house. After graduating from Cornell University in
1911 at age twenty, Lessing went to work at his father's company and in 1920 was
put in charge of the Philadelphia branch. By 1932 he had advanced to chairman
of the board, and seven years later he resigned to devote himself to philanthropy
and collecting.

Rosenwald's career as a collector began with an enthusiasm for prints. By
his midthirties he had the means to indulge his interest in fifteenth-century woodcuts and metal cuts. He acquired important examples at major sales of European
collections in the late 1920s, purchasing some of the rarest block books and incunabula in the world.[139] Although his initial focus was on works produced before
1520, interestingly, Rosenwald made exceptions for books by two distinctive medievalizing makers of *livres d'art*, William Morris and William Blake.

Given his interest in the early history of the illustrated book, it is not surprising that occasionally Rosenwald acquired illuminated manuscripts to supplement his printed book collection. His holdings included a handful of important
Books of Hours, among which were a tiny late-fourteenth-century Parisian Book
of Hours that may have been illuminated by Bourgot Le Noir, daughter of Jean
Le Noir, painter at the court of Charles V (Rosenwald, MS LC BX 2080.A 3 B66
1340) as well as a Horae created at the court of François I (Rosenwald, MS LC
14).[140] Rosenwald also acquired the famous Giant Bible of Mainz (Rosenwald,
MS LC 5), important because of its affinity to the Gutenberg Bible and because its
marginal ornament raises compelling questions about the uses of model books by
both illuminators and printmakers in the period of transition from pen to press.[141]
Splendid though the Rosenwald manuscripts may have been, they are few in
number. It seems that the collector whose family fortune was based in mass-
produced product—sold through printed mail-order catalogues—embraced one
of the earliest and most easily disseminated forms of mass-produced information,
the printed book, over and above the hand-produced codex.[142]

From his first years as a collector, Rosenwald felt a responsibility to share
his holdings with the public.[143] In 1943, only four years after he had retired from
Sears Roebuck to devote himself to his collection, Rosenwald donated his holdings of prints and books, respectively, to the Graphic Arts Collection of the
National Gallery and to the Library of Congress. In the subsequent years he con-

tinued to collect, amassing works to enrich the nation's holdings. Until Rosenwald's death in 1979, the works were kept in Jenkintown (outside Philadelphia) at Alverthorpe, formerly the Rosenwald home, converted into a gallery. Here, the collector often personally welcomed groups of visitors—from schoolchildren to art students to scholars—into the galleries and even encouraged them to handle his precious books.

In 1946, roughly two decades into his career as a collector, Rosenwald began to supplement his print collection with illuminated single leaves and cuttings. He regularly asserted that a collection functions as the mirror of the collector.[144] And indeed his personal expertise in print history and connoisseurship was the basis upon which he formed his library and print collection. The bulk of Rosenwald's sixty-nine illuminations, however, were purchased under the counsel of his friend Erwin Rosenthal, the German manuscript scholar and book dealer who had established himself in Berkeley, California, during the Second World War. Rosenwald tells of his first encounter with Rosenthal's illuminations: "I was so impressed by their inherent beauty and their splendid preservation as well as by Dr. Rosenthal's great knowledge of the subject that I bought many of them."[145] Rosenwald appears to have bought his illuminations not to enrich his personal collection but rather to augment public holdings on the history of the book. Around fifty of the miniatures purchased by Rosenwald were donated in name to the National Gallery within a year of his purchasing them. The rest were granted within four years of their purchase. So in the years that Andrew Mellon and the Wideners were giving their holdings of Renaissance and baroque works to Washington, Rosenwald was enlivening knowledge of illumination in America, welcoming the opportunity to acquire outstanding examples to enrich the country's holdings, although the works were outside the immediate realm of his expertise.[146]

Rosenwald purchased roughly forty-five leaves from Rosenthal, most of them trecento and quattrocento illuminations, many of which were taken from giant choral books executed by outstanding artists such as Niccolò da Bologna, Belbello da Pavia, and the Master of the Dominican Effigies. One leaf by this last master, purchased from Rosenthal, shows Christ and the Virgin enthroned with forty saints (Rosenwald, MGA B-22,128; see figure 139).[147] This large-scale miniature shares compositional elements as well as specific poses and gestures with a painting in the sacristy of Santa Maria Novella. Indeed, the overall format of the leaf recalls Celotti-Ottley illuminated collages; the scene of Christ, the Virgin, and saints functions as the main image, while the floriated border punctuated with medallions of Christ and saints acts as a frame (see chapter 2). The distinction between Rosenwald and the great twentieth-century American collector of single leaves-qua-picture paintings, Robert Lehman, is worth noting: whereas Lehman displayed no interest in the original-manuscript context of his paintinglike leaves, Rosenwald was drawn to miniatures through his enthusiasm for the history of the codex.

The Rosenwald miniatures, however, suggest more than a simple interest in the early book. Whether the collector was aware of it or not, some of his holdings also exemplify nineteenth-century taste for illuminations. Among his purchases were thirteen miniatures excised from a Sevillian antiphonary, dated to the 1430s and attributed to the Master of the Cypresses (possibly identified with Pedro da Toledo).[148] The group is made up of five purely ornamental initials and eight figurative initials—six of King David, one of another Old Testament figure, one of a group of monks at an altar singing—executed in a monumental style that suggests both Italian and Flemish influences. Apparently, in the mid–nineteenth century the cuttings had been bound into an album, along with a fourteenth

139.

**Master of the Dominican Effigies, Christ and Virgin enthroned with forty saints (Italy, circa 1340)**

140.

**Master of the Cypresses, initial *T*, with Benedictine monks singing (Spain, 1430s), from an album bought in Spain in 1849**

miniature of the Resurrected Christ (given to Simon Bening), either by a Madrid dealer or by one W. Sterling, who purchased the album in 1849. We may never know the motivations for the original insertion of the Bruges miniature of Christ with the series of Sevillian fragments. Stylistically they are dissimilar and as a group they present no coherent story or message. We can speculate, however, about the appeal the little composite volume may have held for Rosenwald when he encountered it in the New York gallery of Bernard Rosenthal, son to Erwin. The monumentality and hard edges of the figures in all of the initials in the album suggest a coloristic analogue to the early prints Rosenwald admired. His taste for the early printed book, then, may have drawn him to this group of Sevillian miniatures. The cutting of an intial *T*, for example, presents an enigmatic image of singing monks accompanied by a bearded man who crouches down and drinks from a lion's head fountain (figure 140, plate 33). Here, the crowded, shallow space peopled by animated figures recalls Rosenwald's six prints from a Swabian Passion series (1480–90), to cite one of many possible examples.[149]

Another set of images in the Rosenwald collection speaks to the nineteenth-century interest in illumination and reproductive techniques (figure 77). Three grisaille and gold miniatures created in the style of late-fifteenth-century Flanders were acquired as originals by Rosenwald in the 1940s and 1950s (Rosenwald, NGA B-21, 371–75; and B-21, 367–70). But Nordenfalk did not include the works in his catalogue of the Rosenwald collection after he discovered that they closely follow a series of images in a late-fifteenth-century manuscript created for Louis of Bruges (BnF, MS fr. 181) and deemed the works nineteenth-century copies. Later, however, Wieck demonstrated that the works were not forgeries at all but copies made in good faith as part of the process of creating a chromolithographed facsimile of the Louis of Bruges manuscript produced by Georges Hurtrel in 1870 (see chapter 3).[150] In the album of Sevillian miniatures and these relics of the mechanical reproduction of an earlier age, Rosenwald bequeathed to his country not only specimens of the art of medieval book illustration, but also testaments to the cutting, pasting, and copying practices of nineteenth-century Europe.

**Urban Collections Catch Up**

The impulse to create public holdings of illumination in America was not exclusive to Rosenwald. The New York Public Library, established in 1895, early on gained impressive illuminated pieces. The core collections that originally made up the library, formed from the combined holdings of John Jacob Astor and James Lenox, featured medieval works. Astor had secured select manuscripts and early printed books, and the Lenox library, known primarily for its holdings of important Americana, had gained roughly fifty manuscripts in 1892 from the widow of Robert Leighton Stuart.[151]

But the most spectacular illuminated manuscripts to enter the New York Public Library in its early years were the volumes in the collection of William Augustus Spencer. Spencer had been born in the United States but was educated in Geneva and made his home in Paris. He amassed rich holdings in modern French bindings and illustrated books from the medieval to the modern eras. Included were the early-fourteenth-century English *De la Twyere Psalter*, featuring a pictorial preface of thirteen pages of miniatures formerly in the collection of Henry Yates Thompson, and a richly illuminated Boethius manuscript formerly held by Guyon de Sardière. Impressed by a visit to the work site of the central building of the New York Public Library, Spencer bequeathed his volumes to the city, along with funds to augment the collection.[152] New York gained the prized manuscripts earlier than anyone could have expected. One a return trip to his American homeland in April 1912, Spencer went down with the Titanic.

In the middle decades of the twentieth century, curators at the museums and libraries of important U.S. cities scoured the market for illuminated manuscripts and cuttings, by then considered essential components of a comprehensive and high-quality collection. The illuminated holdings of the Cleveland Museum of Art was founded upon a donation of fourteen leaves to the museum by J.H. Wade between 1923 and 1925.[153] These works range in date from the thirteenth through the fifteenth centuries and stem from both northern and Italian ateliers. Subsequently, the curator, and later director, William Milliken (1889–1978) committed himself to the pursuit of illuminated folia. The sharp eye responsible in 1930 for the acquisition of six outstanding pieces from the Guelph Treasure of medieval objects tended to favor large pieces from the late Middle Ages and Renaissance, mainly of Italian origin. Among the most outstanding of these painting-like works is a 34.9-by-33.7-centimeter initial G with Christ and the Virgin adored by angels, now attributed to Don Silvestro dei Gherarducci and formerly in the collection of Ottley (CMA 30.105).[154] In the fashion of Robert Lehman, Milliken preferred Italian works suitable for mounting, framing, and glazing. As a less-expensive substitute for panel paintings, the legacy of Celotti and Ottley endured within the American museum world.

Boston's public library also began to acquire illuminated manuscripts and leaves and rare books in general in the 1920s. Chiefly responsible for Boston's acquisitions was the Keeper of Rare Books from 1934, Zoltán Haraszti. Intent upon educating his visitors to the medieval past, this Hungarian bibliophile pleaded for rare books for the city of Boston in a 1928 article.[155] Within two decades, Haraszti got his wish. A 1934 reorganization of the library gave special consideration to the library's antiquarian holdings, and in the first years of the 1950s the curator cashed in on several trust funds established to enrich the Rare Books Department, purchasing fifteen illuminated manuscripts and fifteen leaves.[156] Subsequent purchases and gifts resulted in the collection of some sixty single leaves now housed in Boston. Among Haraszti's initial acquisitions were folia from large trecento

Sienese, Florentine, and Venetian antiphonaries, mostly bought from Houpli. A particularly rich example among these pieces is a fragment painted by Niccolò da Bologna featuring the martyrdoms of SS. Stephen, Lawrence, Paul, and Sebastian (Boston Public Library, MS Med. 144 [1569]) and another fourteenth-century German work with a Nativity of the Virgin (MS Med. 156 [1581]).

## Shoppers Consume

If the goal of establishing museums and libraries and mounting exhibitions was to edify and educate a broad American public, nothing could have reached a wider sweep of the urban population than the department store. Neil Harris has articulated the affinities between department stores and museums—both were developed in the late nineteenth century, both displayed items for mass consumption, be it visual or commercial.[157] In major urban centers, the two types of institution often competed for attention, and their exhibition techniques sometimes overlapped. In the early 1890s, as Chicago was preparing to host the World's Columbian Exposition, Marshall Field's underwent a luxurious renovation. Already offering framed paintings and boasting a room devoted to the designs of William Morris, the store added costly Persian carpets, Chippendale furniture, and Chinese rugs and jades.[158] By 1914 it had established a Rare Book Department where both illuminated manuscripts and single leaves were sold.[159] Now anyone could buy books that were formerly the reserve of socialites who could afford a European education and the dealers' prices in the rue de la Paix. "Art these days," asserted the popular magazine *Outlook and Independent* in 1930 "is being bought, not by museums and poor immigrant boys become millionaires, but by Mrs. Smith and Mrs. Jones."[160]

## Dispersal: Illumination Hits the Road

### Otto Ege's Biblioclasm

Surely to allow a thousand people "to have and to hold" an original manuscript leaf, and to get the thrill and understanding that comes only from actual and frequent contact with these art heritages, is justification enough for the scattering of fragments. Few, indeed, can hope to own a complete manuscript book; hundreds, however, may own a leaf.

—OTTO F. EGE, "I AM A BIBLIOCLAST"

The work of Otto F. Ege (1888–1951) offered a variation on programs intended to increase public exposure to illumination. Each of the exhibitions and collections already examined was displayed or housed at a single, fixed institution, its audience drawn from the surrounding area. In Ege's enterprise the action is inverted. This Cleveland-based educator and collector assembled portfolios of single leaves designed to travel the country and bring medieval works to the doorsteps of America. Ege intended the folia that filled his circulating suitcases to represent medieval cultural history as a whole, thereby displaying the European past to an American public that would otherwise have scant opportunity to experience the Middle Ages through concrete objects. Ege also promoted knowledge of medieval manuscripts through his articles in scholarly and popular publications.[161]

Otto F. Ege was born in Reading, Pennsylvania, to a middle-class family. First trained at the Philadelphia School of Industrial Arts, he went on to study art education at New York University, from which he graduated in 1913. Later he directed programs in the training of educators at the Philadelphia Museum School of Industrial Arts and, in the 1920s, became head of the Department of Teacher Training at the Cleveland Museum of Art, where he also served as an instructor in lettering, layout, and typography. He developed summer and weekend programs, gave public lectures on art history and the history of the book, and served on regional arts committees. During the five years before his 1951 suicide, Ege was Dean of the Cleveland Institute of Art.[162]

Although enthusiastic about the medieval book, Ege lacked the financial resources of a Lewis or a Rosenwald. So, rather than buying through private agents or at auction, Ege ferreted out affordable works in European bookshops while chaperoning student trips abroad and scoured the mail-order catalogues of American and European booksellers. By the late 1930s Ege had obtained roughly sixty manuscript volumes in this way as well as over one hundred total incunabula and early printed works. He had also collected hundreds of single leaves, many from Italian and Spanish choir books of the fourteenth, fifteenth, and sixteenth centuries.[163] His nineteen Books of Hours catalogued by De Ricci were supplemented by psalters, choir books, and Bibles, most of which feature little illumination beyond flourished initials, but offer some exquisite calligraphy. Outstanding among his holdings was a richly adorned mid-fifteenth-century Dutch Book of Hours.[164]

Ege's primary motivation for the acquisition of illumination was to gain tools with which to educate the public at large and to raise the caliber of contemporary book design. Whereas enthusiasts from the time of Celotti and Ottley had been excising single leaves and cutting up manuscripts to create picture–painting like isolated images or to gain specimens arrayed within an album, Ege broke apart manuscripts to compile didactic aids in his crusade to educate his audiences. In a 1938 article "I Am a Biblioclast," Ege recounts his initiation into manuscript breaking and offers his justification for such activity.[165] Around 1920, Ege wrote, he found himself bidding at auction for a manuscript he could not afford. When the hammer fell, he had gained the high-priced work. A "well-known Chicago collector" (unnamed by Ege) "tempted" our poor bidder by offering to front the needed funds if Ege would split the manuscript with him. First, insisting that he never again repeated such an undirected and heinous crime against a book, he then presents his personal guidelines for acceptable manuscript breaking: (1) never take apart a museum piece or a unique copy if it is complete; (2) make leaves and sections of manuscripts available to schools, libraries, collections, and individuals; (3) circulate leaf exhibits with supporting educative material to foster interest in fine books, past and present; (4) use the fragments to inspire calligraphers and enthusiasts of the private press to apply older principles to contemporary books while being careful not to blindly imitate past artisans; (5) build a personal collection of the history of the book from ancient Egyptian and Babylonian works to those by contemporary authors. In sum, Ege justifies biblioclastic activities as necessary evils when they foster knowledge of medieval history, art, and culture, and elevate present-day artistic practice.

To expose the public to original examples of the medieval book arts, Ege curated traveling exhibitions. In the 1930s, shows composed of works from his personal collection were sent to museums and other institutions.[166] But Ege left his greatest legacy through the portfolios of single leaves which, in the spirit of the sets of cuttings assembled by the Victoria and Albert Museum (see chapter 4), were intended for mass circulation "from the State of Washington to the State of Massachusetts"[167] and were sold primarily to libraries. Ege's portfolios were filled with matted manuscript leaves and printed sheets. (Occasionally acting as a dealer himself, Ege sometimes included advertisements for the sale of single folia in his boxed sets.) These collections bear titles such as *Original Leaves from Famous Bibles: Nine Centuries, 1121–1935 A.D.* (which contained four medieval manuscript leaves; see figure 141), *Original Leaves from Famous Books: Eight Centuries, 1240–1923 A.D.*

**141.**

*"Twelfth-Century*
*Manuscript Bible," no. 2,*
*Original Leaves from*
*Famous Bibles,*
*Nine Centuries,*
*1121–1935 A.D.*
*Collected and Assembled*
*by Otto F. Ege*
(Cleveland, 1940s)

**142.**

*Beauvais Missal* leaf
(France, circa 1290)

(containing three medieval samples), and *Fifty Original Leaves from Medieval Manuscripts and Fifteen Original Oriental Manuscript Leaves of Six Centuries.*[168]

If, in keeping with his goals as an educator, Ege did not hoard the medieval works he found in the bookstalls of Europe, he nonetheless tended to keep the most richly illuminated—and thus most valuable—folia for his personal collection. One of his more precious pieces was a leaf from the Beauvais Missal, created in France circa 1290. While unilluminated sister leaves from this manuscript toured the country, serving as exquisite examples of late-thirteenth-century script, Ege kept one ornamented folio, featuring an image of a priest before an altar, at home (figure 142). Further testimony to Ege's tendency to hold on to richly adorned pieces and to circulate text pages is found in the works from his collection offered for sale in 1984.[169] An early-fourteenth-century Franco-Flemish lectern Bible, brightly illuminated on every page, was kept fully intact, but leaves from a relatively modestly adorned fifteenth-century Italian volume of Livy's *History of Rome* surface in the portfolios of *Fifty Leaves from Medieval Manuscripts.*[170]

In the portfolios, the descriptive texts that accompany each leaf make plain Ege's pedagogic aim to help his audience to reconstruct an image of the medieval past through the aid of medieval fragments. In *Fifty Original Leaves from Medieval Manuscripts,* for example, each folio is accompanied by two short paragraphs laying out the function of the leaf's parent manuscript, and with cinematic detail that is perhaps more imaginative than accurate, Ege attempts to evoke the manuscript's milieu. Describing a fifteenth-century Italian antiphonal leaf, Ege writes, "Candle grease stains reveal that this small-sized antiphonal was doubtless carried in processions in dimly lighted cathedrals" (no. 27). A fifteenth-century Italian Epistolary bears the meticulously descriptive caption "[the rubrics on the page were inserted] to assist the deacon or sub-deacon in chanting parts of this section of this church service while he was standing on the second step in front of the altar" (no. 37). And Ege informs his students that Books of Hours could be purchased by "the devout and wealthy layman" at bookstalls in front of cathedrals and at shrines on pilgrimage routes (no. 31), these prayer books then becoming "the most treasured possessions [of their owner] . . . not only carried to chapel but . . . often kept at bedside at night" (no. 36).

Ege also served as consultant to a project related to his own mission and sponsored by the publishers of the Grolier Encyclopedia. In the 1950s, in an age of radio, television, film, and comic books, Grolier sought to create an exhibition that would stimulate children to take an interest in the history of writing and the book. A "Magic Carpet on Wheels"—an aluminum trailer—brought "An Exhibition of 4,500 Years of History by the Book of Knowledge" to sites in the United States and Canada that had no museums.[171] Roughly two hundred fragments were laid out to demonstrate the continuous progress of the history of writing from the third millennium B.C.E. to the present. The exhibition opened with cuneiform tablets and a fragment of a papyrus scroll of the Book of Esther. Medieval work was represented by tenth- and eleventh-century fragments and leaves from late-medieval Books of Hours. Modern illuminators like Alberto Sangorski were also represented within the sampling.[172]

Ege sought to popularize knowledge of medieval manuscripts not only through public programs, exhibitions, and portfolios of leaves but also through numerous articles.[173] During his lifetime, he wrote roughly forty pieces on topics from manuscript illumination and the history of the codex to the function of art in education and the design of the modern book. Although he mostly published in journals of education and popular publications such as newspapers and general art magazines, he also had essays in the *College Art Journal, the Journal of the American Institute of Graphic Arts*, and the *American Magazine of Art*. In many of these articles he cast himself as an American follower of Ruskin and Morris. Like Ruskin, Ege argued that the study of the history of art and book design were no frills for dilettantes but important components in the education of the general public as well as designers.[174] In other works Ege evoked Morris's crusade to "strive again for beauty in books," praising "our best present-day printers [for] . . . endeavoring to incorporate beauty [in their works] as did the scribes of the Middle Ages."[175] Ege even directly invokes the Kelmscott Master's "The Ideal Book" in his article "The Modern Book," which bemoans the low state of contemporary book design and advocates a look to the past for inspiration.[176]

In sum, Ege's approach to the medieval book is that of a true American modernist. He takes gatherings of medieval folia, breaks them down into even smaller components, and treats the resultant single leaves as integral works of culture which attest to the spirit of a past age while concurrently functioning as autonomous tools to generate art and book production for the future.

## Mortimer Brandt's Touring Leaves

The impulse to assemble medieval illuminations into a historically coherent package for the enlightenment of Main Street was not exclusive to Ege. In the decades between 1965 and 1986, the collector and art dealer Mortimer Brandt (1905–93) also sent his personal holdings on an extended tour of middle America.[177] In distinction to Ege, this gallery director of means was not limited to purchasing damaged or fragmented works. Rather, with an Old Master paintings and drawings dealership on fashionable Fifty-seventh Street in New York, Brandt had the connoisseur's eye and the wealth to acquire an impressive collection of twenty-nine single leaves and cuttings.[178]

It comes as no surprise that as a dealer of Old Master paintings, Brandt demonstrated little interest in the medieval manuscript as an integral object. Rather, in the manner of Ottley, Celotti, and his own contemporary Robert Lehman, he favored works—particularly Italian works—suitable for mounting and framing. Certain pieces in his collection evoke a specifically Celotti-Ottley-like aesthetic. One pair of sixteenth-century folia, for example, today attributed to a close follower of Cima de Conegliano (given to the circle of Benedetto Bordone in the Brandt-Bober catalogue) fits neatly into the preferred aesthetic of paintings collectors.[179] One leaf features a standing figure of Catherine of Siena surrounded by medallions and panels depicting miraculous scenes from her life. The other presents a central image of St. Dominic surrounded by similar hagiographic episodes. Stylistically, the works recall contemporary monumental Venetian painting, such as the work of Giovanni Bellini and Antonello da Messina. Moreover, compositionally, the leaves bear a remarkable resemblance to the Carracci-like collages sold at the Celotti sale of 1825 (see chapter 2).

Stopping at seventeen venues remote from the major urban centers of this country, Brandt's collection of miniatures circulated for twenty-two years, first stopping in Jacksonville, Florida, and moving on to Louisville, Kentucky; Memphis, Tennessee; Milwaukee, Wisconsin; Wichita, Kansas; Binghamton, New York; Williamstown, Massachusetts; and Athens, Georgia. It then returned to Kentucky, stopping in Lexington, Owensborough, Ashland, Morehead, and Paducah, before visiting Rochester, New York, and making a repeat appearance in Williamstown.

Brandt's friend Harry Bober (1916–88), a professor of medieval art at New York University's Institute of Fine Arts and a collector of single leaves himself, wrote the exhibition catalogue.[180] This work was available at every stop and often was tailored to specific locales with specially printed covers identifying the venue and dates of the exhibition.[181] In some respects, this catalogue echoes Ege. In the introduction, Brandt asserts: "[O]ne may look at reproductions and read about illuminated manuscripts at any time. But no reproductions and no words can tell or show the first essences of this art which only the originals can communicate."[182] But in important ways the Brandt-Bober catalogue distinguishes itself from the written work of the Ohio educator. Whereas Ege focused on the ways in which his leaves would have operated harmoniously within their parent manuscripts, Bober concerned himself with questions natural to a scholar of paintings—iconography, style, visual sources, and provenance.

Bober's emphasis on the paintinglike qualities of Brandt's illuminations is well-demonstrated in his entry on a historiated *A* with a scene of the Presentation of Christ in the Temple from a Pisan choral book from about 1325 to 1350 (no. 16).[183] Unlike Ege, he offers no discussion of the function of the liturgical manuscript in which the initial originally appeared. Instead, Bober first explicates the iconography of the scene, goes on to note that its style resembles the Sienese, and then discusses related works. Notably, the art historian takes special care to argue that the composition and character of the illumination can be seen as a variation on a scene in Duccio's *Maesta* and that the illuminator also seems to have had knowledge of Simone Martini. Discussion of a full-page miniature of a Nativity, excised from a Book of Hours, similarly reads as though it were an entry in a catalogue of paintings (figure 143, plate 34).[184]
Bober praises the artist in terms reminiscent of those typically used to extol the genius of Renaissance masters: "This miniature does not simply illustrate the Nativity, it interprets the event." He goes on to explicate the iconography of the Old Testament figures that frame the main image and, after discussing the decorative programs and functions of Books of Hours, analyzes the mix of medieval and Renaissance styles in the piece. The scholar concludes with a connoisseurial analysis that compares the miniature to the work of the French master Jean Colombe. Although some consideration is given to the original-manuscript context of this miniature, for Bober and Brandt, on the whole, illuminations serve less as tokens of a lost art of the book and more as portable testaments to the past grandeur of painting.

**143.**

**Adoration of the Christ Child (Tours, France, circa 1480–90)**

## ILLUMINATION TRANSFORMS IN THE AMERICAN SCRIPTORIUM

### Olive Frances Rhinelander and Translated Illumination

Similar to the case in Europe, with the development of both a collectorship of and an audience for medieval and Renaissance manuscripts and cuttings, there came a class of professional artists who specialized in modern illumination, executing copies and original creations. These American miniaturists served a market that spanned the extremes between deep knowledge of medieval and Renaissance book production on the one hand and relative ignorance of the original context of illuminated paintings on the other. The productions of Olive Frances Rhinelander (died 1942) catered to the better informed.

Rhinelander was a prominent illuminator working in New York in the 1920s and 1930s. Apparently not content to dabble with boxed sets of paints marketed to ladies of leisure, she undertook extensive personal research into the methods of medieval illuminators. Having studied medieval recipes for the preparation of colors, she used burned grapevine twigs and genuine lapis lazuli to achieve rich purples and blues, and sought out quills that most closely approximated those used by medieval scribes. She achieved public recognition when the Pratt Institute Free Library of Brooklyn held an exhibition of her illuminations in 1933.[186]

Rhinelander was considered so skilled that the most discerning of manuscript collections in America, the Pierpont Morgan Library, acquired her works and even commissioned her to create pieces to serve as exemplars of modern illumination. But though these pieces may have been created by following medieval techniques, they modified their models into works that suited contemporary taste. In one work Rhinelander copied a folio of the Lindau Gospels (Morgan, MS M 688a 2, copy of Morgan, MS M. 1, folio 168; see figures 144 and 145, the outstanding imperial work purchased by Morgan at the outset of his collecting activity). On purple-dyed parchment, in gold Caroline lettering, she gives nine lines of John's Gospel: "In principio erat verbum."[187] The folio, however, is not an exact replica. Similar to Henry Shaw (see chapter 3), Rhinelander "improved" upon her medieval model, editing out the wrinkle that extends from the right margin through the border into the text itself in the original. Further, the modern illumination seems to have been conceived as an autonomous work; roughly half a century after the Celotti-Ottley sale, Rhinelander created a ready-made single leaf suitable for framing. In another project—one that remained unfinished— Rhinelander seems to have sought to recreate a tenth-century manuscript in a twentieth-century mold, for the Pierpont Morgan Library now possesses a box of Rhinelander's purple-stained vellum leaves, three bifolia of which feature an English text of the Gospel of John written in gold capitals. The scribal work imitates another treasure acquired by Pierpont Morgan in his early years of collecting, the tenth-century Golden Gospels (Morgan, MS M. 23).

Rhinelander did not limit herself to emulation and recreation of works associated with the Holy Roman Empire. One of her pieces created for the Morgans presents the text of Psalm 119 executed in the eleventh-century Winchester style of the British Isles. Although it features headings in Latin, the calligraphic verses are presented in English. Another work, with floriated initial and border this time in the style of late-fourteenth-century English manuscript il-

144.

**Olive Frances Rhinelander,
"In principio erat
verbum," copied from the
*Lindau Gospels* (United
States, circa 1924–34)**

145.

***Lindau Gospels* (ninth
century)**

lumination, offers verses addressing the place of faith and love for the Lord in a
modern context: "Oh Love, that maketh heavy burdens light/ Oh Love, that
maketh bitter things most sweet/. . . Not only in Bethlehem of old,/But in the
news and the streets and at our door" (Morgan, MS M. 688a. 4). Offering texts in
modern English (rather than medieval Latin), addressing the contingencies of contemporary urban life, and creating ready-made cuttings, Rhinelander immersed
herself in the styles and techniques of the Middle Ages to create pieces to appeal to
modern sensibilities.

**Coella Lindsay
Ricketts
and Pastiched
Illumination**

Coella Lindsay Ricketts (1860–1941) is a particularly
suitable figure to address at the end of our study. A
collector who exhibited his works and an illuminator
in his own right, he exemplifies several trends we have
examined throughout this book. At the same time the
modern illuminations he and his assistants created typify a wholly American cooption of the medieval past, using that past to lend an aura of authority or mystery to
modern productions.

Ricketts was born and raised in Stockport, Ohio. His youth was spent
assisting his parents with their family farm, but he abandoned agriculture in 1880
when he went to Ohio University in Athens, Ohio, where he studied classics.
Subsequently he moved to Chicago, and in 1885, pursuing a longstanding interest
in penmanship and calligraphy, he opened an engrossing studio, the Scriptorium,
at 38 South Dearborn, where he and his staff created modern illuminated works.
Apparently, he simultaneously pursued a corporate career, serving as vice president
and a director of the Duncan Electric Company, an electrical supplies manufacturing firm in Lafayette, Indiana.[188]

The money he earned from these two ventures allowed Ricketts to nour-
ish his interest in the medieval book (initiated by studying works in the Newberry
Library).[189] During his lifetime he made more than a dozen trips to Europe, where

he purchased manuscripts and cuttings and also undertook meticulous scholarly research in the libraries. He was an early member and supporter of Chicago's Caxton Club, twice serving as its president. Ricketts's lifelong study and promotion of the knowledge of illumination eventually won him an honorary curatorship of manuscripts at the Art Institute of Chicago.

During approximately fifty years of collecting, Ricketts accrued more than a hundred manuscripts and over a thousand manuscript fragments.[190] The manuscripts range in date from the thirteenth to the seventeenth centuries and represent almost every European country, the greatest number being fourteenth- and fifteenth-century Italian works. Although Ricketts maintained that his aim in collecting was to "illustrate the beauty side of written and illuminated manuscripts on vellum of the Mediaeval Ages,"[191] most of his volumes are not heavily adorned with images and seem to have been collected for their calligraphy. Ricketts's holdings of fragments, on the other hand, do offer rich examples of painted work. Dating mostly to the fourteenth and fifteenth centuries, these leaves and cuttings are predominantly from France, Italy, and England. Although Ricketts acquired some of his manuscripts and fragments from American dealers, such as the New York-based Weyhe, many pieces were purchased abroad from von Scherling of Leiden and, in London, from Quaritch and Tregaskis. Indeed, Ricketts developed a close personal relationship with Tregaskis, using his firm as a base at which to receive mail and writing to his daughter of the dealer's failing health.[192]

One of the most compelling aspects of the Ricketts trove is that this collector and illuminator's holdings exemplify key nineteenth-century trends vis-à-vis manuscript illumination as we have tracked them in this study—collaging, copying, and creating. Among the collages Ricketts acquired are samples that exemplify the nineteenth-century taste for works that evoke the golden age of painting (see also chapter 2). For example, he owned one piece that echoes formally the levels of illusionism found in Michelangelo and the Carracci (figure 146). In this work a historiated *O*, perhaps by painter to the Medicis Attavante Attavanti, is framed by a floriated border and two illuminated strips bearing escutcheons that echo the circular form of the main initial. The two round armorials beneath function within an illusionist plane distinct from that of the main image and find visual and conceptual analogs in the tromp l'oeil roundels of the Sistine Chapel and Farnese ceilings (figures 42 and 43). Here, illumination is transformed from ornament into high art.[193]

Other collages acquired by Ricketts evoke a wholly distinctive interest among nineteenth-century collectors of fragments—the impulse to arrange miniatures and initials in capricious new compositions, as evident in nineteenth-century albums. This approach to layout seems to have been at work in four sheets, each adorned with late-fourteenth-century English initials (Lilly, Ricketts MSS I, 10a–d). One of these pages is framed on three sides with a floriated border (figure 147). At the center of the composition, fragments of ornamental vines, which originally must have occupied a manuscript border, are pasted together to create a dominating treelike form. Four flourished letters *C* and *D* are deployed to balance the image. United solely by design elements like tone and line quality, the miniatures making up this collage seemingly were brought together neither to make a narrative point through subject matter nor to demonstrate anything about the historical development of miniature painting, but simply to create a harmonious composition.

Another piece (Lilly, Ricketts MSS I, 18-21; see figure 148) evokes mid-nineteenth-century publications for designers. Here the vertical axis is dominated by a circa-1300 southern French two-tiered historiated *D* and *O* enclosing figures

146.

Attavante Attavanti (?),
(Italy, mid–sixteenth
century), montage of
fragments (England [?],
nineteenth century)

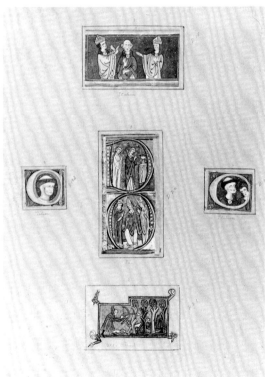

147.

Album page (?),
montage of fragments
(England, nineteenth
century [?])

148.

Historiated initials
*D* and *O*, with a priest
and bishop (France,
fourteenth century),
bishops consecrating an
ecclesiastic (Italy,
fourteenth century),
and a hunt scene
(French Flanders,
fourteenth century),
from an album (?),
montage of fragments

149.

Owen Jones,
*Grammar of Ornament*
(London, 1868), plate 64

of priests and bishops. Above is a fourteenth-century Italian miniature in which two bishops consecrate an ecclesiastic. Balancing the composition at the lateral extremes of the central axis are two initial *C*'s, each enclosing tonsured figures. But at the bottom of the page, breaking with the religious theme of the miniatures above, is a cutting representing a hunt scene from an early-fourteenth-century Franco-Flemish manuscript. The disparate fragments in this piece are united by neither provenance nor subject matter. Rather, the deployment of the images appears to have been inspired by pages such as one in Owen Jones's *Grammar of Ornament* displaying various motifs traced from medieval manuscripts (figure 149; see chapters 3 and 4). The composition equally evokes nineteenth-century album pages such as those assembled by Burckhardt-Wildt (compare figure 41). In collaged and chromolithographed image alike, assorted ornamental details are deployed and arranged into a balanced composition—displayed like rare butterflies laid out for the delectation of enthusiasts.

Many other manuscripts and cuttings in Ricketts's holdings specifically attest to the engrosser's fascination with calligraphy and letter forms. He amassed an extensive collection of writing manuals, many of which inspired Ricketts's own medievalizing creations. Among outstanding examples of late-sixteenth- and seventeenth-century model books for calligraphers is the volume of instruction *Kurtze Unterweissung artlichs annd andeutlichs Schreibens* by Bartholomaeus Horn, a master at the court of Holy Roman Emperor Rudolph II (Newberry, Wing MS ZW 547. H782; see figure 150, plate 35). This precious, six-folio work offers sample letter forms in precise, late-Gothic script with heavily flourished opening initials as well as examples of humanist scripts, letters adorned with birds and human

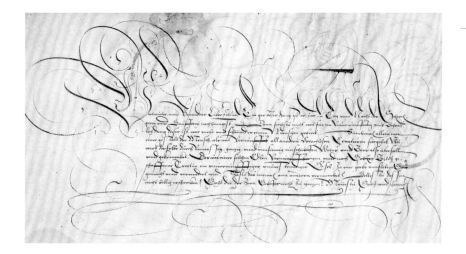

**150.**

**Bartholomaeus Horn, *Kurtze Unterweissung artlichs annd andeutlichs Schreibens*, (Holy Roman Empire, Italy, late sixteenth to early seventeenth centuries)**

faces, and an elaborate composition in micrography framed by ornamental flourishes. Particularly notable is the written address to the work's imperial patron (folio 2v), dominated by flourishes in the late-Gothic style perfected at the German courts.

Ricketts also interested himself in less flamboyant alphabets. One fifteenth-century Italian manuscript presenting a series of specimens must have been a model book for calligraphers (Lilly, Ricketts MSS I, 240; see figure 151). The work is signed by one Guinifortus de Vicomerchato of Milan and dated August 1, 1450 (a series of pages [15v to 19r] contains initials by a slightly later hand). The letters and their accompanying flourishes, isolated from larger texts and laid out row after row, strikingly bring to mind nineteenth-century album pages of cut-and-pasted initials. Indeed, Ricketts may have been aware of the affinities between this manuscript and composite works of the nineteenth century; he took special note of the fact that the book had been seen by Henry Shaw (see chapter

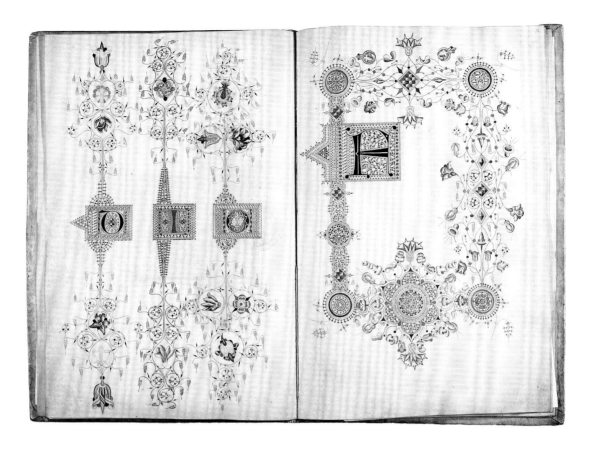

**151.**

Guinifortus de Vicomerchato,
alphabets and calligraphic
specimens (Milan, 1450)

**152.**

Calligraphic alphabet
(late fifteenth century),
initials, with flourishes
(nineteenth century)

3).[194] Yet another scribal manual returns us to the issue of nineteenth-century manipulation of medieval works. On each page of this thirty-six-folio work appears a circa-1470 excised northern Italian initial around which a nineteenth-century collector has added blue and red flourishes (Lilly, Ricketts MSS I, 243, folio 14; see figure 152).

Ricketts's interest in printing and page layout also seems to manifest itself in his acquisition of leaves from the so-called *Bohun Bible*. The history of this mid-fourteenth-century work serves as an incunable of sorts for the treatment of manuscripts examined in our study, for already by 1665, single leaves had been excised from this impressive Bible, perhaps originally bound in four volumes. All the surviving fragments feature eighteenth- and nineteenth-century foliation, indicating that the Bible passed through various hands in those centuries, losing pages along the way. Although the Bodleian Library, with its forty-eight *Bohun Bible* leaves, houses the greatest number of such fragments, many of the folia eventually ended up in private collections in the United States. For example, the Pierpont Morgan Library has two leaves (Morgan, MS M. 741), the Newberry Library owns four (Newberry, MS frag. 62.1–62.4), and the University of Chicago Library houses five (MS 122).[195] In 1930, Ricketts acquired four *Bohun Bible* leaves (Lilly Library, MS Ricketts MSS 15). One of the compelling aspects of the centuries-long enthusiasm for these works is that visually they are distinct from other single leaves popular throughout the nineteenth century. Excised from their original-manuscript context, they do not resemble autonomous small-scale panel paintings. Rather, each featuring two columns of text surrounded by rectilinear borders and punctuated with historiated initials, the leaves seem to have gained their popularity through their handsome overall compositions. The Ricketts piece, with a historiated initial of Baruch writing, is typical of the *Bohun Bible* mise-en-page (figure 153). The harmonious balance of text, image, and ornament was likely to have had particular appeal to the Chicago engrosser, and, interestingly, the design recalls Ricketts's whimsically constructed collages discussed earlier.

As the head of the Scriptorium, Ricketts probably also felt a certain esteem for the great modern illuminator of the nineteenth century Caleb William Wing (see chapter 3), for Ricketts supplemented his holdings of medieval and Renaissance works with pieces by the Brighton master, including two volumes of illuminations that function as ready-made albums from which the text has neatly been excluded, leaving only the specimens of medieval painting. One of these Wing manuscripts consists of eleven folia painted in both the Italian and the Brugeoise styles of the late fifteenth century (Lilly, Ricketts MSS I, MS 139). Ricketts apparently bought the manuscript knowing it was a copy, but his records indicate no interest in discovering the manuscript models used by the modern artist. A second manuscript, created by Wing for his patron John Boykett Jarman (see chapter 3), contains seventeen copies from an early-fifteenth-century French Book of Hours (Lilly, Ricketts MSS I, MS 140; see figure 154, plate 36). In this work Wing appears to have copied directly from a manuscript by the Master of Jean Rolin in the British Library (BL MS. Add. 25695). The depiction of the Annunciation (6r) is particularly skillful. Only details such as the stiff gesture, flat angular face, and disproportionately large nose of the king in the lower right or the awkward lettering of the scrolls in the page's margin betray that this is a modern piece. The great number of hands through which this manuscript passed subsequent to the Jarman sale suggests both a nineteenth-century appreciation for Wing and an enthusiasm for text-free "medieval" illumination regardless of whether the work was produced in the medieval age or not. Ricketts's admiration for the virtuoso modern

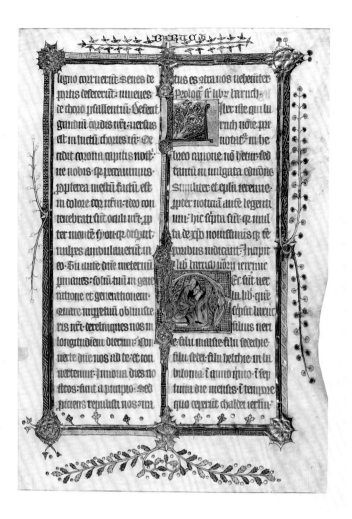

**153.**

*Bohun Bible* leaf with
Baruch writing
(England, circa 1360)

**154.**

Caleb William Wing
Nativity, (England, circa
1858)

inside binding:"[17] beautiful miniatures on vellum with fine borders . . . executed
by the late Mr. Wing for Mr. Jarman at a cost of £10 for each illumination. . . .
A superb specimen of the art of illuminating of the present day."

Today, almost a century after Ricketts was collecting, the taste for Wing
endures. The Lilly Library is the keeper of most of Ricketts's manuscripts and is
thus home to exquisite medieval illuminations by artists such as Pierre Remiet and
Parisian painters in the circle of the Bedford Master. Rather than showcase the
work of one of these artists on the Christmas cards sold in its lobby, however, the
library has chosen to reproduce Wing illuminations on both of its holiday greet-
ings cards. In the early twenty-first century, as in the mid–nineteenth, the familiar
look of a modern painted illumination appeals to general taste.

Ricketts's collection of manuscripts and fragments developed in tandem
with his assiduous study of the works. In this capacity, he fits into the American
impulse to reconstruct a complete history of manuscript illumination for a native
audience. Ricketts sought to educate through two avenues—exhibitions and publications. In 1918 he lent many of his works to a show of manuscripts at the Caxton
Club. In 1929 the Renaissance Society of the University of Chicago exhibited
Ricketts's manuscripts. But Ricketts also undertook a much grander project in his
quest to raise public awareness of illumination. During his many trips abroad he
filled multiple binders with meticulous notes for an extensive history of manuscript
illumination, "The Art of the Scriptorium." For this never-realized work, he and
his assistants painstakingly copied manuscripts that by then had entered the canon
of great works of Western art—the *Book of Durrow*, the *Book of Kells* (figure 155,
plate 37), the Bible of Charles the Bald, the *Ormesby Psalter*.[196] His study was intended to rival Shaw's work *Illuminated Ornaments* (see chapter 3) and to give par-

155.

Coella Lindsay Ricketts,
*Copy of Book of Kells,*
(United States, late
nineteenth to early
twentieth centuries)

## 156

Coella Lindsay Ricketts,
"The Scriptorium"
business card
(United States, late
nineteenth to early
twentieth centuries)

ticular attention to lettering. But unlike his nineteenth-century forebear, Ricketts committed himself to the exact duplication of the illuminations copied for his book. Whereas Shaw prettied up and corrected irregularities in the manuscripts he copied, Ricketts and his assistants fastidiously reproduced every flaw—in a sense documenting the manuscript originals rather than creating new works to suit a modern taste.[197]

In his obsessive approach to recreating the medieval past, Ricketts undertook not only an act of reconstruction but an actual recuperation as well. As leader of his own scriptorium, Ricketts directed his atelier to both copy and create new works precisely following medieval techniques. His notebooks are filled with recipes for gold and colors that revive the methods of medieval scribes and illuminators. Ricketts lived in Chicago, whose Art Institute from 1914 on was committed to industrial design and rapidly developing technology. During the same period studies of manuscripts such as O. Elfrida Saunders's *English Illumination* (1928) used photography to reproduce miniatures as a matter of course.[198] But in an age of mechanical reproduction—when chromolithography and photography had become standard tools of the trade—Ricketts turned his back on technology and donned the mantel of the medieval scribe. Indeed, promoting himself as a bearer of Old World heritage on his business card (figure 156), Ricketts presented himself within the guise of St. Jerome. Seated at his writing desk, a lion at his side, the church father who first translated scripture into the Latin vulgate so that it could be read by a broad audience becomes the ancient counterpart of Ricketts, who, in turn, translated medieval script into an American vernacular.

And Ricketts did not ignore the opportunities of the commercial present. He catered to Chicagoans who, though living in a milieu dominated by skyscrapers and expanding industry, nevertheless found medieval styles appropriate ornament for modern projects. Associated with the venerable secular and ecclesiastical institutions of Europe, medieval ornament and lettering lent an air of prestige to diplomas and official addresses, and these were the stock-in-trade of the Scriptorium. Ricketts's productions were considered so fine that he was chosen to illuminate a centennial invitation for America's most eminent public figure, President Theodore Roosevelt, in 1903.[199] His studio also applied medieval ornamentation to

Christmas cards; in one set, the margins are filled with ornament borrowed from fifteenth-century English workshops, lending an aura of the remote exoticism of the ancient Catholic Church. Like a decal, such adornment could be applied to any address to lend it the weight of Old World authority or to transport the beholder to a fantasy Middle Ages suffused with piety and the mystery of the Church.

But although the Scriptorium produced works in a historiating medieval style, Ricketts also created manuscripts that responded to the hybrid tastes of his American audiences. In 1893, the directors of the German Opera House Company commissioned from Ricketts a hand-illuminated manuscript as a gift celebrating the seventieth birthday of its president, Anton Hesing (Newberry, Wing MS fZW 883. R42; see figure 157). On thick paper with gilded edges, the watercolored work was executed in chemically produced tones. Opening with an engraved portrait of Hesing, the book presents an encomium to the prominent German-American. Written in a variation on Gothic script with letters spaced wide apart for easy legibility, the text—first in German, then in English—expresses the gratitude of Chicago's "German Public" to Hesing for his "indefatigable energy and perseverance in the creation of the Schiller Theater, the crowning work of a lifetime devoted to the earnest furtherance and fearless defense of German culture, customs and ideas in our midst." Works in Ricketts's collection seem to have inspired the manuscript. For example, the textual address to Hesing is flourished in a manner evocative of the fifteenth-century Italian model books (compare figure 151), and the calligraphy recalls the ornamental, late-Gothic Germanic script used in Bartholomaeus Horn's Rudolphine model book (figure 150). One of the manuscript's full-page images features a young blond boy, apparently costumed as a peasant from an eighteenth-century German opera, boldly gesturing toward an image of the Schiller Theater building (figure 158, plate 38). Amid Ricketts's illuminated medieval ornamentation this monument to the future, a newly built Adler and Sullivan skyscraper, is a modern analog of sorts to the portraits of the castles of Jean, duc de Berry, in the *Très Riches Heures*. In this manuscript, in sum, Ricketts collapsed the styles of fifteenth-century Italy, the late-Gothic Holy Roman Empire, and German baroque opera to create a testimonial to the cultural prestige of midwesterners of German descent. He illuminated a monument to European tradition which simultaneously looked to the future among the skyscrapers of America.

**Gertrude Carrier and Illumination in the Modern Market**    One of Ricketts's employees at the Scriptorium was Gertrude Carrier (1902–91), an independent woman who later enjoyed success as a freelance calligrapher and lettering artist. A native of Chicago, Carrier attended the School of the Art Institute, where she studied calligraphy and design with Ernst Detterer, an instructor in lettering who in 1931 became the curator of the John M. Wing Collection at the Newberry Library. Though primarily trained in drafting, upon her graduation Carrier found a position at the Scriptorium. There she worked on exacting facsimiles, such as the copy from the *Book of Kells* (figure 155) created for Ricketts's projected history of the medieval book. After several years with the firm, however, she left to pursue work independently.

Designing everything from liturgical works to greeting cards, department store signage, restaurant interiors, logos, and menus, Carrier applied her training as a manuscript copyist to the needs of a modern commercial society.[200] Some of the works truest to her medieval models were the altar cards she created in the 1950s and 1960s for Catholic churches in the Chicago and Cincinnati areas. These piece

157.

Coella Lindsay Ricketts,
illuminated manuscript
celebrating the seventieth
birthday of Anton Hesing
(United States, 1893)

158.

Coella Lindsay Ricketts,
illuminated manuscript
celebrating the seventieth
birthday of Anton Hesing
(United States, 1893)

display prayers for the liturgy surrounded by skillfully executed borders, often inspired by ornament in the *Book of Kells*. Here, medieval illumination was adopted
as the appropriate vehicle through which to represent the mystery of the Catholic
faith.

But it was not simply the church that sought works stamped with the
authoritative script of the Middle Ages. In the 1970s, Carrier was commissioned to
illuminate a piece presenting the words of Rabbi Hillel in both English and in
Hebrew. In this work, a frame whose form evokes the arched niche of the Holy
Ark, prominently adorned with a Star of David, is executed in a quasi-Iberian,
quasi-English Gothic style. The pious and exotic associations of medieval ornament here are adapted to a Jewish context.

A look at Carrier's work on the Draw Bridge Restaurant in Peoria, Illinois, a theme palace intended to evoke a lost world of knights, queens, and jesters,
underscores the exoticism that medieval ornament has come to signify today (figure 159). Not only did Carrier execute the restaurant's menus and wall decoration,
she assisted in the design of the building itself—complete with crenellated towers
and rose windows. The menu, featuring such delicacies as Sir Galahad's Glory and
Guinivere's Charm, is written in an easily legible variant of Gothic script and ornamented with vignettes peopled with characters like the "Lusty Wench." Carrier
employed her expertise as an illuminator to reconstruct the Middle Ages for the
modern pilgrim to Peoria. In Carrier, the recuperation of illumination in America
is completed. No longer confined within manuscripts and single leaves, medieval
ornament has penetrated popular culture and has moved from being educational to
being kitsch.

**159.**

**Gertrude Carrier,
menu for the
Draw Bridge Restaurant
in Peoria, Illinois
(United States, mid–
twentieth century)**

## Introduction

1. Joy Kenseth, ed., *The Age of the Marvelous*, Hood College of Art, Dartmouth College, 1991, no. 189, p. 422.

2. P. E. Schramm and F. Mutherich, *Denkmale der deutsche Konig und Kaiser*, no. 43 (1962), pp. 130–31; and R. McKitterick, "Charles the Bald and His Library," *English Historical Review* 95 (1980): 28–47.

3. Alan Noel Latimer Munby, *Connoisseurs and Medieval Miniatures, 1750–1850* (Oxford: Claredon Press, 1972).

4. Recently, there has been a surge in studies devoted to modern perceptions of the Middle Ages. Key studies include John Van Engen, ed., *The Past and Future of Medieval Studies* (Notre Dame, Ind.: University of Notre Dame Press, 1994); R. Howard Bloch and Stephen G. Nichols, eds., *Medievalism and the Modernist Temper* (Baltimore: Johns Hopkins University Press, 1996); Kathleen Biddick, *The Shock of Medievalism* (Durham, N.C.: Duke University Press, 1998); Paul Freedman and Gabrielle M. Spiegel, "Medievalisms Old and New: The Rediscovery of Alterity in North American Medieval Studies," *American Historical Review* 103, no. 3 (1998): 677–704.

5. Carl Nordenfalk et al., *Medieval and Renaissance Miniatures from the National Gallery of Art* (Washington, D.C.: National Gallery of Art, 1975).

6. For example, S. Hindman and M. Heinlen, "A Connoisseur's Montage: The *Four Evangelists* Attributed to Gulio Clovio," *Art Institute of Chicago Museum Studies* 17 (1991): 154–78; and Filipp Todini and Milvia Bollati, *Una Collezione di miniature Italiane dal duecento al cinquecento* (Milan, 1993).

7. C. De Hamel, "Cutting up Manuscripts for Pleasure and Profit" (paper presented at the eleventh Sol M. Malkin Lecture in Bibliography, University of Virginia, Charlottesville, 1996), printed in *The Rare Book School 1995 Yearbook*, ed. T. Belanger (Charlottesville, Va., 1996). For De Hamel's work on collectors and connoisseurs of medieval manuscripts, see his *Hidden Friends: A Loan Exhibition of the Comites Latentes Collection of Illuminated Manuscripts from the Bibliothèque Publique et Universitaire, Geneva* (London: Sotheby's, 1985).

8. W. M. Voelkle and R. S. Wieck, introduction to *The Bernard H. Breslauer Collection of Manuscript Illuminations* (New York, 1982): 13–16; and R. S. Weick, "*Folia Fugitiva*: The Pursuit of the Illuminated Manuscript Leaf," *Journal of the Walters Art Gallery* 54 (1996): 233–54.

9. The impact of reproductive technologies has also been the study of much scholarship. Recent interpretive work includes Hillel Schwartz, *The Culture of the Copy: Striking Likenesses, Unreasonable Facsimiles* (New York: Zone Books, 1996); and Carol Armstrong, *Scenes in a Library: Reading the Photograph in the Book, 1843–1875* (Cambridge, Mass.: MIT Press, 1998).

10. See M. Camille, "The *Très Riches Heures*: An Illuminated Manuscript in the Age of Mechanical Reproduction," *Critical Inquiry* 17 (Autumn 1990): 72–107.

11. *Les Très riches heures du Duc de Berry* (Lucerne: Faksimilé-Verlag, 1984).

## "Curiosities"

Epigraphs: Bernard de Montfaucon, *Les Monumens de la monarchie Françoise*, vol. 1 (Paris: J. M. Gandouin, 1729–33), ii; Joseph Strutt, *Sports and Pastimes of the People of England Including Rural and Domestic Recreations, May Games, Mummeries, Shows, Processions, Pageants and Pompous Spectacles from the Earliest Period to the Present time* [circa 1801] (London: Thomas Tegg, 1838), lxvi–lxvii.

1. Alan Noel Latimer Munby, *Connoisseurs and Medieval Miniatures, 1750–1850* (Oxford: Claredon Press, 1972). For observations on Munby's uniqueness, see Antoine Schnapper, "Les 'primitifs français' au temps de Leon de Laborde," in *Hommage à Michel Laclotte* (Paris, 1994), 539.

2. Francis Haskell, *History and Its Images: Art and the Interpretation of the Past* (New Haven, Conn.: Yale University Press, 1993). See also Martin Myrone and Lucy Peltz, eds., *Producing the Past: Aspects of Antiquarian Culture and Practice 1700–1850* (Brookfield, Vt.: Ashgate, 1999).

3. Ibid., 7–8. For other studies that similarly recognize the distinctive nature of early attitudes toward collecting and creating art see the special volume "Art and Curiosity" of *Word & Image* 11, no. 4 (1995).

4. Denis Diderot, *Encyclopédie, ou, Dictionnaire raisonne des sciences, des arts et des metiers par une societe de gens de lettres* (Paris, 1751).

5. On Mabillon, see Rutherford Aris, "Jean Mabillon (1632–1707)," in *Medieval Scholarship: Biographical Studies on the Formation of a Discipline: History*, ed. Helen Damico and Joseph B. Zavadil (New York: Garland Press, 1995), 15–32; Dom Henri Leclerq, "Mabillon," in *Dictionnaire d'archéologie chrétienne et de liturgie* (Paris: Letouzey et Ané, 1931), 427–723; Dom Henri Leclerq, *Mabillon*, 2 vols. (Paris: Letouzy and Ané, 1953–57); J. Vanuxem, "The Theories of Mabillon and Montfaucon on French Sculpture of the Twelfth Century," *Art Studies* 1 (1923); reprint, in *Chartres Cathedral*, ed. Robert Branner (New York, 1969), 168–85.

For recent critical work that places Mabillon in historical context, see Gabriele Bickendorf, "Gustav Friedrich Waagen und der Historismus in der Kunstgeschichte," *Jahrbuch der Berliner Museen* 37 (1995): 23–32. For works by Mabillon, see Jean Mabillon, "Letters and Papers" (Bibliothèque Nationale MSS. lat. 11866, 11902, 12089, 12301, 12777–80, 13067, 13119, 13120, 14187; fr. 17693–700, 19649–59); Jean Mabillon, *De Re Diplomatica, libri VI in quibis quid ad veterum instrumentorum antiquitatem, materiam, scripturam et stilum*, 6 vols. (Paris: L. Billaine, 1681–1704; supplement, 1704; reprint, Paris: C. Robustel, 1704–9; reprint, Naples: Vincentii Ursini, 1789); and M. Valery, *Correspondence inédite de Mabillon et Montfaucon avec l'Italie*, 3 vols. (Paris: Labitte, 1846–47).

On the Maurists in general, see Edmond Martène, *Histoire de la congréga-*

tion de Saint-Maur (Ligugé, Vienne: Abbaye Saint-Martin, 1929–43); David Knowles, *Great Historical Enterprises: Problems in Monastic History* (London: Nelson, 1963); Maarten Ultree, *The Abbey of St. Germain des Pres in the 17th Century: A Powerful Benedictine Monastery* (New Haven, Conn.: Yale University Press, 1981); John McManners, *Church and Society in Eighteenth-Century France*, vol. 1, *The Clerical Establishment and its Social Ramification* (Oxford: Oxford University Press, 1998).

6. *Histoire literaire de la France: ou l'on traite de l'origine et du progres, de la decadence et du retablissement des sciences parmi les Gaulois et parmi les François; du gout et du genie des uns et des autres pour les letres en chaque siecle; de leurs anciennes ecoles; de l'etablissement des universites en France; des principaux colleges; des academies des sciences et des belles lettres; des meilleures bibliotheques anciennes et modernes; des plus celebres imprimeries; et de tout ce qui a un rapport particulier a la literature . . . par des religieux benedictins de la Congregation de S. Maur* (Paris: Palme, 1865–75; reprint, Liechtenstein: Kraus, 1973–74); *Recueil des historiens des Gaules et de la France* (Paris: 1738–1833).

7. Mabillon, *De Re Diplomatica*.

8. Aris, "Jean Mabillon," 15.

9. Jean Mabillon, *De Liturgia Gallicana libri III: In quibus veteris missae: Quae ante annos mille apud Gallos in usu crat, forma ritusque eruuntur ex antiquis monumentis, Lectionario Gallicano hactenus inedito, & tribus missalibus Thomasianis, quae integra referuntur. Accedit Disquisitio de cursu Gallicano, seu de divinorum officiorum origine & progressu in ecclesiis Gallicanis* (Paris: E. Martin et J. Boudot, 1685).

10. See, for example, Mabillon, *De Re Diplomatica*, 373, plate 15.

11. Pierre-Camille Le Moine, *Essai sur l'état des sciences et des arts en Lorraine depuis le premier duc hereditaire jusqu'au règne de Charle III, prouvé par les monuments*, no. 1275 (September 1761; Norway: private collection of Martin Schoyen). See also Marvin L. Colker, "A Palaeographical Album of Pierre-Camille le Moine," *Scriptorium* 47, no. 1 (1993): 56–60.

12. Montfaucon, *Les Monumens*. On Montfaucon, see the classic studies: Emmanuel Broglie, *La société de l'abbaye de Saint-Germain des Près au dix-huitieme siècle: Bernard de Montfaucon et les Bernardins, 1715–1750*, 2 vols. (Paris: E. Plon, 1891); Vanuxem, "Theories of Mabillon and Montfaucon"; André Rostand, "La documentation iconographique des monumens de la monarchie Françoise de Bernard de Montfaucon," *Bulletin de la société de l'Histoire de l'art français* (1932): 104–49; and M. Valery, *Correspondence inédite de Mabillon et Montfaucon avec l'Italie*, 3 vols. (Paris: Labitte, 1846–47). For recent critical work, see Pierre Gasnault, "Un portrait peu connu de Montfaucon," *Bulletin de la Société nationale des antiquaires de France* (1993): 51–60; and Juliette Jesatz, "Bernard de Montfaucon: mauriste et antiquaire: la tentative de l'Antiquité expliquée: 1719–1724," *Ecole nationale des Chartes, Paris, Diplôme d'archiviste paléographe, Positions des thèses* (1995): 169–73.

13. Bernard de Monfaucon, *Palaeographia graeca, sive De ortu progressu literatum graecarium* (Paris, 1708; reprint, Rome: Bibliopola, 1963).

14. Montfaucon, *Les Monumens,* unnumbered: v.

15. Ibid., ii.

16. For the Musée des Monuments, see Louis Charles Jean Courajod, *Alexandre Lenoir, son journal et le Musée des monuments français* (Paris: H. Champion, 1878–87); Christopher M. Greene, "Alexandre Lenoir and the Musée des Monuments Français during the French Revolution," *French Historical Studies* 12 (fall 1981): 200–22; Alexandre Lenoir, *Musée des monumens français; ou Description historique et chronologique des statues en marbre et en bronze, bas reliefs et tombeaux des hommes et des femmes célèbres, pour servir à l'histoire de France . . .* (Paris: Nepveu, 1821); and Dominique Poulot, "Alexandre Lenoir et les musées des monumens français," in *Les Lieux de mémoire,* ed. Pierre Nora (Paris: Gallimard, 1986); translated by Arthur Goldhammer as *Realms of Memory: Rethinking the French Past* (New York: Columbia University Press, 1996), 497–531.

17. Haskell, *History and Its Images,* 242–43.

18. Montfaucon, *Les Monumens,* unnumbered: vi. On Gaignières, see the classic works of Léopold Delisle, "XV: Cabinet de Gaignieres. 1715," in *Le Cabinet des Manuscrits de la Bibliothèque impériale. Etude sur la formation de ce dépôt comprenent les éléments d'une histoire de la calligraphie de la miniature, de la reliure et su commerce des livres à Paris avant l'invention de l'imprimerie* (Paris: Imprimerie Imperiale, 1868–81), 335–56; and Georges Duplessis, "Roger de Gaignières et ses collections iconographiques," *Gazette des Beaux-Arts* 2, no. 12 (1870): 468–88. For recent assessments, see Jean-Bernard de Vaivre, "Sur trois primitifs français du XIVe siècle et le portrait de Jean le Bon," *Gazette des Beaux-Arts* 6, (April 1981): 131–56; Philippe Ariès, *Le temps de l'histoire,* 2d ed. (Paris: Éditions du seuil, 1986), 178–87; Elizabeth A. R. Brown, *The Oxford Collection of Drawings of Roger de Gaignières and the Royal Tombs of Saint-Denis,* vol. 78 (Philadelphia: Transactions of the American Philosophical Society, 1988), part 5; Antoine Schnapper, "Roger de Gaignieres," in *Le géant, la licorne et la tulipe: Collections et collectionneurs dans la France du XVIIe siècle* (Paris: Flammarion, 1988), 291–96; and Max Polonovski, "Deux dessins inédits exécutés pour Roger de Gaignières concernant l'église abbatiale de Saint-Denis," *Bulletin de la Société nationale des antiquaires de France* (1988): 348–56. See also the forthcoming article of Stephen Perkinson, "Interpreting the Louvre Image of John the Good: the Legacy of the Exhibition of *Primitifs françaises* (Paris, 1904)."

19. Delisle, "XV," 335–56.

20. On La Curne de Sainte-Palaye, see Lionel Gossman, *Medievalism and the Ideologies of the Enlightenment. The World and Work of La Curne de Sainte-Palaye* (Baltimore: Johns Hopkins University Press, 1968.

For original works, see Jean Baptiste de La Curne de Sainte-Palaye, "Notices de divers manuscrits de France et d'Italie," 8 vols. in-folio (first version; Moreau, 1654–61), 15 vols. in- quarto

(second version; Moreau, 1662–76 ); Jean Baptiste de La Curne de Sainte-Palaye, "Dictionnaire des antiquités Françoises," 13 vols in-folio (first version; Moreau, 1511–23), 77 vols. in-quarto (second version; Bibliothèque de l'Arsenal, 4277–4353), supplement, 17 vols. in- quarto (Bibliothèque de l'Arsenal 4354–70); Jean Baptiste de La Curne de Sainte-Palaye, 'Jugement de l'Histoire de Froissart,' *Mémoires de litterature tirez des registres d'Académie Royale des inscriptions et Belles Lettres* 13 (1740): 555–79; Jean Baptiste de La Curne de Sainte-Palaye, "Mémoire concernant les principaux monumens de l'histoire de France. Avec la notice & l'histoire des Chroniques de Saint-Denys," *Mémoires de litterature tirez des registres d'Académie Royale des inscriptions et Belles Lettres* 15 (1743): 580–616; Jean Baptiste de La Curne de Sainte-Palaye, "Mémoire concernant la lecture des anciens Romans de Chevalerie," *Mémoires de litterature tirez des registres d'Académie Royale des inscriptions et Belles Lettres* 17 (1751): 787–99; Jean Baptiste de La Curne de Sainte-Palaye, *Lettre à M. de B. (Bachaumont) sur le bon goût dans les arts et dans les lettres* (Paris: 1751 and 1755; reprint, Geneva: Minkoff, 1972); and Jean Baptiste de La Curne de Sainte-Palaye, *Memoires sur l'ancienne chevalerie, considre comme un tablissement politique et militaire* (Paris: La veuve Duchesne, 1781).

21. La Curne de Sainte-Palaye, "Jugement de l'Histoire de Froissart," 574; cited in Haskell, *History and Its Images,* 160.

22. La Curne de Sainte-Palaye, "Mémoire concernant la lecture des anciens Romans de Chevalerie," 794; cited in Haskell, *History and Its Images,* 161.

23. Perhaps "M. Dutertre" is the lawyer Marguerite-Louis-François Duport-Dutertre (1754–93).

24. La Curne de Sainte-Palaye, "Notices de divers manuscrits de France et d'Italie."

25. La Curne de Sainte-Palaye, "Dictionnaire des antiquités Françoises."

26. For Rive's work, see Jean-Joseph Rive, *Essai sur l'art de vérifier l'age des miniatures peintes dans les manuscrits depuis le XIVe jusqu'au XVIIe siècle inclusivement. Prospectus d'un ouvrage* (Paris: Didotaine, 1782); Jean-Joseph Rive, *Catalogue des livres de la Bibliothèque de feu M. le duc de la Vallière. Premiere partie* (Paris: Guillaume de Bure, fils aîné, 1783); Jean- Joseph Rive, *La Chasse aux bibliographes et antiquaires mal-advisés* (London: N. Aphobe, 1788); and Jean-Joseph Rive, *Pieces qui manquent dans la bibliothèque de monsieur le duc de la Valière* (n.p., n.d.).

27. Munby, *Connoisseurs and Medieval Miniatures,* 14.

28. Rive, *Essai sur l'art de verifier l'age des miniatures.*

29. Rive's handwritten descriptions are preserved in the British Library, Add. MS 18850. For more on this project, see Janet Backhouse, "Two Books of Hours of Francis I," *British Museum Quarterly* 31, nos. 3-4 (1967): 90–96, especially 95, note 10. On the sale of the duc de La Vallière's library, see Rive, *Catalogue des livres. Premiere partie.*

30. Rive, *Essai sur l'art,* 4.

31. Ibid., 5.

32. Ibid., 64–68.

33. Ibid., 5.

34. See Claude François Achard, the supposed author, *Chronique Litteraire des ouvrages imprimes et manuscrits de l'Abbé Rive, des secours dans les lettres, que cet abbé a fournis a tant de litterateurs François ou etrangers . . .* (Aix: Eleutheropolis, Imprimerie des Anti-Copet, des Anti-Jean-de Dieu, des Anti-Pascalis, 1790), 9.

35. Rive, *Essai sur l'art,* 12.

36. Ibid., (British Library, Add. MS 15501), plates, with Rive's notes, folios 3v–4r.

37. Ibid., folios 8r–9r.

38. Ibid., folios 45r–46r.

39. Rive, *La Chasse aux bibliographes.*

40. Le Long, *Bibliotheca Sacra,* vol. 1, 316; Rive, *La Chasse aux bibliographes,* 159.

41. Rive, *La Chasse aux bibliographes,* 160.

42. Ibid., 162.

43. John Oldmixion, "An Essay on Criticism as It Regards Design, Thought and Expression, in Prose and Verse" (1728), 18–19. For a discussion of early antiquarian thought in England, see Joan Evans, *A History of the Society of Antiquaries* (Oxford: Oxford University Press for the Society of Antiquaries, 1956).

44. Thomas Astle, *The Origins and Progress of Writing, as Well as Hieroglyphic as Elementary, Illustrated by Engravings Taken from Marbles, Manuscripts and Charters* (London: printed for the author; sold by T. Payne, 1784).

45. Ibid., 195.

46. *The Antiquarian Repertory, a Miscellaneous Assemblage of Topography, History, Biography, Customs, and Manners: Intended to Illustrate and Preserve Serveral Valuable Remains of Old Times. With a Great Many Valuable Additions,* (London, 1807), xii.

47. Humphrey Wanley, *The Diary of Humfrey Wanley, 1672–1726,* ed. C. E. Wright and Ruth C. Wright (London: Bibliographical Society, 1966), 115.

48. Humphrey Wanley, *Letters of Humfrey Wanley: Palaeographer, Anglo-Saxonist, Librarian, 1672–1726,* ed. P. L. Heyworth (Oxford: Claredon Press, 1989), 479. For his correspondence with Bernard de Montfaucon, see p. 425.

49. Rowan Watson, "Medieval Manuscript Fragments," *Archives* 13, no. 58 (autumn 1977): 71.

50. Neil Ripley Ker, *Fragments of Medieval Manuscripts Used as Pastedowns in Oxford Bindings with a Survey of Oxford Binding circa1515–1620* (Oxford: Oxford Bibliographic Society, 1954).

51. Edward Rowe Mores, *Figurae quaedam antiquae ex Caedmonis Monachi paraphraseos in Genesin exemplari pervetusto, in biblioteca Bodleiana, deliate* (London: G. Woodfall, 1754).

52. Biographical information on Strutt can be found in Sir Leslie Stephen and Sir Sidney Lee, eds., *The Dictionary of National Biography,* vol. 19 (Oxford: Oxford University Press, circa 1921–22), 65–67; and the entry by Strutt's son in John Nichols, *Literary Anecdotes of the Eighteenth Century; Comprizing Biographical Memoires of William Bowyer, Printer F.S.A. and Many of His Learned Friends, an Inciden-*

*tal View of the Progress and Advancement of Literature in This Kingdom during the Last Century and Biographical Anecdotes of a Considerable Number of Eminent Writers and Ingenious Artists with a Very Copious Index*, 9 vols. (London: J. Nichols, son and Bently, 1812-16), vol. 5, 665–86. For works by Strutt, see Joseph Strutt, *The Regal and Ecclesiastical Antiquities of England: Containing the Representations of All the English Monarchs from Edward the Confessor to Henry the Eighth, Together with Many of the Great Persons That Were Eminent under Their Several Reigns; the Whole Carefully Collected from Antient [sic] Illuminated Manuscripts* (London: Walter Shropshire, 1777); and Joseph Strutt, *A Complete View of the Dress and Habits of the People of England, from the Establishment of the Saxons in Britain to the Present Time: Illustrated by Engravings Taken from the Most Authentic Remains of Antiquity; to Which Is Prefixed an Introduction, Containing a General Description of the Ancient Habits in Use among Mankind, from Their Earliest Period of Time to the Conclusion of the Seventh Century* (London: J. Nichols, 1796–99. Reissued, London: H. G. Bohn, 1842).

53. Strutt, *Regal and Ecclesiastical Antiquities.*

54. Ibid., unnumbered, 120–24.

55. Barbara Stafford, *Artful Science: Enlightenment Entertainment and the Eclipse of Visual Education* (Boston: MIT Press, 1994), 129.

56. Strutt, *Regal and Ecclesiastical Antiquities,* iii.

57. Ibid., iv.

58. Ibid., iii.

59. Joan Evans, *A History of the Society of Antiquaries* (Oxford: Oxford University Press for the Society of Antiquaries, 1956), 42.

60. Ibid., iv.

61. Joseph Strutt, *Horda Angel-Cynnan; or, A Compleat View of the Manners, Custom, Arms, Habits &c. of the Inhabitants of England, from the Arrival of the Saxons, till the Reign of Henry the Eighth; with a Short Account of the Britons, during the Government of the Romans* (London: J. Nichols, 1774–76; reprint, London: H. G. Bohn, 1842); Strutt, *Complete View.*

62. Ibid., i.

63. Ibid.

64. Ibid. On the "principle of disjunction," see Erwin Panofsky, "Renaissance and Renascences" in *Renaissance and Renascences in Western Art* (Stockholm: Almquist and Wiksell, 1960): 42–113, especially 82–100.

65. Strutt, *Horda Angel-Cynnan,* vol. 1, 180–87.

66. Ibid., vol. 1, 181.

67. Ibid., 182.

68. Quoted in Munby, *Connoisseurs and Medieval Miniatures,* 29. Munby notes that it was the more advanced Douce who added notes on the color and technique of the manuscript.

69. Haskell, *History and Its Images,* figure 172.

70. Strutt, *Sports and Pastimes of the People of England,* lxvi–lxvii.

71. Strutt, *Horda Angel-Cynnan,* vol. 1, iii.

72. Ibid., vol. 3, 181.

73. Cf. the "Advertisement" by

William Hone preceding the 1838 edition of Strutt's *Sports and Pastimes.* Hone states: "The present edition is of a convenient size and at one-sixth the price of the former editions [circa 1801 and circa 1810]."

74. Nichols, *Literary Anecdotes,* vol. 5, 679.

75. Roy Strong, *Recreating the Past: British History and the Victorian Painter* (New York: Thames and Hudson for the Pierpont Morgan Library, 1978; London: Thames and Hudson, 1979), 49–54.

76. Victor Didron, "Des Manuscrits à miniatures," *Annales Archéologiques* 2 (1845): 165–73, especially 165.

77. Strutt, *Sports and Pastimes,* opposite 40. These figures showing archery and slinging are a combination of eleventh-century and thirteenth-century manuscript illumination.

78. For Lenoir's museum, see Caisse Nationale des Monuments Historiques et des Sites, *Le "Gothique" Retrouve avant Viollet-le-Duc. Exposition, Hotel de Sully. 31 octobre 1979–17 février 1980* (Paris: Caisse Nationale des Monuments Historiques et des Sites, 1979.), 75–84; and Haskell, *History and Its Images,* 236–52.

79. Strong, *Recreating the Past,* 50.

80. Stephen and Lee, eds., *Dictionary of National Biography,* vol. 8, 279–82, especially 280.

81. Richard Gough, *Sepulchral Monuments in Great Britain; Applied to Illustrate the History of Families, Manners, Habits and Arts at the Different Periods from the Norman Conquest to the Seventeenth Century: With Introductory Observations,* 2 vols. (London: printed for the author, sold by T. Payne and Son, etc., 1786–96).

82. Richard Gough, *An Account of a Rich Illuminated Missal Executed for John, Duke of Bedford, Regent of France under Henry VI and afterwards in the Possession of the Late Duchess of Portland* (London: J. Nichols for T. Payne, 1794).

83. Janet Backhouse, *The Bedford Hours* (London: British Library, 1990).

84. Munby, *Connoisseurs and Medieval Miniatures,* 4.

85. Ibid., 5. On the Guirlande de Julie, see Irene Frain, *La Guirlande de Julie* (Paris: Robert Laffont for the Bibliothèque Nationale, 1991).

86. See Janet Backhouse, "The Sale of the Luttrell Psalter," in *Antiquaries, Book Collectors and the Circles of Learning,* ed. Robin Meyers and Michael Harris (Winchester: St Paul's Bibliographies, 1996), 113–28. See also Michael Camille, *Mirror in Parchment: The Luttrell Psalter and the Making of Medieval England* (Chicago: University of Chicago Press, 1998).

87. See Gough, *An Account of a Rich Illuminated Missal,* 1.

88. Munby, *Connoisseurs and Medieval Miniatures,* 7.

89. Thomas Frognall Dibdin, *Bibliographical Decameron; or Ten Days of Pleasant Discourse upon Illuminated Manuscripts and Subjects Connected with Early Engraving, Typography and Bibliography,* 3 vols. (London: W. Bulmer, 1817), vol. 1, cxxxviii, footnote.

90. Ibid., vol. 1, cxxxix, footnote.

91. Strutt, *Horda Angel-Cynnan,* vol. 1, iv.

92. On the collections of Charles V, see Léopold Delisle, *Recherches sur la librairie de Charles V* (Paris: H. Champion, 1907); Françoise Autrand, *Charles V, le sage* (Paris: Fayard, 1994); and Danielle Gaborit-Chopin, ed., *L'inventaire du trésor du dauphin, futur Charles V, 1363: Les débuts d'un grand collectionneur* (Paris: Société de L'Histoire de L'Art Française, 1996). On Jean, duc de Berry, see Millard Meiss, *French Painting in the Time of Jean de Berry: The Boucicaut Master,* vol. 3, *National Gallery of Art: Kress Foundation Studies in the History of European Art,* (London: Phaidon, 1968); and Millard Meiss, *French Painting in the Time of Jean de Berry: The Limbourgs and Their Contemporaries* (New York: G. Braziller, 1987). For an introduction to French royal collections, see Marie-Hélène Tesnière, "Medieval Collections of the Bibliothèque Nationale de France: From the Eighth to the Fifteenth Century," in *Creating French Culture: Treasures from the Bibliothèque Nationale de France,* ed. M-H Tesnière et al. (Washington, D.C.: Library of Congress, 1995), 19–127.

93. *Encyclopédie,* IV: 577; quoted by Krzysztof Pomian, *Collectors and Curiosities: Paris and Venice 1500–1800,* trans. Elizabeth Wiles-Portier (Cambridge, U.K.: Polity Press; Cambridge, Mass.: Basil Blackwell, 1990), 55.

94. See Johann Amos Comenius, *Orbis sensualium pictus. Faksimiledruck der Ausgabe Noribergae M. Endter, 1658* (Onasbrück: Otto Zeller, 1964), 200.

95. Bibliothèque Sainte-Geneviève, *Le Cabinet de curiosités de la Bibliothèque Sainte- Geneviève: des origines à nos jours* (Paris: La Bibliothèque, 1989).

96. For more, see Joy Kenseth, ed., *The Age of the Marvelous* (Hanover, N.H.: Hood Museum of Art, 1991); and Werner Muesterberger, *Collecting: An Unruly Passion: Psychological Perspectives* (Princeton, N.J.: Princeton University Press, 1994).

97. Jean-Jaques Charron Menars, *Bibliotheca Menarsiana, ou, Catalogue de la bibliotheque de feu Messire Jean Jaques Charron, Chevalier Marquis de Menars . . .: augmentee & embellie d'un grand nombre de manuscrits, dont les uns sont considerables par leur antiquite & conservation, les autres par la delicatesse des miniatures: en outre cela enrichie de ce qu'il y a de recherche en theologie, de curieux en jurisprudence & en philosophie, d'interessant & de beau en histoire & en belles lettres, & de ce qu'il y a de rares editions parmi les orateurs & poetes, le tout tres bien conditione & quelques uns en grand papier: dont la vent publique se fera* (A La Haye: Chez Abraham de Hondt, 1720); Duc de Rohan and Prince de Soubise, *Catalogue des livres, imprimes et manuscrits, de la bibliotheque de feu Monseigneur le prince de Soubise, marechal de France: dont la vente sera indiquee par affiches au mois de janvier 1789* (Paris: Chez Leclerc, 1788).

98. See especially Claude Jolly, ed., *Histoire des bibliothèques françaises,* 3 vols. (Paris: Promodis-Editions du Cercle de la Librairie, 1988–92).

99. Bernard Quaritch, ed., *Contributions towards a Dictionary of English Book-Collectors, as Also of Some Foreign Collectors Whose Libraries Were Incorporated in English Collections or Whose Books Are Chiefly Met with in England* (London: B. Quaritch, 1892–1921).

100. On de Sardière's manuscripts, see *Catalogue des Livres de la Bibliothèque de feu M.J.B. Denis Guyon, chev. seigneur*

de Sardière, ancien capitaine au Regiment du Roi, l'un des seigneurs du canal de Briare (Paris: Barrois, 1759). On the manuscript holdings of the duc de la Vallière, see Dominique Coq, "Le paragon du bibliophile français: le duc de la Vallière et sa collection," in Histoire des bibliothèques françaises, ed. Jolly, 324.

101. See Rive, Catalogue des livres. Premiere partie, lot 25 (thirteenth-century manuscript Bible), which sold for 67 livres; lot 28 (Fust and Schoeffer, 1462 Bible printed on vellum), which sold for 4,085 livres; and Rive, Catalogue des livres. Premiere partie, vol. 3, lot 4601 (fifteenth-century manuscript of Jean de Coucy chronicle), which sold for 445 livres. See the annotated catalogues of the duc de La Vallière sales in the New York Public Library.

102. Catalogue des Livres de la Bibliothèque de feu M.J.B. Denis Guyon.

103. Ibid., iv.

104. Ibid.

105. Ibid., no. 527.

106. For recent analysis of this manuscript, see Sandra Hindman, "Æsop's Cock and Marie's Hen: Gendered Authorship in Text and Image in Marie de France's Fables," and Susan L. Ward, "Fables for the Court: Illustrations of Marie de France's Fables in Paris, BnF, MS Arsenal 3142," both in Women and the Book: Assessing the Visual Evidence, ed. Lesley Smith and Jane H. M. Taylor (London: British Library, 1997), 45–56 and 190–203, respectively.

107. Catalogue des Livres de la Bibliothèque de feu M.J.B. Denis Guyon. no. 528.

108. Ibid., no. 1474.

109. Catalogue des Livres provenans de la Bibliothèque de M.L.D.D.L.V. [M. le duc de La Vallière] (Paris: Guillaume de Bure, le jeune, 1767); Catalogue des Livres de M*** [e La Vallière], 1773 (Paris: Guillaume de Bure, 1772); Coq, "Le paragon du bibliophile français," 324.

110. Rive, Catalogue des livres. Premiere partie.

111. Rive, Catalogue des livres, Seconde partie.

112. Correspondance de l'abbe Rive avec le libraire aixois Joseph David, 1769, MS 6392 (Paris: Bibliothèque de l'Arsenal).

113. Coq, "Le paragon du bibliophile français," 319.

114. Correspondance de l'abbe Rive avec le libraire aixois Joseph David, MS 6392, folio 72.

115. Charles Blanc, Le trésor de la curiousité tiré des catalogues de vente (Paris: Jules Renouard, 1858), 40.

116. Correspondance de l'abbe Rive avec le libraire aixois Joseph David, October 26, 1771.

117. Blanc, Le trésor de la curiousité tiré, 40–44.

118. Ibid., 43–44.

119. Ibid., 41.

120. See Rive, Catalogue des livres. Premiere partie , vol. 3, lot 4580 (Nicolas Jensen, Justici Historici in Trogi Pompeii Historias, book 43, printed 1470), which sold for 680 livres; and lot 4591 in the same sale (Paul Orosius, Historiographi adversum Christiani nominis

quaerelas, book 7, printed 1471), which sold for 336 livres. See the annotated catalogue of the duc de La Vallière sale in New York, New York Public Library.

121. Rive, Catalogue des livres. Premiere partie, vol. 3, lot 4601 (fifteenth-century manuscript of Jean de Coucy chronicle), which sold for 445 livres.

122. Catalogue des livres imprimés et manuscrits de la Bibliothèque de feu monseigneur le Prince de Soubise, Marechal de France (Paris: Leclerc, 1789), iii.

123. Ibid., v.

124. On the Marquis de Paulmy and his collection, see Bibliothèque de l'Arsenal, "Les Grands Bibliophiles de L'Arsenal et Leurs Collections. Exposition organisee a l'occasion du IIeme congres international des societes de bibliophiles le vendredi 2 septembre 1961," mimeographed publication (Paris: Bibliothèque de l'Arsenal, 1961); Martine Lefèvre and Danielle Muzerelle, "La bibliothèque du marquis de Paulmy," in Histoire des bibliothèques françaises, ed. Jolly, 302–15; Bibliothèque Nationale, "Bibliothèque de L'Arsenal. 1–3, Rue de Sully," in Guide du Lecteur a la Bibliothèque Nationale, a la Mazarine et a l'Arsenal (Paris: Bibliothèque Nationale, 1930), 38–41; and Bibliothèque Nationale, Trésors de la Bibliothèque de l'Arsenal (Paris: Bibliothèque Nationale, 1980).

125. Bibliothèque Nationale, "Bibliothèque de L'Arsenal," 40.

126. Lefèvre and Muzerelle, "La bibliothèque du marquis de Paulmy," 306.

127. Marc-Antoine René de Paulmy Argenson, Bibliothèque universelle des romans, 40 vols. (Paris: Lacombe, 1775–78).

128. De Paulmy Argenson, Bibliothèque universelle des romans, vol. 1, 5.

129. Ibid., 6.

130. Simone Balaye, "La Bibliothèque du Roi, premiere bibliothèque du monde 1664–1789," in Histoire des bibliothèques françaises, ed. Jolly, 209–33.

131. Emmanuel Le Roy Ladurie, introduction to Creating French Culture: Treasures from the Bibliothèque Nationale de France, ed. Marie-Hélène Tesnière and Prosser Gifford (New Haven, Conn.: Yale University Press in association with the Library of Congress and the Bibliothèque Nationale, 1995): 272.

132. Munby, Connoisseurs and Medieval Miniatures, 3–4.

133. Astle, Origins and Progress of Writing.. See also Munby, Connoisseurs and Medieval Miniatures, 27.

134. Horace Walpole, Anecdotes of Painting in England; with Some Account of the Principal Artists; and Incidental Notes on Other Arts; Collected by the Late Mr. George Vertue; and Now Digested and Published from His Original MSS (Strawberry Hill: printed by Thomas Farmer, 1762).

135. Munby, Connoisseurs and Medieval Miniatures, 23.

136. Cf. A Description of the Villa of Mr. Horace Walpole, Youngest Son of Sir Robert Walpole, Earl of Orford at Strawberry Hill near Twickenham, Middlesex (Strawberry Hill: Thomas Kirgate, circa 1784; reprint, London: Gregg Press, 1964), 37–40. See also Peter Hill, Walpole's Art Collection: Horace Walpole's Oil

Paintings, Water Colours and Drawings at Strawberry Hill (Twickenham: Jackson Hill, 1997). See also Munby, Connoisseurs and Medieval Miniatures, 23–24.

137. Massimo Becattini, "La 'Lumiere mysterieue.' Classicismo e Goticismo nel collectioniimo dei 'gessi': il John Soane's Museum di Londra," in Il Medioevo nel calchi della Gipsoteca (Florence, 1994), xv–lix.

138. Not discussed here because he is a seventeenth-century figure but worth mention is Sir. Robert Cotton (1571–1631). Cotton collected illuminated manuscripts, and his books were among the foundation holdings of the British Museum. See Michelle P. Brown, "Sir Robert Cotton, Collector and Connoisseur?" in Illuminating the Book. Makers and Interpreters. Essays in Honour of Janet Backhouse, ed. Michelle P. Brown and Scot McKendrick (London: British Library, 1998): 281–98

139. William Hunter, Anatomia uteri humani gravidi tabulis illustrata: auctore Gulielmo Hunter . . . (The anatomy of the human gravid uterus exhibited in figures, by William Hunter . . .) (Birmingham: J. Baskerville, 1774; reprint, Birmingham: Classics of Medicine, 1980). On Hunter, see Neil Ripley Ker, William Hunter as a Collector of Medieval Manuscripts: The first Edwards Lecture on Palaeography Delivered in the University of Glasgow (Glasgow: University of Glasgow Press, 1983); William Hunter, Dr. William Hunter at the Royal Academy of Arts, ed. Martin Kemp (Glasgow: University of Glasgow Press, 1975)

140. Samuel Ayschough, A Catalogue of the Manuscripts Preserved in the British Museum Including the Collections of Sir Hans Sloane, the Rev. Thomas Birch, and about Five Hundred Volumes Bequeathed, Presented, or Purchased at Various Times (London: printed for the compiler by John Rivington, 1782); Gavin Rylands De Beer, Sir Hans Sloane and the British Museum (London: Oxford University Press, 1953); William R. Sloan, Sir Hans Sloane: Founder of the British Museum: legend and lineage (Helen's Bay, Co. Down: W. R. Sloan, 1981).

141. Ker, William Hunter as a Collector, 7.

142. Ibid., 8.

143. Ibid., appendix A, 13–21.

144. For Count MacCarthy-Reagh's collection, see Clarles Frederick Ingram Ramsden, Richard Wier and Count MacCarthy-Reagh (London: Queen Anne Press, 1953–54); Justin MacCarthy-Reagh, Catalogue des livres rares et precieux de la bibliotheque de feu M. le comte de Mac- Carthy Reagh (Paris: De Bure Freres, 1815).

145. For this episode see M. du Mège, "Notice sur Quelques Manuscrits de la Bibliothèque d'Albi," Histoire et Memoires de L'Academie Royale des Sciences, Inscriptions et Belles-Lettres de Toulouse (1834): 271–74.

146. The Douce Legacy (Oxford: Bodleian Library, 1984) gives the fullest account of this collector; see also Bodleian Library, Francis Douce Centenary, vol. 7, no. 81, The Bodleian Quarterly Record (1934); Douce did not compile a comprehensive list of his acquisitions, but he did keep some memorandum books recording purchases and exchanges. See Douce Legacy, 7 and 132–36.

147. Francis Douce. Illustrations of Shakespeare, and of Ancient Manners: with

*Dissertations on the Clowns and Fools of Shakespeare, on the Collections of Popular Tales entitled Gesta Romanorum and on the English Morris Dance* (London: Longman, Hurst, Rees and Orme, 1807).

148. *Douce Legacy*, 134.

149. Ibid., 135.

150. Ibid., 156, no. 222.

151. Samuel Wells Singer, "Obituary of Francis Douce," *Gentleman's Magazine* (August 1834): 213–17. This obituary was published anonymously, but according to Dibdin, Singer authored it. Thomas Frognall Dibdin, *Reminiscences of a Literary Life*, vol. 2 (London: J. Major, 1836), 776, cited in *Douce Legacy*: vii.

152. Haskell, *History and Its Images*, 372–74; Thomas Wright, *A History of Caricature and Grotesque in Literature and Art. by Thomas Wright . . . the Illustrations from Various Sources, Drawn and Engraved by F. W. Fairholt* (London: Virtue Brothers, 1865); Champfleury (pseud. Jules Fleury), *Histoire de la Caricature au moyen âge* (Paris: 1867–71. 2d ed. issued under title *Histoire de la caricature au moyen-âge et sous la renaissance*, Paris: E. Dentu, 1871).

153. Thomas Frognall Dibdin, *Bibliophobia. Remarks on the Present Languid and Depressed State of Literature and the Book Trade. In a Letter Addressed to the Author of the Bibliomania* (London: H. G. Bohn, 1832), 45.

154. On Dibdin, see Edward John O'Dwyer, *Thomas Frognall Dibdin: Bibliographer and Bibiomaniac Extraordinary, 1776–1847* (Pinner [Mddx.]: Private Libraries Association, 1967; Braswell-Means, 1992). For an introduction to Dibdin's output, see William A Jackson, *Annotated List of the Publications of the Reverend Thomas Frognall Dibdin* (Cambridge: Houghton Library, 1965); Thomas Frognall Dibdin, *Selections* (Metuchen, N.J.: Scarecrow Press, 1978); and J. Windel and K. Pippin, *Thomas Frognall Dibdin, 1776–1847* (New Castle, Del., 1999).

155. Thomas Frognall Dibdin, *Bibliomania, or, Book-Madness: Containing Some Account of the History, Symptoms, and Cure of this Fatal Disease* (London: Longman, Hurst, Rees and Orme, 1809), vol. 1, 109.

156. Dibdin, *Reminiscences of a Literary Life*, vol. 1, 78–120.

157. Dibdin, *Bibliomania*.

158. Thomas Frognall Dibdin, *An Introduction to the Knowledge of Rare and Valuable Editions of the Greek and Roman Classics: Being, in Part, a Tabulated Arrangement from Dr. Harwood's View, &c. : with Notes from Mattaire, De Bure, Dictionnaire Bibliographique, and References to Ancient and Modern Catalogues* (London: Payne, H. Ruff, 1802); *Thomas Frognall Dibdin, Typographical Antiquities: or, The History of Printing in England, Scotland, and Ireland; Containing Memoirs of Our Ancient Printers, and a Register of the Books Printed by Them* (London: William Miller, 1810–19).

159. Thomas Frognall Dibdin, *Bibliomania: or Book Madness; a Bibliographical Romance, in Six Parts; Illustrated with Cuts*, 2d. ed. (London: printed for the author by J. M'Creery, and sold by Messrs. Longman, Hurst, Rees, Orme, and Brown; reprint; London: Club of Old Sticks, 1864).

160. Thomas Frognall Dibdin, *Bibliomania or Book-Madness*, [*circa1811*], (London: Henry G. Bohn, 1842), 179.

161. Dibdin, *Bibliographical Decameron*.

162. Ibid.

163. Ibid., vol. 1, xiii, footnote.

164. Ibid., xxi, footnote.

165. Ibid., xxiii, footnote.

166. Quoted in O'Dwyer, *Thomas Frognall Dibdin*, 26.

167. Dibdin, *Bibliographical Decameron*, vol. 1, xcv–xcvi.

168. Ibid., cviii.

169. Munby, *Connoisseurs and Medieval Miniatures*: 74. See Dibdin, *Bibliographical Decameron*, vol. 1, lxxxiii–xci.

170. Dibdin, *Bibliographical Decameron*, vol. 1, lii–liii.

171. Munby, *Connoisseurs and Medieval Miniatures*, 58.

172. Dibdin, *Bibliographical Decameron*, vol. 1, cxxxiv–cxxxvi.

173. Munby, *Connoisseurs and Medieval Miniatures*, 75.

174. T. F. Dibdin, *Bibliotheca Rosicrusiana: A Catalogue of the Library of an Eminent Bibliographer* [*T. F. Dibdin*] (London: W. Bulmer, 1817).

175. Alan Noel Latimer Munby, "Dibdin's Reference Library: The Sale of 26–28 June 1817," in *Studies in the Book Trade: in Honour of Graham Pollard* (Oxford: Oxford Bibliographical Society, 1975): 279–315.

176. Dibdin, *Bibliophobia*.

177. Dibdin, *Bibliographical Decameron* vol. 1, cxiii–cxv.

178. Ibid., vol. 1, cxi.

## "Specimens"

1. Stanley J. Idzerda, "Iconoclasm during the French Revolution," *American Historical Review* 60 (1954–55): 25.

2. Emmet Kennedy, "Chapter VIII: Vandalism and Conservation," in *A Cultural History of the French Revolution* (New Haven, Conn.: Yale University Press, 1989), 197–220.

3. Kennedy, "Chapter VIII," 201. For the Declaration of the Commission of Monuments, see Bibliothèque Nationale, *1789: Le patrimoine libéré* (Paris: Bibliothèque Nationale, 1989), 130–31.

4. Emmanuel Le Roy Ladurie, introduction to *Creating French Culture: Treasures from the Bibliothèque Nationale de France,* ed. Marie-Hélène Tesnière and Prosser Gifford (New Haven, Conn.: Yale University Press in association with the Library of Congress, Washington, D.C. and the Bibliothèque Nationale de France, Paris, 1995), 273.

5. Henry Barbet de Jouy, *Musée impériale du Louvre. Notice des antiquités . . . composant le Musée des Souverains* (Paris: Charles de Mourgues, 1866), 11–32. The Carolingian manuscripts, described at great length in these pages, are as follows: the Carolingian Charles the Bald Bible, or the Vivian Bible, circa 845 to 846 (BnF MS Lat. 1); *Charles the Bald Psalter* (BnF, MS Lat. 1152); Charlemagne's evangelistary, or the *Godescalc Evangelistary* (BnF, n.a. l. 1203).

There were two thirteenth-century manuscripts: *Psalter of Blanche de Castille and Louis IX* (Paris: Bib. de l'Arsenal MS 1186) and the *Psalter of St. Louis* (BnF, MS lat. 10, 525). There was one fourteenth-century work, the Bible of Charles V (BnF MS français

5707). Other manuscripts include *Heurs de la Croix* owned by Charles VIII and Louis XII (BnF, MS français 5661); *Anne of Brittany Hours* (BnF MS lat. 9474); *Hours of Henry IV*; *Hours of Catherine Médicis*; *Prayerbook of Marie Stuart*, wife of François II (BnF, MS lat. 1405).

6. Dorothy Mackay Quynn, "Art Confiscations of the Napoleonic Wars," *American Historical Review* 50 (1945): 439, citing Albert Sorel, *L'Europe et la révolution française*, 8 vols. (Paris: Plon, 1907–10), 154.

7. Quynn, "Art Confiscations of the Napoleonic Wars," 439; quoting *Moniteur* (October 3, 1796).

8. Marie Pierre Laffitte, "La Bibliothèque Nationale et les 'conquêtes artistiques' de la Révolution et de l'Empire: les manuscrits d'Italie (1796–1815)," *Bulletin du bibliophile*, no. 2 (1989): 273–323; Bibliothèque Nationale, *1789*, 259.

9. Ibid., 279, after A. M. CCLXIX.

10. On the restitution, see Léopold Delisle, "Les archives du Vatican," parts 1 and 2, *Journal des Savants* (July 1892): 429–41; (August 1892): 489–501; and Laffitte, "La Bibliothèque Nationale," 284ff.

11. Bibliothèque Nationale, *1789*, no. 192. 12. Gustav Brunet, *Curiosites bibliographiques et artistiques. Lives, manuscrits et gravures qui, en vente publique, ont depasse le prix de mille francs* (Geneva: Gay, 1867). 13. Quynn, "Art Confiscations of the Napoleonic Wars," 443–44.

12. Gustav Brunet, *Curiosities bibliographiques et artistiques. Livres, manuscrits et gravures qui, en vente publique, ont depasse le prix de mille francs* (Geneva, 1867).

13. Dorothy Mackay Quynn, "Art Confiscations of the Napoleonic Wars," *American Historical Review* 50 (1945): 443-4.

14. Ibid., 454–55, quoting the *Courier* (October 2, 1815).

15. John S. Sartain, *The Reminiscences f a Very Old Man* (New York: D. Appleton,1899), 96; quoted by J. A. Gere, "William Young Ottley as a Collector of Drawings," *British Museum Quarterly* 18, no. 2 (1953): 51.

16. For Celotti's life, see T. J. Brown, "Some Manuscript Fragments Illuminated for Pope Gregory XIII," *British Museum Quarterly* 23, no.1 (1960): 2–5; and G. Valentin, "Literaturberichte und Anzeigen," *Zentralblatt für Bibliothekwesen* 27, nos. 7–8 (July–August 1910): 363–73. Celotti sale catalogues include Abbé Celotti, *Catalogue of the Hebrew, Greek and Latin Antient Manuscripts the Property of Abbé Celotti* (London: Sotheby's, March 14–17, 1825); Abbé Celotti, *Catalogue of a Singularly Rare Collection of Manuscripts on Paper and Vellum in the Oriental, Hebrew, Latin and Italian Languages, together with numerous Superbly Illuminated Missals . . . brought to this Country by the abbé Celotti* (Saibanti and Cononici Manuscripts) (London: Sotheby's, February 26, 1821); Abbé Celotti, *Catalogue of an Extremely Rare and Curious Collection of Italian and Spanish Litera- ture. the Property of the Abbé Celotti* (London: Sotheby's, February 14–21, 1825); and William Young Ottley, *A Catalogue of a Highly Valuable and Extremely Curious Collection of Illumined Miniature Paintings, of the Greatest Beauty, and of Exquisite Finishing, Taken from the Choral

*Books of the Papal Chapel in the Vatican, during the French Revolution: and Subsequently Collected and Brought to This Country by the Abate Celotti,* (London: Christie's, May 26, 1825).

On Ottley's life, see A. Atkinson, "William Young Ottley, Artist and Collector," *Notes and Queries* 174 (April 2, 1938): 236–39; A. A[tkinson], "Further Notes on the Young and Ottley Families," *Notes and Queries* 175 (November 5, 1938): 326–30; A. Atkinson, "Further Notes on the Young and Ottley Families," *Notes and Queries* 175 (November 12, 1938): 344–47; Gere, "William Young Ottley as a Collector of Drawings," 44–53; and E. K. Waterhouse, "Some Notes on William Young Ottley's Collection of Italian Primitives," in *Italian Studies Presented to E. R. Vincent,* ed. C. P. Brand et al. (Cambridge: W. Heffer and Sons, 1962), 272–80.

17. Ottley, *Catalogue of a Highly Valuable and Extremely Curious Collection.*

18. Rowan Watson, "Vandals and Enthusiasts: Views of Illumination in the Nineteenth Century"(London: Victoria and Albert Museum, 1995, desktop publication),16.

19. *Lucca Library. A Catalogue of the Very Celebrated Library of Don Tomaso de Lucca de Cadore* (London: Sotheby's, July 18–26, 1825).

20. Celotti, *Catalogue of the Hebrew, Greek and Latin Ancient Manuscripts.*

21. Celotti, *Catalogue of a Singularly Rare Collection of Manuscripts.*

22. See the introduction of Christopher De Hamel, *Hidden Friends: A Loan Exhibition of the Comites Latentes Collection of Illuminated Manuscripts from the Bibliothèque Publique et Universitaire, Geneva* (London: Sotheby's, 1985).

23. Ottley, *Catalogue of a Highly Valuable and Extremely Curious Collection,* 3.

24. Ibid., 3.

25. A work such as *The Art of Drawing and Painting in Water-colours. Whereby a Stranger to Those Arts May Be Immediately Render'd Capable of Delineating Any View or Prospect with the Utmost Exactness . . . with Instructions for Making Transparent Colours of Every Sort; Partly from Some Curious Personages in Holland, France, and Italy; but Chiefly from a Manuscript of the Great Mr. Boyle* (London: printed for J. Peele, 1731) refers to the art of illuminating prints; Sir William Hamilton, *Supplement to the Campi Phlegraei, Being an Account of the Great Eruption of Mt. Vesuvius in the Month of August, 1779* (Naples, 1779) describing the eruption of Vesuvius mentions five colored plates "illuminated from drawings taken and coloured after nature. " See also the *Oxford English Dictionary* s. v. "Illumination. " A literary magazine could use the word "illumination" in 1843 without any intention to refer to the medieval practice; see *Illuminated Magazine,* ed. Douglas Jerrold (1843–?).

26. Ottley, *Catalogue of a Highly Valuable and Extremely Curious Collection,* 5.

27. Ibid., 27. This collage is also reproduced in Albert Racinet, *L'Ornement polychrome* (Paris, 1873), plate 61; see also n. 144.

28. Gerald Reitlinger, *The Economics of Taste,* 3 vols. (London: Barrie and Rockliff, 1961–70); and Dorothy Lygon and Francis Russell, "Tuscan Primitives in London Sales: 1801–1837," *Burlington Magazine* 122, no. 923 (February 1980): 112–17.

29. *Bibliotheca Towneleiana. A Catalogue of the Curious and Extensive Library of the Late John Townley, esq. Pt. 1.* (London: Evans, June 8–15, 1814), lot 904; *Bibliotheca Splendidissima Rendorpiana. The Entire, Very Elegant and Valuable Library of the Late Learned John Rendorp, esq.* (London: Sotheby's, February 28–March 7, 1825), lot 1334; *Catalogue of the Splendid and Valuable Library of the Rev. Theodore Williams* (London: Stewart, Wheatley and Adlard, April 5–11 and 23–May 2, 1827).

30. For Ottley's sale, see *Catalogue of the Very Beautiful Collection of Highly Finished and Illumined Miniature Paintings, the Property of the Late William Young Ottley, esq.* (London: Sotheby's, May 11–12, 1838).

31. Jean Baptiste Louis Georges Séroux d'Agincourt, *Histoire de l'art par les monumens: depuis sa décadence au IVe siècle jusqu'à son renouvellement au XVIe* (Paris: Treuttel et Würtz, 1823).

32. William Young Ottley, *A Series of Plates Engraved after the Paintings and Sculptures of the most Eminent Masters of the Early Florentine School; intended to illustrate the history of the restoration of the arts of design in Italy. . . .* (London: privately published and sold by Colnaghi, 1826), i (unnumbered).

33. Ibid.

34. Ibid., iii (unnumbered).

35. William Young Ottley, *The Italian School of Design: Being a Series of Facsimiles of Original Drawings by the most Eminent Painters and Sculptors of Italy; with biographical notices of the artists, and observations on their works* (London: Taylor and Hessey, 1823).

36. Gere, "William Young Ottley as a Collector of Drawings," 45.

37. Ottley, *Italian School of Design,* 1.

38. Denys Sutton, "From Ottley to Eastlake," *Apollo* 122, no. 282 (August 1985): 86.

39. *Library of William Roscoe* (Liverpool: Winstanley, August 19–September 3, 1816). On Roscoe, see Michael Compton, "William Roscoe and Early Collectors of Italian Primitives," *Liverpool Libraries, Museums and Art Committee Bulletin* 9 (1960–61): 26–51.

40. *Library of William Roscoe,* advertisement.

41. Henry Fuseli, "Eighth Lecture," in *The Life and Writings of Henry Fuseli,* ed. John Knowles (London: H. Colburn and R. Bentley, 1831), 339.

42. J. Byam Shaw, *Paintings by Old Masters at Christ Church, Oxford* (London: Phaidon, 1967); Christopher Lloyd, comp., *A Catalogue of the Earlier Italian Paintings in the Ashmolean Museum* (Oxford: Clarendon Press, 1977).

43. Quoted in Christopher Lloyd, "Picture Hunting in Italy: Some Unpublished Letters," *Italian Studies* 30 (1975): 51.

44. Quoted in ibid., 52.

45. Ibid., 56.

46. On Waagen, see the proceedings of the1994 symposium, "Gustav Waagen Symposium," *Jahrbuch der Berliner Museen* 37 (1995). For works by Waagen, see Gustav Friedrich Waagen, *Works of Art and Artists in England (1794–1868),* trans. H. E. Lloyd, 3 vols. (London: J. Murray, 1838; reprint, London: Cornmarket, 1970); Gustav Friedrich Waagen, *Treasures of Art in Great Britain: Being an Account of the*

*Chief Collections of Paintings, Drawings, Sculptures, Illuminated Mss.,* 3 vols. (London: J. Murray, 1854).

47. For another instance where Ottley displays an interest in works from the era before the Renaissance, see William Young Ottley, *Observations on a Manuscript in the British Museum, believed to be of the Second or Third Century, and containing Cicero's Translation of the Astronomical Poem by Aratus, accompanied by Drawings of the Constellations: with a preliminary Dissertation in proof of the use of Miniscule Writing by the ancient Romans; and a corrected edition of the Poem itself . . . Communicated . . . in a letter to John Gage* (London: J. B. Nichols, 1835; reprinted in *Archaeologia* 26 [1836]: 47–214). Interestingly (if not surprisingly), here Ottley insists upon the classical qualities of the late-antique miniatures.

48. Quoted in Frank Herrmann, ed., *The English as Collectors: A Documentary Chrestomathy* (New York: Norton, 1972), 184–85.

49. On Soane, see *Description of the house and museum on the north side of Lincoln's-Inn- Fields, the residence of Sir John Soane* (London: James Moyes, 1830); Massimo Becattini, "La 'Lumiere mysterieue. ' Classicismo e Goticismo nel collectioniimo dei 'gessi': il John Soane's Museum di Londra," in *Il Medioevo nel calchi della Gipsoteca* (Florence: Cassa di risparmio, L'Instituto, 1994), xv–lix; Henry Noel Humphreys, *The Book of Ruth: from Holy Scriptures. Enriched with coloured borders, selected from illuminated mss. in the British Museum, Bibliothèque Nationale, Paris, Soane Museum and other Libraries. . . .* (London: Longman, Brown, Green and Longmans, 1850); Eric Millar, "Les manuscrits a peinture de la Bibliothèque du Musee de Sir John Soane, Lincoln's Inn Fields, Londres," *Bulletin de la Societe Francaise de Reproductions de Manuscrits a Peintures* 4, no. 1 (1914–20): 81–149; William Robson-Scott, *The Literary Background of the Gothic Revival in Germany* (Oxford: Clarendon Press, 1965); David Watkin, *Sir John Soane. Enlightenment Thought and the Royal Academy Lectures* (Cambridge: Cambridge University Press, 1996); Iolo A. Williams, "An Identification of Some Early Drawings by John Flaxman," *Burlington Magazine* 102, no. 687 (June 1960): 249.

50. For Soane's views on the Gothic revival, see Watkin, *Sir John Soane.*

51. The association of library and Gothic style is also seen in Frederick William II's Gothic library in the Potsdam Neuer Park, built by Langhans after his visit to Britain in 1775; it is not known whether medieval manuscripts were similarly acquired as furnishings. See Robson-Scott, *Literary Background of the Gothic Revival in Germany.*

52. Alan Noel Latimer Munby, *Connoisseurs and Medieval Miniatures, 1750–1850* (Oxford: Claredon Press, 1972), 23.

53. On Beckford's library before 1823, see William Clarke, *Repertorium Bibliographicum: or, some account of the most celebrated British libraries* (London: W. Clarke, 1819), 203–30; Alan Noel Latimer Munby, *Connoisseurs and Medieval Miniatures, 1750–1850* (Oxford: Clarendon Press, 1972), 10, 77–78; William Beckford, *Life at Fonthill, 1807–1822, with Interludes in Paris and London, from the Correspondence of William Beckford,* trans. and ed. Boyd Alexander (London: R. Hart-Davis, 1957), 174. The Edward III gallery is

illustrated in Clive Wainwright, *The Romantic Interior: The British Collector at Home, 1750–1850, Studies in British Art* (New Haven, Conn.: published for the Paul Mellon Centre for Studies in British Art by Yale University Press, 1989), 114. Beckford collected manuscripts after 1823; most passed to the Earl of Hamilton, whose collection was bought by the German government in 1882; see Seymour De Ricci, *English Collectors of Books and Manuscripts (1530–1930) and Their Marks of Ownership* (Cambridge: Cambridge University Press, 1930), 86.

54. Beckford, *Life at Fonthill,* 174.

55. See the agreeable account of Ian Anstruther, *The Knight and the Umbrella* (London: Geoffrey Bles, 1963). Tournaments held between 1750 and 1839 in Europe and North America are listed on pp. 246–48.

56. Wolfgang Hartmann, *Die historische Festzug: seine Entstehung und Entwicklung im 19. und 20. Jahrhundert* (Munich: Prestel, 1976); see p. 161 for comments on the political role of the festivals.

57. On Phillipps, see Alan Noel Latimer Munby, *Phillipps Studies,* 5 vols. (Cambridge: Cambridge University Press, 1951–60; reprint, London: Sotheby's Parke-Bernet Publications, 1971).

58. There were sixteen sales of the Phillipps library held at Sotheby's between 1886 and 1913: August 1886, January 1889, July 1891, December 1891, July 1892, June 1893, March 1895, June 1896, May 1897, June 1898, June 1899, April–May 1903, June 1908, June 1910, April 1911, and May 1913; and six further Sotheby's sales between 1919 and 1938: June 1919, July 1928, two in. June 1935, June 1936, and June 1938. There were additional sales at Sotheby's and elsewhere between 1946 and 1957. See Munby, *Phillipps Studies,* vol. 5, *The Dispersal of the Phillipps Library.* The Grolier Club, New York, houses a trove of materials relating to Phillipps's library.

59. Munby, *Phillipps Studies,* 2:23–25; 3:138; 4:163.

60. Ibid., 80, quoting Popham.

61. Ibid., 13; Nicolas Barker, *Treasures of the British Library* (New York: Abrams, 1988), 138–39.

62. Waagen, *Treasures of Art in Great Britain,* 205–21. On Holford, see Robert Benson, *The Holford Collection, Westonbirt,* 2 vols. (Oxford: Oxford University Press, 1924); Robert Benson, *The Holford Collection, Dorchester House,* 2 vols. (Oxford: Oxford University Press, 1927); De Ricci, *English Collectors of Books and Manuscripts,* 115ff. The sales of the Holford library took place at Sotheby's on July 12, 1927 (part 1, illuminations on vellum), December 5, 1927 (part 2), March 26, 1928 (part 3), June 4, 1928 (part 4), November 12, 1928 (lots 227–93, imperfect and other books), and July 29, 1929 (lots 1–9: the nine manuscripts not disposed of privately).

63. De Ricci, *English Collectors of Books and Manuscripts,* 117; for the 1838 Ottley sale, see *Catalogue of the Very Beautiful Collection.*

64. See *Catalogue of the Very Celebrated Collection of Works of Art, the Property of Samuel Rogers, Esq. , Deceased; Comprising Ancient and Modern Pictures; Drawings and Engravings; Egyptian, Greek and Roman Antiquities; Greek Vases; Marbles, Bronzes, and Terra-Cottas, and Coins;*

*Also, the Extensive Library; Copies of Rogers's Poems, Illustrated; the Small Service of Plate and Wine* (London: Christie and Manson, April 28, 1856).

65. Ibid.

66. On George Salting, see Sir Leslie Stephen and Sir Sidney Lee, eds., *The Dictionary of National Biography. Supplement, January 1901–December 1911,* vol. 1 (1885-1901; reprints and supplements, 1912-96), 254–56.

67. On the Spitzer sale, see *Catalogue des objets d'art et de haute curiosite antiques, du moyen- âge & de la renaissance, composant l'importante et precieuse Collection Spitzer, dont la vente publique aura lieu a Paris . . . ,* 2 vols. (Paris: E. Menard et Cie, impri. April 17–June 16, 1893); and *Resume du catalogue des objets d'art et de haute curiosite antiques, du Moyen Age et de la Renaissance, composant l'importante et precieuse Collection Spitzer, dont la vente publique aura lieu a Paris, 16 juin 1893* (Paris: E. Menard et Cie, impr., June 16, 1893). On the Musée Spitzer, see Edmond Bonnaffe, *Le musee Spitzer* (Paris: Imprimerie de l'art, 1890).

68 .Thomas Frognall Dibdin, *Bibliographical Decameron; or Ten Days of Pleasant Discourse upon Illuminated Manuscripts and Subjects Connected with Early Engraving, Typography and Bibliography* (London: W. Bulmer, 1817), 1:cxi n.

69. Henry Montanell Lucien, *Hints on Illuminating: With an Essay on the Art of Ornamenting in Gold or Metals* (London: J. Barnard, 1864).

70. See Ottley, *Catalogue of a Highly Valuable and Extremely Curious Collection,* 3.

71. Roger S. Wieck, "Folia Fugitiva: The Pursuit of the Illuminated Manuscript Leaf," *Journal of the Walters Art Gallery* 54 (1996): 233–34.

72. Watson, "Vandals and Enthusiasts, 6.

73. On this phenomenon, see Florence Rionnet, *L'Histoire de l'atelier de moulage du Musée du Louvre (1794–1928)* (Paris: Seuil, 1996).

74. Munby, *Phillipps Studies,* 3:33–35.

75. Christopher De Hamel, "Cutting up Manuscripts for Pleasure and Profit" (paper presented at the eleventh Sol M. Malkin Lecture in Bibliography, Charlottesville, University of Virginia, 1996), in *The Rare Book School 1995 Yearbook,* ed. T. Belanger (Charlottesville, Va.: Rare Book School, 1996).

76. Neil Ripley Ker, *Fragments of Medieval Manuscripts Used as Pastedowns in Oxford Bindings with a Survey of Oxford Binding circa 1515–1620* (Oxford: Oxford Bibliographical Society, 1954). See also Rowan Watson, "Medieval Manuscript Fragments," *Archives* 13, no. 58 (autumn 1977): 61–73; and Robert G. Babcock, *Reconstructing a Medieval Library. Fragments from Lambach* (New Haven, Conn.: Yale University Library, 1993).

77. Bibliothèque Nationale, Departement des Manuscrits, and Leopold Delisle, *Catalogue des manuscrits des fonds Libri et Barrois* (Paris: H. Champion, 1888), lxvii–viii.

78. Karl Morrison, "Interpreting the Fragment," in *Hermeneutics and Medieval Culture* (Albany: State University of New York Press, 1988), 27.

79. Wieck, "Folia Fugitiva," 233.

80. Cécile Scailliérez, "Entre enluminure et peinture: a propos d'un *Paysage*

*avec Saint Jérôme Pénitent* de l'école Ganto-Brugeoise récemment acquis par le Louvre," *Revue du Louvre* 42 (1992): 16–31.

81. François Avril and Nicole Reynaud, *Les manuscrits à peintures en France: 1440–1520* (Paris: Flammarion, Bibliothèque Nationale, 1993), 133. For a comprehensive bibliography and description of this manuscript, see pp. 133–36.

82. See Claude Schaefer, *The Hours of Etienne Chevalier. Jean Fouquet,* with a preface by Charles Sterling (New York: G. Braziller, 1971), 19; and De Hamel, "Cutting up Manuscripts for Pleasure and Profit," 11.

83. For the British Library leaf (add. MS 37421), see Christopher De Hamel, "The 'Rogers' Leaf of the Hours of Etienne Chevalier," in *Illuminating the Book. Makers and Interpreters. Essays in Honour of Janet Backhouse* (London: British Museum, 1998), 250–60.

84. Munby, *Connoisseurs and Medieval Miniatures,* 30.

85. Ottley, *Catalogue of a Highly Valuable and Extremely Curious Collection;* and Ottley, *Catalogue of the Very Beautiful Collection.*

86. Sandra Hindman, *Medieval and Renaissance Miniature Painting* (Akron, Ohio: Bruce Ferrini Rare Books; London: Sam Fogg Rare Books, 1988), 25.

87. For Wallace, see Jonathan J. G. Alexander, *Wallace Collection: Catalogue of Illuminated Manuscript Cuttings* (London: Wallace Collection, 1980).

88. Emmanuelle Brugerolles and David Guillet, *The Renaissance in France: Drawings from the Ecole des Beaux-arts* (Cambridge, Mass.: Harvard University Art Museum; Seattle, Wash.: Distributed by the University of Washington Press, 1995), no. 1.

89. On the Musée de Cluny, see Alain Erlande-Brandenberg, "Le musée des Monuments français et les origines du Musée de Cluny," in *Das kunst- und kulturgeschitliche Museum im 19. Jahrhundert,* ed. Bernward Deneke and Rainer Kahsnitz (Munich: Prestel, 1977), 49–58; Q. Ladonne, *Quand le Moyen Age entré au musée: Monographie du musée du palais des Thermes et de l'hôtel de Cluny (1843–1907),* vol. 7 (Paris: D. E. A. Université Paris, 1992).

90. Yves Brayer, *La Collection Wildenstein* (Paris: Musée Marmottan, n. d.), nos. 204, 181, 69–71, 61, 33, and 34.

91. John Ruskin, *The Diaries of John Ruskin, 1848–1873* (Oxford, 1958), 468–78.

92. See Alice H. R. Hauck, "John Ruskin's Uses of Illuminated Manuscripts and Their Impact on His Theories of Art and Society," (Ph.D. diss., Johns Hopkins University, 1983), 248. See also Alice H. R. Hauck, "John Ruskin's Uses of Illuminated Manuscripts: The Case of the Beaupré Antiphonary, 1853–1856," *Arts Magazine* 56, no. 1 (September 1981): 79–83; James S. Dearden, "John Ruskin, the Collector, with a Catalogue of the Illuminated Manuscripts and Other Manuscripts Formerly in His Collection," *The Library* 5–6, no. 2 (June 1966): 124–54; and James S. Dearden, *Ruskin, Bembridge, and Brantwood: The Growth of the Whitehouse Collection* (Staffordshire, England: Ryburn Publishing, 1994).

93. De Hamel, "Cutting up Manuscripts for Pleasure and Profit," 14. Worth noting is the Book of Hours presently in Philadelphia, formerly in the possession of Ruskin, that has all of its large illuminations excised (Philadelphia: Free Library, Lewis MS. 125). See chapter 5 in this volume, and Edwin Wolf, *A Descriptive Catalogue of the John Frederick Lewis Collection of European Manuscripts in the Free Library of Philadelphia* (Philadelphia: Privately printed, 1937), no. 125.

94. Dibdin, *Bibliographical Decameron,* I:cxi–xii.

95. De Hamel, "Cutting up Manuscripts for Pleasure and Profit."

96. C. E. Wright, "The Elizabethan Society of Antiquaries and the Formation of the Cottonian Library," in *The English Library before 1700,* ed. Francis Wormald and C. E. Wright (London: University of London, Althone Press, 1958), 204–6.

97. Margaret Rickert, *The Reconstructed Carmelite Missal: An English Manuscript of the Late-Fourteenth Century in the British Museum (Additional 29704–5, 44892)* (Chicago: University of Chicago Press, 1952), esp. 18–19 and plate 39.

98. Susan Stewart, *On Longing: Narratives of the Miniature, the Gigantic, the Souvenir, the Collection* (Baltimore: Johns Hopkins University Press, 1984).

99. Victoria and Albert Museum, *Catalogue of the Circulating Collection of Illuminated Manuscripts (Leaves and Cuttings): Selected from the Victoria and Albert Museum, South Kensington,* comp. E. F. Strange (London: Printed for H.M.S.O. by Wyman and Sons, 1908).

100. Compton, "William Roscoe and Early Collectors of Italian Primitives," 68; Munby, *Connoisseurs and Medieval Miniatures,* 68.

101. William Roscoe, *The Life of Lorenzo de' Medici, Called the Magnificent* (London: Printed for A. Strahan, T. Cadell and W. Davies, and J. Edwards, 1796).

102. James H. Marrow et al., *The Golden Age of Dutch Manuscript Painting* (Stuttgart: Belser Verlag, 1989; reprint, New York: George Braziller, 1990), 245ff.

103. Dearden, "John Ruskin, the Collector," 125–26.

104. On Dennistoun, see Hugh Brigstocke, "James Dennistoun's Second European Tour, 1836–1839," *Connoisseur* 184, no. 742 (1973): 240–49; and Hugh Brigstocke, "Memoirs of the Dukes of Urbino: James Dennistoun, Collector and Traveller," *Connoisseur* 198, no. 798 (1978): 316–22. For Dennistoun's own work, see J. Dennistoun, *Memoirs of the Dukes of Urbino, Illustrating the Arms, Arts and Literature of Italy from 1440 to 1630,* 3 vols. (1851; reprint, London: John Lane, 1909).

105. William M. Voelkle and Roger S. Wieck, *The Bernard H. Breslauer Collection of Manuscript Illuminations* (New York: Pierpont Morgan Library, 1992), nos. 67–69.

106. Munby, *Connoisseurs and Medieval Miniatures,* 158.

107. Coutts Lindsay, *Sketches of the History of Christian Art* (London: J. Murray, 1847).

108. Compare John Steegman, *Victorian Taste: A Study of the Arts and Architecture from 1830 to 1870* (Cambridge, Mass.: MIT Press, 1990), 70–71.

109. Wieck, "Folia Fugitiva," 246–47.

110. For further bibliography, see Meta Harrsen, *Central European Manuscripts in the Pierpont Morgan Library* (New York: Pierpont Morgan Library, 1958); Wieck, "Folia Fugitiva," 233–54.

111. On Vasari's *Libro de' Disegni,* see Otto Kurz, "Giorgio Vasari's 'Libro de' Disegni,'" parts 1 and 2, *Old Master Drawings* 45 (June 1937): 1–15; 47 (December 1937): 32–44; and Margaret Morgan Grasselli, ed. , *The Touch of the Artist: Master Drawings from the Woodner Collections* (Washington, D.C.: National Gallery of Art, 1995; distributed by Abrams, 1995), 55–75 (no. 9).

112. Quoted in the original Italian in Kurz, "Giorgio Vasari's 'Libro de' Disegni'"(part 1), 7.

113. Ottley, *Italian School of Design,* commentary for plate 7.

114. Peter Parshall, "The Print Collection of Ferdinand, Archduke of Tyrol," *Jahrbuch des Kunsthistorischen Sammlungen in Wein* 78 (1982): 139–84.

115. Parshall, "Print Collection of Ferdinand," 143.

116. On Dennistoun, see n. 104. See also Munby, *Connoisseurs and Medieval Miniatures,* 158; and Waagen, *Treasures of Art in Great Britain,* 281–82.

117. Dennistoun, *Memoirs of the Dukes of Urbino.*

118. Quoted in Brigstocke, "James Dennistoun's Second European Tour," 247.

119. Ibid.

120. Waagen, *Treasures of Art in Great Britain,* 281–82.

121. Watson, "Vandals and Enthusiasts," 17, no. 29.

122. See Brigstocke, "James Dennistoun's Second European Tour," fig. 4.

123. See Patrick M. De Winter, "Bolognese Miniatures at the Cleveland Museum," *Bulletin of the Cleveland Museum of Art* 70, no. 8 (October 1983): 349; and Aeshlimann, *Arte Lombardo* 14 (1969): 34–35.

124. Quoted in Brigstocke, "James Dennistoun's Second European Tour," 240.

125. Ibid., 242.

126. See Munby, *Connoisseurs and Medieval Miniatures,* 25–26.

127. See John Rigby Hale, *England and the Italian Renaissance. The Growth of Interest in Its History and Art* (London: Faber and Faber, 1954), 131–32.

128. Hale, *England and the Italian Renaissance,* 157 and 161.

129. See Henry Yates Thompson, *A Descriptive Catalogue of Twenty Illuminated Manuscripts, nos. LXXV to XCIV, in the Collection of Henry Yates Thompson* (Cambridge: Cambridge University Press, 1907), 145ff; and Thomas Kren, ed., *Renaissance Painting in Manuscripts: Treasures from the British Museum* (New York: Hudson Hills Press, 1983), 123–31 (no. 16). For the history of this acquisition and sale, see also Brigstocke, "James Dennistoun's Second European Tour," 244–47.

130. Wieck, "Folia Fugitiva," 235.

131. *Early Fifteenth-Century Miniatures,* Alpine Club Gallery, London, May–June 1962. For the denuded album, now private collection, London, see Bloomsbury Books, November 5, 1992, lot 167.

132. Thomas Astle, *The Origins and Progress of Writing, as well as Hieroglyphic as Elementary, Illustrated by Engravings Taken from Marbles, Manuscripts and Charters* (London: printed for the author, sold by T. Payne, 1784); and Munby, *Connoisseurs and Medieval Miniatures,* 27.

133. The firm's file was given by Robert Hoe to the Grolier Club; it would be interesting to trace albums through their catalogues; see De Ricci, *English Collectors of Books and Manuscripts,* esp. 92–93.

134. Benson, *Holford Collection, Westonbirt*; Benson, *Holford Collection, Dorchester House.*

135. Wieck, "Folia Fugitiva," esp. n. 19.

136. See Béatrice Hernad, *Die Graphiksammlung des Humanisten Hartmann Schedel* (Munich: Bayerischen Staatsbibliothek, 1990), nos. 87, 111, and 112.

137. See R. Weick, *European Illuminated Manuscripts* (Turin, 1985).

138. Compton, "William Roscoe and Early Collectors of Italian Primitives," 33.

139. On these collages, see Sandra Hindman and Michael Heinlen, "A Connoisseur's Montage: The *Four Evangelists* Attributed to Gulio Clovio," *The Art Institute of Chicago Museum Studies* 17 (1991): 154–78 and 181–82.

140. One finds a similar echo of the aesthetic of the Carracci ceiling in a collage again featuring a Vincent Raymond miniature, this time showing the birth of John the Baptist. See Voelkle and Wieck, *Bernard H. Breslauer Collection of Manuscript Illuminations,* 224–27 (no. 90).

141. This collage is also addressed in Wieck, "Folia Fugitiva," 242; and Dearden, *Ruskin, Bembridge, and Brantwood,* 170–71.

142. For a case study in the nineteenth-century approach to the reconstruction of medieval stained glass, see Alyce A. Jordan, "Rationalizing the Narrative: Theory and Practice in the Nineteenth-Century Restoration of the Windows of the Sainte-Chapelle," *Gesta* 37, no. 2 (1998): 192–200.

143. O. Du Sartel sale, June 8, 1894, lot 575. See also Hindman, *Medieval and Renaissance Miniature Painting,* 43; and Wieck, "Folia Fugitiva," 242.

144. Racinet, *L'Ornement Polychrome,* I:15–16 ("Appendice sur la chromatique").

**Reproductions**

1. *Oxford English Dictionary,* s.v. "fasimile."

2. J. J. G. Alexander, "Facsimiles, Copies and Variations: The Relationship to the Model in Medieval and Renaissance European Illuminated Manuscripts," in *Retaining the Original: Multiple Originals, Copies and Reproductions,* Studies in the History of Art 20 (Washington, D.C., 1989), 61–72. See also Michael Camille, "The Très Riches Heures: An Illuminated Manuscript in the Age of Mechanical Reproduction," *Critical Inquiry* 17 (autumn 1990): 72–107; and Carl Nordenfalk, *Color of the Middle Ages: A Survey of Book Illumination Based on Color Facsimiles of Medieval Manuscripts* (Pittsburgh, Pa.: University Art Gallery, Henry Clay Frick Fine Arts Building, 1976.).

3. See Edward Rowe Mores, *Figurae quaedam antiquae ex Caedmonis Monachi paraphraseos in Genesin exemplari pervetusto, in biblioteca Bodleiana, deliate* (London: G. Woodfall, 1754). For Rawlinson and Rowe Mores, see Alan Noel Latimer Munby, *Connoisseurs and Medieval Miniatures, 1750–1850* (Oxford: Claredon Press, 1972), 30. For more on antiquarianism in England in the eighteenth and nineteenth centuries, see Joan Evans, *A History of the Society of Antiquaries* (Oxford: Oxford University Press for the Society of Antiquaries, 1956).

4. Alan Noel Latimer Munby, Phillipps Studies, vol. 4 (Cambridge: Cambridge University Press, 1956), 139–41. The Grolier Club, New York City, possesses a trove of materials related to Thomas Phillipps's library. For a recent exhibition of a selection from this material, see E. Holzenberg, *The Middle Hill Press: A Checklist of the Horblitt Collection of Books, Tracts, Leaflets and Broadsides Printed by Sir Thoma Phillipps* (New York: Grolier Club, 1997).

5. See Dominique Poulot, "Alexandre Lenoir et les Musées des Monuments Français," in *Les Lieux de memoire* II, *La Nation* (Paris: Gallimard, 1986): 497–531; and Guy Cogeval, "L'histoire du Musée des Monuments Français," in Patrimoine, temps, espace: Patrimoine en place, patrimoine desplace, ed. F. Furet (Paris: Fayard, 1990).

6. Thomas Frognall Dibdin, *Bibliographical Decameron; or Ten Days of Pleasant Discourse upon Illuminated Manuscripts and Subjects Connected with Early Engraving, Typography and Bibliography* (London: W. Bulmer, 1817), ccxxiv.

7. George Frederic Warner, *Reproductions from Illuminated Manuscripts* (London: British Museum, 1907).

8. For an introduction to the techniques of printing, see Bamber Gascoigne, *How to Identify Prints: A Complete Guide to Manual and Mechanical Processes from Woodcut to Ink Jet* (London: British Museum, 1986).

9. On lithography and chromolithography, see Wilhelm Weber, *A History of Lithography* (London: Thames and Hudson, 1966); Geoffrey Wakeman, *Aspects of Victorian Lithography: Anastatic Printing and Photozincography* (Wymondham, England: Brewhouse Press, 1970); Geoffrey Wakeman, *Victorian Book Illustration: The Technical Revolution* (Norwich: Fletcher and Son for David and Charles Ltd., 1973); and Ruari McLean, *Victorian Book Design and Colour Printing* (London, 1963). For an introduction to the types of lithographed works discussed throughout this chapter, see Allan Dooley, *Author and Printer in Victorian England: Printing Technology Shapes Texts* (Charlottesville: University of Virginia Press, 1992) and Alice H. R. H. Beckwith, *Victorian Bibliomania: The Illuminated Book in Nineteenth-Century Britain* (Providence: Museum of Art, Rhode Island School of Design, 1987).

10. Cf. Lewis Larmore, *Introduction to Photographic Principles* (New York: Dover, 1965); and Aaron Scharf, *Art and Photography* (London: Allen Lane, 1968). For the impact of photography on print production in England, see M. P. Tedeschi, "How Prints Work: Reproductions, Originals and Their Markets in England, 1840–1900" (Ph.D. dissertation, Northwestern University, 1994).

11. On Shaw, see Samuel Redgrave, *A Dictionary of Artists of the English School*

(Amsterdam: G. W. Hissink, 1970), 390; Sir Leslie Stephen and Sir Sidney Lee, eds., The Dictionary of National Biography, vol. 17 (Reprint, Oxford: Oxford University Press, 1917–), 1374–75; William Thomas Lowndes, *The Bibliographer's Manual of English Literature* (London: George Bell, 1875), vol 3, rev. ed. (London: H. G. Bohn), 2371–72; his obituary in *Art Journal*, 1873): 231; and Ruari McLean, "Henry Shaw's Coloured Books and Chiswick Press Colour Printing," in *Victorian Book Design and Colour Printing*, 2d ed. (London: Faber, 1972), 65–71. Much of the material treated in this section is also found in Sandra Hindman, "Facsimiles as Originals: An Unknown Illuminated Manuscript by Henry Shaw," *Journal of the Walters Art Gallery* 54 (1996): 225–32.

12. On the Chiswick Press, see G. Wakeman and G. D. R. Bridson, *A Guide to Nineteenth Century Colour Printers* (Leicestershire: Plough Press, 1975), 22; and Geoffrey Keynes, *William Pickering, Publisher. A Memoir and a Hand-List of His Editions* (London: Fleuron, 1924. Rev. ed., New York: B. Franklin, 1969).

13. On Madden, see especially Robert W. Ackerman and Gretchen P. Akerman, *Sir Frederic Madden. A Biographical Sketch and Bibliography,* (New York and London: Garland, 1979).

14. See Wakeman and Bridson, *Guide to Nineteenth Century Colour Printers*; Keynes, *William Pickering*. The clearest account of the editions is Nordenfalk, *Color of the Middle Ages,* 20–21.

15. These are the prices given by McLean, "Henry Shaw's Coloured Books," 65, subsequently quoted by Nordenfalk, *Color of the Middle Ages,* and Beckwith, *Victorian Bibliomania*; they differ from those given in 1875 by Lowndes and Bohn in *Bibliographer's Manual,* 2371.

16. Nordenfalk, *Color of the Middle Ages,* 20–21; Beckwith, *Victorian Bibliomania,* 30.

17. Nordenfalk, *Color of the Middle Ages,* 20–22; on Shaw and his contemporaries see Munby, *Connoisseurs and Medieval Miniatures,* especially 140–41.

18. On Brooke as a collector, see M. B. Parkes, *The Medieval Manuscripts of Keble College Oxford* (Oxford: Oxford University, Keble College, 1979), xii–xiii; Seymour de Ricci, *English Collectors of Books and Manuscripts (1530–1930) and Their Marks of Ownership* (Cambridge: Cambridge University Press, 1930); and Sir Thomas Brooke, *A Catalogue of Manuscripts and Printed Books Collected by Thomas Brooke, and Preserved at Armitage Bridge House, near Huddersfield,* 2 vols. (London: privately printed, 1891).

19. We thank Sam Carini, Department of Prints and Drawings, Art Institute of Chicago, for his help with our study of the Shaw manuscript

20. Rowan Watson, *Vandals and Enthusiasts. Views of Illumination in the Nineteenth Century* (London: Victoria and Albert Museum, 1995), 10–13.

21. Ibid., 32.

22. Ibid., 32ff.

23. H. Shaw to J. H. Pollen, December 22, 1864, quoted in Watson, *Vandals,* 34.

24. Henry Shaw, *A Catalogue of Illuminated Drawings by Henry Shaw, F.S.A., Author of "Illuminated Ornaments,"*

(London: Christie, Manson and Woods, June 6, 1866). The National Art Library, Victoria and Albert Museum, owns an annotated copy of this catalogue.

25. Shaw, *Catalogue of Illuminated Drawings*. See the copy annotated with prices realized and buyers located in the National Art Library, Victoria and Albert Museum.

26. This is the suggestion of McLean, Victorian Book Design, 68 and 70.

27. See Shaw, *Catalogue of Illuminated Drawings*. The annotated copy in the National Art Library of the Victoria and Albert Museum notes the correspondence between the lots and the museum accession number.

28. See Watson, *Vandals,* 36, mus. nos. 4916, 4917, 4918, 1–9, 4924 (the Boone Portfolio) and London, Christie's, June 6, 1866, lot 76–78, now mus. nos. 5924–26.

29. Watson, Vandals, 32, mus. no. 2958.

30. For the Arundel Society's own sense of its mission, see Frederick W. Maynard, *Descriptive Notice of the Drawings and Publications of the Arundel Society for 1849 to 1868 Inclusive. Illustrated by Photographs of All the Publications, One Fifth Their Original Size, Arranged in Order of Their Issue* (London: J. B. Nichols and Sons, 1869). See also Robin Cooper, "The Popularization of Renaissance Art in Victorian England: The Arundel Society," *Art History,* 1978, 263–92; and T. Harrod, "A Study of the Arundel Society, 1848–1897" (Ph.D. dissertation, Oxford University, 1978); Tanya Harrod, "John Ruskin and the Arundel Society," *Apollo* 127, no. 313 (March 1988): 180–88.

31. Maynard, *Descriptive Notice,* 2.

32. *The Life and Work of Fra Angelico da Fiesole, translated from Vasari . . . with Notes and Twenty-one Plates Illustrative of the Painter's Works* (1849); "The Distribution of Alms by St. Lawrence," after Fra Angelico in the Chapel of Nicholas V in the Vatican (1850); *Four Engravings in a Continuation of the Series of Frescoes by Fra Angelico in the Chapel of Nicholas V in the Vatican* (1850–51); *Two Copperplate Engravings by Herr Schäffer . . . [one of which is a] Continuation of the Series of Frescoes by Fra Angelico in the Chapel of Nicholas V in the Vatican* (1851–52).

33. Cf. Maynard, *Descriptive Notice,* 10; Cooper, "Popularization," 268–71; and Harrod, "John Ruskin," 182.

34. M. Digby Wyatt, *Notices on Sculpture in Ivory, Being a Lecture on the History, Methods and Productions of the Art* (1855).

35. Cooper, "Popularization," 273–6.

36. This Count Cottrell appears to be Charles Cottrell-Dormer. See L. G. Pine, ed., *Burke's Genealogical and Heraldic History of the Landed Gentry,* 7th ed. (London: Burke's Peerage Ltd., 1952), 677; and Stephen and Lee, eds., *Dictionary of National Biography,* vol. 4, 1215–16, especially 1216.

37. Cf. Maynard, *Descriptive Notice,* 24–25.

38. Ibid., 25.

39. Lillian M. C. Randall, Medieval and Renaissance Manuscripts in the Walters Art Gallery, vol. 2, *France, 1420–1540* (Baltimore: Johns Hopkins University Press with the Walters Art Gallery, 1992), 643–44.

40. Cf. Maynard, *Descriptive Notice,* 27–28. For discussions of Liberale da Verona's miniatures, see Enzo Carli, *Miniature di Liberale da Verona dai corali per il Duomo di Siena* (Milan: A. Martello, 1953); and Hans-Joachim Eberhardt, *Die Miniaturen von Liberale da Verona, Girolamo da Cremona und Venturino da Milan in den Chorbüchern des Doms von Siena: Dokumentation, Attribution, Chronolo- gie* (Berlin: Wasmuth, 1983).

41. Watson, *Vandals,* 7–8, no. 2. On Sprega, see Guiseppe Camaiori, "Memorie storiche di Belcaro," *Bulletino senese di storia patria* 3 (1913); and Carlo Sisi and Ettore Spalletti, *La cultura artistica a Siena nell'ottocento* (Siena: Monte dei Paschi di Siena, 1994).

42. Watson, *Vandals,* 7–8, no. 2.

43. Ibid., 7–8 and 29, nos. 2 and 59–60.

44. *Art Journal,* January 1869, 26; cited in Cooper, "Popularization," 263.

45. John Obadiah Westwood, *Fac-similes of the Miniatures and Ornaments of Anglo-Saxon and Irish Manuscripts* (London: B. Quaritch, 1868), ix.

46. John Obadiah Westwood, *Illuminated Illustrations of the Bible Copied from Select Manuscripts of the Middle Ages* (London: William Smith, 1846), 5.

47. Ibid., "The Annunciation," unnumbered page.

48. Ibid., 5 and footnote.

49. J. Backhouse, "A Victorian Connoisseur and His Manuscripts: The Tale of Mr. Jarman and Mr. Wing," *British Museum Quarterly* 32 (1968): 76–92.

50. *Catalogue of the Beautiful Collection of Illuminated Missals and Books of Hours . . . Formed by the Late John Boykett Jarman* (London: Sotheby's, June 13, 1964).

51. London: Victoria and Albert Museum, PDP 7759, facsimile of London: British Library, Arundel MS 157, folio 19, was bought directly from Wing in 1870 for five pounds. Henry Shaw had published a facsimile of this folio in Arundel 157 in 1834 (*Catalogue of manuscripts in the British Museum,* new series, vol. 1, part 1, *The Arundel Manuscripts* [London: British Museum, 1834], plate 7). Our assumption is that in 1870 Wing was selling his own product; it seems unlikely that he engaged in dealing, though he may have been involved in making the facsimile of 1834. There are indications that folios from famous manuscripts, the *Bedford Hours* above all, were independently facsimiled on more than one occasion. Other facsimiles of manuscripts by Wing (London: Victoria and Albert Museum, PDP, 4950–63) were bought from Colnaghi's in 1866 for forty-four pounds, two shillings (or three pounds, three shillings each), a high price but not rivaling those of Henry Shaw, FSA, at the sale of his work in the same year.

52. This collector appears to be Baron Aldenham, Henry Huck Gibbs (1819–1907). See Charles Kidd and David Williamson, eds., *Debrett's Peerage and Baronetage* (London: St. Martin's Press, 1995), 23.

53. See Howard Leathlean, "Henry Noel Humphreys and the Getting-Up of Books in the Mid–Nineteenth Century," *Book Collector* 38, no. 2 (summer 1989): 202, note 42.

54. On Wing's activity in Brighton in general, see David Beevers, ed., *Brighton Revealed through Artists' Eyes, circa 1760–circa 1960* (Brighton: Royal Pavilion, Art Gallery and Museums, 1995), nos. 53–54. Knowledge of Curtis's prospectus, issued in Brighton, with its details of study terms and a page of testimonials, we owe to Ken Spelman, York.

55. Leathlean, "Henry Noel Humphreys and the Getting-Up of Books," 193–209.

56. *Academy* (May 8, 1875): 489.

57. Mary P. Merrifield, *Original Treatises Dating from the XIIth to the XVIIth Centuries on the Arts of Painting in Oil, Miniature, Mosaic and on Glass; of Gilding, Dyeing; and Preparation of Colours and Artificial Gems,* 2 vols. (London: John Murray, 1849).

58. Ibid., vol. 1, v.

59. Ibid., xxxvii.

60. Anna Jameson's most influential text was *Sacred and Legendary Art* (London: Longman, Brown, Green, and Longmans, 1848). On Jameson, see David A. Ludley, "Anna Jameson and D. G. Rossetti: His Use of Her Histories," *Woman's Art Journal* 12, no. 2 (1991–92): 29–33; Sheridan Gilley, "Victorian Feminism and Catholic Art: The Case of Mrs. Jameson," in The Church and the Arts, ed. Diana Wood (Oxford: Blackwell, 1992): 381–91; Adele H. Ernstrom, "Why Should We Be Always Looking Back? 'Christian art' in Nineteenth-Century Historiography in Britain," *Art History* 22, no. 3 (1999): 421–35. The last article also deals with A. W. N. Pugin, discussed in chapter 4.

61. See Jocelyn Bouquillard, "Le comte Auguste de Bastard (1792– 1883): archéologue et imprimeur lithographe" (Ph. D. dissertation, l'École de Chartes, 1995); and Jocelyn Bouquillard, "Les Peintures et ornements des manuscrits du comte de Bastard," *Bulletin du bibliophile,* no. 1 (1996): 108–50.

62. Bouquillard, "Les Peintures et ornements," 114. See Jean-Baptiste-Louis-Georges Séroux d'Agincourt, *Histoire de l'art par les monumens: depuis sa décadence au IVe siècle jusqu' a son renouvellement au XIVe* (Paris: Treuttel et Wurtz, 1823). On Séroux d'Agincourt, see Henri Loyrette, "Séroux d'Agincourt et les origines de l'histoire de l'art médiéval," *Revue de l'art* 48 (1980): 40–56.

63. Bastard d'Estang, "Exposé sommaire de la publication," in *Etudes de symbolique chrétien. Bulletin du Comité de la langue, de l'histoire et des arts de la France, section d'archéologie,* 4 (1857): 902.

64. Cf. Bouquillard, "Les Peintures et ornements," 115–16.

65. Ibid., 116.

66. Ibid., 135. For a tally of the libraries to which the volumes were actually dispersed, see the chart 138–39.

67. Jacques-Charles Brunet, *Manuel du libraire et de l'amateur de livres,* 4th ed., vol. 1 (Paris: Silvestre, 1842), 264; Bouquillard, "Les Peintures et ornements," 143.

68. Jacques-Charles Brunet, *Manuel du libraire et de l'amateur de livres,* 5th ed., vol. 1 (Paris: Firmin-Didot Freres, Fils et Cie, 1860), col. 696–97; Bouquillard, "Les Peintures et ornements," 144.

69. For example, in 1856 a fifteenth-century Book of Hours with seventy-sevn miniatures could go for 440 francs; a less richly illuminated exemplar could go for 100 francs or less. Cf. *Catalogue de livres rares et précieux, manuscits et imprimés, composant la Bibliothèque de M. C. R. ★★★ de Milan* (Paris; L. Potier, 1856), lots 63 and 65. See the annotated copy in Chicago: Newberry Library. As a further point of comparison, at this time a painting attributed to Fra Angelico could go for a mere 75 francs at the 1846 sale of the collection of Cardinal Fesch. See Hippolyte Mireur, *Dictionnaire des ventes d'art faites en France et à l'étranger pendant les XVIIIme et XIXme siècles,* vol. 3 (Paris: Maison d'Editions d'Oeuvres Artistiques, 1911), 151. For Hennin's comments, see Michel Hennin, Les Monuments de l'histoire de France, vol. 2 (Paris: J. F. Delion, 1857): v–vii. On these critiques of Bastard d'Estang's project, see Bouquillard, "Les Peintures et ornements," 144–45.

70. On Curmer, see Maurice Cloche,"Un grand éditeur du XIXe siècle, Léon Curmer," *Arts et métiers graphiques* 33 (1933): 28–36; Gérard Blanchard,"Curmer, ou la leçon d'un grand éditeur romantique," *Le Courrier graphique* 117 (1962): 42–51; and *Un editeur parisien au XIXe siècle. Leon Curmer. Albert Curmer 1911–1912* (n.p.: privately printed, n.d.), a copy of which is in the Bibliothèque Nationale, Paris.

71. Catherine Rosenbaum-Dondaine, *L'Image de piété en France, 1814–1914* (Paris: Muséee-Galerie de la SEITA, 1984): 65 and 70, especially figure 68.

72. Catherine Rosenbaum-Dondaine, "Un siècle et demi de petite imagerie de piété," *Revue de la Bibliothèque Nationale* 6 (December 1982): 25; Bathild Bouniol, *L'Art Chrétien et l'école allemande, avec une notice sur M. Overbeck* (Paris: Ambroise Bray & Schulgen et Schwan, 1856).

73. Subscription details in this and other of Curmer's works are sometimes bound into copies; if they are not, information can be gained from other sources. The copy of the *Imitation* in London (National Art Library, Victoria and Albert Museum) has no subscription details, but the publication is minutely described in Richard Thomson, *A Lecture on Some of the Most Characteristic Features of Illuminated Manuscripts* (London: printed for the London Institution by C. Skipper and East, 1857): 134–35. We have found no publication details for the *Grandes heures de la reine Anne de Bretagne* (Paris, 1861).

74. The appendix volume contains the *Procès-verbal* of August 14 before a notary guaranteeing the restricted print run of 850 copies, with publication details.

75. The publication is described in the *Bulletin du Bibliophile* 15e série (1861): 350–51. The 1872 *Missale Romanum* of Reiss may have been published in a similar way (London: Victoria and Albert Museum, National Art Library 93) 10; the printing of this work is superb and uses a color-printing technique involving woodcuts superior to Curmer's chromolithography.

76. Leopold Carteret, *Le trésor du bibliophile romantique et moderne, 1801–1875,* vol. 3, *Livres illustrés du XIXe siècle* (Paris, 1927), 313, refers to reprintings of the *Imitation.* The serial nature of publication is not mentioned

77. *Le Livre d'heures de la Reine Anne de Bretagne*, 2 vols. (Paris: Curmer, 1861).

78. Ibid., appendix (text volume), 1

79. F. Denis, appendix, *Imitation de Jésus Christ* (Paris: Curmer, 1856–58): 24.

80. Paris Exhibition, *Rapports de Jury 2*, 26e classe, 1252; International Exhibition, 1862, *Medals and Honourable Mentions Awarded by the International Juries* (1862),. 308; Reports on the Paris Universal Exhibition, 1867, vol. 2 (1868), 114.

81. For Engelmann's works, see Godefroy Engelmann, *Manuel du dessinateur lithographe ou description des meilleurs moyens à employer pour faire des dessins sur pierre dans tous les genres connus. Suivie d'une instruction sur le nouveau procédé du lavia lithographique* (Paris: G. Engelmann, 1822); and Godefroy Engelmann, *Traité théoretique et pratique de la lithographie* (Mulhouse, 1839). On Engelmann, see Léon Lang, "Godefroy Engelmann, imprimeur lithographe," in *Trois siècles de l'art alsacien, 1648–1948* (Strasbourg: Editions des Archives Alsaciennes d'Histoire de l'Art, 1948), 159–87; and Léon Lang, *Godefroy Engelmann, imprimeur-lithographe: les incunables, 1814–1817* (Colmar: Editions Alsatia, 1977).

82. Charles Nodier and Justin Taylor, *Voyages pittoresques et romantiques dans l'ancien France* (Paris: Didot l'aine, 1820–57). Cf. Anita Louise Spadafore, "Baron Taylor's *Voyages Pittoresques*" (Ph.D. dissertation, Northwestern University, 1973); and Caisse Nationale des Monuments Historiques et des Sites, *Le "gothique" retrouvé avant Viollet-le-Duc* (Paris: Caisse Nationale des Monuments Historiques et des Sites, 1979), 105–20.

83. See Florence Rionnet, *L'Histoire de l'atelier de moulage du Musée du Louvre (1794–1928)* (Paris: Seuil, 1996).

84. See Eugène Piton, *Famille Firmin-Didot, imprimeurs, libraires, fondeurs, graveurs, papetiers, inventeurs et littérateurs* (Paris: Publications de la Renommée, 1856); André Jammes, *Didotiana* (Paris: Jouve, 1994); and André Jammes ed., *Les Didot. Trois siècles de typographie et de bibliophilie, 1698–1998* (Paris: Bibliothèque Historique de la Ville de Paris, 1998).

85. Paul Lacroix, *Le Moyen Age et la Renaissance*, 5 vols. (Paris: Firmin-Didot, 1848–51). Essay on manuscripts by J. J. Campollion-Figeac in vol. 2.

86. For more on the Firmin-Didot collection and the six-session sale of Ambroise Firmin-Didot's library, see discussion in Jammes, *Didotiana*, 5–12; François Avril, "Les manuscrits de la collection d'Ambroise Firmin-Didot," in Jammes, *Les Didot*, 91–103.

87. Preface to Paul Lacroix, *Les Arts au Moyen Age et à l'époque de la Renaissance* (Paris: Firmin-Didot, 1869), iv. Citation from Paul Lacroix, *The Arts in the Middle Ages and the Renaissance*, revised and rearranged by W. Armstrong (London, 1879; reprint, New York, 1964), viii.

88. Lacroix, *Les Arts au moyen âge*, iv.

89. Paul Lacroix, *Sciences et lettres au moyen âge et à l'époque de la Renaissance* (Paris: Firmin-Didot, 1877).

90. Ibid., iv.

91. On Adolphe Alphonse Gery-Bichard, see Emmanuel Bénézit, *Dictionnaire critique et documentaire des peintures, sculpteurs, dessinateurs et graveurs*,

rev. ed., vol. 6 (Paris: Gründ, 1999), 57; and Ulrich Thieme, *Allgemeines Lexikon der bildenden Künstler*, vol. 13 (Leipzig: E. A. Seemann, 1920), 492. There is also record of a genre painter and watercolorist, Alphonse Joseph Bichard, active in France in the 1870s, but it appears that Gery-Bichard is the more likely candidate for being one of Lacroix's artists. See Bénézit, *Dictionnaire*, vol. 2, 289.

92. Bénézit, *Dictionnaire*, vol. 11, 209; and H. Vollmer et al., *Allgemeines Lexikon der bildenden Künstler*, vol. 27 (Leipzig: E. A. Seemann, 1933), 346.

93. Another artist among those named on the title page of Lacroix's *Sciences et Lettres* can be matched to a name appearing in the historical record—one Emile Florentin Daumont, known as a landscape painter and master of gouache, engraving, and etching. See Bénézit, *Dictionnaire*, vol. 4, 271; and Vollmer et al., *Allgemeines Lexikon*, vol. 8 (Leipzig: E. A. Seemann, 1913), 437. Compère and Werner, also named on Lacroix's title page, are less easy to identify with known figures. The original watercolors we have examined bear the names Le Doux fils, J. Petot, Ch. Chauvet, and Garcia among others. A Jules Adolphe Chauvet, who was an illustrator in Paris in the second half of the nineteenth century, appears in the record, but as yet there is no evidence linking him to the "Ch. Chauvet" active in Lacroix's studio. Likewise an Antonio Garcia y Mencia, watercolorist and painter of allegorical scenes exhibited in Paris (though he was active in Madrid), and there is a possibility (though remote) that this figure can be identified with another of Lacroix's artists. See Bénézit, *Dictionnaire*, vol. 3, 536, and vol. 5, 863. The activity of the painters connected to Lacroix's projects offers an area for further research.

94. See *Catalogue des Livres précieux manuscrits et imprimés faisant partie de la bibliothèque Ambroise Firmin-Didot*, Paris, June 10–14, 1884, lot 76.

95. See *Catalogue des Livres précieux manuscrits et imprimés faisant partie de la bibliothèque Ambroise Firmin-Didot* Paris, June 10–14, 1884, lot 77. Also see Jammes, *Les Didot*: 89–90 (no. 231) and plate 9.

96. *Catalogue des livres rares et précieux . . . faisant partie de la Bibliothèque de M. Ambroise Firmin-Didot*. (Paris: M. Delestre and A. Labitte, June 10–14, 1884), lot 66.

97. Roger S. Wieck, "The Rosenwald *Scribe* Miniature and Its Sister Miniatures: A Case of Mistaken Identity," *Oud Holland* 95, no. 3 (1981): 151–61.

98. Our remarks are based on the copy in London's Victoria and Albert Museum, National Art Library, which has a deluxe binding of velvet with enamel furniture (NAL pressmark 95, GG. 53). Cf. Louis-Charles. Arsenne, *Manuel du peintre*, vol. 1 (Paris: Roret, 1833), 212; and Bruno Foucard, *Le renouveau de la peinture religieuse en France, 1800–1860* (Paris: Arthéna, 1987), 396. On the Hetzel publication, see Henri-Jean Martin and Roger Chartier, eds., *Histoire de l'Edition Française*, vol. 3 (Paris: Promodis, 1985), 177–78 and 181–82.

99. The copy in London's Victoria and Albert Museum, National Art Library, came from the library of the Comte de Chambord and has the label "De la bibliothèque du Comte de Chambord (Henri V de France, duc de Bordeaux)

Né en 1820 *Acquise par Maggs Bros. Ltd. de Londres."*

100. There are copies of the 1838 work in London's Victoria and Albert Museum, National Art Library (pressmark 93. E. 4), and the British Library (C. 25. g. 2, with a variant title page). Aline Guilbert's *Book of Hours* was mentioned in Karl Robert, *Traité practique de l'enluminure* (Paris: Georges Meusnier, 1888), 91; and in Alphonse Labitte, *Les manuscrits et l'art de les orner* (Paris: Charles Mendel, 1893), 380, figure 279. The work was copied from manuscripts in the Bibliothèque Nationale under the direction of the Abbé des Billiers, Canon of Langres, and published by Gruel and Engelmann, éditeurs à Paris, in an edition of five hundred with twelve vellum copies.

101. For the mission of the Musée des Souverains, see H. Barbet de Jouy, *Notice des antiquités, objets du moyen âge, de la renaissance et des temps modernes composant le Musée des Souverains* (Paris: Charles de Mourgues freres, 1866): v–xxviii. We would like to thank Aron Vinegar for his research on this subject.

102. Cf. Kathryn Brush, "Gothic Sculpture as a Locus for the Polemics of National Identity," in Concepts of National Identity in the Middle Ages, ed. Simon Forde, Lesley Johnson and Alan V. Murray (Leeds: Leeds Studies in English, 1995), 189–213. See also Kathryn Brush, "Integration or Segregation among the Disciplines? The Historiography of Gothic Sculpture as Case-Study" in *Artistic Integration in Gothic Buildings*, ed. Virginia C. Raguin, Kathryn Brush, and Peter Draper (Toronto: University of Toronto Press, 1995): 19–40.

103. For Napoleon's acquisitions at the Soltikoff sale, see Bulletin du Bibliophile, 15e série (1861): 353.

104. Manuscripts in the museum were as follows (the numbers are those in the catalogue of de Jouy): no. 23, Charlemagne's Evangelistary, BnF n.a. l. 1203 (*Godescalc Evangelistary*); no. 24, *Charles the Bald Psalter*, BnF MS Latin 1152; no. 25, Bible of Charles the Bald, BnF MS Latin 1 (Vivian Bible); no. 30, *Psalter of Blanche of Castille and St. Louis*, Bib. Arsenal MS 1186; no. 32, *St. Louis Psalter*, BnF MS Latin 10,525; no. 40, Charles V Bible, BnF, MS fr 5707; no. 43, Hours owned by Charles VIII and Louis XII, BnF, MS fr. 5661; no. 51, *Anne of Brittany Hours*, BnF MS Latin 9474; no. 54, *Hours of Marguerite d'Orléans*, sister of François I, acquired by the Musée des Souverains in 1866; no. 63, *Hours of Henri IV*, BnF MS Latin 1171; no. 65, *Hours of Catherine de Médici*; no. 67, prayer book of Marie Stuart, wife of François II, BnF MS Latin 1405; no. 73, statutes of the Ordre du Saint Esprit, BnF MS fr. 4274; no. 74, professions of knights µof the Ordre du Saint Esprit, 1578–1789, BnF n.a. fr. 1993; no. 97, Hours that belonged to Henri IV; no. 111, *Hours of Louis XIV*; no. 128, prayer book of Marie, wife of Louis XV, acquired by the Musée des Souverains in 1864.

105. See Simon Jervis, ed., *Art and design in Europe and America, 1800–1900* (London: Herbert Press, 1987): 62–63.

106. Gerd Krumeich, *Jeanne d'Arc in der Geschichte: Historiographie, Politik, Kultur* (Sigmaringen: J. Thorbecke, 1989), 104–5.

107. Daniel Alcouffe, *Un âge d'or des arts décoratifs, 1814–1848* (Paris: Réunion des Musées Nationaux, 1991): 507–11.

108. Christian Amalvi, *Le Goût du moyen âge* (Paris: Plon, 1996), 192. On the adoption of medieval styles for the monarchist cause earlier in the century during the Restoration, see Richard A. Jackson, *Vive le roi! A History of French Coronation from Charles V to Charles X* (Chapel Hill: University of North Carolina Press, 1984), 191–96.

109. The manuscript (London: Victoria and Albert Museum, National Art Library, MSL 1987/7) is described in Daniel Alcouffe, *Un age d'or*, 464–65, no. 271. We are grateful to Mellerio Joailliers for information from their archives: M. Gallois was a regular client; the bill for the jeweled covers was dated October 1841.

110. The *Annuaire de la pairie et de la noblesse de France*, ed. Borel d'Hauterive, appeared first in 1843. The volume for 1847 described the legal machinery for registering and guaranteeing titles (297–302). In 1814 the ancient nobility could regain their titles, but article 259, guaranteeing against the unauthorized adoption of titles, was not enforced and was dropped from the Code in 1832. In 1848, the *Annuaire* claimed that a rival publication, the *Almanach de Noblesse*, was accepting all titles as authentic. The 690 coats of arms were published in color before 1848 in *Galeries de Versailles, Armoiries de la Salle des Croisades*, with 28 plates (n.d.). On forgeries of this sort, see Nicolas Barker, "Textual Forgery," in Mark Jones, *Fake? The Art of Deception* (London: British Library, 1990), 26. Forged charters purportedly issued by Philip Augustus and Richard Coeur de Lion in Acre were sold at Sotheby's in London, June 23, 1987. See Léopold Delisle, *Bibliothèque de l'École des Chartes* 49 (1888), 304–6, on forgery of this kind. An example of an artificial collection of medieval archival documents made in the nineteenth century for submission in 1867 to the Archives Générales de la Noblesse is the group relating to the de Cusance family, now London: University of London Library, MS 865.

111. Karin Kaudelka-Hanisch, "The Titled Businessman: Prussian Commercial Councillors in the Rhineland and Westphalia during the 19th Century," in The German Bourgeoisie, ed. David Blackburn and Richard Evans (London: Routledge, 1991), 105. Burke's *Peerage* was joined in 1836 by a similar work for the landed gentry, which had reached a fourth edition by 1863. Debrett's *Baronetage*, first published in 1808, had reached a seventh edition by 1839, while the *Peerage*, first published in 1803, had reached its twenty-first edition by 1836 and became an annual, as had *Debrett's Illustrated Peerage* from 1864; a cheap edition was also published from 1865. Debrett's *Illustrated Baronetage and Knightage* was an annual from 1865.

112. The work is described in the catalogue of the *Twenty Eighth Antiquarian Book Fair* (June 23–25, 1988): no. 39, when it was offered for sale by Heribert Tenschert. The printed book may have been the same as the Book of Hours originally printed by Hetzel in 1838.

113. See Claude Savart, "Le livre religieux," in Histoire de l'édition Française, vol. 3, *Le temps des éditeurs* (Paris: Promodis, 1985): 402–7. Many popular

nineteenth- (and twentieth-) century missals and Books of Hours are illustrated in Michel Albaric, ed., *Histoire du Missel français* (Turnhout: Brepols, 1986).

114. On the duc d'Aumale, see Camille, "*Très Riches Heures*." The duc de Chartres was a noted collector of books and manuscripts; see the *Dictionnaire de Biographie Francaise*, vol. 8, 685–86. The inclusion of the duc de Chartres's nineteenth-century Book of Hours in the 1900 Great Exhibition is mentioned in the catalogue of the *Twenty Eighth Antiquarian Book Fair*, no. 39.

115. Munby, *Connoisseurs and Medieval Miniatures*, 143; Bibliothèque Municipale, *L'Art du livre de la restauration au Second Empire, 1815–1852* (Bordeaux: Bibliothèque Municipale, 1938), plate 2; L. Léopold Delisle, "Souvenirs de Jeunesse," in *Recherches sur la librairie de Charles V* (Paris: H. Champion, 1907), xxiii.

116. Miniatures from this celebrated manuscript were copied several times in the nineteenth century. See Catherine Reynolds and Jenny Stratford, "Le manuscrit dit `Le Pontifical de Poitiers,'" *Revue de l'Art* 84 (1989): 61–80. The 1837 miniature with its signature is reproduced in color in *Un trésor gothique. La Chasse de Nivelle* (Paris: Réunion des Musées Nationaux, 1996), 347.

117. Les Evangiles des Dimanches, vol. 3 (Paris: Curmer, 1864), xxviii.

118. Léon Lagrange, "Du rang des femmes dans les arts," *Gazette des Beaux Arts* 8 (1860): 34–5.

119. Henri Bouchot, *L'Art dans la décoration du diplôme. Recueil de 104 documents modernes* (Paris: Henri Laurens, 1901). Bouchot had been a member of the jury at the 1900 Exposition Universelle, judging ephemera produced by printing processes. For Grasset's book, see Gordon N. Ray, The Art of the French Illustrated Book, 1700-1914, vol. 2 (Ithaca, N.Y.: Cornell University Press, 1982), 465–66, no. 357.

120. Patrick Sourget and Elizabeth Sourget, *Manuscrits et livres précieux*, catalogue no. 7 (1991), no. 135.

121. Henri Jadart, "Un enlumineur rémois: Alphonse Lesoeur," *Travaux de l'Académie Nationale de Reims* 135 (1921): 161–66

122. Girodie, André, "Les livres de prières illustrés," *Notes d'Art et archéologie. Revue de la Société de Saint Jean pour l'encouragement de l'art Christien* 2e série, 10e année (1898).

123. Albums of examples, *Modèles d'enluminure appliqués aux objets usuels, Pochettes de l'enlumineur, Livres d'Heures* (in a series Livres à Enluminer), were advertised in Labitte's book of 1893 (Alphonse Labitte, *L'Art de l'enluminure: métier, histoire, pratique* [Paris: H. Laurens, 1893]). Mermet's wares were advertised in the *Coloriste-Enlumineur* (1894). Guillot's series of three albums (*L'Ornementation des manuscrits au moyen ge. Recueil de documents pour l'enluminure*) was published by Laurens in 1893, though earlier editions (circa 1890) had been published by L. Turgis.

124. Robert, *Traité pratique*; Labitte, *L'Art de l'enluminure*; Labitte, *Les manuscrits et l'art*.

125. Martin and Chartier, eds., Histoire de l'Édition Française, vol. 4, 172 and 329.

126. On Maredsous and its "École des métiers," see the bibliography in L. H. Cottineau, *Répertoire Topo-Bibliographique des abbeyes et prieurés*, vol. 2 (Macon, 1937), col. 1744. Illuminated works from the late nineteenth century, most done at the related convent of Maredret, can be seen at the abbey today. (See also chapter 5 for a Maradret manuscript acquired by J. Pierpont Morgan.) After 1900, an Easter missal was illuminated in Art Deco style by Father Vincent Denné.

127. Albert Lecoy de la Marche, *Les manuscrits et la miniature* (Paris: Quantin, 1884), 5, 169, 170, 192, and 244.

128. Alphonse Labitte, ed., *Le Manuscrit* 1 (1894): 97–98 and 109.

129. Emile Goutiére-Vernolle, "Une Renaissance ésperée (L'Enluminure à Nancy)," *La Lorraine Artiste* 10 (1892): 247–49.

130. *Notes d'Art et Archéologie. Revue de la Société Saint-Jean*, 20e année (1908).

131. For a recent examination of this issue, see Jeffrey F. Hamburger, *Nuns as Artists: The Visual Culture of a Medieval Convent* (Berkeley: University of California Press, 1997).

132. Christian Amalvi, "Le défaite, 'mode d'emploi': recherches sur l'utilisation rétrspective du passé dans les rapports franco-allemands en France entre 1870 et 1914,"in *La Guerre de 1870/71 et ses conséquences,* ed. Philippe Levillain and Rainer Riemenschneider (Bonn: Bouvier Verlag, 1990), 451–64.

133. Amalvi, *Le Goût*, 193.

134. René Redmond, *Les droites en France*, 4th ed. (Paris: Aubier Montaigne, 1982): 283.

135. "Appendix," *L'Imitation de Jésus-Christ*, 24.

136. Marius Vachon, *La Guerre artistique avec l'Allemagne: l'organisation de la victoire* (Paris: Payot, 1916).

137. Jean El Gammal, "L'utilisation électorale du passé: 1885–1898," *Revue Historique* 265, no. 537 (1981): 105.

138. Raoul Girardet, *Le Nationalism français, 1871–1914* (Paris: A. Colin, 1966), 17; Thomas Kselman, *Miracles and Prophecies in Nineteenth-Century France* (New Brunswick, N.J.: Rutgers University Press, 1983), 118–20 and 162–65.

139. Christian Amalvi, "Le Révolution au village: jalons pour l'étude de la postérité révolutionnaire dans la France contemporaine, 1871–1914," *History of European Ideas* 13, no. 5 (1991): 560; Redmond, Les droites, 132–33.

140. Rosemonde Sanson, "La `Fête de Jeanne d'Arc' en 1894: controverse et célébration," *Revue d'Histoire Moderne et Contemporaine* 20 (1973): 445.

141. Catherine Rosenbaum-Dondaine, *L'Image de piété*, 83 and 167, nos. 81, 145, and 159.

142. Cf. Gustav Friedrich Waagen, *Treasures of Art in Great Britain: Being an Account of the Chief Collections of Paintings, Drawings, Sculptures, Illuminated Mss*, vol. 1 (London: J. Murray, 1854), 136–222 passim.

143. Cited in Brigitte Buettner, "Panofsky à l'ère de la reproduction Méchanisée: une question de perspec-

tive," *Les Cahiers du Musée nationale de l'art moderne* 53 (1995): 59. See also William Henry Fox Talbot, *The Pencil of Nature* (1844–46; reprint, New York: Da Capo 1969); Joel Snyder and Neill Walsh Allen, "Photography, Vision and Representation," *Critical Inquiry* 2 (1975): 143–69; Walter Benjamin, "Walter Benjamin's Short History of Photography," *Artforum* 15 (February 1977): 46–51; Richard Bolton, ed., *The Contest of Meaning: Critical Histories of Photography* (Cambridge, Mass.: MIT Press, 1989); Patrick Maynard, "Talbot's Technologies: Photographic Depiction, Detection and Reproduction," *Journal of Aesthetics and Art Criticism* 47 (summer 1989): 236–76; Larry J. Schaff, *Out of the Shadows: Herschel, Talbot and the Invention of Photography* (New Haven, Conn., 1992); and Geoffroy Batchen, "The Naming of Photography: 'A Mass of Metaphor,'" *History of Photography* 17 (spring 1993): 22–32.

144. Camille, "*Très Riches Heures,*" 83–84.

145. Paul Durrieu, *Heures de Turin: quarante-cinq feuillets à peintures provenant des Très belles heures de Jean de France* (Paris: P. Renouard, 1902). See also Albert Châtelet, *Jean Van Eyck Enlumineur. Les Heures de Turin et de Milan-Turin* (Strasbourg: Presses Universitaires de Strasbourg, 1993): 47 and passim.

146. Nicolas Barker, *The Publications of the Roxburghe Club, 1814–1962: An Essay with Bibliographical Table* (Cambridge: Roxburghe Club, 1964).

147. See Elmar Mittler and Wilfried Werner, *Codex Manesse. Katalog der Ausstellung vom 12. Juni bis 4. September 1988, Universitätsbibliothek Heidelberg* (Heidelberg: Braus, 1988); Claudia Brinker and Dione Flüher-Kreis. *Die Mannessische Liederhandschrift in Zürich: Exhibition* (Zurich: Schweizerisches Landesmuseum, 1991). For nineteenth-century perceptions of the codex, see Karl Clausberg, *Die Manessische Liederhandschrift* (Cologne: DuMont Buchverlag, 1978).

148. For an early unfinished project reproducing the miniatures in black-and-white lithography, see Bernard Carl Mathieu, *Minnesänger aus der Zeit Hohenstaufen, im vierzehnten Jahrhundert gesammelt von Rudger Maness von Maneck* (Paris, 1850). For other early reproductions of the Manesse Codex, see Friedrich Heinrich von der Hagen, *Bildersaal der altdeutscher Dichter. Bildnisse, Wappen, und Dichter des XII bis XIV. Jahrhunderts: nach Handschriftgemälden, vornamlich der mannesse'schen Sammlung* (Berlin: J. A. Stargardt, 1856); Friedrich Heinrich von der Hagen, "Gemälde in der manesse- 'schen Handschrift von deutschen Dichtern des 12–14. Jahrhunderts," *Abhandlungen der königlichen Akademie der Wissenschaften zu Berlin, Philos.-histor. Kl.* (1853): 517–29. For a good bibliography of the early scholarship on the Manesse Codex, see Rudolf Sillib, Friedich Panzer, and Arthur Haseloff, Die Manessische Lieder-Handschrift. Faksimile-Ausgabe, 7 vols. (Leipzig: Insel-Verlag, 1929).

149. See Léopold Delisle, *Catalogue des manuscrits des fonds Libri et Barrois* (Paris: H. Champion, 1888).

150. See Henri Omont, *Listes des Recueils de Fac-similés et des reproductions de manuscrits conservés à la Bibliothèque Nationale* (Paris: Editions des Bibliothèques Nationales de France, 1935).

151. Paul Eudel, *Trucs et truqueurs: Alterations, fraudes et contrafaçons devoilées* (Paris: Librarie Molière, 1907); Hans Tietz, *Genuine and False: Copies, Imitations, and Forgeries* (New York: Chanticleer Press, 1948); Otto Kurz, *Fakes: A Handbook for Collectors and Students* (London: Faber and Faber, 1948); Otto. Kurz, *Fakes and Forgeries* (Minneapolis: Minneapolis Institute of Art, 1973); Emmanuel Le Roy Ladurie, introduction to *Vrai ou faux? Copier, imiter, falsifier* (Paris: Bibliothèque Nationale, 1988); and Jones, *Fake?*

152. There is a famous history of faked documents. In the fifth century B.C., Herodotus records such a forgery. Famous medieval faked documents include the *Donation of Constantine* and the forged *Decretales of Isadore*. See Barker, "Textual Forgery," in Jones, *Fake?* 22–27. Some possibly forged documents are still under dispute. For example, debate rages to this day over the Vinland map acquired by Yale University in 1965. The work, depicting the New World, purportedly dates to circa A.D.1440, that is, antedating Columbus's voyage west. Some insist upon its authenticity (see R. A. Skelton, Thomas E. Marston, and George D. Painter, *The Vinland Map and the Tartar Relation* [New Haven, Conn.: Yale University Press, 1965]). For a recent assessment, see Laurence Witten, *Vinland's Saga Recalled* (New Haven, Conn.: Yale University Press, 1989). For further examinations of the issue, see Horst Fuhrmann, ed., *Fälschungen im Mittelalter: Internationaler Kongress der Monumenta Germaniae Historica, München 16.–19. September 1986,* 5 vols. (Hannover: Hahnsche Buchhandlung, 1988–90), especially the articles Elizabeth A. R. Brown, "Falsitas pie sive reprehensibilis: Medieval Forgers and Their Intentions, " in vol. 1, 101–20, and Reinhardt Härtel, "Fälschungen im Mittelalter: Geglaubt, verworfen, ver vertuscht, " vol. 3, 29–52. See also Jones, *Fake?* 297–28, no. 329.

153. Jones, *Fake?* 180; Jaap Leeuwenberg, "Early Nineteenth-Century Gothic Ivories." *Aachener Kunstblätter* 39 (1969): 111–48.

154. Durrieu, "L'Exposition des primitifs francais," *Revue de l'Art ancien et moderne,* 15 (January– June 1904): 169–72. See also Paul Eudel, *Le truquage. Les contrefaçons dévoilées* (Paris: E. Dentu, 1887); and *Bulletin de la Société Nationale des Antiquaires de France* (1894): 167.

155. Eudel, *Le truquage,* 265.

156. London: Victoria and Albert Museum, PDP D. 86–1892.

157. Ibid., PDP 3076.

158. London: British Library, Add. MS 31840.

159. Liverpool Art Club, *Exhibition of Illuminated Manuscripts* (Liverpool: The Club, 1876), 56, no. 147, and 60, nos. 173–74.

160. See Jammes, *Didotiana,* 7.

161. For comprehensive studies of the Forger, see William M. Voelkle and Roger S. Wieck, *The Spanish Forger* (New York: Pierpont Morgan Library, 1978); and Curtis Carter and William Voelkle, *The Spanish Forger: Master of Deception* (Milwaukee: Patrick and Beatrice Haggerty Museum of Art, 1987). See also Janet Backhouse, "The 'Spanish Forger,'" *British Museum Quarterly* 33, nos. 1–2 (1968): 65–71; Janet Backhouse, "A Miniature Mas-terpiece by the 'Spanish Forger,'" *Quarto: Abbot Hall Art Gallery Quarterly Bulletin* (January 1975): 8–15; R. L. McGrath, "The Case of the 'Spanish Forger,'" *Dartmouth College Library Bulletin* 7, no. 1 (October 1966): 7–12; Roger S. Wieck, "A 'Late-Medieval' Miniature in the Houghton Library," *Harvard Library Bulletin* 29, no. 2 (April 1981): 212–14; and Jean Preston, "The Spanish Forger," *Kresge Art Museum Bulletin* 5 (1990): 16–21.

162. Durrieu, "L'Exposition," 169–72.

163. Voelkle and Wieck, *Spanish Forger,* 10. See also M. S. Soria, "The So-Called 'French Primitive': An Exposure and a Recantation," *Connoisseur* 117 (1946): 126–27; and Charles Sterling, "Les émules des primitifs," *La Revue de l'art* 21 (1973): 80–93.

164. Voelkle and Wieck, *Spanish Forger,* 76 (appendix 3).

165. Ibid., 12, 65–66.

166. See David F.Hult, "Gaston Paris and the Invention of Courtly Love," in *Medievalism and the Modernist Temper,* eds. R. Howard Bloch and Stephen G. Nichols (Baltimore: Johns Hopkins University Press, 1996), 192–224.

167. Voelkle and Wieck, *Spanish Forger,* 239-42.

168. Voelkle (Voelkle and Wieck, *Spanish Forger,* 10) demonstrates that of the Lacroix volumes published by Fimin-Didot those that provided the greatest number of models for the Forger were *Les arts au moyen âge* (1869); *Mœurs, usages et costumes au moyen âge et à l'époque de la renaissance* (1871); *Vie militaire et religieuse au moyen âge et à l'époque de la renaissance* (1873); *Sciences et lettres* (1877); and *Louis XII et Anne de Bretagne* (1882).

169. Voelkle and Wieck, *Spanish Forger,* 11.

170. See H. Bouchot, *Les primitifs français. Complément documentaire au catalogue officiel de l'exposition* (Paris: Librairie de l'Art Ancien et Moderne, 1904); and forthcoming article of S. Perkinson, "Interpreting the Louvre Image of John the Good: The Legacy of the Exhibition of *Primitifs français* (Paris, 1904)."

171. Voelkle and Wieck, *Spanish Forger,* 11.

172. Ibid.

173. Ibid., 65

174. Ibid., 64–65.

175. Cf. Salomon Reinach, "Two Forged Miniatures of Joan of Arc," *Burlington Magazine* 14, no. 72 (March 1909): 356; and the response of A. Lang, "Two Forged Miniatures of Joan of Arc," *Burlington Magazine* 15, no. 73 (April 1909): 51.

176. Voelkle and Wieck, *Spanish Forger,* 71 (no. OL16). Present location unknown.

177. See L. Quarré-Reybourbon, "Une fausse miniature concernant la ville de Lille," *Mémoire lu à la réunion des Sociétés des Beaux-Arts des Départements, tenu dans l'hémicycle de l'Ecole des Beaux-Arts* (Paris, April 4, 1893): 5–13, plate 21; cited in Voelkle and Wieck, *Spanish Forger,* 72 (no. OL22).

178. Krumeich, *Jeanne d'Arc in der Geschichte,* 194.

179. *Jeanne d'Arc, edition illustré d'après les monuments de l'art depuis le 15e siècle* (Paris: Firmin-Didot, 1876).

180. Labitte, *Les manuscrits et l'art*, figs. 258–60.

181. Reinach, "Two Forged Miniatures."

182. Odile Marcel, *Une éducation française* (Paris: Presses Universitaires de France, 1984), graphically describes the loyalties of this right-wing Catholic environment.

183. Lacroix himself includes discussions of Jews in his publications on the Middle Ages, but in contrast to the anti-Semitic forgeries, he offers a sympathetic assessment. See, for example, Lacroix, *Le Moyen Age et la Renaissance*, vol. 1, "Juifs."

184. For a general discussion see Michael Felmingham, *The Illustrated Gift Book 1880–1930* (Brookfield, Vt.: Ashgate, 1990).

185. See John Obadiah Westwood, "Henry Noel Humphreys," *Academy* 15 (June 21, 1879): 550; G. Wakeman and Bridson, *Guide to Nineteenth-Century Colour Printers*; Michael Shain, "The Irresistible Rise and Fall of the Chromolithograph and the 'Illuminated' Gift Book," *Antiquarian Book Monthly Review* 3, no. 12 (December 1976): 362–71; and Leathlean, "Henry Noel Humphreys and the Getting-Up of Books," 192–209.

186. Henry Noel Humphreys, *Parables of Our Lord* (London: Longman, 1847), i.

187. Henry Noel Humphreys, *The Illuminated Books of the Middle Ages; an Account of the Development and Progress of the Art of Illumination, as a Distinct Branch of Pictorial Ornamentation, from the IVth to the XVIIth Centuries. Illustrated by a Series of Examples, of the Size of the Originals, Selected from the Most Beautiful Mss. of the Various Periods, Executed on Stone and Printed in Colours by Owen Jones* (London: Longman, Brown, Green, and Longmans, 1849; reprint, London: Bracken Books, 1989), 11–15.

188. Henry Noel Humphreys, *The Art of Illumination and Missal Painting: A Guide to Modern Illuminators. Illustrated by a Series of Specimens from Richly Illuminated MSS. of Various Periods, Accompanied by a Set of Outlines to Be Coloured by the Student According to the Theories Developed in the Work* (London: H. G. Bohn, 1849).

189. Humphreys, *Art of Illumination and Missal Painting*, title page.

190. Ibid., 63–64.

191. Beckwith, *Victorian Bibliomania*,. 17–18, no. 2.

192. Cf. H. Leathlean, "Henry Noel Humphreys and Some Pre-Raphaelite Imagery," *Journal of Pre-Raphaelite Studies* 7, no. 2 (May 1987): 41–54.

193. Owen Jones, *The Grammar of Ornament: Illustrated by Examples from Various Styles of Ornament* (London: Day and Son, 1856; reprint, London: B. Quaritch, 1868; reprint, London: Studio Editions, 1986), 1.

194. Humphreys, *Parables of Our Lord*; Henry Noel Humphreys, *Miracles of Our Lord* (London: Longman, 1848).

195. Humphreys, *Miracles*, iii.

196. J. Brodahl, "The Melisende Psalter and Ivories (BL Egerton 1139): An Inquiry into the Status and Collecting of Medieval Art in Early Nineteenth-Century France," (Ph.D. dissertation, Brown University, 1999).

197. Recent publications on Morris include Paul Needham, *William Morris and the Art of the Book* (New York: Pierpont Morgan Library, 1976); William S. Peterson, ed. *The Ideal Book: Essays and Lectures on the Arts of the Book by William Morris* (Berkeley: University of California Press, 1982); Joanna Banham and Jennifer Harris, eds., *William Morris and the Middle Ages: A Collection of Essays together with a Catalogue of Works Exhibited at the Whitworth Art Gallery* (Manchester: Manchester University Press, 1984); Paul Thompson, *The Work of William Morris*, 3rd ed. (Oxford: Oxford University Press, 1991); Stephen F. Eisenman, *Designing Utopia: The Art of William Morris and His Circle* (Katonah, N.Y.: Katonah Museum of Art, 1992); and Linda Parry, ed., *William Morris* (London: Philip Wilson, 1996).

198. See C. Wainwright, "Morris in Context," in William Morris, ed. Parry, 352–61, especially 354.

199. For the most complete account of Morris's manuscripts, see J. Nash, "Calligraphy," in William Morris, ed. Parry, 296–309.

200. On the Wormsley collection, see H. George Fletcher, *The Wormsley Library: A Personal Selection by Sir Paul Getty* (New York: Pierpont Morgan Library, 1999).

201. Nash, "Calligraphy," 298.

202. Parry, ed., *William Morris*, 303, no. N. 4.

203. See Needham, *William Morris*, no. 52.

204. Parry, ed., *William Morris*, 308–9, nos. N. 13 and N. 14.

205. J. Dunlap, "William Morris: Calligrapher," in Needham, *William Morris*, 56; and Parry, ed., *William Morris*, 303, no. N. 5.

206. Parry, ed., *William Morris*, 304, no. N. 6.

207. See the first biography of William Morris, J. W. Mackail's *The Life of William Morris* (London: Longman, Green, 1899; reprint, New York: B. Blom, 1968).

208. Cited in Dunlap, "William Morris: Calligrapher," in Needham, *William Morris*, 68.

209. William Morris, "The Ideal Book" (lecture, 1893), in Morris, *Ideal Book*, ed. Peterson, 67–73.

210. William Morris, *Some Thoughts on the Ornamented Manuscripts of the Middle Ages* (New York: Press of the Woolly Whale, 1934), 1.

211. Ibid., 2.

212. Ibid., 4.

213. Ibid.

214. Ibid., 9–10.

215. See Harris, "William Morris and the Middle Ages," in Banham and Harris, eds., *William Morris and the Middle Ages*, 12–13.

216. Cf. Curt F. Bühler, *The Fifteenth-Century Book: the Scribes, the Printers, the Decorators* (Philadelphia: University of Pennsylvania Press, 1960).

217. William Morris, "The Early Illustration of Printed Books" (lecture, 1895), in Morris, Ideal Book, ed. Peterson, 20.

218. Needham, *William Morris*, 21–22.

219. On Morris's collection of manuscripts, acquired by J. Pierpont Mor-gan, see chapter 5 and Montague Rhodes James, *Catalogue of Manuscripts and Early Printed Books from the Libraries of William Morris, Richard Bennett, Bertram, Fourth Earl of Ashburnham and Other Sources, Now Forming a Portion of the Library of J. Pierpont Morgan* (London: Chiswick Press, 1906–7).

220. Needham, *William Morris*, no. 14, 100.

221. Ibid., no. 15, 100–1.

222. Ibid., no. 23, 102–3.

## Revivals

1. Stuart Piggott, *William Stukeley* (Oxford: Clarendon Press, 1950), 149; Eric Millar, "Les manuscrits à peintures des la Bibliothèque du Musée de Sir John Soane, Lincoln's Inn Field, Londres," *Bulletin de la Société Française de Reproductions de Manuscrits à Peintures*, 4, no. 1 (Paris, 1914–20): 81–49; Alan Noel Latimer Munby, *Connoisseurs and Medieval Miniatures, 1750–1850* (Oxford: Clarendon Press, 1972), 23; on Beckford's library before 1823, see William Clarke, *Repertorium Bibliographicum: or, some account of the most celebrated British libraries* (London, 1819), 203–30; Munby, *Connoisseurs and Medieval Miniatures*, 10, 77–78, 147; William Beckford, *Life at Fonthill, 1807–1822*, trans. and ed. Boyd Alexander (London: R. Hart-Davis, 1957), 174. The Edward III gallery is illustrated in Clive Wainwright, *The Romantic Interior: The British Collector at Home, 1750–1850* (New Haven, Conn.: published for the Paul Mellon Centre for Studies in British Art by Yale University Press, 1989), 114. Beckford collected manuscripts after 1823; most passed to the Earl of Hamilton, whose collection was bought by the German government in 1882; see Seymour De Ricci, *English Collectors of Books and Manuscripts (1530–1930) and Their Marks of Ownership* (Cambridge: Cambridge University Press, 1930), 86

2. The Benedictional joined the canon of important manuscripts early on, being listed in Henry Noel Humphreys's *Illuminated Books of the Middle Ages; an account of the development and progress of the art of illumination, as a distinct branch of pictorial ornamentation, from the IVth to the XVIIth centuries. Illustrated by a series of examples, of the size of the originals, selected from the most beautiful mss. of the various periods, executed on stone and printed in colours by Owen Jones* (London: Longman, Brown, Green and Longmans, 1849; reprint, London: Bracken Books, 1989), 12, where other manuscripts are similarly described in terms of ownership by an aristocrat (see p. 13 for an Italian manuscript "formerly belonging to the Duke of Sussex and now in the British Museum").

3. Beckford, *Life at Fonthill*, 174

4. Curzon's grandfather, Sir Cecil Bishop had claimed the barony, extinct for two hundred years, after much research in 1804; the House of Lords granted him the title in 1810; his daughter Harriet, wife of Robert Curzon (d. 1863), had to settle with her sister to acquire the title, an arrangement sanctioned by the House of Lords in 1829. Robert Curzon became the fourteenth Baron Zouche on the death of his mother, Harriet Curzon, in 1870.

5. For Curzon's armour, see K. N. Watts, "Samuel Pratt and Armour Faking," in *Why Fakes Matter: Essays on*

*Problems of Authenticity* (London: British Museum, 1992), 101. In *The Romantic Interior,* Wainwright describes armor used for decorative purposes. The Maclise painting is discussed in Rebecca Easby, "The Myth of Merrie England," in *History and Community: Essays in Victorian Medievalism,* ed. Florence S. Boos (New York: Garland Publishing Inc, 1992), 70–72. On Curzon and manuscripts, see Munby, *Connoisseurs and Medieval Miniatures,* 83.

6. Alan Noel Latimer Munby, *Phillipps Studies,* 5 vols. (Cambridge: Cambridge University Press, 1952–60; reprint, London: Sotheby's Parke-Bernet Publications, 1971), 2:23–25, 64–72; 3:138; 4:163; Gustav Friedrich Waagen, *Treasures of Art in Great Britain: Being an Account of the Chief Collections of Paintings, Drawings, Sculptures, Illuminated Mss.,* 3 vols. (London: J. Murray, 1854), 2:461; Munby, *Connoisseurs and Medieval Miniatures,* 119; Ian Anstruther, *The Knight and the Umbrella* (London: Geoffrey Bles, 1963).

7. Charles Harvey and Jon Press, *William Morris: Design and Enterprise in Victorian Britain* Manchester: Manchester University Press, 1991), 30; J. Mordaunt Crook et al., *The Strange Genius of William Burgess* (Cardiff, Wales: National Museum of Wales, 1981), 123, 142.

8. Lord Charles Thynne, *A Letter to His Late Parishioners by Lord Charles Thynne, Late Vicar of Longbridge Deverill, and Late Canon of Canterbury Cathedral* (London: Burns and Lambert, 1853). Thynne's copies of the Howard Psalter, Edgar's charter, and the Beauvais Sacramentary are now in the Victoria and Albert Museum, PDP, inv. nos. 4648; 4398; 4391–94.

9. See Phoebe Stanton, "The Sources of Pugin's Contrasts," in *Concerning Architecture: Essays on Architectural Writers and Writing, Presented to Nikolaus Pevsner,* ed. John Summerson (London: Allen Lane, 1968), 120–39. Roland Bonnel ("Medieval Nostalgia in France, 1750–1789: The Gothic Imaginary at the End of the Old Regime," in *Medievalism in Europe,* vol. 5, *Studies in Medievalism,* ed. Leslie J. Workman [Cambridge and Rochester, N.Y.: D. S. Brewer, 1993], 139–63) discusses notions of protection and charity associated with the feudal order in eighteenth-century France.

10. In 1826, at age fourteen, Pugin owned as "MS 3" an early-sixteenth-century prayerbook in Latin and Dutch with etchings of St. Francis; see London, Bloomsbury Book Auctions, sale 246, 12 January 1995, lot 243. The manuscript was subsequently Sam Fogg catalogue no. 16 (March 1995), no. 130.

11. NAL, MSL 1969/5179 and 1969/5176, described in Alexandra Wedgwood, *A.W.N. Pugin and the Pugin family* (London: Victoria and Albert Museum, 1985), 132–40, cat. nos. 109, 110; Margaret Belcher, *A. W. N. Pugin: An Annotated Critical Bibliography* (London: Mansell Publishing Ltd., 1987), 137–39.

12. Belcher, *A.W.N. Pugin,* 68–69. The decoration in, for example, the frontispiece to Pugin's *True Principles of Pointed or Christian Architecture* (London: J. Weale, 1841) is based on acanthus-leaf patterns but is remote from any medieval style of illumination (57).

13. Paul Atterbury and Clive Wainwright, eds., *Pugin: A Gothic Passion*

(New Haven, Conn.: Yale University Press in association with the Victoria and Albert Museum, 1994), 154; letters of 1841 to Michael Forristalm concerning St. George's Cathedral, J. R. Bloxham of Magdalen College, Oxford, and J. F. Russell, member of the Cambridge Camden Society, are reproduced in color in Paul Atterbury, ed., *A. W. N. Pugin: Master of Gothic Revival* (Yale University Press, for the Bard Graduate Center for Studies in the Decorative Arts, New York, 1995), 273, and in *A Gothic Passion,* 107; William Adam, *The Gem of the Peak, or Matlock Bath and Its Vicinity* (London: Longman and Co., 1843) was illuminated with the ancient arms of France (three fleur-de-lis) and the words "à son altesse royal Henri de France, hommage respectueuse de Washington Hibbert, chateau d'Alton, Nov. L'an mdcccxliii" (NAL, pressmark BD 73 – L.1554–1935, identified by the late Clive Wainwright); for the Ushaw manuscript, see *A Gothic Passion,* 154, 155.

14. Phillipps, Ambrose Lisle, trans., *The chronicle of the life of St Elizabeth of Hungary . . . written in French by the Count de Montalembert, peer of France, and now translated into English for the greater glory of God by Ambrose Lisle Phillipps Esquire of Grace Dieu Manor, Leicestershire* (London, 1839). The plates are the same as those in the French edition of 1838. The introduction is decorated with a vignette from the *Grimani Breviary,* an early example of its use. Kingsley's attack was in the preface to his play, *The Saint's Trial* (1848).

15. Ian Ker, *John Henry Newman: A Biography* (New York: Oxford University Press, 1988), 338–39; Owen Chadwick, *The Victorian Church,* 2 vols. (New York: Oxford University Press, 1966–70), 1:418; Raymond Chapman ("Last Enchantments: Medievalism and the Early Anglo-Catholic Movement," in *Medievalism in England,* vol. 4, *Studies in Medievalism,* ed. Leslie J. Workman [Cambridge and Rochester, N.Y.: D. S. Brewer, 1992], 173) contrasts Newman's lack of interest in aesthetics with Pusey's interest in such matters, characteristic of the Ritualist movement. The Trollope novel is cited in James Bentley, *Ritualism and Politics in Victorian Britain* (Oxford and New York: Oxford University Press, 1978), 2.

16. An advertisement for "Keble's Morning Hymn. Containing ten pages of Illuminations, by B.B.B. . . . 15s" occurred in a list of books headed "Illuminated and illustrated works" published by Day and Son, probably in the mid-1860s. The NAL copy is bound with F.M.R., *Emblematic Illumination* (London: Day and Son, n.d., pressmark G29.HH.8). An example of an illuminated edition of Keble's text is *Keble's evening hymn, illustrated by Edith Waring* (London: Day and Son, 1869). An 1875 edition of Keble's work published in London by Bickers and Son with photographic illustrations of pictures by Overbeck was decorated with printed borders reproducing fifteenth-century Italian illuminated manuscripts (NAL pressmark G29.C.93),

17. M. B. Parkes, *The Medieval Manuscripts of Keble College Oxford* (Oxford: Oxford University, Keble College, 1979), vii–xiii.

18. The wedding gift of 1840 is in a private collection. A frontispiece to the ten illuminated sheets has the letter I

made up of architectural Gothic niches containing saints, the letter S wrapped around it; the inscription reads "From her mother 1840." The binding is embroidered in an 1830s "Cathedral" style. The script is a rather careful version of a late-medieval inscriptional Gothic hand; some sheets are written out in a hand of the 1830s used in the law courts. Details of Lady Strange (1788–1862) are given in Louisa Mure, *Recollections of by-gone days* (Privately printed, 1883); the restoration of two books of hours and "a history of the province of Hainalt" is mentioned on p. 62. I am grateful to Janet Backhouse for mentioning the existence of a published biography of Lady Strange to me. Lady Strange's work in the fifteenth-century history of the princes of Hainault, now Boulogne sur Mer, Bibliothèque Municipale, MS 1491, is dated 1846 and 1859; see Francois Avril and Nicole Reynaud, *Les manuscrits à peintures en France: 1440–1520.* (Flammarion, Bibliothèque Nationale, 1993), 78.

19. Raymond Chapman, *The Sense of the Past in Victorian Literature* (New York: St. Martin's Press; London: Croom Helm, 1986), 49. On Yonge, see Julia Courtney, "Charlotte M. Yonge: A Novelist and Her Readers" (Ph.D. diss., University of London, 1989); the manuscript of *The Barnacle* is in the library of Lady Margaret hall, Oxford; the discussion of illumination is derived from W. R. Tymms, *The Art of Illuminating as practised in Europe from the Earliest Times. Illustrated in Borders, Initial Letters and Alphabets. With an essay and instructions by M. D. Wyatt* (London: Day and Sons, 1860), the most authoritative contemporary account of the history of illumination, and of how to do it, then available.

20. F. D. Wacherbarth, *The Revival of Monastic Institutions . . .* (Colchester: W. Totham, 1839), reviewed in *The Athenaeum,* no. 625 (October 19, 1839); Peter Frederick Anson, *The Call of the Cloister. Religious Communities and Kindred Bodies in the Anglican Communion* (London: S. P. C. K., 1955; rev. ed., London: A. W. Campbell, 1964), 220 et seq.

21. This seems to be the implication of Anson, *Call of the Cloister,* 272–73. The books are preserved at Ascor Priory.

22. *Punch* 19 (1850): 163; 20 (1850): 164. In volume 21 (1851), initials copied from those in illuminated manuscripts are used for pieces on "Popery courting persecution," "The slandered king Bomba" (the king of Naples), "Black letters on a Tablet" (the *Tablet* being a Catholic journal published in Dublin), and "Flowers of the Oratory" (on a speech by Newman).

23. *Punch* (May 26, 1849): 216. Alastair Grieve, "Style and Content in Pre-Raphaelite Drawing," in *Pre-Raphaelite Papers,* ed. Leslie Parris (London: Tate Gallery, 1984), 26–27. Lindsay Errington, *Social and Religious Themes in English Art, 1840–1860* (New York: Garland Publishing, 1984), 24–25.

24. Charles Dickens, "Old Lamps for New Ones," *Household Words* (Saturday, June 15, 1850): 265–67. Wornum's essay "Modern Moves in Art" refers to Pre-Raphaelites as the "Young England School; see *Art Journal* (1850): 268, 271. *The Carpenter's Shop* is reproduced in *The Pre-Raphaelites* (London: Tate Gallery with Penguin Books, 1984), 78–79.

25. John Ruskin, *The Works of John Ruskin (the Library Edition)*, ed. E. T. Cook and A. Wedderburn, 39 vols. (London: G. Allen; New York: Longmans, Green, 1903–12), 12:319–327; Julian Treuhertz, "The Pre-Raphaelites and Medieval Illuminated Manuscripts," in *Pre-Raphaelite Papers*, ed. Leslie Parris (London: Tate Gallery, 1984). Millais sometimes accompanied Ruskin to see manuscripts at the British Museum, but it was Ruskin and Morris, with Burne-Jones, rather than Holman Hunt, Collins, or Rosetti, who looked systematically at illuminated manuscripts.

26. Ruskin, *Works*, 12:320–21; *Punch* 20 (1851): 219.

27. William Vaughan, "The Englishness of British Art," *The Oxford Art Journal* 13, no. 2 (1990): 11–23; W. B. Sarsfield Taylor, *The Origin, Progress and Present Condition of the Fine Arts in Great Britain and Ireland*, 2 vols. (London: Whittaker, 1841). Edwin Jewitt (*Manual of Illuminated Missal Painting* [London: J. Barnard, 1860], 17) made the same point, Henry VII's calling on Flemish illuminators leading to a degeneracy of art

28. Humphreys, *Illuminated Books of the Middle Ages*, 5.

29. Tymms, *Art of Illuminating*, 39, 58; Jewitt, *Manual of Illuminated Missal Painting*, 16. See Errington, *Social and Religious Themes in English Art*, 34–36, for naturalism as the province of Protestant art in attacks on Pugin.

30. Longman's calendar for 1845 was reviewed in *The Ecclesiologist* 5 (1846); for William Randle Harrison's frontispiece, see Alice H. R. H. Beckwith, *Victorian Bibliomania. The Illuminated Book in Nineteenth-Century Britain* (Providence, R.I.: Museum of Art, Rhode Island School of Design, 1987), 54 and 66; Charles Blanc, *Grammaire des arts du dessin. . . .* (Paris: Ve J. Renouard, 1867), 631.

31. Joseph Dunlap, "William Morris: Calligrapher," in *William Morris and the Art of the Book*, ed. Paul Needham (New York: Pierpont Morgan Library, 1976), 50ff; John Nash, "Calligraphy," in *William Morris*, ed. Linda Parry (London: Philip Wilson, 1996), 300ff.

32. Vaughan, "The Englishness of British Art," 18.

33. On the gift books, see Ruari McLean, *Victorian Book Design and Colour Printing*, 2d ed. (London: Faber, 1972), chap. 2.

34. G. P. Landow, "*The Art Journal*, 1850–1880: Antiquarians, the Medieval Revival and the Reception of Pre-Raphaelitism," *The Pre-Raphaelite Review* 2, no. 2 (May 1979): 71–76; *Art Journal* (1847): 39; (1959): 223.

35. Humphreys probably saw Arnold's remarks in Arthur P. Stanley, *The Life and Correspondence of Thomas Arnold . . . .*, 2 vols. (New York: C. Scribner's Sons, 1844), 2:403–404. The author of the John Murray *Handbook for Travellers in Central Italy*, pt. 2, *Rome* (London, 1843), was Octavian Blewitt. Dickens reports were published in *Pictures from Italy* (London: Bradbury and Evans, 1846), 195.

36. Vaughan, "The Englishness of British Art," 18.

37. Errington, *Social and Religious Themes in English Art*, 389.

38. William John Loftie, *Lessons in the Art of Illuminating: A Series of Examples*

*Selected from Works in the British Museum, Lambeth Palace Library and the South Kensington Museum; with Practical Instructions and a Sketch of the History of the Art* (London: Blackie and Son, 1885); William John Loftie, *A Plea for Art in the House; with Special Reference to the Economy of Collecting Works of Art, and the Importance of Taste in Education and Words* (London: Macmillan, 1876; reprint, New York: Garland, 1978).

39. John Obadiah Westwood, *Facsimiles of the Miniatures and Ornaments of the Anglo-Saxon and Irish Manuscripts Executed by J. O. Westwood. Drawn on Stone by W. R. Tymms* (London: B. Quaritch, 1868), iv.

40. *Art Journal* (1874): 138 (review of the 1874 Burlington Fine Arts Club exhibition).

41. Kate Flint, "Reading *The Awakening Conscience* Rightly," in *Pre-Raphaelites Reviewed*, ed. Marcia Pointon (Manchester: Manchester University Press, 1989), 45–65.

42. On Alexis-François Rio, see Ronald Lightbown, "The Inspiration of Christian Art," in *Influences in Victorian Art and Architecture*, ed. Sarah Macready and F. H. Thompson (London: Society of Antiquaries, 1985), 11.

43. This is now Reid MS 83 in the Victoria and Albert Museum.

44. Ruskin, *Works*, 5:266, 262; 2:9. Ruskin's use of illumination is conveniently brought together in the thesis of Alice H. R. Hauck (later Beckwith), "John Ruskin's Uses of Illuminated Manuscripts and Their Impact on His Theories on Art and Society" (Ph.D. diss., John Hopkins University, 1983).

45. David Brett, "The Interpretation of Ornament," *Journal of Design History* 1, no. 2 (1988): 106ff.; Ruskin, *Works*, 16:305 (cited in Hauck, "Ruskin's Uses of Illuminated Manuscripts," 202); 12:482, 483, 484, 490. In the lecture of 1859, Ruskin referred to "a little attempt among certain forms of religionists to revive Gothic missal painting, and I have often to protest against the effort to introduce natural flower-painting into the leaves of those missals"; Illumination required "something which shall decorate the writing, which shall make the writing beautiful."

46. See John Unrau, "Ruskin, the Workman and the Savageness of Gothic," in *New Approaches to Ruskin: Thirteen Essays*, ed. Robert Hewison (London: Routledge and Kegan Paul, 1981), 33–50.

47. Catherine W. Morley, *John Ruskin. Late Work: 1870–1890. The Museum and Guild of St. George, An Educational Experiment* (New York: Garland Publishing, 1984), 146.

48. Virginia Surtees, ed., *Reflections of a Friendship: John Ruskin's Letters to Pauline Trevelyan* (London and Boston: Allen and Unwin, 1979); Virginia Surtees, ed., *Sublime and Instructive: Letters from John Ruskin to Louisa, Marchioness of Waterford, Anna Blunden and Ellen Heaton* (London: Joseph, 1972)

49. In F. Delamotte, *Medieval Alphabets and Initials for Illuminators* (London: Lockwood, 1864), iii.

50. For the history of aids to teaching art, see Trevor Fawcett, "Visual Facts and the 19th-Century Art Lecture," *Art History* 6, no. 4 (December 1983). The Oxford teaching materials are described at length in Robert Hewison,

*Ruskin and Oxford: The Art of Education* (Oxford: Clarendon Press; New York: Oxford University Press, 1996). Morley, *John Ruskin. Late Work*, 59, 27.

51. William Morris, *Some Thoughts on the Ornamented Manuscripts of the Middle Ages* (New York: Press of the Woolly Whale, 1934), 4–5; Georgiana Burne-Jones, *Memorials of Edward Burne-Jones*, 2 vols. (London: Macmillan, 1904), 2:99 ss.

52. Society of Antiquaries, Papers, June 1861 (notes made by an unidentified person on an address by Ruskin at the Society's exhibition of illuminated manuscripts).

53. Museum im Gotischen Haus, *Ich schreibe, lese und male ohne Unterlass: Elizabeth, englische Prinzessin und Landgräfin von Hessen-Homburg (1770–1840) als Künstlerin und sammlerin,* (Bad Homburg: Museum im Gotischen Haus, 1995), 78–79. I thank Jane Roberts of the Royal Library, Windsor Castle, for this reference. Princess Elizabeth's work is reproduced in Roberts's book, *Royal Artists from Mary Queen of Scots to the Present Day* (London: Grafton, 1987), plate 23; plate 46 shows work by Princess Alice. The designer Albert Warren, styled "Instructor to the Royal family" in 1860 (Henry Montanell Lucien, *Hints on Illuminating: With an Essay on the Art of Ornamenting in Gold or Metals* [London: J. Barnard, 1864], advertisements at the end of the volume), was supplying the Princess Royal with designs for illumination in December 1855 and February 1857.

54. Victoria and Albert Museum, no. Ph.275.130–1984. See Mark Haworth-Booth, ed., *The Golden Age of British Photography, 1839–1900* (Millerton, N.Y.: Aperture in association with the Philadelphia Museum of Art, 1984), 128.

55. *Linnet's Trial*, 1871 edition, 282–83.

56. The picture is Wellcome Institute Library, Iconographic Collections, accession no. CC 3481, and reproduced in Elisabeth Darby and Nicola Smith, *The Cult of the Prince Consort* (New Haven, Conn.: Yale University Press, 1983), 95.

57. For the press and its background, see William E. Fredeman, "Emily Faithful and the Victoria Press, an Experiment Sociological Bibliography," *The Library* (June 1974); and Sheila R. Herstein, *A Mid-Victorian Feminist. Barbara Leigh Smith Bodichon* (New Haven, Conn.: Yale University Press, 1985), 141ff. A biography of Emily Faithful by James S. Stone (*Emily Faithful, Victorian Champion of Women's Rights* [Toronto: P. D. Meany, 1994]) talks about her being a "household name" (p. 62). Esther Faithful Fleet was still illuminating books in 1900. In that year she gave her son, Ferdinand Francis Fleet (1857–1940), ordained an Anglican priest in 1887, an illuminated book of quotations from the Bible. We thank Peter Cumberlege, great-grandson of Esther Faithful Fleet, for this information.

58. *The Athenaeum*, no. 1185 (July 13, 1850): 743; no. 1412 (November 18, 1854): 1381; and no. 1413 (November 25, 1854): 1432; *Art Journal* (1859): 223; publicity material bound with copies of David Laurent De Lara's *Elementary Instruction in the Art of Illuminating*, 2d. ed. (1857) and 7th edition (London: Longman, Green, Longman, Roberts, and Green, 1863) are in the National Art Library; Delamotte, *Medieval Alphabets*.

59. *Great Exhibition of the Works of Industry of All Nations, 1851. Official Descriptive and Illustrated Catalogue* (London: Spicer Brothers, 1851), 2: nos. 8, 27, 202; Jeffrey Auerbach, *The Great Exhibition of 1851: A Nation on Display* (New Haven, Conn.: Yale University Press, 1999); *Catalogue of the Art Treasures of the United Kingdom Collected at Manchester* (London: Bradbury and Evans, 1857), paintings by ancient masters, nos. 41, 44 (both single leaves from Ottley's collection).

60. Henry Cole, *Fifty Years of Public Service* (1888), 2:227; *The International Exhibition of 1862. The Illustrated Catalogue of the Industrial Department, British Division* (London: For Her Majesty's Commissioners by Clay, Son, and Taylor, 1862), 2:class 18, p. 20; Christopher Dresser, *Development of Ornamental Art in the International Exhibition* (London: Day and Sons, 1862), 187–92; *The Illuminator's Magazine* (London: Barnard and Son, 1862), 109.

61. For Ward's career, see the *Art Journal* (August 1867): 197–98; (1869): 96; his printed sheets were advertised in the *Art Journal* (1863): 82 (EWInsor & Newton, outlines for illuminating); (1867): 175 (Fuller, illuminated texts); (1868): 163 (illuminated designs), 287 (Nelson and Sons, Edinburgh, illuminated texts); the surviving sheet of Ward's is in the Gimingham album (V and L, NAL, MSL 1988/13).

62. Richard Thomson, *A Lecture on Some of the Most Characteristic Features of Illuminated Manuscripts* (London: Printed for the London Institution by C. Skipper and East, 1857), 75–76. On Wing in general, see *Brighton Revealed through Artists' Eyes, c. 1760–c. 1960*, ed. David Beevers (Brighton: Royal Pavilion, Art Gallery and Museums, 1995), cat. nos. 53, 54. I owe my knowledge of Curtis's prospectus, issued in Brighton, with its details of study, terms, and a page of testimonials, to Ken Spelman, York.

63. On chromolithography, see George Ashdown Audsley, *the Art of Chromolithography, Popularly Explained and Illustrated by Forty-four Plates Showing Separate Impressions of All the Stones Employed and All the Progressive Printings in Combination from the First Colour to the Finished Picture* (London: S. L. W., Marston, Searle and Rivington, 1883), with forty-four plates showing what each stone brought to the final image, as well as the image as it developed during the twenty-two impressions. Classes in lithography are mentioned in the *First Report of the Department of Practical Art* (HMSO, 1853), 382; Board of Trade, Department of Science and Art, *A Catalogue of the Museum of Ornamental Art at Marlborough House* (HMSO, 1854), appendix A, p. 88.

64. Victoria and Albert Museum, NAL, MSL 1988/13. Included in the album are heraldic designs, patterned ornament derived from medieval objects of all kinds, and draft pieces of illumination in watercolors. Among samples of printed ornament are an advertisement for De Quincy's works published by James Hogg, the title page of the *Practical Mechanic's Journal* number for the 1862 Great Exhibition in London, and printed illustrated catalogues of Cox and Son, Church Furniture Manufacturers. A bill from Alexander Shapcott, "Artists' Colourman," for pigments supplied to Miss Gimingham, is dated March 1876, London. There are a number of catalogues of stationery suppliers.

65. William Gardner, "High Victorian Taste in Calligraphy and Illumination: The Loyal Addresses Presented to Queen Victoria in 1887," *Journal of the Royal Society of Arts* (July 1987); Edward Offor, *Illuminating Made Easy* (London: J. B. Bunyard, 1865); *Art Journal* (1868): 163.

66. W. G. Collingwood, "Lady Diana's Prayer-Book," *Art Journal* (November 1882): "The modern notion of illuminating is a thick line round and a flat blob in the middle; no wonder we are bored with the result!"

67. For the history of the museum, see most recently Malcolm Baker and Brenda Richardson, eds., *A Grand Design: The Art of the Victoria and Albert Museum* (London: Victoria and Albert Publications with the Baltimore Museum of Art, 1997).

68. Emma Cooper, *Plain Words on the Art and Practice of Illuminating* (London: Gladwell, 1868), 6; Thomas Nichols, *A Handbook for Readers at the British Museum* (London: Longmans, Green, 1866), 95; British Museum, *List of autograph letters, original charters, great seals and manuscripts exhibited to the public in the Department of Manuscripts* (London: British Museum, 1851); the first two printings were August and November 1851; from 1859, these were regular editions.

69. *Proceedings of the Society of Antiquaries, 17 November 1859–June 1861,* second series, vol. 1, 407–408, 410. See Joan Evans, *A History of the Society of Antiquaries* (Oxford: Oxford University Press for the Society of Antiquaries, 1956), 306.

70. *Illuminated Manuscripts Catalogue* (London: Burlington Fine Arts Club, 1874). The exhibition was reviewed in the *Art Journal* (1874): 138–39. The reviewer mentioned the "many single leaves of Italian ornament from the Ottley Collection, lent by Mr Russell."

71. Liverpool Art Club, *Exhibition of Illuminated Manuscripts* (Liverpool: The Club, 1876). Facsimiles of early manuscripts include Kells, Lindisfarne, and an Anglo-Saxon Psalter (nos. 124–29, all owned by Newton).

72. Burlington Fine Arts Club, *Catalogue of a Series of Illuminations from Manuscripts Principally of the Italian and French Schools* (London: Burlington Fine Arts Club, 1886).

73. Sydney Carlyle Cockerell, *Exhibition of Illuminated Manuscripts* (London: Burlington Fine Arts Club, 1908); *Burlington Magazine* 13 (April–September 1908), 128–29.

74. For a detailed study of the collecting of illumination by the South Kensington museum, see Rowan Watson, "Educators, Collectors, Fragments, and the 'Illuminations' Collection at the Victoria and Albert Museum in the 19th century," in *Fragments as Witnesses to Medieval Books and Bookmaking* (Anderson-Lovelace, 2000).

75. Léopold Delisle, *Catalogue des manuscrits des fonds Libri et Barrois* (Paris: H. Champion, 1888), lxvii–lxviii.

76. Today, the single leaves and fragments are kept in the Victoria and Albert Museum's Department of Prints, Drawings and Paintings, where registers are held that give details of their provenance. Details of the complete codices are given in the NAL's *Draft typescript catalogue of illuminated manuscripts;* Neil Ripley Ker (*Medieval Manuscripts in British Libraries* [1967],

1:378–93) describes works dated before 1500.

77. Today, the Victoria and Albert Museum's complete medieval manuscripts are kept in the National Art Library and the single leaves in the Print Room. The only exception to this concerns the fragments from the Circulation department that operated between 1908 and 1979: these fragments are kept in the NAL.

78. On Victoria and Albert Museum, PDP, 800–1894, see Hanns Swarzenski, *Die Deutsche Buchmalerei des 13. Jahrhunderts,* 2 vols. (Berlin: Deutscher Verein für Kunstwissenshaft, 1936), 46 ss.; on 817–1894, see Jonathan J. G. Alexander, ed., *The Painted Page: Italian Renaissance Book Illumination 1450–1550* (London: Royal Academy of Arts; Munich: Prestel, 1994), 26–27, 30; on 816–1894, see Margaret Gibson, T. A. Heslop, and Richard W. Pfaff, eds., *The Eadwine Psalter: Text, Image, and Monastic Culture in Twelfth-Century Canterbury* (London: Modern Humanities Research Association, 1992), 39 ss.

79. A. von Eye, *Das Germanische Museum. Wegweiser* (1853), 20.

80. Victoria and Albert Museum, PDP, D.86–1892.

81. Ibid., PDP, 3076.

82. BL, MS Add. 31840.

83. Liverpool Art Club, *Exhibition of Illuminated Manuscripts,* 56, no. 147; 60, nos. 173, 174.

84. The librarian's report for 1877 in the *Twenty-fifth Report of the Science and Art Department* (HMSO, 1878), 438, mentioned that "a large collection of drawings, illuminations and prints, etc. . . . continues, as heretofore, deposited in the charge of the Art Museum for use in the circulating series." Published in 1908 were the *Catalogue of the Circulating Collection of Illuminated Manuscripts (leaves and cuttings) Selected from the Victoria and Albert Museum, HMSO* (London: Victoria and Albert Museum, 1908), and the *Catalogue of Illuminated Manuscripts, Miniatures, Leaves and Cuttings,* by E. F. Strange with the assistance of Sydney C. Cockerell (HMSO, 1908). A second edition of the latter was published in 1923.

85. Victoria and Albert Museum Archive, Nominal File for Sotheby's, 1899. The facsimiles ware now Victoria and Albert Museum, PDP, D.300–1899 to D.312–1899.

86. *Fifteenth Report of the Science and Art Department of the Committee of Council on Education [for 1867]* (HMSO, 1868), 212; *Sixteenth Report [for 1868]* (1869), 317; *Seventeenth Report [for 1869]* (1870), 369; *Eighteenth Report [for 1870]* (1871), 404. Illuminations do not appear in the list of "Objects copied" in the *Nineteenth Report [for 1871]* (1872), 409. Statistics of this kind were discontinued thereafter. The first statistics of use, in the *Fourteenth Report [for 1866]* (1867), 194, do not mention illuminations: the report commented that the figures did not include "the numerous sketches in note books, etc. which are constantly being made by visitors' but which it would trouble visitors too much to record.

### Reconstructions

Epigraph: Quoted in Anna Wells Rutledge, "Robert Gilmore, Jr.: Baltimore Collector," *Journal of the Walters Art Gallery* 12 (1949): 20.

1. There has been a surge in scholarship on medievalism as a social as well as an artistic phenomenon in the United States. Key investigations of American medievalism include Robin Fleming, "Nineteenth-Century New England's Memory of the Middle Ages," in *Memory and the Middle Ages*, ed. Nancy Netzer and Virginia Reinberg (Chestnut Hill, Mass.: Boston College Museum of Art, 1995), 79–92; Robin Fleming, "Picturesque History and the Medieval in Nineteenth-Century America," *American Historical Review* 100, no. 4 (October 1995): 1061–94; Bernard Rosenthal and Paul E. Szarmach, eds., *Medievalism in American Culture: Papers of the Eighteenth Annual Conference of the Center for Medieval and Early Reniassance Studies* (Binghamton, N.Y.: Center for Medieval and Early Renaissance Studies, State University of New York at Binghamton, 1989); Kathleen Verduin, ed., *Medievalism in North America*, vol. 6 of *Studies in Medievalism* (Cambridge: D. S. Brewer, 1994). On architecture, see K. S. Howe and D. B. Warren, *The Gothic Revival Style in America, 1830–70* (Houston, 1976). A recent exhibition considers the collection of medieval art in the United States, but illumination here remains practically untouched; see Elizabeth Bradford Smith, *Medieval Art in America: Patterns of Collecting, 1800–1940* (University Park, Pa.: Palmer Museum of Art, 1996). See also Edward Kaufman, *Medievalism: An Annotated Bibliography of Recent Research in the Architecture and Art of Britain and North America* (New York: Garland, 1988); select essays in Richard Utz and Tom Shippey, eds., *Medievalism in the Modern World: Essays in Honour of Leslie J. Workman* (Turnhout: Brepols, 1998); Paul Freedman and Gabrielle Spiegel, "Medievalisms Old and New: The Rediscovery of Alterity in North American Medieval Studies," *American Historical Review* 103, no. 3(1998): 677-704; and Kathleen Curran, "The Romanesque Revival: Mural Painting and Protestant Patronage in America," *Art Bulletin* 31 (1999): 693–722.

2. Our discussion of attitudes toward the single leaf in America is indebted to the ground-breaking study of Roger Wieck, "*Folia Fugitiva*: The Pursuit of the Illuminated Manuscript Leaf," *Journal of the Walters Art Gallery* 54 (1996): 233–54.

3. See Rutledge, "Robert Gilmore," 19–39.

4. On Robert Gilmore and his manuscripts, see Smith, *Medieval Art in America*, 24–26, 80–87. For another early collector in America who owned a handful of medieval manuscripts, see J. R. Hall, "William G. Medlicott (1816–1883): An American Book Collector and His Collection," *Harvard Library Bulletin*, n.s. 1, no. 1 (1990): 13–46.

5. It has been suggested that Gilmore's Book of Hours found its way to America through the substantial French population of Charleston, opening the way for speculation about an immigrant populace from France transporting illuminated works to the New World as cultural patrimony. See Smith, *Medieval Art in America*, 82–83.

6. See Gerald Reitlinger, *The Economics of Taste*, 3 vols. (London: Barrie and Rockliff, 1961–70), 1:175–82; 2:226-27. On the development of American taste for European artworks, see René Brimo, *L'évolution du goût aux états-unis*

*d'après l'histoire des collections* (Paris: James Fortune, 1938), particularly 76–100.

7. Press cartoons suggest the potency of the comparison of Morgan with Napoleon. See Neil Harris, "Collective Possession: J. Pierpont Morgan and the American Imagination," in *Cultural Excursions: Marketing Appetites and Cultural Tastes in Modern America* (Chicago: University of Chicago Press, 1990), 275. The analogy is repeated in J. Strouse, *Morgan. American Financier* (New York, 1999), 378.

8. Among the biographies of Morgan, the most useful is the recent work of Strouse, *Morgan*. See also Herbert Livingston Satterlee, *J. Pierpont Morgan: An Intimate Portrait* (New York: Macmillan, 1939), and Francis Henry Taylor, *Pierpont Morgan as Collector and Patron, 1837–1913* (New York: Pierpont Morgan Library, 1970).

9. Wieck, "*Folia Fugitiva*," 246.

10. On this purchase, see Strouse, *Morgan*, 379–81.

11. On the core holdings of Morgan's library, see Montague Rhodes James, *Catalogue of Manuscripts and Early Printed Books from the Libraries of William Morris, Richard Bennett, Bertram fourth Earl of Ashburnham and other sources, now Forming a Portion of the Library of J. Pierpont Morgan* (London: Chiswick Press, 1906–7). See also Meta Harrsen, *Central European Manuscripts in the Pierpont Morgan Library* (New York: Pierpont Morgan Library, 1958).

12. Comte J.-F.-A. Bastard d'Estang, *Histoire de Jésus-Christ en figures, gouaches du XIIe siècle conservées jadis à la collégiale de Saint-Martial de Limoges* (Paris, 1878); *Catalogue des Livres Précieux manuscrits et imprimés faisant partie de la bibliothèque de M. Ambroise Firmin-Didot* (Paris, 1879), no. 10.

13. See Harris, "Collective Possession," 260.

14. Léopold Delisle, "Les Manuscrits de la Bibliothèque de M. Pierpont Morgan," *Journal des Savants* 5, no. 8 (1907): 415–21.

15. On the marginal images in the Luttrell Psalter, see Michael Camille, *Mirror in Parchment: The Luttrell Psalter and the Making of Medieval England* (Chicago: University of Chicago Press, 1998), chap. 1; Michael Camille, "Labouring for the Lord: The Ploughman and the Social Order in the Luttrell Psalter," *Art History* 10, no. 4 (December 1987): 423–54. On the retention of the manuscript in England, see the editorial by R. R. Tatlock, "Editorial: To Avoid a National Disgrace," *Burlington Magazine* 55, no. 321 (December 1929): 271; and J. Backhouse "The Sale of the Luttrell Psalter," in *Antiquaries, Book Collectors and the Circles of Learning*, ed. Robin Meyers and Michael Harris (Winchester: St. Paul's Bibliographies, 1996), 113–28.

16. For the most recent—and revealing—assessment of Greene, see Strouse, *Morgan*, 509–20. See also the entry in *Notable American Women, 1607–1950* (Cambridge, Mass., 1971), 83–84; Pierpont Morgan Library, *The First Quarter Century of the Pierpont Morgan Library. A Retrospective Exhibition in Honor of Belle da Costa Greene* (New York: Pierpont Morgan Library, 1949); and Dorothy E. Miner's foreword in *Studies in Art and Literature for Belle da Costa Greene* (Princeton: Princeton University Press, 1954), ix–xiii.

17. Folio 6 from this work is reproduced in Dorothy E. Miner, *Anastaise and Her Sisters: Women Artists of the Middle Ages* (Baltimore: Walters Art Gallery, 1974), fig. 7.

18. Another manuscript created by this group of nuns, also executed in a fourteenth-century style, shows German troops burning the library at Louvain. See Maurits Smeyers, *L'art de la Miniature flamande du VIIIe au XVIe siècle*, trans. Monique Verbooman (Tournai: La Renaissance du Livre, 1998).

19. See Wieck "*Folia Fugitiva*," 247. See also the comments of D. K. Hill, an early curator at the Walters Art Gallery, "If we were to choose one characteristic in the taste of Henry Walters . . . it would be his feeling for the small object, especially the small sculpturesque object," Dorothy Kent Hill, "William T. Walters and Henry Walters," *Art in America* 32, no. 4 (October 1944): 185.

20. For a biographical essay dealing particularly with Walters's book collections, see Elizabeth Burin, "Henry Walters (September 26, 1848–November 30, 1931)," in *American Book-Collectors and Bibliographers* (Detroit: Bruccoli Clark Layman, 1994), 297–303.

21. Richard B. Gruelle, *Notes Critical and Biographical: Collection of W. T. Walters* (Indianapolis: J. M. Bowles, 1895). See Dorothy E. Miner, "The Publishing Ventures of a Victorian Connoisseur. A Sidelight on William T. Walters," *Papers of the Bibliographical Society of America* 57 (1963): 271–311.

22. By the end of his life, about a third of his medieval-objects collection was made up of enamels and another third was made up of ivory and bone carvings. For a breakdown of Walters's collection of medieval objects, see M. Price, "Henry Walters: Elusive Collector," in *Medieval Art in America*, 131.

23. Lilian M. C. Randall, *France, 1420–1540*, vol. 2, *Medieval and Renaissance Manuscripts in the Walters Art Gallery* (Baltimore: Johns Hopkins University Press in association with the Walters Art Gallery, 1989–92), nos. 109 and 159.

24. E. Burin, "Of Pigs and Parchment," *Journal of the Walters Art Gallery* 49, no. 1 (1996): 4.

25. Eighty-one of the 210 Gruel manuscripts in the Walters collection have bookplates adorned with the initials "G & E," marking their former joint ownership by Gruel and Engelmann. Burin, "Henry Walters," 301.

26. Lilian M. C. Randall, *France, 875–1420*, vol. 1, *Medieval and Renaissance Manuscripts in the Walters Art Gallery* (Baltimore: Johns Hopkins University Press in association with the Walters Art Gallery, 1989–92), no. 98.

27. On Meunier, see F. C. Lonchamp, *Manuel du Bibliophile français (1470–1920)* (Paris, 1927), 1:429–31; and S. T. Prideaux, *Bookbinders and Their Craft* (New York, 1903), 146–50.

28. Grolier Club, *Catalogue of an Exhibition of Illuminated and Painted Manuscripts together with a few Early Printed Books with Illuminations—also some examples of Persian Manuscripts —with plates in Facsimile and an Introductory Essay*. (New York: Grolier Club, 1892). The Meunier-bound Grolier Club catalogue is discussed in Randall, *France, 875–1420*, no. 98; for the likely parent

manuscript for the leaves, see C. W. Dutschke, *Guide to Medieval and Renaissance Manuscripts in the Huntington Library* (San Marino, Calif., 1989), 2:HM 1180.

29. It is worth noting that Walters paid high prices for both of these medieval-style display pieces—the volume adorned with the Boucicaut Master image totaled 350 francs, and the piece adorned with late-fifteenth-century leaves cost 400 francs.

30. For an overview of the entire collection at the Walters Art Gallery, see Denys Sutton, "Editorial: Connoisseur's Haven," *Apollo* 84, no. 58 (December 1966): 422–33. For an addition to the Walters collection relevant specifically to the issues addressed in our study, see Lilian M. C. Randall, "A Ninteenth-Century 'Medieval' Prayerbook Woven in Lyon," in *Art, the Ape of Nature: Studies in Honor of H. W. Janson,* ed. Moshe Barasch and Lucy Freeman Sandler (New York: Abrams, 1981), 651–68.

31. See Claire Richter Sherman, "Dorothy Eugenia Miner (1904–1973): The Varied Career of a Medievalist: Scholar and Keeper of Manuscripts, Librarian and Editor at the Walters Art Gallery," in *Women as Interpreters of the Visual Arts, 1820–1979,* ed. Claire Richter Sherman with Adele M. Holcomb (Westport, Conn., 1981), 377–409; Ursula E. McCracken, Lilian M. C. Randall, and Richard H. Randall, eds., *Gatherings in Honor of Dorothy E. Miner* (Baltimore: Walters Art Gallery, 1974); and the notice on Miner in *Notable American Women. The Modern Period.* (Cambridge, Mass., 1980), 479–81.

32. In their efforts to reunite single leaves with their parent manuscripts, the Walters Art Gallery has recently acquired five leaves originally belonging to the fourteenth-century English Botiller or Butler Hours (MS. W. 105) and a single folia that matches a fifteenth-century book of proverbs from Savoy (MS. W. 313). Burin, "Pigs and Parchment," 4–5.

33. The most recent study of the Conradin Bible is Rebecca W. Corrie, "The Conradin Bible, MS. 152, the Walters Art Gallery: Manuscript Illumination in a Thirteenth-Century Italian Atelier," (Ph.D. diss., Harvard University, 1986), book forthcoming. Discussion of the modern history of the manuscript is summarized in Rebecca W. Corrie, "The Conradin Bible: Since 'Since De Ricci'," *Journal of the Walters Art Gallery* 40 (1982): 13–24. In a 1994 article, Corrie amends and corrects her earlier discussions of the Conradin Bible single leaves ("The Conradin Bible and the Problem of Court Ateliers in Southern Italy in the Thirteenth Century," in *Intellectual Life at the Court of Frederick II Hohenstaufen,* ed. William Tronzo [Washington, D.C.: National Gallery of Art, 1994]: 34 n. 11). See also Dorothy E. Miner, "The Conradin Bible. A Masterpiece of Italian Illumination," *Apollo* 84, no. 58 (December 1966): 470–75; and Dorothy E. Miner, "Since De Ricci—Western Illuminated Manuscripts Acquired since 1934," pt. 2, *Journal of the Walters Art Gallery* 31–32 (1968–69): 87–92.

34. On the Olschkis and the Rosenthals, see Bernard M. Rosenthal, "Cartel, Clan or Dynasty? The Olschkis and the Rosenthals 1859–1976," *Harvard Library Bulletin* 25, no. 4 (October 1977): 381–98.

35. In its present condition, the Conradin Bible opens with the Book of Daniel and continues through a nearly complete New Testament text. At the back of the manuscript, the opening books of the Old Testament (missing about half their leaves) have been bound in.

36. Miner, "Conradin Bible," 475 n. 2. See also Corrie, "Conradin Bible," 13.

37. For the acquisition of many of these fragments by the Walters Art Gallery, see Miner, "Since De Ricci," 87–92.

38. Sotheby's, *Illuminated Miniatures and Single Leaves from the Ninth to the Sixteenth Century* (London: Sotheby's, July 14, 1981), lots 12–16.

39. Filippo Todini and Milvia Bollati, *Una collezione di miniature italiane dal duecento al cinquecento* (Milan: Studio nella Longari, 1993), 12–17.

40. Sotheby's, *Illuminated Miniatures,* lots 10–12.

41. Quoted by Lee Edmonds Grove, "Robert Hoe III, 1839–1909," in *Grolier 75: A Biographical Retrospective to Celebrate the Seventy-Fifth Anniversary of the Grolier Club in New York* (New York: Grolier Club, 1959), 26.

42. On the Grolier Club, see discussion of early exhibitions below; and Grolier Club, *The Grolier Club, 1884–1984: Its Library, Exhibitions & Publications* (New York: Grolier Club, 1984).

43. For an overview of Hoe's holdings, see Oscar Albert Bierstadt, *The Library of Robert Hoe: A Contribution to the History of Bibliophilism in America* (New York: Duprat, 1895). See also note 44 below.

44. *Catalogue of the Library of Robert Hoe of New York. Illuminated Manuscripts, Incunabula, Historical Bindings, Early English Literature, Rare Americana, French Illustrated Books, Eighteenth-Century English Authors, Autographs, Manuscripts, etc.* (New York: Anderson Auction Company, 1911–12). For a narrative account of the contest over handling the sale between the American Art Association and Anderson, see Wesley Towner, *The Elegant Auctioneers* (New York: Hill and Wang, 1970), 258–65.

45. Between 1903 and 1909, Hoe had funded a series of volumes, each dealing with a separate aspect of his collection, but the sixteen privately produced catalogues of the library had been printed in limited runs and were not widely known outside a small circle of bibliophiles. The volume dealing with Hoe's manuscripts is Carolyn Shipman, *Catalogue of Manuscripts Comprising a Portion of the Library of Robert Hoe* (New York: Duprat, 1909).

46. *Catalogue of the Library of Robert Hoe,* 1: no. 2137; now Morgan Library, M.677. The richly illuminated manuscript, containing 150 miniatures (some of which the catalogue attributed to Fouquet) had formerly been in the collection of Ambroise Firmin-Didot; see *Catalogue des livres rares et précieux . . . faisant partie de la Bibliothèque de M. Ambroise Firmin-Didot* (Paris: M. Delestre and A. Labitte, June 10–14, 1884 ), no. 17.

47. *Catalogue of the Library of Robert Hoe,* 1, no. 2127; for Cortlandt Field Bishop collection, see Seymour De Ricci and W. J. Wilson, *Census of Medieval and Renaissance Manuscripts in the United States and Canada* (New York:

H. W. Wilson, 1935), 1654, no. 2; C. F. Bishop sale, April 25, 1938, now Philadelphia Museum of Art. See also Towner, *Elegant Auctioneers,* 278.

48. See D. C. Dickinson, *Henry E. Huntington's Library of Libraries* (San Marino, Calif., 1995), esp. 40–50.

49. *Catalogue of the Library of Robert Hoe,* 1, no. 2132 (now Huntington Library HM 1126); no. 2138 (sold to Felix M. Warburg); see De Ricci and Wilson, *Census,* 1851, no. 13; present whereabouts unknown.

50. See *Catalogue of the Library of Robert Hoe,* 1, no. 2134 for Book of Hours from Angers; no. 2142 for Book of Hours by G. Tory; no. 2146 for Josephus History; and no. 2154 for Burgundian Mirouer Historial.

51. *Catalogue of the Library of Robert Hoe,* 1, no. 2168; now Huntington Library HM 60 (sold to Huntington in 1918). For Hoe library description of the manuscript, see Bierstadt, *Library of Robert Hoe,* 16–18; and Shipman, *Catalogue of Manuscripts,* 153–55.

52. *New York Times,* May 7, 1911, 1.

53. Ibid., May 8, 1991, 3.

54. Ibid., May 9, 1911, 20.

55. Ibid., May 10, 1911, 8; and May 11, 1911, 10.

56. See Dutschke, *Huntington Library,* HM 60.

57. *Catalogue of the Library of Robert Hoe,* 1, no. 2153, present whereabouts unknown. We have been unable to match any of Hoe's albums definitively with the albums examined in chapter 2.

58. Ibid., 4, no. 2361, present whereabouts unknown.

59. Ibid., no. 2362.

60. For Minns's own account of her collecting activity, see the preface to her sale in *The Notable Collection of Miss Susan Minns of Boston, Mass. Books, Bookplates, Coins, Curios, Prints, Illuminated Manuscripts and Horae Illustrative of the "Dance of Death."* New York: American Art Galleries, May 2–3, 1922.

61. *Collection of Miss Susan Minns,* 425, now in the Lewis Collection, Philadelphia, cf. E. Wolf, *A Descriptive Catalogue of the John Frederick Lewis Collection of European Manuscripts in the Free Library of Philadelphia* (Philadelphia: Privately printed, 1937), no. 113.

62. *Collection of Miss Susan Minns,* no. 405, present whereabouts unknown.

63. Ibid., no. 408, now New York Public Library: 17.

64. Minns, preface to *Collection of Miss Susan Minns,* ii (unnumbered).

65. Manuscripts from the Minns sale were also purchased by American collectors—five by Philadelphian John Frederick Lewis and one by C. L. Ricketts of Chicago—both discussed below.

66. "Museum of Death bought for Louvain," *New York Times,* May 4, 1922, 14.

67. John Frederick Lewis, "Christopher Columbus" (lecture presented for the United Italian Societies of Philadelphia, Philadelphia, October 12, 1892), 6.

68. On selections from Lewis's print collection, see Federal Art Project, Works Progress Administration, *Master*

*Prints from the John F. Lewis Collection of the Pennsylvania Academy of Fine Arts* (Washington, D.C., Federal Art Project, Works Progress Administration, 1939). For Lewis's historical interest in the development of printmaking, see his "'Schrotblätter': or, Prints in the 'Manière criblée,'" (paper presented to the Numismatic and Antiquarian Society, Philadelphia, 1904) and his "'Teigdrücke'—Prints in Paste" (paper presented to the Numismatic and Antiquarian Society, Philadelphia, 1904).

69. On Lewis's Western manuscripts, see Edwin Wolf, *A Descriptive Catalogue of the John Frederick Lewis Collection of European Manuscripts in the Free Library of Philadelphia* (Philadelphia: Privately printed, 1937). On Philadelphia collectors of illuminated manuscripts in general, see James R. Tanis, *Leaves of Gold: Treasures of Illuminated Manuscripts from Philadelphia Collections* (Philadelphia: Philadelphia Museum of Art, 2001).

70. *Collection of Miss Susan Minns*, 421.

71. Wolf, *Catalogue of the John Frederick Lewis Collection*, 140, no. 125.

72. See Janet Backhouse, "A Victorian Connoisseur and His Manuscripts. The Tale of Mr. Jarman and Mr. Wing," *British Library Quarterly* 32 (1968): 84–85.

73. This little-studied collection of leaves is the subject of only one article, Meta Harrsen, "Mediaeval and Renaissance Miniatures in the John Frederick Lewis Collection in Philadelphia," *Scriptorium* 14, no. 1 (1960): 75–79.

74. See B. W. Meijer, ed., *Italian Drawings from the Rijksmuseum, Amsterdam,* trans. P. Spring (Florence, 1995), 89.

75. For the parent manuscript, see E. Martini, *Catalogo di manoscritti greci esistenti nelle biblioteche italiane* (Milan, 1893), 141–46. On the Lewis leaves, see Harold R. Willoughby, "Vagrant Folios from Family 2400 in the Free Library of Philadelphia," *Byzantion* 15 (1940–41): 126–32; and Harold R. Willoughby, "Stray New Testament-Psalter Leaves Identified," *Journal of Biblical Literature* 16 (March 1942): 57–60.

76. This collection, now housed in the Free Library, Philadelphia, is catalogued in Muhammed Ahmed Simsar, *Oriental Manuscripts of the John Frederick Lewis Collection in the Free Library of Philadelphia* (Baltimore: J. H. Furst, 1937).

77. In keeping with the philanthropic tendencies of the day, Lewis left his collections to the public institutions of Philadelphia. His engravings went to the Pennsylvania Academy of Fine Arts, and his portraits and the medieval and Eastern manuscripts and cuttings went to the Free Library.

78. The papers of John Frederick Lewis dating from 1878 to 1932 are housed at the American Philosophical Society, Philadelphia. From 1903 through 1932, there are numerous letters from book dealers concerning offers and purchases. They are, however, disappointingly vague—often mentioning illuminated manuscripts but rarely describing them. In 1987 the Archives of American Art microfilmed a selection of the letters, focusing particularly on Lewis's affiliation with the Pennsylvania Academy of Fine Arts and his involvement with the contemporary art scene.

79. Lewis, "Christopher Columbus."

80. This insight is offered by Wieck in "Folia Fugitiva," 236.

81. Lewis owned two other extra-illustrated copies of W. Blades, *The Enemies of Books* [AL 025.8 B56; AL 025.8 B561]. We would like to thank Russell Maylone of Special Collections, Deering Library, Northwestern University, for bringing these extra-illustrated copies of Blades to our attention.

82. We wish to thank Martha Repman, formerly of the Rare Books Collection at the Free Library, for bringing the multiple grangerized volumes owned by Lewis to our attention. These volumes are: E. M. Thompson, *English Illuminated Manuscripts* (London, 1895) [AL 096 T371]; J. W. Bradley, *Illuminated Manuscripts. Little Books on Art* (London, 1905)[AL 096 B72]; W. Blades, *Enemies of Books* (London, 1880) [AL 025.8 B53]; W. Blades, *Enemies of Books* (London, 1880) [AL 025.8 B56]; W. Blades, *Enemies of Books.* (London, 1880) [AL 025.8 B562]; F. Madan, *Books in Manuscript* (London, 1893) [AL 091 M261]; F. Madan, *Books in Manuscript* (London, 1893) [AL 091 M2612]; E. Quaile, *Illuminated Manuscripts: their Origin, History and Characteristics. A sketch* (Liverpool, 1897) [AL 096 Q2]; W. de Gray Birch, *Early Drawings and Illuminations. An introduction to the study of illuminated manuscripts with a dictionary of subjects in the British Museum* (London, 1879) [AL 096 B531]; W. de Gray Birch, *Early Drawings and Illuminations with a Dictionary of Subjects* (London, 1873) [AL 096 B53]; H. Shaw, *The Art of Illumination,* 2d. ed. (London, 1870) [AL 096 Sh2].

83. De Ricci and Wilson's *Census,* 2037, no. 308 indicates that three works by the Spanish Forger—a flight into Egypt (M 31:34), an initial *N* with a coronation of a queen (M 49:10), and the historiated *G* with female saint, attendant, and reliquary in a boat (M 49:11)—were stored together. See William M. Voelkle and Roger S. Wieck, *The Spanish Forger* (New York: Pierpont Morgan Library, 1978), L58, L60, and L61.

84. In 1928 Robert Lehman catalogued the 105 most important works in the family holdings in a deluxe, folio-sized work produced in Paris with a press run of only three hundred copies for private distribution. Robert Lehman, *The Philip Lehman Collection, New York* (Paris: Calmann-Lévy, 1928). The Lehman collection has long been recognized for its excellence. In 1954 the Metropolitan Museum held an exhibition of the works, and two years later Lehman accepted an invitation from the French government to exhibit the masterpieces of the collection at the Orangerie, an honor never before —nor since—bestowed on a single collector. See Musée de l'Orangerie, *Exposition de la collection Lehman de New York* (Paris: Editions des musées nationaux, 1957). Three years later, in an equally unprecedented move, Lehman lent almost 600 objects in his collection to the Cincinnati Art Museum. See Cincinnati Art Museum, *The Lehman Collection, New York* (Cincinnati: Cincinnati Art Museum, 1959). The Lehman family house was subsequently converted into a private museum open to the public, and at Robert Lehman's death in 1969, the collection, nearly 3,000 objects, was donated to the Metropolitan Museum, to be housed

in a special wing. On Lehman's Italian paintings, see John Pope-Hennessy, *The Robert Lehman Collection,* vol. 1, *Italian Paintings* (New York: Metropolitan Museum of Art, 1987). On Northern paintings in Lehman's collection, see Charles Sterling et al., *The Robert Lehman Collection,* vol. 2, *Fifteenth- to Eighteenth-Century European Paintings* (New York: Metropolitan Museum of Art, 1998).

85. See Cincinnati Art Museum, *Lehman Collection,* nos. 328 and 322; and Sandra Hindman et al., *The Robert Lehman Collection. Vol. 4, Illuminations* (New York: Metropolitan Museum of Art, 1997), no. 21.

86. Hindman et al., *Robert Lehman,* nos. 6, 7, and 24. See also De Ricci and Wilson, *Census,* 1702, A.1 a–d; 1703, A.14 and 10, A.30 a–f; 1704, A.3; 1706, A.21; 1707, A.12; 1708, A.4; 1710, A.8; 1711, A.5a, A.17; 1713, A.6; 1714, A.9; 1717, A.5d; 1718, A.2.

87. Hindman et al., *Robert Lehman,* nos. 1 and 21; and De Ricci and Wilson, *Census,* 1702, C.32; and 1709, D.28; Hindman et al., *Robert Lehman,* nos. 2 (esp. n. 2), 3 (esp. n. 1), 9, and 10; and De Ricci and Wilson, *Census,* 1718, C.12; 1712, C.13; 1717, B.21.

88. Pope-Hennessy, *Italian Paintings,* 95.

89. Ibid., 85.

90. Hindman et al., *Robert Lehman,* no. 11.

91. Sterling et al., *European Paintings,* no. 20. Cf. Cécile Scaillièrez, "Entre enluminure et peinture: a propos d'un *Paysage avec Saint Jérôme pénitent* de l'école Ganto-Brugeoise récemment acquis par le Louvre," *Revue du Louvre* 42 (1992): 16–31.

92. For cuttings from Maggs, see Hindman et al., *Robert Lehman,* nos. 15 (which passed through Olschki before Lehman purchased it), 17, and 26; De Ricci and Wilson, *Census,* 1706, B.22; 1712, D.17 and D.4.

93. Hindman et al., *Robert Lehman,* no. 19.

94. George Szabo, *Masterpieces of Italian Drawing in the Robert Lehman Collection, the Metropolitan Museum of Art* (New York: Hudson Hill Press, 1983), no 14; and K. Christiansen, L. B. Kanter, and C. B. Strehlke, *Painting in Renaissance Siena, 1420–1500* (New York, 1988), no. 68.

95. Szabo, *Masterpieces of Italian Drawing,* 53.

96. See Hindman et al., *Robert Lehman,* no. 13.

97. See Elizabeth A. Peterson and Alison Stones, "The Book Goes Public," *Carnegie Magazine* 54, no. 8 (March–April 1989): 30–35. Obituary of Howard A. Noble, *Pittsburgh Post Gazette,* May 2, 1964. We would like to thank Alison Stones for generously providing us with information on Howard A. Noble.

98. *The Astor Collection of Illuminated Manuscripts* (London: Sotheby's, June 21, 1988).

99. See Hindman et al., *Robert Lehman,* no. 25. The other nine works are no longer in the Lehman holdings. See De Ricci and Wilson, *Census,* 1714–17, nos. C19–27. For the Lord Northwick

100. For Celotti sale, see William Young Ottley. *A Catalogue of a Highly Valuable and Extremely Curious Collection*

of Illumined Miniature Paintings, of the
Greatest Beauty, and of Exquisite Finishing, Taken from the Choral Books of the
Papal Chapel in the Vatican, during the
French Revolution: and Subsequently Collected and Brought to This Country by the
Abate Celotti (London: Christie's, May
26, 1825), lot 51; for Ottley sale, see
Catalogue of the Very Beautiful Collection
of Highly Finished and Illumined Miniature Paintings, the Property of the Late
William Young Ottley, Esq. (London:
Sotheby's, May 11–12, 1838). De Ricci
and Wilson, Census, 1717, no. C.25,
now New York, private collection.

101. See Lehman, Philip Lehman Collection.

102. On De Ricci's experience, see S.
De Ricci, "Les Amateurs de livres anciens en France de 1900 à 1925," Bulletin du Bibliophile, no. 3 (1926): 1–12.

103. De Ricci and Wilson, Census,
supplement 1962. A computerized update of De Ricci and Wilson's Census,
called The Uncatalogued Manuscript Control Center (formerly the Union Manuscript Computer Catalogue), is currently
in process under the direction of
Melissa Conway and Lisa Fagin Davis
(Website: members.aol.com/dericci/
umcc/umcc.html). A further computerized census update, called The
Medieval Manuscript Project, is also un-
derway.

104. De Ricci and Wilson, Census, x.

105. On Bryan, see Russell Lynes, The
Tastemakers (New York: Harper, 1954),
42–44; William George Constable, Art
Collecting in the United States: An Out-
line of a History (London: Thomas
Nelson and Sons, 1964), 29–30; and
Brimo, L'évolution du goût, 65.

106. Most of Bryan's Italian primitives
were purchased from Parisian collector
Artaud de Montor, whose Considerations sur l'état de la peinture en Italie,
1808, essentially was a catalogue of his
collection of primitives acquired in
Italy in the wake of the Napoleonic
wars.

107. Thomas Jefferson Bryan and
Richard Grant White, Companion to
the Bryan Gallery of Christian Art (New
York: Baker, Godwin, 1853): see for
example, iv and 5.

108. Apparently the society did little to
promote the collection or to encourage public study of it. Ultimately,
against the explicit conditions of the
gift, many of the paintings were dispersed in sales of 1971, 1980, and 1995.

109. On Jarves, see Francis Steegmuller, The Two Lives of James Jackson
Jarves (New Haven, Conn.: Yale University Press, 1951); Lynes, Tastemakers,
48–62; Constable, Art Collecting in the
United States, 31–39; Brimo, L'évolution
du goût, 65–67.

110. See Osvald Sirén, A Descriptive
Catalogue of the Pictures in the Jarves Collection Belonging to Yale University (New
Haven, Conn.: Yale University Press,
1916); Richard Offner, Italian Primitives
at Yale University: Comments and Revisions (New Haven, Conn.: Yale University Press, 1927); David Arnheim et
al., Italian Primitives: The Case History of
a Collection and Its Conservation (New
Haven, Conn.: Yale University Press,
1972).

111. James Jackson Jarves, Art Hints:
Architecture, Sculpture, and Painting
(New York: Sampson Low, Son,
1855); James Jackson Jarves, Art Studies:
The "Old Masters" of Italy (New York:
Derby and Jackson, 1861). On Jarves's
dependence on Ruskin, see the letter

reproduced in Steegmuller, Two Lives
of James Jackson Jarves, 152–53. Saarinen
maintains that ultimately, Jarves's writings were not widely circulated and he
influenced few. See Aline B. Saarinen,
The Proud Possessors. The Lives, Times
and Tastes of some Adventurous American
Art Collectors (New York: Random
House, 1958; reprint, New York: Vintage Books, 1969), xxii. Elizabeth
Bradfor Smith, on the other hand, optimistically asserts that Jarves was widely read in his day. See Smith, Medieval
Art in America, 28.

112. James Jackson Jarves, Art
Thoughts: The Experiences and Observations of an American Amateur in Europe
(New York: Hurd and Houghton,
1869), 230.

113. Ibid., 231.

114. See C. Snay, "Medieval Art in
American Popular Culture: Mid-Nineteenth-Century American Travelers in
Europe," in Medieval Art in America,
ed, Smith, 35–40.

115. See Fleming, "Picturesque History," 1064–8, and Fleming, "Nineteenth-Century New England's
Memory," 79–83.

116. T. J. Jackson Lears, No Place of
Grace: Antimodernism and the Transformation of American Culture 1880–1920
(Chicago: University of Chicago Press,
1981).

117. For recent work on Henry Adams
and a "feminine" middle ages, see Kim
Moreland, "Henry Adams, the Medieval Lady and the 'New Woman,'"
CLIO 18, no. 3 (spring 1989): 291–
305; and Nancy Comley, "Henry
Adams' Feminine Fictions: The Economics of Maternity," American Literary
Realism 22, no. 1 (fall 1989): 3–16.

118. See, for example, Eileen Boris,
Art and Labor: Ruskin, Morris and the
Craftsman Ideal in America (Philadel-
phia: Temple University Press, 1986);
Roger B. Stein, John Ruskin and Aes-
thetic Thought in America, 1840–1900
(Cambridge, Mass.: Harvard University
Press, 1967); and Lears, No Place of
Grace, 60–96.

119. Lears, No Place of Grace, 66–73.

120. Ibid., 163.

121. On the development of the Clois-
ters, see Hubert Landais, "The Clois-
ters or the Passion for the Middle
Ages," in The Cloisters: Studies in
Honor of the Fiftieth Anniversary, ed.
Elizabeth C. Parker (New York: Met-
ropolitan Museum of Art, 1992),
41–48; and William H. Forsyth, "Five
Crucial People in the Building of the
Cloisters," in The Cloisters, 51–62.

122. W. Irwin, E. C. May, and J.
Hotchkiss, A History of the Union
League Club of New York City (New
York, 1952), 92–99.

123. Union League Club, Illuminated
Books and Manuscripts, Old Masters and
Modern Paintings (New York: Union
League Club, 1890). We would like to
thank Wendy Bellion for bringing this
exhibition to our attention.

124. Ibid., ii.

125. Ibid., iii–iv.

126. Brayton Ives, quoted in J. T.
Winterich, The Grolier Club, 1884–1950:
An Informal History (New York:
Grolier Club, 1950): 7–8. On the his-
tory of the club see Grolier Club, The
Grolier Club, 1884–1984, its Library, Ex-
hibitions & Publications (New York:
Grolier Club, 1984).

127. On exhibitions at the Grolier
Club, see G. T. Tanselle, "Exhibi-
tions," and A. Asaf, "Exhibitions and
Meetings, 1884–1983," both in Grolier
Club, Grolier Club, 1884–1984. For the
first Grolier Club exhibition of manu-
scripts, see Transactions of the Grolier
Club, vol. 1 (1884).

128. Winterich, Grolier Club, 1884–
1950, 16.

129. Also included were three groups
of cuttings (nos. 83, 85, and 89), two
albums of cuttings (no. 87 and 94),
and a collage (no. 52)—a piece offered
at the Celotti sale, featuring a Crucifixion by Clovio (see chapter 2).

130. See V. G. Simkhovitch, "Exhibition of Illuminated Manuscripts," Columbia University Quarterly 9 (1906–7):
44–46; on the history of manuscripts at
Columbia, see Robert Somerville,
"The Origins of Columbia University's Collection of Medieval and Renaissance Manuscripts," in Renaissance
Society and Culture, ed. J. Monfasani
and Ronald G. Musto (New York:
Italica Press, 1991), 289–300. See also
Jane E. Rosenthal, "Illuminated Manuscripts at Columbia University," in
Medieval and Renaissance Manuscripts at
Columbia University, ed. Beatrice Ter-
rien-Somerville (New York: Columbia
University Libraries, 1991), 27–38.

131. Charles Rufus Morey, History of
the Art of Illumination. Special Exhibits
in the Princeton University Library
(Princeton: Princeton University Press,
1916), 109.

132. Morey, History of the Art of Illumination, 111.

133. On the Guelph treasure and its
history in the United States, see O.
van Falke, R. Schmidt, and G. Swarzenski, eds., The Guelph Treasure: The
Sacred Relics of Brunswick Cathedral
formerly in the Possession of the Ducal
House of Brunswick-Lüneburg, trans. S.
M. Welch. (Frankfurt am Main, 1930);
and P. M. De Winter, The Sacral Treasure of the Guelphs. A Special Issue of the
Bulletin of the Cleveland Museum of Art
72, no. 1 (March 1985).

134. Cockerell, quoted in Charles F.
McCombs, Illuminated Manuscripts from
the Pierpont Morgan Library. Catalogue
of an Exhibition Held at the New York
Public Library (New York: New York
Public Library, 1934), 4.

135. Charles Rufus Morey, Pierpont
Morgan Library. Exhibition of Illuminated
Manuscripts Held at the New York Public
Library. Catalogue of the Manuscripts
by Belle da Costa Greene and Meta P.
Harrsen (New York: Pierpont Morgan
Library, 1934).

136. Morey, Pierpont Morgan Library, ii,
v, viii, ix, xi, xiii, xv.

137. In 1935, at the time of publication
of De Ricci and Wilson's Census, the
pre-1500 manuscripts of the Library of
Congress were sparsely illuminated at
best. For example, most of its eight
Books of Hours contained only a
handful of miniatures, and the group
of roughly fifty fragments acquired by
the Library in the late 1920s were un-
adorned. De Ricci and Wilson, Census, 179–266.

138. On Rosenwald as benefactor of
the Library of Congress, see W. Matheson, "Lessing J. Rosenwald 'A Splendidly Generous Man,'" Quarterly
Journal of the Library of Congress 37,
no. 1 (winter 1980): 3–24. See also Library of Congress, The Rosenwald Collection. A Catalogue of Illustrated Books

NOTES

295

and Manuscripts, of Books from Celebrated Presses, and of Bindings and Maps, 1150–1950 (Washington, D.C.: Library of Congress, 1954); Elizabeth Mongan, Rosenwald Collection: An Exhibition of Recent Acquisitions (Washington, 1950); and Library of Congress, Vision of a Collector. The Lessing J. Rosenwald Collection of the Library of Congress (Washington, D.C.: Library of Congress, 1991).

139. On Rosenwald's as a print collector, see R. Fine, Lessing J. Rosenwald. Tribute to a Collector (Washington, D.C.: National Gallery of Art, 1982); and Fred Ferretti, "The Treasure of Jenkintown, Pa.: Lessing Rosenwald's 25,000 Prints," Art News 72, no. 3 (March 1973): 43–45. For Rosenwald's own account of his developing interest in printed books, see Lessing J. Rosenwald, "The Formation of the Rosenwald Collection," Quarterly Journal of the Library of Congress 3, no. 1 (October 1945): 54; and Lessing J. Rosenwald, Recollections of a Collector (Jenkintown, Pa.: Alverthorpe Gallery, 1976). On the relationship between the collector and the bookseller Rosenbach, see Rosenbach Museum and Library, Rosenwald and Rosenbach: Two Philadelphia Bookmen (Philadelphia, 1983).

140. L. M. C. Randall, "Horae Beatae Mariae Virginis (Edith G. Rosenwald Hours)," in Library of Congress, Vision of a Collector, 3–5. For more on Rosenwald's medieval and Renaissance illuminated manuscripts, see Library of Congress, Vision of a Collector, 3–14, and Library of Congress, The Rosenwald Collection, 1–4. See also R. Wieck, "Horae Beatae Mariae ad usum Romanum. [France], 1524," in Vision of a Collector, 13–14.

141. A. Shestack, "Biblia Latina (Giant Bible of Mainz)," in Vision of a Collector, 6–7.

142. For highlights of Rosenwald's collection as a whole, see F. R. Goff, "Catalogue of Fine Books and Manuscripts Selected for Exhibition at the Library of Congress from the Lessing J. Rosenwald Collection," Library of Congress Quarterly Journal of Current Acquisitions 3, no. 1 (October 1945): 5–51. See also the catalogue of the collection, Library of Congress, The Lessing J. Rosenwald Collection: A Catalogue of the Gifts of Lessing J. Rosenwald to the Library of Congress, 1943 to 1975 (Washington, D.C., 1977). On the richness of the Rosenwald collection, its broad scholarly interest and research potential, see Sandra Hindman, ed., The Early Illustrated Book. Essays in Honor of Lessing J. Rosenwald (Washington, D.C.: Library of Congress, 1982).

143. In 1929, just a few years into his print collecting enterprise, he lent two hundred Rembrandt prints to the Art Alliance of Philadelphia; in 1931 he lent seventy-five prints spanning the centuries from the fifteenth to the early twentieth to the Print Club of Philadelphia. See Print Club of Philadelphia, Five Centuries of Print Making from the Collection of Lessing J. Rosenwald (Philadelphia, 1931). Rosenwald also increasingly lent throughout the 1930s.

144. For Rosenwald's own accounts of his collecting activity, see Rosenwald, Recollections of a Collector. This memoir offers little insight into Rosenwald's collection of illumination. Indeed, the single significant mention

of a manuscript or leaf in this work refers not to Rosenwald's personal holdings but to those of the Rosenbach Foundation in Philadelphia.

145. L. J. Rosenwald, preface to Medieval and Renaissance Miniatures from the National Gallery of Art, by Carl Nordenfalk et al. (Washington, D.C.: National Gallery of Art, 1975), viii.

146. The complete collection of miniatures was exhibited at the National Gallery in 1975; see Nordenfalk et al., Medieval and Renaissance Miniatures.

147. Ibid., no. 8.

148. Ibid., no. 46; and University of Notre Dame Art Gallery, Medieval Manuscripts from the Lessing J. Rosenwald Collection (South Bend, Ind.: University of Notre Dame Art Gallery, 1972), 24–31.

149. R. S. Field. Fifteenth Century Woodcuts and Metalcuts from the National Gallery of Art (Washington, D.C., 1965), nos. 18–23.

150. Roger S. Wieck, "The Rosenwald Scribe Miniature and Its Sister Miniatures: A Case of Mistaken Identity," Oud Holland 95, no. 3 (1981): 151–61.

151. On the formation of the New York Public Library, see H. M. Lydenberg, History of the New York Public Library (New York, 1923); for Astor's manuscripts, see 89–90. For Stuart's collection, see Catalogue of the Library of Robert L. Stuart (New York, 1884).

152. See New York Public Library, The Spencer Collection of Illustrated Books (New York: New York Public Library, 1928).

153. W. M. Milliken, "Illuminated Miniatures in the Cleveland Museum of Art," Bulletin of the Cleveland Museum of Art 12 (1925): 62.

154. For Ottley sale, see Catalogue of the Very Beautiful Collection, lot 182. See L. Kanter, Painting and Illumination in Early Renaissance Florence, 1300–1450 (New York, 1995), no. 16.

155. Z. Haraszti, "Medieval Manuscripts" and "Medieval Manuscripts in the Library," More Books. The Bulletin of the Boston Public Library 3, no. 2 (March 1928): 56.

156. On the 1934 reorganization, see W. M. Whitehill, Boston Public Library. A Centennial History (Cambridge, Mass., 1956), 230–31. On Haraszti's acquisitions in the early 1950s, see Z. Haraszti, "Notable Purchases," The Boston Public Library Quarterly 7, no. 2 (April 1955): 72–91; "Twenty-five Years of the Treasure Room," The Boston Public Library Quarterly 7, no. 3 (July 1955): 115–27; and "Additions to the Rare Book Department," The Boston Public Library Quarterly 9, no. 2 (April 1957): 59–72.

157. N. Harris, "Museums, Merchandising and Popular Taste: The Struggle for Influence," in Cultural Excursions, 56–81.

158. L. Wendt and H. Kogan, Give the Lady What She Wants! The Story of Marshall Field & Company (Chicago, 1952), 212 and 218.

159. For the establishment of the Rare Book Department, see Wendt and Kogan, Story of Marshall Field, 308.

160. Z. F. Popkin, "Art: Three Aisles Over," Outlook and Independent (November 26, 1930): 503.

161. We would like to thank Christine Geisler Andrews for her research on Otto Ege.

162. There exists a "microfilm memorial" to Ege at the Reading Public Library, Reading, Pennsylvania, presented by the Reading Public High School class of 1907.

163. Some of the works in Ege's collection were sold after his death by Cleveland dealer Peter Keisogloff (No printed catalogue of these holdings exists). A portion of the Ege manuscripts were included in the sale Western Manuscripts and Miniatures (London: Sotheby's, December 11, 1984). Some Ege manuscripts and leaves can now be found at the Cleveland Public Library (Bible and rare book portfolios and over a dozen single leaves from Ege's collection, including many large choral sheets); some leaves are now in the possession of Akron dealer, Bruce Ferrini.

164. James H. Marrow et al., The Golden Age of Dutch Manuscript Painting (Stuttgart: Belser, 1989; New York: George Braziller, 1990), no. 66.

165. O. Ege, "I am a Biblioclast," Avocations: A Magazine of Hobbies and Leisure 1 (March 1938): 518.

166. Ibid.; De Ricci and Wilson, Census, 1937.

167. Ege, "I am a Biblioclast," 518.

168. Portfolios of Otto F. Ege's Fifty Original Leaves from Medieval Manuscripts (n.p., n.d.) can now be found at the Walter's Art Gallery (MS. W.814), The Cleveland Public Library, and Case Western Reserve University.

169. Western Manuscripts and Miniatures, London, Sotheby's, December 11, 1984.

170. Western Manuscripts and Miniatures, lots 39 and 51. When Ege purchased the Livy in 1950, the work was described as having "upwards of 300 leaves." At the time of the posthumous sale at Sotheby's, the book had only 240 folios.

171. We wish to thank Bronwen Wilson for her research on the Grolier "Magic Carpet on Wheels."

172. Ultimately, half of the Grolier Encyclopedia collection went to Kansas City and in 1955 the St. Louis Public Library acquired half of the collection.

173. A list of these publications is available at the Cleveland Public Library.

174. See, for example, Otto F. Ege, "The Most Beautiful Book in the World," School Arts Magazine 21, no. 8 (April 1922): 447–50, which deals with the Book of Kells.

175. Otto F. Ege, "Manuscripts of the Middle Ages," American Magazine of Art 23, no. 5 (November 1931): 380.

176. Otto F. Ege, "The Modern Book," School Arts Magazine 46, no. 6 (March 1947): 218–22.

177. For a brief introduction to Mortimer Brandt, see Wieck, "Folia Fugitiva," 8.

178. Today the Brandt collection of illuminations is dispersed. The works were temporarily put on deposit at the Walters Art Gallery, but in 1988 the entire collection was purchased by dealers Sam Fogg and Bruce Ferrini and has since been sold off. Among

those who bought Brandt folios was single-leaf collector, Bernard Breslauer. See William M. Voelkle and Roger S. Wieck, *The Bernard H. Breslauer Collection of Manuscript Illuminations,* ed. Maria Francesca P. Saffiotti (New York: Pierpont Morgan Library, 1992), no. 33.

179. Henry Bober, *The Mortimer Brandt Collection of Medieval Manuscript Illuminations* (Hatfield Herts: Stellar Press, 1966), nos. 27 and 28; Michael J. Heinlen, *Medieval and Renaissance Miniature Painting* (Akron and London, 1989), no. 19. Present whereabouts unknown.

180. Bober, *Mortimer Brandt Collection.*

181. For Bober's biography, see B. D. Boehm, "Necrology: Harry Bober (1915–1988)," *Gesta* 28, no. 1 (1989): 103–5.

182. Bober, introduction to *Mortimer Brandt Collection,* 3.

183. Bober, *Mortimer Brandt Collection,* no. 16.

184. Ibid., no. 5, now in the collection of the Billy Graham Center Museum, Wheaton, Ill.

185. Moira Collins and Judy Chambliss, "Gertrude Carrier in Her Own Words . . . " *Chicago Calligraphy Collective Letter* (summer 1995): 18.

186. See Rhinelander's obituary, *New York Times,* June 13, 1942, 15.

187. There is some confusion as to the precise dating of Rhinelander's copies of Morgan manuscripts M.1 and M.23. The Morgan Library catalogue dates the copies to "about 1924" but the back of the leaves state, "Written and illuminated by Olive Frances Rhinelander in New York, USA in 1934."

188. Edward F. Rothschild, "Medieval Manuscript Illumination. The Renaissance Society Sponsors Exhibition," *University of Chicago Magazine* 22 (1929–30): 193. We would like to thank Robert Williams for bringing this article to our attention. Gertrude Carrier, a former student of Ricketts to be discussed subsequently, offhandedly mentions that at one time Ricketts was also a professional bookkeeper; Collins and Chambliss, "Gertrude Carrier," 14.

189. Ricketts was not the only Chicago collector with a taste for things medieval. Martin A. Ryerson, Kate Sturgis Buckingham, and George Franklin Harding also acquired medieval and Renaissance objects in the decades around the turn of the twentieth century and donated them to Chicago institutions. None of these collectors, however, was particularly interested in illuminated manuscripts or cuttings. See Neil Harris, "Midwestern Medievalism: Three Chicago Collectors," in *Fenway Court,* vol. 27, *Cultural Leadership in America. Art Matronage and Patronage* (Boston: Trustees of the Isabella Stewart Gardner Museum, 1997), 104–23. We would like to thank Andrew Walker for bringing this article to our attention.

190. In 1961 the Lilly Library at the University of Indiana acquired the bulk of Ricketts's manuscripts and cuttings, as well as his original illuminations. Ricketts's outstanding collection of writing manuals as well as other manuscripts went to the John M. Wing Foundation on the History of Printing at the Newberry Library, Chicago. The Newberry Library also retains the Ricketts Collecting Papers, which consist of notes on the manuscripts that he acquired. We would like to thank Paul Gehl, Wing Curator at the Newberry Library for bringing this collection to our attention. In 1930 the Renaissance Society at the University of Chicago sponsored an exhibition of Ricketts's manuscripts, supplemented by facsimiles. See Rothschild, "Medieval Manuscript Illumination," 192–95.

191. Letter to Herbert L. Putnam, in response to De Ricci and Wilson, *Census* inquiry, July 29, 1930. Lilly Library, Ricketts MSS. III, Correspondence.

192. Letter from Ricketts to his daughter Julia, written from London, November 2, 1926. Lilly Library, Ricketts MSS. III, Correspondence.

193. De Ricci and Wilson, *Census,* 633, no. 108, obtained from Tregaskis, cat. 764, December 1, 1914, n. 28. Ricketts owned other works that attested to his interest in collages evoking "grand manner" painting. For example, he possessed a "Composite Leaf" made up of late-fifteenth- century Italian borders from manuscripts that had appeared in the Celotti sale (see chapter 2). See Celotti sale, see Ottley, *Catalogue of a Highly Valuable and Extremely Curious Collection,* no. 44; De Ricci and Wilson, *Census,* 632, no. 104, present whereabouts unknown.

194. See De Ricci and Wilson, *Census,* 655, no. 240.

195. Lucy Freeman Sandler, *Gothic Manuscripts, 1285–1385* (London: Harvey Miller, 1986), 2: no. 132.

196. The notebooks and facsimiles for this unfinished project are now housed at the Lilly Library, Ricketts MSS. III.

197. Rothschild, "Medieval Manuscript Illumination," 193.

198. O. Elfrida Saunders, *English Illumination* (New York, 1928).

199. Reported in the *Chicago Tribune,* April 26, 1903.

200. The Newberry Library houses Gertrude Carrier's papers, which include notebooks from art history classes that she attended at The Art Institute of Chicago (some from the lectures of Helen Gardner), sketches and mock-ups, and personal correspondence. We would like to thank Paul Gehl for bringing this collection to our attention.

**1. Manuscript (Gradual)**
(Italy, fifteenth century; binding,
1599). *Evanston, Ill.: Northwestern University, The Charles Deering McCormick Library of Special Collections Western MS 43.*

**2. Cutout fragment**
(Florence, 1392–99), by Don Silvestro dei Gherarducci.
Historiated initial *C*, with a prophet, from a gradual made for San Michele a Murano in Venice.
PROVENANCE: Acquired by the Victoria and Albert Museum, London, before 1863.
LITERATURE: Laurence B. Kanter et al., *Painting and Illumination in Early Renaissance Florence, 1300–1450* (New York: Metropolitan Museum of Art, 1994), 161.
*London: The Victoria and Albert Museum, PDP, 431.*
(figure 30)

**3. Single leaf**
(England, mid–twelfth century).
Scenes from the Life of Christ from a Bible or psalter created at the monastery of Bury St. Edmunds.
PROVENANCE: Formerly in the collection of W. Y. Ottley.
LITERATURE: C. R. Dodwell, *Pictorial Arts of the West, 800–1200* (New Haven, Conn.: Yale University Press, 1993), 336–37, 432; C. M. Kauffmann, *Romanesque Manuscripts, 1066–1190* (London: Harvey Miller, 1975), no. 66.
*New York: The Pierpont Morgan Library, M. 521.*
(figure 20)

**4. Single leaf**
(England, circa 1240), William de Brailes.
Scenes from the infancy of Christ. This leaf was pasted into an extra-illuminated Thomas Frognall Dibdin, *Bibliographical Decameron* (1817).
LITERATURE: Richard Marks and Nigel J. Morgan, *The Golden Age of English Manuscript Painting, 1200–1500* (New York: Braziller, 1981), plate 5; Nigel J. Morgan, *Early Gothic Manuscripts (I) 1190–1250* (London: Harvey Miller, 1982), 14, 16, 32, 118–19.
*New York: The Pierpont Morgan Library, M. 913.*
(figure 18)

**5. Cutout fragments**
(Italy, thirteenth century).
From the *Conradin Bible* (Baltimore: The Walters Art Gallery, WAG MS 152).
LITERATURE: Filippo Todini and Milvia Bollati, *Una collezione di miniature italiane dal Duecento al Cinquecento* (Milan: Studio nella Longari, 1993), 12–17.
*Milan: The Longari Collection.*
(figure 31)

**6. Single leaf**
(England, circa 1360). Baruch writing (was folio 261) from the so-called *Bohun Bible.* As early as 1665 single leaves had already been extracted from this multivolume Bible.
PROVENANCE: Collection of C. L. Ricketts.
LITERATURE: Lucy Freeman Sandler, *Gothic Manuscripts, 1285–1385,* vol. 2, no. 132 (London: Harvey Miller, 1986).
*Bloomington, Ind.: The Lilly Library, Ricketts MSS I, 15.*
(figure 153)

**7. Montage of fragments**
(Italy, sixteenth century; assembled pre-1825), by Giulio Clovio or follower.
Miniatures (Evangelists and decoration) excised from a Sistine Chapel choir

book. The choir book was dismembered circa 1796, reassembled in England, before 1825.
PROVENANCE: Among the collages sold at the Celotti-Ottley sale, London, Christie's, May 26, 1825; collection of Firmin-Didot.
LITERATURE: Reproduced in Albert Racinet, *L'Ornement Polychrome* (Paris: Firmin- Didot, 1873), plate 61; Sandra Hindman and Michael Heinlen, "A Connoisseur's Montage: The *Four Evangelists* Attributed to Gulio Clovio," *Art Institute of Chicago Museum Studies* 17 (1991): figure 3, appendix 2.
*New York: The Pierpont Morgan Library, M. 270.*
(figure 22)

**8. Photograph of Sistine Chapel ceiling** (Rome, 1508–12), by Michelangelo.
Prophet Zachariah, in spandrel of the Sistine Chapel ceiling.
(figure 42)

**9. Montage of fragments**
(Rome, early sixteenth century; assembled pre-1825).
Miniatures (decollation of St. Paul and decoration) excised from a Sistine Chapel choir book. Choir book dismembered (circa 1796), reassembled in England (pre-1825).
PROVENANCE: Among the collages sold at the Celotti-Ottley sale, London, Christie's, May 26, 1825; acquired by the Victoria and Albert Museum, London, with the Salting Collection in 1910.
LITERATURE: William M. Voelkle and Roger S. Wieck, *The Bernard H. Breslauer Collection of Manuscript Illuminations,* edited by Maria Francesca P. Saffiotti (New York: Pierpont Morgan Library, 1992), figure 11.
*London: The Victoria and Albert Museum, PDP, E.4578-1910.*
(figure 23)

**10. Single leaf**
(Italy, circa 1572), by Giulio Clovio.
Miniature, Crucifixion.
LITERATURE: Sandra Hindman and Michael Heinlen, "A Connoisseur's Montage: The *Four Evangelists* Attributed to Gulio Clovio," *Art Institute of Chicago Museum Studies* 17 (1991): figure 5.
*New York: The Brooklyn Museum, Gift of A. Augustus Healy (11.499).*
(figure 24)

**11. Album**
(Hungary, circa 1300–50; assembled seventeenth century). Miniatures, scenes from the life of St. Bartholomew, cut and reconfigured in an album; already bound as a picture album in 1630 when presented by Giovanni Battista Saluzzo to Angelo Saluzzo.
PROVENANCE: Collection of Saluzzo family; purchased in 1909 by J. P. Morgan from Rossi.
LITERATURE: Meta Harrsen, *Central European Manuscripts in the Pierpont Morgan Library* (New York: Pierpont Morgan Library, 1958), no. 35.
*New York: The Pierpont Morgan Library, M.360,0 folio 20.*
(figure 37)

**12. Montage of fragments**
(France, late fifteenth century, and Italy, late fourteenth century; assembled nineteenth century).
Miniatures, the Annunciation and the Adoration of the Magi, by the Master of the Geneva Latini or a follower (Rouen, circa 1480); miniatures of heads, constituting frame, by Nicolò di Giacomo da

Bologna (Bologna, circa 1370). Montage perhaps assembled by O. Du Sartel (Paris [?], circa 1880).
PROVENANCE: Sale of O. Du Sartel, Paris, June 8, 1894, lot 575; London, Sotheby's, December 2, 1986, lot 13.
*Literature:* Sandra Hindman, *Medieval and Renaissance Miniature Painting* (Akron, Ohio: Ferrini, 1988), no. 43.
*United States: private collection.*
(figure 46)

**13. Montage of fragments**
(France, late fifteenth century, and Italy, early sixteenth century; assembled nineteenth century).
Miniature, Virgin and Child, by Simon Marmion (France, late fifteenth century) in decorative frame by Attavante Attavanti (Italy, early sixteenth century). Montage assembled in the nineteenth century.
PROVENANCE: Collection of Frederic Spitzer, sold in sale of his collection, Paris, April 17– June 16, 1893.
*Toledo, Ohio: The Toledo Museum of Art, Frederick B. and Kate L. Shoemaker Fund, 1939.501.*
(figure 26)

**14. Montage of fragments**
(France, circa 1250; assembled nineteenth century).
Historiated initials from a pocket Bible, cut out and arranged like a Gothic stained-glass window (nineteenth century).
PROVENANCE: Bought by the Victoria and Albert Museum, London, at Sotheby's, March 19, 1909, lot 235.
*London: The Victoria and Albert Museum, PDP, E.2126-1909 to 2141-1909.*
(figure 45)

**15. Cutout fragment**
(Lorraine, France, circa 1295).
Miniature (*The Woman Clothed with the Sun and the Dragon*) from Apocalypse manuscript formerly in the Burckhardt-Wildt Collection.
PROVENANCE: Peter Birmann, Basel; Daniel Burckhardt-Wildt; London: Sotheby's, April 25, 1983, lot 50.
LITERATURE: Patrick M. De Winter, "Visions of the Apocalypse in Medieval England and France," *Bulletin of the Cleveland Museum of Art* 70, no. 10 (December 1983): 396–417.
*Cleveland, Ohio: The Cleveland Museum of Art. Purchase John L. Severance Fund, 1983.73.2.a.*
(figure 40)

**16. Cutout fragment**
(Italy, fourteenth century).
Historiated initial *M*, with Christ crucified in a church, a bishop catching his blood, elders and two beggars.
PROVENANCE: Collection of James Dennistoun (1803–55); bought by J. C. Robinson for the Victoria and Albert Museum, London, 1855.
*London: The Victoria and Albert Museum, PDP, 2991.*
(figure 36)

**17. Dennistoun album**
(England, nineteenth century).
PROVENANCE: Collection of James Dennistoun (1803–55); bought by Sir Kenneth Clark.
*Private collection.*
(figure 38)

**18. Single leaf**
(Italy, circa 1860).
Initial *R*, copied from the fifteenth-century choir book of San Marco, Florence (Museo di San Marco, Graduale B, inv. 516, circa 3). The original illumination

was attributed to Fra Angelico in the nineteenth century; today, it is given to Zanobi Strozzi.
PROVENANCE: Made for Count Cottrell and passed by him to the Arundel Society; passed to the National Gallery, London, in 1889 or 1895, made a gift in 1899; passed as a loan to the Victoria and Albert Museum, London, in 1906, made a gift in 1996.
LITERATURE: Renzo Chiarelli, *I Codici Miniati del Museo di San Marco a Firenze* (Florence: Bonachi, 1968).
*London: The Victoria and Albert Museum, PDP, E.120-1996.*
(figure 55)

19. **Single leaf**
(Siena, Italy, circa 1863), by Ernesto Sprega.
Copy of a historiated initial *L*, Miracle of the Loaves and Fishes, by Liberale da Verona, in a fifteenth-century choir book from Siena cathedral.
PROVENANCE: Purchased by the Victoria and Albert Museum, London, from the Arundel Society in 1866.
*London: The Victoria and Albert Museum, PDP, 4594.*
(figure 58)

20. **Single leaf**
(Siena, Italy, circa 1863), by Ernesto Sprega.
Copy of a historiated initial *C*, with St. Lawrence and two angels, by Liberale da Verona, in a choir book (fifteenth century) from Siena cathedral.
PROVENANCE: Purchased by the Victoria and Albert Museum, London, from the Arundel Society in 1866.
*London: The Victoria and Albert Museum, PDP, 4596.*
(figure 57)

21. **Single leaf**
(Siena, Italy, circa 1863), by Ernesto Sprega.
Copy of a historiated initial *D*, Christ's Entry into Jerusalem, by Liberale da Verona in a choir book (fifteenth century) from Siena cathedral.
PROVENANCE: Bought by the Victoria and Albert Museum, London, from the Arundel Society in 1866.
*London: The Victoria and Albert Museum, PDP, 4595.*
(figure 59)

22. **Single leaf**
(London, early 1860s), by Henry Shaw.
Copy of a "carpet page" in the *Lindisfarne Gospels* (BL, MS Cotton Nero D.iv*).
PROVENANCE: Bought by the Victoria and Albert Museum, London, in 1866.
*London: The Victoria and Albert Museum, PDP, 5862.*
(figure 51)

23. **Single leaf**
(London, early 1860s), by Henry Shaw.
Historiated initial *B*, Tree of Jesse. Copy of a leaf from the *Howard Psalter* (fourteenth century), English manuscript (London: BL Arundel MS 83, folio 14).
PROVENANCE: Bought by the Victoria and Albert Museum, London, in 1866.
*London: The Victoria and Albert Museum, PDP, 5863.*
(figure 52)

24. **Single leaf and fragments**
(England, circa 1860), by Henry Shaw.
Copy of border frame and ornament from a manuscript illuminated by "Appolonius Bonfratelis di Capranica Capellae," dated 1564, belonging to Samuel Rogers, now in the British Library.
*London: The Victoria and Albert Museum, PDP, 5924 and 5926.*
(figure 53)

25. **Single leaves**
(France, nineteenth century).
Handmade copies of miniatures, Queen of Sheba before Solomon and Old Testament scene, from the *Grimani Breviary* (Venice, Biblioteca San Marco).
PROVENANCE: Collection of Ambroise Firmin-Didot, sale of his collection, Paris, June 1884, lot 77.
LITERATURE: André Jammes, ed., *Les Didot. Trois siècles de typographie et de bibliophile, 1698–1998* (Paris: Bibliothèque Historique de la Ville de Paris, 1998), no. 231; Paul Lacroix, *Moeurs et usages au moyen âge* (Paris: Firmin-Didot, 1877).
*France: private collection.*
(figure 75)

26. **Single leaf**
(Italy, late fifteenth century), by Francesco Bettini for Cardinal Domenico Della Rovere.
Historiated initial *S*, Presentation of Christ in the Temple, from the *Della Rovere Missal*, water damaged.
LITERATURE: Jonathan J. G. Alexander, *The Painted Page* (Munich: Prestel, 1994), 60–61, no. 6.
*New York: The Pierpont Morgan Library, M. 306, folio 78v.*
(figure 63)

27. **Single leaf**
(England, circa 1870), by Caleb William Wing (1801–75).
Historiated initial *S*, Presentation of Christ in the Temple. Copy from a leaf of the *Della Rovere Missal* (New York: Pierpont Morgan Library, M. 306, folio 78v) before it suffered water damage; signed by Francesco Bettini. Probably made when the manuscript was owned by John Boykett Jarman.
PROVENANCE: Bought by the Victoria and Albert Museum, London, at Sotheby's, March 11, 1899.
*London: The Victoria and Albert Museum, PDP, D.310-1899.*
(figure 64)

28. **Single leaves**
(England, before 1865), by Lord Charles Thynne.
Pages copied from tenth- and eleventh-century manuscripts owned by Reverend Walter Sneyd.
PROVENANCE: Bought by the Victoria and Albert Museum, London, in 1865.
*London: The Victoria and Albert Museum, PDP, 4391-1392, 4392-1392, 4393-1392, 4394-1392.*
(figure 104)

29. *Elementary Instruction in the Art of Illuminating and Missal Painting on Vellum, a Guide to Modern Illuminators* (London: Ackermann and Company, 1857), by David Laurent de Lara, "Illuminating Artist to the Queen."
Illumination manual, with illustrations printed in gold and colors and outlines for copying for the student.
*Evanston, Ill.: Northwestern University, The Charles Deering McCormick Library of Special Collections, 745 L382.*
*Ann Arbor: University of Michigan Graduate Library, ND 3310 .L38 1986.*
(figure 117)

30. **Single leaf**
(England, before 1866), by Caleb William Wing (1801–1875).
Historiated *D*, Christ calling Peter and Paul, copied from a north Italian choir book (1470s or 1480s).
PROVENANCE: Bought by the Victoria and Albert Museum, London, from Colnagi and Company, picture dealers, in 1866.
*London: The Victoria and Albert Museum, PDP, 4950.*
(figure 65)

31. **Photograph of boxed set of paints for illuminating**
(England, nineteenth century).
Paintbox from the London firm George Rowney & Co.
*Baltimore: The Walters Art Gallery, acc. no. 66.2.*
(figure 118)

32. *The Art of Illumination and Missal Painting: A Guide to Modern Illuminators. Illustrated by a Series of Specimens from Richly Illuminated MSS. of Various Periods, Accompanied by a Set of Outlines to Be Coloured by the Student According to the Theories Developed in the Work* (London: H. G. Bohn, 1849), by Henry Noel Humphreys.
*Chicago: The Newberry Library, Wing ZP 8452.50.*
(figures 94 and 95)

33. *Liber precationum quas Carolus Calvus imperator* (Ingolstadt: David Sartori, 1583).
Early woodcut facsimile of the prayerbook of Charles the Bald.
*Evanston, Ill.: Northwestern University, The Charles Deering McCormick Library of Special Collections, 242.802 C 4751.*
(figure 2)

34. *Les Monumens de la monarchie françoise qui comprenent l'histoire de France avec les figures de chaque règne que l'injure des tems à épargnées, vol. 3* (Paris: J. M. Gandouin, 1729–33), by Bernard de Montfaucon.
*Evanston, Ill.: Northwestern University, The Charles Deering McCormick Library of Special Collections, L944 M791.*
(figures 7 and 8)

35. *A Complete View of the Dress and Habits of the People of England, from the Establishment of the Saxons in Britain to the Present Time: Illustrated by Engravings Taken from the Most Authentic Remains of Antiquity; to Which Is Prefixed an Introduction, Containing a General Description of the Ancient Habits in Use among Mankind, from Their Earliest Period of Time to the Conclusion of the Seventh Century* (London: J. Nichols, 1796–99; reissued, London: H. G. Bohn, 1842), by Joseph Strutt.
*Evanston, Ill.: Northwestern University Library, The Charles Deering McCormick Library of Special Collections, L391 S927.*
(figures 11 and 13)

36. *Sports and Pastimes of the People of England. Including the Rural and Domestic Recreations, May Games, Mummeries, Shows, Processions, Pageants, and Pompous Spectacles, from the Earliest Period to the Present Time*, 2d ed. (London: Thomas Tegg, 1838), by Joseph Strutt.
*Evanston, Ill.: Northwestern University Library, 790 S927.*

37. *Bibliographical Decameron; or Ten Days of Pleasant Discourse upon Illuminated Manuscripts and Subjects Connected with Early Engraving, Typography and Bibliography* (London: W. Bulmer and Company, 1817), by Thomas Frognall Dibdin.
LITERATURE: Edward John O'Dwyer, *Thomas Frognall Dibdin: Bibliographer and Bibliomaniac Extraordinary, 1776–1847* (Pinner [Mddx.]: Private Libraries Association, 1967; Braswell-Means, 1992).
*Evanston, Ill.: Northwestern University, The Charles Deering McCormick Library of Special Collections, L090 D544.*
(figures 17 and 19)

38. *Illuminated Ornaments Selected from Manuscripts and Early Printed Books from the Sixth to the Seventeenth Centuries* (London: William Pickering, 1830–33), by Henry Shaw (1800–73).

LITERATURE: Sandra Hindman, "Facsimiles as Originals: An Unknown Illuminated Manuscript by Henry Shaw," *Journal of the Walters Art Gallery* 54 (1996), 225–32.
*Evanston, Ill.: Northwestern University, The Charles Deering McCormick Library of Special Collections, F745.67 M179i.*
(figure 56).

39. *Peintures et ornements des manuscrits, classés dans un ordre chronologique, pour servir à l'histoire des arts du dessin depuis le I'VE siècle de l'ère jusqu'à la fin du XVIe* (Paris: privately printed, 1837–46).
Published by Comte Auguste de Bastard d'Estang.
LITERATURE: Jocelyn Bouquillard, "Les Peintures et ornements des manuscrits du comte de Bastard. Histoire d'une entreprise de reproductions lithographiques d'enluminures sous la Monarchie de Juillet," *Bulletin du bibliophile*, no. 1 (1996), 108–50.
*Evanston, Ill.: Northwestern University, The Charles Deering McCormick Library of Special Collections, F745.67B 324P.*
(figure 67)

40. *Statuts de l'Ordre de Saint-Esprit au droit desir, ou du noeud institue à Naples en 1354 par Louis d'Anjou ... roi de Jerusalem, de Naples et de Sicile. Manuscrit du XIVme siècle conservé au Louvre dans le Musée des souverains français avec une Notice sur la peinture des miniatures et la description du manuscrit par M. le comte Horace de Viel-Castel* (Paris: Engelmann et Graf, 1853).
Chromolithographed facsimile.
*Evanston, Ill.: Northwestern University Library, F091 065.*
(figure 72)

41. *Livre d'heures complet (Heures nouvelles)* (Paris: Hetzel, 1837; Paris: Curmer, 1842).
Chromolithographed medievalizing prayerbook with illustrations by the painter Gérard-Séguin; ornaments by the architect Daniel Ramée; published by Hetzel; later reissued by Léon Curmer with engravings by Adrien Féart and others.
*London: The Victoria and Albert Museum, MSL 1986/154.*
(figure 78)

42. *Le Livre d'heures de la Reine Anne de Bretagne* (Paris: Curmer, 1861).
Chromolithographed facsimile of *Book of Hours of Anne of Brittany* (Paris: BnF MS Lat. 9474).
*Notre Dame: University of Notre Dame Library, the Medieval Institute, ND3363 A613.*
(figures 69–70)

43. **Album** (France, nineteenth century), by M. Hendschel, M. Gewundel, M. Lavril, and A. Racinet, Père.
Album of experiments in reproductive technology connected to the chromolithographed facsimile of Fouquet's *Hours of Etienne Chevalier* (Paris: Léon Curmer, 1864–66).
PROVENANCE: Firmin-Didot archives.
*France: private collection.*
(figures 69 and 70)

44. *Oeuvre de Jehan Fouqet. Heures de Maistre Estienne Chevalier. Texte restitué par M. l'abbé Delaunay, curé de St. Etienne du Mont* (Paris: Curmer, 1866).
Chromolithographed facsimile published by Léon Curmer.
*Chicago: The Newberry Library, Case *W 01 .F 815.*
(figure 71)

45. **Preparatory artwork** (London, circa 1861), by Owen Jones. Artwork for the chromolithographed edition of the *Victoria Psalter* (London: Day and Son, 1861).
*London: The Victoria and Albert Museum, MSL 1952/458.*
(figure 97)

46. *Victoria Psalter* (London, 1861), by Owen Jones. Chromolithographed medievalizing psalter with original embossed leather binding.
*Evanston, Ill.: Northwestern University, The Charles Deering McCormick Library of Special Collections, *L223.2E 1861.*
(figure 98)

47. *The Grammar of Ornament: Illustrated by Examples from Various Styles of Ornament* (London: Day and Son, 1856; reprint, London: B. Quaritch, 1868), by Owen Jones.
*Evanston, Ill.: Northwestern University, The Charles Deering McCormick Library of Special Collections, L740.9 J77.*
(figure 149)

48. **Illuminated notebook** (England, 1832), by Augustus Welby Northmore Pugin.
"The Shrine," illuminated page with a list of reliquaries.
LITERATURE: Alexandra Wedgwood, *A. W. N. Pugin and the Pugin Family, Catalogues of Architectural Drawings in the Victoria and Albert Museum* (London: Victoria and Albert Museum, 1985), 132–36, no. 109.
*London: The Victoria and Albert Museum, MSL 1969-5179.*
(figure 106)

49. **Illuminated notebook** (England, 1833), by Augustus Welby Northmore Pugin. "St. Margaret's Chapel," illuminated ornament based on Romanesque and fourteenth-century Italian examples.
LITERATURE: Alexandra Wedgewood, *A. W. N. Pugin and the Pugin Family, Catalogues of Architectural Drawings in the Victoria and Albert Museum* (London: Victoria and Albert Museum, 1985), 137–140, no. 119.
*London: The Victoria and Albert Museum, MSL 1969/5176.*
(figure 107)

50. **Single leaf** (Flanders, circa 1290).
Historiated initial O, Betrayal of Christ. From the *Beaupré-lez-Grammont Antiphoner.* Choir books from Beaupré were on the London art market in the 1860s, and John Ruskin owned and distributed many leaves. The Victoria and Albert leaves were said to have been rescued from the Strasbourg Library, which destroyed in 1870, by A. Pickert of Nuremberg.
PROVENANCE: Given by A. Pickert to the Victoria and Albert Museum, London, in 1872.
LITERATURE: A. Brounts, *Manuscrits datés conservés en Belgique*, vol. 1 (1968), 25, no. 23.
*London: The Victoria and Albert Museum, PDP, 7939.*
(figure 29)

51. **Single leaf** (Scotland, 1886–87), by Phoebe Traquaire.
*The Dream*, written and illuminated in Edinburgh (1886–87). John Ruskin praised this work in a letter to Traquaire.
*London: The Victoria and Albert Museum, MSL. 1936/1765.*
(figure 124)

52. **Manuscript** (England, 1871), by William Morris, translator, scribe, illuminator.
*The Story of Kormak.*
LITERATURE: Paul Needham ed., *William Morris and the Art of the Book* (New York: The Pierpont Morgan Library, 1976), no. 52.
*New York: The Pierpont Morgan Library, M. A. 1804.*
(figure 101)

53. **Manuscript** (England, 1870), by William Morris, Charles Fairfax Murray, George Wardle, and Edward Burne-Jones.
*A Book of Verse*, illuminated manuscript of twenty-five of Morris's poems presented to Giorgiana Burne-Jones (August 26, 1870). Illustration of "The Youths" by Burne-Jones; remaining illuminations by Fairfax Murray. Ornaments for the first ten pages by George Wardle; ornaments for pages 11 to 55 by Morris. Calligraphy by Morris.
LITERATURE: Parry, Linda, ed., *William Morris* (London: Philip Wilson, 1996), no. N. 5
*London: The Victoria and Albert Museum, MSL 1953/131.*
(figures 102 and 103)

54. **Manuscript** (Paris, 1844).
Financed by ladies of Legitimist sympathies made for the Comte de Chambord, the pretender to the throne of France, when he became head of the Bourbon family.
LITERATURE: Simon Jervis, *Art and Design in Europe and America, 1800–1900* (London: Herbert Press, 1987).
*London: The Victoria and Albert Museum, MSL 1984/68.*
(figure 79)

55. **Manuscript** (Paris, 1835–42).
*Gallois Hours*, made for Louis-Jules Gallois, Comte de Naives. Miniatures signed by Auguste Ledoux and Charles Leblanc; jeweled covers by François Mellerio; binding by Alphonse Simier, "relieur du roi."
LITERATURE: Marin Breslauer, *Catalogue 108*, no. 51; *National Art Collections Fund Review* (1987), 135; *Un age d'or des arts décoratifs, 1814–1848* (Paris: Réunion des Musées Nationaux, 1991), 464–65.
*London: The Victoria and Albert Museum, MSL 1987/7.*
(figure 80)

56. *Le Coloriste Enlumineur* (Paris, 1894).
Model for illuminating Joan of Arc, published by Desclée de Brouwer for the Société de Saint Augustin.
PROVENANCE: Purchased by the NAL, Victoria and Albert Museum, London, in 1894.
*London: The Victoria and Albert Museum, G29.AA.12.13.*
(figure 81)

57. **Manuscript** (England, nineteenth century), by Caleb William Wing.
Facsimile of the *Roman de la Rose* in the British Library (Harley MS 4425), illuminations by Caleb William Wing and calligraphy by Midolle; created for Delepierre.
*Chicago: The Newberry Library, Case MS Y 7675.R7184.*
(figure 66)

58. *Te Deum Laudamus* (London: Victoria Press, 1863), by Esther Faithful Fleet.
Printed by Emily Faithful at the Victoria Press, London; dedicated to Queen Victoria.

London: The Victoria and Albert Museum, MSL 1982/4235.
(figure 116)

59. Single leaf
(Ireland, 1877).
Illuminated address, presented to William Reed by the employees of Messers Edward Shaw and Company, Flax Spinning Mills (Celbridge, County Kildare, Ireland, 1877).
London: The Victoria and Albert Museum, MSL 1984/69/2.
(figure 122)

60. Single leaf
(Liverpool, England, 1900), by James Orr Marples.
Illuminated address recording the Liverpool Council's decision of September 5, 1900, to accept the gift of the late Hugh Frederick Hornby's art library; the address was presented to Mrs. Matilda Madden.
London: The Victoria and Albert Museum, MSL 1985/15.
(figure 123)

61. Manuscript in jeweled binding
(England, twentieth century).
Jeweled binding by Sangorski and Sutcliff, housing "Some Odes" by John Keats. Made for the Grolier Society, New York City. Colophon signed by Howell (circa 1910–20).
Philadelphia: Rare Book Department, The Free Library of Philadelphia, John Frederick Lewis Collection, additions.
(figure 100)

62. Single leaf
(France, nineteenth century), by the Spanish Forger.
Seated Ruler with Two Women and a Standing Saint.
LITERATURE: William M. Voelkle with Roger S. Wieck, The Spanish Forger (New York: Pierpont Morgan Library, 1978), L41.
New York: The Pierpont Morgan Library M. 786c.
(figure 85)

63. Manuscript
(France, fifteenth and nineteenth centuries).
Book of Hours (France, fifteenth century), illuminations added by Spanish Forger (late nineteenth century).
United States: private collection.
(figure 86)

64. Sciences et lettres au moyen âge et à l'époque de la renaissance
(Paris: Firmin-Didot, 1877), by Paul Lacroix.
Chromolithographic publication that provided the source for many of the Spanish Forger's miniatures.
Evanston, Ill.: Northwestern University Library, L709 L 147.
(figure 88)

65. Watercolor drawing
(France, nineteenth century), by Garcia.
Watercolor copy of full-page illumination from a fifteenth-century Burgundian manuscript, used as model for illustrations in publications by Paul Lacroix, published by Firmin-Didot, Paris.
Provenance: Firmin-Didot archives.
France: private collection.
(figure 89)

66. Sciences et lettres au moyen âge et à l'époque de la renaissance
(Paris: Firmin-Didot, 1877), by Paul Lacroix.
Chicago: University of Chicago, The Joseph Regenstein Library, CB 351.L14.
(figure 73)

67. Watercolor drawing
(France, nineteenth century), by H. Bichard.
Copy of illumination of Henri d'Albret, roi de Navarre, from a manuscript in the Bibliothèque de l'Arsenal (BN Bibliothèque de l'Arsenal, MS 5096, folio 1), used as a model for chromolithographed frontispiece of Paul Lacroix, Sciences et lettres au moyen âge et à l'époque de la Renaissance (Paris: Firmin-Didot, 1877).
Provenance: Firmin-Didot archives.
France: private collection.
(figure 74)

68. Single leaf
(France, nineteenth century), by a Forger.
Miniatures, Life of Saint Louis in Eight Scenes.
LITERATURE: William M. Voelkle with Roger S. Wieck, The Spanish Forger (New York: The Pierpont Morgan Library, 1978), OL11.
New York: The Pierpont Morgan Library, M. 786b.
(figure 91)

69. Manuscript
(France, fifteenth and nineteenth centuries).
Book of Hours, use of Coutances; an unfinished manuscript with six miniatures and twelve calendar illustrations added by a nineteenth-century forger.
LITERATURE: William M. Voelkle with Roger S. Wieck, The Spanish Forger (New York: The Pierpont Morgan Library, 1978), 12–13, OM2.
New York: The Pierpont Morgan Library, M. 54.
(figures 84 and 90)

70. Three autoradiographs and a transparency of a single leaf
(United States, twentieth century).
Technical analysis of a single leaf (folio 86) from M. 54 of New York's Pierpont Morgan Library demonstrates that the makeup of the green pigment in the miniature includes a compound only present in commercially made pigments after 1814.
LITERATURE: William M. Voelkle with Roger S. Wieck, The Spanish Forger (New York: The Pierpont Morgan Library, 1978), 12–13, OM2.
New York: The Pierpont Morgan Library.
(figure 83)

71. Single leaf
(Augsburg, Germany, 1494–95, and England [?] nineteenth century), by George Beck.
Full-page miniature, Saints Ulrich and Afra, removed from a psalter (Augsburg, Staatsbibliothek, Cod. in-folio 49a) in the nineteenth century and overpainted to suit contemporary taste.
PROVENANCE: Collection of Crawford, sold 1891; bought by the Victoria and Albert Museum, London, from Quaritch, 1892.
London: The Victoria and Albert Museum, PDP, D.86-1892.
(figure 82)

72. Manuscript
(France, circa 1200).
Miniatures, the Life of Christ (Vie de Jesus Christ).
PROVENANCE: Owned and reproduced by Bastard d'Estang in Peintures et ornements des manuscrits (Paris, 1837–46); collection of Ambroise Firmin-Didot, sale of his library, Paris, May 26–31, 1879, lot 10.
New York: The Pierpont Morgan Library, M. 44.
(figure 68)

73. Manuscript and fragments
(England, fifteenth century).
Illuminated version of John Gower's

Confessio Amantis, which originally featured 198 miniatures. In the late eighteenth century Thomas Worth cut out nine miniatures and sold them to Sir John Fenn. The Pierpont Morgan Library eventually purchased the mutilated manuscript and acquired the extracted miniatures.
PROVENANCE: Collection of Peter le Neve (1661–1729); collection of Thomas Martin of Palgrave (1697–1771); collection of Thomas Worth; collection of Brigg Price Fountain of Narford; acquired by Quaritch in 1902.
New York: The Pierpont Morgan Library, M. 126.
(figure 28)

74. Illuminated manuscript
(Belgium, 1914–15), by the nuns of the Abbey of Maredret, Belgium.
Nuptial Mass in French and Latin with large and marginal illuminations in the fourteenth-century style was created in the opening years of World War I. Marginalia include images of ships with American flags and knights defending Belgium from zeppelins.
LITERATURE: Dorothy E. Miner, Anastaise and Her Sisters: Women Artists of the Middle Ages (Baltimore: Walters Art Gallery, 1974), figure 7.
New York: The Pierpont Morgan Library, M. 658.
(figures 125 and 126)

75. Extra-illustrated book
(England, late nineteenth century).
Volume of William Blades, The Enemies of Books (London: Trübner, 1888), interleaved with manuscript and printed fragments and initials.
PROVENANCE: Collection of John Frederick Lewis.
Philadelphia: Rare Book Department, The Free Library of Philadelphia, John Frederick Lewis Collection, AL025.8B562.
(figures 133 and 134)

76. Single leaf
(Constantinople, twelfth century).
Illumination, standing figure of Moses, from a lectionary.
PROVENANCE: Collection of John Frederick Lewis.
LITERATURE: Harold R. Willoughby, "Stray New Testament-Psalter Leaves Identified," Journal of Biblical Literature 16, no. 1 (March 1942), 57–60; and Harold R. Willoughby, "Vagrant Folios from Family 2400 in the Free Library of Philadelphia," Byzantion 15 (1940–41), 126–32.
Philadelphia: Rare Book Department, The Free Library of Philadelphia, John Frederick Lewis Leaves M 44:28.
(figure 132)

77. Single leaf
(France, nineteenth century), by the Spanish Forger.
Historiated initial G, with a female saint, an attendant, and a reliquary in a boat.
PROVENANCE: Collection of John Frederick Lewis.
LITERATURE: William M. Voelkle and Roger S. Wieck, The Spanish Forger (New York: The Pierpont Morgan Library, 1978), L61.
Philadelphia: Rare Book Department, The Free Library of Philadelphia, John Frederick Lewis Leaves M 49:11.
(figure 120)

78. Single leaf
(Flanders, circa 1522–23), by Simon Bening.
Illumination, St. Gertrude of Nivelles, excised from the Hours of Albrecht of Brandenburg. Sister leaves in the Robert Lehman Collection of the Metropolitan Museum of Art and elsewhere.

LITERATURE: Sandra Hindman et al., *The Robert Lehman Collection*, vol. 4, *Illuminations* (New York: Metropolitan Museum of Art, 1997), no. 13.
*Pittsburgh: The Carnegie Museum of Art, bequest of Howard A. Noble, 1964, 64.11.6.*
(figure 137)

79. Single leaf
(United States, circa 1924–34), by Olive Francis Rhinelander.
"In principio erat verbum," copy of Carolingian script in Lindau Gospels (New York: The Pierpont Morgan Library, M. 1, folio 168).
*New York: The Pierpont Morgan Library, M.688 a 2.*
(figure 144)

80. Manuscript
(England, circa 1858), by Caleb William Wing (1801–75).
Seventeen illuminations copied from fifteenth-century Books of Hours from Bruges and Italy, painted for John Boykett Jarman, and acquired by Coella Lindsay Ricketts, who inscribed the work with the colophon "a superb specimen of the art of illuminating of the present day."
PROVENANCE: Collection of John Boykett Jarman; collection of C. L. Ricketts.
*Bloomington, Ind.: The Lilly Library, MS 140.*
(figure 154)

81. Montage of fragments
(France, Italy, Flanders, fourteenth century; assembled nineteenth century).
Historiated initials *D* and *O,* with a priest and a bishop (France, fourteenth century); bishops consecrating an ecclesiastic (Italy, fourteenth century); and a hunt scene (French Flanders, fourteenth century). Collage perhaps assembled by C. L. Ricketts.
*Bloomington, Ind.: The Lilly Library, Ricketts MSS I D18-21.*
(figure 148)

82. Single leaf
(United States, twentieth century), by Coella Lindsay Ricketts and his Scriptorium.
Illumination copying the *Book of Kells.*
*Bloomington, Ind.: The Lilly Library, Ricketts MSS III, "The Book."*
(figure 155)

83. Manuscript
(Chicago, 1893), by Coella Lindsay Ricketts.
Presented to Anton Hesing on his seventieth birthday, 1893. Commissioned by the directors of the German Opera House Company.
*Chicago: The Newberry Library, Wing MS fZW883.R42.*
(figures 157 and 158)

84. Calligraphy model book
(Prague or Vienna, 1598), by Bartholomaeus Horn, master at the court of Emperor Rudolf II.
PROVENANCE: Collection of C. L. Ricketts.
*Chicago: The Newberry Library, Wing MS ZW547.H782.*
(figure 150)

85. Single leaf
(Tours, France, circa 1480–90).
Adoration of the Christ Child.
PROVENANCE: Collection of Mortimer Brandt.
*Wheaton, Ill.: The Billy Graham Center Museum, 1290-2.*
(figure 143)

86. Single leaf
(France, circa 1290).
From the *Beauvais Missal.* Other leaves from this manuscript are included in Otto F. Ege, *Fifty Original Leaves from Medieval Manuscripts* (mid-1940s), no. 10.
PROVENANCE: Owned and broken by Otto F. Ege.
*Oberlin, Ohio: The Allen Memorial Art Museum, Richard Lee Ripin and R.T. Miller, Jr. Fund, 1993, 93.16.*
(figure 142)

87. Original leaves from famous Bibles (nine centuries, a.d. 1121–1935), collected and assembled by Otto F. Ege
(Cleveland, 1940s).
Portfolio box with leaves annotated by Otto F. Ege: no. 2, "Twelfth-Century Manuscript Bible (circa 1150, France)"; no. 4, "Leaf from a Paris Bible (circa 1310, France)"; table of contents. Mounted leaves from dismembered manuscripts with printed commentary.
*Cleveland, Ohio: Ingalls Library, The Cleveland Museum of Art Library, Gift of Frank H. Teagle Jr., Rare H81/E29A.*
(figure 141)

88. *Les Très Riches Heures* du duc de Berry
(Lucerne: Faksimilé-Verlag Luzern, 1984).
Deluxe modern facsimile of *Très Riches Heures* of Jean, duc de Berry, the fifteenth-century French manuscript housed at Musée Condé, Chantilly (MS 65).
*Ithaca, N.Y.: Cornell University Library, Rare Books ND 3363.B53 T 779++ 1984 comm.*
(figure 4)

89. Magazine reproduction
(United States, January 5, 1948).
*Life* magazine, February calendar page from *Très Riches Heures* of Jean, duc de Berry (folio 2v), with genitalia of peasants effaced.
*Evanston, Ill.: Northwestern University, The Charles Deering McCormick Library of Special Collections, F051 L722.*
(figure 3)

90. Computer with CD-ROMs of illuminated manuscripts
(United States, twenty-first century).
Interactive installation allowing museum visitors to turn manuscript pages electronically.
*Evanston, Ill.: The Mary and Leigh Block Museum of Art.*

# BIBLIOGRAPHY

## Manuscript Sources

Chicago: Newberry Library, Wing Modern Manuscripts. "Coella Lindsay Ricketts Collecting Papers."

London: British Library. MS Add. 15501. Abbé Rive, Essai sur l'art de verifier l'age des miniatures peintes dans les manuscrits depuis le XIVe jusqu'au XVIIe siècle inclusivement. Prospectus d'un ouvrage. Plates, with Rive's notes. 1782.

London: British Library. MS Add. 18850. Abbé Rive.

Oslo and London: Martin Schoyen Collection, no. 1275. Pierre-Camille Le Moine, "Essai sur état des sciences et des arts en Lorraine depuis le premier duc hereditaire jusqu'au règne de Charle III, prouvé par les monuments." September 1761.

Paris: Bibliothèque de l'Arsenal. MSS 4277–4353, Moreau 1511–23, 13 vols. in-folio (first version), and supplement 4354–7077, 17 vols. in-quarto (second version). Jean Baptiste de La Curne de Sainte-Palaye, "Dictionnaire des antiquités françoises."

Paris: Bibliothèque de l'Arsenal. Moreau 1654–61, 8 vols. in-folio (first version), Moreau 1662–76, 15 vols. in-quarto (second version). Jean Baptiste de La Curne de Sainte-Palaye, "Notices de divers manuscrits de France et d'Italie."

Paris: Bibliothèque de l'Arsenal. MS 6392. Correspondance de l'abbe Rive avec le libraire aixois Joseph David.

Paris: Bibliothèque Nationale. MSS lat. 11866, 11902, 12089, 12301, 12777–80, 13067, 13119, 13120, 14187; fr. 17693–700, 19649–59. Jean Mabillon, "Letters and Papers."

## Sale Catalogues

1759. Catalogue des Livres de la Bibliothèque de feu M.J.B. Denis Guyon, chev. seigneur de Sardière, ancien capitaine au Regiment du Roi, l'un des seigneurs du canal de Briare. Paris: Barrois.

1767. Catalogue des Livres provenans de la Bibliothèque de M.L.D.D.L.V. [M. Le duc de la Vallière]. Paris: Guillaume de Bure, le jeune.

1769. Supplément à la bibliographie instructive ou Catalogue des livres du cabinet de feu M. Louis Jean Gaignat. Paris: Guillaume de Bure.

1772. Catalogue des Livres de M*** [De la Vallière], 1773. Paris: Guillaume de Bure.

1783. Jean-Joseph Rive. Catalogue des livres de la Bibliothèque de feu M. le duc de la Vallière. Premiere partie. Paris: Guillaume de Bure, fils aîné.

1789. Catalogue des livres imprimés et manuscrits de la Bibliothèque de feu monseigneur le Prince de Soubise, Marechal de France. Paris: Leclerc.

1804. Select and Valuable Collections of Italian, French and Flemish Pictures the Genuine Property of a Collector of Refined Taste . . . Celebrated Masters of the Great Italian Schools and a Few Unique Specimens of Early Florentine. London: Christie's, May 12.

1814. Bibliotheca Towneleiana: A Catalogue of the Curious and Extensive Library of the Late John Townley, Esq. Pt. 1. London: Evans, June 8–15.

1815. Valuable Library of James Edwards. London: Evans, April 5–10.

1816. Library of William Roscoe. Liverpool: Winstanley, August 19–September 3.

1821. Catalogue of a Singularly Rare Collection of Manuscripts on Paper and Vellum in the Oriental, Hebrew, Latin and Italian Languages, together with Numerous Superbly Illuminated Missals ... Brought to This Country by the Abbé Celotti. Saibanti and Cononici Manuscripts. London: Sotheby's, February 26.

1824. Catalogue of the Principle Part of Italian, French, Flemish, Dutch and English Pictures and Also the Very Celebrated Antique Marble Bas-Relief . . . the Property of Sir G. Osborne Page Turner. London: Christie's, June 7–8.

1824. Catalogue of the Splendid, Curious and Extensive Library of the Late Sir Mark Masterman Sykes. London: Evans, May 11–22, May 28–June 3, June 21–29.

1825. Bibliotheca Splendidissima Rendorpiana. The Entire, Very Elegant and Valuable Library of the Late Learned John Rendorp, Esq. London: Sotheby's, February 28–March 7.

1825. Catalogue of the Valuable and More Select Part of the Italian, French, Flemish and Dutch Pictures, a Few Drawings by Old Masters, Books on Art and Books of Prints . . . of Mr. Urbino Pizzetta. London: Christie's, April 15–16.

1825. William Young Ottley. A Catalogue of a Highly Valuable and Extremely Curious Collection of Illumined Miniature Paintings, of the Greatest Beauty, and of Exquisite Finishing, Taken from the Choral Books of the Papal Chapel in the Vatican, during the French Revolution: And Subsequently Collected and Brought to This Country by the Abate Celotti. London: Christie's, May 26.

1825. Lord Berwick's Pictures. A Catalogue of the Genuine and Valuable Collection of Paintings by the Most Distinguished Masters of the Italian, Dutch and Flemish Schools, the Property of the Rt. Hon. Lord Berwick. And Also the Collection of . . . a Foreign Nobleman. London: Phillips, June 7.

1825. Lucca Library. A Catalogue of the Very Celebrated Library of Don Tomaso de Lucca de Cadore. London: Sotheby's, July 18–26.

1826. Catalogue of a Singularly Curious and Valuable Selection from the Library of a Gentleman. London, June 9–17.

1827. Catalogue of the Splendid and Valuable Library of the Rev. Theodore Williams. London: Stewart, Wheatley and Adlard, April 5–11, April 23–May 2.

1830. Catalogue of the Very Choice Library of William Simonds Higgs, Esq. London: Sotheby's, April 26–28.

1831. Catalogue of a Valuable and Singularly Rare Collection of Books, the Property of a Nobleman. London: Sotheby's, August 12–13.

1838. Catalogue of the Very Beautiful Collection of Highly Finished and Illuminated Miniature Paintings, the Property of the Late William Young Ottley, Esq. London: Sotheby's, May 11–12.

1856. Catalogue de livres rares et précieux, manuscits et imprimés, composant la Bibliothèque de M. C. R. *** de Milan. Paris: L. Potier.

1856. Catalogue of the Very Celebrated Collection of Works of Art, the Property of Samuel Rogers, Esq., Deceased; Comprising Ancient and Modern Pictures; Drawings and Engravings; Egyptian, Greek and Roman Antiquities; Greek Vases; Marbles, Bronzes, and Terra-Cottas, and Coins; also, the Extensive Library; Copies of Rogers's Poems, Illustrated; the Small Service of Plate and Wine. London: Christie and Manson, April 28.

1866. A Catalogue of Illuminated Drawings by Henry Shaw, F.S.A., Author of "Illuminated Ornaments." London: Christie, Manson and Woods, June 6.

1879. Catalogue des Livres rares et précieux . . . faisant partie de la Bibliothèque de M. Ambroise Firmin-Didot. Paris: M. Delestre and A. Labitte, May 26–31.

1884. Catalogue des livres rares et précieux . . . faisant partie de la Bibliothèque de M. Ambroise

1893. Catalogue des objects d'art et de haute curiosite antiques, du moyen-age & de la renaissance, composant l'importante et precieuse Collection Spitzer, dont la vente publique aura lieu a Paris. 2 vols. Paris: Menard et Cie, April 17–June 16.

1893. Resume du catalogue des objets d'art et de haute curiosite antiques, du Moyen Age et de la Renaissance, composant l'importante et precieuse Collection Spitzer, dont la vente publique aura lieu a Paris, 16 juin 1893. Paris: E. Menard et Cie, June 16.

1911–12. Catalogue of the Library of Robert Hoe of New York. Illuminated Manuscripts, Incunabula, Historical Bindings, Early English Literature, Rare Americana, French Illustrated Books, Eighteenth-Century English Authors, Autographs, Manuscripts, Etc. New York: Anderson Auction Company.

1913. Edouard Rahir. La Vente Robert Hoe. Paris: Librairie Henri Leclerc.

1922. The Notable Collection of Miss Susan Minns of Boston, Mass. Books, Bookplates, Coins, Curios, Prints, Illuminated Manuscripts and Horae Illustrative of the "Dance of Death." New York: American Art Galleries, May 2–3.

1964. Catalogue of the Beautiful Collection of Illuminated Missals and Books of Hours . . . Formed by the Late John Boykett Jarman. London: Sotheby's, June 13.

1981. Illuminated Miniatures and Single Leaves from the Ninth to the Sixteenth Century. London: Sotheby's, July 14.

1983. Catalogue of Single Leaves and Miniatures from Western Illuminated Manuscripts. London: Sotheby's, April 25.

1984. Paintings and Works of Art from the Collections of the late Lord Clark of Saltwood O. M., C. H., K. C. B. London: Sotheby's, July 3.

## Secondary Sources

Achard, Claude Francois. Chronique Litteraire des ouvrages imprimes et manuscrits de l'Abbe Rive, des secours dans les lettres, que cet abbe a fournis a tant de litterateurs francois ou etrangers. Aix: Eleutheropolis, Imprimerie des Anti-Copet, des Anti-Jean-de Dieu, des Anti-Pascalis, 1790.

Ackerman, Robert W., and Gretchen P. Ackerman. Sir ric Madden: A Biographical Sketch and Bibliography. New York: Garland, 1979.

Adam, William. The Gem of the Peak, or Matlock Bath and Its Vicinity. London: Longman, 1843.

Aho, Gary L. William Morris, a Reference Guide. Boston: G. K. Hall, 1985.

Albaric, Michel, ed. Histoire du Missel français. Turnhout: Brepols, 1986.

Alcouffe, Daniel. Un Age d'or des arts décoratifs, 1814–1848. Paris: Réunion des Musées Nationaux, 1991.

Alexander, Jonathan J. G. "Facsimiles, Copies, and Variations: The Relationship to the Model in Medieval and Renaissance European Illuminated Manuscripts." In Retaining the Original: Multiple Originals, Copies, and Reproduc-

*tions,* edited by K. Preciado, 61–72. Washington, D.C.: National Gallery of Art, 1989.

———. *Wallace Collection. Catalogue of Illuminated Manuscript Cuttings.* London: Wallace Collection, 1980.

Alexander, Jonathan J. G., ed. *The Painted Page: Italian Renaissance Book Illumination 1450–1550.* London: Royal Academy of Arts; Munich: Prestel, 1994.

Amalvi, Christian. "Le défaite, 'mode d'emploi': recherches sur l'utilisation rétrospective du passé dans les rapports franco-allemands en France entre 1870 et 1914." In *La Guerre de 1870/71 et ses conséquences,* edited by Philippe Levillain and Rainer Riemenschneider, 451–64. Bonn: Bouvier Verlag, 1990.

———. *Le Goût du moyen âge.* Paris: Plon, 1996.

———. "Le Révolution au village: jalons pour l'étude de la postérité révolutionnaire dans la France contemporaine, 1871–1914." *History of European Ideas* 13, no.5 (1991): 545–70.

Anson, Peter rick. *The Call of the Cloister: Religious Communities and Kindred Bodies in the Anglican Communion.* London: SPCK, 1955. Rev. ed. London: A. W. Campbell, 1964.

Anstruther, Ian. *The Knight and the Umbrella.* London: Geoffrey Bles, 1963.

*The Antiquarian Repertory, a Miscellaneous Assemblage of Topography, History, Biography, Customs, and Manners: Intended to Illustrate and Preserve Several Valuable Remains of Old Times, with a Great Many Valuable Additions.* London: printed and published for E. Jeffery, 1807.

Ariès, Philippe. *Le temps de l'histoire.* 2d ed. Paris: Editions du Seuil, 1986.

Aris, Rutherford. "Jean Mabillon (1632–1707)." In *Medieval Scholarship: Biographical Studies on the Formation of a Discipline.* Vol. 1, *History,* edited by Helen Damico and Joseph B. Zavadil, 15–32. New York: Garland Press, 1995.

Armstrong, Carol. *Scenes in a Library: Reading the Photograph in the Book, 1843–1875.* Cambridge, Mass.: MIT Press, 1998.

Arnheim, David, et al. *Italian Primitives: The Case History of a Collection and its Conservation.* New Haven, Conn.: Yale University Art Gallery, 1972.

Arsenne, Louis-Charles. *Manuel du peintre et du sculpteur.* 2 vols. Paris: Roret, 1833.

*The Art of Drawing and Painting in Watercolours. Whereby a Stranger to Those Arts May Be Immediately Render'd Capable of Delineating Any View or Prospect with the Utmost Exactness . . . With Instructions for Making Transparent Colours of Every Sort; Partly from Some Curious Personages in Holland, France, and Italy; but Chiefly from a Manuscript of the Great Mr. Boyle.* London: printed for J. Peele, 1731.

Arundel Society. *An Alphabet: Capital Letters Selected from the Illuminations of Italian Choral Books of the Fifteenth and Sixteenth Centuries. Engraved in Outline with One Letter Printed in Colours.* London: Arundel Society, 1862.

Astle, Thomas. *The Origins and progress of writing, as well as hieroglyphic as elementary, illustrated by engravings taken from marbles, manuscripts and charters.* London: printed for the author, sold by T. Payne, 1784.

*The Astor Collection of Illuminated Manuscripts.* London: Sotheby's, June 21, 1988.

Atkinson, A. "Further Notes on the Young and Ottley Families." *Notes and Queries* 175 (November 5, 1938): 326–30.

———. "Further Notes on the Young and Ottley Families." *Notes and Queries* 175 (November 12, 1938): 344–47.

———. "William Young Ottley, Artist and Collector." *Notes and Queries* 174 (April 2, 1938): 236–39.

Atterbury, Paul, ed. *A. W. N. Pugin, Master of Gothic Revival.* New Haven, Conn.: Yale University Press for the Bard Graduate Center for Studies in the Decorative Arts, New York, 1995.

Atterbury, Paul, and Clive Wainwright, eds. *Pugin: A Gothic Passion.* New Haven, Conn.: Yale University Press in association with the Victoria and Albert Museum, 1994.

Audsley, George Ashdown. *The Art of Chromolithography, Popularly Explained and Illustrated by Fourty-Four Plates Showing Separate Impressions of all the Stones Employed and All the Progressive Printings in Combination from the First Colour to the Finished Picture.* London: SLW, Marston, Searle and Rivington, 1883.

Auerbach, Jeffrey. *The Great Exhibition of 1851: A Nation on Display.* New Haven, Conn.: Yale University Press, 1999.

Avril, François, and Nicole Reynaud. *Les manuscrits à peintures en France: 1440–1520.* Paris: Flammarion, Bibliothèque Nationale, 1993.

Ayscough, Samuel. *A Catalogue of the Manuscripts Preserved in the British Museum Including the Collections of Sir Hans Sloane, the Rev. Thomas Birch, and about Five Hundred Volumes Bequeathed, Presented, or Purchased at Various Times.* London: printed for the compiler by John Rivington, 1782.

J. Backhouse "The Sale of the Luttrell Psalter," in *Antiquaries, Book Collectors and the Circles of Learning,* ed. Robin Meyers and Michael Harris (Winchester: St. Paul's Bibliographies, 1996), 113–28.

Backhouse, Janet. "A Miniature Masterpiece by the 'Spanish Forger.'" *Quarto: Abbot Hall Art Gallery Quarterly Bulletin* (January 1975): 8–15.

———. "The Sale of the Luttrell Psalter." In *Antiquaries, Book Collectors and the Circles of Learning,* edited by Robin Meyers and Michael Harris, 113–28. Winchester: St. Paul's Bibliographies, 1996.

"The Sale of the Luttrell Psalter," in *Antiquaries, Book Collectors and the Circles of Learning,* ed. Robin Meyers and Michael Harris (Winchester: St. Paul's Bibliographies, 1996), 113–28.

———. "The 'Spanish Forger.'" *British Museum Quarterly* 33, nos. 1–2 (1968): 65–71.

———. "Two Books of Hours of Francis I." *British Museum Quarterly* 31, nos. 3–4 (1967): 90–96.

———. "A Victorian Connoisseur and His Manuscripts: The Tale of Mr. Jarman and Mr. Wing." *British Library Quarterly* 32 (1968): 76–92.

Baker, Malcolm, and Brenda Richardson, eds. *A Grand Design: The Art of the Victoria and Albert Museum.* London: Victoria and Albert Publications with the Baltimore Museum of Art, 1997.

Banham, Joanna, and Jennifer Harris, eds. *William Morris and the Middle Ages: A Collection of Essays together with a Catalogue of Works Exhibited at the Whitworth Art Gallery.* Manchester: Manchester University Press, 1984.

Barbet de Jouy, Henry. *Musée impériale du Louvre. Notice des antiquités . . . composant le Musée des Souverains.* Paris: Charles de Mourgues, 1868.

———. *Notice des antiquités, objets du moyen âge, de la renaissance et des temps modernes composant le Musée des Souverains.* Paris: Charles de Mourgues Freres, 1866.

Barclay, David. "Medievalism and Nationalism in Nineteenth-Century Germany." In *Medievalism in Europe,* edited by Leslie J. Workman, 5–22. Cambridge: D. S. Brewer, 1993.

Barker, Nicolas. *The Publications of the Roxburghe Club, 1814–1962: An Essay with Bibliographical Table.* Cambridge: Roxburghe Club, 1964.

———. *Treasures of the British Library.* New York: Abrams, 1988.

Bastard d'Estang, Jean-François-Auguste."Exposé sommaire de la publication." In *Etudes de symbolique chrétien. Bulletin du Comité de la langue, de l'histoire et des arts de la France* 4 (1857): 902.

———. "Exposé sommaire de la publication." *Etudes de symbolique chrétien. Bulletin du Comité de la langue, de l'histoire et des arts de la France* 4 (1857): 902.

———. *Histoire de Jésus-Christ en figures, gouaches du XIIe siècle conservées jadis à la collégiale de Saint-Martial de Limoges.* Paris, 1878.

———. *Peintures et ornements des manuscrits, classés dans un ordre chronologique, pour servir à l'histoire des arts du dessin depuis le IVe siècle de l'ère jusqu'à la fin du XVIe.* Paris: privately printed, 1837–46.

Batchen, Geoffroy. "The Naming of Photography: 'A Mass of Metaphor.'" *History of Photography* 17 (spring 1993): 22–32.

Bates, David. "Léopold Delisle (1826–1910)." In *Medieval Scholarship: Biographical Studies on the Formation of a Discipline.* Vol. 1, *History,* edited by Helen Damico and Joseph B. Zavadil, 101–13. New York: Garland Press, 1995.

Becattini, Massimo. "La 'Lumiere mysterieue.' Classicismo e Goticismo nel collectioniimo dei 'gessi': il John Soane's Museum di Londra." In *Il Medioevo nel calchi della Gipsoteca.* Florence: Cassa di risparmio, L'Instituto, 1993.

Becker, Jean-Jacques, and Stéphane Audoin-Rouzeau. *La France, la nation, la guerre, 1850–1920.* Paris: SEDES, 1995.

Beckford, William. *Life at Fonthill, 1807–1822, with Interludes in Paris and London, from the Correspondence of William Beckford.* Translated and edited by Boyd Alexander. London: R. Hart-Davis, 1957.

Beckwith, Alice H. R. H. *Victorian Bibliomania: The Illuminated Book in Nineteenth-Century Britain.* Providence: Museum of Art, Rhode Island School of Design, 1987.

Beckford, William. *Life at Fonthill, 1807–1822.* Translated and edited by Boyd Alexander. London: R. Hart-Davis, 1957.

Beevers, David, ed. *Brighton Revealed through Artists' Eyes, circa 1760–circa 1960.* Brighton: Royal Pavilion, Art Gallery and Museums, 1995.

Belcher, Margaret. *A. W. N. Pugin: An Annotated Critical Bibliography.* London: Mansell Publishing Ltd., 1987.

Bénézit, Emmanuel. *Dictionnaire critique et documentaire des peintures, sculpteurs, dessinateurs et graveurs.* Rev. ed. Paris: Gründ, 1999.

Benjamin, Walter. "Walter Benjamin's Short History of Photography." *Artforum* 15 (February 1977): 46–51.

Benson, Robert. *The Holford Collection: Dorchester House.* 2 vols. Oxford: University Press, 1927.

———. *The Holford Collection: Westonbirt.* 2 vols. Oxford: University Press, 1924.

Bentley, James. *Ritualism and Politics in Victorian Britain.* Oxford and New York: University Press, 1978.

"Bibliothèque de l'Arsenal: 1–3, Rue de Sully." In *Guide du Lecteur a la Bibliothèque Nationale, a la Mazarine et a l'Arsenal,* 38–42. Paris: A. Morance, 1930.

Bibliothèque de l'Arsenal. *Les Grands Bibliophiles De L'Arsenal et Leurs Collections. Exposition organisée a l'occasion du IIeme congres international des societes de bibliophiles le vendredi 2 septembre 1961.* Paris: Bibliothèque de l'Arsenal, 1961.

Bibliothèque Municipale. *L'Art du livre de la restauration au Second Empire, 1815–1852.* Bordeaux: Bibliothèque Municipale, 1938.

Bibliothèque Nationale. *1789. Le patrimoine libéré.* Paris: Bibliothèque Nationale, 1989.

———. *Trésors de la Bibliothèque de l'Arsenal.* Paris: Bibliothèque Nationale, 1980.

Bibliothèque Sainte-Geneviève. *Le Cabinet de curiosités de la Bibliothèque Sainte-Geneviève: des origines à nos jours.* Paris: La Bibliothèque, 1989.

Biddick, Kathleen. *The Shock of Medievalism.* Durham, N.C.: Duke University Press, 1998.

Bierstadt, Oscar Albert. *The Library of Robert Hoe: A Contribution to the History of Bibliophilism in America.* New York: Duprat, 1895.

Blades, William. *The Enemies of Books.* London: Trübner, 1888.

Blanc, Charles. *Grammaire des arts du dessin.* Paris: J. Renouard, 1867.

———. *Le trésor de la curiosité tiré des catalogues de vente.* Paris: Jules Renouard, 1858.

Blanchard, Gérard. "Curmer, ou la leçon d'un grand éditeur romantique." *Courrier graphique* 117 (1962): 42–51.

Bloch, R. Howard, and Stephen G. Nichols, eds. *Medievalism and the Modernist Temper.* Baltimore: Johns Hopkins University Press, 1996.

Blumer, M. L. "La Commision pour la recherche des objets de sciences et arts en Italie, 1796–1797," *Révolution française* (1934): 62–88, 124–50, 222–59.

Board of Trade, Department of Science and Art. *A Catalogue of the Museum of Ornamental Art at Marlborough House.* HMSO, 1854.

Bober, Harry. *The Mortimer Brandt Collection of Medieval Manuscript Illuminations.* Hatfield Herts: Stellar Press, 1966.

Boehm, B. D. "Necrology: Harry Bober (1915–1988)," *Gesta* 28, no. 1 (1989): 103–5.

Bolton, Richard, ed. *The Contest of Meaning: Critical Histories of Photography.* Cambridge, Mass.: MIT Press, 1989.

Bonnaffe, Edmond. *Le musee Spitzer.* Paris: Imprimerie de l'Art, 1890.

Bonnel, Roland. "Medieval Nostalgia in France, 1750–1789: The Gothic Imaginary at the End of the Old Regime." In *Medievalism in Europe,* edited by Leslie J. Workman, 139–63. Cambridge: D. S. Brewer, 1993.

Borenius, Tancred. "The Rediscovery of the Primitives." *Quarterly Review* 475 (April 1923): 258–70.

Boris, Eileen. *Art and Labor: Ruskin, Morris and the Craftsman Ideal in America.* Philadelphia: Temple University Press, 1986.

Bouchot, Henri. *L'Art dans la décoration du diplôme: Recueil de 104 documents modernes.* Paris: Henri Laurens, 1901.

———. *Les primitifs français. Complément documentaire au catalogue officiel de l'exposition.* Paris: Librairie de l'Art Ancien et Moderne, 1904.

Bouchot, Henri, et al., eds. *Exposition des primitifs français au palais du Louvre et à la Bibliothèque Nationale.* Paris: Palais du Louvre et Bibliothèque Nationale, 1904.

Bouniol, Bathild. *L'Art Chrétien et l'école allemande, avec une notice sur M. Overbeck.* Paris: Ambroise Bray & Schulgen et Schwan, 1856.

Bouquillard, Jocelyn. "Le comte Auguste de Bastard (1792–1883): archéologue et imprimeur lithographe." Ph.D. dissertation, Ecole des chartes, 1995.

———. "Les Peintures et ornements des manuscrits du comte de Bastard. Histoire d'une entreprise de reproductions lithographiques d'enluminures sous la Monarchie de Juillet." *Bulletin du bibliophile,* no. 1 (1996): 108–50.

Boyer, Ferdinand. *Le monde des arts en Italie et la France de la Révolution et de l'Empire: Etudes et recherches.* Turin: Società Editrice Internazionale, 1970.

Brett, David. "The Interpretation of Ornament." *Journal of Design History* 1, no. 2 (1988): 103–11.

Brigstocke, Hugh. "James Dennistoun's Second European Tour, 1836–1839." *Connoisseur* 184, no. 742 (1973): 240–49.

———. "Memoirs of the Dukes of Urbino: James Dennistoun, Collector and Traveller." *Connoisseur* 198, no. 798 (1978): 316–22.

Brimo, René. *L'évolution du goût aux Etats-Unis d'après l'histoire des collections.* Paris: James Fortune, 1938.

Brinker, Claudia, and Dione Flüher-Kreis. *Die Manessische Liederhandschrift in Zürich: Exhibition.* Zürich: Schweizerisches Landesmuseum, 1991.

British Museum. *Catalogue of Manuscripts in the British Museum.* New series. Vol. 1, part 1. *The Arundel Manuscripts.* London: British Museum, 1834.

———. *List of Autograph Letters, Original Charters, Great Seals and Manuscripts Exhibited to the Public in the Department of Manuscripts.* London: British Museum, 1851.

Brodahl, J. "The Melisende Psalter and Ivories (BL Egerton 1139): An Inquiry into the Status and Collecting of Medieval Art in Early Nineteenth-Century France." Ph.D. dissertation, Brown University, 1999.

Broglie, Emmanuel. *La société de l'abbaye de Saint-Germain des Près au dix-huitieme siècle: Bernard de Montfaucon et les Bernardins, 1715–1750.* 2 vols. Paris: E. Plon, 1891.

Brooke, Sir Thomas. *A Catalogue of Manuscripts and Printed Books Collected by Thomas Brooke, and Preserved at Armitage House, near Huddersfield.* 2 vols. London: privately printed, 1891.

Brown, Elizabeth A. R. "Falsitas pie sive reprehensibilis: Medieval Forgers and Their Intentions." In *Fälschungen im Mittelalter: Internationaler Kongress der Monumenta Germaniae Historica, München 16.–19. September 1986,* edited by Horst Fuhrmann. Vol. 1, 101–20. Hannover: Hahnsche Buchhandlung, 1988–90.

Brown, T. J. "Some Manuscript Fragments Illuminated for Pope Gregory XI-II." *British Museum Quarterly* 23, no. 1 (1960): 2–5.

Brugerolles, Emmanuelle, and David Guillet. *The Renaissance in France: Drawings from the Ecole des Beaux-arts.* Cambridge, Mass.: Harvard University Art Museum, 1995.

Brunet, Gustave. *Curiosites bibliographiques et artistiques. Livres, manuscrits et gravures qui, en vente publique, ont depasse le prix de mille francs.* Geneva: Gay, 1867.

Brunet, Jacques-Charles. *Manuel du libraire et de l'amateur de livres.* 4th ed. 5 vols. Paris: Silvestre, 1842–44.

———. *Manuel du libraire et de l'amateur de livres.* 5th ed. 6 vols. Paris: Firmin-Didot Freres, Fils et Cie, 1860–65.

Brush, Kathryn. "Gothic Sculpture as a Locus for the Polemics of National Identity." In *Concepts of National Identity in the Middle Ages,* edited by Simon Forde, Lesley Johnson, and Alan V. Murray, 189–213. Leeds: Leeds Studies in English, 1995.

———. "Integration or Segregation among the Disciplines? The Historiography of Gothic Sculpture as Case-Study." In *Artistic Integration in Gothic Buildings,* edited by Virginia C. Raguin, Kathryn Brush, and Peter Draper, 19–40. Toronto: University of Toronto Press, 1995.

Bryan, Thomas Jefferson. *Catalogue of the Bryan Gallery of Christian Art from the Earliest Masters to the Present Time.* New York: George F. Nesbitt, 1852.

Bryan, Thomas Jefferson, and Richard Grant White. *Companion to the Bryan Gallery of Christian Art.* New York: Baker, Godwin, 1853.

Buettner, Brigitte. "Panofsky à l'ère de la reproduction Méchanisée: une question de perspective." *Les Cahiers du Musée nationale de l'art moderne* 53 (1995): 57–78.

Bühler, Curt F. *The Fifteenth-Century Book: The Scribes, the Printers, the Decorators.* Philadelphia: University of Pennsylvania Press, 1960.

Burch, Robert M. *Colour Printing and Colour Printers.* London: I. Pitman, 1910. Reprint, with an introduction by Joan M. Friedman, New York: Garland, 1981.

Burckhardt-Werthemann, Daniel. "Die Basler Kunstsammler des 18. Jahrhunderts." *Jahresbericht des Basler Kunstvereins* (1901): 3–69.

Burin, Elizabeth. "Henry Walters (September 26, 1848–November 30, 1931)." In *American Book-Collectors and Bibliographers,* 297–303. Detroit: Bruccoli Clark Layman, 1994.

———. "Of Pigs and Parchment" *Journal of the Walters Art Gallery* 49, no. 1 (1996): 4.

Burlington Fine Arts Club. *Catalogue of a Series of Illuminations from Manuscripts Principally of the Italian and French Schools.* London: Burlington Fine Arts Club, 1886.

Burlington Fine Arts Club. *Illuminated Manuscripts Catalogue.* London: Burlington Fine Arts Club, 1874.

Burne-Jones, Georgiana. *Memorials of Edward Burne-Jones.* 2 vols. London: Macmillan, 1904.

Caisse Nationale des Monuments Historiques et des Sites. *Le "Gothique" Retrouvé avant Viollet-le-Duc. Exposition, Hotel de Sully. 31 octobre 1979–17 février 1980.* Paris: Caisse Nationale des Monuments Historiques et des Sites, 1979.

Camaiori, Guiseppe. "Memorie storiche di Belcaro." *Bulletino senese di storia patria* 3 (1913).

Camille, Michael. "Labouring for the Lord: The Ploughman and the Social Order in the Luttrell Psalter." *Art History* 10, no. 4 (December 1987): 423–54.

————. *Mirror in Parchment: The Luttrell Psalter and the Making of Medieval England* (Chicago: University of Chicago Press, 1998).

————. "The *Très Riches Heures*: An Illuminated Manuscript in the Age of Mechanical Reproduction." *Critical Inquiry* 17 (autumn 1990): 72–107.

Carington, Dorothy. "Cardinal Fesch, a Grand Collector." *Apollo* 86, no. 69 (1967): 346–57.

Carli, Enzo. *Miniature di Liberale da Verona dai corali per il Duomo di Siena.* Milan: A. Martello, 1953.

Carter, Curtis, and William Voelkle. *The Spanish Forger: Master of Deception.* Milwaukee: Patrick and Beatrice Haggerty Museum of Art, 1987.

Carteret, Leopold. *Le trésor du bibliophile romantique et moderne, 1801–1875.* 4 vols. Paris, 1924–28.

*Catalogue of the Art Treasures of the United Kingdom Collected at Manchester.* London: Bradbury and Evans, 1857.

*Catalogue of the Library of Robert L. Stuart* (New York, 1884).

Chadwick, Owen. *The Victorian Church.* 2 vols. New York: Oxford University Press, 1966–70.

Champfleury [Jules Fleury, pseud.]. *Histoire de la Caricature au Moyen Age.* Paris, 1867–1871. 2d ed., *Histoire de la caricature au moyen-âge et sous la renaissance.* Paris: E. Dentu, 1871.

Chandler, Alice. *A Dream of Order: The Medieval Ideal in Nineteenth-Century English Literature.* Lincoln: University of Nebraska Press, 1970; London: Routledge and Kegan Paul, 1971.

Chapman, Raymond. "Last Enchantments: Medievalism and the Early Anglo-Catholic Movement." In *Medievalism in England,* edited by Leslie J. Workman, 173. Vol. 4. Studies in Medievalism, 1992.

————. *The Sense of the Past in Victorian Literature.* New York: St. Martin's Press; London: Croom Helm, 1986.

Chartier, Roger. *The Cultural Origins of the French Revolution.* Translated by Lydia G. Cochrane. Durham, N.C.: Duke University Press, 1991.

Châtelet, Albert. *Jean Van Eyck Enlumineur: Les Heures de Turin et de Milan-Turin.* Strasbourg: Presses Universitaires de Strasbourg, 1993.

Chaudonneret, Marie-Claude. *Fleury Richard et Pierre Révoil: La peinture troubadour.* Paris: Arthena, 1980.

Christiansen, K., L. B. Kanter, and C. B. Strehlke. *Painting in Renaissance Siena,* *1420–1500,* New York: Metropolitan Museum of Art, 1988.

Cincinnati Art Museum. *The Lehman Collection, New York.* Cincinnati: Cincinnati Art Museum, 1959.

Clarke, William. *Repertorium Bibliographicum: Or, Some Account of the Most Celebrated British Libraries.* London: W. Clarke, 1819.

Clausberg, Karl. *Die Manessische Liederhandschrift.* Cologne: DuMont Buchverlag, 1978.

Cloche, Maurice. "Un grand éditeur du XIXe siècle, Léon Curmer." *Arts et métiers graphiques* 33 (1933): 28–36.

Cockerell, Sydney Carlyle. *Exhibition of Illuminated Manuscripts.* London: Burlington Fine Arts Club, 1908.

Cogeval, Guy. "L'histoire du Musée des Monuments Français." In *Patrimoine, temps, espace: Patrimoine en place, patrimoine desplace,* edited by F. Furet. Paris: Fayard, 1990.

Cole, Henry. *Fifty Years of Public Work of Sir Henry Cole, K. C. B.* London: G. Bell, 1884.

Colker, Marvin L. "A Palaeographical Album of Pierre-Camille le Moine." *Scriptorium* 47, no. 1 (1993): 56–60.

Collingwood, W. G. "Lady Diana's Prayer-Book." *Art Journal,* 1882, 337–39.

Collins, Moira, and Judy Chambliss. "Gertrude Carrier in Her Own Words." *Chicago Calligraphy Collective Letter* (summer 1995): 13–18.

Comley, Nancy. "Henry Adams' Feminine Fictions: The Economics of Maternity." *American Literary Realism* 22, no. 1 (fall 1989): 3–16.

Compton, Michael. "William Roscoe and Early Collectors of Italian Primitives." *Liverpool Libraries, Museums and Art Committee Bulletin* 9 (1960–61): 26–51.

Comstock, Helen. "The Robert Lehman Collection of Miniatures." *International Studio* 86, no. 359 (April 1927): 47–57.

Constable, William George. *Art Collecting in the United States of America: An Outline of a History.* London: Thomas Nelson and Sons, 1964.

Cooper, Emma. *Plain Words on the Art and Practice of Illuminating.* London: Gladwell, 1868.

Cooper, Robyn. "The Popularization of Renaissance Art in Victorian England: The Arundel Society." *Art History,* 1978, 263–92.

Coq, Dominique. "Le parangon du bibliophile français: le duc de la Vallière et sa collection." In *Histoire des bibliothèques françaises. Les bibliothèques sous l'Ancien Régime, 1530–1789,* edited by Claude Jolly, 316–31. Paris: Promodis-Editions du Cercle de la Librairie, 1988.

Corrie, Rebecca W. "The Conradin Bible, MS 152, the Walters Art Gallery: Manuscript Illumination in a Thirteenth-Century Italian Atelier." Ph.D. dissertation, Harvard University, 1986.

————. "The Conradin Bible and the Problem of Court Ateliers in Southern Italy in the Thirteenth Century." In *Intellectual Life at the Court of rick II Hohenstaufen,* edited by William Tronzo, 16–39. Washington, D.C.: National Gallery of Art, 1994.

————. "The Conradin Bible: Since 'Since De Ricci.'" *Journal of the Walters Art Gallery* 40 (1982): 13–24.

Courajod, Louis Charles Jean. *Alexandre Lenoir, son journal et le Musée des monuments français.* 3 vols. Paris: H. Champion, 1878–87.

Courtney, Julia. "Charlotte M. Yonge: A Novelist and Her Readers." Ph.D. dissertation, University of London, 1989.

Crook, J. Mordaunt, et al. *The Strange Genius of William Burges.* Cardiff: National Museum of Wales, 1981.

Cumming, Elizabeth. *Phoebe Anna Traquaire.* Edinburgh: Scottish National Portrait Gallery, 1993.

Curran, Kathleen. "The Romanesque Revival: Mural Painting and Protestant Patronage in America." *Art Bulletin* 31 (1999): 693–722.

Damico, Helen, and Joseph B. Zavadil, eds. *Medieval Scholarship: Biographical Studies on the Formation of a Discipline.* Vol. 1, *History.* New York: Garland Press, 1995.

Darby, Elisabeth, and Nicola Smith. *The Cult of the Prince Consort.* New Haven, Conn.: Yale University Press, 1983.

D'Argenson, A. R. Voyer et al. *Bibliothèque universelle des romans.* 112 vols. Paris, 1775–1789. Reprint, Geneve: Slatkine Reprints, 1969.

Davies, H. E. "Sir John Charles Robinson (1824–1913): His Role as a Connoisseur and Creator of Public and Private Collections." Ph.D. dissertation, University of Oxford, 1992.

Dearden, James S. "John Ruskin, the Collector, with a Catalogue of the Illuminated and Other Manuscripts Formerly in His Collection." *Library* 5–6, no. 2 (June 1966): 124–54.

De Beer, Gavin Rylands. *Sir Hans Sloane and the British Museum.* London: Oxford University Press, 1953.

Debray, Régis, ed. *La France à l'Exposition universelle, Séville 1992: facettes d'une nation.* Paris: Flammarion, 1992.

De Hamel, Christopher. "Cutting up Manuscripts for Pleasure and Profit." Paper presented at the eleventh Sol M. Malkin Lecture in Bibliography, Charlottesville, University of Virginia, 1996. In *The Rare Book School 1995 Yearbook,* edited by T. Belanger. Charlottesville, Va.: Rare Book School, 1996.

————. *Hidden Friends: A Loan Exhibition of the Comites Latentes Collection of Illuminated Manuscripts from the Bibliothèque Publique et Universitaire, Geneva.* London: Sotheby's, 1985.

De Laborde, Léon. "Additions au tome premier. Peinture." Supplement to *La Renaissance des arts à la cour de France. Etudes sur le siezième siècle.* Paris, 1855.

————. *La Renaissance des arts à la cour de France. Etudes sur le siezième siècle. Tome premier. Peinture.* Paris: L. Potier, 1850. Supplement, *Additions au tome premier. Peinture.* Paris, 1855. Reprint, Geneva: Slatkine Reprints, 1970.

————. *Les Ducs de Bourgogne. Etudes sur les lettres, les arts et l'industrie pendant le XVe siècle et plus particulièrement dans les Pays-Bas et le duché de Bourgogne. Seconde partie, Preuves.* Paris: Plon, 1849–52.

Delamotte, F. *Medieval Alphabets and Initials for Illuminators.* London: Lockwood, 1864.

De Lara, David Laurent. *Elementary Instruction in the Art of Illuminating and Missal Painting on Vellum.* 2d ed. 1857. 7th ed., London: Longman, Green, Longman, Roberts, and Green, 1863.

Delisle, Léopold. *Catalogue des manuscrits des fonds Libri et Barrois.* Paris: H. Champion, 1888.

———. *Le Cabinet des Manuscrits de la Bibliothèque impériale. Étude sur la formation de ce dépôt comprenent les éléments d'une histoire de la calligraphie de la miniature, de la reliure et su commerce des livres à Paris avant l'invention de l'imprimerie.* 3 vols. and atlas. Paris: Imprimerie Imperiale, 1868–81.

———. "Les archives du Vatican. Parts 1 and 2." *Journal des Savants* (July 1892): 429–41; (August 1892): 489–501.

———. "Les Livres d'heures du duc de Berry." *Gazette des beaux-arts* 2, no. 29 (1884): 97–110, 281–92, 391–405.

———. "Les Manuscrits de la Bibliothèque de M. Pierpont Morgan." *Journal des Savants* 5, no. 8 (August 1907): 415–21.

———. *Les manuscrits des fonds Libri et Barrois à la Bibliothèque Nationale.* Paris: H. Champion, 1888.

———. "Souvenirs de Jeunesse." In *Recherches sur la librairie de Charles V.* 2 vols., xxi–xxvii. Paris: H. Champion, 1907.

Deneke, Bernward, and Rainer Kahsnitz, eds. *Das kunst- und kulturgeschichtliche Museum im 19. Jahrhundert.* Munich: Prestel, 1977.

Denis, F. *Imitation de Jésus Christ.* Paris: Curmer, 1856–58.

Denis, Rafael Cardoso. "The Educated Eye and the Industrial Hand: Art and Design Instruction for the Working Classes in Mid-Victorian Britain." Ph.D. dissertation, University of London, 1995.

Dennistoun, James. *Memoirs of the Dukes of Urbino, Illustrating the Arms, Arts and Literature of Italy from 1440 to 1630.* 3 vols. 1851. Reprint, London: John Lane, 1909.

Denon, Vivant. *Travels in Upper and Lower Egypt during the Campaigns of General Bonaparte.* London: B. Crosby, 1802. Reprint, London: Darf, 1986.

De Ricci, Seymour. *English Collectors of Books and Manuscripts (1530–1930) and Their Marks of Ownership.* Cambridge: Cambridge University Press, 1930.

———. "Les Amateurs de livres anciens en France de 1900 à 1925." *Bulletin du Bibliophile,* no. 3 (1926): 1–12.

De Ricci, Seymour, and W. J. Wilson. *Census of Medieval and Renaissance Manuscripts in the United States and Canada.* New York: H. W. Wilson, 1935. Supplement by Christopher Urdahl Faye and William Henry Bond. New York: Bibliographical Society of America, 1962.

De Vaivre, Jean-Bernard. "Sur trois primitifs français du XIVe siècle et le portrait de Jean le Bon." *Gazette des beaux-arts* 6, (April 1981): 131–56.

De Winter, Patrick M. "Bolognese Miniatures at the Cleveland Museum." *Bulletin of the Cleveland Museum of Art* 70, no. 8 (October 1983): 314–51.

———. *The Sacral Treasure of the Guelphs. A Special Issue of the Bulletin of the Cleveland Museum of Art* 72, no. 1 (March 1985).

———. "Visions of the Apocalypse in Medieval England and France." *Bulletin of the Cleveland Museum of Art* 70, no. 10 (December 1983): 396–417.

Dibdin, Thomas Frognall. *Bibliographical Decameron; or Ten Days of Pleasant Discourse upon Illuminated Manuscripts and Subjects Connected with Early Engraving, Typography and Bibliography.* 3 vols. London: W. Bulmer, 1817.

———. *Bibliomania, or, Book-Madness: Containing Some Account of the History, Symptoms, and Cure of this Fatal Disease.* Vol. 1, 109. London: Longman, Hurst, Rees, and Orme, 1809. 2d ed., *Bibliomania: or Book Madness; a Bibliographical Romance, in Six Parts; Illustrated with Cuts.* London: printed for the author by J. M'Creery and sold by Messrs. Longman, Hurst, Rees, Orme, and Brown. Reprint, London: Club of Old Sticks, 1864.

———. *Bibliophobia. Remarks on the Present Languid and Depressed State of Literature and the Book Trade. In a Letter Addressed to the Author of the Bibliomania.* London: H. G. Bohn, 1832.

———. *Bibliotheca Rosicrusiana: a Catalogue of the Library of an Eminent Bibliographer [T. F. Dibdin].* London: W. Bulmer, 1817.

———. *An Introduction to the Knowledge of Rare and Valuable Editions of the Greek and Roman Classics: Being, in Part, a Tabulated Arrangement from Dr. Harwood's View, &C.: with Notes from Mattaire, De Bure, Dictionnaire Bibliographique, and References to Ancient and Modern Catalogues.* London: Payne, H. Ruff, 1802.

———. *Reminiscences of a Literary Life.* London: J. Major, 1836.

———. *Selections.* Metuchen, N.J.: Scarecrow Press, 1978.

———. *Typographical Antiquities: Or, the History of Printing in England, Scotland, and Ireland; Containing Memoirs of Our Ancient Printers, and a Register of the Books Printed by Them.* 4 vols. London: William Miller, 1810–19.

Dickens, Charles. "Old Lamps for New Ones." *Household Words* (June 15, 1850): 265–67.

Dickinson, Donald C. *Henry E. Huntington's Library of Libraries* (San Marino, Calif., 1995).

———. "An Overland Book Trail from New York to California." *AB Bookman's Weekly* 91, no. 6 (1993): 456–72.

Diderot, Denis. *Encyclopédie, ou, Dictionnaire raisonne des sciences, des arts et des metiers par une societe de gens de lettres.* Paris, 1751.

Dooley, Allan. *Author and Printer in Victorian England: Printing Technology Shapes Texts.* Charlottesville: University of Virginia Press, 1992.

*The Douce Legacy.* Oxford: Bodleian Library, 1984.

Dresser, Christopher. *Development of rnamental Art in the International Exhibition.* London: Day and Sons, 1862.

Driskel, Michael. *Representing Belief: Religion, Art and Society in Nineteenth-Century France.* University Park: Penn State University Press, 1992.

Du Mège, Alexandre. "Notice sur Quelques Manuscrits de la Bibliothèque d'Albi." *Histoire et Memoires de L'Academie Royale des Sciences, Inscriptions et Belles-Lettres de Toulouse* (1834): 271–74.

Duplessis, Georges. "Roger de Gaignières et ses collections iconographiques." *Gazette des beaux-arts* 2, no. 12 (1870): 468–88.

Duro, Paul. "'Un Livre Ouvert à l'Instruction': Study Museums in Paris in the Nineteenth Century." *Oxford Art Journal* 10, no. 1 (1987): 44–58.

Durrieu, Paul. "L'Exposition des primitifs francais." *Revue de l'Art ancien et moderne* 15 (January–June 1904): 169–72.

———. *Heures de Turin: quarante-cinq feuillets à peintures provenant des Très belles heures de Jean de France.* Paris: P. Renouard, 1902.

Durrieu, Paul, and Jean-J. Marquet de Vasselot. "Les manscrits à miniatures des Héroïdes d'Ovide, traduite par St.-Gelais et un grand miniaturiste français du XVIe siècle." *L'Artiste* 7 (May 1894): 331–47.

Du Sommerard, Alexandre. *Les arts au moyen âge.* 5 vols. Paris: Hôtel de Cluny, 1838–46.

Dutschke, C. W. *Guide to Medieval and Renaissance Manuscripts in the Huntington Library.* San Marino, Calif., 1989.

Easby, Rebecca. "The Myth of Merrie England." In *History and Community: Essays in Victorian Medievalism,* edited by Florence S. Boos, 70–72. New York: Garland Publishing, 1992.

Eberhardt, Hans-Joachim. *Die Miniaturen von Liberale da Verona, Girolamo da Cremona und Venturino da Milan in den Chorbüchern des Doms von Siena: Dokumentation, Attribution, Chronologie.* Berlin: Wasmuth, 1983.

*Un editeur parisien au XIXe siècle. Leon Curmer. Albert Curmer 1911–1912.* N.p.: privately printed, n.d.

Ege, Otto F. "I Am a Biblioclast." *Avocations: A Magazine of Hobbies and Leisure* 1 (March 1938): 516–21.

———. "Manuscripts of the Middle Ages." *American Magazine of Art* 23, no. 5 (November 1931): 375–80.

———. "The Modern Book." *School Arts Magazine* 46, no. 6 (March 1947): 218–22.

———. "The Most Beautiful Book in the World." *School Arts Magazine* 21, no. 8 (April 1922): 447–50.

Ege, Otto F., compiler and annotater. *Fifty Original Leaves from Medieval Manuscripts.* N.p, n.d.

"Ege, Otto F., Microfilmed Memorial." Presented by the Reading High School Class of 1907 to the Reading Public Library, Reading, Pa.

Eisenman, Stephen F. *Designing Utopia: The Art of William Morris and His Circle.* Katonah, N.Y.: Katonah Museum of Art, 1992.

El Gammal, Jean. "L'utilisation électorale du passé: 1885–1898." *Revue Historique* 265, no. 537 (1981): 103–30.

Elkins, James. "From Original to Copy and Back Again." *British Journal of Aesthetics* 33, no. 2 (April 1993): 113–20.

Engelmann, Godefroy. *Manuel du dessinateur lithographe ou description des meilleurs moyens à employer pour faire des dessins sur pierre dans tous les genres connus. Suivie d'une instruction sur le nouveau procédé du lavia lithographique par G. Engelmann, directeur de la Société Lithographique de Mulhouse.* Paris: G. Engelmann, 1822.

———. *Traité théorotique et pratique de la lithographie.* Mulhouse: P. Baret, 1839.

Erlande-Brandenberg, Alain. "Le musée des Monuments français et les origines du Musée de Cluny." In *Das kunst- und kulturgeschichtliche Museum im 19. Jahrhundert,* edited by Bernward Deneke and Rainer Kahsnitz, 49–58. Munich: Prestel, 1977.

Ernstrom, Adele H. "Why Should We Be Always Looking Back? 'Christian Art' in Nineteenth-Century Historiography in Britain." *Art History* 22, no. 3 (1999): 421–35.

Errington, Lindsay. *Social and Religious Themes in English Art, 1840–1860.* New York: Garland, 1984.

Eudel, Paul. *Le truquage. Les contrefaçons dévoilées.* Paris: E. Dentu, 1887.

———. *Trucs et truqueurs: Alterations, fraudes et contrafaçons devoilées.* Paris: Librarie Molière, 1907.

*Les Evangiles des Dimanches.* Vol. 3. Paris: Curmer, 1864.

Musée de l'Orangerie. *Exposition de la collection Lehman de New York.* Paris: Éditions des Musées Nationaux, 1957.

Evans, Joan. *A History of the Society of Antiquaries.* Oxford: Oxford University Press for the Society of Antiquaries, 1956.

Fawcett, Trevor. "Visual Facts and the 19th-Century Art Lecture." *Art History* 6, no. 4 (December 1983): 442–60.

Federal Art Project, Works Progress Administration. *Master Prints from the John F. Lewis Collection of the Pennsylvania Academy of Fine Arts.* Washington, D.C.: Federal Art Project, Works Progress Administration, 1939.

Felmingham, Michael. *The Illustrated Gift Book 1880–1930.* Brookfield,Vt.: Ashgate, 1990.

Ferretti, Fred. "The Treasure of Jenkintown, Pa.: Lessing Rosenwald's 25,000 Prints," *Art News* 72, no. 3 (March 1973): 43–45.

Field, R. S. *Fifteenth Century Woodcuts and Metalcuts from the National Gallery of Art.* Washington, D.C., 1965.

Fine, R. *Lessing J. Rosenwald: Tribute to a Collector.* Washington, D.C.: National Gallery of Art, 1982.

Firmenich-Richartz, Eduard. *Sulpiz und Melchior Boisserée als Kunstsammler. ein Beitrag zur Geschichte der Romantik.* Jena: E. Diederich, 1916.

*First Report of the Department of Practical Art* (HMSO, 1853), 382.

Fleming, Robin. "Nineteenth-Century New England's Memory of the Middle Ages." In *Memory and the Middle Ages,* edited by Nancy Netzer and Virginia Reinberg, 77–92. Chestnut Hill, Mass.: Boston College Museum of Art, 1995.

———. "Picturesque History and the Medieval in Nineteenth-Century America." *American Historical Review* 100, no. 4 (October 1995): 1061–94.

Fletcher, H. George. *The Wormsley Library: A Personal Selection by Sir Paul Getty.* New York: Pierpont Morgan Library, 1999.

Flint, Kate. "Reading *The Awakening Conscience* Rightly." In *Pre-Raphaelites Reviewed,* edited by Marcia Pointon, 45–65. Manchester: Manchester University Press, 1989.

Forsyth, William H. "Five Crucial People in the Building of the Cloisters." In *The Cloisters: Studies in Honor of the Fiftieth Anniversary,* edited by Elizabeth C. Parker, 51–62. New York: Metropolitan Museum of Art, 1992.

Foucart, Bruno. *Le renouveau de la peinture religieuse en France, 1800–1860.* Paris: Arthéna, 1987.

Fox, Daniel M. *Engines of Culture: Philanthropy and Art Museums.* Madison: Department of History, University of Wisconsin, 1963.

Frain, Irene. *La Guirlande de Julie.* Paris: Robert Laffont for the Bibliothèque Nationale, 1991.

*Francis Douce Centenary.* Vol. 7, no. 81, *The Bodleian Quarterly Record,* 1934.

Fredeman, William E. "Emily Faithful and the Victoria Press, an Experiment Sociological Bibliography," *Library* (June 1974).

Freedman, Paul, and Gabrielle M. Spiegel. "Medievalisms Old and New: The Rediscovery of Alterity in North American Medieval Studies." *American Historical Review* 103, no. 3 (1998): 677–704.

Fuhrmann, Horst, ed. *Fälschungen im Mittelalter. Internationaler Kongress der Monumenta Germaniae Historica, München 16.–19. September 1986.* 5 vols. Hannover: Hahnsche Buchhandlung, 1988–90.

Fuseli, Henry. "Eighth Lecture." In *The Life and Writings of Henry Fuseli,* edited by John Knowles. London: H. Colburn and R. Bentley, 1831.

Gardner, William. "High Victorian Taste in Calligraphy and Illumination: The Loyal Addresses Presented to Queen Victoria in 1887." *Journal of the Royal Society of Arts* (July 1987).

Garmier, Jean-François. "Le goût du moyen âge chez les collectionneurs lyonnais du XIXe siècle." *Revue de l'art* 47 (1980): 53–64.

Gascoigne, Bamber. *How to Identify Prints: A Complete Guide to Manual and Mechanical Processes from Woodcut to Ink Jet.* London: Thames and Hudson, 1986.

George, Albert J. *The Didot Family and the Progress of Printing.* Syracuse: Syracuse University Press, 1961.

Georgel, Chantal, ed. *La Jeunesse des Musées: Les musées de France au XIXe siècle.* Paris: Éditions de la Réunion des Musées Nationaux, 1994.

———. "The Museum as Metaphor in Nineteenth-Century France." In *Museum Culture: Histories, Discourses, Spectacles,* edited by Daniel J. Sherman and Irit Rogoff, 113–22. Minneapolis: University of Minnesota Press, 1994.

Gere, J. A. "William Young Ottley as a Collector of Drawings." *British Museum Quarterly* 18, no. 2 (1953): 44–53.

Gibson, Margaret, T. A. Heslop, and Richard W. Pfaff, eds. *The Eadwine Psalter: Text, Image, and Monastic Culture in Twelfth-Century Canterbury.* London: Modern Humanities Research Association, 1992.

Gilley, Sheridan. "John Keble and the Victorian Churching of Romanticism." In *An Infinite Complexity: Essays in Romanticism,* edited by J. R. Watson, 226–39. Edinburgh: Edinburgh University Press for the University of Durham, 1983.

———. "Victorian Feminism and Catholic Art: The Case of Mrs. Jameson." In *The Church and the Arts,* edited by Diana Wood, 381–91. Oxford: Blackwell, 1992.

Girardet, Raoul. *Le Nationalism français, 1871–1914.* Paris: A. Colin, 1966.

Girodie, André. "Les livres de prières illustrés." *Notes d'Art et archéologie. Revue de la Société de Saint Jean pour l'encouragement de l'art chrétien,* 2e série, 10e année (1898).

Goff, F. R. "Catatogue of Fine Books and Manuscripts Selected for Exhibition at the Library of Congress from the Lessing J. Rosenwald Collection." *Library of Congress Quarterly Journal of Current Acquisitions* 3, no. 1 (October 1945): 5–51.

Gossman, Lionel. *Medievalism and the Ideologies of the Enlightenment. The World and Work of La Curne de Sainte-Palaye.* Baltimore: Johns Hopkins Press, 1968.

Gough, Richard. *An Account of a Rich Illuminated Missal Executed for John, Duke of Bedford, Regent of France under Henry VI and Afterwards in the Possession of the Late Duchess of Portland.* London: J. Nichols for T. Payne, 1794.

———. *Sepulchral Monuments in Great Britain; Applied to Illustrate the History of Families, Manners, Habits and Arts at the Different Periods from the Norman Conquest to the Seventeenth Century. With Introductory Observations.* 2 vols. London: printed for the author, sold by T. Payne and Son, etc., 1786–96.

Gould, Cecil. *Trophy of Conquest. The Musée Napoleon and the Creation of the Louvre.* London: Faber and Faber, 1965.

Goutiére-Vernolle, Emile. "Une Renaissance éspérée (L'Enluminure à Nancy)." *La Lorraine Artiste* 10 (1892): 247–49.

Grasselli, Margaret Morgan, ed. *The Touch of the Artist: Master Drawings from the Woodner Collections.* Washington, D.C.: National Gallery of Art, 1995.

*Great Exhibition of the Works of Industry of All Nations, 1851: Official Descriptive and Illustrated Catalogue.* 3 vols. London: Spicer Brothers, 1851.

Greene, Christopher M. "Alexandre Lenoir and the Musée des Monuments Français during the French Revolution." *French Historical Studies* 12 (autumn 1981): 200–22.

Grieve, Alastair. "Style and Content in Pre-Raphaelite Drawing." In *Pre-Raphaelite Papers,* edited by Leslie Parris, 23–43. London: Tate Gallery, 1984.

Grolier Club. *Catalogue of an Exhibition of Illuminated and Painted Manuscripts Together with a Few Early Printed Books with Illuminations—also Some Examples of Persian Manuscripts—with Plates in Facsimile and an Introductory Essay.* New York: Grolier Club, 1892.

———. *The Grolier Club, 1884–1984: Its Library, Exhibitions and Publications.* New York: Grolier Club, 1984.

Grove, Lee Edmonds. "Robert Hoe III, 1839–1909." In *Grolier 75: A Biographical Retrospective to Celebrate the Seventy-Fifth Anniversary of the Grolier Club in New York,* 24–26. New York: Grolier Club, 1959.

Gruelle, Richard B. *Notes Critical and Biographical: Collection of W. T. Walters.* Indianapolis: J. M. Bowles, 1895.

Hale, John Rigby. *England and the Italian Renaissance: The Growth of Interest in Its History and Art.* London: Faber and Faber, 1954.

Hall, J. R. "William G. Medlicott (1816–1883): An American Book Collector and His Collection." *Harvard Library Bulletin,* n.s. 1, no. 1 (1990): 13–46.

Halleur, G. C. Hermann. *The Art of Photography. Instructions in the Art of Producing Photographic Pictures in Any Colour, and on Any Material, for the Use of Beginners; and Also of Persons Who Have Already Attained Some Proficiency in the Art; and of Engravers on Copper, Stone, Wood, Etc.* Translated by G. L. Strauss. London: John Weale, 1854.

Hamburger, Jeffrey F. *Nuns as Artists: The Visual Culture of a Medieval Convent.* Berkeley: University of California Press, 1997.

Hamilton, Sir William. *Supplement to the Campi Phlegraei, Being an Account of the Great Eruption of Mt. Vesusvius in the Month of August, 1779.* Naples, 1779.

Haraszti, Zoltán. "Additions to the Rare Book Department," *The Boston Public Library Quarterly* 9, no. 2 (April 1957): 59–72.

———. "Medieval Manuscripts" and "Medieval Manuscripts in the Library," *More Books: The Bulletin of the Boston Public Library* 3, no. 2 (March 1928): 56.

———. "Notable Purchases," *The Boston Public Library Quarterly* 7, no. 2 (April 1955): 72–91.

———. "Twenty-five Years of the Treasure Room," *The Boston Public Library Quarterly* 7, no. 3 (July 1955): 115–27; and

Harris, Neil. "Collective Possession: J. Pierpont Morgan and the American Imagination." In *Cultural Excursions: Marketing Appetites and Cultural Tastes in Modern America,* 250–75. Chicago: University of Chicago Press, 1990.

———. "Midwestern Medievalism: Three Chicago Collectors." In *Fenway Court.* Vol. 27, *Cultural Leadership in America: Art Matronage and Patronage,* 104–23. Boston: Trustees of the Isabella Stewart Gardner Museum, 1997.

Harrod, Tanya. "John Ruskin and the Arundel Society." *Apollo* 127, no. 313 (March 1988): 180–88.

———. "A Study of the Arundel Society, 1848–1897." Ph.D. dissertation, Oxford University, 1978.

Harrsen, Meta. *Central European Manuscripts in the Pierpont Morgan Library.* New York: Pierpont Morgan Library, 1958.

———. "Mediaeval and Renaissance Miniatures in the John Frederick Lewis Collection in Philadelphia." *Scriptorium* 14, no. 1 (1960): 75–79.

Härtel, Reinhardt. "Fälschungen im Mittelalter: Geglaubt, verworfen, vertuscht." In *Fälschungen im Mittelalter: Internationaler Kongress der Monumenta Germaniae Historica, München 16.–19. September 1986,* edited by Horst Fuhrmann. Vol. 3, 29–52. Hannover: Hahnsche Buchhandlung, 1988–90.

Hartmann, Wolfgang. *Die historische Festzug: seine Entstehung und Entwicklung im 19. und 20. Jahrhundert.* Munich: Prestel, 1976.

Harvey, Charles, and Jon Press. *William Morris: Design and Enterprise in Victorian Britain.* Manchester: Manchester University Press, 1991.

Haskell, Francis. *History and Its Images: Art and the Interpretation of the Past.* New Haven, Conn.: Yale University Press, 1993.

———. *Rediscoveries in Art: Some Aspects of Taste, Fashion and Collecting in England and France.* London: Phaidon, 1976.

Hauck, Alice H. R. "John Ruskin's Uses of Illuminated Manuscripts: The Case of the Beaupré Antiphonary, 1853–1856." *Arts Magazine* 56, no. 1 (September 1981): 79–83.

———. "John Ruskin's Uses of Illuminated Manuscripts and Their Impact on His Theories of Art and Society." Ph.D. dissertation, Johns Hopkins University, 1983.

Haworth-Booth, Mark, ed. *The Golden Age of British Photography, 1839–1900.* Millerton, N.Y.: Aperture in Association with the Philadelphia Museum of Art, 1984.

Hazen, Allen T. *A Catalogue of Horace Walpole's Library.* New Haven, Conn.: Yale University Press, 1969.

Heinlen, Michael J. *Medieval and Renaissance Miniature Painting.* Akron and London, 1989.

Hennin, Michel. *Les Monuments de l'histoire de France.* 10 vols. Paris: J. F. Delion, 1856–63.

Herrmann, Frank, ed. *The English as Collectors: A Documentary Chrestomathy.* New York: Norton, 1972.

Herstein, Sheila R. *A Mid-Victorian Feminist: Barbara Leigh Smith Bodichon.* New Haven, Conn.: Yale University Press, 1985.

Hewison, Robert. *Ruskin and Oxford: The Art of Education.* Oxford: Clarendon Press; New York: Oxford University Press, 1996.

Hill, Dorothy Kent. "William T. Walters and Henry Walters." *Art in America* 32, no. 4 (October 1944): 178–86.

Hindman, Sandra. "Facsimiles as Originals: An Unknown Illuminated Manuscript by Henry Shaw." *Journal of the Walters Art Gallery* 54 (1996): 225–32.

———. *Medieval and Renaissance Miniature Painting.* Akron, Ohio: Bruce Ferrini Rare Books; London: Sam Fogg Rare Books, 1988.

Hindman, Sandra, ed. *The Early Illustrated Book: Essays in Honor of Lessing J. Rosenwald.* Washington, D.C.: Library of Congress, 1982.

Hindman, Sandra, and James Douglas Farquar. *Pen to Press: Illustrated Manuscripts and Printed Books in the Age of the First Century of Printing.* College Park, Md.: Art Department, University of Maryland, 1977.

Hindman, Sandra, and Michael Heinlen. "A Connoisseur's Montage: The *Four Evangelists* Attributed to Gulio Clovio." *Art Institute of Chicago Museum Studies* 17 (1991): 154–78, 181–82.

Hindman, Sandra, et al. *The Robert Lehman Collection.* Vol. 4, *Illuminations.* New York: Metropolitan Museum of Art, 1997.

*Histoire literaire de la France: ou l'on traite de l'origine et du progres, de la decadence et du retablissement des sciences parmi les Gaulois et parmi les Francois; du gout et du genie des uns et des autres pour les letres en chaque siecle; de leurs anciennes ecoles; de l'establissement des universites en France; des principaux colleges; des academies des sciences et des belles lettres; des meilleures bibliotheques anciennes et modernes; des plus celebres imprimeries; et de tout ce qui a un rapport particulier a la literature... par des religieux benedictins de la Congregation de S. Maur.* Paris: Palme, 1865–75. Reprint, Liechtenstein: Kraux, 1973–74.

Hobson, Anthony. "Appropriations from Foreign Libraries during the French Revolution and Empire." *Bulletin du bibliophile,* no. 2 (1986): 255–72.

Holzenberg, E. *The Middle Hill Press: A Checklist of the Horblitt Collection of Books, Tracts, Leaflets and Broadsides Printed by Sir Thomas Phillipps.* New York: Grolier Club, 1997.

Hourticque, Louis. *Le génie de la France, illustrations de l'auteur.* Paris: Presses universitaires de France, 1943.

Howe, K. S., and D. B. Warren. *The Gothic Revival Style in America, 1830–70.* Houston, 1976.

Hult, David F. "Gaston Paris and the Invention of Courtly Love." In *Medievalism and the Modernist Temper,* edited

by R. Howard Bloch and Stephen G. Nichols, 192–224. Baltimore: Johns Hopkins University Press, 1996.

Humphreys, Henry Noel. *The Art of Illumination and Missal Painting: A Guide to Modern Illuminators. Illustrated by a Series of Specimens from Richly Illuminated MSS. of Various Periods, Accompanied by a Set of Outlines to Be Coloured by the Student According to the Theories Developed in the Work.* London: H. G. Bohn, 1849.

———. *The Book of Ruth: from Holy Scriptures. Enriched with Coloured Borders, Selected from Illuminated Mss. In the British Museum, Bibliothèque Nationale, Paris, Soane Museum and Other Libraries.* London: Longman, Brown, Green and Longmans, 1850.

———. *The Illuminated Books of the Middle Ages; an Account of the Development and Progress of the Art of Illumination, as a Distinct Branch of Pictorial Ornamentation, from the IVth to the XVIIth Centuries. Illustrated by a Series of Examples, of the Size of the Originals, Selected from the Most Beautiful Mss. of the Various Periods, Executed on Stone and Printed in Colours by Owen Jones.* London: Longman, Brown, Green, and Longmans, 1849. Reprint, London: Bracken Books, 1989.

———. *Illuminated Calendar for M.DC-CC.XL.VI.* London: Longman, 1846.

———. *Illuminated Illustrations of Froissart: Selected from the Ms. in the Bibliothèque Royale, Paris, and from Other Sources.* London: William Smith, 1845.

———. *Miracles of Our Lord.* London: Longman, 1848.

———. *The Origin and Progress of the Art of Writing.* London: Ingram, Cooke, 1853.

———. *Parables of our Lord.* London: Longman, 1847.

———. *The Penitential Psalms.* London: Day and Son, 1861.

———. *Ten Centuries of Art. Its Progress in Europe from the IXth to the XIXth Century. With a Glance at the Artistic Works Classical Antiquity and Concluding Considerations on the Probable Influence of the Great Exhibition, and on the Present State and Future Prospects of Art in Great Britain.* London: Grant and Griffith, St. Paul's Churchyard, 1852.

Hunter, William. *Anatomia uteri humani gravidi tabulis illustrata: auctore Gulielmo Hunter . . . (The Anatomy of the Human Gravid Uterus Exhibited in Figures, by William Hunter . . .).* Birmingham: J. Baskerville, 1774. Reprint, Birmingham: Classics of Medicine, 1980.

———. *Dr. William Hunter at the Royal Academy of Arts.* Edited by Martin Kemp. Glasgow: University of Glasgow Press, 1975.

Idzerda, Stanley J. "Iconoclasm during the French Revolution." *American Historical Review* 60 (1954–55): 13–26.

*Illuminator's Magazine.* London: Barnard and Son, 1862.

International Exhibition of 1862. *The Illustrated Catalogue of the Industrial Department, British Division.* 4 vols. London: For Her Majesty's Commissioners by Clay, Son, and Taylor, 1862.

Irwin, W., E. C. May, and J. Hotchkiss. *A History of the Union League Club of New York City.* New York, 1952.

Jackson, Richard A. *Vive le roi! A History of French Coronation from Charles V to Charles X.* Chapel Hill: University of North Carolina Press, 1984.

Jackson, William A. *Annotated List of the Publications of the Reverend Thomas Frognall Dibdin.* Cambridge: Houghton Library, 1965.

Jadart, Henri, "Un enlumineur rémois: Alphone Lesueur." *Travaux de l'Académie Nationale de Reims* 135 (1921): 161–66.

James, Montague Rhodes. *Catalogue of Manuscripts and Early Printed Books from the Libraries of William Morris, Richard Bennett, Bertram Fourth Earl of Ashburnham and Other Sources, Now Forming a Portion of the Library of J. Pierpont Morgan.* London: Chiswick Press, 1906–7.

Jameson, Anna. *Sacred and Legendary Art.* London: Longman, Brown, Green, and Longmans, 1848.

Jammes, André. *Didotiana.* Paris: Jouve, 1994.

Jammes, André, ed. *Les Didot. Trois siècles de typographie et de bibliophilie, 1698–1998.* Paris: Bibliothèque Historique de la Ville de Paris, 1998.

Jarves, James Jackson. *Art Hints: Architecture, Sculpture, and Painting.* London: Sampson Low, Son, 1855.

———. *Art Studies: The "Old Masters" of Italy.* New York: Derby and Jackson, 1861.

———. *Art Thoughts: The Experiences and Observations of an American Amateur in Europe.* New York: Hurd and Houghton, 1869.

*Jeanne d'Arc, edition illustré d'après les monuments de l'art depuis le 15e siècle.* Paris: Firmin-Didot, 1876.

Jervis, Simon, ed. *Art and Design in Europe and America, 1800–1900.* London: Herbert Press, 1987.

Jewitt, Edwin. *Manual of Illuminated Missal Painting.* London: J. Barnard, 1860.

Jolly, Claude, ed. *Histoire des bibliothèques françaises.* 3 vols. Paris: Promodis-Editions du Cercle de la Librairie, 1988–92.

Jones, Mark. *Fake? The Art of Deception.* London: British Library, 1990.

Jones, Owen. *Book of Common Prayer and Administration of the Sacraments and Other Rites and Ceremonies of the Church: According to the Use of the United Church of England and Ireland.* London: John Murray, 1850.

———. *The Grammar of Ornament: Illustrated by Examples from Various Styles of Ornament.* London: Day and Son, 1856. Reprint, London: B. Quaritch, 1868. Reprint, London: Studio Editions, 1986.

———. *Holy Matrimony.* London: Longman, 1849.

———. *One Thousand and One Initial Letters.* London: Day and Son, 1864.

———. *The Psalms of David.* London: Day, 1845.

———. *The Sermon on the Mount: Gospel of St. Matthew, Chapters V, Vi, Vii. Illuminated by W. & G. Audsley, Architects, Liverpool; Illustrated by Charles Rolt; Chromolithographed by W.R. Tymms.* London: Longman, 1844.

———. *The Song of Songs.* London: Longman, 1849.

Jordan, Alyce A. "Rationalizing the Narrative: Theory and Practice in the Nineteenth-Century Restoration of the Windows of the Sainte-Chapelle." *Gesta* 37, no. 2 (1998): 192–200.

Kanter, Laurence B., et al. *Painting and Illumination in Early Renaissance Florence, 1300–1450.* New York: Metropolitan Museum of Art, 1994.

Kaudelka-Hanisch, Karin. "The Titled Businessman: Prussian Commercial Councillors in the Rhineland and Westphalia during the 19th Century." In *The German Bourgeoisie,* edited by David Blackburn and Richard Evans, 87–114. London: Routledge, 1991.

Kaufman, Edward. *Medievalism: An Annotated Bibliography of Recent Research in the Architecture and Art of Britain and North America.* New York: Garland, 1988.

Keble, John. *The Christian Year: Thoughts in Verse for the Sundays and Holydays throughout the Year.* Oxford: John Henry and James Parker, 1859.

———. *Keble's Evening Hymn, Illustrated by Edith Waring.* London: Day and Son, 1869.

Kemp, Wolfgang. *The Desire of My Eyes: The Life and Work of John Ruskin.* Translated by Jan van Heurck. New York: Farrar, Straus and Giroux, 1983.

Kennedy, Emmet. "Chapter VIII: Vandalism and Conservation." In *A Cultural History of the French Revolution,* 197–220. New Haven, Conn.: Yale University Press, 1989.

———. *A Cultural History of the French Revolution.* New Haven, Conn.: Yale University Press, 1989.

Kenseth, Joy, ed. *The Age of the Marvelous.* Hanover, N.H.: Hood Museum of Art, 1991.

Ker, Ian. *John Henry Newman: A Biography.* New York: Oxford University Press, 1988.

Ker, Neil Ripley. *Fragments of Medieval Manuscripts Used as Pastedowns in Oxford Bindings with a Survey of Oxford Binding circa 1515–1620.* Oxford: Oxford Bibliographic Society, 1954.

———. *Medieval Manuscripts in British Libraries,* no. 1 (1967):378–93.

———. *William Hunter as a Collector of Medieval Manuscripts: The First Edwards Lecture on Palaeography Delivered in the University of Glasgow.* Glasgow: University of Glasgow Press, 1983.

Keynes, Geoffrey. *William Pickering, Publisher. A Memoir and a Hand-List of His Editions.* London: Fleuron, 1924. Rev. ed., New York: B. Franklin, 1969.

Kidd, Charles, and David Williamson, eds. *Debrett's Peerage and Baronetage.* London: St. Martin's Press, 1995.

Kren, Thomas, ed. *Renaissance Painting in Manuscripts: Treasures from the British Library.* New York: Hudson Hills Press, 1983.

Krumeich, Gerd. *Jeanne d'Arc in der Geschichte: Historiographie, Politik, Kultur.* Sigmaringen: J. Thorbecke, 1989.

Kselman, Thomas. *Miracles and Prophecies in Nineteenth-Century France.* New Brunswick, N.J.: Rutgers University Press, 1983.

Kurz, Otto. *Fakes: A Handbook for Collectors and Students.* London: Faber and Faber, 1948.

———. *Fakes and Forgeries.* Minneapolis: Minneapolis Institute of Art, 1973.

———. "Giorgio Vasari's 'Libro de'Disegni.'" Parts 1 and 2. *Old Master Drawings* 45 (June 1937): 1–15; 47 (December 1937): 32–44.

Labitte, Alphonse. *L'Art de l'enluminure: métier, histoire, pratique.* Paris: H. Laurens, 1893.

———. *Les manuscrits et l'art de les orner. Ouvrage historique et pratique.* Paris: Charles Mendel, 1893.

Lacroix, Paul. *The Arts in the Middle Ages and the Renaissance.* Revised and rearranged by W. Armstrong. London, 1879. Reprint, New York, 1964.

———. *Le Moyen Age et la Renaissance, histoire et description des mœurs et usages, du commerce et de l'industrie, des sciences, des arts, des littératures et des beaux-arts en Europe.* 5 vols. Paris: Firmin-Didot, 1848–51.

———. *Les Arts au Moyen Age et à l'époque de la Renaissance.* Paris: Firmin-Didot, 1877.

———. *Moeurs, usages, et costumes au moyen âge et à l'époque de la Renaissance; ouvrage illustré de quinze planches chromolithographiques exécutés par F. Kellerhoven et de quatre cent quarante graveurs.* Paris: Firmin-Didot, 1877.

———. *Sciences et lettres au moyen âge et à l'époque de la Renaissance.* Paris: Firmin-Didot, 1877.

La Curne de Sainte-Palaye, Jean Baptiste de. "Jugement de l'Histoire de Froissart." *Mémoires de litterature tirez des registres d'Académie Royale des inscriptions et Belles Lettres* 13 (1740): 555–79.

———. *Lettre à M. de B. (Bachaumont) sur le bon goût dans les arts et dans les lettres.* Paris, 1751, 1755. Reprint, Geneva: Minkoff Reprint, 1972.

———. "Mémoire concernant la lecture des anciens Romans de Chevalerie." *Mémoires de litterature tirez des registres d'Académie Royale des inscriptions et Belles Lettres* 17 (1751): 787–99.

———. "Mémoire concernant les principaux monumens de l'histoire de France. Avec la notice & l'histoire des Chroniques de Saint-Denys." *Mémoires de litterature tirez des registres d'Académie Royale des inscriptions et Belles Lettres* 15 (1743): 580–616.

———. *Mémoires sur l'ancienne chevalerie, considre comme un tablissement politique et militaire.* Paris: La Veuve Duchesne,1781.

Ladonne, Q. *Quand le Moyen Age entré au musée: Monographie du musée du palais des Thermes et de l'hôtel de Cluny (1843–1907).* Vol. 7. Paris: D.E.A. Université Paris, 1992.

Ladurie, Emmanuel Le Roy. Introduction to *Creating French Culture: Treasures from the Bibliothèque Nationale de France,* edited by Marie-Hélène Tesnière and Prosser Gifford. New Haven, Conn.: Yale University Press, Library of Congress, and Bibliothèque Nationale, 1995.

———. Introduction to *Vrai ou faux? Copier, imiter, falsifier.* Paris: Bibliothèque Nationale, 1988.

Laffitte, Marie Pierre. "La Bibliothèque Nationale et les 'conquêtes artistiques' de la Révolution et de l'Empire: les manuscrits d'Italie (1796–1815)." *Bulletin du bibliophile,* no. 2 (1989): 273–323.

Lagrange, Léon. "Du rang des femmes dans les arts." *Gazette des beaux-arts* 8 (1860): 30–43.

Landais, Hubert. "The Cloisters or the Passion for the Middle Ages." In *The Cloisters: Studies in Honor of the Fiftieth Anniversary,* edited by Elizabeth C. Parker, 41–48. New York: Metropolitan Museum of Art, 1992.

Landow, George P. "*The Art Journal,* 1850–1880: Antiquarians, the Medieval Revival and the Reception of Pre-Raphaelitism." *The Pre-Raphaelite Review* 2, no. 2 (May 1979): 71–76.

Lang, A. "Two Forged Miniatures of Joan of Arc." *Burlington Magazine* 15, no. 73 (April 1909): 51.

Lang, Léon. "Godefroy Engelmann, imprimeur lithographe." In *Trois siècles d'art alsacien, 1648–1948,* 159–87. Strasbourg: Editions des Archives Alsaciennes d'Histoire de l'Art, 1948.

———. *Godefroy Engelmann, imprimeur-lithographe: les incunables, 1814–1817.* Colmar: Editions Alsatia, 1977.

Larmore, Lewis. *Introduction to Photographic Principles.* New York: Dover, 1965.

Latham, David. *An Annotated Critical Bibliography of William Morris.* London: Harvester Wheatsheaf, 1991.

Lears, T. J. Jackson. *No Place of Grace: Antimodernism and the Transformation of American Culture 1880–1920.* Chicago: University of Chicago Press, 1981.

Leathlean, Howard. "Henry Noel Humphreys and Some Pre-Raphaelite Imagery." *Journal of Pre-Raphaelite Studies* 7, no. 2 (May 1987): 41–54.

———. "Henry Noel Humphreys and the Getting-Up of Books in the Mid–Nineteenth Century." *Book Collector* 38, no. 2 (summer 1989): 192–209.

Leclerq, Dom Henri. "Mabillon." In *Dictionnaire d'archéologie chrétienne et de liturgie,* 427–723. Paris: Letouzey et Ané, 1931.

———. *Mabillon.* 2 vols. Paris: Letouzey et Ané, 1953–57.

Lecoy de la Marche, Albert. *Les manuscrits et la miniature.* Paris: Quantin, 1884.

Leeuwenberg, Jaap. "Early Nineteenth-Century Gothic Ivories." *Aachener Kunstblätter* 39 (1969): 111–48.

Lefèvre, Martine, and Danielle Muzerelle. "La bibliothèque du marquis de Paulmy." In *Histoire des bibliothèques françaises: Les bibliothèques sous l'Ancien Régime, 1530–1789,* edited by Claude Jolly, 302–15. Paris: Promodis-Editions du Cercle de la Librairie, 1988.

Lehman, Robert. *The Philip Lehman Collection, New York.* Paris: Calmann-Lévy, 1928.

Lenoir, Alexandre. *Musée des monumens français; ou Description historique et chronologique des statues en marbre et en bronze, bas reliefs et tombeaux des hommes et des femmes célèbres, pour servir à l'histoire de France.* Paris: Nepveu, 1821.

Levine, Lawrence W. *Highbrow/Lowbrow: The Emergence of Cultural Hierarchy in America.* Cambridge, Mass.: Harvard University Press, 1988.

Lewis, John Frederick. "Christopher Columbus." Lecture presented for the United Italian Societies of Philadelphia, Philadelphia, Philadelphia, October 12, 1892.

———. "Papers." Philadelphia: American Philosophical Society, 1987. Microfilm of art correspondence compiled by the Archives of American Art.

———. "'Schrotblätter': or, Prints in the 'Manière criblée.'" Paper presented to the Numismatic and Antiquarian Society, Philadelphia, 1904.

———. "'Teigdrücke'—Prints in Paste." Paper presented to the Numismatic and Antiquarian Society, Philadelphia, 1904.

Library of Congress. *The Rosenwald Collection. A Catalogue of Illustrated Books and Manuscripts, of Books from Celebrated Presses, and of Bindings and Maps, 1150–1950.* Washington, D.C.: Library of Congress, 1954.

———. *Vision of a Collector. The Lessing J. Rosenwald Collection of the Library of Congress.* Washington, D.C.: Library of Congress, 1991.

Lightbown, Ronald. "The Inspiration of Christian Art." In *Influences in Victorian Art and Architecture,* edited by Sarah Macready and F. H. Thompson, 3–40. London: Society of Antiquaries, 1985.

Lindsay, Coutts. *Sketches of the History of Christian Art.* London: J. Murray, 1847.

Liverpool Art Club. *Exhibition of Illuminated Manuscripts.* Liverpool: The Club, 1876.

*Le Livre d'heures de la Reine Anne de Bretagne.* 2 vols. Paris: Curmer, 1861.

Lloyd, Christopher. "Picture Hunting in Italy: Some Unpublished Letters." *Italian Studies* 30 (1975): 42–68.

Lloyd, Christopher, comp. *A Catalogue of the Earlier Italian Paintings in the Ashmolean Museum.* Oxford: Clarendon Press, 1977.

Loftie, William John. *Lessons in the Art of Illuminating: A Series of Examples Selected from Works in the British Museum, Lambeth Palace Library and the South Kensington Museum; with Practical Instructions and a Sketch of the History of the Art.* London: Blackie and Son, 1885.

———. *A Plea for Art in the House; with Special Reference to the Economy of Collecting Works of Art, and the Importance of Taste in Education and Words.* London: Macmillan, 1876. Reprint, New York: Garland, 1978.

Lonchamp, F. C. *Manuel du Bibliophile français (1470–1920).* Paris, 1927.

Lowndes, William Thomas. *The Bibliographer's Manual of English Literature.* Vol 3. London: George Bell, 1875. Rev. ed. London: H. G. Bohn.

Loyrette, Henri. "Séroux d'Agincourt et les origines de l'histoire de l'art médiéval." *Revue de l'art* 48 (1980): 40–56.

Lucien, Henry Montanell. *Hints on Illuminating: With an Essay on the Art of Ornamenting in Gold or Metals.* London: J. Barnard, 1864.

Ludley, David A. "Anna Jameson and D. G. Rossetti: His Use of Her Histories." *Woman's Art Journal* 12, no. 2 (1991–92): 29–33.

Lydenberg, H. M. *History of the New York Public Library.* New York, 1923.

Lygon, Dorothy, and Francis Russell. "Tuscan Primitives in London Sales: 1801–1837." *Burlington Magazine* 122, no. 923 (February 1980): 112–17.

Lynes, Russell. *The Tastemakers.* New York: Harper, 1954. Reprint, Westport, Conn.: Greenwood Press, 1983.

Mabillon, Jean. *De liturgia Gallicana libri III: In quibus veteris missae: Quae ante annos mille apud Gallos in usu crat, forma ritusque eruuntur ex antiquis monumentis, Lectionario Gallicano hactenus inedito, & tribus missalibus Thomasianis, quae integra referuntur. Accedit Disquisitio de cursu Gallicano, seu de divinorum officiorum origine & progressu in ecclesiis Gallicanis.* Paris: E. Martin et J. Boudot, 1685.

———. *De re Diplomatica, libri VI in quibis quid ad veterum instrumentorum antiquitatem, materiam, scripturam et stilum.* 6 vols. Paris: L. Billaine, 1681–1704. Supplement, 1704. Reprint, Paris: C. Robustel, 1704–9. Reprint, Naples: Vincentii Ursini.

MacCarthy-Reagh, Justin, compte de. *Catalogue des livres rares et precieux de la bibliotheque de feu M. le comte de Mac-*

Carthy-Reagh. Paris: De Bure Freres, 1815.

Mackail, J. W. *The Life of William Morris.* London: Longman, Green, 1899. Reprint, New York: B. Blom, 1968.

Mainardi, Patricia. "Assuring the Empire of the Future: The 1798 Fête de la Liberté." *Art Journal,* summer 1989, 155–63.

Marcel, Odile. *Une éducation française.* Paris: Presses Universitaires de France, 1984.

Marrow, James H. et al., *The Golden Age of Dutch Manuscript Painting.* Stuttgart: Belser, 1989; New York: George Braziller, 1990.

Martin, Henri-Jean, and Roger Chartier. *Histoire de l'edition française.* Paris: Promodis, 1983–.

Martin, Henri-Jean, and Roger Chartier, eds. *Histoire de l'édition française. Le temps des éditeurs. Du Romantisme à la Belle Époque.* Paris: Promidis, 1985.

Matheson, William. "Lessing J. Rosenwald 'A Splendidly Generous Man.'" *Quarterly Journal of the Library of Congress* 37, no. 1 (winter 1980): 3–24.

Mathieu, Bernard Carl. *Minnesänger aus der Zeit Hohenstaufen, im vierzehnten Jahrhundert gesammelt von Rudger Maness von Maneck.* Paris, 1850.

Maynard, Frederick W. *Descriptive Notice of the Drawings and Publications of the Arundel Society for 1849 to 1868 Inclusive. Illustrated by Photographs of All the Publications, One Fifth Their Original Size, Arranged in Order of Their Issue.* London: J. B. Nichols and Sons, 1869.

———. *Descriptive Notice of the Drawings and Publications of the Arundel Society from 1869 to 1873 Inclusive, Being a Continuation of ("Twenty Years of the Arundel Society"). Illustrated by Photographs of All the Publications Arranged in the Order of Their Issue.* London: J. B. Nichols and Sons, 1873.

Maynard, Patrick. "Talbot's Technologies: Photographic Depiction, Detection and Reproduction." *Journal of Aesthetics and Art Criticism* 47 (summer 1989): 236–76.

McCombs, Charles F. *Illuminated Manuscripts from the Pierpont Morgan Library. Catalogue of an Exhibition Held at the New York Public Library.* New York: New York Public Library, 1934.

McCracken, Ursula E., Lilian M. C. Randall, and Richard H. Randall, eds. *Gatherings in Honor of Dorothy E. Miner.* Baltimore: Walters Art Gallery, 1974.

McGrath, R. L. "The Case of the 'Spanish Forger.'" *Dartmouth College Library Bulletin* 7, no. 1 (October 1966): 7–12.

McKitterick, R. "Charles the Bald and his Library." *English Historical Review* 95 (1980): 28–47.

McLean, Ruari. "Henry Shaw's Coloured Books and Chiswick Press Colour Printing." In *Victorian Book Design and Colour Printing,* 65–71. London: Faber, 1972.

———. *Victorian Book Design and Colour Printing.* 2d ed. London: Faber, 1972.

McManners, John. *Church and Society in Eighteenth-Century France.* Vol. 1, *The Clerical Establishment and its Social Ramification.* Oxford: Oxford University Press, 1998.

Meijer, B. W., ed., *Italian Drawings from the Rijksmuseum, Amsterdam,* translated by P. Spring. Florence, 1995.

Meiss, Millard. *French Painting in the Time of Jean de Berry: The Boucicaut Master.* Vol. 3, *National Gallery of Art: Kress Foundation Studies in the History of European Art.* London: Phaidon, 1968.

———. *French Painting in the Time of Jean de Berry: The Limbourgs and Their Contemporaries.* New York: G. Braziller, 1987.

Merrifield, Mary P. *Original Treatises Dating from the XIIth to the XVIIth Centuries on the Arts of Painting in Oil, Miniature, Mosaic and on Glass; of Gilding, Dyeing; and Preparation of Colours and Artificial Gems.* 2 vols. London: John Murray, 1849.

Millar, Eric. "Les manuscrits a peinture de la Bibliothèque du Musee de Sir John Soane, Lincoln's Inn Fields, Londres." *Bulletin de la Societe Francaise de Reproductions de Manuscrits a Peintures* 4, no. 2 (1914–20): 81–149.

Milliken, W. M. "Illuminated Miniatures in the Cleveland Museum of Art." *Bulletin of the Cleveland Museum of Art* 12 (1925): 62.

Miner, Dorothy E. *Anastaise and Her Sisters: Women Artists of the Middle Ages.* Baltimore: Walters Art Gallery, 1974.

———. "The Conradin Bible. A Masterpiece of Italian Illumination." *Apollo* 84, no. 58 (December 1966): 470–75.

———. "The Publishing Ventures of a Victorian Connoisseur: A Sidelight on William T. Walters." *Papers of the Bibliographical Society of America* 57 (1963): 271–311.

———. "Since De Ricci—Western Illuminated Manuscripts Acquired since 1934." *Journal of the Walters Art Gallery* 29–30 and 31–32 (1966–67 and 1968–69): 29–30 and 41–115.

Miner, Dorothy E., ed. *Studies in Art and Literature for Belle da Costa Greene.* Princeton: Princeton University Press, 1954.

Mireur, Hippolyte. *Dictionnaire des ventes d'art faites en France et à l'étranger pendant les XVIIIme et XIXme siècles.* 7 vols. Paris: Maison d'Editions d'Oeuvres Artistiques, 1911.

Mittler, Elmar, and Wilfried Werner. *Codex Manesse. Katalog der Ausstellung vom 12. Juni bis 4. September 1988, Universitätsbibliothek Heidelberg.* Heidelberg: Braus, 1988.

Mongan, Elizabeth. *Rosenwald Collection: An Exhibition of Recent Acquisitions.* Washington, D.C.: National Gallery of Art, 1950.

Monnier, Gérard. *L'art et ses institution en France, de la révolution à nos jours.* Paris: Gallimard, 1995.

Montfaucon, Bernard de. *Les Monumens de la monarchie françoise qui comprennent l'histoire de France avec les figures de chaque règne que l'injure des tems à épargnées.* 5 vols. Paris: J. M. Gandouin, 1729–33.

———. *Palaeographica graeca, sive de ortu progressu literatum graecarium.* Paris: Apud Ludovicum Guerin, 1708. Reprint, Rome: Bibliopola, 1963.

Moreland, Kim. "Henry Adams, the Medieval Lady and the 'New Woman.'" *CLIO* 18, no. 3 (spring 1989): 291–305.

Mores, Edward Rowe. *Figurae quaedam antiquae ex Caedmonis Monachi paraphraseos in Genesin exemplari pervetusto, in biblioteca Bodleiana, deliate.* London: G. Woodfall, 1754.

Morey, Charles Rufus. *History of the Art of Illumination. Special Exhibits in the Princeton University Library.* Princeton,

N.J.: Princeton University Library, 1916.

———. *Pierpont Morgan Library. Exhibition of Illuminated Manuscripts Held at the New York Public Library.* Catalogue by Belle da Costa Greene and Meta P. Harrsen. New York: Pierpont Morgan Library, 1934.

Morley, Catherine W. *John Ruskin. Late Work: 1870–1890. The Museum and Guild of St George, an Educational Experiment.* New York: Garland Publishing, 1984.

Morris, William. *Hopes and Fears for Art.* London: Ellis and White, 1882. Reprint, Bristol, England: Thoemmes Press, 1994.

———. *The Ideal Book: Essays and Lectures on the Arts of the Book by William Morris.* Edited by William S. Peterson. Berkeley and Los Angeles: University of California Press, 1982.

———. *A Note by William Morris on His Aims in Founding the Kelmscott Press, Together with a Short Description of the Press by S.c. Cockerell, & an Annotated List of the Books Printed Thereat.* Hammersmith: Kelmscott Press, 1898. Reprint, New York: A. Schram, 1969.

———. *Some Thoughts on the Ornamented Manuscripts of the Middle Ages.* New York: Press of the Woolly Whale, 1934.

Morrison, Karl. "Interpreting the Fragment." In *Hermeneutics and Medieval Culture.* Edited by Patrick J. Gallacher and Helen Damico, 27–37. Albany: State University of New York Press, 1988.

Morrison, Karl F. "Henry Adams (1838–1918)." In *Medieval Scholarship. Biographical Studies on the Formation of a Discipline.* Vol. 1, *History,* edited by Helen Damico and Joseph B. Zavadil, 115–30. New York: Garland, 1995.

Morrissey, Robert. "Charlemagne." In *Les lieux de mémoire,* edited by Pierre Nora. Paris: Gallimard, 1984–92.

———. "Charlemagne." *Realms of Memory: Rethinking the French Past.* Translated by Arthur Goldhammer. New York: Columbia University Press, 1996.

Muensterberger, Werner. *Collecting: An Unruly Passion. Psychological Perspectives.* Princeton: Princeton University Press, 1994.

Munby, Alan Noel Latimer. *Connoisseurs and Medieval Miniatures, 1750–1850.* Oxford: Clarendon Press, 1972.

———. "Dibdin's Reference Library. The Sale of 26–28 June 1817." In *Studies in the Book Trade: In Honour of Graham Pollard,* edited by R. W. Hunt, I. G. Philip, and R. J. Roberts, 279–315. Oxford: Oxford Bibliographical Society, 1975.

———. "The Earl and the Thief." In *Essays and Papers,* edited by Nicholas Barker, 175–91. London: Scolar Press, 1978.

———. *Phillipps Studies.* 5 vols. Cambridge: Cambridge University Press, 1951–60. Reprint, London: Sotheby's Parke-Bernet Publications, 1971.

———. "The Triumph of Delisle." In *Essays and Papers,* edited by Nicholas Barker, 193–205. London: Scolar Press, 1977.

Müntz, Eugène. "Les annexions de collections d'art ou des bibliothèques et leur rôle dans les relations internationales principalement pendant la Révolution française." Parts 1–3. *Revue d'histoire diplomatique* 8 (1894): 481–97; 9 (1895): 375–95; 10 (1896): 481–508.

Mure, Louisa. *Recollections of by-gone days.* Privately printed, 1883.

Musée des Beaux-arts. *Les Muses de Messidor. Peintres et sculpteurs Lyonnais de la Révolution à l'Empire.* Lyon: Musée des Beaux-arts, 1989.

Musée des Beaux-arts de Nantes. *Les années romantiques. La peinture française de 1815 à 1850.* Paris: Réunion des Musées Nationaux, 1995.

Musée Royal. *Notices des tableaux des écoles primitives de l'Italie, de l'Allemagne, et de plusieurs autres tableaux de diff(rentes écoles, exposés dans le grand salon du Musée royal, ouvert le 25 juillet 1814.* Paris: L.-P. Dubray, 1814.

Museum im Gotischen Haus. *Ich schreibe, lese und male ohne Unterlass: Elizabeth, englische Prinzessin und Landgräfin von Hessen-Homburg (1770–1840) als Künstlerin und sammlerin.* Bad Homburg: Museum im Gotischen Haus, 1995.

Naudé, Gabriel. *Advis pour dresser une bibliothèque présenté à Mgr le président de Mesmes.* Paris: n.p., 1627.

Naumann, Robert. *Führer durch die Ausstellung von handschriften und Druckwerken auf der Stadtsbibliothek zu Leipzig.* Leipzig: C. P. Melzer, 1859.

Needham, Paul, ed. *William Morris and the Art of the Book.* New York: Pierpont Morgan Library, 1976.

New York Public Library. *The Spencer Collection of Illustrated Books.* New York: New York Public Library, 1928.

Nichols, John. *Literary Anecdotes of the Eighteenth Century; Comprizing Biographical Memoires of William Bowyer, Printer F.S.A. and Many of His Learned Friends, an Incidental View of the Progress and Advancement of Literature in This Kingdom during the Last Century and Biographical Anecdotes of a Considerable Number of Eminent Writers and Ingenious Artists with a Very Copious Index.* 9 vols. London: J. Nichols, Son and Bently, 1812–16.

Nichols, Thomas. *A Handbook for Readers at the British Museum.* London: Longman, Green, 1866.

Nodier, Charles, and Justin Taylor. *Voyages pittoresques et romantiques dans l'ancienne France.* 19 vols. Paris: Didot l'Aine, 1820–78.

Nora, Pierre, ed. *Les Lieux de mémoire.* Paris: Gallimard, 1984–92.

———. *Realms of Memory: Rethinking the French Past.* Translated by Arthur Goldhammer. New York: Columbia University Press, 1996.

Nordenfalk, Carl. *Color of the Middle Ages: A Survey of Book Illumination Based on Color Facsimiles of Medieval Manuscripts.* Pittsburgh, Pa.: University Art Gallery, Henry Clay Frick Fine Arts Building, 1976.

Nordenfalk, Carl, et al. *Medieval and Renaissance Miniatures from the National Gallery of Art.* Washington, D.C.: National Gallery of Art, 1975.

*Notable American Women: The Modern Period.* Cambridge, Mass., 1980.

O'Dwyer, Edward John. *Thomas Frognall Dibdin: Bibliographer and Bibliomaniac Extraordinary, 1776–1847.* Pinner (Mddx.): Private Libraries Association, 1967; Braswell-Means, 1992.

Offner, Richard. *Italian Primitives at Yale University: Comments and Revisions.* New Haven, Conn.: Yale University Press, 1927.

Offor, Edward. *Illuminating Made Easy.* London: J. B. Bunyard, 1865.

Oldmixion, John. *An Essay on Criticism as It Regards Design, Thought and Expres-*

sion, in Prose and Verse. London: Printed by J. Pemberton, 1728.

Omont, Henri. Listes des Recueils de Fac-similés et des reproductions de manuscrits conservés à la Bibliothèque Nationale. Paris: Editions des Bibliothèques Nationales de France, 1935.

Ottley, William Young. A Descriptive Catalogue of the Pictures in the National Gallery. London: W. Nicol, 1835.

———. The Italian School of Design: Being a Series of Fac-similes of Original Drawings by the Most Eminent Painters and Sculptors of Italy; with Biographical Notices of the Artists, and Observations on Their Works. London: Taylor and Hessey, 1823.

———. Observations on a Manuscript in the British Museum, Beleived to Be of the Second or Third Century, and Containing Cicero's Translation of the Astronomical Poem by Aratus, Accompanied by Drawings of the Constellations: with a Preliminary Dissertation in Proof of the Use of Miniscule Writing by the Ancient Romans; and a Corrected Edition of the Poem Itself... Communicated ... in a Letter to John Gage. London: J. B. Nichols, 1835. Reprinted in Archaeologia 26 (1836): 47–214.

———. A Series of Plates Engraved after the Paintings and Sculptures of the Most Eminent Masters of the Early Florentine School; Intended to Illustrate the History of the Restoration of the Arts of Design in Italy. London: privately published and sold by Colnaghi, 1826.

Panofsky, Erwin. "The First Page of Giorgio Vasari's 'Libro.'" In Meaning in the Visual Arts, 169–225. Woodstock, N.Y.: Overlook Press, 1974. First published in Städel-Jahrbuch 6 (1930): 25–72.

Parkes, M. B. The Medieval Manuscripts of Keble College Oxford. Oxford: Oxford University, Keble College, 1979.

Parris, Leslie, ed. Pre-Raphaelite Papers. London: Tate Gallery, 1984.

Parry, Linda, ed. William Morris. London: Philip Wilson, 1996.

Parshall, Peter. "The Print Collection of Ferdinand, Archduke of Tyrol." Jahrbuch des Kunsthistorischen Sammlungen in Wein 78 (1982): 139–84.

Perkinson, S. "Interpreting the Louvre Image of John the Good: The Legacy of the Exhibition of Primitifs français (Paris, 1904)." Forthcoming.

Peterson, Elizabeth A., and Alison Stones, "The Book Goes Public," Carnegie Magazine 54, no. 8 (March–April 1989): 30–35.

Peterson, William S., ed. The Ideal Book: Essays and Lectures on the Arts of the Book by William Morris. Berkeley: University of California Press, 1982.

Phillipps, Ambrose Lisle, trans. The Chronicle of the Life of St Elizabeth of Hungary . . . Written in French by the Count De Montalembert, Peer of France, and Now Translated into English for the Greater Glory of God by Ambrose Lisle Phillipps Esquire of Grace Dieu Manor, Leicestershire. London: n. p., 1839.

Pierpont Morgan Library. The First Quarter Century of the Pierpont Morgan Library: A Retrospective Exhibition in Honor of Belle da Costa Greene. New York: Pierpont Morgan Library, 1949.

———. In August Company: The Collections of the Pierpont Morgan Library. New York: Pierpont Morgan Library, 1993.

Piggott, Stuart. William Stukeley. Oxford: Clarendon Press, 1950.

Pine, L. G., ed. Burke's Genealogical and Heraldic History of the Landed Gentry. 7th ed. London: Burke's Peerage Ltd., 1952.

Piton, Eugène. Famille Firmin-Didot, imprimeurs, libraires, fondeurs, graveurs, papetiers, inventeurs et littérateurs. Paris: Publications de la Renommée, 1856.

Pointon, Marcia, ed. Pre-Raphaelites Reviewed. Manchester: Manchester University Press, 1989.

Pomian, Krzysztof. Collectors and Curiosities: Paris and Venice 1500–1800. Translated by Elizabeth Wiles-Portier. Cambridge, U.K.: Polity Press; Cambridge, Mass.: Basil Blackwell, 1990.

Pope-Hennessy, John. The Robert Lehman Collection. Vol. 1. Italian Paintings. New York: Metropolitan Museum of Art, 1987.

Popkin, Z. F. "Art: Three Aisles Over." Outlook and Independent (November 26, 1930): 503.

Poulot, Dominique. "Alexandre Lenoir et les musées des monumens français." In Les Lieux de mémoire, edited by Pierre Nora, 497–531. Paris: Gallimard, 1986.

———. "Alexandre Lenoir." Realms of Memory: Rethinking the French Past, translated by Arthur Goldhammer. New York: Columbia University Press, 1996.

The Pre-Raphaelites. London: Tate Gallery with Penguin Books, 1984.

Preston, Jean. "The Spanish Forger." Kresge Art Museum Bulletin 5 (1990): 16–21.

Previtali, Giovanni. La fortuna dei primitivi dal Vasari ai neoclassici. Turin: Einaudi, 1964.

Price, M. "Henry Walters: Elusive Collector," in Medieval Art in America, edited by Elizabeth Bradford Smith, University Park, Pa: Palmer Museum of Art, 1996.

Prideaux, S. T. Bookbinders and Their Craft. New York, 1903.

Print Club of Philadelphia, Five Centuries of Print Making from the Collection of Lessing J. Rosenwald. Philadelphia, 1931.

Pugin, Augustus Welby Northmore. An Apology for the Revival of Christian Architecture in England. London: John Weale, 1843. Reprint, Frome, Somerset: Butler and Tanner, 1969.

———. Contrasts; or, a Parallel between the Noble Edifices of the Fourteenth and Fifteenth Centuries, and Similar Buildings of the Present Day, Showing the Present Decay of Taste, Accompanied by Appropriate Text. London: Pugin, 1836. Rev. ed. London: C. Dolman, 1841. Reprint, New York: Humanities Press, 1969.

———. Floriated Ornament: A Series of Thirty-One Designs. London: Henry G. Bohn, 1849. Reprint, Somerset: Richard Dennis, Shepton Beauchamp, 1994.

———. Glossary of Ecclesiastical Ornament and Costume, Compiled and Illustrated from Antient Authorities and Examples. London: Henry G. Bohn, 1844.

———. True Principles of Pointed or Christian Architecture. London: J. Weale, 1841.

Quaritch, Bernard, ed. Contributions Towards a Dictionary of English Book-collectors, as Also of Some Foreign Collectors Whose Libraries Were Incorporated in English Collections or Whose Books Are Chiefly Met with in England. London: B. Quaritch, 1892–1921.

Quarré-Reybourbon, L. "Une fausse miniature concernant la ville de Lille." Mémoire lu à la réunion des Sociétés des Beaux-Arts des Départements, tenu dans l'hémicycle de l'Ecole des Beaux-Arts (Paris, April 4, 1893): 5–13.

Quynn, Dorothy Mackay. "Art Confiscations of the Napoleonic Wars." American Historical Review 50 (1945): 437–60.

Rahir, Edouard. La Vente Robert Hoe. Paris: Librairie Henri Leclerc, 1913.

Ramsden, Charles Frederick Ingram. Richard Wier and Count MacCarthy-Reagh. London: Queen Anne Press, 1953–54.

Randall, Lilian M. C. "Horae Beatae Mariae Virginis (Edith G. Rosenwald Hours)." In Library of Congress, Vision of a Collector: The Lessing J. Rosenwald Collection of the Library of Congress. Washington, D.C.: Library of Congress, 1991.

———. Medieval and Renaissance Manuscripts in the Walters Art Gallery. 2 vols. Baltimore: Johns Hopkins University Press with the Walters Art Gallery, 1989–92.

———. "A Ninteenth-Century 'Medieval' Prayerbook Woven in Lyon." In Art, the Ape of Nature: Studies in Honor of H.W. Janson, edited by Moshe Barasch and Lucy Freeman Sandler, 651–68. New York: Abrams, 1981.

Ray, Gordon N. The Art of the French Illustrated Book, 1700–1914. 2 vols. Ithaca, N.Y.: Cornell University Press, 1982.

Redgrave, Samuel. A Dictionary of Artists of the English School. Amsterdam: G. W. Hissink, 1970.

Redmond, René. Les droits en France. 4th ed. Paris: Aubier Montaigne, 1982.

Reinach, Salomon. "Copies des chefs d'oeuvres." Revue archéologique 34 (1931): 289–99.

———. "Two Forged Miniatures of Joan of Arc." Burlington Magazine 14, no. 72 (March 1909): 356.

Reitlinger, Gerald. The Economics of Taste. 3 vols. London: Barrie and Rockliff, 1961–70.

Reynolds, Catherine, and Jenny Stratford. "Le manuscrit dit 'Le Pontifical de Poitiers.'" Revue de l'Art 84 (1989): 61–80.

Rickert, Margaret. The Reconstructed Carmelite Missal: An English Manuscript of the Late-Fourteenth Century in the British Museum (Additional 29704–5, 44892). Chicago: University of Chicago Press, 1952.

Rionnet, Florence. L'Histoire de l'atelier de moulage du Musée du Louvre (1794–1928). Paris: Seuil, 1996.

Rive, Jean-Joseph. Essai sur l'art de verifier l'age des miniatures peintes dans les manuscrits depuis le XIVe jusqu'au XVIIe siècle inclusivement. Prospectus d'un ouvrage. Paris: Didot Aine, 1782.

———. La Chasse aux bibliographes et antiquaires mal-avisés. London: N. Aphobe, 1788.

———. Pieces qui manquent dans la bibliothèque de monsieur le duc de la Valière. N.p., n.d.

Robert, Karl. Traité pratique de l'enluminure des livres d'heures, canons d'autel, images et gravures. Paris: Georges Meusnier, 1888.

Roberts, Jane. Royal Artists from Mary Queen of Scots to the Present Day. London: Grafton, 1987.

Robinson, John Charles. The Museum of Art: Introductory Address to the Science and

Art Department and the South Kensington Museum. Vol. 5. London: South Kensington Museum, 1858.

Robinson, John Charles, ed. Catalogue of the Special Exhibition of Works of Art of the Medieval, Renaissance, and more Recent Periods, on Loan at the South Kensington Museum. London: George E. Eyre and William Spottiswoode for HMSO, 1862.

Robson-Scott, William. D. The Literary Background of the Gothic Revival in Germany. Oxford: Clarendon Press, 1965.

Rosenbach Museum and Library. Rosenwald and Rosenbach: Two Philadelphia Bookmen. Philadelphia, 1983.

Roscoe, William. The Life of Lorenzo de' Medici, Called the Magnificent. London: printed for A. Strahan, T. Cadell and W. Davies, and J. Edwards, 1796.

Rosenbaum-Dondaine, Catherine. L'Image de piété en France, 1814–1914. Paris: Musée-Galerie de la SEITA, 1984.

———."Un siècle et demi de petite imagerie de piété." Revue de la Bibliothèque Nationale 6 (December 1982): 24–34.

Rosenthal, Bernard M. "Cartel, Clan or Dynasty? The Olschkis and the Rosenthals, 1859–1976." Harvard Library Bulletin 25, no. 4 (October 1977): 381–98.

Rosenthal, Bernard, and Paul E. Szarmach, eds. Medievalism in American Culture: Papers of the Eighteenth Annual Conference of the Center for Medieval and Early Reniassance Studies. Binghamton, N.Y.: Center for Medieval and Early Renaissance Studies, State University of New York at Binghamton, 1989.

Rosenthal, Jane E. "Illuminated Manuscripts at Columbia University." In Medieval and Renaissance Manuscripts at Columbia University. Edited by Beatrice Terrien-Somerville. New York: Columbia University Libraries, 1991, 27–38.

Rosenwald, Lessing J. "The Formation of the Rosenwald Collection." Quarterly Journal of the Library of Congress 3, no. 1 (October 1945): 53–62.

———. "The Mirror of the Collector." Quarterly Journal of the Library of Congress 22, no. 3 (July 1965): 160–69.

———. Recollections of a Collector. Jenkintown, Pa.: Alverthorpe Gallery, 1976.

Rostand, André. "La documentation iconographique des monumens de la monarchie françoise de Bernard de Montfaucon." Bulletin de la société de l'Histoire de l'art français (1932): 104–49.

Rothschild, Edward F. "Medieval Manuscript Illumination. The Renaissance Society Sponsors Exhibition." University of Chicago Magazine 22 (1929–30): 192–95.

Ruskin, John. Praeterita: The Autobiography of John Ruskin. Oxford: Oxford University Press, 1978.

———. The Works of John Ruskin. Library ed. Edited by E. T. Cook and A. Wedderburn. 39 vols. London: G. Allen; New York: Longmans, Green, 1903–12.

Rutledge, Anna Wells. "Robert Gilmore, Jr.: Baltimore Collector." Journal of the Walters Art Gallery 12 (1949): 19–39.

Saarinen, Aline B. The Proud Possessors. The Lives, Times and Tastes of Some Adventurous American Art Collectors. New York: Random House, 1958. Reprint, New York: Vintage Books, 1969.

Saenger, Paul, and Michael Heinlen. "Incunable Description and Its Implica-

tion for the Analysis of Fifteenth-Century Reading Habits." In Printing the Written Word: The Social History of Books, Circa 1450–1520, edited by Sandra Hindman, 225–58. Ithaca, N.Y.: Cornell University Press, 1991.

Sandler, Lucy Freeman. Gothic Manuscripts, 1285–1385, 2 vols. London: Harvey Miller, 1986.

Sanson, Rosemonde. "La 'Fête de Jeanne d'Arc' en 1894: controverse et célébration." Revue d'Histoire Moderne et Contemporaine 20 (1973): 444–63.

Sartain, John S. The Reminiscences of a Very Old Man. New York: D. Appleton, 1899.

Satterlee, Herbert Livingston. J. Pierpont Morgan: An Intimate Portrait. New York: Macmillan, 1939.

Saunders, O. Elfrida. English Illumination. New York, 1928.

Saunier, Charles. Les Conquêtes artistiques de la Révolution et de l'Empire. Paris: H. Laurens, 1902.

Savart, Claude. "Le livre religieux." In Le temps des éditeurs. Vol. 3 of Histoire de l'édition Française, edited by Henri-Jean Martin and Roger Chartier, 402–7. Paris: Promodis, 1983–.

Scailliérez, Cécile. "Entre enluminure et peinture: a propos d'un Paysage avec Saint Jérôme Pénitent de l'école Ganto-Brugeoise récemment acquis par le Louvre." Revue du Louvre 42 (1992): 16–31.

Schaefer, Claude. The Hours of Etienne Chevalier: Jean Fouquet. With a preface by Charles Sterling. New York: G. Braziller, 1971.

Schaefer, Claude, Christopher De Hamel, and Jean-Yves Ribault. "Du nouveau sur les Heures d'Étienne Chevalier illustrées par Fouquet." Gazette des beaux-arts 6, no. 123 (December 1981): 193–200.

Schaff, Larry J. Out of the Shadows: Herschel, Talbot and the Invention of Photography. New Haven, Conn., 1992.

Scharf, Aaron. Art and Photography. London: Allen Lane, 1968.

Shaw, Henry. Alphabets, Numerals and Devices of the Middle Ages. London: B. Quaritch, 1845.

———. Dresses and Decorations of the Middle Ages. 2 vols. London: William Pickering, 1843.

———. Encyclopaedia of Ornament. London: William Pickering, 1836–42.

———. Hand Book of Mediaeval Alphabets and Devices. 2d ed. London: William Pickering, 1856.

———. Handbook of the Art of Illumination as Practised during the Middle Ages: With a Description of the Metals, Pigments and Processes Employed by the Artists at Different Periods. London: Bell and Daldy, 1866.

———. Illuminated Ornaments Selected from Manuscripts and Early Printed Books from the Sixth to the Seventeenth Centuries. Descriptions by Frederic Madden. London: William Pickering, 1830–33.

Shaw, J. Byam. Paintings by Old Masters at Christ Church, Oxford. London: Phaidon, 1967.

Sherman, Claire Richter. "Dorothy Eugenia Miner (1904–1973): The Varied Career of a Medievalist: Scholar and Keeper of Manuscripts, Librarian and Editor at the Walters Art Gallery." In Women as Interpreters of the Visual Arts, 1820–1979, edited by Claire Richter

Sherman with Adele M. Holcomb, 377–409. Westport, Conn., 1981.

———. The Portraits of Charles V of France (1338–1380). Vol. 20 of Monographs on Archaeology and the Fine Arts. New York: New York University Press for the College Art Association of America, 1969.

Sherman, Daniel J. Worthy Monuments: Art Museums and the Politics of Culture in Nineteenth-Century France. Cambridge, Mass.: Harvard University Press, 1989.

Shestack, A. "Biblia Latina (Giant Bible of Mainz)." In Vision of a Collector. The Lessing J. Rosenwald Collection of the Library of Congress. Washington, D.C.: Library of Congress, 1991.

Shipman, Carolyn. Catalogue of Manuscripts Comprising a Portion of the Library of Robert Hoe. New York: Duprat, 1909.

Sillib, Rudolf, Friedrich Panzer, and Arthur Haseloff. Die Manessische Lieder-Handschrift. Faksimile-Ausgabe. 7 vols. Leipzig: Insel-Verlag, 1929.

Silver, Joel. "Robert Hoe and His Library." AB Bookman's Weekly 95, no. 15 (April 10, 1995): 1574–82.

Simkhovitch, V. G. "Exhibition of Illuminated Manuscripts." Columbia University Quarterly 9 (1906–7): 44–46.

Simsar, Muhammed Ahmed. Oriental Manuscripts of the John Frederick Lewis Collection in the Free Library of Philadelphia. Baltimore: J. H. Furst, 1937.

Sirn, Osvald. A Descriptive Catalogue of the Pictures in the Jarves Collection Belonging to Yale University. New Haven, Conn.: Yale University Press, 1916.

Sisi, Carlo, and Ettore Spalletti. La cultura artistica a Siena nell'ottocento. Siena: Monte dei Paschi di Siena, 1994.

Skelton, R. A., Thomas E. Marston, and George D. Painter. The Vinland Map and the Tartar Relation. New Haven, Conn.: Yale University Press, 1965.

Sloan, William R. Sir Hans Sloane: Founder of the British Museum: Legend and Lineage. Down, N. Ireland: W. R. Sloan, 1981.

Smeyers, Maurits. L'art de la Minaiture flamande du VIIIe au XVIe siècle. Translated by Monique Verboomen. Tournai: La Renaissance du Livre, 1998.

Smith, Elizabeth Bradford. Medieval Art in America: Patterns of Collecting, 1800–1940. University Park, Pa.: Palmer Museum of Art, 1996.

Snay, C. "Medieval Art in American Popular Culture: Mid- Nineteenth-Century American Travelers in Europe." In Medieval Art in America, edited by Elizabeth Bradford Smith University Park, Pa: Palmer Museum of Art, 1996.

Snyder Joel, and Neill Walsh Allen. "Photography, Vision and Representation" Critical Inquiry 2 (1975): 143–69.

Soane, John, Sir. Description of the House and Museum on the North Side of Lincoln's-inn-fields, the Residence of Sir John Soane. London: James Moyes, 1830.

Somerville, Robert. "The Origins of Columbia University's Collection of Medieval and Renaissance Manuscripts." In Renaissance Society and Culture: Essays in Honor of Eugene F. Rice, edited by John Monfasani and Ronald G. Musto, 289–300. New York: Italica Press, 1991.

Sorel, Albert. L'Europe et la révolution française. 8 vols. Paris: Plon, 1907–10.

Soria, M. S. "The So-Called 'French Primitive': An Exposure and a Recantation." *Connoisseur* 117 (1946): 126–27.

Sourget, Patrick, and Elizabeth Sourget. *Manuscrits et livres précieux,* catalogue no. 7 (1991).

Sotheby's, *Illuminated Miniatures and Single Leaves from the Ninth to the Sixteenth Century.* London: Sotheby's, July 14, 1981.

Spadafore, Anita Louise. "Baron Taylor's *Voyages Pittoresques.*" Ph.D. dissertation, Northwestern University, 1973.

Spies, Gerd. "Die Kunst- und kulturgeschichtlichen Lokal- und Regionalmuseen. Zeiten, auslösende Faktoren, Initiatoren der Gründungen." In *Das kunst- und kulturgeschichtliche Museum im 19. Jahrhundert,* edited by Bernward Deneke and Rainer Kahsnitz, 77–81. Munich: Prestel, 1977.

Stafford, Barbara. *Artful Science: Enlightenment Entertainment and the Eclipse of Visual Education.* Boston: MIT Press, 1994.

Stanley, Arthur P. *the Life and Correspondence of Thomas Arnold.* 2 vols. New York: C. Scribner's Sons, 1844.

Stanton, Phoebe. *Pugin.* London: Thames and Hudson, 1971.

———. "The Sources of Pugin's Contrasts." In *Concerning Architecture: Essays on Architectural Writers and Writing, Presented to Nikolaus Pevsner,* edited by John Summerson, 120–39. London: Allen Lane, 1968.

*Statuts de l'Ordre de Saint-Esprit au droit desir, ou du noeud institue à Naples en 1354 par Louis d'Anjou … roi de Jerusalem, de Naples et de Sicile. Manuscrit du XIVme siècle conservé au Louvre dans le Musée des souverains français avec une Notice sur la peinture des miniatures et la description du manuscrit par M. le comte Horace de Viel-Castel.* Paris: Engelmann et Graf, 1853.

Steegmuller, Francis. *The Two Lives of James Jackson Jarves.* New Haven, Conn.: Yale University Press, 1951.

Stein, Roger B. *John Ruskin and Aesthetic Thought in America, 1840–1900.* Cambridge, Mass.: Harvard University Press, 1967.

Stephen, Sir Leslie, and Sir Sidney Lee, eds. *The Dictionary of National Biography: 1885–90.* Reprint, Oxford: Oxford University Press, 1917–90.

Sterling, Charles. "Les émules des primitifs." *La Revue de l'art* 21 (1973): 80–93.

Sterling, Charles, et al. *The Robert Lehman Collection.* Vol. 2, *Fifteenth- to Eighteenth-Century European Paintings.* New York: Metropolitan Museum of Art, 1998.

Stewart, Susan. *On Longing: Narratives of the Miniature, the Gigantic, the Souvenir, the Collection.* Baltimore: Johns Hopkins University Press, 1984.

Stone, James S. *Emily Faithful, Victorian Champion of Women's Rights.* Toronto: P. D. Meany, 1994.

Stonehouse, John Harrison. *The Story of the Great Omar, Bound by Francis Longinus Sangorski, and Its Tragic Loss.* London: Piccadilly Fountain Press, 1933.

Strange, E. F. *Catalogue of the Circulating Collection of Illuminated Manuscripts (Leaves and Cuttings): Selected from the Victoria and Albert Museum, South Kensington.* London: printed for H.M.S.O. by Wyman and Sons, 1908.

Strong, Roy. *Recreating the Past: British History and the Victorian Painter.* New York: Thames and Hudson for the Pierpont Morgan Library, 1978; London: Thames and Hudson, 1979.

Strouse, Jean *Morgan. American Financier.* New York: Random House, 1999.

Strutt, Joseph. *A Complete View of the Dress and Habits of the People of England, from the Establishment of the Saxons in Britain to the Present Time: Illustrated by Engravings Taken from the Most Authentic Remains of Antiquity; to Which Is Prefixed an Introduction, Containing a General Description of the Ancient Habits in Use among Mankind, from Their Earliest Period of Time to the Conclusion of the Seventh Century.* London: J. Nichols, 1796–99. Reprint, London: H. G. Bohn, 1842.

———. *Horda Angel-Cynnan; or, A Compleat View of the Manners, Custom, Arms, Habits &c. of the Inhabitants of England, from the Arrival of the Saxons, till the Reign of Henry the Eighth; with a Short Account of the Britons, during the Government of the Romans.* London: J. Nichols, 1774–76. Reprint, London: H. G. Bohn, 1842.

———. *The Regal and Ecclesiastical Antiquities of England: Containing the Representations of All the English Monarchs from Edward the Confessor to Henry the Eighth, Together with Many of the Great Persons That Were Eminent under Their Several Reigns; the Whole Carefully Collected from Antient Illuminated Manuscripts.* London: Walter Shropshire, 1777.

Sulzberger, Suzanne. *La Réhabilitation des primitifs Flamands, 1802–1867.* Brussels: Académie Royale de Belgique, 1961.

Surtees, Virginia, ed. *Reflections of a Friendship: John Ruskin's Letters to Pauline Trevelyan.* London and Boston: Allen and Unwin, 1979.

———. *Sublime and Instructive: Letters from John Ruskin to Louisa, Marchioness of Waterford, Anna Blunden and Ellen Heaton.* London: Joseph, 1972.

Sutton, Denys. "Editorial: Connoisseur's Haven." *Apollo* 84, no. 58 (December 1966): 422–33.

———. "Editorial: The English and Early Italian Art." *Apollo* 81, no. 38 (April 1965): 254–56.

———. "From Ottley to Eastlake." *Apollo* 122, no. 282 (August 1985): 84–95.

Swarzenski, Hanns. *Die Deutsche Buchmalerei des 13.Jahrhunderts.* 2 vols. Berlin: Deutscher Verein für Kunstwissenshaft, 1936.

Szabo, George. *Masterpieces of Italian Drawing in the Robert Lehman Collection, the Metropolitan Museum of Art.* New York: Hudson Hill Press, 1983.

Talbot, William Henry Fox. *The Pencil of Nature.* 1844–46. Reprint, New York: Da Capo, 1969.

Tanis, James R. *Leaves of Gold: Treasures of Illuminated Manuscripts from Philadelphia Collections.* Philadelphia: Philadelphia Museum of Art, 2001.

Tatlock, R. R. "Editorial: To Avoid a National Disgrace." *Burlington Magazine* 55, no. 321 (December 1929): 271.

Taylor, Francis Henry. *Pierpont Morgan as Collector and Patron, 1837–1913.* New York: Pierpont Morgan Library, 1970.

Taylor, W. B. Sarsfield. *The Origin, Progress and Present Condition of the Fine Arts in Great Britain and Ireland.* 2 vols. London: Whittaker, 1841.

Tedeschi, Martha P. "How Prints Work: Reproductions, Originals, and Their Markets in England, 1840–1900."

Ph.D. dissertation, Northwestern University, 1994.

Thieme, Ulrich. *Allgemeines Lexikon der bildenden Künstler.* Leipzig: E. A. Seemann, 1920.

Thierhoff, Bianca. "Ferdinand Franz Wallraf—ein Sammler des "pädagogischen Zeitalters." In *Lust und Verlust: Kölner Sammler zwischen Trikolore und Preußenadler,* edited by Hiltrud Kier and Frank Günter Zehnder, 389–405. Cologne: Wienand and Museen der Stadt Köln, 1995.

Thompson, Henry Yates. *A Descriptive Catalogue of Twenty Illuminated Manuscripts, Nos. LXXV to XCIV, in the Collection of Henry Yates Thompson.* Cambridge: Cambridge University Press, 1907.

Thompson, Paul. *The Work of William Morris.* 3d ed. Oxford: Oxford University Press, 1991.

Thomson, Richard. *A Lecture on Some of the Most Characteristic Features of Illuminated Manuscripts.* London: printed for the London Institution by C. Skipper and East, 1857.

Thynne, Lord Charles. *A Letter to His Late Parishioners by Lord Charles Thynne, Late Vicar of Longbridge Deverill, and Late Canon of Canterbury Cathedral.* London: Burns and Lambert, 1853.

Tietz, Hans. *Genuine and False: Copies, Imitations, and Forgeries.* New York: Chanticleer Press, 1948.

Todini, Filippo and Milvia Bollati. *Una collezione di miniature italiane dal Duecento al Cinquecento.* Milan: Studio nella Longari, 1993.

Török, Gyöngyi. "Neue Folii aus dem 'Ungarischen Anjou-Legendarium.'" *Zeitschrift für Kunstgeschichte* 55, no. 4 (1992): 565–77.

Towner, Wesley. *The Elegant Auctioneers.* New York: Hill and Wang, 1970.

Trachtenberg, Alan. *The Incorporation of America: Culture and Society in the Gilded Age.* New York: Hill and Wang, 1982.

Julian Treuhertz, "The Pre-Raphaelites and Medieval Illuminated Manuscripts," in *Pre-Raphaelite Papers,* ed Leslie Parris (London: Tate Gallery, 1984).

Twyman, Michael. *Lithography 1800–1850: The Techniques of Drawing on Stone in England and France and Their Application in Works of Topography.* Oxford: Oxford University Press, 1970.

———. *Printing 1770–1970: An Illustrated History of Its Development and Uses in England.* London: Eyre and Spottiswoode, 1970.

Tymms, William Robert. *The Art of Illuminating as Practised in Europe from the Earliest Times. Illustrated in Borders, Initial Letters and Alphabets. With an Essay and Instructions by M. D. Wyatt.* London: Day and Son, Ltd., 1860.

Ultree, Maarten. *Abbey of St. Germain des Pres in the Seventeenth Century: A Powerful Benedictine Monastery.* New Haven, Conn.: Yale University Press, 1981.

Union League Club. *Illuminated Books and Manuscripts, Old Masters and Modern Paintings.* New York: Union League Club, 1890.

University of Notre Dame Art Gallery. *Medieval Manuscripts from the Lessing J. Rosenwald Collection.* South Bend, IN: University of Notre Dame Art Gallery, 1972.

Unrau, John. "Ruskin, the Workman and the Savageness of Gothic." In *New Approaches to Ruskin: Thirteen Essays*, edited by Robert Hewison, 33–50. London: Routledge and Kegan Paul, 1981.

*Un trésor gothique. La Chasse de Nivelle.* Paris: Réunion des Musées Nationaux, 1996.

Utz, Richard, and Tom Shippey, eds. *Medievalism in the Modern World: Essays in Honour of Leslie J. Workman.* Turnhout: Brepols, 1998.

Vachon, Marius. *La Guerre artistique avec l'Allemagne: l'organisation de la victoire.* Paris: Payot, 1916.

Valentin, G. "Literaturberichte und Anzeigen." *Zentralblatt für Bibliothekwesen* 27, no. 7–8 (July–August 1910): 363–73.

Valery, M. *Correspondence inédite de Mabillon et Montfaucon avec l'Italie.* 3 vols. Paris: Labitte, 1846–47.

Van Engen, John, ed. *The Past and Future of Medieval Studies.* Notre Dame, Ind.: University of Notre Dame Press, 1994.

van Falke, O., R. Schmidt, and G. Swarzenski, eds., *The Guelph Treasure: The Sacred Relics of Brunswick Cathedral Formerly in the Possession of the Ducal House of Brunswick-Lüneburg,* translated by S. M. Welch. Frankfurt am Main, 1930.

Vanuxem, Jacques. "The Theories of Mabillon and Montfaucon on French Sculpture of the Twelfth Century," *Art Studies* 1 (1923). Reprinted in *Chartres Cathedral,* edited by Robert Branner. New York, 1969, 168–85.

Varry, Dominique. "Les confiscations révolutionnaires." In *Histoire des bibliothèques françaises. Les bibliothèques de la Révolution et du XIXe siècle, 1789–1914,* edited by Dominique Varry, 8–27. Paris: Promodis-Editions du Cercle de la Librairie, 1991.

Vaughan, William. "The Englishness of British Art." *Oxford Art Journal* 13, no. 2 (1990): 11–23.

————. *German Romantic Painting.* New Haven, Conn.: Yale University Press, 1980.

Verduin, Kathleen, ed. *Medievalism in North America.* Vol. 6 of *Studies in Medievalism.* Cambridge: D. S. Brewer, 1994.

Viardot, Jean. "Naissance de la bibliophilie: les cabinets de livres rares." In *Histoire des bibliothèques françaises. Les bibliothèques sous l'Ancien Régime, 1530–1789,* edited by Claude Jolly, 268–89. Paris: Promodis-Editions du Cercle de la Librairie, 1988.

Victoria and Albert Museum. *Catalogue of the Circulating Collection of Illuminated Manuscripts (Leaves and Cuttings) Selected from the Victoria and Albert Museum, HMSO.* London: Victoria and Albert Museum, 1908.

Voelkle, William M., with Roger S. Wieck. *The Spanish Forger.* New York: Pierpont Morgan Library, 1978.

Voelkle, William M., and Roger S. Wieck. *The Bernard H. Breslauer Collection of Manuscript Illuminations,* assisted by Maria Francesca P. Saffiotti. New York: Pierpont Morgan Library, 1992.

Von der Hagen, Friedrich Heinrich. *Bildersaal der altdeutscher Dichter: Bildnisse, Wappen, und Dichter des XII bis XIV. Jahrhunderts: nach Handschriftgemälden, vornamlich der manesse'schen Sammlung.* Berlin: J. A. Stargardt, 1856.

————. "Gemälde in der manesse'schen Handschrift von deutschen Dichtern des 12–14. Jahrhunderts." *Abhandlungen der königlichen Akademie der Wissenschaften zu Berlin, Philos.-histor. Kl.* (1853): 517–29.

Von Eye, A. *Das Germanische Museum. Wegweiser.* 1853.

Waagen, Gustav Friedrich. *Treasures of Art in Great Britain: Being an Account of the Chief Collections of Paintings, Drawings, Sculptures, Illuminated Mss.* 3 vols. London: J. Murray, 1854.

————. *Works of Art and Artists in England (1794–1868).* Translated by H. E. Lloyd. 3 vols. London: J. Muray, 1838. Reprint, London: Cornmarket, 1970.

Wacherbarth, F. D. *The Revival of Monastic Institutions.* Colchester: W. Totham, 1839.

Wainwright, Clive. *The Romantic Interior: The British Collector at Home, 1750–1850, Studies in British Art.* New Haven, Conn.: Yale University Press for the Paul Mellon Centre for Studies in British Art, 1989.

Wakeman, G., and G. D. R. Bridson. *A Guide to Nineteenth Century Colour Printers.* Leicestershire: Plough Press, 1975.

Wakeman, Geoffrey. *Aspects of Victorian Lithography: Anastatic Printing and Photozincography.* Wymondham, England: Brewhouse Press, 1970.

————. *Victorian Book Illustration: The Technical Revolution.* Norwich: Fletcher and Son for David and Charles Ltd., 1973.

Wallon, Henri Alexandre. *Jeanne d'Arc, édition illustré d'après les monuments de l'art depuis le 15ème siècle jusqu'à nos jours.* Paris: Firmin-Didot, 1876.

Walpole, Horace. *Anecdotes of Painting in England; with Some Account of the Principal Artists; and Incidental Notes on Other Arts; Collected by the Late Mr. George Vertue; and Now Digested and Published from His Original MSS.* Strawberry Hill: printed by Thomas Farmer, 1762.

Walsdorf, John J. *William Morris in Private Press and Limited Editions: A Descriptive Bibliography of Works by and about William Morris, 1891–1981.* Phoenix, AZ: Oryx Press, 1983.

Wanley, Humphrey. *The Diary of Humfrey Wanley, 1672–1726.* Edited by C. E. Wright and Ruth C. Wright. London: Bibliographical Society, 1966.

————. *Letters of Humfrey Wanley: Palaeographer, Anglo-Saxonist, Librarian, 1672–1726.* Edited by P. L. Heyworth. Oxford: Clarendon Press, 1989.

Warner, George Frederic. *Reproductions from Illuminated Manuscripts.* London: British Museum, 1907.

Waterhouse, E. K. "Some Notes on William Young Ottley's Collection of Italian Primitives." In *Italian Studies Presented to E.R. Vincent,* edited by Charles Peter Brand et al., 272–80. Cambridge: W. Heffer and Sons, 1962.

Watson, Rowan. "The Chambord Missal." In *Art and Design in Europe and America, 1800–1900,* edited by Simon Jervis, 62–63. New York: E. P. Dutton, 1987.

————."The Illuminated Manuscript in the Age of Photographic Reproduction." In *Making the Medieval Book. Techniques of Production.* Edited by Linda

L. Brownrigg, 133–43. Los Altos Hills, Calif.: Anderson-Lovelace, 1995.

————. "Educators, Collectors, Fragments and the 'Illuminations' Collection at the Victoria and Albert Museum in the Nineteenth Century." In *Interpreting and Collecting Fragments of Medieval Books.* Edited by Linda L. Brownrigg and Margaret M. Smith, 21–46. Los Altos Hills, Calif.: Anderson-Lovelace, 2000.

————. "Medieval Manuscript Fragments." *Archives* 13, no. 58 (autumn 1977): 61–73.

————. "New Uses for Medieval Art: Some Illuminated Manuscripts Produced in Paris in the 1840s." Paper presented at "A la recherche de la mémoire. Le patrimoine culturel." *Actes du colloque organisé par la Section des Bibliothèques d'Art de l'IFLA,* Paris, Munich, August 16–19, 1989.

————. *Vandals and Enthusiasts: Views of Illumination in the Nineteenth Century.* London: Victoria and Albert Museum, 1995. Desktop publication.

Watts, K. N. "Samuel Pratt and Armour Faking." In *Why Fakes Matter: Essays on Problems of Authenticity.* London: British Museum, 1992.

Weber, Wilhelm. *A History of Lithography.* London: Thames and Hudson, 1966.

Wedgwood, Alexandra. *A. W. N. Pugin and the Pugin Family.* London: Victoria and Albert Museum, 1985.

Wendt, L., and H. Kogan, *Give the Lady What She Wants! The Story of Marshall Field and Company.* Chicago, 1952.

Westfehling, Uwe. "Ferdinand Franz Wallraf als Graphiksammler." In *Lust und Verlust: Kölner Sammler zwischen Trikolore und Preußenadler,* edited by Hiltrud Kier and Frank Günter Zehnder, 407–16. Cologne: Wienand and Museen der Stadt Köln, 1995.

Westwood, John Obadiah. *Fac-similes of the Miniatures and Ornaments of the Anglo-Saxon and Irish Manuscripts Executed by J.O. Westwood. Drawn on Stone by W. R. Tymms.* London: B. Quaritch, 1868.

————. "Henry Noel Humphreys." *Academy* 15 (June 21, 1879): 550.

————. *Illuminated Illustrations of the Bible: Copied from Select Manuscripts of the Middle Ages.* London: William Smith, 1846.

Whitehill, W. M. *Boston Public Library. A Centennial History* (Cambridge, Mass., 1956), 230–31.

Wieck, Roger S. "*Folia Fugitiva*: The Pursuit of the Illuminated Manuscript Leaf." *Journal of the Walters Art Gallery* 54 (1996): 233–54.

————. "Horae Beatae Mariae ad usum Romanum. [France], 1524.In Library of Congress, *Vision of a Collector: The Lessing J. Rosenwald Collection of the Library of Congress.* Washington, D.C.: Library of Congress, 1991.

————. "A 'Late-Medieval' Miniature in the Houghton Library." *Harvard Library Bulletin* 29, no. 2 (April 1981): 212–14.

————. "The Rosenwald *Scribe* Miniature and Its Sister Miniatures: A Case of Mistaken Identity." *Oud Holland* 95, no. 3 (1981): 151–61.

Williams, Iolo A. "An Identification of Some Early Drawings by John Flaxman," *Burlington Magazine* 102, no. 687 (June 1960): 246–50.

Willoughby, Harold R. "The Rocke-feller McCormick Manuscript and What Became of It." In *A Bibliographical Record*. Chicago: New Testament De-partment, University of Chicago, 1943.

————. "Stray New Testament-Psalter Leaves Identified." *Journal of Biblical Lit-erature* 16, no. 1 (March 1942): 57–60.

————. "Vagrant Folios from Family 2400 in the Free Library of Philadel-phia." *Byzantion* 15 (1940–41): 126–32.

Windel, John and Karma Pippin. *Thomas Frognall Dibdin, 1776–1847*. New Castle, Del.: Oak Knoll, 1999.

Winterich, John T. *The Grolier Club, 1884–1950: An Informal History*. New York: Grolier Club, 1950.

————. *The Grolier Club, 1884–1967: An Informal History*. New York: Grolier Club, 1967.

Witten, Laurence. *Vinland's Saga Recalled*. New Haven, Conn.: Yale Uni-versity Press, 1989.

Wolf, Edwin. *A Descriptive Catalogue of the John Frederick Lewis Collection of Euro-pean Manuscripts in the Free Library of Philadelphia*. Philadelphia: privately printed, 1937.

Wolfram, Eddie. *History of Collage: An Anthology of Collage, Assemblage and Event Structures*. New York: Macmillan, 1975.

Wright, C. E. "The Elizabethan Society of Anitquaries and the Formation of the Cottonian Library." In *The English Li-brary before 1700*, edited by Francis Wormald and C. E. Wright, 176–212. London: University of London, Althone Press, 1958.

Wright, Thomas. *A History of Caricature and Grotesque in Literature and Art. . . . The Illustrations from Various Sources, Drawn and Engraved by F. W. Fairholt*. London: Virtue Brothers, 1865.

Wyatt, Matthew Digby. *Notices on Sculp-ture in Ivory, Being a Lecture on the History, Methods and Productions of the Art*. Lon-don: Arundel Society, 1956.